Lecture Notes in Computer Science 14441

Founding Editors

Gerhard Goos
Juris Hartmanis

Editorial Board Members

Elisa Bertino, *Purdue University, West Lafayette, IN, USA*
Wen Gao, *Peking University, Beijing, China*
Bernhard Steffen ⓘ, *TU Dortmund University, Dortmund, Germany*
Moti Yung ⓘ, *Columbia University, New York, NY, USA*

The series Lecture Notes in Computer Science (LNCS), including its subseries Lecture Notes in Artificial Intelligence (LNAI) and Lecture Notes in Bioinformatics (LNBI), has established itself as a medium for the publication of new developments in computer science and information technology research, teaching, and education.

LNCS enjoys close cooperation with the computer science R & D community, the series counts many renowned academics among its volume editors and paper authors, and collaborates with prestigious societies. Its mission is to serve this international community by providing an invaluable service, mainly focused on the publication of conference and workshop proceedings and postproceedings. LNCS commenced publication in 1973.

Jian Guo · Ron Steinfeld
Editors

Advances in Cryptology – ASIACRYPT 2023

29th International Conference on the Theory
and Application of Cryptology and Information Security
Guangzhou, China, December 4–8, 2023
Proceedings, Part IV

 Springer

Editors
Jian Guo 🆔
Nanyang Technological University
Singapore, Singapore

Ron Steinfeld 🆔
Monash University
Melbourne, VIC, Australia

ISSN 0302-9743   ISSN 1611-3349 (electronic)
Lecture Notes in Computer Science
ISBN 978-981-99-8729-0   ISBN 978-981-99-8730-6 (eBook)
https://doi.org/10.1007/978-981-99-8730-6

This Springer imprint is published by the registered company Springer Nature Singapore Pte Ltd.
The registered company address is: 152 Beach Road, #21-01/04 Gateway East, Singapore 189721, Singapore

Paper in this product is recyclable.

Preface

The 29th Annual International Conference on the Theory and Application of Cryptology and Information Security (Asiacrypt 2023) was held in Guangzhou, China, on December 4–8, 2023. The conference covered all technical aspects of cryptology, and was sponsored by the International Association for Cryptologic Research (IACR).

We received an Asiacrypt record of 376 paper submissions from all over the world, and the Program Committee (PC) selected 106 papers for publication in the proceedings of the conference. Due to this large number of papers, the Asiacrypt 2023 program had 3 tracks.

The two program chairs were supported by the great help and excellent advice of six area chairs, selected to cover the main topic areas of the conference. The area chairs were Kai-Min Chung for Information-Theoretic and Complexity-Theoretic Cryptography, Tanja Lange for Efficient and Secure Implementations, Shengli Liu for Public-Key Cryptography Algorithms and Protocols, Khoa Nguyen for Multi-Party Computation and Zero-Knowledge, Duong Hieu Phan for Public-Key Primitives with Advanced Functionalities, and Yu Sasaki for Symmetric-Key Cryptology. Each of the area chairs helped to lead discussions together with the PC members assigned as paper discussion lead. Area chairs also helped to decide on the submissions that should be accepted from their respective areas. We are very grateful for the invaluable contribution provided by the area chairs.

To review and evaluate the submissions, while keeping the load per PC member manageable, we selected a record size PC consisting of 105 leading experts from all over the world, in all six topic areas of cryptology. The two program chairs were not allowed to submit a paper, and PC members were limited to submit one single-author paper, or at most two co-authored papers, or at most three co-authored papers all with students. Each non-PC submission was reviewed by at least three reviewers consisting of either PC members or their external sub-reviewers, while each PC member submission received at least four reviews. The strong conflict of interest rules imposed by IACR ensure that papers are not handled by PC members with a close working relationship with the authors. There were approximately 420 external reviewers, whose input was critical to the selection of papers. Submissions were anonymous and their length was limited to 30 pages excluding the bibliography and supplementary materials.

The review process was conducted using double-blind peer review. The conference operated a two-round review system with a rebuttal phase. After the reviews and first round discussions the PC selected 244 submissions to proceed to the second round and the authors were then invited to participate in an interactive rebuttal phase with the reviewers to clarify questions and concerns. The remaining 131 papers were rejected, including one desk reject. The second round involved extensive discussions by the PC members. After several weeks of additional discussions, the committee selected the final 106 papers to appear in these proceedings.

The eight volumes of the conference proceedings contain the revised versions of the 106 papers that were selected. The final revised versions of papers were not reviewed again and the authors are responsible for their contents.

The PC nominated and voted for two papers to receive the Best Paper Awards, and one paper to receive the Best Early Career Paper Award. The Best Paper Awards went to Thomas Espitau, Alexandre Wallet and Yang Yu for their paper "On Gaussian Sampling, Smoothing Parameter and Application to Signatures", and to Kaijie Jiang, Anyu Wang, Hengyi Luo, Guoxiao Liu, Yang Yu, and Xiaoyun Wang for their paper "Exploiting the Symmetry of Z^n: Randomization and the Automorphism Problem". The Best Early Career Paper Award went to Maxime Plancon for the paper "Exploiting Algebraic Structure in Probing Security". The authors of those three papers were invited to submit extended versions of their papers to the Journal of Cryptology. In addition, the program of Asiacrypt 2023 also included two invited plenary talks, also nominated and voted by the PC: one talk was given by Mehdi Tibouchi and the other by Xiaoyun Wang. The conference also featured a rump session chaired by Kang Yang and Yu Yu which contained short presentations on the latest research results of the field.

Numerous people contributed to the success of Asiacrypt 2023. We would like to thank all the authors, including those whose submissions were not accepted, for submitting their research results to the conference. We are very grateful to the area chairs, PC members and external reviewers for contributing their knowledge and expertise, and for the tremendous amount of work that was done with reading papers and contributing to the discussions. We are greatly indebted to Jian Weng and Fangguo Zhang, the General Chairs, for their efforts in organizing the event and to Kevin McCurley and Kay McKelly for their help with the website and review system. We thank the Asiacrypt 2023 advisory committee members Bart Preneel, Huaxiong Wang, Kai-Min Chung, Yu Sasaki, Dongdai Lin, Shweta Agrawal and Michel Abdalla for their valuable suggestions. We are also grateful for the helpful advice and organization material provided to us by the Eurocrypt 2023 PC co-chairs Carmit Hazay and Martijn Stam and Crypto 2023 PC co-chairs Helena Handschuh and Anna Lysyanskaya. We also thank the team at Springer for handling the publication of these conference proceedings.

December 2023

Jian Guo
Ron Steinfeld

Organization

General Chairs

Jian Weng   Jinan University, China
Fangguo Zhang   Sun Yat-sen University, China

Program Committee Chairs

Jian Guo   Nanyang Technological University, Singapore
Ron Steinfeld   Monash University, Australia

Program Committee

Behzad Abdolmaleki   University of Sheffield, UK
Masayuki Abe   NTT Social Informatics Laboratories, Japan
Miguel Ambrona   Input Output Global (IOHK), Spain
Daniel Apon   MITRE Labs, USA
Shi Bai   Florida Atlantic University, USA
Gustavo Banegas   Qualcomm, France
Zhenzhen Bao   Tsinghua University, China
Andrea Basso   University of Bristol, UK
Ward Beullens   IBM Research Europe, Switzerland
Katharina Boudgoust   Aarhus University, Denmark
Matteo Campanelli   Protocol Labs, Denmark
Ignacio Cascudo   IMDEA Software Institute, Spain
Wouter Castryck   imec-COSIC, KU Leuven, Belgium
Jie Chen   East China Normal University, China
Yilei Chen   Tsinghua University, China
Jung Hee Cheon   Seoul National University and Cryptolab Inc,
     South Korea
Sherman S. M. Chow   Chinese University of Hong Kong, China
Kai-Min Chung   Academia Sinica, Taiwan
Michele Ciampi   University of Edinburgh, UK
Bernardo David   IT University of Copenhagen, Denmark
Yi Deng   Institute of Information Engineering, Chinese
     Academy of Sciences, China

Patrick Derbez University of Rennes, France
Xiaoyang Dong Tsinghua University, China
Rafael Dowsley Monash University, Australia
Nico Döttling Helmholtz Center for Information Security,
 Germany
Maria Eichlseder Graz University of Technology, Austria
Muhammed F. Esgin Monash University, Australia
Thomas Espitau PQShield, France
Jun Furukawa NEC Corporation, Japan
Aron Gohr Independent Researcher, New Zealand
Junqing Gong ECNU, China
Lorenzo Grassi Ruhr University Bochum, Germany
Tim Güneysu Ruhr University Bochum, Germany
Chun Guo Shandong University, China
Siyao Guo NYU Shanghai, China
Fuchun Guo University of Wollongong, Australia
Mohammad Hajiabadi University of Waterloo, Canada
Lucjan Hanzlik CISPA Helmholtz Center for Information
 Security, Germany
Xiaolu Hou Slovak University of Technology, Slovakia
Yuncong Hu Shanghai Jiao Tong University, China
Xinyi Huang Hong Kong University of Science and
 Technology (Guangzhou), China
Tibor Jager University of Wuppertal, Germany
Elena Kirshanova Technology Innovation Institute, UAE and I. Kant
 Baltic Federal University, Russia
Eyal Kushilevitz Technion, Israel
Russell W. F. Lai Aalto University, Finland
Tanja Lange Eindhoven University of Technology, Netherlands
Hyung Tae Lee Chung-Ang University, South Korea
Eik List Nanyang Technological University, Singapore
Meicheng Liu Institute of Information Engineering, Chinese
 Academy of Sciences, China
Guozhen Liu Nanyang Technological University, Singapore
Fukang Liu Tokyo Institute of Technology, Japan
Shengli Liu Shanghai Jiao Tong University, China
Feng-Hao Liu Florida Atlantic University, USA
Hemanta K. Maji Purdue University, USA
Takahiro Matsuda AIST, Japan
Christian Matt Concordium, Switzerland
Tomoyuki Morimae Kyoto University, Japan
Pierrick Méaux University of Luxembourg, Luxembourg

Mridul Nandi	Indian Statistical Institute, Kolkata, India
María Naya-Plasencia	Inria, France
Khoa Nguyen	University of Wollongong, Australia
Ryo Nishimaki	NTT Social Informatics Laboratories, Japan
Anca Nitulescu	Protocol Labs, France
Ariel Nof	Bar Ilan University, Israel
Emmanuela Orsini	Bocconi University, Italy
Adam O'Neill	UMass Amherst, USA
Morten Øygarden	Simula UiB, Norway
Sikhar Patranabis	IBM Research, India
Alice Pellet-Mary	CNRS and University of Bordeaux, France
Edoardo Persichetti	Florida Atlantic University, USA and Sapienza University, Italy
Duong Hieu Phan	Telecom Paris, Institut Polytechnique de Paris, France
Josef Pieprzyk	Data61, CSIRO, Australia and ICS, PAS, Poland
Axel Y. Poschmann	PQShield, UAE
Thomas Prest	PQShield, France
Adeline Roux-Langlois	CNRS, GREYC, France
Amin Sakzad	Monash University, Australia
Yu Sasaki	NTT Social Informatics Laboratories, Japan
Jae Hong Seo	Hanyang University, South Korea
Yaobin Shen	UCLouvain, Belgium
Danping Shi	Institute of Information Engineering, Chinese Academy of Sciences, China
Damien Stehlé	CryptoLab, France
Bing Sun	National University of Defense Technology, China
Shi-Feng Sun	Shanghai Jiao Tong University, China
Keisuke Tanaka	Tokyo Institute of Technology, Japan
Qiang Tang	University of Sydney, Australia
Vanessa Teague	Thinking Cybersecurity Pty Ltd and the Australian National University, Australia
Jean-Pierre Tillich	Inria, Paris, France
Yosuke Todo	NTT Social Informatics Laboratories, Japan
Alexandre Wallet	University of Rennes, Inria, CNRS, IRISA, France
Meiqin Wang	Shandong University, China
Yongge Wang	UNC Charlotte, USA
Yuyu Wang	University of Electronic Science and Technology of China, China
Qingju Wang	Telecom Paris, Institut Polytechnique de Paris, France

Benjamin Wesolowski	CNRS and ENS Lyon, France
Shuang Wu	Huawei International, Singapore, Singapore
Keita Xagawa	Technology Innovation Institute, UAE
Chaoping Xing	Shanghai Jiao Tong University, China
Jun Xu	Institute of Information Engineering, Chinese Academy of Sciences, China
Takashi Yamakawa	NTT Social Informatics Laboratories, Japan
Kang Yang	State Key Laboratory of Cryptology, China
Yu Yu	Shanghai Jiao Tong University, China
Yang Yu	Tsinghua University, Beijing, China
Yupeng Zhang	University of Illinois Urbana-Champaign and Texas A&M University, USA
Liangfeng Zhang	ShanghaiTech University, China
Raymond K. Zhao	CSIRO's Data61, Australia
Hong-Sheng Zhou	Virginia Commonwealth University, USA

Additional Reviewers

Amit Agarwal
Jooyoung Lee
Léo Ackermann
Akshima
Bar Alon
Ravi Anand
Sarah Arpin
Thomas Attema
Nuttapong Attrapadung
Manuel Barbosa
Razvan Barbulescu
James Bartusek
Carsten Baum
Olivier Bernard
Tyler Besselman
Ritam Bhaumik
Jingguo Bi
Loic Bidoux
Maxime Bombar
Xavier Bonnetain
Joppe Bos
Mariana Botelho da Gama
Christina Boura
Clémence Bouvier
Ross Bowden

Pedro Branco
Lauren Brandt
Alessandro Budroni
Kevin Carrier
André Chailloux
Suvradip Chakraborty
Debasmita Chakraborty
Haokai Chang
Bhuvnesh Chaturvedi
Caicai Chen
Rongmao Chen
Mingjie Chen
Yi Chen
Megan Chen
Yu Long Chen
Xin Chen
Shiyao Chen
Long Chen
Wonhee Cho
Qiaohan Chu
Valerio Cini
James Clements
Ran Cohen
Alexandru Cojocaru
Sandro Coretti-Drayton

Anamaria Costache
Alain Couvreur
Daniele Cozzo
Hongrui Cui
Giuseppe D'Alconzo
Zhaopeng Dai
Quang Dao
Nilanjan Datta
Koen de Boer
Luca De Feo
Paola de Perthuis
Thomas Decru
Rafael del Pino
Julien Devevey
Henri Devillez
Siemen Dhooghe
Yaoling Ding
Jack Doerner
Jelle Don
Mark Douglas Schultz
Benjamin Dowling
Minxin Du
Xiaoqi Duan
Jesko Dujmovic
Moumita Dutta
Avijit Dutta
Ehsan Ebrahimi
Felix Engelmann
Reo Eriguchi
Jonathan Komada Eriksen
Andre Esser
Pouria Fallahpour
Zhiyong Fang
Antonio Faonio
Pooya Farshim
Joël Felderhoff
Jakob Feldtkeller
Weiqi Feng
Xiutao Feng
Shuai Feng
Qi Feng
Hanwen Feng
Antonio Flórez-Gutiérrez
Apostolos Fournaris
Paul Frixons

Ximing Fu
Georg Fuchsbauer
Philippe Gaborit
Rachit Garg
Robin Geelen
Riddhi Ghosal
Koustabh Ghosh
Barbara Gigerl
Niv Gilboa
Valerie Gilchrist
Emanuele Giunta
Xinxin Gong
Huijing Gong
Zheng Gong
Robert Granger
Zichen Gui
Anna Guinet
Qian Guo
Xiaojie Guo
Hosein Hadipour
Mathias Hall-Andersen
Mike Hamburg
Shuai Han
Yonglin Hao
Keisuke Hara
Keitaro Hashimoto
Le He
Brett Hemenway Falk
Minki Hhan
Taiga Hiroka
Akinori Hosoyamada
Chengan Hou
Martha Norberg Hovd
Kai Hu
Tao Huang
Zhenyu Huang
Michael Hutter
Jihun Hwang
Akiko Inoue
Tetsu Iwata
Robin Jadoul
Hansraj Jangir
Dirmanto Jap
Stanislaw Jarecki
Santos Jha

Ashwin Jha

Dingding Jia

Yanxue Jia

Lin Jiao

Daniel Jost

Antoine Joux

Jiayi Kang

Gabriel Kaptchuk

Alexander Karenin

Shuichi Katsumata

Pengzhen Ke

Mustafa Khairallah

Shahram Khazaei

Hamidreza Amini Khorasgani

Hamidreza Khoshakhlagh

Ryo Kikuchi

Jiseung Kim

Minkyu Kim

Suhri Kim

Ravi Kishore

Fuyuki Kitagawa

Susumu Kiyoshima

Michael Klooß

Alexander Koch

Sreehari Kollath

Dimitris Kolonelos

Yashvanth Kondi

Anders Konring

Woong Kook

Dimitri Koshelev

Markus Krausz

Toomas Krips

Daniel Kuijsters

Anunay Kulshrestha

Qiqi Lai

Yi-Fu Lai

Georg Land

Nathalie Lang

Mario Larangeira

Joon-Woo Lee

Keewoo Lee

Hyeonbum Lee

Changmin Lee

Charlotte Lefevre

Julia Len

Antonin Leroux

Andrea Lesavourey

Jannis Leuther

Jie Li

Shuaishuai Li

Huina Li

Yu Li

Yanan Li

Jiangtao Li

Song Song Li

Wenjie Li

Shun Li

Zengpeng Li

Xiao Liang

Wei-Kai Lin

Chengjun Lin

Chao Lin

Cong Ling

Yunhao Ling

Hongqing Liu

Jing Liu

Jiahui Liu

Qipeng Liu

Yamin Liu

Weiran Liu

Tianyi Liu

Siqi Liu

Chen-Da Liu-Zhang

Jinyu Lu

Zhenghao Lu

Stefan Lucks

Yiyuan Luo

Lixia Luo

Jack P. K. Ma

Fermi Ma

Gilles Macario-Rat

Luciano Maino

Christian Majenz

Laurane Marco

Lorenzo Martinico

Loïc Masure

John McVey

Willi Meier

Kelsey Melissaris

Bart Mennink

Charles Meyer-Hilfiger
Victor Miller
Chohong Min
Marine Minier
Arash Mirzaei
Pratyush Mishra
Tarik Moataz
Johannes Mono
Fabrice Mouhartem
Alice Murphy
Erik Mårtensson
Anne Müller
Marcel Nageler
Yusuke Naito
Barak Nehoran
Patrick Neumann
Tran Ngo
Phuong Hoa Nguyen
Ngoc Khanh Nguyen
Thi Thu Quyen Nguyen
Hai H. Nguyen
Semyon Novoselov
Julian Nowakowski
Arne Tobias Malkenes Ødegaard
Kazuma Ohara
Miyako Ohkubo
Charles Olivier-Anclin
Eran Omri
Yi Ouyang
Tapas Pal
Ying-yu Pan
Jiaxin Pan
Eugenio Paracucchi
Roberto Parisella
Jeongeun Park
Guillermo Pascual-Perez
Alain Passelègue
Octavio Perez-Kempner
Thomas Peters
Phuong Pham
Cécile Pierrot
Erik Pohle
David Pointcheval
Giacomo Pope
Christopher Portmann

Romain Poussier
Lucas Prabel
Sihang Pu
Chen Qian
Luowen Qian
Tian Qiu
Anaïs Querol
Håvard Raddum
Shahram Rasoolzadeh
Divya Ravi
Prasanna Ravi
Marc Renard
Jan Richter-Brockmann
Lawrence Roy
Paul Rösler
Sayandeep Saha
Yusuke Sakai
Niels Samwel
Paolo Santini
Maria Corte-Real Santos
Sara Sarfaraz
Santanu Sarkar
Or Sattath
Markus Schofnegger
Peter Scholl
Dominique Schröder
André Schrottenloher
Jacob Schuldt
Binanda Sengupta
Srinath Setty
Yantian Shen
Yixin Shen
Ferdinand Sibleyras
Janno Siim
Mark Simkin
Scott Simon
Animesh Singh
Nitin Singh
Sayani Sinha
Daniel Slamanig
Fang Song
Ling Song
Yongsoo Song
Jana Sotakova
Gabriele Spini

Marianna Spyrakou

Lukas Stennes

Marc Stoettinger

Chuanjie Su

Xiangyu Su

Ling Sun

Akira Takahashi

Isobe Takanori

Atsushi Takayasu

Suprita Talnikar

Benjamin Hong Meng Tan

Ertem Nusret Tas

Tadanori Teruya

Masayuki Tezuka

Sri AravindaKrishnan Thyagarajan

Song Tian

Wenlong Tian

Raphael Toledo

Junichi Tomida

Daniel Tschudi

Hikaru Tsuchida

Aleksei Udovenko

Rei Ueno

Barry Van Leeuwen

Wessel van Woerden

Frederik Vercauteren

Sulani Vidhanalage

Benedikt Wagner

Roman Walch

Hendrik Waldner

Han Wang

Luping Wang

Peng Wang

Yuntao Wang

Geng Wang

Shichang Wang

Liping Wang

Jiafan Wang

Zhedong Wang

Kunpeng Wang

Jianfeng Wang

Guilin Wang

Weiqiang Wen

Chenkai Weng

Thom Wiggers

Stella Wohnig

Harry W. H. Wong

Ivy K. Y. Woo

Yu Xia

Zejun Xiang

Yuting Xiao

Zhiye Xie

Yanhong Xu

Jiayu Xu

Lei Xu

Shota Yamada

Kazuki Yamamura

Di Yan

Qianqian Yang

Shaojun Yang

Yanjiang Yang

Li Yao

Yizhou Yao

Kenji Yasunaga

Yuping Ye

Xiuyu Ye

Zeyuan Yin

Kazuki Yoneyama

Yusuke Yoshida

Albert Yu

Quan Yuan

Chen Yuan

Tsz Hon Yuen

Aaram Yun

Riccardo Zanotto

Arantxa Zapico

Shang Zehua

Mark Zhandry

Tianyu Zhang

Zhongyi Zhang

Fan Zhang

Liu Zhang

Yijian Zhang

Shaoxuan Zhang

Zhongliang Zhang

Kai Zhang

Cong Zhang

Jiaheng Zhang

Lulu Zhang

Zhiyu Zhang

Chang-An Zhao
Yongjun Zhao
Chunhuan Zhao
Xiaotong Zhou
Zhelei Zhou

Zijian Zhou
Timo Zijlstra
Jian Zou
Ferdinando Zullo
Cong Zuo

Sponsoring Institutions

- Gold Level Sponsor: Ant Research
- Silver Level Sponsors: Sansec Technology Co., Ltd., Topsec Technologies Group
- Bronze Level Sponsors: IBM, Meta, Sangfor Technologies Inc.

Contents – Part IV

Quantum Random Oracle Model

Cryptanalysis of Post-quantum
and Public-Key Systems

A New Approach Based on Quadratic Forms to Attack the McEliece Cryptosystem

Alain Couvreur[1], Rocco Mora[2], and Jean-Pierre Tillich[2(✉)]

[1] Inria Saclay, LIX, CNRS UMR 7161, École Polytechnique, 1 rue Honoré d'Estienne
d'Orves, 91120 Palaiseau Cedex, France
`alain.couvreur@inria.fr`
[2] Inria Paris, 2 rue Simone Iff, 75012 Paris, France
`{rocco.mora,jean-pierre.tillich}@inria.fr`

Abstract. We introduce a novel algebraic approach for attacking the
McEliece cryptosystem which is currently at the 4-th round of the NIST
competition. The contributions of the article are twofold. (1) We present
a new distinguisher on alternant and Goppa codes working in a much
broader range of parameters than [FGO+11]. (2) With this approach we
also provide a polynomial–time key recovery attack on alternant codes
which are distinguishable with the distinguisher [FGO+11].

These results are obtained by introducing a subspace of matrices representing quadratic forms. Those are associated with quadratic relations
for the component-wise product in the dual of the Goppa (or alternant)
code of the cryptosystem. It turns out that this subspace of matrices contains matrices of unusually small rank in the case of alternant or Goppa
codes (2 or 3 depending on the field characteristic) revealing the secret
polynomial structure of the code. MinRank solvers can then be used to
recover the secret key of the scheme. We devise a dedicated algebraic
modeling in characteristic 2 where the Gröbner basis techniques to solve
it can be analyzed. This computation behaves differently when applied
to the matrix space associated with a random code rather than with a
Goppa or an alternant code. This gives a distinguisher of the latter code
families, which contrarily to the one proposed in [FGO+11] working only
in a tiny parameter regime is now able to work for code rates above $\frac{2}{3}$.
It applies to most of the instantiations of the McEliece cryptosystem in
the literature. It coincides with the one of [FGO+11] when the latter
can be applied (and is therefore of polynomial complexity in this case).
However, its complexity increases significantly when [FGO+11] does not
apply anymore, but stays subexponential as long as the co-dimension
of the code is sublinear in the length (with an asymptotic exponent
which is below those of all known key recovery or message attacks). For
the concrete parameters of the McEliece NIST submission [ABC+22],
its complexity is way too complex to threaten the cryptosystem, but is

This work was partly funded by the French Agence Nationale de la Recherche
through the France 2023 ANR project ANR-22-PETQ-0008PQ-TLS and the ANR-
21-CE390009-BARRACUDA.

© International Association for Cryptologic Research 2023
J. Guo and R. Steinfeld (Eds.): ASIACRYPT 2023, LNCS 14441, pp. 3–38, 2023.
https://doi.org/10.1007/978-981-99-8730-6_1

smaller than known key recovery attacks for most of the parameters of the submission. This subspace of quadratic forms can also be used in a different manner to give a polynomial time attack of the McEliece cryptosystem based on generic alternant codes or Goppa codes provided that these codes are distinguishable by the method of [FGO+11], and in the Goppa case we need the additional assumption that its degree is less than $q - 1$, where q is the alphabet size of the code.

1   Introduction

The McEliece Cryptosystem

The McEliece encryption scheme [McE78], which is only a few months younger than RSA [RSA78], is a code-based cryptosystem built upon the family of binary Goppa codes. It is equipped with very fast encryption and decryption algorithms and has very small ciphertexts but large public key size. Contrarily to RSA which is broken by quantum computers [Sho94], it is also widely viewed as a viable quantum-safe cryptosystem. A variation of this public key cryptosystem intended to be IND-CCA secure and an associated key exchange protocol [ABC+22] is one of the three remaining code-based candidates in the fourth round of the NIST post-quantum competition on post-quantum cryptography. Its main selling point for being standardized is that it is the oldest public key cryptosystem which has resisted all possible attacks be they classical or quantum so far, this despite very significant efforts to break it.

The consensus right now about this cryptosystem is that key-recovery attacks that would be able to exploit the underlying algebraic structure are way more expensive than message-recovery attacks that use decoding algorithms for generic linear codes. Because of this reason, the parameters of McEliece encryption scheme are chosen according to the latest algorithms for decoding a linear code. This is also actually another selling point for this cryptosystem, since despite significant efforts on improving the algorithms for decoding linear codes, all the classical algorithms for performing this task are of exponential complexity and this exponent has basically only decreased by less than 20 percent for most parameters of interest after more than 60 years of research [Pra62, Ste88, Dum89, CC98, MMT11, BJMM12, MO15, BM17]. The situation is even more stable when it comes to quantum algorithms [Ber10, KT17].

Key Recovery Attacks

The best key recovery attack has not changed for many years. It was given in [LS01] and consists in checking all Goppa polynomials and all possible supports with the help of [Sen00]. Its complexity is also exponential with an exponent which is much bigger than the one obtained for message recovery attacks. There has been some progress on this issue, not on the original McEliece cryptosystem, but on variations of it. This concerns very high rate binary Goppa codes for devising signature schemes [CFS01], non-binary Goppa codes over large alphabets [BLP10, BLP11], or more structured versions of the McEliece system, based on quasi-cyclic alternant codes [BCGO09, CBB+17] (a family of algebraic codes containing Goppa codes retaining the essential algebraic features of Goppa codes) or on quasi-dyadic Goppa codes such as [MB09, BLM11, BBB+17].

The quasi-cyclic or quasi-dyadic alternant/Goppa codes have been attacked in [FOPT10, GUL09, BC18] by providing a suitable algebraic modeling for the secret key and then solving the algebraic system with Gröbner bases techniques. This algebraic modeling tries to recover the underlying polynomial structure of these codes coming from the underlying generalized Reed-Solomon structure by using just an arbitrary generator matrix of the alternant or Goppa code which is given by the public key of the scheme. This is basically the secret key of the scheme. It allows to decode the alternant or Goppa code and therefore all possible ciphertexts. Recall that a generalized Reed-Solomon code is defined by

Definition 1 (Generalized Reed-Solomon (GRS) code). *Let* $\boldsymbol{x} = (x_1, \ldots, x_n) \in \mathbb{F}^n$ *be a vector of pairwise distinct entries and* $\boldsymbol{y} = (y_1, \ldots, y_n) \in \mathbb{F}^n$ *a vector of nonzero entries, where* $\mathbb{F}$ *is a finite field. The* generalized Reed-Solomon (GRS) code *over* $\mathbb{F}$ *of dimension* k *with* support $\boldsymbol{x}$ *and* multiplier $\boldsymbol{y}$ *is*

$$\mathbf{GRS}_k(\boldsymbol{x}, \boldsymbol{y}) \overset{def}{=} \{(y_1 P(x_1), \ldots, y_n P(x_n)) \mid P \in \mathbb{F}[z], \deg P < k\}.$$

Alternant codes are defined as subfield subcodes of GRS codes, meaning that an alternant code $\mathscr{A}$ of length n is defined over some field $\mathbb{F}_q$ whereas the underlying GRS code $\mathscr{C}$ is defined over an extension field $\mathbb{F}_{q^m}$ of degree m. The alternant code is defined in this case as the set of codewords of the GRS code whose entries all belong to the subfield $\mathbb{F}_q$, *i.e.* $\mathscr{A} = \mathscr{C} \cap \mathbb{F}_q^n$. Rather than trying to recover the polynomial structure of the underlying GRS code, the algebraic attack in [FOPT10] actually recovers the polynomial structure of the *dual code*. Recall that the dual code of a linear code is defined by

Definition 2 (dual code). *The dual* $\mathscr{C}^\perp$ *of a linear code* $\mathscr{C}$ *of length* n *over* $\mathbb{F}_q$ *is the subspace of* $\mathbb{F}_q^n$ *defined by* $\mathscr{C}^\perp \overset{def}{=} \{\boldsymbol{d} \in \mathbb{F}_q^n : \boldsymbol{d} \cdot \boldsymbol{c} = 0, \ \forall \boldsymbol{c} \in \mathscr{C}\}$, *where* $\boldsymbol{d} \cdot \boldsymbol{c} = \sum_{i=1}^n c_i d_i$ *with* $\boldsymbol{c} = (c_i)_{1 \leqslant i \leqslant n}$ *and* $\boldsymbol{d} = (d_i)_{1 \leqslant i \leqslant n}$.

The dual code of an alternant code has also a polynomial structure owing to the fact that the dual of a GRS code is actually a GRS code:

Proposition 1 ([MS86, Theorem 4, p. 304]). *Let* $\mathbf{GRS}_r(\boldsymbol{x}, \boldsymbol{y})$ *be a GRS code of length* n. *Its dual is also a GRS code. In particular* $\mathbf{GRS}_r(\boldsymbol{x}, \boldsymbol{y})^\perp = \mathbf{GRS}_{n-r}(\boldsymbol{x}, \boldsymbol{y}^\perp)$, *with* $\boldsymbol{y}^\perp \overset{def}{=} \left(\frac{1}{\pi'_x(x_1)y_1}, \ldots, \frac{1}{\pi'_x(x_n)y_n} \right)$, *where* $\pi_x(z) \overset{def}{=} \prod_{i=1}^n (z - x_i)$ *and* π'_x *is its derivative.*

It is actually the dual of the underlying GRS code which serves to define the multiplier and the support of an alternant code as shown by

Definition 3 (alternant code). *Let $n \leqslant q^m$, for some positive integer m. Let* $\mathbf{GRS}_r(\boldsymbol{x}, \boldsymbol{y})$ *be the GRS code over $\mathbb{F}_{q^m}$ of dimension r with support $\boldsymbol{x} \in \mathbb{F}_{q^m}^n$ and multiplier $\boldsymbol{y} \in (\mathbb{F}_{q^m}^*)^n$. The alternant code with support $\boldsymbol{x}$ and multiplier $\boldsymbol{y}$, degree r over $\mathbb{F}_q$ is*

$$\mathscr{A}_r(\boldsymbol{x}, \boldsymbol{y}) \stackrel{def}{=} \mathbf{GRS}_r(\boldsymbol{x}, \boldsymbol{y})^\perp \cap \mathbb{F}_q^n = \mathbf{GRS}_{n-r}(\boldsymbol{x}, \boldsymbol{y}^\perp) \cap \mathbb{F}_q^n.$$

The integer m is called extension degree *of the alternant code.*

It is much more convenient to recover with an algebraic modeling the support and the multiplier of the dual of the underlying GRS code because *any* codeword $\boldsymbol{c}$ of the alternant code $\mathscr{A}_r(\boldsymbol{x}, \boldsymbol{y})$ is readily seen to be orthogonal to any codeword $\boldsymbol{d}$ of $\mathbf{GRS}_r(\boldsymbol{x}, \boldsymbol{y})$, *i.e.* $\boldsymbol{c} \cdot \boldsymbol{d} = 0$. The algebraic modeling of [FOPT10] is based on such equations where the unknowns are the entries of $\boldsymbol{x}$ and $\boldsymbol{y}$. Goppa codes can be recovered from this approach too, since they are particular alternant codes:

Definition 4 (Goppa code). *Let $\boldsymbol{x} \in \mathbb{F}_{q^m}^n$ be a support vector and $\Gamma \in \mathbb{F}_{q^m}[z]$ a polynomial of degree r such that $\Gamma(x_i) \neq 0$ for all $i \in \{1, \ldots, n\}$. The Goppa code of degree r with support $\boldsymbol{x}$ and Goppa polynomial Γ is defined as $\mathscr{G}(\boldsymbol{x}, \Gamma) \stackrel{def}{=} \mathscr{A}_r(\boldsymbol{x}, \boldsymbol{y})$, where $\boldsymbol{y} \stackrel{def}{=} \left(\frac{1}{\Gamma(x_1)}, \ldots, \frac{1}{\Gamma(x_n)} \right)$.*

The algebraic modeling approach of [FOPT10] worked because the quasi cyclic/dyadic structure allowed to reduce drastically the number of unknowns of the algebraic system when compared to the original McEliece cryptosystem. A variant of this algebraic modeling was introduced in [FPdP14] to attack certain parameters of the variant of the McEliece cryptosystem [BLP10, BLP11] based on wild Goppa codes/wild Goppa codes incognito. It only involves equations on the multiplier $\boldsymbol{y}$ of the Goppa code induced by the wild Goppa structure. The McEliece cryptosystem based on plain binary Goppa codes seems immune to both the approaches of [FOPT10] and [FPdP14]. The first one because the degree and the number of variables of the resulting system are most certainly too big to make such an approach likely to succeed if not at the cost of a very high exponential complexity (but this has to be confirmed by a rigorous analysis which is hard to perform because Gröbner bases techniques perform here very differently from a generic system). The second one because this modeling does not apply to binary Goppa codes. In particular, it needs a very small extension degree and a code alphabet size that are prime powers rather than prime.

It was also found that Gröbner bases techniques when applied to the algebraic system [FOPT10] behaved very differently when the system corresponds to a Goppa code instead of a random linear code of the same length and dimension. This approach led to [FGO+11] that gave a way to distinguish high-rate Goppa codes from random codes. It is based on the kernel of a linear system related to the aforementioned algebraic system. It was shown there to have an unexpectedly high dimension when instantiated with Goppa codes or the more general family of alternant codes rather than with random linear codes. Another interpretation was later on given to this distinguisher in [MP12], where it was proved that the kernel dimension is related to the dimension of the square of the dual of the Goppa code. Very recently, [MT22] revisited [FGO+11] and gave rigorous bounds for the dimensions of the square codes of Goppa or alternant codes and a better insight into the algebraic structure of these squares. The component-wise/Schur product/square of codes is defined from the component-wise/Schur product $\boldsymbol{a} \star \boldsymbol{b} \stackrel{\text{def}}{=} (a_1 b_1, \ldots, a_n b_n)$ of vectors $\boldsymbol{a} = (a_i)_{1 \leqslant i \leqslant n}$ and $\boldsymbol{b} = (b_i)_{1 \leqslant i \leqslant n}$ by

Definition 5. *The* component-wise product *of codes* $\mathscr{C}, \mathscr{D} \subseteq \mathbb{F}^n$ *is defined as*

$$\mathscr{C} \star \mathscr{D} \stackrel{\text{def}}{=} \langle \boldsymbol{c} \star \boldsymbol{d} \mid \boldsymbol{c} \in \mathscr{C}, \boldsymbol{d} \in \mathscr{D} \rangle_{\mathbb{F}}.$$

If $\mathscr{C} = \mathscr{D}$, *we call* $\mathscr{C}^{\star 2} \stackrel{\text{def}}{=} \mathscr{C} \star \mathscr{C}$ *the* square code *of* $\mathscr{C}$.

The reason why Goppa codes behave differently from random codes for this product is essentially because the underlying GRS code behaves very abnormally with respect to the component-wise product. Indeed,

Proposition 2 ([CGG+14]). *Let* $\mathbf{GRS}_k(\boldsymbol{x}, \boldsymbol{y})$ *be a GRS code with support* $\boldsymbol{x}$, *multiplier* $\boldsymbol{y}$ *and dimension* k. *We have* $\mathbf{GRS}_k(\boldsymbol{x}, \boldsymbol{y})^{\star 2} = \mathbf{GRS}_{2k-1}(\boldsymbol{x}, \boldsymbol{y} \star \boldsymbol{y})$. *Hence, if* $k \leqslant \frac{n+1}{2}$, $\dim_{\mathbb{F}_{q^m}}(\mathbf{GRS}_k(\boldsymbol{x}, \boldsymbol{y}))^{\star 2} = 2k - 1$.

On the other hand, random linear codes behave very differently, because they attain with probability close to 1 [CCMZ15] the general upper bound on the dimension given by $\dim_{\mathbb{F}} \mathscr{C}^{\star 2} \leqslant \min \left(n, \binom{\dim_{\mathbb{F}} \mathscr{C} + 1}{2} \right)$. In other words, the dimension of the square of a random linear code scales quadratically as long as the dimension is $k = \mathcal{O}(\sqrt{n})$ and attains after this the full dimension n, whereas the dimension of the square of a GRS code of dimension k increases only linearly in k. This peculiar property of GRS codes survives in an attenuated form in the square of the dual of an alternant/Goppa code as shown by [MT22].

This tool was also instrumental in another breakthrough in this area, namely that for the first time a polynomial attack [COT14, COT17] was found on the McEliece scheme when instantiated with Goppa codes. This was done by using square code considerations. However, this attack required very special parameters to be carried out: (i) the extension degree should be 2, (ii) the Goppa code should be a wild Goppa code. It is insightful to remark that this attack exploits the unusually low dimension of the square of wild Goppa codes when their dimension is low enough whereas the distinguisher of [FGO+11] actually uses the small dimension of the square of the *dual* of a Goppa or alternant code. The dual of such codes has a much more involved structure, in particular it loses a lot of the nice polynomial structure of the Goppa code (this was essential in the attack performed in [COT14]). This is probably the reason why for a long time the distinguisher of [FGO+11] has not turned into an actual attack. However, recently in [BMT23] it has been found out that in certain cases (i) very small field size $q = 2$ or $q = 3$ over which the code is defined, (ii) being a *generic alternant code* rather than being in the special case of Goppa code, (iii) being in the region of parameters where the distinguisher of [FGO+11] applies, then this distinguisher can actually be turned into a polynomial-time attack.

Note that [BMT23] also made some crucial improvements in the algebraic modeling of [FOPT10] (in particular by adding low-degree equations that take into account that the multiplier and support of the alternant/Goppa code should satisfy certain constraints).

A New Approach

A First Idea: Non Generic Quadratic Relations on the Extended Dual Alternant/Goppa Code. We devise in this work a radically new approach toward attacking the McEliece cryptosystem when it is based on alternant or Goppa codes. This leads to two new contributions: (1) a new distinguisher on alternant and Goppa codes and (2) a polynomial time key-recovery attack on the alternant and part of the Goppa codes that are distinguishable by [FGO+11]. Both exploit the structure of the extension over a larger field of the dual of an alternant/Goppa code. The extension of a code over a field extension is given by

Definition 6 (Extension of a code over a field extension). *Let $\mathscr{C}$ be a linear code over $\mathbb{F}_q$. We denote by $\mathscr{C}_{\mathbb{F}_{q^m}}$ the $\mathbb{F}_{q^m}$-linear span of $\mathscr{C}$ in $\mathbb{F}_{q^m}^n$.*

Definition 7 (Image of a code by the Frobenius map). *Let $\mathscr{C} \subseteq \mathbb{F}_{q^m}$ be a code, we define $\mathscr{C}^{(q)} \overset{def}{=} \{(c_1^q, \ldots, c_n^q) \mid (c_1, \ldots, c_n) \in \mathscr{C}\}$.*

It turns out that the extension of the dual of an alternant code actually contains GRS codes and their images by the Frobenius map:

Proposition 3 ([BMT23]). *Let $\mathscr{A}_r(\boldsymbol{x}, \boldsymbol{y})$ be an alternant code over $\mathbb{F}_q$. Then $\left(\mathscr{A}_r(\boldsymbol{x}, \boldsymbol{y})^{\perp}\right)_{\mathbb{F}_{q^m}} = \sum_{j=0}^{m-1} \mathbf{GRS}_r(\boldsymbol{x}, \boldsymbol{y})^{(q^j)} = \sum_{j=0}^{m-1} \mathbf{GRS}_r(\boldsymbol{x}^{q^j}, \boldsymbol{y}^{q^j})$.*

Observe now that a GRS code contains non-zero codewords c_1, c_2, c_3 satisfying a very peculiar property, namely

$$c_1 \star c_3 = c_2^{\star 2}. \tag{1}$$

This can be seen by choosing $c_1 = \boldsymbol{y}\boldsymbol{x}^a = (y_i x_i^a)_{1 \leqslant i \leqslant n}$, $c_2 = \boldsymbol{y}\boldsymbol{x}^b = (y_i x_i^b)_{1 \leqslant i \leqslant n}$ and $c_3 = \boldsymbol{y}\boldsymbol{x}^c = (y_i x_i^c)_{1 \leqslant i \leqslant n}$ for any a, b, c in $[\![0, r-1]\!]$ satisfying $b = \frac{a+c}{2}$. Such a relation is unlikely to hold in a random linear code of dimension k, unless it is of rate k/n close to 1. Therefore the dual code of our alternant or Goppa code contains very peculiar codewords. The issue is now how to find them?

A New Concept: The Code of Quadratic Relations. Equation (1) can be viewed as a quadratic relation between codewords. There is a natural object that can be brought in that encodes in a natural way quadratic relations

Definition 8 (Code of quadratic relations). *Let $\mathscr{C}$ be an $[n, k]$ linear code over $\mathbb{F}$ and let $\mathcal{V} = \{\boldsymbol{v}_1, \ldots, \boldsymbol{v}_k\}$ be a basis of $\mathscr{C}$. The **code of relations between the Schur's products with respect to** $\mathcal{V}$ is*

$$\mathscr{C}_{rel}(\mathcal{V}) \overset{def}{=} \{\boldsymbol{c} = (c_{i,j})_{1 \leqslant i \leqslant j \leqslant k} \mid \sum_{i \leqslant j} c_{i,j} \boldsymbol{v}_i \star \boldsymbol{v}_j = 0\} \subseteq \mathbb{F}^{\binom{k+1}{2}}.$$

Such an element $c = (c_{i,j})_{1 \leqslant i \leqslant j \leqslant k}$ of $\mathscr{C}_{\mathrm{rel}}(\mathcal{V})$ defines a quadratic form as

$$Q_c(x_1, \cdots, x_k) = \sum_{i \leqslant j} c_{i,j} x_i x_j.$$

When a basis $\mathcal{V}$ containing the aforementioned c_i's is chosen, there exists an element in $\mathscr{C}_{\mathrm{rel}}(\mathcal{V})$ whose associated quadratic form is of the form $x_i x_j - x_\ell^2$ (for $v_i = c_1$, $v_j = c_3$, $v_\ell = c_2$). In other words, this quadratic form is of rank 3 (in odd characteristic). To find such non–generic elements in $\mathscr{C}_{\mathrm{rel}}(\mathcal{V})$, it is convenient to represent the elements of $\mathscr{C}_{\mathrm{rel}}(\mathcal{V})$ as matrices corresponding to the bilinear map given by the polar form of the quadratic form, i.e. the matrix $\boldsymbol{M}_c$ corresponding to $c \in \mathscr{C}_{\mathrm{rel}}(\mathcal{V})$ that satisfies for all $\boldsymbol{x}$ and $\boldsymbol{y}$ in $\mathbb{F}_{q^m}^k$

$$\boldsymbol{x} \boldsymbol{M}_c \boldsymbol{y}^\intercal = Q_c(\boldsymbol{x} + \boldsymbol{y}) - Q_c(\boldsymbol{x}) - Q_c(\boldsymbol{y}). \tag{2}$$

This definition allows to have a matrix definition of the quadratic form which works both in odd characteristic and characteristic 2 and which satisfies the crucial relation (3) when the basis is changed. Note that $\boldsymbol{M}_c$ is symmetric in odd characteristic, whereas it is skew-symmetric in characteristic 2.

Remark 1. By *skew symmetric* matrices in characteristic 2 we mean symmetric matrices with zero diagonal.

Definition 9 (Matrix code of relations). *Let $\mathscr{C}$ be an $[n, k]$ linear code over $\mathbb{F}$ and let $\mathcal{V} = \{v_1, \ldots, v_k\}$ be a basis of $\mathscr{C}$. The **matrix code of relations between the Schur's products with respect to** $\mathcal{V}$ is*

$$\mathscr{C}_{mat}(\mathcal{V}) \overset{def}{=} \{\boldsymbol{M}_c = (m_{i,j})_{\substack{1 \leqslant i \leqslant k \\ 1 \leqslant j \leqslant k}} \mid c = (c_{i,j})_{1 \leqslant i \leqslant j \leqslant k} \in \mathscr{C}_{rel}(\mathcal{V})\} \subseteq \mathbf{Sym}(k, \mathbb{F}),$$

where $\boldsymbol{M}_c$ is defined as $m_{i,j} \overset{def}{=} m_{j,i} \overset{def}{=} c_{i,j}, i \neq j$ and $m_{i,i} \overset{def}{=} 2c_{i,i}, 1 \leqslant i \leqslant k$.

The previous discussion shows that if $\mathcal{V}$ contains the triple c_1, c_2, c_3, then there exists a matrix of rank 3 in the matrix code of relations in odd characteristic. Note that the matrix is of rank 2 in characteristic 2 since the polar form corresponding to the quadratic form $Q(\boldsymbol{x}) = x_i x_j - x_\ell^2$ is given by $(x_i + y_i)(x_j + y_j) - (x_\ell + y_\ell)^2 - x_i x_j + x_\ell^2 - y_i y_j + y_\ell^2 = x_i y_j + x_j y_i$.

Now the point is that even if we do not have a basis containing the c_i's, there are still rank 3 (or 2) matrices in the matrix code of relations. This holds because a change of basis basically amounts to a congruent matrix code. Indeed if $\mathcal{A}$ and $\mathcal{B}$ are two different bases of the same code, there exists (see Proposition 4) an invertible $\boldsymbol{P} \in \mathbb{F}^{k \times k}$ such that

$$\mathscr{C}_{\mathrm{mat}}(\mathcal{A}) = \boldsymbol{P}^\intercal \mathscr{C}_{\mathrm{mat}}(\mathcal{B}) \boldsymbol{P}. \tag{3}$$

Therefore for any choice of basis, there exists a rank 3 matrix in the corresponding matrix code of relations. Finding such matrices can be viewed as a MinRank problem for rank 3 with symmetric matrices.

Problem 1 (Symmetric MinRank problem for rank r). Let $M_1, \cdots, M_K$ be K symmetric matrices in $\mathbb{F}^{N \times N}$. Find an $M \in \langle M_1, \cdots, M_K \rangle_{\mathbb{F}}$ of rank r.

Of course, the dimension of the matrix code could be so large that there are rank 3 (or 2) matrices which are here by chance and which are not induced by these unusual quadratic relations between codewords of the GRS code. We will study this problem and will give in Sect. 4 bounds on the parameters of the problem which rule out this possibility. Basically, the parameters that we will encounter for breaking McEliece-type systems will avoid this phenomenon.

A Dedicated Algebraic Approach for Finding Rank 2 Elements in a Skew-Symmetric Matrix Code. There are many methods which can be used to solve the MinRank problem, be they combinatorial [GC00], based on an algebraic modeling and solving them with Gröbner basis or XL type techniques, such as [KS99, FLP08, FSEDS10, VBC+19, BBC+20] or hybrid methods [BBB+22]. Basically all of them can be adapted to the symmetric MinRank problem. One of the most attractive methods for solving the problem for the parameters we have is the Support Minors approach introduced in [BBC+20]. Unfortunately due to the symmetric or skew-symmetric form of the matrix space, solving the corresponding system with the proposed XL type approach behaves very differently from a generic matrix space and its complexity seems very delicate to predict. For this reason, we have devised another way of solving the corresponding MinRank problem in characteristic 2. First, we took advantage that the algebraic system describing the variety of skew-symmetric matrices of rank $\leqslant 2$ has already been studied in the literature and Gröbner bases are known. Next, we add to this Gröbner basis the linear equations expressing that the skew-symmetric matrix should also belong to the matrix code of relations. This allows us to understand the complexity of solving the corresponding algebraic system. It turns out that the Gröbner basis computation behaves very differently when applied to the skew-symmetric matrix space associated with a random code rather than with a Goppa or an alternant code. This clearly yields a way to distinguish a Goppa code or more generally an alternant code from a random code. Contrarily to the distinguisher that has been devised in [FGO+11] which works only for a very restricted set of parameters, this new distinguisher basically works already for rates above $\frac{2}{3}$. This concerns an overwhelming proportion of code parameters that have been proposed (and all parameters of the NIST submission [ABC+22]). Interestingly enough, for the code parameters where [FGO+11] works, our new distinguisher coincides with it. Despite the fact that its complexity increases significantly when [FGO+11] does not apply anymore, it stays subexponential as long as the co-dimension of the code is sublinear in the length. Interestingly enough in this regime, its asymptotic exponent is below those of all known key recovery or message attacks. For the concrete parameters of the McEliece NIST submission [ABC+22], its complexity is too complex to threaten the cryptosystem, but is smaller than known key recovery attacks for most of the parameters of the submission.

A New Attack Exploiting Rank Defective Matrices in the Matrix Code of Relations. There is another way to exploit this matrix code which consists in observing that for a restricted set of code parameters (i) the degree r of the alternant code is less than $q + 1$ or $q - 1$ in the Goppa case, (ii) the code is distinguishable with the method of [FGO+11], a rank defective matrix in the matrix code of relations leaks information on the secret polynomial structure of the code. This can be used to mount a simple attack by just (i) looking for such matrices by picking enough random elements in the matrix code and verifying if they are rank defective (ii) and then exploiting the information gathered here to recover the support and multiplier of the alternant/Goppa code.

Summary of the Contributions. In a nutshell, our contributions are

- We introduce a new concept, namely the matrix code of quadratic relations which can be derived from the extended dual of the Goppa/alternant code for which we want to recover the polynomial structure. This is a subspace of symmetric or skew-symmetric matrices depending on the field characteristic over which the code is defined which has the particular feature of containing very low-rank matrices (rank 3 in odd characteristic, rank 2 in characteristic 2) which are related to the secret key of the corresponding McEliece cryptosystem.
- We devise a dedicated algebraic approach for finding these low-rank matrices in characteristic 2 when this subspace of matrices is formed by skew-symmetric matrices. It takes advantage of the fact that we know a Gröbner basis for the algebraic system expressing the fact that a skew-symmetric matrix is of rank $\leqslant 2$ based on the nullity of all minors of size greater than 2. This system can be solved with the help of Gröbner bases techniques. It turns out that the solving process behaves differently when applied to the matrix code of quadratic relations associated with a random linear code rather than with a Goppa or an alternant code. This gives a way to distinguish a Goppa code or more generally an alternant code from a random code which contrarily to the distinguisher of [FGO+11, FGO+13] works for virtually all code parameters relevant to cryptography (recall that the latter works only for very high rate Goppa or alternant codes). Moreover, the complexity of this system solving can be analyzed and an upper bound on the complexity of the distinguisher can be given. It is polynomial in the same regime of parameters when the distinguisher of [FGO+11] works. Even if its complexity increases significantly outside this regime, it is less complex than all known attacks in the sublinear co-dimension regime. For the concrete NIST submission parameters [ABC+22] its complexity is very far away from representing a threat, but is below the known key attacks for most of these parameters. This can be considered as a breakthrough in this area.
- Rank defective elements in this matrix space also reveal something about the hidden polynomial structure of the Goppa or alternant code in a certain parameter regime, namely when (i) the degree r of the alternant code is less than $q + 1$ or $q - 1$ in the Goppa case, (ii) the code is distinguishable with the

method of [FGO+11]. We use this to give a polynomial-time attack in such a case by just looking for rank defective elements with a random search. This complements nicely the polynomial attack which has been found in [BMT23] which also needs that the code is distinguishable with [FGO+11], but works in the reverse parameter regime $r \geqslant q+1$ (and has also additional restrictions, code alphabet size either binary or ternary and it does not work for Goppa codes). Note that in conjunction with the filtration of [BMT23], this new attack works for *any* distinguishable generic alternant code. This gives yet another example of a case when the distinguisher of [FGO+11] turns into an actual attack of the scheme.

Important Note. Proofs of all results and more experimental results can be found at [CMT23].

2   Notation and Preliminaries

2.1   Notation

General Notation. $[a, b]$ indicates the closed integer interval between a and b. We will make use of two notations for finite fields, $\mathbb{F}_q$ denotes the finite field with q elements, but sometimes we do not indicate the size of it when it is not important to do so and simply write $\mathbb{F}$. Instead, a general field (not necessarily finite) is denoted by $\mathbb{K}$ and its algebraic closure by $\overline{\mathbb{K}}$.

Vector and Matrix Notation. Vectors are indicated by lowercase bold letters x and matrices by uppercase bold letters M. Given a function f acting on $\mathbb{F}$ and a vector $x = (x_i)_{1 \leqslant i \leqslant n} \in \mathbb{F}$, the expression $f(x)$ is the component-wise mapping of f on x, i.e. $f(x) = (f(x_i))_{1 \leqslant i \leqslant n}$. We will even apply this with functions f acting on $\mathbb{F} \times \mathbb{F}$: for instance for two vectors x and y in $\mathbb{F}^n$ and two positive integers a and b we denote by $x^a y^b$ the vector $(x_i^a y_i^b)_{1 \leqslant i \leqslant n}$. We will use the same operation over matrices, but in order to avoid confusion with the matrix product, we use for a matrix $A = (a_{i,j})_{i,j}$ the notation $A^{(q)}$ which stands for the entries of A all raised to the power q, i.e. the entry (i, j) of $A^{(q)}$ is equal to $a_{i,j}^q$. The scalar product between $x = (x_i)_{1 \leqslant i \leqslant n} \in \mathbb{F}^n$ and $y = (y_i)_{1 \leqslant i \leqslant n} \in \mathbb{F}^n$ is denoted by $x \cdot y$ and is defined by $x \cdot y = \sum_{i=1}^{n} x_i y_i$.

Symmetric and Skew-Symmetric Matrices. The set of $k \times k$ symmetric matrices over $\mathbb{F}$ is denoted by $\mathbf{Sym}(k, \mathbb{F})$, whereas the corresponding set of skew-symmetric matrices is denoted by $\mathbf{Skew}(k, \mathbb{F}_q)$.

Vector Spaces. Vector spaces are indicated by $\mathscr{C}$. For two vector spaces $\mathscr{C}$ and $\mathscr{D}$, the notation $\mathscr{C} \oplus \mathscr{D}$ means that the two vector spaces are in direct sum, i.e. that $\mathscr{C} \cap \mathscr{D} = \{0\}$. The $\mathbb{F}$-linear space generated by $x_1, \ldots, x_m \in \mathbb{F}^n$ is denoted by $\langle x_1, \ldots, x_m \rangle_{\mathbb{F}}$.

Codes. A linear code $\mathscr{C}$ of length n and dimension k over $\mathbb{F}$ is a k dimensional subspace of $\mathbb{F}^n$. We refer to it as an $[n, k]$-code.

Ideals. Ideals are indicated by calligraphic $\mathcal{I}$. Given a sequence S of polynomials, $\mathcal{I}(S)$ refers to the polynomial ideal generated by such sequence. Given the polynomials $f_1, \ldots, f_m$, we denote by $\mathcal{I}(f_1, \ldots, f_m)$ the ideal generated by them. The variety associated with a polynomial ideal $\mathcal{I} \subseteq \mathbb{K}[x_1, \ldots, x_n]$ is indicated by $\boldsymbol{V}(\mathcal{I})$ and defined as $\boldsymbol{V}(\mathcal{I}) = \{\boldsymbol{a} \in \overline{\mathbb{K}}^n \mid \forall f \in \mathcal{I}, \; f(\boldsymbol{a}) = 0\}$.

2.2   Distinguishable Alternant or Goppa Code

We will frequently use here the term *distinguishable alternant/Goppa* (in the sense of [FGO+11]) code. They are defined as

Definition 10 (Square–distinguishable alternant/Goppa code). *A (generic) alternant code $\mathscr{A}_r(\boldsymbol{x}, \boldsymbol{y})$ of length n over $\mathbb{F}_q$ and extension degree m is said to be* square–distinguishable *if*

$$n > \binom{rm+1}{2} - \frac{m}{2}(r-1)\left((2e_{\mathscr{A}}+1)r - 2\frac{q^{e_{\mathscr{A}}+1}-1}{q-1}\right) \qquad (4)$$

where $e_{\mathscr{A}} \overset{def}{=} \max\{i \in \mathbb{N} \mid r \geqslant q^i + 1\} = \lfloor \log_q(r-1) \rfloor$.
A Goppa code $\mathscr{G}(\boldsymbol{x}, \Gamma)$ of the same parameters is said to be square–distinguishable *if*

$$n > \binom{rm+1}{2} - \frac{m}{2}(r-1)(r-2), \qquad\qquad\qquad \text{if } r < q-1 \quad (5)$$

$$n > \binom{rm+1}{2} - \frac{m}{2}r\left((2e_{\mathscr{G}}+1)r - 2(q-1)q^{e_{\mathscr{G}}-1}-1\right), \qquad \text{otherwise,} \quad (6)$$

where $e_{\mathscr{G}} \overset{def}{=} \min\{i \in \mathbb{N} \mid r \leqslant (q-1)^2 q^i\} + 1 = \left\lceil \log_q\left(\frac{r}{(q-1)^2}\right)\right\rceil + 1$.

This definition is basically due to the fact that there is a way to distinguish such codes from random codes in this case [FGO+11]. For our purpose, it is better to use the point of view of [MT22] and to notice that they are distinguishable because the computation of the dimension of the square of the dual code leads to a result which is different from n and $\binom{rm+1}{2}$ (which is the expected dimension of the square of a dual code of dimension rm). This is shown by

Theorem 1 ([MT22]). *Let $e_{\mathscr{A}}$ and $e_{\mathscr{G}}$ be defined as in Definition 10. For an alternant code $\mathbb{F}_q$ of length n and extension degree m we have*

$$\dim_{\mathbb{F}_q}(\mathscr{A}_r(\boldsymbol{x}, \boldsymbol{y})^{\perp})^{*2} \leqslant \min\left\{n, \binom{rm+1}{2} - \frac{m}{2}(r-1)\left((2e_{\mathscr{A}}+1)r - 2\frac{q^{e_{\mathscr{A}}+1}-1}{q-1}\right)\right\}.$$
$$(7)$$

For a Goppa code $\mathscr{G}(\boldsymbol{x}, \Gamma)$ of length n over $\mathbb{F}_q$ with Goppa polynomial $\Gamma(X) \in \mathbb{F}_{q^m}[X]$ of degree r we have

$$\dim(\mathscr{G}(\boldsymbol{x}, \Gamma)^{\perp})^{*2} \leqslant \min\left\{n, \binom{rm+1}{2} - \frac{m}{2}(r-1)(r-2)\right\}, \quad \text{if } r < q-1 \qquad (8)$$

$$\dim(\mathscr{G}(\boldsymbol{x}, \Gamma)^{\perp})^{*2} \leqslant \min\left\{n, \binom{rm+1}{2} - \frac{m}{2}r\left((2e_{\mathscr{G}}+1)r - 2(q-1)q^{e_{\mathscr{G}}-1}-1\right)\right\}, \quad \text{otherwise.} \quad (9)$$

3   Invariants of the Matrix Code of Quadratic Relations

3.1   Changing the Basis

The fundamental objects that we have introduced, namely the code of relations $\mathscr{C}_{rel}(\mathcal{V})$ and the corresponding matrix code $\mathscr{C}_{mat}(\mathcal{V})$ both depend on the basis $\mathcal{V}$ which is chosen. However, all these matrix codes are isometric for the rank metric, namely the metric d between matrices given by $d(\boldsymbol{X}, \boldsymbol{Y}) \overset{\text{def}}{=} \mathbf{Rank}(\boldsymbol{X} - \boldsymbol{Y})$. This holds because of the following result:

Proposition 4. *Let $\mathcal{A}$ and $\mathcal{B}$ be two bases of a same $[n, k]$ $\mathbb{F}$-linear code $\mathscr{C}$, with $\mathbb{F}$. Then $\mathscr{C}_{mat}(\mathcal{A})$ and $\mathscr{C}_{mat}(\mathcal{B})$ are isometric matrix codes, i.e. there exists $\boldsymbol{P} \in \mathbf{GL}_k(\mathbb{F})$ such that*

$$\mathscr{C}_{mat}(\mathcal{A}) = \boldsymbol{P}^{\mathsf{T}}\mathscr{C}_{mat}(\mathcal{B})\boldsymbol{P}. \tag{10}$$

The matrix $\boldsymbol{P}$ coincides with the change of basis matrix between $\mathcal{A}$ and $\mathcal{B}$.

This Proposition is proved in [CMT23, Appendix B]. This result implies that there are several fundamental quantities which stay invariant when considering different bases, such as for instance

– the distribution of ranks $\{n_i, 0 \leqslant i \leqslant k\}$ where n_i is the number of matrices in $\mathscr{C}_{mat}(\mathcal{V})$ of rank i;
– the dimension of $\mathscr{C}_{mat}(\mathcal{V})$, more precisely:

Proposition 5. *Let $\mathscr{C} \subseteq \mathbb{F}^n$ be an $[n, k]$ linear code with ordered basis $\mathcal{V}$. Then*

$$\dim_{\mathbb{F}} \mathscr{C}_{mat}(\mathcal{V}) = \dim_{\mathbb{F}} \mathscr{C}_{rel}(\mathcal{V}) = \binom{k+1}{2} - \dim_{\mathbb{F}} \mathscr{C}^{\star 2}.$$

(this result is proved in [CMT23, §3])

We will sometime avoid specifying the basis, and simply write $\mathscr{C}_{mat}$, when referring to invariants for the code.

4   Low-Rank Matrices in $\mathscr{C}_{mat}$

4.1   Low-Rank Matrices from Quadratic Relations in [FGO+13]

By Proposition 4, all the matrix codes $\mathscr{C}_{mat}(\mathcal{B})$ are isometric for any choice of basis $\mathcal{B}$. We will be interested here in showing that the matrix code of quadratic relations associated to the extension over $\mathbb{F}_{q^m}$ of the dual of an alternant code $\mathscr{A}_r(\boldsymbol{x}, \boldsymbol{y})$ defined over $\mathbb{F}_q$ contains many low rank matrices. This is due to the fact that this code contains the GRS codes $\mathbf{GRS}_r(\boldsymbol{x}^{q^i}, \boldsymbol{y}^{q^i})$ for all $i \in [\![0, m-1]\!]$ (Proposition 3). This will be clear if we choose the basis appropriately. We can namely choose the following ordered basis, that we call *canonical basis*:

$$\mathcal{A} = (a_0, \cdots, a_{r-1}, a_0^q, \cdots, a_{r-1}^q, \cdots, a_0^{q^{m-1}}, \cdots, a_{r-1}^{q^{m-1}})$$
$$= (\boldsymbol{y}, \boldsymbol{xy}, \ldots, \boldsymbol{x}^{r-1}\boldsymbol{y}, \ldots, \boldsymbol{y}^{q^{m-1}}, (\boldsymbol{xy})^{q^{m-1}}, \ldots, (\boldsymbol{x}^{r-1}\boldsymbol{y})^{q^{m-1}}). \tag{11}$$

There are simple quadratic relations between the $a_i^{q^j}$ owing to the trivial algebraic relations introduced in [FGO+13]: $(x^a y)^{q^l} \star (x^b y)^{q^u} = (x^c y)^{q^l} \star (x^d y)^{q^u}$ if $aq^l + bq^u = cq^l + dq^u$. This amounts to the quadratic relation between the basis elements

$$a_a^{q^l} \star a_b^{q^u} - a_c^{q^l} \star a_d^{q^u} = 0. \tag{12}$$

It is readily seen that matrix of $\mathscr{C}_{\mathrm{mat}}(\mathcal{B})$ corresponding to this quadratic relation is of rank 4 with the exception of the case $c = d$ and $l = u$ where it is of rank 3 (odd characteristic) or rank 2 (characteristic 2). Indeed, if we reorder the basis $\mathcal{B}$ such that it starts with $a_a^{q^l}, a_b^{q^l}, a_c^{q^l}$, then it is readily seen that the matrix $M \in \mathscr{C}_{\mathrm{mat}}(\mathcal{B})$ corresponding to (12) has only zeros with the exception of the first 3×3 block M' which is given by

$$M' = \begin{bmatrix} 0 & 1 & 0 \\ 1 & 0 & 0 \\ 0 & 0 & -2 \end{bmatrix} \text{ (odd characteristic)}, \quad M' = \begin{bmatrix} 0 & 1 & 0 \\ 1 & 0 & 0 \\ 0 & 0 & 0 \end{bmatrix} \text{ (characteristic 2)}.$$

This leads to the following fact

Fact 1. *Consider the alternant code $\mathscr{A}_r(\boldsymbol{x}, \boldsymbol{y})$ of extension degree m and let $\mathscr{C}_{\mathrm{mat}}(\mathcal{A})$ be the corresponding matrix code associated to the basis choice (11). Let $l \in [\![0, m-1]\!]$ and a, b, c in $[\![0, r-1]\!]$ be such that $a+b = 2c$. Then the matrix of $\mathscr{C}_{\mathrm{mat}}(\mathcal{A})$ corresponding to the quadratic relation $a_a^{q^l} \star a_b^{q^l} - \left(a_c^{q^l}\right)^{\star 2} = 0$ is of rank 3 in odd characteristic and of rank 2 in characteristic 2.*

This already shows that there are many rank 2 or 3 matrices in $\mathscr{C}_{\mathrm{mat}}$ corresponding to an alternant code. But it will turn out some subsets of the set of rank $\leqslant 2$ matrices of $\mathscr{C}_{\mathrm{mat}}$ form a vector space of matrices. Moreover, depending on the fact that the alternant code has a Goppa structure we will have even more low rank matrices as we show below. We namely have in characteristic 2

Proposition 6. *Let $\mathscr{A}_r(\boldsymbol{x}, \boldsymbol{y})$ be an alternant code of extension degree m and order r over a field of characteristic 2. Then $\mathscr{C}_{\mathrm{mat}}$ contains $\lfloor \frac{r-1}{2} \rfloor$-dimensional subspaces of rank-($\leqslant 2$) matrices. If $\mathscr{A}_r(\boldsymbol{x}, \boldsymbol{y})$ is a binary Goppa code with a square-free Goppa polynomial, then $\mathscr{C}_{\mathrm{mat}}$ contains $(r-1)$-dimensional subspaces of rank-($\leqslant 2$) matrices.*

We can also give a lower bound on the number of such matrices as shown by

Proposition 7. *Let $\mathscr{A}_r(\boldsymbol{x}, \boldsymbol{y})$ be an alternant code in characteristic 2 and extension degree m. The matrix code of quadratic relationships $\mathscr{C}_{\mathrm{mat}}$ contains at least $\Omega(m(q^{m(r-2)})$ matrices of rank 2.*

In the particular case of binary Goppa codes associated to a square-free polynomial (i.e. the standard choice in a McEliece cryptosystem) we have

Proposition 8. *Let $\mathscr{G}(\boldsymbol{x}, \Gamma)$ be a binary Goppa code of extension degree m with Γ a square-free polynomial of degree r. Then $\mathscr{C}_{\mathrm{mat}}$ contains at least $m\frac{(q^{mr}-1)(q^{m(r-1)}-1)}{q^{2m}-1}$ matrices of rank 2.*

These propositions are proved in [CMT23, Appendix C.1]. It also turns out that for the "canonical" choice mentioned above (namely when choosing the basis $\mathcal{A}$ given in (11)) under certain circumstances, $\mathscr{C}_{\mathrm{mat}}$ contains the subspace of block diagonal skew symmetric matrices with blocks of size r

Proposition 9. *Let $\mathscr{G}(\boldsymbol{x}, \Gamma)$ be a binary $[n, n-rm]$ Goppa code with Γ a square-free polynomial of degree r and let $\mathcal{A}$ be the canonical basis of $\mathscr{G}(\boldsymbol{x}, \Gamma)_{\mathbb{F}_{q^m}}^{\perp}$ given in (11) with $\boldsymbol{y} = \frac{1}{\Gamma(\boldsymbol{x})}$. Then $\mathscr{C}_{mat}(\mathcal{A})$ contains the space of block-diagonal skew-symmetric matrices with $r \times r$ blocks.*

4.2 The Random Case

We have described in the previous subsection a family of matrices in $\mathscr{C}_{\mathrm{mat}}(\mathcal{A})$ with a small rank. In particular, we found rank 3 matrices for odd characteristic and rank 2 matrices for even characteristic. In the case of binary Goppa codes with square-free Goppa polynomial, the subspace generated by such rank 2 matrices is even bigger. Since the two codes $\mathscr{C}_{\mathrm{mat}}(\mathcal{A})$ and $\mathscr{C}_{\mathrm{mat}}(\mathcal{B})$ have the same weight distribution, the same number of low-rank matrices must exist for $\mathscr{C}_{\mathrm{mat}}(\mathcal{B})$ as well. We may wonder if such low-rank matrices exist in the matrix code of relationships $\mathscr{C}_{\mathrm{mat}}(\mathcal{R})$ of an $[n, rm]$ random $\mathbb{F}_{q^m}$-linear code $\mathscr{R}$ with basis $\mathcal{R}$. This can be determined by computing the Gilbert-Varshamov distance d_{GV} for spaces of symmetric (resp. skew-symmetric) matrices, which is the smallest d such that $|\mathscr{C}_{\mathrm{mat}}(\mathcal{R})||B_d^{(\mathbf{Sym})}| \geqslant |\mathbf{Sym}(rm, \mathbb{F}_{q^m})|$ (resp. $card\mathscr{C}_{\mathrm{mat}}(\mathcal{R})|B_d^{(\mathbf{Skew})}| \geqslant |\mathbf{Skew}(rm, \mathbb{F}_{q^m})|$) where $B_d^{(\mathbf{Sym})}$ (resp. $B_d^{(\mathbf{Skew})}$) is the ball of radius d (with respect to the rank metric) of the space of symmetric (resp. skew-symmetric) matrices. The rationale of this definition is that it can be proved that for a random linear code $\mathscr{C}$ the probability of having a non zero matrix of rank $\leqslant d$ in $\mathscr{C}$ is upper-bounded by the ratio $\frac{|\mathscr{C}||B_d^{(\mathbf{Sym})}|}{|\mathbf{Sym}(rm, \mathbb{F}_{q^m})|}$ in the symmetric case. A similar bound holds in the skew-symmetric case. In a low dimension scenario, more precisely when $\binom{rm+1}{2} \leqslant n$, the code $\mathscr{C}_{\mathrm{mat}}(\mathcal{R})$ is expected to be trivial. This corresponds indeed to the square distinguishable regime. We will then assume $\binom{rm+1}{2} > n$.

Proposition 10. *Let $\mathscr{R} \subset \mathbb{F}_{q^m}^n$ be a random code of dimension rm with basis $\mathcal{R}$ and let $\binom{rm+1}{2} > n$. Under the assumption that $\mathscr{C}_{mat}(\mathcal{R})$ has the same rank weight distribution as a random linear matrix code, it contains matrices of rank $\leqslant d$ with non-negligible probability iff $n \leqslant drm - \binom{d}{2}$ (symmetric case), or $n \leqslant (d+1)rm - \binom{d+1}{2}$ (skew-symmetric case, characteristic 2, d even).*

This proposition is proved in [CMT23, Appendix C.2]. In particular, we expect rank-3 symmetric matrices in $\mathscr{C}_{\mathrm{mat}}(\mathcal{R})$ in odd characteristic or rank-2 skew-symmetric matrices in $\mathscr{C}_{\mathrm{mat}}(\mathcal{R})$ in characteristic 2 for

$$n \leqslant 3rm - 3. \qquad (13)$$

We observe that for all security levels of Classic McEliece [ABC+22], the code rate is such that $n = \alpha rm$ with $\alpha \in (3.5, 5)$. This means that any algorithm that finds low-rank matrices in $\mathscr{C}_{\mathrm{mat}}(\mathcal{R})$ represents a distinguisher between Goppa codes (and more in general alternant codes) and random linear codes for Classic McEliece rates.

5   A New Distinguisher of Alternant and Goppa Codes in Characteristic 2

We are going to focus here on the particular case of characteristic 2 where we want to find rank 2 matrices in the matrix code of quadratic relations. We are going to consider a particular algebraic modeling for finding matrices of this kind for which we can estimate the running time of Gröbner bases algorithms for solving it. We will show that the behavior of the Gröbner basis computation is quite different when applied to the matrix code corresponding to an alternant (or a Goppa) code rather than to the matrix code corresponding to a random code of the same dimension and length as the alternant/Goppa code. This provides clearly a distinguisher of an alternant or Goppa code whose complexity can be estimated. Interestingly enough, it coincides with the square distinguisher of [FGO+11] for the parameters where the latter applies, but it also permits to distinguish other parameters and can distinguish Goppa or alternant codes of rate in the range $[\frac{2}{3}, 1]$, contrarily to the former which works only for rate extremely close to 1.

5.1   A Modeling Coming from the Pfaffian Ideal

We are first going to give an algebraic modelling expressing that a skew-symmetric matrix M with arbitrary entries is of rank $\leqslant 2$. To do so, we express the fact that all minors of size 4 should be zero. This implies that M should be of rank $\leqslant 2$, because any skew-symmetric matrix is of even rank and therefore cannot have rank 3. In other words, let us consider the generic skew-symmetric matrix $M = (m_{i,j})_{i,j} \in \mathbf{Skew}(s, \mathbb{F}_{q^m})$, whose entries $m_{i,j}$ with $1 \leqslant i < j \leqslant s$ are independent variables. Let $\boldsymbol{m} = (m_{i,j})_{1 \leqslant i < j \leqslant s}$. We will write sometimes $m_{j,i}$ with $i < j$, this must just be seen as an alias for $m_{i,j}$ and not as another variable. We denote by $\mathbf{Minors}(M, d)$ the set of all minors of M of size d. The set of specializations of M that provide rank 2 matrices is the variety of the determinantal ideal generated by $\mathbf{Minors}(M, 3)$. We refer the reader to [MS05, § 15.1] Since there do not exist rank 3 matrices in $\mathbf{Sym}(s, \mathbb{F}_{q^m})$, the ideal generated by $\mathbf{Minors}(M, 4)$ leads to the same variety.

The homogeneous ideal $\mathcal{I}(\mathbf{Minors}(M, 2l))$ is not radical. The determinant of a generic skew-symmetric matrix of size $2l \times 2l$ is the square of a polynomial of degree l, called *Pfaffian* [Wim12, § 1.1]. It is well-known that the corresponding radical ideal is generated by the square roots of a subset of minors, namely those corresponding to a submatrix with the same subset for row and column indexes. Note that such matrices are skew-symmetric as well, and thus their determinant is the square of a Pfaffian polynomial. In particular, we define

Definition 11 (Pfaffian ideal for rank 2). *The Pfaffian ideal of rank 2 for M in characteristic 2 is*

$$\mathcal{P}_2(M) \overset{\text{def}}{=} \mathcal{I}\left(m_{i,j}m_{k,l} + m_{i,k}m_{j,l} + m_{i,l}m_{j,k} \mid 1 \leqslant i < j < k < l \leqslant s\right), \quad (14)$$

We have

Proposition 11 ([HT92, Theorem 5.1]). *The basis $\{m_{i,j}m_{k,l} + m_{i,k}m_{j,l} + m_{i,l}m_{j,k} \mid 1 \leqslant i < j < k < l \leqslant s\}$ is a Gröbner basis of $\mathcal{P}_2(M)$ with respect to a suitable order.*

Another straightforward result, proved in [CMT23, §5.1], is that

Proposition 12. *We have $V(\mathcal{P}_2(M)) = V(\mathcal{I}(\mathbf{Minors}(M, 4)))$.*

Our modeling takes advantage of the deep knowledge we have about this ideal. We express now the fact that a matrix M of size s belongs to some matrix code $\mathscr{C}_{\text{mat}}$ associated to an $[n, k]$ code (which implies that $s = n - k$ since we are looking at quadratic relations on the *dual* code) by $t \overset{\text{def}}{=} \binom{s}{2} - \dim \mathscr{C}_{\text{mat}}$ linear equations $L_1 = 0, \ldots, L_t = 0$ linking the $m_{i,j}$'s. The algebraic modeling we use to express that an element M of $\mathscr{C}_{\text{mat}}$ is of rank $\leqslant 2$ uses these t linear equations and the Gröbner basis of the Pfaffian ideal. In other words, we have the following algebraic modeling

Modeling 1 ($M \in \mathscr{C}_{mat}$, $\mathbf{Rank}(M) \leqslant 2$)

- $\binom{s}{4}$ *quadratic equations $m_{i,j}m_{k,l} + m_{i,k}m_{j,l} + m_{i,l}m_{j,k} = 0$ where $1 \leqslant i < j < k < l \leqslant s$*
- $t \overset{\text{def}}{=} \binom{s}{2} - \dim \mathscr{C}_{mat}$ *linear equations $L_1 = 0, \ldots, L_t = 0$ linking the m_{ij}'s expressing the fact that M belongs to $\mathscr{C}_{mat}$.*

5.2   Gröbner Bases and Hilbert Series

We will be interested in computing the Hilbert series of the ideal corresponding to Modeling 1 because it will turn out to behave differently depending on the code we use for defining the associated matrix code $\mathscr{C}_{\text{mat}}$. This will lead to a distinguisher of alternant or Goppa codes. Given a homogeneous ideal $\mathcal{I} \in \mathbb{K}[z]$, $z = (z_1, \ldots, z_n)$, the Hilbert function of the ring $R = \mathbb{K}[z]/\mathcal{I}$ is defined as

$$HF_R(d) \overset{\text{def}}{=} \dim_{\mathbb{K}}(R) = \dim_{\mathbb{K}}(\mathbb{K}[z]_d) - \dim_{\mathbb{K}}(\mathcal{I}_d),$$

where $\mathbb{K}[z]_d = \{f \in \mathbb{K}[z] \mid \deg(f) = d\}$ and $\mathcal{I}_d = \mathcal{I} \cap \mathbb{K}[z]_d$. Then the Hilbert series of R is the formal series $HS_R(t) \overset{\text{def}}{=} \sum_{d \geqslant 0} HF_R(d) t^d$. We are interested in computing individual terms $HF_R(d)$. This can be done by computing the rank of the Macaulay matrix at degree d by taking m generators of the ideal $\mathcal{I}$ (see [CMT23, Appendix A]). An upper bound on its cost can therefore be derived directly from [BFS15, Proposition 1]:

Proposition 13. *Let* $F = \{f_1, \ldots, f_m\} \subset \mathbb{K}[z_1, \ldots, z_n]$ *be a homogeneous system. Let* $\mathcal{I}$ *be the corresponding ideal. The term* $HF_R(d)$ *of degree* d *of the Hilbert function of* $R = \mathbb{K}[\boldsymbol{z}]/\mathcal{I}$ *can be computed in time bounded by*

$$\mathcal{O}\left(md\binom{n+d-1}{d}^{\omega}\right),$$

where ω *is the linear algebra exponent.*

Fortunately, the Hilbert function for our Pfaffian ideal is known. We define the quotient ring $R(\boldsymbol{M}) = \mathbb{F}_{q^m}[\boldsymbol{m}]/\mathcal{P}_2(\boldsymbol{M})$. The Hilbert function (or equivalently the Hilbert series) of $R(\boldsymbol{M})$ is well-known:

Proposition 14 ([GK04, (from) Theorem 1]). *Let* $\boldsymbol{M} = (m_{i,j})_{i,j}$ *be the generic* $s \times s$ *skew-symmetric matrix over* $\mathbb{F}$. *Then* $\dim \boldsymbol{V}(\mathcal{P}_2(\boldsymbol{M})) = 2s - 3$ *and*

$$HF_{R(\boldsymbol{M})}(d) = \binom{s+d-2}{d}^2 - \binom{s+d-2}{d+1}\binom{s+d-2}{d-1} = \frac{1}{s+d-1}\binom{s+d-1}{d+1}\binom{s+d-1}{d},$$

$$HS_{R(\boldsymbol{M})}(z) = \frac{\sum_{d=0}^{s-3}\left(\binom{s-2}{d}^2 - \binom{s-3}{d-1}\binom{s-1}{d+1}\right)z^d}{(1-z)^{2s-3}}.$$

Modeling 1 adds linear equations to it expressing the fact that the matrix should also be in the matrix code of quadratic relations. There is one handy tool that allows to compute the Hilbert series obtained by enriching with polynomials an ideal whose Hilbert series is known.

Proposition 15 ([Bar04, Lemma 3.3.2]). *As long as there are no reductions to 0 in the F5 algorithm, the Hilbert function* $HF_{\mathbb{K}[\boldsymbol{x}]/\mathcal{I}(f_1,\ldots,f_m)}(d)$ *satisfies the following recursive formula:*

- $HF_{\mathbb{K}[\boldsymbol{x}]/\mathcal{I}(f_1,\ldots,f_m)}(d) = HF_{\mathbb{K}[\boldsymbol{x}]/\mathcal{I}(f_1,\ldots,f_{m-1})}(d) - HF_{\mathbb{K}[\boldsymbol{x}]/\mathcal{I}(f_1,\ldots,f_{m-1})}(d - \deg(f_m))$.

Essentially, reductions to 0 in F5 [Fau02] correspond to "non generic" reductions to 0 and experimentally we have not observed this behavior for Modeling 1 when we add the linear equations expressing that $\boldsymbol{M}$ belongs to the matrix code $\mathscr{C}_{\mathrm{mat}}$ of relations associated to a random linear code.

5.3 Analysis of the Hilbert Series for the Pfaffian Ideal

We will from now on consider that the matrix code $\mathscr{C}_{\mathrm{mat}}$ of quadratic relations is associated to a code $\mathscr{C}$ over $\mathbb{F}_{q^m}$ of parameters $[n, mr]$ which are the same as those of the extended dual code $\mathscr{A}_r(\boldsymbol{x}, \boldsymbol{y})_{\mathbb{F}_{q^m}}^{\perp}$ of an alternant code $\mathscr{A}_r(\boldsymbol{x}, \boldsymbol{y})^{\perp}$ of length n over $\mathbb{F}_q$ and extension degree m which we assume to be of generic dimension $k = n - mr$. We will from now on also assume that the $[n, mr]$ code $\mathscr{C}$ we consider satisfies $\dim \mathscr{C}^{*2} = n$. Equivalently, we suppose that the code is not square distinguishable and will look for another and more powerful distinguisher. This corresponds to the generic case of a random code as soon as $\binom{rm+1}{2} \geqslant n$

and to duals of alternant codes/Goppa codes that are not square–distinguishable. Recall that, from Proposition 5,

$$\dim_{\mathbb{F}_{q^m}} \mathscr{C}_{\mathrm{mat}}(\mathcal{V}) = \binom{mr+1}{2} - \dim_{\mathbb{F}_{q^m}} \mathscr{C}^{\star 2} = \binom{mr}{2} + mr - n = \binom{mr}{2} - k,$$

where $k \stackrel{\mathrm{def}}{=} n - rm$ is given above and corresponds to the dimension of the alternant code we are interested in. Notice that k is also the cardinality of the set of independent linear equations expressing in Modeling 1 that the $rm \times rm$ matrix M belongs to $\mathscr{C}_{\mathrm{mat}}$ since $\binom{rm}{2} - \dim \mathscr{C}_{\mathrm{mat}} = k$. We are now going to show that the Hilbert function of the ring $\mathbb{F}_{q^m}[\boldsymbol{m}]/(\mathcal{P}(\boldsymbol{M}) + \langle L_i \rangle_i)$ differs starting from some degree $\bar{d}$ depending on how the linear relations L_i's are defined (coming from $\mathscr{C}_{\mathrm{mat}}$ associated to a random $\mathscr{C}$ or to the extended dual of an alternant or Goppa code). We will assume that the parameters of our matrix code are such that we do not expect a matrix or rank 2 when $\mathscr{C}$ is random, which according to Proposition 10 holds as soon as $n > 3rm - 3$, *i.e.* essentially for $k/n > 2/3$.

Random Case. We assume that there are no reductions to 0 in F5 and that we can apply inductively Proposition 15

$$HF_{\mathbb{K}[z]/(\mathcal{I}+\mathcal{I}(L_1,\ldots,L_\ell))}(d) = HF_{\mathbb{K}[z]/(\mathcal{I}+\mathcal{I}(L_1,\ldots,L_{\ell-1}))}(d) - HF_{\mathbb{K}[z]/(\mathcal{I}+\mathcal{I}(L_1,\ldots,L_{\ell-1}))}(d-1)$$

$$= \cdots = \sum_{i=0}^{d} (-1)^i \binom{\ell}{i} HF_{\mathbb{K}[z]/\mathcal{I}}(d-i).$$

This holds as long as there are no reductions to 0 in F5. When there are, we expect that the Hilbert series at this degree is zero, which means that the induction formula when adding a polynomial f to $\mathcal{I}$ should be

$$HF_{\mathbb{K}[z]/(\mathcal{I}+\mathcal{I}(f))}(d) = \max(HF_{\mathbb{K}[z]/\mathcal{I}}(d) - HF_{\mathbb{K}[z]/\mathcal{I}}(d - \deg(f)), 0).$$

This leads to the following conjecture, supported by extensive experiments for several choices of matrix code dimension and matrix size.

Conjecture 1 (Random case). *Let $L_1, \ldots, L_k$ be the $k = n - rm$ linear relations relative to the matrix code $\mathscr{C}_{\mathrm{mat}}$ associated to a random $[n, rm]$-code as above. Let $\mathcal{P}_2^+(\boldsymbol{M}) \stackrel{\mathrm{def}}{=} \mathcal{P}_2(\boldsymbol{M}) + \mathcal{I}(L_1, \ldots, L_k)$. If $HF_{\mathbb{F}[m]/\mathcal{P}_2^+(\boldsymbol{M})}(d') > 0$ for all $d' < d$, then*

$$HF_{\mathbb{F}[\boldsymbol{m}]/\mathcal{P}_2^+(\boldsymbol{M})}(d) = \max\left(0, \sum_{i=0}^{d}(-1)^i \binom{k}{i} HF_{\mathbb{F}[\boldsymbol{m}]/\mathcal{P}_2(\boldsymbol{M})}(d-i)\right)$$

$$= \max\left(0, \sum_{i=0}^{d} \frac{(-1)^i}{rm+d-i-1}\binom{k}{i}\binom{rm+d-i-1}{d-i+1}\binom{rm+d-i-1}{d-i}\right). \quad (15)$$

Otherwise $HF_{\mathbb{F}[\boldsymbol{m}]/\mathcal{P}_2^+(\boldsymbol{M})}(d) = 0$.

Because we assume that Modeling 1 has only zero for solution in the case of a random code, there exists a d such that $HF_{\mathbb{F}[\boldsymbol{m}]/\mathcal{P}_2^+(\boldsymbol{M})}(d) = 0$. Experiments (see [CMT23, Appendix D.2]) lead to conjecture the following behavior:

Conjecture 2. *Let $\mathscr{C}_{mat}$ be the matrix code of relations originated by a random $[n, rm]$ code as above. Let $\mathcal{P}_2^+(M)$ the corresponding Pfaffian ideal and $d_{reg} = \min\{d : HF_{\mathbb{F}[m]/\mathcal{P}_2^+(M)}(d) = 0\}$. Then $d_{reg} \sim c\frac{(rm)^2}{n-rm}$ for a constant c equal or close to $\frac{1}{4}$.*

The value d_{reg} is known in the literature as the **degree of regularity**.

Alternant/Goppa Case. In the alternant/Goppa case however the Hilbert series never vanishes because the variety of solutions has always positive dimension. We can even lower its dimension by a rather large quantity. The proof of the next proposition can be found in [CMT23, §5.3].

Proposition 16. *Let $\mathscr{C}_{mat}$ be the matrix code of quadratic relations corresponding to the extended dual of an $[n, n - rm]$ binary Goppa code with a square-free Goppa polynomial. Let $\mathcal{P}_2^+(M)$ be the corresponding Pfaffian ideal. Then $\dim V(\mathcal{P}_2^+(M)) \geqslant 2r - 3$.*

More in general, we can upper bound the dimension of the variety using the following proposition, whose proof is given in [CMT23, Appendix D.1].

Proposition 17. *Let $\mathscr{C}_{mat}$ be the matrix code of quadratic relations corresponding to the extended dual of an $[n, n-rm]$ alternant code over a field of characteristic 2. Let $\mathcal{P}_2^+(M)$ be the corresponding Pfaffian ideal. Then $\dim V(\mathcal{P}_2^+(M)) \geqslant r - 2$.*

Remark 2. Equalities in the two previous propositions were met in the experiments we performed. Note that, comparing with Proposition 6, the Pfaffian ideal contains subspaces of dimension roughly half the dimension of the variety.

Now, as a consequence of the variety not being trivial, we have the following result, whose proof can be found in [CMT23, §5.3].

Proposition 18. *Let $\mathscr{C}_{mat}$ be the matrix code of quadratic relations corresponding to the extended dual of an $[n, n - rm]$ alternant code. Let $\mathcal{P}_2^+(M)$ be the corresponding Pfaffian ideal. For all $d \in \mathbb{N}$, $HF_{\mathbb{F}[m]/\mathcal{P}_2^+(M)}(d) > 0$.*

Computing the Hilbert function up to some degree d provides a distinguisher as soon as it assumes a different value depending on whether it refers to random or alternant/Goppa codes. Thanks to Proposition 18, this will happen at the latest at the degree of regularity d_{reg} corresponding to a random code.

An Extension of the Distinguisher of [FGO+11]. All these considerations lead to a very simple distinguisher of alternant or more specifically of Goppa codes, we compute for a code $HF_{\mathbb{F}_{q^m}[m]/\mathcal{P}_2^+(M)}(d)$ at a certain degree (where $\mathcal{P}_2^+(M)$ is the associated Pfaffian ideal), and say that it does not behave like a random code if this Hilbert function evaluated at degree d does not coincide with the formula we expect from a random code which is given in Conjecture 1. This leads us to the following definition

Definition 12 (*d*-distinguishable). *An* $[n, rm]$ $\mathbb{F}_{q^m}$*-linear code $\mathscr{C}$ is said to be d-distinguishable from a generic $[n, rm]$ linear code over $\mathbb{F}_{q^m}$ when the following holds*

$$HF_{\mathbb{F}_{q^m}[m]/\mathcal{P}_2^+(M)}(d) \neq \max\left(0, \sum_{i=0}^{d} \frac{(-1)^i}{rm+d-i-1}\binom{n-rm}{i}\binom{rm+d-i-1}{d-i+1}\binom{rm+d-i-1}{d-i}\right)$$

where $\mathcal{P}_2^+(M)$ is the Pfaffian ideal associated to $\mathscr{C}$.

Note that in general $HF_{\mathbb{F}_{q^m}[m]/\mathcal{P}_2^+(M)}(1) = \dim_{\mathbb{F}_{q^m}} \mathscr{C}_{\mathrm{mat}}(\mathcal{B})$, hence a different evaluation of the Hilbert function in degree 1 witnesses an unusually large dimension of $\mathscr{C}_{\mathrm{mat}}(\mathcal{B})$ and consequently an atypically small dimension of the square code. Indeed, this corresponds to the square distinguisher from [FGO+11]. Being 1-distinguishable is therefore being square-distinguishable. In this sense, this new distinguisher generalizes the square-distinguisher of [FGO+11].

We can readily find examples of codes which are not square-distinguishable (*i.e.* 1-distinguishable), but are distinguishable for higher values of d. We provide parameters of 2-distinguishable alternant/Goppa codes in [CMT23, §5.3].

For the time being, we have only a limited understanding of how $HF_{\mathbb{F}[m]/\mathcal{P}_2^+(M)}(d)$ behaves for alternant/Goppa codes. However in the case of binary square-free Goppa code, *i.e.* those used in McEliece's schemes, we can significantly improve upon the $HF_{\mathbb{F}[m]/\mathcal{P}_2^+(M)}(d) > 0$ lower bound as shown by

Theorem 2. *Let $\mathscr{G}(x, \Gamma)$ be a non distinguishable binary $[n, k = n-rm]$ Goppa code with Γ a square-free polynomial of degree r and extension degree m. Let $\mathcal{P}_2^+(M)$ be the corresponding Pfaffian ideal. Then, for all $d > 0$,*

$$HF_{\mathbb{F}_{2^m}[m]/\mathcal{P}_2^+(M)}(d) \geqslant m\left(\binom{r+d-2}{d}^2 - \binom{r+d-2}{d+1}\binom{r+d-2}{d-1}\right).$$

The proof is given in [CMT23, Appendix D]. Theorem 2 has some theoretical interest, because it shows that the distinguisher can be further improved by analyzing the matrix code of relations obtained from a Goppa code.

5.4   Complexity of Computing the Distinguisher and Comparison with Known Key and Message Attacks

Complexity of Computing the Distinguisher. The complexity of computing the distinguisher is upper-bounded by using Proposition 13

Proposition 19. *The computation of $HF_{\mathbb{F}_{q^m}[m]/\mathcal{P}_2^+(M)}(d)$ for the Pfaffian ideal associated to an $[n, mr]$-code has complexity*

$$\mathcal{O}\left(d\left(n-rm+\binom{rm}{4}\right)\left(\frac{\binom{rm}{2}+d-1}{d}\right)^{\omega}\right),$$

where ω is the linear algebra exponent.

However, in the case at hand, we can use Wiedemann's algorithm [Wie86], because (i) we know the Hilbert function for the Pfaffian ideal associated to an $[n, mr]$ random code, and know when it is equal to 0, namely for $d = d_{\text{reg}}$, (ii) we only have to check whether at degree $d = d_{\text{reg}}$ the Macaulay matrix $\text{Mac}(F, d_{\text{reg}})$ has a non zero kernel, (iii) this Macaulay matrix is sparse, since the Pfaffian equations contain only 3 quadratic monomials, and therefore the number of entries in a row of $\text{Mac}(F, d_{\text{reg}})$ is upper-bounded with the number of nonzero entries of the polynomial $m^\alpha L(m)$, where m is the variable vector of the matrix entries, $L = 0$ is one of the k linear equations and α is a multi-index exponent of multi-degree $d_{\text{reg}} - 1$. This quantity clearly coincides with the number of nonzero entries of L itself and can be upper bounded by $\binom{rm}{2} - k + 1$ thanks to Gaussian elimination. There is another point that is potentially problematic for applying Wiedemann's algorithm. It is the fact that the Macaulay matrix (call it M) is non square (it has more rows than columns). The standard trick consisting in choosing randomly a subset of rows so that the resulting submatrix is square does not work here, because there are many small subsets of rows in the Macaulay matrix M that are not linearly independent. The effect of this is that this strategy typically tends to give rank defective submatrices even if the whole matrix is not rank defective. There is an easy way to settle this issue in the case at hand. Let us say that the Macaulay matrix has a rows and b columns. We choose a random matrix N in $\mathbb{F}_{q^m}^{b \times a}$ with row weight $\approx$ the average column weight w_2 of M and column weight close to the average row weight w_1 of M. If we use the sparseness of M to perform the multiplication (which is something we do here), multiplication by N has the same cost as multiplication by M. We claim that in the case at hand, $N \cdot M$ has typically the same rank as a random square matrix when M is of full rank, which would give the following behavior.

Conjecture 1. If M is of full rank b, $\text{prob}(\mathbf{Rank}(N \cdot M) = b) = 1 - \mathcal{O}(q^{-m})$.

We run a few experiments for various field sizes that all indicated that this simple heuristic predicts indeed the right behavior. This gives that the cost of multiplication in Wiedemann's algorithm can be bounded by $\mathcal{O}(a \cdot w_1 + b \cdot w_2)$. Since $a \cdot w_1 = b \cdot w_2$ we can bound the overall cost of Wiedemann's algorithm by $\mathcal{O}(a \cdot b \cdot w_1) = \mathcal{O}(bN)$ where N is the number of non zero elements in the Macaulay matrix. From these considerations, we obtain

Proposition 20. *Checking whether a code is an alternant code or a generic linear code can be performed with a complexity upper-bounded by*

$$\mathcal{O}\left(\left(\left(\binom{rm}{2} - k + 1\right)(n - rm)\binom{\binom{rm}{2} + d_{\text{reg}} - 2}{d_{\text{reg}} - 1} + 3\binom{rm}{4}\binom{\binom{rm}{2} + d_{\text{reg}} - 3}{d_{\text{reg}} - 2}\right)\binom{\binom{rm}{2} + d_{\text{reg}} - 1}{d_{\text{reg}}}\right).$$
(16)

Complexity of the Standard Approach for Key Recovery. Recall that it consists in guessing the irreducible Goppa polynomial Γ and the support set of coordinates. After that, the Support Splitting Algorithm (SSA) [Sen00] checks whether the public code is permutation equivalent to the guessed Goppa code. The total complexity of this approach can be estimated as

$$\mathcal{O}\left(\frac{\binom{q^m}{n}}{r}\sum_{a\mid r}\mu(a)(q^m)^{\frac{r}{a}}\right), \tag{17}$$

where μ is the Möbius function. We refer to [CMT23, §5.4] for more details.

Comparison of Distinguisher with the Key-Attack. The comparison of all the methods we have just presented is given in Table 1 with respect to Classic McEliece parameters. We remark that, using sparse linear algebra, we can improve upon the classical method for all parameters except those for category 5. Note that in this case the Goppa code is full-support and therefore the support coordinates do not need to be guessed, leading to a big improvement upon non-full support instances. However, our distinguisher suffers less than the standard key-recovery algorithm from taking instances that are not full support. Indeed, if we consider the same r and m used in Category 5, but a smaller length n, then our distinguisher approach outperforms the previous one. In fact, this can be seen directly from Category 3, which shares the same r and m with Category 5, but it is not full support.

Table 1. Computational cost comparison between *this* distinguisher and retrieving the permutation equivalence

Category	n	r	m	d_{reg}	R	classical key-recovery $\mathbb{C}=\frac{\binom{2^m}{n}}{r}\sum_{a\mid r}\mu(a)(2^m)^{\frac{r}{a}}$	dense linear algebra $\mathbb{C}=\binom{rm}{4}d_{\mathrm{reg}}\left(\frac{\binom{rm}{2}-k+d_{\mathrm{reg}}-1}{d_{\mathrm{reg}}}\right)^{\omega}$	sparse linear algebra $\mathbb{C}$ as in (16)
1	3488	64	12	84	0.7798	$2^{2476}\cdot 2^{762}=2^{3238}$	2^{3141}	2^{2229}
2	4608	96	13	212	0.7292	$2^{8093}\cdot 2^{1241}=2^{9334}$	2^{7931}	2^{5642}
3	6688	128	13	229	0.7512	$2^{5629}\cdot 2^{1657}=2^{7286}$	2^{9030}	2^{6423}
4	6960	119	13	169	0.7777	$2^{4997}\cdot 2^{1540}=2^{6537}$	2^{6779}	2^{4820}
5	8192	128	13	154	0.7969	$2^0\cdot 2^{1657}=2^{1657}$	2^{6329}	2^{4499}

We also remark that our distinguishing modeling works for any alternant code, while the classical key-recovery procedure described here is specific for Goppa codes. Indeed, guessing a valid pair of support $\boldsymbol{x}$ and multiplier $\boldsymbol{y}$ for a generic alternant code is dramatically more costly for two reasons. First of all, the n multiplier coordinates y_i's are independent and do not have a compact representation through a degree-r polynomial. Moreover, in order to guess a correct code permutation, the support and multiplier coordinate indexes must correspond.

In Fig. 1 we show the growth of the degree of regularity d_{reg} for a random $[n=2^m, n-rm]$ code, for fixed m. The graph is defined on the integer interval whose endpoints are given by the smallest value of r for which [FGO+11] is not

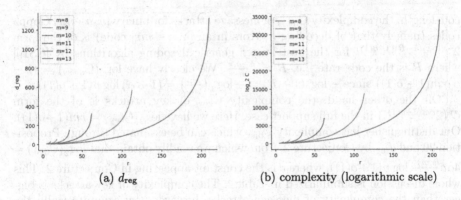

(a) d_{reg} (b) complexity (logarithmic scale)

Fig. 1. Growth of the degree regularity in function of r for fixed m

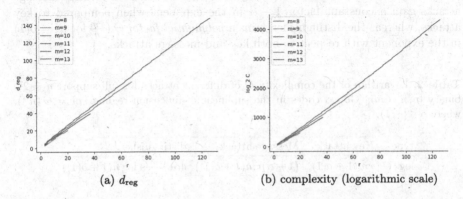

(a) d_{reg} (b) complexity (logarithmic scale)

Fig. 2. Degree of regularity and complexity cost with respect to sparse linear algebra for the fixed rate $R = 4/5$

able to distinguish a binary Goppa code and the largest value for which this new modeling is able to distinguish respectively. Note that in this case the rate is decreasing. On the other hand, Fig. 2 provides the degree of regularity d_{reg} and the complexity estimate using sparse linear algebra, for m fixed, r growing and $n = 5rm$, *i.e.* for the fixed rate $R = 4/5$. The domain of the graph is computed in the same way as for Fig. 1.

Sublinear Regime. It is insightful to study the asymptotic complexity of distinguishing an $[n, rm]$-code in the sublinear regime, when the dimension rm is sublinear in the codelength n and to compare it with key and message attacks. Assume that $rm = \Theta(n^\alpha)$ where $\alpha \in [\frac{1}{2}, 1)$. We will also be interested in the case where the code is a binary Goppa code. To simplify a little bit the discussion and to minimize the complexity of the known key attack, we will assume that we have a Goppa code of full support, i.e. $n = 2^m$.

A binary Goppa code of length n, extension degree m and degree r allows to correct r errors. Because the number of errors to decode is sublinear in the codelength, the complexity C_{mess} of message attacks for binary $[n, n-mr]$ Goppa codes (namely that of decoding r errors in an $[n, n-mr]$ code) is of the form $2^{-r\log_2(1-R)(1+o(1))}$ for the best known generic decoding algorithms by [CS16] where R is the code rate, i.e. $R = \frac{n-mr}{n}$. We clearly have $\log_2(C_{\text{mess}}) = (1-\alpha)rm(1 + o(1))$ since $-\log_2(1-R) = -\log_2\left(\frac{rm}{n}\right) = (1-\alpha)\log n(1 + o(1))$.

On the other hand, the complexity C_{key} of key attacks is of the form $\mathcal{O}\left(2^{rm(1+o(1))}\right)$ in the full support case. Here we have $\log_2(C_{\text{key}}) = rm(1+o(1))$. Our distinguisher has complexity C_{dist} which can be estimated through Proposition 20 and d_{reg} by Conjecture 2, from which we readily obtain that $\log_2(C_{\text{dist}}) = 4\alpha c\frac{(rm)^2}{n}\log n(1+o(1))$, where c is the constant appearing in Conjecture 2. This whole discussion is summarized in Table 2. The complexity of key attacks is bigger than the complexity of message attacks, however now asymptotically the complexity of the distinguisher is *significantly lower* than both attacks: message attacks gain a constant factor $1 - \alpha$ in the exponent when compared to key attacks, whereas the distinguisher gains a *polynomial factor* $\Theta\left(\frac{rm}{n}\log n\right) = o(1)$ in the exponent with respect to both key and message attacks.

Table 2. Logarithm of the complexity C of different attacks for full support $n = 2^m$ binary $[n, n - mr]$ Goppa codes in the sublinear codimension regime $rm = \Theta(n^\alpha)$, where $\alpha \in [\frac{1}{2}, 1)$.

type	Key attack	Message attack	distinguisher
$\log_2 C$	$rm(1 + o(1))$	$(1-\alpha)rm(1 + o(1))$	$4\alpha c\frac{(rm)^2}{n}\log n(1 + o(1))$

6 An Attack on Distinguishable Random Alternant Codes, Without the Use of Gröbner Bases

We are going to present now a polynomial time attack on square-distinguishable generic alternant codes defined over $\mathbb{F}_q$ as soon as the degree r satisfies $r < q+1$ by using this new notion of the matrix code of quadratic relations. We also recall that a square-distinguishable alternant code must have degree $r \geqslant 3$ [FGO+11]. If we combine this together with the filtration technique of [BMT23] which allows to compute from a square-distinguishable alternant code of degree r satisfying $r \geqslant q+1$ an alternant code with the same support but of degree $r-1$, we obtain an attack on all square-distinguishable generic alternant codes. This is a big improvement on the attack presented in [BMT23] which needed two conditions to hold: (1) a square-distinguishable alternant code, (2) q is either 2 or 3. Moreover [BMT23] could not handle the subcase where the alternant code is actually a Goppa code, whereas our new attack is able to treat this case at least in the case $r < q - 1$. We present in Table 3 a summary of the attacks. The reason why for the time being the square-distinguishable Goppa codes are out of reach, is that

Table 3. Summary of the attacks against square-distinguishable codes. The column q corresponds to the restrictions on q for the attack to work and the column r has the same meaning for the parameter r.

code	technique/paper	$r(\geqslant 3)$	q
(generic) square-distinguishable alternant code	[BMT23]	any	$\in \{2,3\}$
(generic) square-distinguishable alternant code	this paper	$< q+1$	any
(generic) square-distinguishable alternant code	this paper + filtration techn. of [BMT23]	any	any
square-distinguishable Goppa codes	this paper	$< q-1$	any

the filtration technique of [BMT23] for reducing the degree of the code does not work for the special case of Goppa codes.

Thus, from now on, we will consider an alternant code $\mathscr{A}_r(\boldsymbol{x}, \boldsymbol{y}) \subseteq \mathbb{F}_q^n$ of extension degree m which is such that $r < q+1$. For generic alternant codes, this corresponds to the square-distinguisher case with $e = 0$. If instead the alternant code is also Goppa, then we restrict ourselves to the case of $r < q-1$. We will show now how to recover $\boldsymbol{x}$ and $\boldsymbol{y}$ from the knowledge of a generator matrix of this code by making use of the matrix code of quadratic relations associated to the extended dual code over $\mathbb{F}_{q^m}$.

The Idea

We first present the underlying idea by picking the canonical basis $\mathcal{A}$ of (11) and the parity-check matrix $\boldsymbol{H}_\mathcal{A}$ of $\mathscr{A}_r(\boldsymbol{x}, \boldsymbol{y})_{\mathbb{F}_{q^m}}$ whose rows correspond to the elements of $\mathcal{A}$ in that same order. We also assume q is odd for now. The crucial point is that, with the assumption of a square-distinguishable generic alternant code (resp. Goppa code) with $r < q+1$ (resp. $r < q-1$), the analysis provided in [FGO+11] implies that the matrix code is generated by *all and only* relations of the kind

$$\boldsymbol{y}^{q^l} \boldsymbol{x}^{aq^l} \star \boldsymbol{y}^{q^l} \boldsymbol{x}^{bq^l} = \boldsymbol{y}^{q^l} \boldsymbol{x}^{cq^l} \star \boldsymbol{y}^{q^l} \boldsymbol{x}^{dq^l}$$

where l is arbitrary in $[\![0, m-1]\!]$ and a, b, c, d in $[\![0, r-1]\!]$ such that $a+b = c+d$. This corresponds to the quadratic relation $\boldsymbol{a}_a^{q^l} \star \boldsymbol{a}_b^{q^l} - \boldsymbol{a}_c^{q^l} \star \boldsymbol{a}_d^{q^l} = 0$. The related code of relations $\mathscr{C}_{\text{mat}}(\mathcal{A})$ has therefore a block diagonal structure with blocks of size r, i.e., for each element in $\boldsymbol{A} \in \mathscr{C}_{\text{mat}}(\mathcal{A})$, we have

$$A = \begin{bmatrix} A_{0,0} & & & \\ & A_{1,1} & & 0 \\ & & \ddots & \\ 0 & & & A_{m-1,m-1} \end{bmatrix} \tag{18}$$

where the diagonal blocks $A_{i,i}$ are symmetric and of size r. Clearly $\mathbf{Rank}(A_{i,i}) \leqslant r$ and, because of the block diagonal shape, $\mathbf{Rank}(A) = \sum_i \mathbf{Rank}(A_{i,i})$. Now assume that A happens to be minimally rank defective, i.e. $\mathbf{Rank}(A) = rm - 1$. It means that for exactly one index $j \in [\![0, m-1]\!]$, $\mathbf{Rank}(A_{j,j}) = r - 1$, and for all $i \in [\![0, m-1]\!] \setminus \{j\}$, $\mathbf{Rank}(A_{i,i}) = r$. We consider the left kernel of (the map corresponding to) the matrix A, simply denoted by $\ker(A)$. Note that, if we identify row vectors with column vectors, left and right kernels are the same in this case, as A is symmetric. Since $\mathbf{Rank}(A) = rm - 1$, we have $\dim(\ker(A)) = 1$. Let $v = (v_0, \dots, v_{m-1}) \in \mathbb{F}_{q^m}^{rm}$ be a generator of $\ker(A)$, with $v_i \in \mathbb{F}_{q^m}^r$. Because of the block diagonal structure of A, v must satisfy $v = (0_r, \dots, 0_r, v_j, 0_r, \dots, 0_r)$. In other words, the computation of this nullspace provides information about the position of the vectors generating a single GRS code $\mathbf{GRS}_r(x^{q^j}, y^{q^j})$. The key idea is that if enough of such vectors are found, a basis of the corresponding GRS code can be retrieved.

6.1   Choosing $\mathcal{B}$ with a Special Shape

Consider an ordered basis

$$\mathcal{B} = (b_0, \dots, b_{r-1}, b_0^q, \dots, b_{r-1}^q, \dots, b_0^{q^{m-1}}, \dots, b_{r-1}^{q^{m-1}}) \tag{19}$$

of $\mathscr{A}_r(x, y)_{\mathbb{F}_{q^m}}^{\perp}$. Such a basis can be computed by drawing $b_0, \dots, b_{r-1} \in \mathscr{A}_r(x, y)_{\mathbb{F}_{q^m}}^{\perp}$ at random, applying the Frobenius map $m - 1$ times and checking if the obtained family generates $\mathscr{A}_r(x, y)_{\mathbb{F}_{q^m}}^{\perp}$, or equivalently if its dimension is rm. If not, draw another r-tuple $b_0, \dots, b_{r-1}$ at random until the construction provides a basis. We remark that even sampling a basis as in (19) does not provide a basis with the same properties of $\mathcal{A}$, i.e. $(b_0, \dots, b_{r-1})$ is not an ordered basis of $\mathbf{GRS}_r(x, y)$, except with negligible probability.

When $\mathcal{B}$ is chosen as in (19), the transition matrix P has a special shape.

Lemma 1. *The matrix P is blockwise Dickson. That is to say, there exist $P_0, \dots, P_{m-1} \in \mathbb{F}_{q^m}^{r \times r}$ such that*

$$P = \begin{bmatrix} P_0 & P_1 & \cdots & P_{m-1} \\ P_{m-1}^{(q)} & P_0^{(q)} & \cdots & P_{m-2}^{(q)} \\ \vdots & \vdots & \ddots & \vdots \\ P_1^{(q^{m-1})} & P_2^{(q^{m-1})} & \cdots & P_0^{(q^{m-1})} \end{bmatrix}. \tag{20}$$

Let $S \in \mathbf{GL}_{mr}(\mathbb{F}_{q^m})$ be the right r-cyclic shift matrix, *i.e.*

$$S \overset{\text{def}}{=} \begin{bmatrix} I_r & & & \\ & I_r & & 0 \\ & 0 & \ddots & \\ & & & I_r \\ I_r & & & \end{bmatrix}. \tag{21}$$

Note that $S^{-1} = S^{\mathsf{T}}$ is the left r-cyclic shift matrix. The block-wise Dickson structure of P can be re-interpreted as follows:

Proposition 21. *Let S be defined as in (21) and P satisfy the blockwise Dickson structure of (20). Then $P = S^{\mathsf{T}} P^{(q)} S$.*

The following result will also be used frequently in what follows

Proposition 22. *Whenever a basis $\mathcal{B}$ has the form given in (19), $\mathscr{C}_{mat}(\mathcal{B})$ is stable by the operation $M \longmapsto S^{\mathsf{T}} M^{(q)} S$.*

The proof is given in [CMT23, Appendix E]. Note that $S^{(q^i)} = S$ for any i. By applying i times the map $M \longmapsto S^{\mathsf{T}} M^{(q)} S$, we obtain $M \longmapsto (S^{\mathsf{T}})^i M^{(q^i)} (S)^i$. We say that M and $(S^{\mathsf{T}})^i M^{(q^i)} (S)^i$ are *blockwise Dickson shift* of each other.

6.2   The Full Algorithm with Respect to a Public Basis $\mathcal{B}$

Algorithm 1 provides a sketch of the attack in the case of odd chacteristic field size. We will then justify why this algorithm is supposed to work with non-negligible probability, elaborate on some subroutines (as sampling matrices of rank $rm - 1$). The adaptation to the even characteristic case is treated in [CMT23, Appendices E8, E.9, E.10]. We now show the structure of the attack. Starting form a public basis, compute a basis as in (19), as already explained above. Similarly to $H_{\mathcal{A}}$, we define $H_{\mathcal{B}}$ as the parity-check matrix of $\mathscr{A}_r(x, y)_{\mathbb{F}_{q^m}}$ whose rows correspond to the elements of $\mathcal{B}$ in that same order. The correctness of the whole algorithm follows immediately from the following propositions whose proofs can be found in [CMT23, Appendix E]. The first one explains why when we have one kernel element in Algorithm 1 at line 6 we can find $m - 1$ other ones.

Proposition 23. *Let v be in the kernel of a matrix B in $\mathscr{C}_{mat}(\mathcal{B})$ of rank $rm-1$. Then $v^q S, \ldots, v^{q^{m-1}} S^{m-1}$ are $m - 1$ elements that are also kernel elements of matrices in $\mathscr{C}_{mat}(\mathcal{B})$ of rank $rm - 1$ which are respectively $S^{\mathsf{T}} B^{(q)} S, \cdots, (S^{\mathsf{T}})^{m-1} B^{(q^{m-1})} S^{m-1}$.*

Then we are going to give a description of the space $\mathcal{V}$ produced in line 17. Basically this a vector space of elements that correspond to a similar GRS code, in the following sense.

Algorithm 1. Sketch of the attack in odd characteristic

Input: (a basis of) an alternant code $\mathscr{A}_r(\boldsymbol{x}, \boldsymbol{y})$
Output: a pair $(\boldsymbol{x}', \boldsymbol{y}')$ of support and multiplier for $\mathscr{A}_r(\boldsymbol{x}, \boldsymbol{y})$

1: Choose a basis $\mathcal{B} = (\boldsymbol{b}_0, \ldots, \boldsymbol{b}_{r-1}, \ldots, \boldsymbol{b}_0^{q^{m-1}}, \ldots, \boldsymbol{b}_{r-1}^{q^{m-1}})$ for $\mathscr{A}_r(\boldsymbol{x}, \boldsymbol{y})^{\perp}_{\mathbb{F}_{q^m}}$
2: $\mathscr{S}_{aux} \leftarrow \{0\}$
3: **repeat**
4:    Sample $\boldsymbol{B} \in \mathscr{C}_{\mathrm{mat}}(\mathcal{B})$ of rank $rm - 1$ at random
5:    $\boldsymbol{v} \leftarrow$ generator of $\ker(\boldsymbol{B})$
6:    $\mathscr{S}_{aux} \leftarrow \mathscr{S}_{aux} + \left\langle \boldsymbol{v}, \boldsymbol{v}^q \boldsymbol{S}, \ldots, \boldsymbol{v}^{q^{m-1}} \boldsymbol{S}^{m-1} \right\rangle_{\mathbb{F}_{q^m}}$
7: **until** $\dim_{\mathbb{F}_{q^m}} \mathscr{S}_{aux} = (r-1)m$
8: Sample $\boldsymbol{B}_1 \in \mathscr{C}_{\mathrm{mat}}(\mathcal{B})$ of rank $rm - 1$ at random
9: $\boldsymbol{u}_1 \leftarrow$ generator of $\ker(\boldsymbol{B}_1)$
10: $\mathscr{V} \leftarrow \langle \boldsymbol{u}_1 \rangle$
11: **for** $j \in [\![2, r]\!]$ **do**
12:    Sample $\boldsymbol{B}_j \in \mathscr{C}_{\mathrm{mat}}(\mathcal{B})$ of rank $rm - 1$ at random
13:    $\boldsymbol{u}_j \leftarrow$ generator of $\ker(\boldsymbol{B}_j)$
14:    **repeat**
15:       $\boldsymbol{u}_j \leftarrow \boldsymbol{u}_j^q \boldsymbol{S}$
16:    **until** $\dim_{\mathbb{F}_{q^m}} \mathscr{S}_{aux} + \langle \boldsymbol{u}_1, \boldsymbol{u}_j \rangle = (r-1)m + 1$
17:    $\mathscr{V} \leftarrow \mathscr{V} + \langle \boldsymbol{u}_j \rangle$
18: $\mathscr{D} \leftarrow \mathscr{V}^{\perp}$
19: $\mathscr{G} \leftarrow \mathscr{D}$
20: **for** $j \in [\![1, m-2]\!]$ **do**
21:    $\mathscr{D} \leftarrow \mathscr{D}^{(q)} \boldsymbol{S}$
22:    $\mathscr{G} \leftarrow \mathscr{G} \cap \mathscr{D}$
23: Apply the Sidelnikov-Shestakov attack [SS92] on $\mathscr{G} \cdot \boldsymbol{H}_{\mathcal{B}}$
24: Return the support-multiplier pair $(\boldsymbol{x}', \boldsymbol{y}')$ found from Sidelnikov-Shestakov attack

---

Definition 13. *Let $\mathcal{A}, \mathcal{B}$ be the two bases introduced before and $\boldsymbol{P}$ the change of basis, i.e. $\boldsymbol{H}_{\mathcal{B}} = \boldsymbol{P} \boldsymbol{H}_{\mathcal{A}}$. Let $\boldsymbol{u}_1, \boldsymbol{u}_2 \in \mathbb{F}_{q^m}^{rm}$ be two vectors such that*

$$\forall t \in \{1, 2\}, \quad \boldsymbol{u}_t (\boldsymbol{P}^{-1})^{\mathsf{T}} \boldsymbol{P}^{-1} \boldsymbol{H}_{\mathcal{B}} \in \mathbf{GRS}_r(\boldsymbol{x}, \boldsymbol{y})^{q^{j_t}}$$

*for some values $j_t \in [\![0, m-1]\!]$. We say that $\boldsymbol{u}_1$ and $\boldsymbol{u}_2$ **correspond to the same GRS code with respect to the basis** $\mathcal{B}$ if and only if $j_1 = j_2$.*

Two vectors $\boldsymbol{u}_1$ and $\boldsymbol{u}_2$ obtained by computing the nullspaces of rank $rm - 1$ matrices may or may not correspond to the same GRS code. In any case, from them, we can easily exhibit two vectors corresponding to the same GRS code by choosing among their shifts $\boldsymbol{u}_t^{q^i} \boldsymbol{S}^i$. More precisely, we have

Proposition 24. *Let $\mathcal{A}, \mathcal{B}$ be the two bases introduced before and $\boldsymbol{P}$ the change of basis, i.e. $\boldsymbol{H}_{\mathcal{B}} = \boldsymbol{P} \boldsymbol{H}_{\mathcal{A}}$. Let $\boldsymbol{u}_1, \boldsymbol{u}_2 \in \mathbb{F}_{q^m}^{rm}$ be two vectors such that*

$$\forall t \in \{1, 2\}, \quad \boldsymbol{u}_t (\boldsymbol{P}^{-1})^{\mathsf{T}} \boldsymbol{P}^{-1} \boldsymbol{H}_{\mathcal{B}} \in \mathbf{GRS}_r(\boldsymbol{x}, \boldsymbol{y})^{(q^{j_t})}$$

for some values $j_t \in [\![0, m-1]\!]$. There exists a unique $l \in [\![0, m-1]\!]$ such that $\boldsymbol{u}_1$ and $\boldsymbol{u}_2^{q^l} \boldsymbol{S}^l$ correspond to the same GRS code.

To detect which shift of $\boldsymbol{u}_2$ corresponds to the same GRS code of $\boldsymbol{u}_1$, we rely on the following proposition.

Proposition 25. *Let* $\boldsymbol{v}_1, \dots, \boldsymbol{v}_{r-1}, \boldsymbol{u}_1, \boldsymbol{u}_2 \in \mathbb{F}_{q^m}^{rm}$ *be the generators of the kernels of* $\boldsymbol{B}_1, \dots, \boldsymbol{B}_{r-1}, \boldsymbol{B}', \boldsymbol{B}'' \in \mathscr{C}_{mat}(\mathcal{B})$ *respectively, for randomly sampled matrices of rank* $rm - 1$. *Define*

$$\mathscr{S}_{aux} \overset{def}{=} \left\langle \boldsymbol{v}_j^{q^l} \boldsymbol{S}^l \mid j \in [\![1, r-1]\!], l \in [\![0, m-1]\!] \right\rangle_{\mathbb{F}_{q^m}}.$$

If the following conditions are satisfied:

- $\dim_{\mathbb{F}_{q^m}} \mathscr{S}_{aux} = (r-1)m$ *(i.e. the* $(r-1)m$ *vectors that generate* $\mathscr{S}_{aux}$ *are linearly independent);*
- $\dim_{\mathbb{F}_{q^m}} \mathscr{S}_{aux} + \langle \boldsymbol{u}_t \rangle_{\mathbb{F}_{q^m}} = (r-1)m + 1, \quad t = 1, 2;$

then the two following statements are equivalent:

1. $\dim_{\mathbb{F}_{q^m}} \mathscr{S}_{aux} + \left\langle \boldsymbol{u}_1, \boldsymbol{u}_2^{q^l} \boldsymbol{S}^l \right\rangle_{\mathbb{F}_{q^m}} = (r-1)m + 1;$
2. $\boldsymbol{u}_1$ *and* $\boldsymbol{u}_2^{q^l} \boldsymbol{S}^l$ *correspond to the same GRS code with respect to* $\mathcal{B}$.

We are therefore able to construct a space of dimension r whose elements all correspond to a same GRS code. Then we use

Proposition 26. *Let* $j \in [\![0, m-1]\!]$. *Let* $\mathscr{V}_j$ *be the* $[rm, r]$ *linear code generated by* r *linearly independent vectors corresponding to the same GRS code* $\mathbf{GRS}_r(\boldsymbol{x}, \boldsymbol{y})^{(q^j)}$ *with respect to* $\mathcal{B}$. *Then the linear space* $\mathscr{V}_j^{\perp}$ *orthogonal to* $\mathscr{V}_j$ *is such that*

$$\mathscr{V}_j^{\perp} \boldsymbol{H}_{\mathcal{B}} = \sum_{i \in [\![0,m-1]\!] \setminus \{j\}} \mathbf{GRS}_r(\boldsymbol{x}, \boldsymbol{y})^{(q^i)}. \tag{22}$$

Given $\mathscr{V}_j^{\perp}$, the other codes $\mathscr{V}_i^{\perp} \boldsymbol{H}_{\mathcal{B}}$ that are sums of $m-1$ GRS codes can be obtained according to the following chain of equalities

$$\sum_{i \in [\![0,m-1]\!] \setminus \{j+l \bmod m\}} \mathbf{GRS}_r(\boldsymbol{x}, \boldsymbol{y})^{(q^i)} = \left(\sum_{i \in [\![0,m-1]\!] \setminus \{j\}} \mathbf{GRS}_r(\boldsymbol{x}, \boldsymbol{y})^{(q^i)} \right)^{(q^l)}$$

$$= (\mathscr{V}_j^{\perp} \boldsymbol{H}_{\mathcal{B}})^{(q^l)} = (\mathscr{V}_j^{\perp})^{(q^l)} \boldsymbol{H}_{\mathcal{B}}^{(q^l)} = (\mathscr{V}_j^{\perp})^{(q^l)} \boldsymbol{S} \boldsymbol{H}_{\mathcal{B}}.$$

After this, we are ready to compute a basis of a GRS code.

Proposition 27. *Let* $\mathscr{V}_j^{\perp}$ *be a linear space satisfying Eq. (22), for all* $j \in [\![0, m-1]\!]$. *Then with the standard assumption that all* $\mathbf{GRS}_r(\boldsymbol{x}, \boldsymbol{y})^{(q^j)}$ *are in direct sum, we obtain, for any* $j \in [\![0, m-1]\!]$,

$$\mathbf{GRS}_r(\boldsymbol{x}, \boldsymbol{y})^{(q^j)} = \bigcap_{i \in [\![0,m-1]\!] \setminus \{j\}} \mathscr{V}_i^{\perp} \boldsymbol{H}_{\mathcal{B}}.$$

At this point, it is sufficient to run the Sidelnikov-Shestakov [SS92] attack on the GRS code. This algorithm takes as input the basis of a GRS code and returns as output a valid pair of support and multiplier for it. Thanks to Propositions 3 and 27, this is also a valid pair for the alternant/Goppa code, thus concluding the key-recovery attack. The runtime of the Sidelnikov-Shestakov attack is $\mathcal{O}(n^3)$.

Remark 3. In the q odd case, the only exception to what was said until now occurs for $r = 3$. In this case a non-full rank diagonal block $\boldsymbol{B}_{j,j}$ becomes the null block, because there are no matrices of rank 1 or 2. In this case, the kernel of a rank $r(m-1) = 3m - 3$ matrix is a three-dimensional subspace, which immediately provides the subspace $\mathscr{V}_j$ from which to recover the associated GRS codes.

How to Sample Matrices in $\mathscr{C}_{\mathrm{mat}}(\mathcal{B})$ of Rank $rm - 1$

This is the most costly part of the algorithm. We address here the case of odd characteristic, as the case of even characteristic needs an ad hoc discussion and is treated in [CMT23, Appendix E]. It is not too difficult to estimate that the density of rank $rm - 1$ matrices inside $\mathscr{C}_{\mathrm{mat}}(\mathcal{B})$ is of order q^{-m} and therefore it is desirable to have a better technique than just a brute force approach. More precisely, we take two matrices $\boldsymbol{D}_1, \boldsymbol{D}_2$ at random in $\mathscr{C}_{\mathrm{mat}}(\mathcal{B})$ and solve over $\mathbb{F}_{q^m}$ the equation $\det(w\boldsymbol{D}_1 + \boldsymbol{D}_2) = 0$. The determinant $\det(w\boldsymbol{D}_1 + \boldsymbol{D}_2)$ is a univariate polynomial of degree rm and since w is taken over $\mathbb{F}_{q^m}$ we can expect to have solutions with non-negligible probability. A root w_0 of $\det(w\boldsymbol{D}_1 + \boldsymbol{D}_2)$ determines a matrix $w_0\boldsymbol{D}_1 + \boldsymbol{D}_2$ whose rank is strictly smaller than rm but not necessarily equal to $rm - 1$. However, the rank $rm - 1$ is by far the most likely outcome. Repeating the process enough times ($\Theta(1)$ times on average) then provides a matrix of rank $rm - 1$.

6.3   Complexity

The bottelneck of the attack is the computation of rank $rm - 1$ matrices in $\mathscr{C}_{\mathrm{mat}}(\mathcal{B})$ which is explained in the previous paragraph. The computation of the polynomial $\det(w\boldsymbol{D}_1 + \boldsymbol{D}_2)$ can be done by choosing rm distinct elements $\alpha_1, \ldots, \alpha_{rm}$ of $\mathbb{F}_{q^m}$, compute the values $\det(\alpha_1\boldsymbol{D}_1 + \boldsymbol{D}_2), \ldots, \det(\alpha_{rm}\boldsymbol{D}_1 + \boldsymbol{D}_2)$ and then recover the polynomial $\det(w\boldsymbol{D}_1 + \boldsymbol{D}_2)$ by interpolation. This represents the calculation of $rm = \mathcal{O}(n)$ determinants of $rm \times rm$ matrices and hence a cost $\mathcal{O}(n^{\omega+1})$, where ω is the complexity exponent of linear algebra. Once this polynomial (in the variable w) is computed, the cost of the root–finding step is negligible compared to that of the previous calculation.

Since the latter process should be repeated $\mathcal{O}(n)$ times, we get an overall complexity of $\mathcal{O}(n^{\omega+2})$ operations in $\mathbb{F}_{q^m}$.

7   Conclusion

A General Methodology for Studying the Security of the McEliece Cryptosystem with Respect to Key–Recovery Attacks. Trying to find an attack on the key of the McEliece scheme based on Goppa codes, has turned out over the years to be a formidable problem. The progress on this issue has basically been non existent for many years and it was for a long time judged that the McEliece scheme was immune against this kind of attacks. This changed a little bit when many variants of the original McEliece came out, either by turning to a slightly larger class of codes namely the alternant codes which retain the main algebraic structure of the Goppa code and/or adding additional structure on it [BCGO09, BBB+17], changing the alphabet [BLP10, BLP11], or going to extreme parameters [CFS01]. This has lead to devise many tools to attack these variants such as algebraic modeling to recover the alternant stucture of a Goppa code which is basically enough to recover its structure [FOPT10], using square code considerations [COT14, COT17, BC18], or trying to solve a simpler problem which is to distinguish these algebraic codes from random codes [FGO+11, FGO+13, MT22]. We actually believe that in order to make further progress on this very hard problem, it is desirable to move away now from studying particular schemes proposed in the literature, by exploring and developing systematically tools for solving this problem and study the region of parameters (alphabet size q, code length n, degree r of the code, extension degree m) where these methods work. We suggest the following research plan

- Studying the slightly more general problem of attacking alternant codes might be the right way to go because it retains the essential algebraic features of Goppa codes and it allows to find attacks that might not work in the subcase of Goppa codes where the additional structure can be a nuisance. An example which is particularly enlightening here is the recent work [BMT23] (attack on generic alternant codes in a certain parameter regime which amazingly does not work in the particular case of Goppa codes where the additional structure prevents the attack to work).
- A particularly fruitful research thread is to study the potentially easier problem of finding a distinguisher for alternant/Goppa codes first.
- Turn later on this distinguisher into an attack (such as [BMT23] for the distinguisher of [FGO+11]).

This is the research plan we have followed to some extent here.

A Distinguisher in Odd Characteristic. It is clear that any algebraic modeling for solving the symmetric MinRank problem for rank 3 could be used to attack the problem in odd characteristic. The Support Minors modeling of [BBC+20] would be for instance a good candidate for this. The difficulty is here to predict the complexity of system solving, since the fact that the matrices are symmetric gives many new linear dependencies that do not happen in the generic MinRank case. This is clearly a promising open problem.

Turning the Distinguisher of Sect. 5 into an Attack. The Pfaffian modeling for the distinguisher can be used in principle to attack the key-recovery problem as well. This problem is strictly harder than just distinguishing because of the algebraic structure in the code $\mathscr{C}_{mat}(\mathcal{A})$ that is much stronger than in $\mathscr{C}_{mat}(\mathcal{R})$ (random case). In particular, rank 2 matrices are found at a potentially larger degree than $\bar{d}$ at which the Hilbert function in the random case becomes 0. The fact that the solution space is very large, in particular it contains a rather large vector space (see Sect. 4), suggests though that we can safely specialize a rather large number of variables to speed up the system solving. Once a rank 2 matrix is found, the attack is not finished yet, but it is tempting to conjecture that the main bottleneck is to find such a matrix first and that some of the tools developed in the attack given in Sect. 6 might be used to finish the job.

Indeed, since rank 2 matrices in $\mathscr{C}_{mat}(\mathcal{A})$ are identically zero outside the main block diagonal, we can consider a matrix subcode spanned by many of them, obtained by solving the Pfaffian system with different specializations. This subcode will have a block diagonal shape and that is why the attack of the last section is expected to apply on such subspace.

Acknowledgement. The authors would like to thank the anonymous reviewers, the shepherd and Daniel J. Bernstein for their comments and their help in improving the quality of the paper.

References

[ABC+22] Albrecht, M., et al.: Classic McEliece (merger of Classic McEliece and NTS-KEM) (2022). https://classic.mceliece.org. Fourth round finalist of the NIST post-quantum cryptography call

[Bar04] Bardet, M.: Étude des systèmes algébriques surdéterminés. Applications aux codes correcteurs et à la cryptographie. Ph.D. thesis, Université Paris VI (2004). http://tel.archives-ouvertes.fr/tel-00449609/en/

[BBB+17] Banegas, G., et al.: DAGS: key encapsulation for dyadic GS codes (2017). https://csrc.nist.gov/CSRC/media/Projects/Post-Quantum-Cryp tography/documents/round-1/submissions/DAGS.zip. First round submission to the NIST post-quantum cryptography call

[BBB+22] Bardet, M., Briaud, P., Bros, M., Gaborit, P., Tillich, J.-P.: Revisiting algebraic attacks on MinRank and on the rank decoding problem (2022). arXiv:2208.05471

[BBC+20] Bardet, M., et al.: Improvements of algebraic attacks for solving the rank decoding and MinRank problems. In: Moriai, S., Wang, H. (eds.) ASIACRYPT 2020. LNCS, vol. 12491, pp. 507–536. Springer, Cham (2020). https://doi.org/10.1007/978-3-030-64837-4_17

[BC18] Barelli, É., Couvreur, A.: An efficient structural attack on NIST submission DAGS. In: Peyrin, T., Galbraith, S. (eds.) ASIACRYPT 2018. LNCS, vol. 11272, pp. 93–118. Springer, Cham (2018). https://doi.org/10.1007/978-3-030-03326-2_4

[BCGO09] Berger, T.P., Cayrel, P.-L., Gaborit, P., Otmani, A.: Reducing key length of the McEliece cryptosystem. In: Preneel, B. (ed.) AFRICACRYPT 2009. LNCS, vol. 5580, pp. 77–97. Springer, Heidelberg (2009). https://doi.org/10.1007/978-3-642-02384-2_6

[Ber10] Bernstein, D.J.: Grover vs. McEliece. In: Sendrier, N. (ed.) PQCrypto 2010. LNCS, vol. 6061, pp. 73–80. Springer, Heidelberg (2010). https://doi.org/10.1007/978-3-642-12929-2_6

[BFS15] Bardet, M., Faugère, J.-C., Salvy, B.: On the complexity of the F_5 Gröbner basis algorithm. J. Symbolic Comput. **70**, 49–70 (2015)

[BJMM12] Becker, A., Joux, A., May, A., Meurer, A.: Decoding random binary linear codes in $2^{n/20}$: how $1 + 1 = 0$ improves information set decoding. In: Pointcheval, D., Johansson, T. (eds.) EUROCRYPT 2012. LNCS, vol. 7237, pp. 520–536. Springer, Heidelberg (2012). https://doi.org/10.1007/978-3-642-29011-4_31

[BLM11] Barreto, P.S.L.M., Lindner, R., Misoczki, R.: Monoidic codes in cryptography. In: Yang, B.-Y. (ed.) PQCrypto 2011. LNCS, vol. 7071, pp. 179–199. Springer, Heidelberg (2011). https://doi.org/10.1007/978-3-642-25405-5_12

[BLP10] Bernstein, D.J., Lange, T., Peters, C.: Wild McEliece. In: Biryukov, A., Gong, G., Stinson, D.R. (eds.) SAC 2010. LNCS, vol. 6544, pp. 143–158. Springer, Heidelberg (2011). https://doi.org/10.1007/978-3-642-19574-7_10

[BLP11] Bernstein, D.J., Lange, T., Peters, C.: Wild McEliece incognito. In: Yang, B.-Y. (ed.) PQCrypto 2011. LNCS, vol. 7071, pp. 244–254. Springer, Heidelberg (2011). https://doi.org/10.1007/978-3-642-25405-5_16

[BM17] Both, L., May, A.: Optimizing BJMM with nearest neighbors: full decoding in $2^{2/21n}$ and McEliece security. In: WCC Workshop on Coding and Cryptography (2017)

[BMT23] Bardet, M., Mora, R., Tillich, J.-P.: Polynomial time key-recovery attack on high rate random alternant codes. CoRR, abs/2304.14757 (2023)

[CBB+17] Couvreur, A., et al.: Big Quake (2017). https://bigquake.inria.fr. NIST Round 1 submission for Post-Quantum Cryptography

[CC98] Canteaut, A., Chabaud, F.: A new algorithm for finding minimum-weight words in a linear code: application to McEliece's cryptosystem and to narrow-sense BCH codes of length 511. IEEE Trans. Inf. Theory **44**(1), 367–378 (1998)

[CCMZ15] Cascudo, I., Cramer, R., Mirandola, D., Zémor, G.: Squares of random linear codes. IEEE Trans. Inf. Theory **61**(3), 1159–1173 (2015)

[CFS01] Courtois, N.T., Finiasz, M., Sendrier, N.: How to achieve a McEliece-based digital signature scheme. In: Boyd, C. (ed.) ASIACRYPT 2001. LNCS, vol. 2248, pp. 157–174. Springer, Heidelberg (2001). https://doi.org/10.1007/3-540-45682-1_10

[CGG+14] Couvreur, A., Gaborit, P., Gauthier-Umaña, V., Otmani, A., Tillich, J.-P.: Distinguisher-based attacks on public-key cryptosystems using Reed-Solomon codes. Des. Codes Cryptogr. **73**(2), 641–666 (2014)

[CMT23] Couvreur, A., Mora, R., Tillich, J.-P.: A new approach based on quadratic forms to attack the McEliece cryptosystem. arXiv preprint arXiv:2306.10294 (2023)

[COT14] Couvreur, A., Otmani, A., Tillich, J.-P.: New identities relating wild Goppa codes. Finite Fields Appl. **29**, 178–197 (2014)

[COT17]   Couvreur, A., Otmani, A., Tillich, J.-P.: Polynomial time attack on wild McEliece over quadratic extensions. IEEE Trans. Inf. Theory **63**(1), 404–427 (2017)

[CS16]   Canto Torres, R., Sendrier, N.: Analysis of information set decoding for a sub-linear error weight. In: Takagi, T. (ed.) PQCrypto 2016. LNCS, vol. 9606, pp. 144–161. Springer, Cham (2016). https://doi.org/10.1007/978-3-319-29360-8_10

[Dum89]   Dumer, I.: Two decoding algorithms for linear codes. Probl. Inf. Transm. **25**(1), 17–23 (1989)

[Fau02]   Faugère, J.-C.: A new efficient algorithm for computing Gröbner bases without reduction to zero: F5. In: Proceedings ISSAC 2002, pp. 75–83. ACM Press (2002)

[FGO+11]   Faugère, J.-C., Gauthier, V., Otmani, A., Perret, L., Tillich, J.-P.: A distinguisher for high rate McEliece cryptosystems. In: Proceedings of the IEEE Information Theory Workshop, ITW 2011, Paraty, Brasil, pp. 282–286 (2011)

[FGO+13]   Faugère, J.-C., Gauthier, V., Otmani, A., Perret, L., Tillich, J.-P.: A distinguisher for high rate McEliece cryptosystems. IEEE Trans. Inf. Theory **59**(10), 6830–6844 (2013)

[FLP08]   Faugère, J.-C., Levy-dit-Vehel, F., Perret, L.: Cryptanalysis of MinRank. In: Wagner, D. (ed.) CRYPTO 2008. LNCS, vol. 5157, pp. 280–296. Springer, Heidelberg (2008). https://doi.org/10.1007/978-3-540-85174-5_16

[FOPT10]   Faugère, J.-C., Otmani, A., Perret, L., Tillich, J.-P.: Algebraic cryptanalysis of McEliece variants with compact keys. In: Gilbert, H. (ed.) EUROCRYPT 2010. LNCS, vol. 6110, pp. 279–298. Springer, Heidelberg (2010). https://doi.org/10.1007/978-3-642-13190-5_14

[FPdP14]   Faugère, J.-C., Perret, L., de Portzamparc, F.: Algebraic attack against variants of McEliece with Goppa polynomial of a special form. In: Sarkar, P., Iwata, T. (eds.) ASIACRYPT 2014. LNCS, vol. 8873, pp. 21–41. Springer, Heidelberg (2014). https://doi.org/10.1007/978-3-662-45611-8_2

[FSEDS10]   Faugère, J.-C., El Din, M.S., Spaenlehauer, P.-J.: Computing loci of rank defects of linear matrices using Gröbner bases and applications to cryptology. In: International Symposium on Symbolic and Algebraic Computation, ISSAC 2010, Munich, Germany, 25–28 July 2010, pp. 257–264 (2010)

[GC00]   Goubin, L., Courtois, N.T.: Cryptanalysis of the TTM cryptosystem. In: Okamoto, T. (ed.) ASIACRYPT 2000. LNCS, vol. 1976, pp. 44–57. Springer, Heidelberg (2000). https://doi.org/10.1007/3-540-44448-3_4

[GK04]   Ghorpade, S.R., Krattenthaler, C.: The Hilbert series of Pfaffian rings. In: Christensen, C., Sathaye, A., Sundaram, G., Bajaj, C. (eds.) Algebra, Arithmetic and Geometry with Applications, pp. 337–356. Springer, Heidelberg (2004). https://doi.org/10.1007/978-3-642-18487-1_22

[GUL09]   Gauthier-Umaña, V., Leander, G.: Practical key recovery attacks on two McEliece variants. IACR Cryptology ePrint Archive, Report 2009/509 (2009)

[HT92]   Herzog, J., Trung, N.V.: Gröbner bases and multiplicity of determinantal and Pfaffian ideals. Adv. Math. **96**(1), 1–37 (1992)

[KS99]   Kipnis, A., Shamir, A.: Cryptanalysis of the HFE public key cryptosystem by relinearization. In: Wiener, M. (ed.) CRYPTO 1999. LNCS, vol.

1666, pp. 19–30. Springer, Heidelberg (1999). https://doi.org/10.1007/3-540-48405-1_2

[KT17] Kachigar, G., Tillich, J.-P.: Quantum information set decoding algorithms. In: Lange, T., Takagi, T. (eds.) PQCrypto 2017. LNCS, vol. 10346, pp. 69–89. Springer, Cham (2017). https://doi.org/10.1007/978-3-319-59879-6_5

[LS01] Loidreau, P., Sendrier, N.: Weak keys in the McEliece public-key cryptosystem. IEEE Trans. Inf. Theory **47**(3), 1207–1211 (2001)

[MB09] Misoczki, R., Barreto, P.S.L.M.: Compact McEliece keys from Goppa codes. In: Jacobson, M.J., Rijmen, V., Safavi-Naini, R. (eds.) SAC 2009. LNCS, vol. 5867, pp. 376–392. Springer, Heidelberg (2009). https://doi.org/10.1007/978-3-642-05445-7_24

[McE78] McEliece, R.J.: A Public-Key System Based on Algebraic Coding Theory, pp. 114–116. Jet Propulsion Lab, 1978. DSN Progress Report 44

[MMT11] May, A., Meurer, A., Thomae, E.: Decoding random linear codes in $\tilde{\mathcal{O}}(2^{0.054n})$. In: Lee, D.H., Wang, X. (eds.) ASIACRYPT 2011. LNCS, vol. 7073, pp. 107–124. Springer, Heidelberg (2011). https://doi.org/10.1007/978-3-642-25385-0_6

[MO15] May, A., Ozerov, I.: On computing nearest neighbors with applications to decoding of binary linear codes. In: Oswald, E., Fischlin, M. (eds.) EUROCRYPT 2015. LNCS, vol. 9056, pp. 203–228. Springer, Heidelberg (2015). https://doi.org/10.1007/978-3-662-46800-5_9

[MP12] Márquez-Corbella, I., Pellikaan, R.: Error-correcting pairs for a public-key cryptosystem. CBC 2012, Code-based Cryptography Workshop (2012). http://www.win.tue.nl/ruudp/paper/59.pdf

[MS86] MacWilliams, F.J., Sloane, N.J.A.: The Theory of Error-Correcting Codes. North-Holland, Amsterdam (1986)

[MS05] Miller, E., Sturmfels, B.: Combinatorial Commutative Algebra. Graduate Texts in Mathematics, vol. 227. Springer, New York (2005)

[MT22] Mora, R., Tillich, J.-P.: On the dimension and structure of the square of the dual of a Goppa code. In: Workshop on Coding Theory and Cryptography, WCC 2022 (2022)

[Pra62] Prange, E.: The use of information sets in decoding cyclic codes. IRE Trans. Inf. Theory **8**(5), 5–9 (1962)

[RSA78] Rivest, R.L., Shamir, A., Adleman, L.M.: A method for obtaining digital signatures and public-key cryptosystems. Commun. ACM **21**(2), 120–126 (1978)

[Sen00] Sendrier, N.: Finding the permutation between equivalent linear codes: the support splitting algorithm. IEEE Trans. Inf. Theory **46**(4), 1193–1203 (2000)

[Sho94] Shor, P.W.: Algorithms for quantum computation: discrete logarithms and factoring. In: Goldwasser, S. (ed.) FOCS, pp. 124–134 (1994)

[SS92] Sidelnikov, V.M., Shestakov, S.O.: On the insecurity of cryptosystems based on generalized Reed-Solomon codes. Discrete Math. Appl. **1**(4), 439–444 (1992)

[Ste88] Stern, J.: A method for finding codewords of small weight. In: Cohen, G., Wolfmann, J. (eds.) Coding Theory 1988. LNCS, vol. 388, pp. 106–113. Springer, Heidelberg (1989). https://doi.org/10.1007/BFb0019850

[VBC+19] Verbel, J., Baena, J., Cabarcas, D., Perlner, R., Smith-Tone, D.: On the complexity of "superdetermined" minrank instances. In: Ding, J., Steinwandt, R. (eds.) PQCrypto 2019. LNCS, vol. 11505, pp. 167–186. Springer, Cham (2019). https://doi.org/10.1007/978-3-030-25510-7_10

[Wie86] Wiedemann, D.: Solving sparse linear equations over finite fields. IEEE
         Trans. Inf. Theory **32**(1), 54–62 (1986)
[Wim12] Wimmer, M.: Algorithm923: efficient numerical computation of the Pfaf-
         fian for dense and banded skew-symmetric matrices. ACM Trans. Math.
         Softw. **38**(4) (2012)

Solving the Hidden Number Problem for CSIDH and CSURF via Automated Coppersmith

Jonas Meers[✉] [iD] and Julian Nowakowski [iD]

Ruhr-University Bochum, Bochum, Germany
{jonas.meers,julian.nowakowski}@rub.de

Abstract. We define and analyze the Commutative Isogeny Hidden Number Problem which is the natural analogue of the Hidden Number Problem in the CSIDH and CSURF setting. In short, the task is as follows: Given two supersingular elliptic curves E_A, E_B and access to an oracle that outputs some of the most significant bits of the CDH of two curves, an adversary must compute the shared curve $E_{AB} = \mathsf{CDH}(E_A, E_B)$.

We show that we can recover E_{AB} in polynomial time by using Coppersmith's method as long as the oracle outputs $\frac{13}{24} + \varepsilon \approx 54\%$ (CSIDH) and $\frac{31}{41} + \varepsilon \approx 76\%$ (CSURF) of the most significant bits of the CDH, where $\varepsilon > 0$ is an arbitrarily small constant. To this end, we give a purely combinatorial restatement of Coppersmith's method, effectively concealing the intricate aspects of lattice theory and allowing for near-complete automation. By leveraging this approach, we attain recovery attacks with ε close to zero within a few minutes of computation.

Keywords: Coppersmith · Isogenies · CSIDH · CSURF · Hidden Number Problem

1 Introduction

The Hidden Number Problem (HNP) introduced by Boneh and Venkatesan [5] asks to compute a hidden number α given many tuples $(t_i, \mathsf{MSB}_k(\alpha \cdot t_i \mod p))$ for randomly chosen $t_i \in \mathbb{Z}_p^*$. Here, we denote by $\mathsf{MSB}_k(x)$ the k most significant bits of x. One of the applications of the hidden number problem is the assessment of the bit security of the Diffie-Hellman key exchange over $\mathbb{Z}_p^*$. More concretely, the task can be rephrased as follows: compute the shared Diffie-Hellman key $g^{ab} = \mathsf{CDH}(g^a, g^b) \in \mathbb{Z}_p^*$ given access to an oracle $\mathcal{O}_{\mathsf{MSB}_k}$ that on input $h \in \mathbb{Z}_p^*$ outputs the k most significant bits of $\mathsf{CDH}(g^a, h)$. The famous result by Boneh and Venkatesan states that one can recover g^{ab} in polynomial time if $k \geq \sqrt{\log p}$. Therefore, the $\sqrt{\log p}$ most significant bits of the shared key g^{ab} are as hard to compute as the whole key. The existence of the oracle $\mathcal{O}_{\mathsf{MSB}_k}$ is typically motivated by side-channel attacks and it has recently been shown that such

© International Association for Cryptologic Research 2023
J. Guo and R. Steinfeld (Eds.): ASIACRYPT 2023, LNCS 14441, pp. 39–71, 2023.
https://doi.org/10.1007/978-981-99-8730-6_2

oracles exist in practice [35, 41]. Furthermore, the hidden number problem can be used to cryptanalyze ECDSA, Intels Software Guard Extensions (SGX), DSA and qDSA [2, 6, 17, 19, 37, 47].

The seminal result by Boneh and Venkatesan inspired many follow-up works that investigated different variants of the hidden number problem, for example in the context of Elliptic Curve Diffie-Hellman [4, 26, 44, 53]. As it turns out, the Elliptic Curve Hidden Number Problem (EC-HNP) is already much harder to solve and requires different techniques. In particular, Boneh, Halevi and Howgrave-Graham propose in [3] to use *Coppersmith's method* [13, 14] to solve EC-HNP for $k \geq 0.98 \log p$ and curves defined over $\mathbb{F}_p$. More recently, this approach was further improved, making it feasible to solve EC-HNP for $k \geq \frac{1}{d+1} \log p$ and any fixed $d > 0$ [54].[1] Here the key ingredient is (a very involved variant of) Coppersmith's method.

The recent advent of quantum computers completely bypasses the bit security statements of the (elliptic curve) Diffie-Hellman key exchange since the discrete logarithm problem for groups can be solved in quantum polynomial time due to Shor's algorithm [45]. To thwart this issue, many post-quantum secure alternatives have been proposed. One popular approach is based on *isogenies* which are rational maps between (supersingular) elliptic curves. In some settings, isogenies give rise to cryptographic group actions in the sense of [1] which behave very similarly to exponentiation in prime order groups. Due to this (syntactical) similarity, many protocols and results from the Diffie-Hellman context have been adapted to the isogeny setting (for example [20, 28, 29, 55]). However, this is not the case for the bit security of isogeny based key exchanges. One of the few results in that area studies the bit security of the SIDH key exchange and states that computing one component of the secret j-invariant of a curve is as hard as computing both components [22]. Due to the recent devastating attacks on SIDH [8, 31, 40], however, the statement about its bit security is now obsolete. Apart from SIDH there still exist (non-interactive) key exchanges based on isogenies that are still believed to be post-quantum secure. The most prominent examples are CSIDH [10] and CSURF [7], both of which are based on the group action of fractional ideals on the set of supersingular elliptic curves over $\mathbb{F}_p$. These key exchanges are not affected by the attacks on SIDH, yet very little is known about their bit security.

1.1 Our Contributions

In this work, we close this gap and analyze the hardness of the Commutative Isogeny Hidden Number Problem (CI-HNP) for CSIDH and CSURF, which can be informally stated as follows:

---

[1] Note that if d is not fixed the runtime of the algorithm is in fact super-exponential in d.

Commutative Isogeny Hidden Number Problem (Informal). Given two public curves E_A, E_B defined over $\mathbb{F}_p$ and access to an oracle $\mathcal{O}_{\mathsf{MSB}_k}$ that on input two elliptic curves E, E' outputs $\mathsf{MSB}_k(\mathsf{CDH}(E, E'))$, recover the shared curve $E_{AB} = \mathsf{CDH}(E_A, E_B)$.

SOLVING CI-HNP. Our first major contribution is a (heuristic) polynomial time algorithm based on Coppersmith's method that recovers the shared curve E_{AB} for $k = (\frac{13}{24} + \varepsilon)n$ (CSIDH) and $k = (\frac{31}{41} + \varepsilon)n$ (CSURF), where $n = \log p$ and $\varepsilon > 0$ is an arbitrarily small constant. We remark that our results do not yield an *unconditional* bit security statement for the respective non-interactive key exchanges due to the heuristic nature of Coppersmith's method. Nevertheless, our result implies that (under some constraints) computing the $\frac{13}{24}n$ (CSIDH) and $\frac{31}{41}n$ (CSURF) most significant bits of the shared curve E_{AB} is as hard as solving CDH and quantumly as hard as solving DLOG due to the quantum equivalence of the latter two assumptions [52].

AUTOMATED COPPERSMITH. As our second major contribution, we give a significantly simplified reformulation of Coppersmith's method. This allows us to automate Coppersmith's method almost entirely, and to easily apply it to CI-HNP. This is in stark contrast to almost all previous Coppersmith-type results, which typically required highly involved lattice constructions that had to be fine-tuned using ad-hoc techniques. (See, e.g., May's recent survey [32] and the references therein.) Our approach, on the other hand, only requires to specify which monomials we want to include in our lattice basis. For any given set of monomials our approach then automatically (and efficiently) constructs the corresponding *optimal* lattice.

We also give a simple automated strategy for selecting these monomials. While this strategy might not always yield optimal results, it performs well in practice, and allows us to derive our bounds for CI-HNP. Furthermore, it enables another interesting application: For any given system of polynomial equations our algorithm can (under some reasonable heuristics) *automatically* derive upper bounds on the size of the roots that can be recovered by Coppersmith's method – a process that prior to our work involved a lot of manual effort. Our reformulation of Coppersmith's method is not specific to the application at hand and might therefore be of independent interest.

IMPLEMENTATION. As our third contribution we provide an efficient open source implementation of our automated variant of Coppersmith's method in SageMath. The source code is available at

https://github.com/juliannowakowski/automated-coppersmith.

Using this implementation, we run our algorithm for CI-HNP on cryptographically sized instances with bitsize $n = 512, 1024, 1792$. Our experimental results verify the correctness of our heuristic algorithm, and show that we come close to the asymptotic bounds of $k = \frac{13}{24}n \approx 0.542n$ and $k = \frac{31}{41}n \approx 0.756n$ in a matter of minutes.

1.2   Technical Details and Related Work

Similar to the case of EC-HNP we use Coppersmith's method to recover the least significant bits of the Montgomery coefficient of the shared curve E_{AB}. To this end, we define polynomial relations between the Montgomery coefficient of E_{AB} and the Montgomery coefficients of its d-isogenous neighboring curves, essentially replicating the behaviour of the *modular polynomials* but for the case of Montgomery coefficients. We then embed the partial information from the oracle $\mathcal{O}_{\mathsf{MSB}_k}$ in the coefficients of these polynomials by querying $\mathcal{O}_{\mathsf{MSB}_k}$ on specific input. As a consequence, we can construct a system of polynomial equations that has a common small root in the Montgomery coefficient of the curve E_{AB}. In a last step, this small root is found by Coppersmith's method.

COMPARISON WITH HNP AND EC-HNP. In their original work Boneh and Venkatesan use lattice reduction techniques to solve HNP over $\mathbb{Z}_p^*$ [5]. More specifically, given many oracle queries one derives an underdetermined system of *linear* equations that is subsequently encoded into a lattice. By solving a closest vector problem in the lattice one obtains the secret value. With EC-HNP it is already much harder to implement this approach as the system of equations is inherently *nonlinear*. In fact, each query to the oracle results in a bivariate polynomial of total degree 3. The secret value is then encoded in a common small root of these polynomials, and recovered via Coppersmith's method [54]. Nevertheless, both HNP and EC-HNP have in common that one can get arbitrarily many equations by querying the oracle $\mathcal{O}_{\mathsf{MSB}_k}$ as many times as needed. Phrased differently, the system of polynomial equations – while still being underdetermined – can be made arbitrarily large. Furthermore, each polynomial in the system of equations has the same *shape*.

Unfortunately, in the case of CI-HNP neither of the two properties hold. In both the CSIDH and CSURF settings, each curve has for any given degree d at most two d-isogenous neighbours defined over $\mathbb{F}_p$. Hence, if we wish to make many such oracle queries we necessarily have to use isogenies of higher degree, which in turn result in high-degree polynomial relations. Therefore, we are left with a choice: either have few polynomials of low degree or have many polynomials with very high degree. Additionally, by changing the degree of the isogeny one obtains polynomials of a different *shape*, making optimizations very challenging.

RECOVERY RATES. Curiously, the recovery rates between CSIDH and CSURF differ quite significantly. It turns out that the reason for this is an order-3 subgroup of the ideal class group $cl(\mathcal{O})$ in the CSIDH setting that is not present in CSURF. Subsequently, in the CSIDH setting we are able to construct *more* polynomial relations which have *smaller* degree compared to the CSURF setting. Since Coppersmith's method performs best for polynomials with low degree, this results in a better recovery rate. It is worth mentioning that in the context of analyzing the security of the CSIDH key exchange the same order-3 subgroup is also responsible for reducing the security of the key exchange by a factor of $\frac{1}{3}$ [11,38].

COMPARISON WITH SIDH. The Isogeny Hidden Number Problem has been considered before by Galbraith, Petit, Shani and Ti in the context of SIDH [22]. However, their approach only applies to SIDH due to the fact that in this setting the resulting polynomial equations are defined over $\mathbb{F}_{p^2}$. If we let $\mathbb{F}_{p^2} = \mathbb{F}_p(\theta)$ where $\theta^2 \in \mathbb{F}_p$ denotes some quadratic non-residue, then any equation $f(j) = 0$ over $\mathbb{F}_{p^2}$ results in *two* equations over $\mathbb{F}_p$: for $f(j) = f_{\mathsf{real}}(j) + f_{\mathsf{im}}(j) \cdot \theta = 0$, we must have $f_{\mathsf{real}}(j) = 0$ and $f_{\mathsf{im}}(j) = 0$ simultaneously. This trick in combination with the modular polynomial allowed the authors of [22] to build a system of two polynomial equations in two unknowns which can be solved exactly. Subsequently the authors were able to recover one component of the secret j-invariant given an oracle that returns the other component.

This approach is not applicable to CSIDH and CSURF as in this context the polynomial relations are necessarily defined over $\mathbb{F}_p$. We therefore have to resort back to heavy machinery like Coppersmith's method to solve systems of polynomial equations.

COPPERSMITH'S METHOD. To solve a system of polynomial equations, Coppersmith's method requires as input a set of well-chosen *shift-polynomials*. Crucially, these shift-polynomials f_i must satisfy several technical constraints imposed by Coppersmith's method while simultaneously minimizing the determinant of a certain matrix. Concretely, the matrix has as entries the coefficient vectors of the f_i. In the process of selecting the f_i a ripple effect can occur where a locally optimal choice of a single f_i leads to an overall larger determinant. We observe, however, that choosing *globally optimal* f_i can be fully automated once we fix the set of monomials over which the f_i are defined. Therefore, the only non-trivial task is choosing a "good" set of monomials. The subsequent optimal construction of the f_i then reduces to a purely combinatorial strategy, somewhat similar to the celebrated *Jochemsz-May* strategy [27]. However, we significantly improve on Jochemsz-May since we can handle *systems* of polynomial equations, whereas their strategy only handles *single* polynomial equations. This is particularly useful for the application at hand as in the case of CI-HNP we must deal with such a system of polynomial equations.

COMPUTING ASYMPTOTIC BOUNDS. Similar to the construction of the shift-polynomials, the task of determining asymptotic upper bounds for Coppersmith's method is typically very time-consuming and has to be performed manually each time a new set of polynomials is considered. Moreover, the proof that a given asymptotic bound holds is oftentimes convoluted. We overcome both issues by combining our automated variant of Coppersmith's method with *polynomial interpolation*. More specifically, given a system of polynomial equations our algorithm determines (under some reasonable heuristics) the size of the largest root that can be recovered. This upper bound may not be optimal with respect to the given system of polynomial equations, but nevertheless serves as a good starting point. We demonstrate the usefulness of this approach in the main body of this paper. In addition, the accompanying proof is easy to verify but crucially relies on the correctness of the heuristic. Fortunately, it appears that from the output of our algorithm it is always possible to extract a rigorous proof of correctness that does not involve the aforementioned heuristic. This task, however, requires manual work.

1.3 Outline of the Paper

The paper is organized as follows: In Sect. 2 we give some basic preliminaries for CSIDH, CSURF and Coppersmith's method. Our new formulation of Coppersmith's method is described in Sect. 3 and proven in Sect. 4. In Sect. 5 we show how to solve CI-HNP and discuss the quantum hardness of simulating $\mathcal{O}_{\mathsf{MSB}_k}$. In Sect. 6 we give results on the practical recovery rate of our heuristic algorithm, which experimentally verify its correctness. We conclude our work in Sect. 7 where we also state some open problems.

2   Preliminaries

We use the notation $x \xleftarrow{\$} \mathcal{X}$ to indicate that x is uniformly sampled from a set $\mathcal{X}$. By $\log n$ we denote the base 2 logarithm of n. For a prime p with $p \equiv 3$ mod 4 and a square $a \in \mathbb{F}_p$ we further define $\sqrt{a} \in \mathbb{F}_p$ to be the unique square root of a which is itself again a square. It can be computed as $\sqrt{a} = a^{(p+1)/4}$ mod p. For a n-bit prime p and an integer $x \in \mathbb{Z}_p$ we denote by $\mathsf{MSB}_k(x)$ the k most significant bits of x, i.e. the integer t such that $0 \le x - t \cdot 2^{n-k} < p/2^k$.

2.1   Elliptic Curves and Isogenies

The following facts about isogenies are mostly taken from Silverman [46].

Let $E/\mathbb{F}_p$ be an elliptic curve over a finite field $\mathbb{F}_p$ with p an odd prime. We denote the point at infinity with ∞_E. For an extension field $\mathbb{K} \supseteq \mathbb{F}_p$ we denote the set of $\mathbb{K}$-rational points by $E(\mathbb{K})$. An elliptic curve is called *supersingular* if $\#E(\mathbb{F}_p) = p + 1$ and *ordinary* otherwise.

An isogeny is a morphism $\varphi : E \to E'$ between elliptic curves E, E' such that $\varphi(\infty_E) = \infty_{E'}$. The degree of φ is its degree as a morphism and we call φ *separable* if $p \nmid \deg \varphi$. An isogeny can be expressed as a fraction of polynomials and we call two elliptic curves *isogenous* if there exists an isogeny between them. An isogeny is called an isomorphism if it has an inverse (which may be defined over the algebraic closure of $\mathbb{F}_p$). In that case the inverse is again an isogeny. One can check whether two elliptic curves are isomorphic by comparing their *j-invariant*, which is a simple algebraic expression in the coefficients of the curve equation.

An isogeny from E to itself is called an *endomorphism*. The set $\mathrm{End}(E)$ of endomorphisms of E (defined over the algebraic closure) forms a ring under addition and composition and is thus called the *endomorphism ring*. We denote by $\mathrm{End}_p(E)$ the subring defined over $\mathbb{F}_p$, which is an order in the imaginary quadratic field $\mathbb{Q}(\sqrt{-p})$ if E is supersingular.

Any isogeny $\varphi : E \to E'$ is automatically a group homomorphism from E to E' and as such its kernel is a finite subgroup of E. In the case where φ is separable we have that $\deg \varphi = \#\ker \varphi$. Conversely, any finite subgroup $G \subset E$ corresponds to a separable isogeny $\varphi : E \to E'$ with kernel $\ker \varphi = G$ that is unique up to post-composition with an isomorphism. Since E' is uniquely determined by $\ker \varphi$ (again up to isomorphism), we write $E' = E/G$ from now on. One can compute φ and E/G via Vélus formula [51], which can be evaluated in time polynomial in the size of the kernel.

For an integer n we denote the multiplication-by-n map by $[n]$, which is an endomorphism of E. Its kernel is the n-torsion subgroup $E[n] = \{P \in E : [n]P = \infty_E\}$. Another important endomorphism is the Frobenius endomorphism π_E, sending $(x, y) \in E$ to $(x^p, y^p) \in E$. In the case where E is supersingular it satisfies $\pi_E \circ \pi_E = -p$, implying that $\mathbb{Z}[\sqrt{-p}] \subseteq \mathrm{End}_p(E)$.

2.2 Group Actions from Isogenies

Currently there exist two popular constructions for an isogeny-based group action, namely CSIDH [10] and CSURF [7]. They mainly differ in the choice of $\mathrm{End}_p(E)$. Indeed, if $p \equiv 3 \mod 4$ and E is supersingular there are two choices for $\mathrm{End}_p(E)$, namely $\mathbb{Z}[\sqrt{-p}]$ and $\mathbb{Z}[(1+\sqrt{-p})/2]$. The following section is mostly based on [7,10], however we also incorporate some recent suggestions related to CSURF stated in [12].

CSIDH. Let $p = 4 \cdot \ell_1 \dots \ell_n - 1$ be a prime where the ℓ_i are small odd primes. Fix the order $\mathcal{O} = \mathbb{Z}[\pi]$, where $\pi = \sqrt{-p}$ is the Frobenius endomorphism. Let $\mathcal{E}\ell\ell_p(\mathcal{O})$ be the set of supersingular elliptic curves E defined over $\mathbb{F}_p$ with endomorphism ring $\mathrm{End}_p(E) \cong \mathcal{O}$ (called the *floor*). The ideal class group $cl(\mathcal{O})$ acts on the set $\mathcal{E}\ell\ell_p(\mathcal{O})$ in the following way: to each $\mathfrak{a} \subseteq \mathcal{O}$ we can associate the subgroup

$$E[\mathfrak{a}] := \bigcap_{\varphi \in \mathfrak{a}} \{P \in E : \varphi(P) = \infty_E\} \subseteq E.$$

Here, we view φ as an endomorphism of E through the isomorphism $\mathrm{End}_p(E) \cong \mathcal{O}$.

Theorem 1 (Theorem 4.5 of [43]). *The map*

$$\star : cl(\mathcal{O}) \times \mathcal{E}\ell\ell_p(\mathcal{O}) \to \mathcal{E}\ell\ell_p(\mathcal{O}),$$

sending $([\mathfrak{a}], E)$ *to* $\mathfrak{a} \star E := E/E[\mathfrak{a}]$ *is a well-defined free and transitive group action.*

Observe that because $p \equiv -1 \mod \ell_i$ the ideal (ℓ_i) splits in $\mathbb{Z}[\pi]$ as $(\ell_i) = \langle \ell_i, \pi-1 \rangle \langle \ell_i, \pi+1 \rangle$. Additionally, since $\#E(\mathbb{F}_p) = p+1$ each curve in $\mathcal{E}\ell\ell_p(\mathcal{O})$ has an $\mathbb{F}_p$-rational point $P_\to$ generating a subgroup of order ℓ_i, which corresponds to the ideal $\mathfrak{l}_i = \langle \ell_i, \pi - 1 \rangle$. Therefore, the action $\star$ can be computed efficiently for the ideals $\mathfrak{l}_i$ by finding $P_\to$ and then applying Vélu's formula. A similar reasoning applies to the ideal $\bar{\mathfrak{l}}_i = \langle \ell_i, \pi+1 \rangle$ where the only difference is that the generating

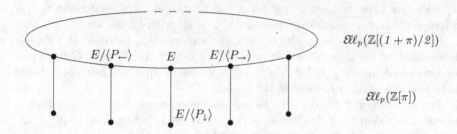

Fig. 1. The 2-isogeny graph for a prime $p \equiv 7 \mod 8$.

point $P_{\leftarrow}$ of order ℓ_i has its x-coordinate in $\mathbb{F}_p$ but its y-coordinate outside of $\mathbb{F}_p$. Therefore, the CSIDH group action can be evaluated efficiently for ideals of the form $\prod \mathfrak{l}_i^{e_i}$, where the e_i are from a small range $[-B, B]$.

For each E on the floor there exists a unique $A \in \mathbb{F}_p$ called the Montgomery *coefficient* such that E is isomorphic to the curve $E_A : y^2 = x^3 + Ax^2 + x$ [10, Proposition 8]. The curve E_A is called the Montgomery *form* of E and we denote by $\mathcal{M}_p(\mathcal{O})$ the set of Montgomery coefficients of curves in $\mathcal{Ell}_p(\mathcal{O})$. We can now see the group action $\star$ equivalently as a group action

$$\star : cl(\mathcal{O}) \times \mathcal{M}_p(\mathcal{O}) \to \mathcal{M}_p(\mathcal{O}), \tag{1}$$

where we identify each $A \in \mathcal{M}_p(\mathcal{O})$ with the curve E_A. By slight abuse of notation we denote this action by $\star$ as well.

Lastly, we define $E_0 : y^2 = x^3 + x$ to be the starting curve of the group action. Indeed, E_0 has endomorphism ring $\mathbb{Z}[\pi]$ and therefore lives on the floor.

CSURF. Let $p = 4 \cdot \ell_0 \dots \ell_n - 1$ be a prime such that $\ell_0 = 2$ and the ℓ_i are small odd primes for $i > 0$. Fix the order $\mathcal{O} = \mathbb{Z}[(1+\pi)/2]$ where again $\pi = \sqrt{-p}$ is the Frobenius endomorphism and $\mathcal{Ell}_p(\mathcal{O})$ is the set of supersingular elliptic curves with endomorphism ring $\mathcal{O}$ (which is now called the *surface*). The ideal class group $cl(\mathcal{O})$ acts in a very similar way on $\mathcal{Ell}_p(\mathcal{O})$. In fact, the action of the ideals $\mathfrak{l}_i$ with $i > 0$ can be evaluated.in the same way as in CSIDH. The only difference is that the ideal (2) now splits in $\mathbb{Z}[(1+\pi)/2]$ as $(2) = \langle 2, (\pi-1)/2 \rangle \langle 2, (\pi+1)/2 \rangle$ due to the congruence $p \equiv 7 \mod 8$.

This means that there are two additional ideals $\mathfrak{l}_0$ and $\bar{\mathfrak{l}}_0$ available for the group action. In contrast to the odd degree isogenies, for each $E \in \mathcal{Ell}_p(\mathcal{O})$ there are now *three* points of order 2 with x-coordinate in $\mathbb{F}_p$. It turns out that $\mathfrak{l}_0$ is generated by a point $P_{\rightarrow}$ of order 2 whose four halves are all $\mathbb{F}_p$-rational. Similarly, the four halves of the point $P_{\leftarrow}$ generating $\bar{\mathfrak{l}}_0$ have x-coordinate in $\mathbb{F}_p$ but y-coordinate outside of $\mathbb{F}_p$. The remaining point $P_{\downarrow}$ of order two has its four halves completely outside of $\mathbb{F}_p$ and quotienting out $\langle P_{\downarrow} \rangle$ results in a curve on the floor (see Fig. 1). In order to compute the action of $\mathfrak{l}_0$ and $\bar{\mathfrak{l}}_0$, one first finds the corresponding point of order 2 and then applies Vélu's formula. In accordance with the literature, we call the isogenies generated by $P_\leftarrow$ and $P_\rightarrow$ *horizontal*, whereas the isogeny generated by $P_\downarrow$ is called *vertical*.

Another difference to CSIDH is that there are now two isomorphic curves in Montgomery form for each $E \in \mathcal{Ell}_p(\mathcal{O})$ [7, Corollary 1]. To make the choice unique one can choose the curve $E_A : y^2 = x^3 + Ax^2 + x$ such that $A \pm 2$ are both squares[2] in $\mathbb{F}_p$. As before, let $\mathcal{M}_p(\mathcal{O})$ denote the set of such Montgomery coefficients. We again have a group action

$$\star : cl(\mathcal{O}) \times \mathcal{M}_p(\mathcal{O}) \to \mathcal{M}_p(\mathcal{O}), \qquad (2)$$

where $A \in \mathcal{M}_p(\mathcal{O})$ is identified with E_A.

Lastly, we set the starting curve to be $E_{3/\sqrt{2}} : y^2 = x^3 + (3/\sqrt{2})x^2 + x$, which has endomorphism ring $\mathbb{Z}[(1 + \pi)/2]$. Note that due to the convention on modular square roots, we also have that

$$\frac{3}{\sqrt{2}} \pm 2 = \frac{1}{\sqrt{2}}(3 \pm 2\sqrt{2}) = \frac{1}{\sqrt{2}}(1 \pm \sqrt{2})^2$$

are both squares.

Remark 1. In [7] it was suggested to identify $E \in \mathcal{Ell}_p(\mathcal{O})$ with its corresponding Montgomery$^-$ form $E_A^- : y^2 = x^3 + Ax^2 - x$ as it uniquely represents the isomorphism class of E [7, Proposition 4]. However, this suggestion was later revoked due to slower low-level arithmetics on Montgomery$^-$ curves [12, p. 12]. Additionally, one uses regular Montgomery curves to compute the action of the 2-isogenies anyway [7, Algorithm 1], which is why we choose to work with regular Montgomery curves as well.

2.3   Cryptographic Assumptions and Protocols

The CSIDH and CSURF group action can be used to instantiate a non-interactive key exchange (NIKE) similar to the Hashed Diffie-Hellman key exchange over prime-order groups (see Fig. 2). In the Random Oracle Model its passive security relies on the hardness of the following two problems, which go back to Couveignes (who called them Vectorization and Parallelization) [16]. Both definitions apply to the CSIDH and CSURF setting.

Definition 1 (Discrete Logarithm Problem (DLOG)). *Let $E \in \mathcal{Ell}_p(\mathcal{O})$ be a fixed starting curve and $[\mathfrak{a}] \xleftarrow{\$} cl(\mathcal{O})$. Given the tuple $(E, \mathfrak{a} \star E)$, recover $[\mathfrak{a}]$.*

Definition 2 (Computational Diffie-Hellman Problem (CDH)). *Let $E \in \mathcal{Ell}_p(\mathcal{O})$ be a fixed starting curve and $[\mathfrak{a}], [\mathfrak{b}] \xleftarrow{\$} cl(\mathcal{O})$. Given the tuple $(E, \mathfrak{a} \star E, \mathfrak{b} \star E)$, compute $\mathfrak{ab} \star E$.*

---

[2] This actually guarantees that $P_\rightarrow = (0, 0)$.

$$\boxed{\begin{array}{ll}
\textbf{Alice A} & \textbf{Bob B} \\
\mathsf{sk_A} = [\mathfrak{a}] \xleftarrow{\$} cl(\mathcal{O}) & \mathsf{sk_B} = [\mathfrak{b}] \xleftarrow{\$} cl(\mathcal{O}) \\
\mathsf{pk_A} = \mathfrak{a} \star M & \mathsf{pk_B} = \mathfrak{b} \star M \\
\\
\multicolumn{2}{c}{K := \mathsf{H}(\mathfrak{b} \star \mathsf{pk_A}) = \mathsf{H}(\mathfrak{a} \star \mathsf{pk_B}) = \mathsf{H}(\mathfrak{ab} \star M)}
\end{array}}$$

Fig. 2. Non-interactive key exchange based on CSIDH/CSURF where M is the Montgomery coefficient of a fixed starting curve and $\mathsf{H} : \{0,1\}^* \to \{0,1\}^\lambda$ is a hash function.

Remark 2. In the following we leave out the starting curve E as long as there is no ambiguity.

Galbraith et al. showed that for efficiently computable group actions, CDH is equivalent to DLOG in a quantum setting [21]. Their reduction assumes a perfect adversary $\mathcal{A}$ against CDH, i.e. an adversary with success probability 1, which is then used to construct a quantum adversary against DLOG. Moreover, they assume that the action of a random element $[\mathfrak{a}] \xleftarrow{\$} cl(\mathcal{O})$ can be computed efficiently, which in general is not the case for the CSIDH and CSURF group action. Furthermore, it is currently not known how to sample an element $[\mathfrak{a}]$ uniformly at random for arbitrary parameter sets.

More recently, their result was improved by Montgomery and Zhandry who showed that the equivalence also holds for any adversary $\mathcal{A}$ having a non-negligible success probability [36]. The authors also gave some mild evidence that the equivalence holds for *restricted effective group actions* (of which CSIDH and CSURF are instantiations, see also [1]), but this result only holds for generic adversaries making classical queries to a group action oracle.

In the special case of the CSIDH and CSURF group action, Wesolowski showed that CDH and DLOG are quantumly equivalent under the generalized Riemann hypothesis [52].

2.4 Polynomials

Let $x_1, \ldots, x_k$ be symbolic variables. A *monomial* is a product of the form $x_1^{i_1} \cdot \ldots \cdot x_k^{i_k}$, where $i_1, \ldots, i_k \in \mathbb{N}$. In particular, a product of the form $c \cdot x_1^{i_1} \cdot \ldots \cdot x_k^{i_k}$, where $c \neq 1$, is not a monomial. Let $f(x_1, \ldots, x_k) = \sum_{i_1, \ldots, i_k \in \mathbb{N}} \alpha_{i_1, \ldots, i_k} \cdot x_1^{i_1} \cdot \ldots \cdot x_k^{i_k}$ be a polynomial with coefficients $\alpha_{i_1, \ldots, i_k} \in \mathbb{Z}$. We say that $x_1^{i_1} \cdot \ldots \cdot x_k^{i_k}$ is a *monomial of* f, if $\alpha_{i_1, \ldots, i_k} \neq 0$. If all monomials of f are elements of some set $\mathcal{M}$, then we say that f *is defined over* $\mathcal{M}$. We denote by $\deg(f)$ the *total degree* of f, i.e.,

$$\deg(f) := \max_{\alpha_{i_1, \ldots, i_k} \neq 0} (i_1 + \ldots + i_k).$$

The degree of some finite set of polynomials $\mathcal{F} \subseteq \mathbb{Z}[x_1, \ldots, x_k]$ is defined as

$$\deg(\mathcal{F}) := \max_{f \in \mathcal{F}} \deg(f).$$

The norm of f, denoted $\|f\|$, is defined as the Euclidean norm of its coefficient vector, i.e.,

$$\|f\| := \sqrt{\sum_{i_1,\dots,i_k \in \mathbb{N}} \alpha_{i_1,\dots,i_k}^2}.$$

Definition 3. *For a set of polynomials $\mathcal{F} \subset \mathbb{Z}[x_1,\dots,x_k]$, we define the set of its integer roots as*

$$Z_{\mathbb{Z}}(\mathcal{F}) := \left\{ r = (r_1,\dots,r_k) \in \mathbb{Z}^k \mid \forall f \in \mathcal{F} : f(r) = 0 \right\}.$$

Similarly, for parameters $M, X_1,\dots,X_k \in \mathbb{N}$, we define the corresponding set of its small modular roots as

$$Z_{M,X_1,\dots,X_k}(\mathcal{F}) := \left\{ r = (r_1,\dots,r_k) \in \mathbb{Z}^k \,\middle|\, \begin{array}{l} \forall f \in \mathcal{F} : f(r) \equiv 0 \mod M, \\ \forall j : |r_j| \le X_j \end{array} \right\}.$$

For a finite set $\mathcal{F} = \{f_1,\dots,f_n\}$, we may abuse notation and write

$$Z_{\mathbb{Z}}(f_1,\dots,f_n) := Z_{\mathbb{Z}}(\mathcal{F}),$$
$$Z_{M,X_1,\dots,X_k}(f_1,\dots,f_n) := Z_{M,X_1,\dots,X_k}(\mathcal{F}).$$

Definition 4. *Let $\mathcal{M}$ be a set of monomials. A* monomial order *(on $\mathcal{M}$) is a total order $\prec$ on $\mathcal{M}$, that satisfies the following two properties:*

1. *For every $\lambda \in \mathcal{M}$, it holds that $1 \prec \lambda$.*
2. *If $\lambda_1 \prec \lambda_2$, then $\lambda \cdot \lambda_1 \prec \lambda \cdot \lambda_2$ for every monomial $\lambda \in \mathcal{M}$.*

We frequently use the *lexicographic monomial order* $\prec_{\mathsf{lex}}$. The *leading monomial* of a polynomial f (with respect to some monomial order $\prec$) is the unique monomial λ of f, which satisfies $\lambda' \prec \lambda$ for every monomial λ' of f. The coefficient of the leading monomial is called *leading coefficient*. If the monomial order is clear from the context, we denote by $\mathsf{LM}(f)$ and $\mathsf{LC}(f)$ the leading monomial and the leading coefficient of f, respectively. Notice that for any two polynomials f, g we have

$$\mathsf{LM}(fg) = \mathsf{LM}(f)\mathsf{LM}(g), \tag{3}$$
$$\mathsf{LC}(fg) = \mathsf{LC}(f)\mathsf{LC}(g). \tag{4}$$

If $\mathsf{LC}(f) = 1$, then we say that f is *monic*.

2.5 Lattices

A *(full-rank) lattice* is a set of the form $\mathcal{L}(\mathbf{B}) := \mathbf{B} \cdot \mathbb{Z}^d$, where $\mathbf{B} \in \mathbb{R}^{d \times d}$ is an invertible matrix. We call $\mathbf{B}$ a *basis matrix* of $\mathcal{L}(\mathbf{B})$ and say that $\mathcal{L}(\mathbf{B})$ is the lattice generated by the columns of $\mathbf{B}$. The value d is called the *dimension* of $\mathcal{L}(\mathbf{B})$. The *determinant* of $\mathcal{L}(\mathbf{B})$ is defined as $\det \mathcal{L}(\mathbf{B}) := |\det \mathbf{B}|$. We call two basis matrices $\mathbf{B}_1, \mathbf{B}_2 \in \mathbb{R}^{d \times d}$ *equivalent*, if $\mathcal{L}(\mathbf{B}_1) = \mathcal{L}(\mathbf{B}_2)$. For equivalent basis matrices $\mathbf{B}_1, \mathbf{B}_2$ it holds that $\det \mathcal{L}(\mathbf{B}_1) = \det \mathcal{L}(\mathbf{B}_2)$. The *norm* of a lattice vector $\mathbf{v} \in \mathcal{L}(\mathbf{B})$, denoted $\|\mathbf{v}\|$, is the Euclidean norm.

The famous LLL lattice-reduction Algorithm [30] computes on input of a lattice basis $\mathbf{B} = (b_{i,j})_{1 \leq i \leq j \leq d} \in \mathbb{Z}^{d \times d}$ an equivalent basis in time polynomial in d and $\max_{i,j} \log(|b_{i,j}|)$, consisting of relatively short lattice vectors:

Lemma 1. *Let* $\mathbf{B} = (\mathbf{b}_1, \ldots, \mathbf{b}_d)$ *be an LLL-reduced basis of a d-dimensional lattice* $\Lambda \subseteq \mathbb{Z}^d$ *and let* $M, m \in \mathbb{N}$, *such that* $\log(M) \geq d \geq m$. *Suppose that*

$$\det(\Lambda) \leq M^{(m-k)d}$$

holds for some $k \leq d$. *Then*

$$\|\mathbf{b}_i\| < \frac{M^m}{\sqrt{d}}$$

holds for every $i = 1, \ldots, k$.

A proof for Lemma 1 is given in the full version of the paper.

3   Coppersmith's Method

In this section, we introduce our significantly simplified reformulation of Coppersmith's method. In Sect. 3.1, we recall the high-level idea behind Coppersmith's method, as well as the heuristic, that is used in almost all Coppersmith-type results. After that, we give in Sect. 3.2 a purely combinatorial reformulation and show how this allows us to automate Coppersmith's method almost entirely. As an application of our reformulation, we derive in Sect. 3.3 two new Coppersmith-type bounds, which we use in Sect. 5 to prove our results for CI-HNP.

3.1   High Level Idea

Suppose we are given a modulus $M \in \mathbb{N}$, polynomials $f_1, \ldots, f_n \in \mathbb{Z}_M[x_1, \ldots, x_k]$ and bounds $X_1, \ldots, X_k \in \mathbb{N}$. If the bounds are sufficiently small (and k is fixed), then Coppersmith's method finds all small modular roots

$$r \in Z_{M, X_1, \ldots, X_k}(f_1, \ldots, f_n)$$

in time polynomial in $\log(M)$.

The main idea behind Coppersmith's method is to transform the system of polynomial equations defined by the f_i's over $\mathbb{Z}_M$ into an efficiently solvable system of equations defined over $\mathbb{Z}$. To this end, Coppersmith's method uses lattice-based techniques to construct k polynomials $h_1, \ldots, h_k \in \mathbb{Z}[x_1, \ldots, x_k]$, such that all small modular roots of the f_i's are also integer roots of the h_i's, i.e.,

$$Z_{M, X_1, \ldots, X_k}(f_1, \ldots, f_n) \subseteq Z_{\mathbb{Z}}(h_1, \ldots, h_k).$$

Given the h_i's, we can efficiently compute all small modular roots r as follows:

In the univariate setting, where $k = 1$, we simply compute all roots of h_1 over $\mathbb{R}$ using standard techniques (such as Newton's method or the Sturm sequence) and then output those that lie in $Z_{M,X_1}(f_1,\ldots,f_n)$. In the multivariate setting, where $k > 1$, we follow a Gröbner basis based approach. Here, we first compute the Gröbner basis of the ideal $\mathfrak{a} := (h_1,\ldots,h_k) \subseteq \overline{\mathbb{Q}}[x_1,\ldots,x_k]$. Assuming that the variety of $\mathfrak{a}$ is zero-dimensional (which is usually the case in practice) we then efficiently obtain $Z_{\mathbb{Z}}(h_1,\ldots,h_k)$ from the Gröbner basis, again using standard techniques. Finally, from $Z_{\mathbb{Z}}(h_1,\ldots,h_k)$ we efficiently obtain $Z_{M,X_1,\ldots,X_k}(f_1,\ldots,f_n)$.

The Coppersmith Heuristic. Unfortunately, there is no *provable* guarantee that the variety of $\mathfrak{a}$ is zero-dimensional. In the multivariate setting, Coppersmith's method thus relies on the following (well-established) heuristic.

Heuristic 1 (Coppersmith Heuristic). *The polynomials obtained from Coppersmith's method generate an ideal of a zero-dimensional variety.*

While one can deliberately construct polynomials $f_1,\ldots,f_n$ and moduli M for which Heuristic 1 fails (see, e.g., [15, Section 12]), the heuristic holds for most instances arising in practice.

Nevertheless, we stress that it is important to verify the correctness of Heuristic 1 experimentally, since there are a few instances known for which the heuristic unexpectedly fails (see, e.g., the discussion on [48] in [34, Section 4]). We verify the correctness of Heuristic 1 for our algorithm for CI-HNP in Sect. 6.

Constructing $h_1,\ldots,h_k$. To construct the polynomials $h_1,\ldots,h_k$, Coppersmith's method requires as input a set of polynomials $\mathcal{F} \subset \mathbb{Z}[x_1,\ldots,x_k]$ satisfying certain technical constraints. (The h_i's are then computed as integer linear combinations of the elements of $\mathcal{F}$.) Construction of $\mathcal{F}$ is often difficult and usually done in an ad-hoc fashion. Furthermore, proving that a given set $\mathcal{F}$ satisfies the required technical constraints is often very tedious.

To overcome these issues, we introduce in the following Sect. 3.2 our novel and automated approach to Coppersmith's method, which allows us to greatly simplify construction of $\mathcal{F}$.

3.2 Coppersmith's Method Automated

The main idea behind our automated approach to Coppersmith's method is the following Definition 5. It allows us to abstract away all technicalities arising from lattice theory in Coppersmith's method and to replace them by purely combinatorial constraints.

Definition 5. *Let $\mathcal{M}$ be a finite set of monomials, and let $\prec$ be a monomial order on $\mathcal{M}$. A set of polynomials $\mathcal{F}$ is called $(\mathcal{M}, \prec)$-suitable, if:*

1. Every $f \in \mathcal{F}$ is defined over $\mathcal{M}$.

2. *For every monomial $\lambda \in \mathcal{M}$ there is a unique polynomial $f \in \mathcal{F}$ with leading monomial λ (with respect to $\prec$).*

If $\mathcal{F}$ is $(\mathcal{M}, \prec)$-suitable and $\lambda \in \mathcal{M}$, then we denote by $\mathcal{F}[\lambda]$ the unique polynomial $f \in \mathcal{F}$ with leading monomial λ.

We note that similar but less general constraints on $\mathcal{F}$ have first been used in [33, Lemma 4]. Definition 5 now allows us to compactly formulate Coppersmith's method as follows.

Theorem 2 (Coppersmith's Method). *Suppose we are given a modulus $M \in \mathbb{N}$, polynomials $f_1, \ldots, f_n \in \mathbb{Z}_M[x_1, \ldots, x_k]$ and bounds $0 \leq X_1, \ldots, X_k \leq M$, where $k = \mathcal{O}(1)$. Furthermore, suppose we are given an integer $m \in \mathbb{N}$, a set of monomials $\mathcal{M}$, a monomial order $\prec$ on $\mathcal{M}$, and an $(\mathcal{M}, \prec)$-suitable set of polynomials $\mathcal{F} \subseteq \mathbb{Z}_{M^m}[x_1, \ldots, x_k]$ with*

$$Z_{M, X_1, \ldots, X_k}(f_1, \ldots, f_n) \subseteq Z_{M^m, X_1, \ldots, X_k}(\mathcal{F}). \tag{5}$$

If the conditions

$$\prod_{\lambda \in \mathcal{M}} |\mathsf{LC}(\mathcal{F}[\lambda])| \leq \frac{M^{(m-k)|\mathcal{M}|}}{\prod_{\lambda \in \mathcal{M}} \lambda(X_1, \ldots, X_k)}, \tag{6}$$

$\log(M) \geq |\mathcal{M}| \geq m$ and $|\mathcal{M}| \geq k$ *hold, then we can compute all*

$$r \in Z_{M, X_1, \ldots, X_k}(f_1, \ldots, f_n)$$

in time polynomial in $\deg(\mathcal{F}) \cdot \log(M)$, under Heuristic 1 for $k > 1$.

A proof for Theorem 2 is given in Sect. 4. The algorithm behind Theorem 2 is given in Algorithm 1.

Algorithm 1: Coppersmith's Method.

Input: Integers $M, m \in \mathbb{N}$, polynomials $f_1, \ldots, f_n \in \mathbb{Z}_M[x_1, \ldots, x_k]$, bounds $0 \leq X_1, \ldots, X_k \leq M$, set of monomials $\mathcal{M}$, monomial order $\prec$ on $\mathcal{M}$, and a $(\mathcal{M}, \prec)$-suitable set of polynomials $\mathcal{F} \subseteq \mathbb{Z}_{M^m}[x_1, \ldots, x_k]$, satisfying the constraints of Theorem 2.

Output: All $r \in Z_{M, X_1, \ldots, X_k}(f_1, \ldots, f_n)$.

1 Construct an $|\mathcal{M}| \times |\mathcal{M}|$ basis matrix $\mathbf{B}$, whose columns are the coefficient vectors of the polynomials $\mathcal{F}[\lambda](X_1 x_1, \ldots, X_k x_k)$, where $\lambda \in \mathcal{M}$.

2 LLL-reduce $\mathbf{B}$.

3 Interpret the first k column of the resulting matrix as coefficient vectors of polynomials $h_i(X_1 x_1, \ldots, X_k x_k)$.

4 Compute the Gröbner basis of $\left(h_1(x_1, \ldots, x_k), \ldots, h_k(x_1, \ldots, x_k) \right)$.

5 **return** all $r \in Z_{\mathbb{Z}}(h_1, \ldots, h_k) \cap Z_{M, X_1, \ldots, X_k}(f_1, \ldots, f_n)$.

Given a modulus $M \in \mathbb{N}$, polynomials $f_1, \ldots, f_n \in \mathbb{Z}_M[x_1, \ldots, x_k]$ and bounds $X_1, \ldots, X_k \in \mathbb{N}$, Theorem 2 now suggests the following simple approach for computing all small modular roots $r \in Z_{M, X_1, \ldots, X_k}(f_1, \ldots, f_n)$:

1. Pick a set of monomials $\mathcal{M}$ in $x_1, \ldots, x_k$ with $|\mathcal{M}| \geq k$, a monomial order $\prec$ on $\mathcal{M}$, and an $m \in \mathbb{N}$, such that $\log(M) \geq |\mathcal{M}| \geq m$.
2. Pick an $(\mathcal{M}, \prec)$-suitable set of polynomials $\mathcal{F} \subseteq \mathbb{Z}_{M^m}[x_1, \ldots, x_k]$, satisfying Eqs. (5) and (6).
3. Apply Theorem 2/Algorithm 1 to compute all $r \in Z_{M, X_1, \ldots, X_k}(f_1, \ldots, f_n)$.

As we show below, choosing an *optimal* $\mathcal{F}$ can be automated entirely, once $\mathcal{M}$, m and $\prec$ are fixed. Furthermore, choosing m and $\prec$ is very easy. In our new approach all difficulties of Coppersmith's method thus boil down the much simpler task of choosing $\mathcal{M}$.

Below, we also describe a very simple and automated strategy for choosing $\mathcal{M}$. While this strategy does not always yield optimal results, it still performs well in practice.

Choosing $\mathcal{F}$. Suppose we have already chosen $\mathcal{M}$, $\prec$ and m. The set $\mathcal{F}$ then has to satisfy the following three conditions:

1. It has to be $(\mathcal{M}, \prec)$-suitable,
2. it has to satisfy Eq. (5),
3. it has to satisfy Eq. (6).

Satisfying Eq. (5) is easy: Like in all other Coppersmith-type results, we simply construct $\mathcal{F}$ using so-called *shift-polynomials*, i.e., polynomials of the form

$$p_{[j_1, \ldots, j_k, i_1, \ldots, i_n]} := x_1^{j_1} \cdot \ldots \cdot x_k^{j_k} \cdot f_1^{i_1} \cdot \ldots \cdot f_n^{i_n} \cdot M^{m-(i_1 + \ldots + i_n)}, \qquad (7)$$

for some appropriately chosen integers $j_1, \ldots, j_k, i_1, \ldots, i_n \in \mathbb{N}$, where $i_1 + \ldots + i_n \leq m$. Since for any $r \in Z_{M, X_1, \ldots, X_k}(f_1, \ldots, f_n)$ we have

$$f_1^{i_1}(r) \cdot \ldots \cdot f_n^{i_n}(r) \equiv 0 \mod M^{i_1 + \ldots + i_n},$$

it then holds that

$$p_{[j_1, \ldots, j_k, i_1, \ldots, i_n]}(r) \equiv 0 \mod M^m.$$

The resulting $\mathcal{F} := \{p_{[j_1, \ldots, j_k, i_1, \ldots, i_n]}\}_{j_1, \ldots, j_k, i_1, \ldots, i_n}$ thus satisfies Eq. (5).

For satisfying Eq. (6), notice that the right hand side in Eq. (6) does not depend on $\mathcal{F}$. For fixed $\mathcal{M}$, $\prec$, and m, Eq. (6) thus simply requires that the product of (the absolute values of) the leading coefficients of the polynomials in $\mathcal{F}$ is smaller than some constant. Making the mild assumption that the f_i's are monic, it follows from Eq. (4) that the leading coefficient of the shift-polynomial $p_{[j_1, \ldots, j_k, i_1, \ldots, i_n]}$ from Eq. (7) is

$$\mathsf{LC}\left(p_{[j_1, \ldots, j_k, i_1, \ldots, i_n]}\right) = M^{m-(i_1 + \ldots + i_n)}.$$

Hence, the larger the sum $i_1 + \ldots + i_n$ gets, the smaller gets the leading coefficient of the corresponding shift-polynomial. To satisfy Eq. (6), we thus have to take shift polynomials $p_{[j_1, \ldots, j_k, i_1, \ldots, i_n]}$ with as large $i_1 + \ldots + i_n$ as possible.

Finally, to ensure that $\mathcal{F}$ is $(\mathcal{M}, \prec)$-suitable, we have to include for every monomial $\lambda \in \mathcal{M}$ one shift-polynomial $p_{[j_1, \ldots, j_k, i_1, \ldots, i_n]}$ in $\mathcal{F}$, such that

1. the leading monomial of $p_{[j_1,\ldots,j_k,i_1,\ldots,i_n]}$ is λ, and
2. $p_{[j_1,\ldots,j_k,i_1,\ldots,i_n]}$ is defined over $\mathcal{M}$.

From Eq. (3) it easily follows that the shift-polynomials, which satisfy these conditions, are exactly the polynomials of the form

$$f_{[\lambda,i_1,\ldots,i_n]} := \frac{\lambda}{\mathsf{LM}(f_1)^{i_1} \cdot \ldots \cdot \mathsf{LM}(f_n)^{i_n}} \cdot f_1^{i_1} \cdot \ldots \cdot f_n^{i_n} \cdot M^{m-(i_1+\ldots+i_n)}, \qquad (8)$$

where

1. $\mathsf{LM}(f_1)^{i_1} \cdot \ldots \cdot \mathsf{LM}(f_n)^{i_n}$ divides λ, and
2. $f_{[\lambda,i_1,\ldots,i_n]}$ is defined over $\mathcal{M}$.

Hence, to construct an *optimal* set of shift-polynomials, we simply have to enumerate all such shift-polynomials $f_{[\lambda,i_1,\ldots,i_n]}$ and then include for every $\lambda \in \mathcal{M}$ one shift-polynomial in $\mathcal{F}$, that maximizes the sum $i_1 + \ldots + i_n$.

A formal description of this approach is given in Algorithm 2. The runtime of Algorithm 2 is $\mathcal{O}(|\mathcal{M}| \cdot m^n)$, which – for fixed n – is polynomial in our main parameter $\log(M)$, since by construction $m \le |\mathcal{M}| \le \log(M)$.

A somewhat optimized implementation of the algorithm is available in our GitHub repository. As we show in Sect. 6, our implementation is very efficient, even for cryptographically-sized instances.

Algorithm 2: Constructing an optimal set $\mathcal{F}$.

Input: Set of monomials $\mathcal{M}$, monomial order $\prec$ on $\mathcal{M}$, monic polynomials
$f_1,\ldots,f_n$, and integer $m \in \mathbb{N}$.
Output: $(\mathcal{M},\prec)$-suitable set of shift-polynomials $\mathcal{F}$, satisfying Eq. (5), and
minimizing the left hand side in Eq. (6).

1   $\mathcal{F} := \emptyset$
2   **for** $\lambda \in \mathcal{M}$ **do**
3   Enumerate all shift-polynomials $f_{[\lambda,i_1,\ldots,i_n]}$, as in Eq. (8), such that
      $\mathsf{LM}(f)^{i_1} \cdot \ldots \cdot \mathsf{LM}(f)^{i_n}$ divides λ, and $f_{[\lambda,i_1,\ldots,i_n]}$ is defined over $\mathcal{M}$.
4   Among all such $f_{[\lambda,i_1,\ldots,i_n]}$ pick one that maximizes $i_1 + \ldots + i_n$ and include
      it in $\mathcal{F}$.
5   **end**
6   **return** $\mathcal{F}$

Choosing $\prec$. The choice of $\prec$ is usually of secondary importance in Coppersmith's method, and simply choosing the lexicographic order $\prec_{\mathsf{lex}}$ will suffice in most applications. Indeed, if we were to restate all known Coppersmith-type results from the literature using the language of our new Theorem 2, then almost all results would use $\prec_{\mathsf{lex}}$ as monomial order.[3]

---

[3] However, we note that some results, which deeply exploit the algebraic structure of the underlying polynomials $f_1,\ldots,f_n$ via *unravelled linearization* [24], e.g., [33,49, 50], would require more involved monomial orders.

Choosing m and $\mathcal{M}$. Instead of choosing one fixed m and $\mathcal{M}$, we define an increasing sequence $\mathcal{M}_1 \subset \mathcal{M}_2 \subset \mathcal{M}_3 \subset \ldots$ of sets of monomials. While the Coppersmith-type literature strongly suggests that there is no *fully* automated strategy for choosing the $\mathcal{M}_i$'s, it appears that defining

$$\mathcal{M}_i := \left\{ \lambda \mid \lambda \text{ is a monomial of } f_1^{j_1} \cdot \ldots \cdot f_n^{j_n}, 0 \leq j_1, \ldots, j_n \leq i \right\} \tag{9}$$

$$m_i := i \cdot n, \tag{10}$$

often provides a good starting point, which one then may further optimize by incorporating special properties of the underlying polynomials $f_1, \ldots, f_n$.

The condition from Eq. (6), under which Coppersmith's method is successful, then typically translates to an inequality of the form

$$X_1^{\alpha_1} \cdot \ldots \cdot X_k^{\alpha_k} \leq M^{\delta - \varepsilon}, \tag{11}$$

for some constants $\alpha_1, \ldots, \alpha_k, \delta \geq 0$ and some $\varepsilon > 0$ that tends to 0 as $\mathcal{M}_i$ increases. (In other words, the larger we pick $\mathcal{M}_i$, the better Coppersmith's method performs.)

For the best possible result, we thus always pick the largest $\mathcal{M}_i$ that satisfies the condition $|\mathcal{M}_i| \leq \log(M)$ (which is imposed by Theorem 2). A typical Coppersmith-type result thus is a bound on the X_i's as in Eq. (11), where the error term ε vanishes as $M \to \infty$.

Computing Asymptotic Bounds. Once we have chosen our sequence of sets $\mathcal{M}_i$, we can use Algorithm 2 to construct – for any fixed $\mathcal{M}_i$ and $m_i := i \cdot n$ – a corresponding optimal set of shift-polynomials $\mathcal{F}_i$. Given $\mathcal{F}_i$, $\mathcal{M}_i$ and m_i, we may then derive from Eq. (6) a bound on $X_1, \ldots, X_k$, under which Coppersmith's method successfully recovers the desired small roots.

However, in practice one usually is not interested in the performance of Coppersmith's method for one fixed i, but rather in its asymptotic performance, i.e., usually it is desirable to obtain asymptotic bounds as in Eq. (11). Luckily, Algorithm 2 also allows us to derive such asymptotic bounds via polynomial interpolation as follows:

It turns out that the terms in Eq. (6) grow in practice as

$$M^{(m-k)|\mathcal{M}_i|} = M^{p_{\mathcal{M}}(m_i)}, \tag{12}$$

$$\prod_{\lambda \in \mathcal{M}_i} |\mathsf{LC}(\mathcal{F}_i[\lambda])| = M^{p_{\mathcal{F}}(m_i)} \tag{13}$$

$$\prod_{\lambda \in \mathcal{M}_i} \lambda(X_1, \ldots, X_k) = X_1^{p_1(m_i)} \cdot \ldots \cdot X_k^{p_k(m_i)}, \tag{14}$$

where $p_{\mathcal{M}}, p_{\mathcal{F}}, p_1, \ldots, p_k$ are polynomials of degree $k + 1$. Based on this observation, we simply run Algorithm 2 on $\mathcal{M}_1, \ldots, \mathcal{M}_{k+2}$ to construct $k + 2$ sets of shift-polynomials $\mathcal{F}$. Given $\mathcal{M}_1, \ldots, \mathcal{M}_{k+2}$ and the corresponding $\mathcal{F}_i$'s, we obtain the values of the polynomials $p_{\mathcal{F}}, p_{\mathcal{M}}, p_1, \ldots, p_k$ on $k + 2$ different inputs. Using polynomial interpolation, we then easily construct $p_{\mathcal{M}}, p_{\mathcal{F}}, p_1, \ldots, p_k$.

Denoting the leading coefficients of the polynomials by $\ell_\mathcal{M}, \ell_\mathcal{F}, \ell_1, \ldots, \ell_k$, Eq. (6) then translates to an asymptotic bound

$$X_1^{\ell_1} \cdot \ldots \cdot X_k^{\ell_k} \leq M^{\ell_\mathcal{M} - \ell_\mathcal{F} - \varepsilon}, \tag{15}$$

for some $\varepsilon > 0$ that vanishes as m increases, similar to Eq. (11).

When defining $\mathcal{M}_i$ and m_i as in Eqs. (9) and (10), it is easy to see that exponents in Eqs. (12) and (14) indeed grow as polynomials in m_i. However, *proving* that the same also holds for Eq. (13) appears to be difficult. Therefore, we require the following heuristic assumption.

Heuristic 2. *Let $f_1, \ldots, f_n \in \mathbb{Z}[x_1, \ldots, x_k]$, let $\prec$ be a monomial order on $x_1, \ldots, x_k$, and define*

$$\mathcal{M}_i := \left\{ \lambda \mid \lambda \text{ is a monomial of } f_1^{j_1} \cdot \ldots \cdot f_n^{j_n}, 0 \leq j_1, \ldots, j_n \leq i \right\}$$

$$m_i := i \cdot n,$$

for $i \in \mathbb{N}$. Then there exists a polynomial $p(m)$ of degree $k+1$, such that for any set $\mathcal{F}_i$, that is obtained from Algorithm 2 on input $(\mathcal{M}_i, \prec, (f_1, \ldots, f_n), m_i)$, it holds that

$$\prod_{\lambda \in \mathcal{M}_i} |\mathsf{LC}(\mathcal{F}_i[\lambda])| = M^{p(m_i)}.$$

In practice, Heuristic 2 always seems to hold. It is in an interesting open problem to further explore this behavior of Algorithm 2.

We note that in order to increase confidence in Heuristic 2 for any given set of polynomials $\{f_1, \ldots, f_n\}$, one may construct significantly more than $k+2$ sets $\mathcal{M}_i$ with corresponding sets of shift-polynomials $\mathcal{F}_i$. If the polynomial interpolation then still yields a polynomial of degree $k+1$, this serves as a very strong indication of the correctness of Heuristic 2.

If one still wishes to rigorously prove asymptotic bounds, i.e. without Heuristic 2, then one can proceed as follows: We run Algorithm 2 on $\mathcal{M}_1, \ldots, \mathcal{M}_{k+2}$, but instead of using polynomial interpolation, we (manually) look for patterns in the algorithms output, i.e., we look for patterns in the resulting sets of shift-polynomials $\mathcal{F}_i$. From these patterns, we then derive formulas that describe for any given $\mathcal{M}_i$ the corresponding set $\mathcal{F}_i$. Finally, these formulas allow us to derive an asymptotic bound as in Eq. (15).[4]

Clearly, this approach is significantly less automated than our polynomial interpolation approach based on Heuristic 2. However, due to the use of Algorithm 2 it is arguably still much simpler than most previous approaches to Coppersmith's method.

---

[4] We note that this approach is similar to the integer programming approach recently introduced by May, Nowakowski and Sarkar [33, Remark 1].

3.3   Applications of Our Automated Approach

Let us now use our automated approach to Coppersmith's method to derive two new Coppersmith-type bounds, which we use in the subsequent Sect. 5 to prove our results for CI-HNP.

Theorem 3. *Suppose we are given a modulus $M \in \mathbb{N}$, polynomials*

$$f(x, y, z) := xy + f_1 x + f_2 y + f_3,$$
$$g(x, y, z) := yz + g_1 y + g_2 z + g_3,$$
$$h(x, y, z) := xz + h_1 x + h_2 z + h_3,$$

for some constants $f_i, g_i, h_i \in \mathbb{Z}$, bounds $X, Y, Z \in \mathbb{N}$, and an arbitrarily small constant $\varepsilon > 0$. If M is sufficiently large, and

$$XYZ < M^{11/8-\varepsilon},$$

then we can compute all $r \in Z_{M,X,Y,Z}(f, g, h)$ in time polynomial in $\log(M)$, under Heuristics 1 and 2.

Proof. Following our strategy from Sect. 3.2, we choose a parameter $i \in \mathbb{N}$, define

$$\mathcal{M}_i := \left\{ \lambda \mid \lambda \text{ is a monomial of } f^{j_1} g^{j_2} h^{j_3}, 0 \le j_1, j_2, j_3 \le i \right\}$$
$$m_i = i \cdot 3,$$

and equip the elements in $\mathcal{M}_i$ with the lexicographic monomial order $\prec_{\mathsf{lex}}$ on x, y, z. Note that the constraints $|\mathcal{M}_i| \ge m_i$ and $|\mathcal{M}_i| \ge 3$ from Theorem 2 are trivially satisfied. For sufficiently large M, the additional constraint $\log(M) \ge |\mathcal{M}_i|$ is also satisfied.

It is easy to see that

$$M^{(m-3)|\mathcal{M}_i|} = M^{p_{\mathcal{M}}(m_i)},$$

$$\prod_{\lambda \in \mathcal{M}_i} \lambda(X, Y, Z) = X^{p_X(m_i)} \cdot Y^{p_Y(m_i)} \cdot Z^{p_Z(m_i)},$$

for some polynomials $p_{\mathcal{M}}, p_X, p_Y, p_Z$ of degree 4. Under Heuristic 2, we also have

$$\prod_{\lambda \in \mathcal{M}_i} |\mathsf{LC}(\mathcal{F}_i[\lambda])| = M^{p_{\mathcal{F}}(m_i)}$$

for some polynomial $p_{\mathcal{F}}$ of degree 4, where $\mathcal{F}_i$ denotes the output of Algorithm 2 on input $(\mathcal{M}_i, \prec_{\mathsf{lex}}, (f, g, h), m_i)$.

We run Algorithm 2 for $i = 1, \ldots, 5$. From the output of the algorithm, we obtain the following values:

Using polynomial interpolation, we obtain

$$p_{\mathcal{M}}(m_i) = \frac{8}{27} m_i^4 + o(m_i^4),$$

$$p_{\mathcal{F}}(m_i) = \frac{13}{81} m_i^4 + o(m_i^4),$$

$$p_X(m) = p_Y(m_i) = p_Z(m_i) = \frac{8}{81} m_i^4 + o(m_i^4).$$

m_i	$p_\mathcal{M}(m_i)$	$p_\mathcal{F}(m_i)$	$p_X(m_i)$	$p_Y(m_i)$	$p_Z(m_i)$
3	0	50	27	27	27
6	375	439	250	250	250
9	2058	1767	1029	1029	1029
12	6561	4946	2916	2916	2916
15	15972	11200	6655	6655	6655

Hence, the condition from Eq. (6) becomes

$$X^{8/81}Y^{8/81}Z^{8/81} < M^{8/27-13/81-\varepsilon} = M^{11/81-\varepsilon}$$

for some $\varepsilon > 0$ that vanishes as m (or equivalently M) increases. Taking the $\frac{8}{81}$-th root and replacing ε by $\frac{81}{8}\varepsilon$ in the above inequality, we obtain

$$XYZ < M^{11/8-\varepsilon},$$

as required.   □

In the full version of the paper, we show that Theorem 3 remains correct even when removing Heuristic 2 from the theorem. (However removing the heuristic comes at the cost of a significantly more complicated proof and manual effort.) We see this as a strong indication of the correctness of Heuristic 2.

Theorem 4. *Suppose we are given a modulus $M \in \mathbb{N}$, polynomials*

$$f(x,y,z) := x^2 + f_1 xy^2 + f_2 xy + f_3 x + f_4 y^2 + f_5 y + f_6,$$
$$g(x,y,z) := z^2 + g_1 x^2 z + g_2 xz + g_3 z + g_4 x^2 + g_5 x + g_6,$$

for some bounds $f_i, g_i \in \mathbb{Z}$, bounds $X, Y, Z \in \mathbb{N}$, and an arbitrarily small constant $\varepsilon > 0$. If M is sufficiently large, and

$$XYZ < M^{30/41-\varepsilon},$$

then we can compute all $r \in Z_{M,X,Y,Z}(f,g,h)$ in time polynomial in $\log(M)$, under Heuristics 1 and 2.

The proof of Theorem 4 is analogous to that of Theorem 3 and therefore omitted. A rigorous but involved proof that does not require Heuristic 2 is given in the full version of the paper.

The ε-term in Theorems 3 and 4. Previous works on Coppersmith's method often (implicitly) assume that one can easily eliminate the ε-term in Coppersmith-type bounds. However, as we discuss in the full version of the paper, when dealing with systems of *multivariate* equations (as in Theorems 3 and 4), the ε-term is inherent and eliminating it requires sub-exponential (but super-polynomial) runtime.

4 Proof for Theorem 2

The main idea behind Coppersmith's method is the following simple Lemma 2. Intuitively, it states that small modular roots of a polynomial h with small coefficients are actually integer roots of h.

Lemma 2 (Håstad [23], Howgrave-Graham [25]). *Let* $h(x_1, \ldots, x_k)$ *be a polynomial with at most d monomials, and let* $M^m, X_1, \ldots, X_k \in \mathbb{N}$. *Suppose h has a root* $r = (r_1, \ldots, r_k)$ *modulo* M^m, *satisfying* $|r_i| \leq X_i$ *for every* $i = 1, \ldots, k$. *If*

$$\|h(X_1 x_1, \ldots, X_k x_k)\| < \frac{M^m}{\sqrt{d}},$$

then $h(r_1, \ldots, r_k) = 0$ *holds over the integers.*

As discussed in Sect. 3.1, given a set of polynomials $\mathcal{F}$, Coppersmith's method efficiently computes all small modular roots $r \in Z_{M,X_1,\ldots,X_k}(\mathcal{F})$ by constructing a set of k-polynomials $\{h_1, \ldots, h_k\}$ such that

$$Z_{M,X_1,\ldots,X_k}(\mathcal{F}) \subseteq Z_{\mathbb{Z}}(h_1, \ldots, h_k).$$

To this end, Coppersmith's method uses LLL lattice reduction to construct the h_i's as small-norm integer linear combinations of the $f \in \mathcal{F}$. By Lemma 2 every r then is an integer root of the h_i's, as required.

Using this observation we now prove Theorem 2, which for the sake of readability we recall below.

Theorem 2 (Coppersmith's Method). *Suppose we are given a modulus $M \in \mathbb{N}$, polynomials* $f_1, \ldots, f_n \in \mathbb{Z}_M[x_1, \ldots, x_k]$ *and bounds* $0 \leq X_1, \ldots, X_k \leq M$, *where* $k = \mathcal{O}(1)$. *Furthermore, suppose we are given an integer* $m \in \mathbb{N}$, *a set of monomials* $\mathcal{M}$, *a monomial order* $\prec$ *on* $\mathcal{M}$, *and an* $(\mathcal{M}, \prec)$-*suitable set of polynomials* $\mathcal{F} \subseteq \mathbb{Z}_{M^m}[x_1, \ldots, x_k]$ *with*

$$Z_{M,X_1,\ldots,X_k}(f_1, \ldots, f_n) \subseteq Z_{M^m,X_1,\ldots,X_k}(\mathcal{F}). \tag{5}$$

If the conditions

$$\prod_{\lambda \in \mathcal{M}} |\mathsf{LC}(\mathcal{F}[\lambda])| \leq \frac{M^{(m-k)|\mathcal{M}|}}{\prod_{\lambda \in \mathcal{M}} \lambda(X_1, \ldots, X_k)}, \tag{6}$$

$\log(M) \geq |\mathcal{M}| \geq m$ *and* $|\mathcal{M}| \geq k$ *hold, then we can compute all*

$$r \in Z_{M,X_1,\ldots,X_k}(f_1, \ldots, f_n)$$

in time polynomial in $\deg(\mathcal{F}) \cdot \log(M)$, *under Heuristic 1 for* $k > 1$.

Proof. For every $i = 1, \ldots, |\mathcal{M}|$, let λ_i denote the i-th smallest monomial in $\mathcal{M}$ (with respect to $\prec$). For every $\lambda \in \mathcal{M}$, we denote by $\mathbf{f}_\lambda \in \mathbb{Z}^{|\mathcal{M}|}$ the coefficient vector of $\mathcal{F}[\lambda](X_1x_1,\ldots,X_kx_k)$, where the i-th coordinate of $\mathbf{f}_\lambda$ is the coefficient of λ_i in $\mathcal{F}[\lambda](X_1x_1,\ldots,X_kx_k)$.

We construct an $|\mathcal{M}| \times |\mathcal{M}|$ lattice basis matrix $\mathbf{B}$, where the i-th column of $\mathbf{B}$ is the vector $\mathbf{f}_{\lambda_i}$. Since λ_i is the leading monomial of $\mathcal{F}_{\lambda_i}$, the i-th entry of $\mathbf{f}_{\lambda_i}$ equals $\mathsf{LC}(\mathcal{F}_{\lambda_i}) \cdot \lambda_i(X_1,\ldots,X_k)$. Further, for every $j > i$ the j-th entry of $\mathbf{f}_{\lambda_i}$ equals 0, since $\lambda_i \prec \lambda_j$. Hence, $\mathbf{B}$ is a triangular matrix with determinant

$$\det \mathbf{B} = \prod_{\lambda \in \mathcal{M}} \mathsf{LC}(\mathcal{F}[\lambda]) \cdot \lambda(X_1,\ldots,X_k).$$

Together with Eq. (6) this implies

$$\det \mathcal{L}(\mathbf{B}) \le M^{(m-k)|\mathcal{M}|}. \tag{16}$$

We compute an LLL-reduced basis $\mathbf{B}_{\mathsf{LLL}} = (\mathbf{b}_1,\ldots,\mathbf{b}_{|\mathcal{M}|})$ of $\mathcal{L}(\mathbf{B})$. From $\log(M) \ge |\mathcal{M}| \ge m$, Lemma 1 and Eq. (16) it follows that the first k columns $\mathbf{b}_1,\ldots,\mathbf{b}_k$ of $\mathbf{B}_{\mathsf{LLL}}$ have norm

$$\|\mathbf{b}_1\|,\ldots,\|\mathbf{b}_k\| < \frac{M^m}{\sqrt{|\mathcal{M}|}}. \tag{17}$$

Notice, since $|\mathcal{M}| \ge k$, the matrix $\mathbf{B}_{\mathsf{LLL}}$ indeed has at least k columns.

By definition of $\mathbf{B}$, every vector $\mathbf{b}_i$ from the LLL-reduced basis is the coefficient vector of some polynomial $h_i(X_1x_1,\ldots,X_kx_k)$, such that

$$h_i(x_1,\ldots,x_k) = \sum_{\lambda \in \mathcal{M}} \alpha_{i,\lambda} \mathcal{F}[\lambda](x_1,\ldots,x_k), \tag{18}$$

for some $\alpha_{i,\lambda} \in \mathbb{Z}$. Let $r \in Z_{M,X_1,\ldots,X_k}(f_1,\ldots,f_n)$. Since

$$Z_{M,X_1,\ldots,X_k}(f_1,\ldots,f_n) \subseteq Z_{M^m,X_1,\ldots,X_k}(\mathcal{F}),$$

it follows from Eq. (18) that

$$h_i(r) \equiv \sum_{\lambda \in \mathcal{M}} \alpha_{i,\lambda} \mathcal{F}[\lambda](r) \equiv 0 \mod M^m.$$

Together with Eq. (17) and Lemma 2, this implies that r is a root of $h_1,\ldots,h_k$ have r over the integers. Hence,

$$Z_{M,X_1,\ldots,X_k}(f_1,\ldots,f_n) \subseteq Z_{\mathbb{Z}}(h_1,\ldots,h_k).$$

Since the entries of $\mathbf{B}$ are upper bounded by polynomials of degree at most $d := \deg(\mathcal{F})$ in M^m, the runtime of LLL to compute $\mathbf{B}_{\mathsf{LLL}}$ is polynomial in $d \cdot m \cdot \log(M) \le d \log(M)^2$ and $|\mathcal{M}| \le \log(M)$. Hence, we can compute $h_1,\ldots,h_k$ in time polynomial in $d \cdot \log(M)$, as required.

Finally, if $k = 1$, we efficiently obtain all $r \in Z_{M,X_1,\ldots,X_k}(f_1,\ldots,f_n)$, by computing all integer roots of h_1 and then outputting only those that lie in $Z_{M,X_1,\ldots,X_k}(f_1,\ldots,f_n)$. If $k > 1$, we efficiently obtain all such r's under Heuristic 1 from the Gröbner basis of $\mathfrak{a} := (h_1,\ldots,h_k)$, which we can compute in polynomial time, since $k = \mathcal{O}(1)$. □

5   The Commutative Isogeny Hidden Number Problem

In this section we use the results developed in Sect. 3 to solve the Commutative Isogeny Hidden Number Problem. We assume that an elliptic curve is always represented by its corresponding Montgomery coefficient. That is, oracles or algorithms that take as input an elliptic curve always expect the Montgomery coefficient of said curve. The same principle applies to the output of such an oracle or algorithm. This means that we mainly work with the group action from Eq. (1) and Eq. (2), respectively.

We now define the main computational problem, which applies to both CSIDH and CSURF where we (implicitly) set the prime p, the order $\mathcal{O}$ and the starting curve M accordingly.

Definition 6 (Commutative Isogeny Hidden Number Problem (CI-HNP$_k$)). *Let p be an n-bit prime and let $k < n$ be a positive integer. Further let $[\mathfrak{a}], [\mathfrak{b}] \xleftarrow{\$} cl(\mathcal{O})$. Assume that there exists an oracle $\mathcal{O}_{\mathsf{MSB}_k}$ that on input two Montgomery coefficients $M_0, M_1 \in \mathcal{M}_p(\mathcal{O})$ computes*

$$\mathcal{O}_{\mathsf{MSB}_k}(M_0, M_1) := \mathsf{MSB}_k(\mathsf{CDH}(M_0, M_1)).$$

Given the tuple $(\mathfrak{a} \star M, \mathfrak{b} \star M)$ and access to $\mathcal{O}_{\mathsf{MSB}_k}$, the task is to recover $\mathfrak{ab} \star M$.

Remark 3. Because we can write

$$M_{\mathfrak{ab}} := \mathfrak{ab} \star M = \mathcal{O}_{\mathsf{MSB}_k}(\mathfrak{a} \star M, \mathfrak{b} \star M) \cdot 2^{n-k} + m_{\mathfrak{ab}} \tag{19}$$

for some $m_{\mathfrak{ab}} < 2^{n-k}$ we focus on recovering $m_{\mathfrak{ab}}$ from now on.

In the next sections we give an algorithm $\mathcal{A}$ that solves CI-HNP$_k$ for both CSIDH and CSURF. Like many algorithms that solve a flavour of the hidden number problem, $\mathcal{A}$ proceeds in two stages:

1. Query the oracle $\mathcal{O}_{\mathsf{MSB}_k}$ on specific input, obtaining a set of bivariate polynomial equations that have a common small root in $m_{\mathfrak{ab}}$.
2. Use Coppersmith's method to solve the system of equations, yielding the common root $m_{\mathfrak{ab}}$.

We remark that the second stage is the same for both CSIDH and CSURF. Furthermore, for the results in the following sections it is actually sufficient to have a *static* oracle. That is, an oracle where one of the inputs to the oracle is fixed, i.e.

$$\mathcal{O}_{\mathsf{MSB}_k}(M') := \mathsf{MSB}_k(\mathsf{CDH}(M', \mathfrak{b} \star M))$$

with $\mathfrak{b}$ as in Definition 6.

5.1   Solving CI-HNP for CSIDH

Let $p \equiv 3 \mod 8$ be a prime and $\mathcal{O} = \mathbb{Z}[\pi]$. Our goal is to find polynomial relations between neighboring Montgomery curves similar to what the modular polynomial provides for j-invariants. A variant of Vélu's formula dedicated to Montgomery curves provides a good starting point.

Theorem 5 (Proposition 1 in [39]). *Let $E_A : y^2 = x^3 + Ax^2 + x$ with $A^2 \neq 4$ be a Montgomery curve defined over $\mathbb{F}_p$ and let $G \subset E_A(\overline{\mathbb{F}}_p)$ be a finite subgroup such that $(0,0) \notin G$. Further define φ to be a separable isogeny with $\ker \varphi = G$. Then there exists a Montgomery curve $E_B : y^2 = x^3 + Bx^2 + x$ such that, up to isomorphism, $\varphi : E_A \to E_B$ and*

$$B = \tau(A - 3\sigma), \qquad where \ \tau = \prod_{P \in G \setminus \{\infty\}} x_P, \qquad \sigma = \sum_{P \in G \setminus \{\infty\}} \left(x_P - \frac{1}{x_P} \right).$$

By expanding the equation for B we immediately get a polynomial that relates two isogenous Montgomery coefficients to each other. Evidently, Theorem 5 can handle isogenies of almost arbitrary degree d and therefore could be used to derive polynomials describing the neighborhood of any two d-isogenous curves. To keep the total degree of the polynomial low, however, it is beneficial to look at isogenies of small degree. It is therefore natural to consider 3-isogenies as they have the smallest kernel amongst those isogenies admissible by the CSIDH group action. Moreover, removing the unwanted variables $\{x_P\}_{P \in G \setminus \{\infty\}}$ can be done via the 3-*division polynomial* (for a precise definition see [9]) and a resultant computation.

In the case of 3-isogenies this approach yields polynomial relations of total degree 6. However, we can improve on this by instead considering *4-isogenies*. In fact, the ideal (4) splits in $\mathbb{Z}[\pi]$ as $\overline{\mathfrak{l}} = \langle 4, \pi - 1 \rangle \langle 4, \pi + 1 \rangle$. Most notably, the ideal $\mathfrak{l}$ has order 3 which is a direct result of using the class group of the non-maximal order $\mathbb{Z}[\pi]$ [11,38]. Hence the following formulas are only applicable to the CSIDH setting.

Proposition 1 (Theorem 7 in [38]). *Let $A \in \mathcal{M}_p(\mathbb{Z}[\pi])$ be the Montgomery coefficient of the curve $E_A \in \mathcal{Ell}_p(\mathbb{Z}[\pi])$. The two 4-isogenous curves of E_A in $\mathcal{Ell}_p(\mathbb{Z}[\pi])$ are*

$$E_B : y^2 = x^3 + Bx^2 + x, \qquad where \ B = 2\frac{A - 6}{A + 2}$$

and

$$E_C : y^2 = x^3 + Cx^2 + x, \qquad where \ C = 2\frac{A + 6}{2 - A}.$$

It is immediately evident that due to their simple form, the 4-isogeny formulas result in polynomial relations of degree only 2.

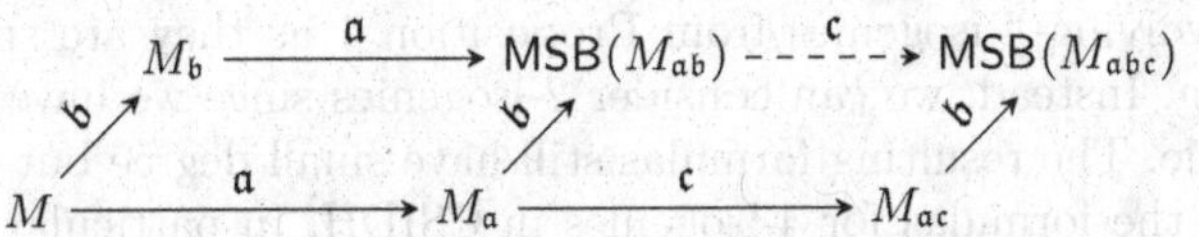

Fig. 3. Visualization of the general strategy where $\mathfrak{c}$ is an ideal of small norm (i.e. an isogeny of small degree). Here, $\mathcal{O}_{\mathsf{MSB}_k}$ allows us to compute the most significant bits of M_{ab} and M_{abc}, which are connected by the same ideal $\mathfrak{c}$.

Corollary 1. *The Montgomery coefficients A, B and C from Proposition 1 satisfy the relations*

$$2A - AB - 2B - 12 = 0,$$
$$2C - AC - 2A - 12 = 0 \text{ and}$$
$$2B - BC - 2C - 12 = 0.$$

Proof. This is a simple restatement of Proposition 1 where the third formula is derived from the first two by taking the resultant with respect to A. □

Remarkably, due to the small order of $\mathfrak{l}$ we get *three* relations between A and its 4-isogenous neighbors B and C that all have the same total degree. This is particularly interesting as we can usually only hope to craft two polynomial relations of the same degree between A and its d-isogenous neighbors. The reason for this is that the two neighboring curves B and C are in general d^2-isogenous, resulting in a third polynomial relation of larger degree. As it turns out, Coppersmith's method strongly benefits from having a third relation of the same total degree, which in turn allows us to solve CI-HNP$_k$ for a smaller value k.

Theorem 6. *Let $p \equiv 3 \mod 8$ be a n-bit prime, and let $\varepsilon > 0$ be an arbitrarily small constant. There exists a PPT algorithm $\mathcal{A}$ that solves CI-HNP$_k$ in the CSIDH setting for $k = (\frac{13}{24} + \varepsilon)n$ under Heuristic 1.*

Proof. Let (M_a, M_b) be an instance of CI-HNP$_k$. The algorithm $\mathcal{A}$ proceeds as follows: First, it uses Proposition 1 to compute the 4-isogenous neighbors of M_a, which we denote by M_{ac} and $M_{a\eth}$ respectively. It then submits the queries $\mathcal{O}_{\mathsf{MSB}_k}(M_a, M_b)$ and $\mathcal{O}_{\mathsf{MSB}_k}(M_{ac}, M_b)$, which yield the most significant bits of $M_{ab} = \mathsf{CDH}(M_a, M_b)$ and $M_{abc} = \mathsf{CDH}(M_{ac}, M_b)$ (see Fig. 3). Since the group action is commutative we have that M_{ab} and M_{abc} are 4-isogenous as well, thus satisfying the first equation in Corollary 1. The same process is repeated for $M_{a\eth}$, yielding the most significant bits of $M_{ab\eth}$. Finally, by using Eq. (19) we can rewrite the resulting equations in terms of the least significant bits m_{ab}, m_{abc} and $m_{ab\eth}$, which are now small roots of size $p^{11/24}$ of the respective polynomials. $\mathcal{A}$ then finds these small roots via Theorem 3. □

5.2 Solving CI-HNP for CSURF

Let $p \equiv 7 \mod 8$ be a prime and $\mathcal{O} = \mathbb{Z}[(1+\pi)/2]$. We use a very similar strategy compared to Sect. 5.1 to craft the polynomials. Unfortunately, we cannot use the same trick involving 4-isogenies from Proposition 1 as they are specific to the CSIDH setting. Instead, we can consider 2-isogenies since we have the ideals $\mathfrak{l}_0$ and $\bar{\mathfrak{l}}_0$ available. The resulting formulas still have small degree but cannot quite compete with the formulas for 4-isogenies in CSIDH. In particular, the ideal $\mathfrak{l}_0$ has very large order, meaning that we only get two relations between a curve and its 2-isogenous neighbors.

Recall that the point $P_\rightarrow = (0,0)$ has order 2 and corresponds to the ideal $\mathfrak{l}_0$. In order to compute the image curve of the vertical isogeny with kernel $\langle P_\rightarrow \rangle$ we use the following formula from [18, Equation (18)].

Proposition 2. *Let $A \in \mathcal{M}_p(\mathbb{Z}[(1 + \pi)/2])$ be the Montgomery coefficient of the curve E_A and let $P_\rightarrow = (0,0)$. The curve $E_A/\langle P_\rightarrow \rangle$ is isomorphic to a Montgomery curve E_B that can be written as*

$$E_B : y^2 = x^3 + Bx^2 + x, \qquad where \ B = \frac{A + 6}{2\sqrt{A + 2}}.$$

Note that $A + 2$ is a square by definition. Squaring both sides and rearranging terms yields a bivariate polynomial of total degree 3.

Corollary 2. *Let the notation be as in Proposition 2. The Montgomery coefficients A and B satisfy*

$$A^2 + 12A - 4B^2A - 8B^2 + 36 = 0.$$

The formula above only applies to the vertical isogeny generated by the point $P_\rightarrow$. However, one can treat the other vertical isogeny generated by $P_\leftarrow \neq (0,0)$ similarly by observing that if $E' = E/\langle P_\leftarrow \rangle$, then $E \cong E'/\langle P_\rightarrow \rangle$. We thus get almost the same formula as in Corollary 2 where the only difference is that the coefficient A now takes the role of the image curve.

Corollary 3. *Let $A \in \mathcal{M}_p(\mathbb{Z}[(1 + \pi)/2])$ be the Montgomery coefficient of E_A and let E_C be the Montgomery curve isomorphic to $E_A/\langle P_\leftarrow \rangle$. Then the Montgomery coefficients A and C satisfy*

$$C^2 + 12C - 4A^2C - 8A^2 + 36 = 0.$$

Observe that in Corollary 3 the monomials involving the Montgomery coefficient A are quite different compared to Corollary 2. This is in stark contrast to the CSIDH setting (in particular Corollary 1) where in the first two equations the monomials involving A are almost identical (up to sign). This "asymmetry" in the polynomials is undesirable for Coppersmith's method. In combination with the fact that we only have two relations instead of three, we have to increase the value k significantly in order to solve CI-HNP$_k$ for CSURF.

Theorem 7. *Let $p \equiv 7 \mod 8$ be a n-bit prime, and let $\varepsilon > 0$ be an arbitrarily small constant. There exists a PPT algorithm $\mathcal{A}$ that solves CI-HNP$_k$ in the CSURF setting for $k = (\frac{31}{41} + \varepsilon)n$ under Heuristic 1.*

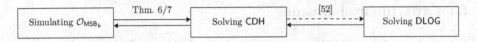

Fig. 4. Overview of the reduction from simulating the oracle $\mathcal{O}_{\mathsf{MSB}_k}$ to DLOG. Dashed lines denote quantum reductions.

Proof. The algorithm $\mathcal{A}$ proceeds like in the previous section. Given an instance $(M_{\mathfrak{a}}, M_{\mathfrak{b}})$ of CI-HNP$_k$, $\mathcal{A}$ first computes the 2-isogenous coefficients $M_{\mathfrak{ac}}$ and $M_{\mathfrak{ad}}$ by quotienting out $\langle P_{\rightarrow}\rangle$ and $\langle P_{\leftarrow}\rangle$ on $M_{\mathfrak{a}}$, respectively. It then submits the oracle queries $\mathcal{O}_{\mathsf{MSB}_k}(M_{\mathfrak{a}}, M_{\mathfrak{b}})$ and $\mathcal{O}_{\mathsf{MSB}_k}(M_{\mathfrak{ac}}, M_{\mathfrak{b}})$, which yield the most significant bits of the coefficients $M_{\mathfrak{ab}} = \mathsf{CDH}(M_{\mathfrak{a}}, M_{\mathfrak{b}})$ and $M_{\mathfrak{abc}} = \mathsf{CDH}(M_{\mathfrak{ac}}, M_{\mathfrak{b}})$. Lastly it uses Eq. (19) to express the equation from Corollary 2 in terms of $m_{\mathfrak{ab}}$ and $m_{\mathfrak{abc}}$, where $m_{\mathfrak{ab}}$ and $m_{\mathfrak{abc}}$ are now small roots of size $p^{10/41}$ of the corresponding polynomial. The same process is repeated with the curve $M_{\mathfrak{ad}}$ and Corollary 3. The small root $m_{\mathfrak{ab}}$ is then found by Coppersmith's method and the bound for k follows from Theorem 4. Note that the monomials in Theorem 4 differ slightly from those appearing in Corollary 2 and Corollary 3 due to the substitution mentioned in Eq. (19). $\qquad\square$

5.3 Hardness of Simulating $\mathcal{O}_{\mathsf{MSB}_k}$

The results from the previous sections can be directly used to analyze the hardness of simulating the oracle $\mathcal{O}_{\mathsf{MSB}_k}$. More concretely, simulating $\mathcal{O}_{\mathsf{MSB}_k}$ is quantumly as hard as solving DLOG due to the equivalence of CDH and DLOG in the CSIDH/CSURF setting. For simplicity we state the following result only for CSIDH, the statement and proof for CSURF is completely analogous.

Corollary 4. *Let $p \equiv 3 \mod 4$ be an n-bit prime, $\mathcal{O} = \mathbb{Z}[\pi]$ and $k = (\frac{13}{24} + \varepsilon)n$ for some arbitrary small constant $\epsilon > 0$. Assume that there exists an efficient (possibly quantum) algorithm $\mathcal{A}$ with*

$$\Pr[\mathcal{A}(\mathfrak{a} \star M, \mathfrak{b} \star M) = \mathcal{O}_{\mathsf{MSB}_k}(\mathfrak{a} \star M, \mathfrak{b} \star M)] = 1$$

where $[\mathfrak{a}], [\mathfrak{b}] \xleftarrow{\$} cl(\mathcal{O})$. Then there exists an efficient quantum algorithm $\mathcal{B}$ solving DLOG in the CSIDH setting under Heuristic 1.

Proof. The reduction is straightforward and depicted in Fig. 4. In a first step, we use our algorithm developed in Theorem 6 to transform the algorithm $\mathcal{A}$ into an algorithm $\mathcal{A}'$ solving CDH under Heuristic 1. In a second step we can simply use $\mathcal{A}'$ (which still has success probability 1) together with the techniques developed by [52] to construct the algorithm $\mathcal{B}$ solving DLOG. $\qquad\square$

We currently require $\mathcal{A}$ to simulate $\mathcal{O}_{\mathsf{MSB}_k}$ perfectly. This is a direct consequence of the fact that there is no obvious way to re-randomize the inputs to the oracle $\mathcal{O}_{\mathsf{MSB}_k}$ such that we still get meaningful information about the neighboring curves of $\mathfrak{ab} \star M$.

6   Experimental Results

We implemented our new automated variant of Coppersmith's method from Theorem 2 in SageMath and used it to run our algorithms from Theorems 6 and 7 in practice.

CSIDH and CSURF Results. We ran our algorithms from Theorems 6 and 7 using SageMath 9.7 on an AMD EPYC 7763 processor with 128 physical and 256 logical cores. As Table 1 shows, our algorithms perform well in practice and we come close to our asymptotic bounds of $k = \frac{13}{24}n \approx 0.542n$ and $k = \frac{31}{41}n = 0.756n$ in a matter of minutes.

Table 1. Experimental results for CSIDH/Theorem 6 (top) and CSURF/Theorem 7 (bottom) with n-bit prime p and k-bit MSB oracle, averaged over 10 runs each. The columns m and $|\mathcal{M}|$ show the parameters m and $|\mathcal{M}|$ used in Coppersmith's method. The columns $\mathcal{F}$, LLL and GB show the required runtime for constructing the set $\mathcal{F}$, running LLL and computing the Gröbner basis, respectively. For every n and m, the table shows the smallest k for which our algorithms were able to solve CI-HNP$_k$.

n	k (known bits)	m	$|\mathcal{M}|$ (lattice dim.)	Runtime $\mathcal{F}$	LLL	GB
512	318 (62.11%)	3	27	< 1 s	<1 s	<1 s
512	302 (58.98%)	6	125	<1 s	30 s	5 s
512	297 (58.00%)	9	343	2 s	8 min	56 s
1024	634 (61.91%)	3	27	<1 s	1 s	1 s
1024	601 (58.69%)	6	125	<1 s	39 s	9 s
1024	589 (57.52%)	9	343	3 s	10 min	2 min
1792	1108 (61.83%)	3	27	<1 s	1 s	1 s
1792	1051 (58.65%)	6	125	<1 s	50 s	15 s
1792	1028 (57.37%)	9	343	3 s	13 min	3 min

n	k (known bits)	m	$|\mathcal{M}|$ (lattice dim.)	Runtime $\mathcal{F}$	LLL	GB
512	438 (85.55%)	2	33	<1 s	1 s	<1 s
512	419 (81.84%)	4	165	<1 s	52 s	4 s
512	405 (79.10%)	6	469	1 s	16 min	34 s
1024	874 (85.35%)	2	33	<1 s	1 s	<1 s
1024	830 (81.05%)	4	165	<1 s	1 min	6 s
1024	808 (78.91%)	6	469	1 s*	22 min	57 s
1792	1528 (85.27%)	2	33	<1 s	2 s	1 s
1792	1451 (80.97%)	4	165	<1 s	2 min	7 s
1792	1412 (78.79%)	6	469	1 s	31 min	2 min

In every experiment Heuristic 1 was valid, i.e., we were always able to extract the unknowns from the Gröbner basis. This confirms the correctness of our heuristic algorithms.

Implementation Details. For constructing the set of shift-polynomials $\mathcal{F}$, we used in our experiments a slightly optimized implementation of Algorithm 2. Instead of simply enumerating *all* possible shift-polynomials in Step 3 of the algorithm, our implementation iterates over a carefully crafted tree of shift-polynomials. The tree is constructed only implicitly, and our implementation automatically detects (and ignores) some branches that are not worth visiting. This results in a significant speed-up in practice.

The LLL lattice reduction step was performed using the recently published **flatter** algorithm [42], which significantly outperforms SageMath's native implementation of LLL (which internally calls FPLLL).

For the Gröbner basis computation, we used SageMath's native Gröbner basis algorithm (which internally calls **Singular**) to compute Gröbner bases over small finite fields $\mathbb{F}_2, \mathbb{F}_3, \mathbb{F}_5, \mathbb{F}_7 \ldots$, and then recovered the desired roots via Chinese remaindering.

7 Conclusion

In this work we analyzed the Commutative Isogeny Hidden Number Problem and solved it for $k = \frac{13}{24}n$ (CSIDH) and $k = \frac{31}{41}n$ (CSURF) by using a new and automated variant of Coppersmith's method. Since the recovery rate for CSURF is much worse compared to CSIDH, we conclude that in the context of side-channel attacks, CSURF offers more resilience against exposing the most significant bits of the shared key. Even more generally it seems to be advisable that the class group $cl(\mathcal{O})$ does not contain a small order subgroup, which is in line with previous observations [11,38].

Furthermore, we gave a purely combinatorial restatement of Coppersmith's method that allows for near complete automation. In particular, we identified a single step in Coppersmith's method that, when optimized, yields provably optimal results. We implemented our variant of Coppersmith's method in SageMath and demonstrated its practicality by using it to solve the Commutative Isogeny Hidden Number Problem. In particular, we gave highly simplified proofs for the recovery bound of our algorithm that only rely on a mild heuristic.

Open Problems. Lastly we state some open problems. Improving the recovery bound for either CSIDH or CSURF would of course be desirable. Apart from incremental improvements coming from an improved Coppersmith lattice the only other natural option seems to be to incorporate higher-degree isogenies. This would yield more polynomial relations at the expense of higher total degrees of said polynomials. It is currently not known whether this trade-off can be used to increase the overall recovery rate. Alternatively, finding a completely different approach to solving CI-HNP would be very intriguing.

Secondly, any improvements to Corollary 4 would be welcome, either by extending the reduction to adversaries with non-negligible success probability or by removing the condition on CSIDH/CSURF being effective group actions.

Thirdly, proving Heuristic 2 (even in some special cases) would be very interesting as it would yield an efficient algorithm that can derive provably correct recovery bounds.

Acknowledgements. We would like to thank Sabrina Kunzweiler for her helpful discussions and pointing us to the 4-isogenies in the CSIDH setting. Jonas Meers was funded by the Deutsche Forschungsgemeinschaft (DFG, German Research Foundation) under Germany's Excellence Strategy - EXC 2092 CASA - 390781972. Julian Nowakowski is funded by the DFG grant 465120249.

References

1. Alamati, N., De Feo, L., Montgomery, H., Patranabis, S.: Cryptographic group actions and applications. In: Moriai, S., Wang, H. (eds.) ASIACRYPT 2020. LNCS, vol. 12492, pp. 411–439. Springer, Cham (2020). https://doi.org/10.1007/978-3-030-64834-3_14

2. Aranha, D.F., Fouque, P.-A., Gérard, B., Kammerer, J.-G., Tibouchi, M., Zapalowicz, J.-C.: GLV/GLS decomposition, power analysis, and attacks on ECDSA signatures with single-bit nonce bias. In: Sarkar, P., Iwata, T. (eds.) ASIACRYPT 2014. LNCS, vol. 8873, pp. 262–281. Springer, Heidelberg (2014). https://doi.org/10.1007/978-3-662-45611-8_14

3. Boneh, D., Halevi, S., Howgrave-Graham, N.: The modular inversion hidden number problem. In: Boyd, C. (ed.) ASIACRYPT 2001. LNCS, vol. 2248, pp. 36–51. Springer, Heidelberg (2001). https://doi.org/10.1007/3-540-45682-1_3

4. Boneh, D., Shparlinski, I.E.: On the unpredictability of bits of the elliptic curve Diffie-Hellman scheme. In: Kilian, J. (ed.) CRYPTO 2001. LNCS, vol. 2139, pp. 201–212. Springer, Heidelberg (2001). https://doi.org/10.1007/3-540-44647-8_12

5. Boneh, D., Venkatesan, R.: Hardness of computing the most significant bits of secret keys in Diffie-Hellman and related schemes. In: Koblitz, N. (ed.) CRYPTO 1996. LNCS, vol. 1109, pp. 129–142. Springer, Heidelberg (1996). https://doi.org/10.1007/3-540-68697-5_11

6. Breitner, J., Heninger, N.: Biased nonce sense: lattice attacks against weak ECDSA signatures in cryptocurrencies. In: Goldberg, I., Moore, T. (eds.) FC 2019. LNCS, vol. 11598, pp. 3–20. Springer, Cham (2019). https://doi.org/10.1007/978-3-030-32101-7_1

7. Castryck, W., Decru, T.: CSIDH on the surface. In: Ding, J., Tillich, J.-P. (eds.) PQCrypto 2020. LNCS, vol. 12100, pp. 111–129. Springer, Cham (2020). https://doi.org/10.1007/978-3-030-44223-1_7

8. Castryck, W., Decru, T.: An efficient key recovery attack on SIDH. In: Hazay, C., Stam, M. (eds.) Part V. LNCS, vol. 14008, pp. 423–447. Springer, Heidelberg (2023). https://doi.org/10.1007/978-3-031-30589-4_15

9. Castryck, W., Decru, T., Vercauteren, F.: Radical isogenies. In: Moriai, S., Wang, H. (eds.) ASIACRYPT 2020. LNCS, vol. 12492, pp. 493–519. Springer, Cham (2020). https://doi.org/10.1007/978-3-030-64834-3_17

10. Castryck, W., Lange, T., Martindale, C., Panny, L., Renes, J.: CSIDH: an efficient post-quantum commutative group action. In: Peyrin, T., Galbraith, S. (eds.) ASIACRYPT 2018. LNCS, vol. 11274, pp. 395–427. Springer, Cham (2018). https://doi.org/10.1007/978-3-030-03332-3_15

11. Castryck, W., Panny, L., Vercauteren, F.: Rational isogenies from irrational endo-
    morphisms. In: Canteaut, A., Ishai, Y. (eds.) EUROCRYPT 2020. LNCS, vol.
    12106, pp. 523–548. Springer, Cham (2020). https://doi.org/10.1007/978-3-030-
    45724-2_18
12. Castryk, W.: CSIDH on the surface (csurf) (2021). https://homes.esat.kuleuven.
    be/~wcastryc/summer_school_csurf.pdf
13. Coppersmith, D.: Finding a small root of a bivariate integer equation; factoring
    with high bits known. In: Maurer, U. (ed.) EUROCRYPT 1996. LNCS, vol. 1070,
    pp. 178–189. Springer, Heidelberg (1996). https://doi.org/10.1007/3-540-68339-
    9_16
14. Coppersmith, D.: Finding a small root of a univariate modular equation. In: Mau-
    rer, U. (ed.) EUROCRYPT 1996. LNCS, vol. 1070, pp. 155–165. Springer, Heidel-
    berg (1996). https://doi.org/10.1007/3-540-68339-9_14
15. Coppersmith, D.: Small solutions to polynomial equations, and low exponent
    RSA vulnerabilities. J. Cryptol. **10**(4), 233–260 (1997). https://doi.org/10.1007/
    s001459900030
16. Couveignes, J.M.: Hard homogeneous spaces. Cryptology ePrint Archive, Report
    2006/291 (2006). https://eprint.iacr.org/2006/291
17. Dall, F., et al.: CacheQuote: efficiently recovering long-term secrets of SGX EPID
    via cache attacks. IACR TCHES **2018**(2), 171–191 (2018). https://doi.org/10.
    13154/tches.v2018.i2.171-191, https://tches.iacr.org/index.php/TCHES/article/
    view/879
18. De Feo, L., Jao, D., Plût, J.: Towards quantum-resistant cryptosystems from
    supersingular elliptic curve isogenies. Cryptology ePrint Archive, Report 2011/506
    (2011). https://eprint.iacr.org/2011/506
19. De Mulder, E., Hutter, M., Marson, M.E., Pearson, P.: Using Bleichenbache's solu-
    tion to the hidden number problem to attack nonce leaks in 384-Bit ECDSA.
    In: Bertoni, G., Coron, J.-S. (eds.) CHES 2013. LNCS, vol. 8086, pp. 435–452.
    Springer, Heidelberg (2013). https://doi.org/10.1007/978-3-642-40349-1_25
20. Duman, J., Hartmann, D., Kiltz, E., Kunzweiler, S., Lehmann, J., Riepel, D.:
    Group action key encapsulation and non-interactive key exchange in the QROM.
    In: Agrawal, S., Lin, D. (eds.) Part II. LNCS, vol. 13792, pp. 36–66. Springer,
    Heidelberg (2022). https://doi.org/10.1007/978-3-031-22966-4_2
21. Galbraith, S., Panny, L., Smith, B., Vercauteren, F.: Quantum equivalence of the
    DLP and CDHP for group actions. Cryptology ePrint Archive, Report 2018/1199
    (2018). https://eprint.iacr.org/2018/1199
22. Galbraith, S.D., Petit, C., Shani, B., Ti, Y.B.: On the security of supersingu-
    lar isogeny cryptosystems. In: Cheon, J.H., Takagi, T. (eds.) ASIACRYPT 2016.
    LNCS, vol. 10031, pp. 63–91. Springer, Heidelberg (2016). https://doi.org/10.1007/
    978-3-662-53887-6_3
23. Hastad, J.: N using RSA with low exponent in a public key network. In: Williams,
    H.C. (ed.) CRYPTO 1985. LNCS, vol. 218, pp. 403–408. Springer, Heidelberg
    (1986). https://doi.org/10.1007/3-540-39799-X_29
24. Herrmann, M., May, A.: Attacking power generators using unravelled linearization:
    when do we output too much? In: Matsui, M. (ed.) ASIACRYPT 2009. LNCS,
    vol. 5912, pp. 487–504. Springer, Heidelberg (2009). https://doi.org/10.1007/978-
    3-642-10366-7_29
25. Howgrave-Graham, N.: Approximate integer common divisors. In: Silverman, J.H.
    (ed.) CaLC 2001. LNCS, vol. 2146, pp. 51–66. Springer, Heidelberg (2001). https://
    doi.org/10.1007/3-540-44670-2_6

26. Jao, D., Jetchev, D., Venkatesan, R.: On the bits of elliptic curve Diffie-Hellman keys. In: Srinathan, K., Rangan, C.P., Yung, M. (eds.) INDOCRYPT 2007. LNCS, vol. 4859, pp. 33–47. Springer, Heidelberg (Dec (2007)

27. Jochemsz, E., May, A.: A strategy for finding roots of multivariate polynomials with new applications in attacking RSA variants. In: Lai, X., Chen, K. (eds.) ASIACRYPT 2006. LNCS, vol. 4284, pp. 267–282. Springer, Heidelberg (2006). https://doi.org/10.1007/11935230_18

28. Kawashima, T., Takashima, K., Aikawa, Y., Takagi, T.: An efficient authenticated key exchange from random self-reducibility on CSIDH. In: Hong, D. (ed.) ICISC 2020. LNCS, vol. 12593, pp. 58–84. Springer, Cham (2021). https://doi.org/10.1007/978-3-030-68890-5_4

29. de Kock, B., Gjøsteen, K., Veroni, M.: Practical isogeny-based key-exchange with optimal tightness. In: Dunkelman, O., Jacobson, Jr., M.J., O'Flynn, C. (eds.) SAC 2020. LNCS, vol. 12804, pp. 451–479. Springer, Cham (2021). https://doi.org/10.1007/978-3-030-81652-0_18

30. Lenstra, A.K., Lenstra, H.W., Lovász, L.: Factoring polynomials with rational coefficients. Math. Ann. **261**, 515–534 (1982)

31. Maino, L., Martindale, C., Panny, L., Pope, G., Wesolowski, B.: A direct key recovery attack on SIDH. In: Hazay, C., Stam, M. (eds.) Part V. LNCS, vol. 14008, pp. 448–471. Springer, Heidelberg (2023). https://doi.org/10.1007/978-3-031-30589-4_16

32. May, A.: Lattice-based integer factorisation: an introduction to coppersmith's method. In: Computational Cryptography: Algorithmic Aspects of Cryptology, pp. 78–105. London Mathematical Society Lecture Note Series, Cambridge University Press (2021)

33. May, A., Nowakowski, J., Sarkar, S.: Partial key exposure attack on short secret exponent CRT-RSA. In: Tibouchi, M., Wang, H. (eds.) ASIACRYPT 2021. LNCS, vol. 13090, pp. 99–129. Springer, Cham (2021). https://doi.org/10.1007/978-3-030-92062-3_4

34. May, A., Nowakowski, J., Sarkar, S.: Approximate divisor multiples - factoring with only a third of the secret CRT-exponents. In: Dunkelman, O., Dziembowski, S. (eds.) Part III. LNCS, vol. 13277, pp. 147–167. Springer, Heidelberg (2022). https://doi.org/10.1007/978-3-031-07082-2_6

35. Merget, R., Brinkmann, M., Aviram, N., Somorovsky, J., Mittmann, J., Schwenk, J.: Raccoon attack: finding and exploiting most-significant-bit-oracles in TLS-DH(E). In: Bailey, M., Greenstadt, R. (eds.) USENIX Security 2021, pp. 213–230. USENIX Association (2021)

36. Montgomery, H., Zhandry, M.: Full quantum equivalence of group action DLog and CDH, and more. In: Agrawal, S., Lin, D. (eds.) Part I. LNCS, vol. 13791, pp. 3–32. Springer, Heidelberg (2022). https://doi.org/10.1007/978-3-031-22963-3_1

37. Nguyen, P.Q.: The dark side of the hidden number problem: Lattice attacks on DSA. In: Lam, K.Y., Shparlinski, I., Wang, H., Xing, C. (eds.) Cryptography and Computational Number Theory, vol. 20, pp. 321–330. Birkhäuser Basel, Basel (2001). https://doi.org/10.1007/978-3-0348-8295-8_23

38. Onuki, H., Takagi, T.: On collisions related to an ideal class of order 3 in CSIDH. In: Aoki, K., Kanaoka, A. (eds.) IWSEC 2020. LNCS, vol. 12231, pp. 131–148. Springer, Cham (2020). https://doi.org/10.1007/978-3-030-58208-1_8

39. Renes, J.: Computing isogenies between Montgomery curves using the action of (0,0). Cryptology ePrint Archive, Report 2017/1198 (2017). https://eprint.iacr.org/2017/1198

40. Robert, D.: Breaking SIDH in polynomial time. In: Hazay, C., Stam, M. (eds.) Part V. LNCS, vol. 14008, pp. 472–503. Springer, Heidelberg (2023). https://doi.org/10.1007/978-3-031-30589-4_17

41. Ryan, K., Heninger, N.: Cryptanalyzing MEGA in six queries. Cryptology ePrint Archive, Report 2022/914 (2022). https://eprint.iacr.org/2022/914

42. Ryan, K., Heninger, N.: Fast practical lattice reduction through iterated compression. Cryptology ePrint Archive, Report 2023/237 (2023). https://eprint.iacr.org/2023/237

43. Schoof, R.: Nonsingular plane cubic curves over finite fields. J. Comb. Theory, Ser. A **46**(2), 183–211 (1987). https://doi.org/10.1016/0097-3165(87)90003-3

44. Shani, B.: On the bit security of elliptic curve Diffie–Hellman. In: Fehr, S. (ed.) PKC 2017. LNCS, vol. 10174, pp. 361–387. Springer, Heidelberg (2017). https://doi.org/10.1007/978-3-662-54365-8_15

45. Shor, P.W.: Algorithms for quantum computation: discrete logarithms and factoring. In: 35th FOCS, pp. 124–134. IEEE Computer Society Press (1994). https://doi.org/10.1109/SFCS.1994.365700

46. Silverman, J.H.: The Arithmetic of Elliptic Curves. Graduate texts in mathematics, Springer, Dordrecht (2009). https://doi.org/10.1007/978-0-387-09494-6, https://cds.cern.ch/record/1338326

47. Takahashi, A., Tibouchi, M., Abe, M.: New Bleichenbacher records: fault attacks on qDSA signatures. IACR TCHES **2018**(3), 331–371 (2018). https://doi.org/10.13154/tches.v2018.i3.331-371, https://tches.iacr.org/index.php/TCHES/article/view/7278

48. Takayasu, A., Kunihiro, N.: Partial key exposure attacks on CRT-RSA: better cryptanalysis to full size encryption exponents. In: Malkin, T., Kolesnikov, V., Lewko, A.B., Polychronakis, M. (eds.) ACNS 2015. LNCS, vol. 9092, pp. 518–537. Springer, Cham (2015). https://doi.org/10.1007/978-3-319-28166-7_25

49. Takayasu, A., Lu, Y., Peng, L.: Small CRT-exponent RSA revisited. In: Coron, J.-S., Nielsen, J.B. (eds.) EUROCRYPT 2017. LNCS, vol. 10211, pp. 130–159. Springer, Cham (2017). https://doi.org/10.1007/978-3-319-56614-6_5

50. Takayasu, A., Lu, Y., Peng, L.: Small CRT-exponent RSA revisited. J. Cryptol. **32**(4), 1337–1382 (2019). https://doi.org/10.1007/s00145-018-9282-3

51. Vélu, J.: Isogénies entre courbes elliptiques. Comptes-Rendus de l'Académie des Sci. **273**, 238–241 (1971)

52. Wesolowski, B.: Orientations and the supersingular endomorphism ring problem. In: Dunkelman, O., Dziembowski, S. (eds.) Part III. LNCS, vol. 13277, pp. 345–371. Springer, Heidelberg (2022). https://doi.org/10.1007/978-3-031-07082-2_13

53. Xu, J., Hu, L., Sarkar, S.: Cryptanalysis of elliptic curve hidden number problem from PKC 2017. Des. Codes Crypt. **88**(2), 341–361 (2020). https://doi.org/10.1007/s10623-019-00685-y

54. Xu, J., Sarkar, S., Wang, H., Hu, L.: Improving bounds on elliptic curve hidden number problem for ECDH key exchange. In: Agrawal, S., Lin, D. (eds.) Part III. LNCS, vol. 13793, pp. 771–799. Springer, Heidelberg (2022). https://doi.org/10.1007/978-3-031-22969-5_26

55. Yoneyama, K.: Post-quantum variants of ISO/IEC standards: compact chosen ciphertext secure key encapsulation mechanism from isogeny. In: Proceedings of the 5th ACM Workshop on Security Standardisation Research Workshop, SSR 2019, pp. 13–21. Association for Computing Machinery, New York, NY, USA (2019). https://doi.org/10.1145/3338500.3360336

Memory-Efficient Attacks on Small LWE Keys

Andre Esser[1] , Rahul Girme[2], Arindam Mukherjee[2(✉)] ,
and Santanu Sarkar[2]

[1] Technology Innovation Institute, Abu Dhabi, UAE
andre.esser@tii.ae
[2] Department of Mathematics, Indian Institute of Technology Madras, Chennai, India
rahulgirme3@gmail.com, ma18d004@smail.iitm.ac.in, santanu@iitm.ac.in

Abstract. The LWE problem is one of the prime candidates for building the most efficient post-quantum secure public key cryptosystems. Many of those schemes, like Kyber, Dilithium or those belonging to the NTRU-family, such as NTRU-HPS, -HRSS, BLISS or GLP, make use of small max norm keys to enhance efficiency. The presumably best attack on these schemes is a hybrid attack, which combines combinatorial techniques and lattice reduction. While lattice reduction is not known to be able to exploit the small max norm choices, May recently showed (Crypto 2021) that such choices allow for more efficient combinatorial attacks.

However, these combinatorial attacks suffer enormous memory requirements, which render them inefficient in realistic attack scenarios and, hence, make their general consideration when assessing security questionable. Therefore, more memory-efficient substitutes for these algorithms are needed. In this work, we provide new combinatorial algorithms for recovering small max norm LWE secrets using only a polynomial amount of memory. We provide analyses of our algorithms for secret key distributions of current NTRU, Kyber and Dilithium variants, showing that our new approach outperforms previous memory-efficient algorithms. For instance, considering uniformly random ternary secrets of length n we improve the best known time complexity for polynomial memory algorithms from $2^{1.063n}$ down-to $2^{0.926n}$. We obtain even larger gains for LWE secrets in $\{-m, \ldots, m\}^n$ with $m = 2, 3$ as found in Kyber and Dilithium. For example, for uniformly random keys in $\{-2, \ldots, 2\}^n$ as is the case for Dilithium we improve the previously best time from $2^{1.742n}$ down-to $2^{1.282n}$.

Our fastest algorithm incorporates various different algorithmic techniques, but at its heart lies a nested collision search procedure inspired by the Nested-Rho technique from Dinur, Dunkelman, Keller and Shamir (Crypto 2016). Additionally, we heavily exploit the representation technique originally introduced in the subset sum context to make our nested approach efficient.

A. Esser—Supported by the Deutsche Forschungsgemeinschaft (DFG, German Research Foundation) - Project-ID MA 2536/12.

J. Guo and R. Steinfeld (Eds.): ASIACRYPT 2023, LNCS 14441, pp. 72–105, 2023.
https://doi.org/10.1007/978-981-99-8730-6_3

Keywords: Learning with Errors · nested collision search ·
representation technique · polynomial memory

1   Introduction

The Learning with Errors (LWE) problem is one of the most promising candidates for post-quantum cryptographic constructions. Given a matrix $\mathbf{A} \in \mathbb{Z}_q^{n \times n}$ and a vector $\mathbf{b} = \mathbf{As} - \mathbf{e} \in \mathbb{Z}_q^n$, where $\mathbf{e}$ is a short error vector, the problem asks to recover the secret vector $\mathbf{s}$. The LWE problem is known to be as hard as some worst case lattice problems, which made it an attractive choice as foundation for several efficient cryptographic systems [6,9,21,29,34,36,37]. The most efficient of these schemes rely on ring variants of LWE, which exploit the algebraic structure of the underlying rings to represent the matrix $\mathbf{A}$ [9,30]. Further, some schemes restrict the error term $\mathbf{e}$, as well as the vector $\mathbf{s}$, to vectors with small max norm [6,14,23,28]. Crystals-Kyber [9], which is going to be standardised by NIST, for example, samples key and error from a centered binomial distribution, which in turn results in small max norm key and error of norm 2 or 3. NTRU-type schemes go even further and choose ternary secrets with coefficients in $\{0, \pm 1\}$, i.e., with max norm 1. Usually, these are efficiency driven decisions, whose security argument is based on the lack of faster algorithms to solve these variants, since lattice reduction is not known to be able to exploit small max norm. However, the best attack on ternary LWE keys is considered to be a combination of combinatorial attacks and lattice reduction, known as *the hybrid attack* introduced by Howgrave-Graham [26]. Internally, this attack balances the complexity of an involved meet-in-the-middle and a lattice reduction step. Therefore, progress on combinatorial attacks has a strong potential to affect parameter selection for those schemes. Putting the focus on the NTRU-family of schemes and its variants we concentrate in this work on LWE with ternary secrets. However, our attacks also translate well to higher max norm variants as we showcase by an application to LWE keys as found in Kyber and Dilithium (see Sect. 6).

Intuitively, it is clear that small max norm keys with reduced search space of size $\mathcal{D}$ allow for faster combinatorial attacks that rely on enumerating possible keys. However, for a long time, the best combinatorial algorithm was a basic meet-in-the-middle attack by Odlyzko from 1996, mentioned in the original NTRU paper [25], achieving a running time of $\mathcal{D}^{0.5}$. Recently, May [31] showed how to adapt advanced techniques from solving the subset sum problem to the small max norm LWE setting. This results in significant improvements of the running time to approximately $\mathcal{D}^{0.25}$ for ternary LWE keys.

However, the biggest obstacle of all combinatorial approaches, including the results by May and its recent adaptation to the cases of Kyber and Dilithium [22], is their huge memory complexity, which is as high as their time complexity. Even if such large amounts of memory should be ever available, the slowdown emerging from accessing such large-scale memories is likely to render those algorithms inefficient.

In contrast, in this work we provide new (heuristic) algorithms for solving the LWE problem with small max norm secrets using only *polynomial memory*. Polynomial memory algorithms are of crucial importance to cryptanalysis for multiple reasons. On the one hand, they allow for very efficient implementations on inherently memory constrained platforms such as FPGAs or even more commonly used GPUs [5,15,32,33]. Practical record computations, therefore, often start from a low-memory algorithm, with only polynomial memory requirement, which is then supported by the available memory if possible [10,18,38]. Further, aiming at near- to mid-term quantum cryptanalytic implementations, the focus has to be on low-memory algorithms.

Our algorithms almost achieve the same running time as Odlyzko's meet-in-the-middle, i.e., $\mathcal{D}^{0.5}$, while in contrast only using a negligible amount of memory. Our fastest construction is based on a variety of different techniques, but at its heart lies a nested collision search procedure inspired by the nested rho technique from [13], which is also the foundation of the fastest (heuristic) polynomial space algorithm for subset sum [17]. Our analyses, thereby, rely only on mild heuristics, which are frequently applied and experimentally verified in the context of collision search and the representation technique. Asymptotically our approach outperforms pure lattice enumeration, which has also only polynomial space requirements, but comes at a running time of $2^{cn \log n}$, where c is a constant and n the LWE dimension [3,20]. In contrast our algorithms' running times are single exponential in the LWE dimension, i.e., of the form $2^{c'n}$ for a constant c'. Further, we significantly improve the constant c' in comparison to previously suggested memoryless algorithms based on conventional collision search techniques, such as [31,39].

With respect to concrete, currently proposed parameters, pure combinatorial attacks, such as Odlyzko's, May's and ours, are quite far from competing against pure lattice strategies.[1] Hence, our attacks, analogous to those of May [31], do not invalidate security claims of currently suggested parameters as we improve primarily on the memory complexity. However, advances on those attacks, on one hand, strengthen our understanding of the hardness of those problems by providing clean combinatorial upper bounds; especially they clarify the effect of the sparsity of the secret, heavily exploited by those strategies, showing that overly sparse choices might lead to unwanted drops in security. Furthermore and probably most importantly, combinatorial attacks have a huge potential to improve the Hybrid attack by replacing Odlyzko's meet-in-the-middle with faster routines, such as, May's [31], or more memory-efficient strategies, such as ours. However, replacing Odlyzko's is not possible in a plug-and-play manner as detailed and posed as an open question in [31]. Since then the problem has been actively investigated by multiple recent works [7,24], and once a clear consensus is reached, we also expect practical implications of our attacks.

---

[1] Best runtime results from May [31] are slightly less than the square of current lattice complexities.

Our Contribution. We first revisit basic collision search techniques for solving the ternary LWE problem introduced by van Vredendaal [39] and recently refined by May [31] to set the baseline for our new algorithmic improvements. In this context, as a small initial contribution, we provide a single framework from which the algorithms of [39] as well as all variations given in [31] can be obtained as different instantiations.

We then introduce our novel nested collision search algorithm that leads to significant runtime improvements over previous approaches. In terms of the search space size $\mathcal{D}$ our nested algorithm applied to ternary LWE achieves approximately a running time of $\mathcal{D}^{0.55}$, which is just slightly higher than the running time of Odlyzko's meet-in-the-middle but reduces the memory from $\mathcal{D}^{0.5}$ to a negligible amount. In comparison, the polynomial memory technique of van Vredendaal obtains a running time of $\mathcal{D}^{0.75}$, while May obtains roughly $\mathcal{D}^{0.65}$.[2] For keys following distributions as in Kyber, we get even closer to meet-in-the-middle's running time by reaching $\mathcal{D}^{0.513}$ and $\mathcal{D}^{0.508}$ respectively. We illustrate the running time exponent of our algorithm on ternary LWE in comparison to van Vredendaal and May as a function of the Hamming weight w of the solution in Fig. 1. We observe that our technique outperforms both previous methods for all choices of the weight. Furthermore, in contrast to May's method, our technique follows the natural behavior of a reduced time complexity for high weights, i.e., when the search space starts decreasing again.

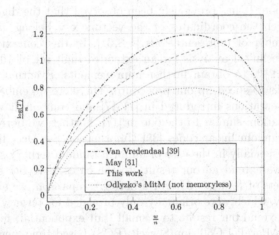

Fig. 1. Runtime exponents c as a function of the relative weight w/n for different polynomial memory algorithms and Odlyzko's MitM, with memory equal to time. The running time is of the form $T = 2^{cn+o(n)}$.

On the technical side, we employ multiple techniques to make the nested approach functional and efficient. Methods based on conventional collision search

---

[2] Since May's algorithm performance is worse towards high weights, we considered for this comparison only weights $w/n \leq \frac{2}{3}$.

rely on Odlyzko's hash function to eliminate **e** from the LWE identity. This gives an exact identity which can then be formulated as collision search problem. However, while the solution forms a collision between the defined functions by construction, not necessarily every collision leads to the solution. Therefore, the collision search needs to be re-applied an exponential number of times until a collision is found that gives rise to the solution.

In a nutshell, we replace the iterative application of the collision search by another layer of collision search. While this increases the time to perform a single (two-layer) collision search, it is compensated by eliminating the need for multiple iterations, as a single (two-layer) collision search suffices to identify the solution. Unfortunately, Odlyzko's hash function is not well compatible with our nested approach. First, it is not additive, which is crucial to enable the nesting and its output of only n bits is not sufficient for both collision searches. However, we circumvent this problem by adapting a guessing strategy introduced in [31] in the context of non-polynomial space algorithms. Here, we first guess $r := \frac{n}{\log n}$ coordinates of **e**, which can be done in subexponential time $\mathcal{O}(3^r)$. We then use the resulting exact identity to identify in the first layer collision search those elements $(\mathbf{x}, \mathbf{y})$ that fulfill the LWE identity $\mathbf{A}(\mathbf{x} + \mathbf{y}) = \mathbf{b} + \mathbf{e}$ on the r known coordinates. In the second layer, we may then again rely on Odlyzko's hash function to extract the solution, similar to the conventional methods. Further, to make the nesting efficient, we incorporate the representation technique from subset sum [27], which allows to increase the number of collisions that give rise to the solution. It has previously been observed that the digit set, i.e., the alphabet to which the coordinates of the vectors $\mathbf{x}, \mathbf{y}$ belong, plays a crucial role for the number of representations [4,8,31]. In this context, we also provide the quite technical analysis for an extended digit set of $\{0, \pm 1, \pm 2\}$, i.e., $\mathbf{x}, \mathbf{y} \in \{0, \pm 1, \pm 2\}^n$, to obtain further improvements. Eventually, we use several further tricks to speed up our procedure. Therefore we embed the concept of partial representations introduced in [11,17] and combine it with an initial instance permutation, similar to the one in [17]. Further, we borrow techniques from decoding random linear codes [35] (Information Set Decoding) to obtain improvements, especially in the case of uniform random ternary secrets.

Eventually, we extend all our results to the cases of Kyber and Dilithium involving digit sets of $\{-3, \ldots, 3\}$. For a better comparison, we also extend the results from May, which were originally only provided for ternary keys.

Further, we extend our results to a small (but exponential) memory setting by introducing a Parallel Collision Search (PCS) based time-memory trade-off. This reflects the practical scenario where even low memory devices provide a certain (small) amount of memory.

Heuristic Assumptions. When applied to random LWE instances our algorithms rely only on standard assumptions in the context of collision search and representation based algorithms, which have been extensively verified in multiple prior works [13,17,18,27]. However, we also provide experimental data that verify those assumptions in our precise setting in the full version of this work [16].

An application of our results to structured LWE instances, as found in Kyber, Dilithium or NTRU, further requires the assumption that the introduced structure does not affect the behavior of our algorithms. Note that this assumption is common in the analysis of combinatorial algorithms in the LWE context [22,31] and was recently made more explicit by Glaser-May [22]. Also, a similar assumption is required in the related code-based setting when applying such algorithms to structured candidates like BIKE or HQC, which has held true in extensive practical experiments [18,19].

Source Code. The source code of all our implementations is available at https:// github.com/arindamIITM/Small-LWE-Keys.

Outline. In Sect. 2 we give basic notations and definitions including the formalization of the ternary LWE problem and we recall standard techniques for collision search. Subsequently, in Sect. 3 we give a framework for methods solving LWE via conventional collision search from which we derive the algorithms of van Vredendaal and May. We give our main result, the nested-collision technique together with several improvements in Sect. 4. In Sect. 5 we conclude the ternary analysis with a detailed comparison of our new method and previous approaches, while in Sect. 6 we provide runtime results of our attacks applied to Kyber and Dilithium keys. Eventually, we present a time-memory trade-off for small but exponential amounts of memory in Sect. 7.

2 Preliminaries

We denote vectors as bold lower case and matrices as bold upper case letters. For a vector $\mathbf{x}$ and an integer ℓ we denote by $\pi_\ell(\mathbf{x}) := (x_1, \ldots, x_\ell)$ the canonical projection to the first ℓ coordinates of $\mathbf{x}$. For a vector $\mathbf{s} \in \mathbb{Z}_q^n$ its Hamming weight or just weight is defined as the number of non-zero coordinates of $\mathbf{s}$.

2.1 Complexity Statements

For complexity statements we use standard Landau notation, where $\tilde{\mathcal{O}}$-notation suppresses polylogarithmic factors. In this context, we frequently use the well known approximation for multinomial coefficients that can be derived from Stirling's formula

$$\binom{n}{k_1 n, \ldots, k_p n} = \tilde{\mathcal{O}}\left(2^{H(k_1, \ldots, k_p)n}\right), \tag{1}$$

where H denotes the Shannon entropy function $H(k_1, \ldots, k_p) = -\sum_1^p k_i \log_2(k_i)$ with $\sum_1^p k_i = 1$. Since k_p is fully determined by the remaining k_i's we define the following notation $\binom{n}{k_1 n, \ldots, k_{p-1} n, \cdot} := \binom{n}{k_1 n, \ldots, k_p n}$.

2.2 LWE and Ternary Vectors

In this work, we focus on LWE instances with max norm one, i.e., ternary secrets and errors. However, in principle our techniques extend to any constant max norm, as we show by application to LWE with secrets in $\{-m, \ldots, m\}^n$ for $m = 2, 3$ in Sect. 6.

Definition 1 (Ternary LWE problem). *Let $n \in \mathbb{N}$ and $q = poly(n)$. Given a matrix $\mathbf{A} \in \mathbb{Z}_q^{n \times n}$, a vector $\mathbf{b} \in \mathbb{Z}_q^n$ and an integer w the ternary LWE problem asks to find a vector $\mathbf{s} \in \{-1, 0, 1\}^n$ of weight w satisfying the LWE identity $\mathbf{As} = \mathbf{b} + \mathbf{e} \mod q$, where $\mathbf{e} \in \{-1, 0, 1\}^n$ is an arbitrary ternary vector.*

Motivated by cryptographic constructions our definition covers only square matrices $\mathbf{A}$, even though our results extend well to the non-square case. Further, we restrict the modulus $q = \text{poly}(n)$ which is proven to be a hard regime and larger choices might allow for faster attacks [2].

In our analysis we assume all entries of the matrix $\mathbf{A}$ are drawn independently and uniformly at random from $\mathbb{Z}_q$. Note that, apart from ring LWE instantiations this is generally the case and we do not exploit the ring structure in our attacks. Moreover, we only consider the case of balanced weight-w solutions, i.e., solutions with the same amount of $w/2$ entries equal to 1 and $w/2$ entries equal to -1. Most NTRU-type instantiations, such as NTRU, GLP, and BLISS, use balanced weight secrets by default. But even if the proportion of ones and minus ones should be unknown, our attacks can easily be generalized by iterating our procedures for each possible proportion. For constant max norm secrets this results at most in a polynomial overhead. In this context, we denote the set of ternary vectors of length n and balanced weight w as $\tau^n(w/2)$, that is,

$$\tau^n(w/2) = \{\mathbf{s} \in \{0, \pm1\}^n : \mathbf{s} \text{ has } w/2 \text{ many 1-entries} \wedge w/2 \text{ many } (-1)\text{-entries}\}.$$

Odlyzko's Hash Function. In the context of the LWE problem, Odlyzko made use of a locality sensitive hash function that eliminates the unknown ternary vector $\mathbf{e}$ from the LWE identity. For a vector $x \in \mathbb{Z}_q^n$ the hash function maps each coordinate $x_i \in \{-\lfloor q/2 \rfloor, \ldots, 0, \ldots, \lfloor q/2 \rfloor\}$ to its sign. More precisely let us define $\hbar : \mathbb{Z}_q^n \to \{0, 1\}^n$ in the following way. For $\mathbf{x} \in \mathbb{Z}_q^n$ we coordinate-wise assign the binary hash label $\hbar(\mathbf{x})_i$ where,

$$\hbar(\mathbf{x})_i = \begin{cases} 0, & \text{if } x_i < 0 \\ 1, & \text{if } x_i \geq 0 \end{cases}$$

Note that, as long as $\mathbf{e}$ does not cause the signs of both sides of the LWE identity to diverge we have $\hbar(\mathbf{As}) = \hbar(\mathbf{b})$. Such a divergence can only happen if there are coordinates equal to -1 or $\lfloor q/2 \rfloor$ present in $\mathbf{As}$ or $\mathbf{b}$, which are called *edge cases*. Therefore, split the ternary $\mathbf{e} = \mathbf{e}_1 - \mathbf{e}_2$ with $\mathbf{e}_i \in \{0, 1\}^n$ and rewrite the LWE identity as $\mathbf{As} + \mathbf{e}_2 = \mathbf{b} + \mathbf{e}_1$. Now the addition of $\mathbf{e}_i$ can only cause a sign flip for the mentioned edge cases of -1 or $\lfloor q/2 \rfloor$ coordinates.

2.3   Collision Search

Let $f : S \to S$ be any random function on S. Then a collision in f defines a tuple $(y_1, y_2) \in S^2$ with $f(y_1) = f(y_2)$. Such a collision can be found using $\mathcal{O}(\sqrt{|S|})$ evaluations of f and polynomial memory. The standard technique is to create a chain of invocations of the function f from a random starting point x. That is iterating $f(x)$, $f^2(x)$, $f^3(x)$, ..., until a repetition occurs, which is found via a cycle detection algorithm. Let $f^k(x)$ be the first repeated value in the chain and let $f^{k+l}(x)$ be its second appearance (compare to Fig. 2). We denote the output of a collision finding algorithm on f with starting point x as $\text{RHO}(f, x)$ which gives the colliding inputs. More precisely,

$$\text{RHO}(f, x) = (f^{k-1}(x), f^{k+l-1}(x)).$$

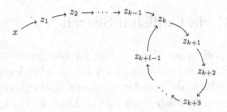

Fig. 2. Application of RHO - function for f with starting point x. $f^i(x)$ is denoted by z_i.

The technique also extends to finding collisions between two different functions, i.e., two random functions $f_1 : S \to S$ and $f_2 : S \to S$. Therefore we define another function $F : S \to S$ as

$$F(x) = \begin{cases} f_1(x), & \text{if } g(x) = 0 \\ f_2(x), & \text{if } g(x) = 1 \end{cases}$$

where $g : S \to \{0, 1\}$ is a random function. Now we search for collisions in F using the previously discussed method. A collision (y_1, y_2) in F, i.e., $F(y_1) = F(y_2)$, yields a collision between f_1 and f_2 iff $g(y_1) \neq g(y_2)$, which happens with probability $\frac{1}{2}$. In case of $g(y_1) = g(y_2)$, one might (deterministically) change the starting point and reapply the procedure. Since, in expectation, this results only in a constant factor overhead, we conveniently write $\text{RHO}(f_1, f_2, x)$ to denote the collision (y_1, y_2) between f_1 and f_2 reachable from starting point x still using $\mathcal{O}(\sqrt{|S|})$ evaluations of the function F.

Note that several starting points x might lead to the same collision (y_1, y_2), for instance any point $z_1, \ldots, z_{k-1}$ in Fig. 2 produces the same collision (z_{k-1}, z_{k+l-1}). To obtain (heuristic) independence between different calls to the RHO function we introduce randomizations of the functions called flavors.

Definition 2 (Flavour of a function). *Let $f : S \to S$ be a function and $P_t : S \to S$ be a family of bijective functions indexed by $t \in \mathbb{N}$. Then the tth flavour of f is defined as*

$$f^{[t]}(x) := P_t(f(x)).$$

A collision (y_1, y_2) in $f^{[t]}$ satisfies

$$f^{[t]}(y_1) = f^{[t]}(y_2) \quad \Leftrightarrow \quad P_t(f(y_1)) = P_t(f(y_1)) \quad \Leftrightarrow \quad f(y_1) = f(y_2).$$

Hence, (y_1, y_2) is a collision in f itself. When searching for collisions in randomly flavored functions, i.e., for random choices of t, we (heuristically) assume that different invocations of the RHO-function produce independent and uniformly at random drawn collisions form the set of all collisions. This is a standard assumption in the context of collision search [4,13,17] which has been verified experimentally multiple times [13,17] in different settings.

3   Solving LWE via Collision Search

For didactic reasons and to set the baseline for our improvements, let us start by recalling the memory-less attacks given by van Vredendaal [39] and more recently by May [31] which are based on conventional collision search.

Let us first give a general framework for this kind of attack, which later allows to instantiate the different algorithms. Recall the LWE identity

$$\mathbf{As} = \mathbf{b} + \mathbf{e} \quad \bmod q, \tag{2}$$

where $\mathbf{A}, \mathbf{b}$ are known. We split $\mathbf{s} = \mathbf{s}_1 + \mathbf{s}_2$ in the sum of two addends, where $\mathbf{s}_i \in \mathcal{T}_i$.[3] Further, we define the two functions $f_i \colon \mathcal{T}_i \to \{0,1\}^\ell$, $i = 1, 2$ where

$$f_1 \colon \mathbf{x} \mapsto \pi_\ell\big(\hbar(\mathbf{Ax})\big) \quad \text{and} \quad f_2 \colon \mathbf{x} \mapsto \pi_\ell\big(\hbar(\mathbf{b} - \mathbf{Ax})\big).$$

Hence, the functions output the first ℓ bits of Odlyzko's hash function applied to the respective input. Note that, as long as we restrict to no edge cases regarding the hash function $\hbar$ (see Sect. 2), any tuple $(\mathbf{s}_1, \mathbf{s}_2)$ that sums to $\mathbf{s}$ forms a collision between the functions f_1 and f_2. The algorithms now search for collisions in f_1, f_2 until they find a collision $(\mathbf{x}, \mathbf{y})$ for which $\mathbf{A}(\mathbf{x} + \mathbf{y}) - \mathbf{b}$ and $\mathbf{x} + \mathbf{y}$ are both ternary, and then outputs $\mathbf{s} = \mathbf{x} + \mathbf{y}$.

Remark 1 (Hashing back to the range). Technically, for a collision search procedure as outlined in Sect. 2 to work, the used functions need to have same domain and range, as they are iteratively applied to their own output. However, for simplicity of notation, we only ensure that domain and range have the same size in all our algorithms. Prior to applying the functions to their own output, one would apply a bijective mapping from the range to the domain, i.e., here from $\{0,1\}^\ell$ to $\mathcal{T}_i$.

Algorithm 1: COLLISION-SEARCH

Input: $(\mathbf{A}, \mathbf{b}) \in \mathbb{Z}_q^{n \times n} \times \mathbb{Z}_q^n$, positive integer $w \leq n$
Output: $\mathbf{s} \in \tau^n(w/2)$ such that $\mathbf{e} = \mathbf{As} - \mathbf{b} \mod q \in \{-1, 0, 1\}^n$

1 $\ell := \log |T_1|$
2 **repeat**
3   choose random flavour for f_1, f_2
4   choose random starting point $\mathbf{v} \in \{0, 1\}^\ell$
5        $(\mathbf{z}_1, \mathbf{z}_2) \leftarrow \text{RHO}(f_1, f_2, \mathbf{v})$
6 **until** $\mathbf{z}_1 + \mathbf{z}_2 \in \tau^n(w/2) \wedge \mathbf{A}(\mathbf{z}_1 + \mathbf{z}_2) - \mathbf{b} \in \{-1, 0, 1\}^n$
7 **return** $\mathbf{s} = \mathbf{z}_1 + \mathbf{z}_2$

Correctness of Algorithm 1. To ensure that our functions have domain and range of same size we choose $\ell := \log |T_1|$ and guarantee $|T_1| = |T_2|$ by our later choice of T_1, T_2.

Note that for any $\mathbf{s}_1, \mathbf{s}_2$ that sums to $\mathbf{s}$ we have $f_1(\mathbf{s}_1) = f_2(\mathbf{s}_2)$, as long as there is no edge case among the lower ℓ coordinates of $\mathbf{As}_1$ and $\mathbf{b} - \mathbf{As}_2$, i.e. an $\mathbb{Z}_q$ coordinate equal to $\lfloor q/2 \rfloor$ or -1. In [39] it was shown, that the probability of no edge case occurring for such a pair is constant. Therefore as long as the function domains include at least a single *representation* of $\mathbf{s}$, i.e., a pair $(\mathbf{s}_1, \mathbf{s}_2) \in T_1 \times T_2$ with $\mathbf{s} = \mathbf{s}_1 + \mathbf{s}_2$, there is a collision that leads to the solution with constant probability. Now, by the standard assumption that the collisions sampled by the algorithm for different function flavors are independent and uniform, the algorithm is able to find this collision and hence, succeeds with constant probability.

Complexity of Algorithm 1. If f_1, f_2 behave like random functions, we expect that there exists a total amount of

$$\frac{|T_1| \cdot |T_2|}{|\{0, 1\}^\ell|} = \frac{|T_1|^2}{|T_1|} = |T_1|$$

collisions, between them, since $\ell := \log |T_1|$ and $|T_1| = |T_2|$. Further, we know that finding one of these collisions takes time $\tilde{\mathcal{O}}\left(\sqrt{|T_1|}\right)$. If now there exist R representations of $\mathbf{s}$, i.e., pairs $(\mathbf{s}_1, \mathbf{s}_2) \in T_1 \times T_2$ that sum to $\mathbf{s}$, we expect that after finding $\frac{|T_1|}{R}$ collisions, we found one that is a representation of $\mathbf{s}$. Finding these $\frac{|T_1|}{R}$ collisions takes expected time

$$T = \tilde{\mathcal{O}}\left(|T_1|/R \cdot \sqrt{|T_1|}\right) = \tilde{\mathcal{O}}\left(|T_1|^{3/2}/R\right).$$

Remark 2 (Random behavior of the functions). All algorithms following this framework are based on the heuristic assumption that the constructed functions behave like random functions with respect to collision search and the total number of existing collisions. This assumption has been verified experimentally

---

[3] The precise choice of T_i depends on the specific instantiation and is described later.

various times in different settings [1,12,13,17,38]. We provide additional experimental evidence for its validity in our precise setting in the full version of this work [16].

The different algorithms from [31,39] now differ in their choice of function domains T_i.

Van Vredendaal's Instantiation. Van Vredendaal [39] chooses a meet in the middle split of $\mathbf{s}$, i.e.,

$$T_1 := \{(\mathbf{x}, 0^{n/2}) \mid \mathbf{x} \in \tau^{n/2}(w/4)\}$$
$$T_2 := \{(0^{n/2}, \mathbf{x}) \mid \mathbf{x} \in \tau^{n/2}(w/4)\}.$$

The algorithm assumes that the -1 and 1 entries of $\mathbf{s}$ distribute evenly on both sides. Note that if this is not the case one might re-randomize the initial instance by permuting columns of $\mathbf{A}$, as $\mathbf{AP}$, with solution $\mathbf{P}^{-1}\mathbf{s}$, where $\mathbf{P}$ is a permutation matrix. The expected amount of random permutations until we obtain the desired weight distribution is

$$\frac{\binom{n}{w/2,w/2,\cdot}}{\binom{n/2}{w/4,w/4,\cdot}^2} = \text{poly}(n),$$

which vanishes in our asymptotic notation. For evenly distributed $\mathbf{s}$ and this specific choice of domains T_i, we have clearly only one representation $(\mathbf{s}_1, \mathbf{s}_2) \in T_1 \times T_2$ of $\mathbf{s}$, i.e., $R = 1$. Since the domain size is determined as

$$|T_1| = \mathcal{O}\binom{n/2}{w/4, w/4, \cdot}.$$

the time complexity of Algorithm 1 for van Vredendaal's choice of domains becomes

$$T_{\text{v-V}} = \tilde{\mathcal{O}}\left(|T_1|^{3/2}/R\right) = \tilde{\mathcal{O}}\left(\binom{n/2}{w/4, w/4, \cdot}^{3/2}\right) = \tilde{\mathcal{O}}\left(2^{3H(\omega/2,\omega/2,\cdot)n/4}\right),$$

where $\omega := w/n$.

May's Instantiations. May gives three different instantiations for T_i, called REP-0, REP-1 and REP-2. For all choices the weight of the vectors distributes over the full n coordinates. The difference then lies in the precise choice of weight and the digit set. Let us start with the most simple REP-0 variant.

REP-0 *Instantiation.* Here the domains are chosen as

$$T_1 = T_2 := \tau^n(w/4),$$

which results in a domain size of

$$|\mathcal{T}_i| = \mathcal{O}\binom{n}{w/4, w/4, \cdot}.$$

Note that when representing $\mathbf{s} = \mathbf{s}_1 + \mathbf{s}_2$ with $\mathbf{s}_i \in \mathcal{T}_i$, we can obtain a 1 (resp. a -1) coordinate only as $1 + 0$ or $0 + 1$ (resp. $-1 + 0$ or $0 - 1$), while a 0 only as $0 + 0$. Therefore the number of representations amounts to

$$R = \binom{w/2}{w/4}^2.$$

as we can freely choose $w/4$ out of $w/2$ of the ones to be represented as $1 + 0$ while the rest is represented as $0 + 1$ (and analogously for the -1's).

The time complexity is then given as

$$T_{\text{REP-0}} = \tilde{\mathcal{O}}\left(|\mathcal{T}_i|^{3/2}/R\right) = \tilde{\mathcal{O}}\left(2^{\left(3H(w/4, w/4, \cdot)/2 - \omega\right)n}\right),$$

where again $\omega := w/n$.

REP-1 *Instantiation.* The REP-1 instantiation increases the weight of the vectors to $w/2 + 2d$ for some small d, that has to be optimized, i.e.,

$$\mathcal{T}_1 = \mathcal{T}_2 := \tau^n(w/4 + d).$$

Similar to before we have

$$|\mathcal{T}_i| = \mathcal{O}\binom{n}{w/4 + d, w/4 + d, \cdot}.$$

The benefit of the increased weight lies in an increased number of representations. As now it is possible to represent a zero coordinate in $\mathbf{s} = \mathbf{s}_1 + \mathbf{s}_2$ not only as $0 + 0$ but also via $-1 + 1$ and $1 + (-1)$. In total, this leads to

$$R = \binom{w/2}{w/4}^2 \binom{n - w}{d, d, \cdot},$$

as we represent d zeros via $-1 + 1$, d as $1 + (-1)$ and $n - w - 2d$ as $0 + 0$. In total the time complexity of this approach then becomes

$$T_{\text{REP-1}} = \tilde{\mathcal{O}}\left(|\mathcal{T}_i|^{3/2}/R\right) = \tilde{\mathcal{O}}\left(2^{\left(3H(w/4 + \delta, w/4 + \delta, \cdot)/2 - \omega - (1 - \omega)H\left(\delta/(1 - \omega), \delta/(1 - \omega), \cdot\right)\right)n}\right),$$

where $d = \delta n$.

REP-2 *Instantiation.* In the REP-2 instantiation May defines the vectors no longer over $\{-1, 0, 1\}^n$ but over $\{-2, -1, 0, 1, 2\}^n$. Again the additional -2 and 2 entries lead to more representations. However, the analysis becomes quite technical. We give an extended analysis of this representation approach for our nested algorithm in Sect. 4.3 and an analysis of an extension to REP-3 in the appendix. For a complexity analysis specific to May's instantiation we refer to [31]. In Fig. 3 we illustrate the runtime exponents of the algorithms by May and van Vredendaal.

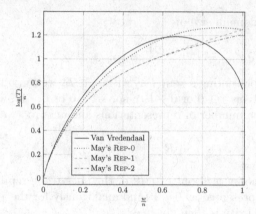

Fig. 3. Comparison between van Vredendaal's instantiation and May's instantiations.

4   Nested Collision Search for LWE

So far the collision search algorithm solves the LWE identity only on a projection after applying Odlyzko's hash function. To eventually identify the solution among all candidates that satisfy this less restrictive identity, the collision search procedure is repeated an exponential amount of times. In other words, a brute force technique is applied to isolate the solution.

Our nested collision search procedure now replaces the brute force step by a second collision search. While one might hope that a single collision $(\mathbf{x}, \mathbf{y})$ would then suffice to solve the problem, usually $\mathbf{x}, \mathbf{y}$ do not sum to a ternary vector, i.e., $\mathbf{x} + \mathbf{y} \notin \{-1, 0, 1\}^n$. Therefore the algorithm still needs to iterate over multiple collisions. However, as soon as $\mathbf{x} + \mathbf{y} \in \{-1, 0, 1\}^n$, it implies that $\mathbf{s} = \mathbf{x} + \mathbf{y}$ is the solution.

Let us start again with a general framework before discussing our concrete instantiations. For the two-layer approach, we split the solution into four summands $\mathbf{s} = \mathbf{s}_1 + \mathbf{s}_2 + \mathbf{s}_3 + \mathbf{s}_4$. This implies

$$\mathbf{A}(\mathbf{s}_1 + \mathbf{s}_2 + \mathbf{s}_3 + \mathbf{s}_4) = \mathbf{b} + \mathbf{e} \qquad\qquad \mathrm{mod}\ q$$
$$\Leftrightarrow\ \mathbf{A}(\mathbf{s}_1 + \mathbf{s}_2) \qquad = \mathbf{b} - \mathbf{A}(\mathbf{s}_3 + \mathbf{s}_4) + \mathbf{e} \quad \mathrm{mod}\ q.$$

Further, for now we assume that we know the first 2ℓ coordinates of $\mathbf{e}$. Then we obtain

$$\pi_{2\ell}\big(\mathbf{A}(\mathbf{s}_1 + \mathbf{s}_2)\big) = \mathbf{b}' - \pi_{2\ell}\big(\mathbf{A}(\mathbf{s}_3 + \mathbf{s}_4)\big) \quad \mathrm{mod}\ q, \qquad (3)$$

where $\mathbf{b}' := \pi_{2\ell}(\mathbf{b} + \mathbf{e})$ is known. This *layer-2 identity* will later be used to identify $(\mathbf{s}_1, \mathbf{s}_2)$ and $(\mathbf{s}_3, \mathbf{s}_4)$ among a set of candidates. Further let $\mathbf{r} := \pi_{\ell}\big(\mathbf{A}(\mathbf{s}_1 + \mathbf{s}_2)\big)$ be the lower ℓ coordinates of the left side of this layer-2 identity. Then we obtain our two *layer-1 identities* as

$$\pi_{\ell}(\mathbf{A}\mathbf{s}_1) = \mathbf{r} - \pi_{\ell}(\mathbf{A}\mathbf{s}_2) \qquad\qquad \mathrm{mod}\ q$$
$$\pi_{\ell}(\mathbf{A}\mathbf{s}_3) = \pi_{\ell}(\mathbf{b}') - \mathbf{r} - \pi_{\ell}(\mathbf{A}\mathbf{s}_4) \quad \mathrm{mod}\ q. \qquad (4)$$

Now let us define the functions f_1, f_2 and f_3, f_4 used for collision search on layer one, where $f_i \colon \mathcal{T}_i \to \mathbb{Z}_q^\ell$ as

$$f_1, f_3 \colon \mathbf{x} \mapsto \pi_\ell(\mathbf{Ax}), \quad f_2 \colon \mathbf{x} \mapsto \mathbf{r} - \pi_\ell(\mathbf{Ax}) \quad \text{and} \quad f_4 \colon \mathbf{x} \mapsto \pi_\ell(\mathbf{b'}) - \mathbf{r} - \pi_\ell(\mathbf{Ax}).$$
(5)

Note that the value of $\mathbf{r}$ is not known a priori; hence the algorithm iterates over random choices of $\mathbf{r}$ until it succeeds. By definition any representation $(\mathbf{s}_1, \mathbf{s}_2, \mathbf{s}_3, \mathbf{s}_4)$ of $\mathbf{s}$ with $\pi_\ell(\mathbf{A}(\mathbf{s}_1 + \mathbf{s}_2)) = \mathbf{r}$ satisfies the layer-1 (and layer-2) identities and furthermore yields collisions in our functions f_i. Namely $(\mathbf{s}_1, \mathbf{s}_2)$ forms a collision between the functions f_1, f_2, while $(\mathbf{s}_3, \mathbf{s}_4)$ forms a collision in f_3, f_4. While not every collision is a representation, we can sample candidates for $\mathbf{s}_1, \mathbf{s}_2$ (resp. $\mathbf{s}_3, \mathbf{s}_4$) by finding collisions between f_1, f_2 (resp. f_3, f_4).

Every collision, regardless of being a representation or not, already fulfills one of the layer-1 identities (Eq. (4)) (depending if the collision is between f_1, f_2 or f_3, f_4). Furthermore, note that any tuple $(\mathbf{y}_1, \mathbf{y}_2, \mathbf{y}_3, \mathbf{y}_4)$ where $(\mathbf{y}_1, \mathbf{y}_2)$ is a collision in f_1, f_2 and $(\mathbf{y}_3, \mathbf{y}_4)$ a collision in f_3, f_4, already fulfills the layer-2 identity (Eq. (3)) on the lower ℓ coordinates. Therefore just consider the summation of both layer-1 identities from Eq. (4).

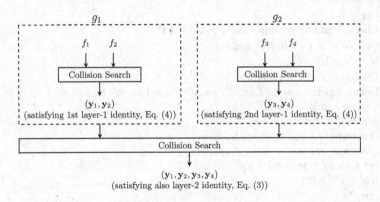

Fig. 4. Schematic illustration of multiple-layer collision search.

We now apply a second collision search to identify those pairs of collisions that jointly satisfy the layer-2 identity on all 2ℓ coordinates. This process is illustrated in Fig. 4.

Let $\vartheta_\ell \colon \mathbb{Z}_q^k \to \mathbb{Z}_q^\ell$, $k \geq 2\ell$ be the projection to the coordinates of the vector indexed by $\ell + 1$ to 2ℓ, i.e., for $\mathbf{x} = (x_1, \ldots, x_k)$ we let $\vartheta_\ell(\mathbf{x}) := (x_{\ell+1}, \ldots, x_{2\ell})$. Now we are ready to define the *second layer functions* $g_i \colon \mathbb{Z}_q^\ell \to \mathbb{Z}_q^\ell$, $i = 1, 2$. These functions take as input a starting point of a collision search procedure between the layer-1 functions f_{2i-1}, f_{2i} and compute the colliding entries $\mathbf{y}_{2i-1}, \mathbf{y}_{2i}$ reachable from that starting point. Finally they output the upper ℓ coordinates of the corresponding value of the layer-2 identity for $(\mathbf{y}_{2i-1}, \mathbf{y}_{2i})$. More formally, we have

$$g_1 : \mathbf{x} \mapsto \vartheta_\ell(\mathbf{A}(\mathbf{y}_1 + \mathbf{y}_2)), \text{ where } (\mathbf{y}_1, \mathbf{y}_2) = \text{RHO}(f_1^{[\mathbf{x}]}, f_2^{[\mathbf{x}]}, \mathbf{x}) \quad \text{and}$$

$$g_2 : \mathbf{x} \mapsto \vartheta_\ell(\mathbf{b}') - \vartheta_\ell(\mathbf{A}(\mathbf{y}_3 + \mathbf{y}_4)), \text{ where } (\mathbf{y}_3, \mathbf{y}_4) = \text{RHO}(f_3^{[\mathbf{x}]}, f_4^{[\mathbf{x}]}, \mathbf{x}). \quad (6)$$

Note that here we flavour the inner functions f_i deterministically via the starting point used for collision search (see Definition 2), similar to [13,17]. In this way g_1, g_2 stay deterministic, as required for the general collision search procedure, while we obtain (heuristic) independence of returned collisions from the inner functions.

The general algorithm is outlined in Algorithm 2 as pseudocode and visually illustrated in Fig. 5. The smaller *Rho*-structures in the figure represent the layer-1 collision search, while the layer-2 search is formed as a big *Rho* using multiple layer-1 collision searches.

Algorithm 2: NESTED-COLLISION-SEARCH

Input: $(\mathbf{A}, \mathbf{b}) \in \mathbb{Z}_q^{n \times n} \times \mathbb{Z}_q^n$, positive integer $w \leq n$
Output: $\mathbf{s} \in \tau^n(w/2)$ such that $\mathbf{e} = \mathbf{As} - \mathbf{b} \mod q \in \{-1, 0, 1\}^n$

1 Let f_i and g_j be as defined in Eqs. (5) and (6)
2 $\ell := \frac{\log_q |\tau^n(w/2)|}{2}$
3 **repeat**
4 | Choose random permutation $\mathbf{P}$, $\mathbf{A}' \leftarrow \mathbf{AP}$
5 | Choose $\mathbf{e}' \in \{-1, 0, 1\}^{2\ell}$ randomly
6 | $\mathbf{b}' \leftarrow \pi_{2\ell}(\mathbf{b}) + \mathbf{e}'$
7 | Choose $\mathbf{r}, \mathbf{z} \in \mathbb{Z}_q^\ell$ randomly
8 | Define functions as in Eqs. (5) and (6) based on $\mathbf{A}', \mathbf{b}'$ and $\mathbf{r}$
9 | Choose random flavour for g_1, g_2
10 | $(\mathbf{z}_1, \mathbf{z}_2) \leftarrow \text{RHO}(g_1, g_2, \mathbf{z})$
11 | Compute $(\mathbf{y}_1, \mathbf{y}_2) = \text{RHO}(f_1, f_2, \mathbf{z}_1)$
12 | Compute $(\mathbf{y}_3, \mathbf{y}_4) = \text{RHO}(f_3, f_4, \mathbf{z}_2)$
13 | Set $\mathbf{s}' = \mathbf{y}_1 + \mathbf{y}_2 + \mathbf{y}_3 + \mathbf{y}_4$
14 **until** $\mathbf{s}' \in \tau^n(w/2)$
15 **return** $\mathbf{Ps}'$

4.1 Analysis of Nested Collision Search

Correctness. First note the permuted instance defined by $\mathbf{A}' = \mathbf{AP}$ has solution $\mathbf{s}' = \mathbf{P}^{-1}\mathbf{s}$. Hence, once this solution is found we have to return $\mathbf{s} = \mathbf{Ps}'$.

We have already shown, that any representation $(\mathbf{s}_1, \mathbf{s}_2, \mathbf{s}_3, \mathbf{s}_4)$ of the solution $\mathbf{s}$ for the correct choice of $\mathbf{r} = \pi_\ell(\mathbf{A}(\mathbf{s}_1 + \mathbf{s}_2))$ and the correct guess for $\mathbf{e}' = \pi_{2\ell}(\mathbf{e})$ satisfies the layer-1 and layer-2 identities (compare to Eq. (3) and Eq. (4)). Further, we know that such a representation forms a collision in g_1, g_2. Therefore by sampling independent and uniformly random collisions between g_1 and g_2 we

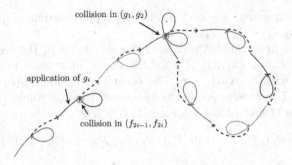

collision in (g_1, g_2)

application of g_i

collision in (f_{2i-1}, f_{2i})

Fig. 5. Illustration of the nested collision search. Different colors identify different function flavors. Dashed arrows indicate mapping from collisions to starting points (Color figure online).

can find $\mathbf{s}$, given there exist at least one representation (which will be ensured by the choice of $\mathcal{T}_i$ later). Again we obtain heuristic independence of the sampled collisions by the choice of random flavors in each iteration.

It remains to show that after finding a collision $(\mathbf{x}_1, \mathbf{x}_2)$ in g_1, g_2 for which the value $\mathbf{s}' = \mathbf{y}_1 + \mathbf{y}_2 + \mathbf{y}_3 + \mathbf{y}_4 \in \tau^n(w/2)$, i.e., $\mathbf{s}'$ is a ternary vector of weight w, it suffices to conclude that $\mathbf{s}'$ is a solution. Therefore note that the expected number of elements from $\tau^n(w/2)$ that fulfill the layer-2 identity is by the randomness of $\mathbf{A}$

$$\frac{|\tau^n(w/2)|}{q^{2\ell}} = 1,$$

since we choose $\ell = \frac{\log_q |\tau^n(w/2)|}{2}$. Hence, once such an element is found, we conclude that it is $\mathbf{s}$. This proves correctness under the same heuristic used by the algorithms based on conventional collision search (see Remark 2).

Note that the specific choice of ℓ implies that the range of all functions is of size $q^\ell = \sqrt{|\tau^n(w/2)|}$. Hence, to allow for collision search, we have to ensure

$$|\mathcal{T}_i| \stackrel{!}{=} q^\ell = \sqrt{|\tau^n(w/2)|} \qquad (7)$$

by our choice of function domains $\mathcal{T}_i$.

Complexity. For a representation $(\mathbf{s}_1, \mathbf{s}_2, \mathbf{s}_3, \mathbf{s}_4)$ of $\mathbf{s}$ with $\mathbf{s}_i \in \mathcal{T}_i$ let

$$\mathbf{s} = \underbrace{\mathbf{s}_1 + \mathbf{s}_2}_{\mathbf{a}_1} + \underbrace{\mathbf{s}_3 + \mathbf{s}_4}_{\mathbf{a}_2}. \qquad (8)$$

In our analysis we consider only those representations where $\mathbf{a}_i \in \mathcal{D}_i$ for some set $\mathcal{D}_i$, which we refer to as *mid-level domains*.[4] Let us assume that there exist R_2 different representations $(\mathbf{a}_1, \mathbf{a}_2) \in \mathcal{D}_1 \times \mathcal{D}_2$ of the solution $\mathbf{s}$. Further assume that

---

[4] The concrete choice of $\mathcal{D}_i$, similar to the function domains $\mathcal{T}_i$, depends on the instantiation and is specified later.

any such $\mathbf{a}_1$ (analogously any such $\mathbf{a}_2$) has R_1 representations $(\mathbf{s}_1, \mathbf{s}_2) \in \mathcal{T}_1 \times \mathcal{T}_2$ (analogously $(\mathbf{s}_3, \mathbf{s}_4) \in \mathcal{T}_3 \times \mathcal{T}_4$).

Consider one iteration of Algorithm 2. We denote by $E_\mathbf{r}$ the event that there exist a representation $(\mathbf{a}_1, \mathbf{a}_2)$ of $\mathbf{s}$ for the choice of $\mathbf{r}$ made in line 7, i.e., a representation with $\pi_\ell(\mathbf{A}\mathbf{a}_1) = \mathbf{r}$. The event of guessing $\pi_{2\ell}(\mathbf{e})$ correctly we denote by $E_\mathbf{e}$. Eventually, we denote the event that the tuple $(\mathbf{y}_1, \mathbf{y}_2, \mathbf{y}_3, \mathbf{y}_4)$ obtained in line 11 and 12 is a representation of $\mathbf{s}$ by $E_\mathbf{s}$. Then we expect

$$\Pr\left[E_\mathbf{e} \cap E_\mathbf{r} \cap E_\mathbf{s}\right]^{-1} = \left(\Pr\left[E_\mathbf{e}\right] \cdot \Pr\left[E_\mathbf{r} \mid E_\mathbf{e}\right] \cdot \Pr\left[E_\mathbf{s} \mid E_\mathbf{e} \cap E_\mathbf{r}\right]\right)^{-1}$$

iterations of the loop until success.

The probability of guessing the correct $\mathbf{e}'$ in line 5 of Algorithm 2 is $q_\mathbf{e} = 3^{-2\ell} = 3^{-\log_q |\tau^n(w/2)|}$. Since $q = \text{poly}(n)$ and $|\tau^n(w/2)| = 2^{cn}$ for some constant c, it follows that

$$q_3 := \Pr\left[E_\mathbf{e}\right] = 3^{-2\ell} = 2^{-\Theta\left(\frac{n}{\log n}\right)}.$$

Further, by the randomness of $\mathbf{A}$, we have

$$q_2 := \Pr\left[E_\mathbf{r} \mid E_\mathbf{e}\right] = \frac{R_2}{q^\ell}.$$

Now given $E_\mathbf{e} \cap E_\mathbf{r}$ there exists a representation $(\mathbf{a}_1, \mathbf{a}_2)$. As both, $\mathbf{a}_1$ and $\mathbf{a}_2$, have R_1 different representations $(\mathbf{s}_1, \mathbf{s}_2)$ and $(\mathbf{s}_3, \mathbf{s}_4)$, we find a total of $(R_1)^2$ pairs of representations that together lead to $\mathbf{a}_1, \mathbf{a}_2$. Recall that each such pair fulfills the layer-1 and layer-2 identities and, hence, forms a collision between the functions g_1, g_2. Therefore, a random collision in the functions g_1, g_2 leads to $\mathbf{s}$ with probability

$$q_1 := \Pr\left[E_\mathbf{s} \mid E_\mathbf{e} \cap E_\mathbf{r}\right] = \frac{(R_1)^2}{q^\ell},$$

as by Remark 2 there exist a total of q^ℓ collisions between g_1 and g_2.

Eventually, the time per iteration of the loop is dominated by the collision search between g_1 and g_2. This collision search requires $\mathcal{O}(q^{\frac{\ell}{2}})$ evaluations of those functions. Now for each evaluation a collision search between f_1, f_2 (resp. f_3, f_4) with time complexity $\tilde{\mathcal{O}}\left(q^{\frac{\ell}{2}}\right)$ is performed. Hence the time per iteration is $\tilde{\mathcal{O}}\left(q^{\frac{\ell}{2}} \cdot q^{\frac{\ell}{2}}\right) = \tilde{\mathcal{O}}\left(q^\ell\right)$.

Overall this leads to time complexity

$$T = (q_1 q_2 q_3)^{-1} \cdot q^\ell = \left(\frac{|\tau^n(w/2)|^{\frac{3}{2}}}{(R_1)^2 \cdot R_2}\right)^{1+o(1)} = \left(\frac{\binom{n}{w/2, w/2, \cdot}^{\frac{3}{2}}}{(R_1)^2 \cdot R_2}\right)^{1+o(1)}. \tag{9}$$

Remark 3. Note that the heuristic specified in Remark 2 must fail if there are significantly more collisions between the constructed functions than there would be between random functions. Precisely, this is the case if $(R_1)^2 > q^\ell$, since there are $(R_1)^2$ collisions caused by representations in the second layer functions, while for random functions we would expect q^ℓ collisions. However, we actively prevent this due to an appropriate choice of function domains ensuring $R_1 < q^{\frac{\ell}{2}}$.

A Different Analysis Approach. Another way to derive the time complexity of Algorithm 2 is via directly computing the probability that the sampled tuple $(\mathbf{y}_1, \mathbf{y}_2, \mathbf{y}_3, \mathbf{y}_4)$ sums to a ternary vector. We provide this alternative analysis in the full version of this work [16].

Use of Odlyzko's Hash Function. Our construction does not rely on Odlyzko's hash function but instead guesses 2ℓ coordinates of $\mathbf{e}$ to obtain an exact identity on these coordinates. For the first layer this is necessary to ensure that any pair of collisions between f_1, f_2 and f_3, f_4 jointly satisfy the layer-2 identity on the lower ℓ coordinates. This is because the exact identities in contrast to Odlyzko's hash function are additive, i.e., adding both identities from Eq. (4) results in a valid identity. Note that, for the second layer, we could apply Odlyzko's hash function rather than relying on the exact identity on the subsequent ℓ coordinates. Then guessing ℓ rather than 2ℓ bits of $\mathbf{e}$ would suffice. However, as this only improves second order terms we decided for ease of exposition to not rely on Odlyzko's hash function at all.

4.2   Concrete Instantiations

Next we give a first concrete instantiation for Algorithm 2, i.e., we specify the choice of function domains $\mathcal{T}_i$ and the mid level domains $\mathcal{D}_i$. We start with a choice of domains representing ternary vectors analogously to the REP-1 instantiation given in Sect. 3.

Nested-1 Instantiation. Recall that for the nested collision search besides the function domains $\mathcal{T}_i$ we have to specify the sums we aim to obtain on the middle level, i.e., the mid-level domains D_i of the $\mathbf{a}_i$ from Eq. (8). We consider for the D_i ternary vectors of length n with balanced weight $p_2 := w/4 + d_2$, where d_2 is an optimization parameter.

The function domains $\mathcal{T}_i$ are then chosen as all ternary vectors of length n and balanced weight $p_1 := p_2/2 + d_1 = w/8 + d_2/2 + d_1$, where d_1 has again to be optimized. In summary, we have

$$\mathcal{D}_i := \tau^n(p_2) \quad \text{and} \quad \mathcal{T}_i := \tau^n(p_1)$$

This gives function domains of size

$$|\mathcal{T}_i| = \binom{n}{p_1, p_1, \cdot}.$$

Let us now determine the number of representations R_1, R_2. Recall that R_2 is the amount of different $(\mathbf{a}_1, \mathbf{a}_2) \in D_1 \times D_2$ that sums to the solution $\mathbf{s}$. Hence, we have

$$R_2 = \binom{w/2}{w/4}^2 \binom{n-w}{d_2, d_2, \cdot},$$

as $\mathbf{s} \in \tau^n(w/2)$. Furthermore, each element of $\mathbf{a}_1$ respectively $\mathbf{a}_2$ has

$$R_1 = \binom{p_2}{p_2/2}^2 \binom{n - 2p_2}{d_1, d_1, \cdot}$$

representations as the sum of elements from $\mathcal{T}_i$.

Now plugging R_1 and R_2 into Eq. (9) gives the running time $T_{\text{Nested-1}}$ of this instantiation.

To obtain the runtime exponent c in $T_{\text{Nested-1}} = 2^{cn}$, we again approximate the involved binomial and multinomial coefficients via Eq. 1. Further we model $d_1 = \delta_1 n$ and $d_2 = \delta_2 n$ for $\delta_i \in [0, 1]$. Eventually we obtain c by minimizing over the choice of δ_1, δ_2 under the constraint on the function domain's size given in Eq. 7. For this minimization we use a numerical optimizer provided by the *scipy* python library, inspired by the code used for numerical optimization in [8]. The code used to run the numerical optimization for all our algorithms is available at https://github.com/arindamIITM/Small-LWE-Keys.

Remark 4 (Optimization Accuracy). In general these kind of numerical optimizers do not guarantee to find a global minimum, but instead might return only a local minimum or miss optimal parameters slightly. However, to increase the confidence in the optimality of the returned value, we minimized over thousands of runs of the optimizer on random starting points and multiple different formulations of the problem, until no further improvement could be obtained.

Note that for $w \geq 0.64$ even for $d_1 = d_2 = 0$, which minimizes the function domains we have $|\mathcal{T}_i| > \sqrt{|\tau^n(w/2)|}$. Therefore we do not obtain further instantiations as we can not satisfy Eq. 7. In the following, we make use of the concept of partial representations to allow for an adaptive scaling of the function domain size.

Nested-1$^+$ Instantiation. We now split the vectors of the domains into two parts, a disjoint part of length $(1 - \gamma)n$ and a joint part of length γn (compare to Fig. 6).

Precisely, for $\gamma \in [0, 1]$ we define the function domains $\mathcal{T}_i$ as

$$\mathcal{T}_1 = \tau^{\bar{\gamma}n/4}(\bar{\gamma}w/8) \times \quad 0 \quad \times \quad 0 \quad \times \quad 0 \quad \times \tau^{\gamma n}(p_1),$$
$$\mathcal{T}_2 = \quad 0 \quad \times \tau^{\bar{\gamma}n/4}(\bar{\gamma}w/8) \times \quad 0 \quad \times \quad 0 \quad \times \tau^{\gamma n}(p_1),$$
$$\mathcal{T}_3 = \quad 0 \quad \times \quad 0 \quad \times \tau^{\bar{\gamma}n/4}(\bar{\gamma}w/8) \times \quad 0 \quad \times \tau^{\gamma n}(p_1),$$
$$\mathcal{T}_4 = \quad 0 \quad \times \quad 0 \quad \times \quad 0 \quad \times \tau^{\bar{\gamma}n/4}(\bar{\gamma}w/8) \times \tau^{\gamma n}(p_1),$$

where $\bar{\gamma} = 1 - \gamma$ and $p_1 := \gamma w/8 + d_2/2 + d_1$. This gives function domain sizes of

$$|\mathcal{T}_i| = \binom{\bar{\gamma}n/4}{\bar{\gamma}w/8, \bar{\gamma}w/8, \cdot} \binom{\gamma n}{p_1, p_1, \cdot}.$$

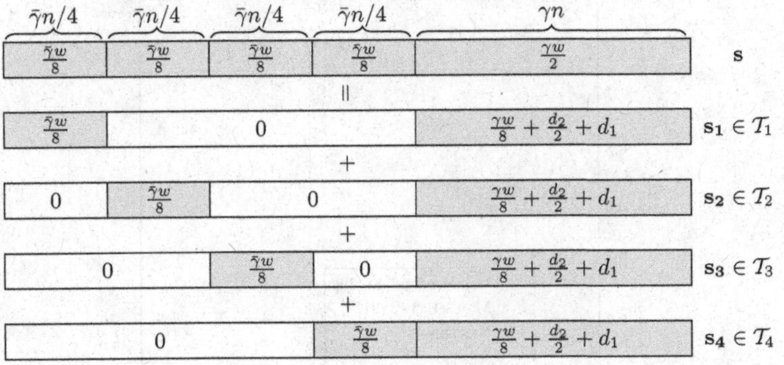

Fig. 6. Weight distribution of function domains using partial representations. Gray areas indicate regions of fixed balanced-ternary weight, where $\bar{\gamma} := 1 - \gamma$

Analogously, to the previous instantiation we define the domains D_i on the middle level as

$$\mathcal{D}_1 = \tau^{\bar{\gamma}n/4}(\bar{\gamma}w/8) \times \tau^{\bar{\gamma}n/4}(\bar{\gamma}w/8) \times \quad 0 \quad \times \quad 0 \quad \times \tau^{\gamma n}(p_2),$$
$$\mathcal{D}_2 = \quad 0 \quad \times \quad 0 \quad \times \tau^{\bar{\gamma}n/4}(\bar{\gamma}w/8) \times \tau^{\bar{\gamma}n/4}(\bar{\gamma}w/8) \times \tau^{\gamma n}(p_2),$$

where $p_2 = \gamma w/4 + d_2$.

To be able to construct the solution, we assume that on all five parts the weight of the solution is distributed proportionally. This can be achieved by the permutation in line 4 of Algorithm 2. Again, as for the van Vredendaal instantiation from Sect. 3, this causes only a small polynomial overhead.

Observe that as before we hope that on the jointly enumerated part (now of size γn) the vectors of weight p_1 add up to weight p_2. Further recall, that on the disjoint weight part of length $\bar{\gamma}n = (1 - \gamma)n$ we have only a single representation of any element from $(\tau^{\bar{\gamma}n}(\bar{\gamma}w/8))^4$. Hence, the number of representations is similar as before, but takes into account the reduced length of γn, where representations exist. For representations from the middle level we get

$$R_2 = \binom{\gamma w/2}{\gamma w/4}^2 \binom{\gamma(n-w)}{d_2, d_2, \cdot},$$

while every element on the middle level has $R_1 = \binom{p_2}{p_2/2}^2 \binom{\gamma n - 2p_2}{d_1, d_1, \cdot}$ many representations.

Similar as before we obtain the running time $T_{\text{NESTED-1+}}$ of this instantiation using Eq. 9. Again, we obtain the runtime exponent c by approximating the multinomial coefficients, letting $d_1 = \delta_1 n, d_2 = \delta_2 n$ and finally minimizing over the choice of δ_1, δ_2 and γ. The obtained runtime exponents of both our instantiations NESTED-1 and NESTED-1$^+$ are given in Fig. 7 in comparison to the exponents of van Vredendaal's as well as May's Rep-2 instantiation of the basic collision search. We observe that NESTED-1$^+$ significantly outperforms all other

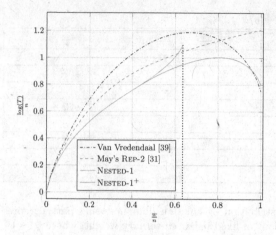

Fig. 7. Runtime exponents of NESTED-1 and NESTED-1$^+$ instantiations compared to previous work.

instantiations for almost all choices of the weight w. Only for a weight w close to n, i.e. w/n close to one, van Vredendaal's algorithm offers a slightly better running time. In comparison to May's representation based instantiations our nested approach has the natural property that for large weights, with decreased search space size, the running time also decreases again.

We also observe that NESTED-1$^+$ not only extends NESTED-1 to weights $w/n > 0.64$, it also offers runtime improvements in the regime $w/n \geq 0.44$. This value of $w/n = 0.44$ marks the point from where the γ-parameter of the NESTED-1$^+$ instantiation is chosen smaller than one to fulfill the correctness constraint from Eq. (7). The ability to control the domain sizes by γ instead of having to decrease the representation parameters d_1 and d_2 results in the superiority of NESTED-1$^+$ over NESTED-1 in this regime.

4.3   Exploiting the Permutation

Next, we show how to improve the algorithm by aiming at a non-proportional weight distribution induced by the permutation. Then we give two further instantiations for the function domains one based on REP-1-like representations and one exploiting the REP-2 concept.

Recall that by our choice of function domains (see Eq. (7)), as soon as we find a collision between the second-layer functions g_i, that leads to an $\mathbf{s}' \in \tau^n(w/2)$ it implies that $\mathbf{s}'$ is a solution. In our previous instantiation NESTED-1$^+$, we introduced a disjoint weight part, which automatically leads to elements of the desired form on a $(1 - \gamma)$ fraction of the coordinates. In other words a collision between g_1 and g_2 leading to an $\mathbf{s}' \notin \tau^n(w/2)$ is always caused by the coordinates in the jointly enumerated part not adding up as desired.

The idea is now to exploit the permutation to distribute a higher fraction of the weight on the disjoint part in the solution $\mathbf{P}^{-1}\mathbf{s}$ of the permuted instance. Since, in turn the decreased weight on the joint part increases the probability that elements add up to ternary vectors, as desired.

More precisely, instead of obtaining the proportional ternary weight of γw on the γn-part and $(1-\gamma)w/4$ in each of the four disjoint parts we aim at weight $\beta\gamma w$ on the joint part and $(1 - \beta\gamma)w/4$ on the disjoint parts for some positive $\beta \in [\frac{w-(1-\gamma)n}{\gamma w}, 1]$. The lower bound on β just ensures that the length of the disjoint parts is larger or equal to the weight, i.e., $(1 - \beta\gamma)w/4 \leq (1 - \gamma)n/4$. Note that once we assume the solution $\mathbf{s}' = \mathbf{P}^{-1}\mathbf{s}$ to the permuted instance in this form, the search space changes from $\tau^n(w/2)$ to

$$
D := \left(\tau^{\bar{\gamma}n/4}\big((1 - \beta\gamma)w/8\big)\right)^4 \times \tau^{\gamma n}(\beta\gamma w/2),
$$

where $\bar{\gamma} := 1 - \gamma$. This means the size of the search space reduces to

$$
|D| = \binom{\bar{\gamma}n/4}{(1-\gamma\beta)w/8,\, (1-\gamma\beta)w/8,\, \cdot}^4 \binom{\gamma n}{\beta\gamma w/2,\, \beta\gamma w/2,\, \cdot}.
$$

In turn the expected amount of elements from D that satisfy the second-layer identity Eq. (3) is $\frac{|D|}{q^{2\ell}}$. Hence, to guarantee that there exists only one such element in expectation we have to choose $\ell = \frac{\log_q |D|}{2}$. In other words, the constraint from Eq. (7) now changes to

$$
|\mathcal{T}_i| \overset{!}{=} \sqrt{|D|}. \tag{10}
$$

While the analysis from Sect. 4.1 in principle still holds, we need to account for the probability of the weight being distributed as desired. Note that this probability can be expressed as

$$
q_4 := \Pr[\mathbf{P}^{-1}\mathbf{s} \in D] = \frac{|D|}{|\tau^n(w/2)|}.
$$

Hence, in total the algorithm needs to be iterated q_4^{-1} times more often. Together with the changed value of ℓ we obtain (compare to Eq. 9)

$$
T = (q_1 q_2 q_3 q_4)^{-1} q^\ell = \left(\frac{|D|^{\frac{1}{2}} \cdot |\tau^n(w/2)|}{(R_1)^2 R_2}\right)^{1+o(1)}. \tag{11}
$$

Nested-1* Instantiation Let us first consider an instantiation using again the REP-1 concept for representations. We now choose according to the changed weight distribution adapted function domains as shown in Fig. 8.

More formally, we let

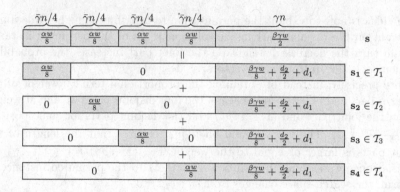

Fig. 8. Weight distribution of function domains for NESTED-1* instantiation. Gray regions are of fixed balanced-ternary weight, with $\alpha := 1 - \beta\gamma$

$$
\begin{aligned}
\mathcal{T}_1 &= \tau^{\bar{\gamma}n/4}(\alpha w/8) \times && 0 && \times && 0 && \times && 0 && \times \tau^{\gamma n}(p_1), \\
\mathcal{T}_2 &= 0 && \times \tau^{\bar{\gamma}n/4}(\alpha w/8) \times && 0 && \times && 0 && \times \tau^{\gamma n}(p_1), \\
\mathcal{T}_3 &= 0 && \times 0 && \times \tau^{\bar{\gamma}n/4}(\alpha w/8) \times && 0 && \times \tau^{\gamma n}(p_1), \\
\mathcal{T}_4 &= 0 && \times 0 && \times 0 && \times \tau^{\bar{\gamma}n/4}(\alpha w/8) \times \tau^{\gamma n}(p_1),
\end{aligned}
$$

where $\bar{\gamma} := 1 - \gamma$, $\alpha := (1 - \beta\gamma)$ and $p_1 := \beta\gamma w/8 + d_2/2 + d_1$. This gives function domain sizes of

$$
|\mathcal{T}_i| = \binom{\bar{\gamma}n/4}{\alpha w/8, \alpha w/8, \cdot} \binom{\gamma n}{p_1, p_1, \cdot}.
$$

Accordingly, we adjust the mid-level domains to

$$
\begin{aligned}
\mathcal{D}_1 &= \tau^{\bar{\gamma}n/4}(\alpha w/8) \times \tau^{\bar{\gamma}n/4}(\alpha w/8) \times && 0 && \times && 0 && \times \tau^{\gamma n}(p_2), \\
\mathcal{D}_2 &= 0 && \times 0 && \times \tau^{\bar{\gamma}n/4}(\alpha w/8) \times \tau^{\bar{\gamma}n/4}(\alpha w/8) \times \tau^{\gamma n}(p_2),
\end{aligned}
$$

with $p_2 := \beta\gamma w/4 + d_2$ In turn this leads to an amount of

$$
R_2 = \binom{\beta\gamma w/2}{\beta\gamma w/4}^2 \binom{\gamma(n - \beta w)}{d_2, d_2, \cdot},
$$

representations of the solution as sum of elements from D_1, D_2. Furthermore, every element from D_1 (resp. D_2) as sum of elements from $\mathcal{T}_1, \mathcal{T}_2$ (resp. $\mathcal{T}_3, \mathcal{T}_4$) has

$$
R_1 = \binom{p_2}{p_2/2}^2 \binom{\gamma n - 2p_2}{d_1, d_1, \cdot}
$$

representations.

We now obtain the running time $T^*_{\text{NESTED-1}}$ via Eq. (11). As before we approximate the multinomial coefficients via Eq. (1) and perform a numerical optimization to obtain the runtime exponent c in $T^*_{\text{NESTED-1}} = 2^{cn}$. Here, we minimize c over the choice of β, γ, δ_1 and δ_2, where $d_1 = \delta_1 n$ and $d_2 = \delta_2 n$, while ensuring the constraint given in Eq. (10).

Nested-2* Instantiation. Eventually, we provide an instantiation using REP-2 like representations, i.e., function and mid level domains whose vectors have coordinates in $\{-2, -1, 0, 1, 2\}$ (see Fig. 9). This increases the number of representations at the cost of quite technical analysis. While in principle it is possible to extend the digit set further, previous results on subset sum [8] and LWE [31] indicate that the runtime quickly converges. For the formal definition of our function domains, let us first extend the definition of $\tau^n(\cdot)$ to $\tau^n_2(a,b) := \{\mathbf{x} \in \{\pm 2, \pm 1, 0\}^n : |\mathbf{x}|_1 = |\mathbf{x}|_{-1} = a \wedge |\mathbf{x}|_2 = |\mathbf{x}|_{-2} = b\}$, where $|\mathbf{x}|_i := |\{j \mid x_j = i\}|$.

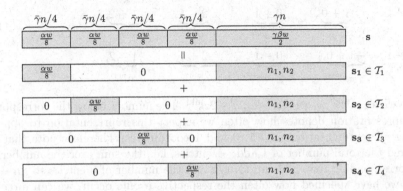

Fig. 9. Weight distribution of function domains for NESTED-2* instantiation. Gray regions with single numbers indicate parts with fixed balanced-ternary weight, where $\alpha := 1 - \beta\gamma$. Gray parts with two numbers n_1, n_2 contain n_1 1s, n_1 −1s, n_2 2s, n_2 −2s and rest zeros.

The function domains are then defined as

$$\mathcal{T}_1 = \tau^{\bar{\gamma}n/4}(\alpha w/8) \times \quad 0 \quad \times \quad 0 \quad \times \quad 0 \quad \times \tau^{\gamma n}_2(n_1, n_2),$$
$$\mathcal{T}_2 = \quad 0 \quad \times \tau^{\bar{\gamma}n/4}(\alpha w/8) \times \quad 0 \quad \times \quad 0 \quad \times \tau^{\gamma n}_2(n_1, n_2),$$
$$\mathcal{T}_3 = \quad 0 \quad \times \quad 0 \quad \times \tau^{\bar{\gamma}n/4}(\alpha w/8) \times \quad 0 \quad \times \tau^{\gamma n}_2(n_1, n_2),$$
$$\mathcal{T}_4 = \quad 0 \quad \times \quad 0 \quad \times \quad 0 \quad \times \tau^{\bar{\gamma}n/4}(\alpha w/8) \times \tau^{\gamma n}_2(n_1, n_2),$$

where $\bar{\gamma} := 1 - \gamma$ and $\alpha := (1 - \beta\gamma)$, while we derive the precise form of n_1 and n_2 later. This gives function domain sizes of

$$|\mathcal{T}_i| = \binom{\bar{\gamma}n/4}{\alpha w/8, \alpha w/8, \cdot} \binom{\gamma n}{n_1, n_1, n_2, n_2, \cdot}.$$

Accordingly, we adjust the mid-level domains to

$$\mathcal{D}_1 = \tau^{\bar{\gamma}n/4}(\alpha w/8) \times \tau^{\bar{\gamma}n/4}(\alpha w/8) \times \quad 0 \quad \times \quad 0 \quad \times \tau_2^{\gamma n}(n_1^{\mathrm{mid}}, n_2^{\mathrm{mid}}),$$
$$\mathcal{D}_2 = \quad 0 \quad \times \quad 0 \quad \times \tau^{\bar{\gamma}n/4}(\alpha w/8) \times \tau^{\bar{\gamma}n/4}(\alpha w/8) \times \tau_2^{\gamma n}(n_1^{\mathrm{mid}}, n_2^{\mathrm{mid}}),$$

while again we postpone determining $n_1^{\mathrm{mid}}, n_2^{\mathrm{mid}}$ to the analysis of the number of representations.

Let us start by determining the number of representations of the ternary weight-ω solution $\mathbf{s}$ as sum of elements from $\mathcal{D}_1, \mathcal{D}_2$. Recall that we only have representations on the last γn coordinates, where we assume $\mathbf{s}$ to have weight $\hat{w} := \gamma\beta w$. To represent a $-1, 0$ or 1 of the solution we have the following possibilities

$$
\begin{array}{llllll}
0: & \underbrace{0+0,}_{m^{\mathrm{mid}}} & \underbrace{1-1,}_{z_1^{\mathrm{mid}}} & \underbrace{-1+1,}_{z_1^{\mathrm{mid}}} & \underbrace{2-2,}_{z_2^{\mathrm{mid}}} & \underbrace{-2+2,}_{z_2^{\mathrm{mid}}} \\[1.5em]
1: & \underbrace{1+0,}_{\frac{\hat{w}}{4}-o^{\mathrm{mid}}} & \underbrace{0+1,}_{\frac{\hat{w}}{4}-o^{\mathrm{mid}}} & \underbrace{2-1,}_{o^{\mathrm{mid}}} & \underbrace{-1+2,}_{o^{\mathrm{mid}}} & \qquad (12) \\[1.5em]
-1: & \underbrace{-1+0,}_{\frac{\hat{w}}{4}-o^{\mathrm{mid}}} & \underbrace{0-1,}_{\frac{\hat{w}}{4}-o^{\mathrm{mid}}} & \underbrace{-2+1,}_{o^{\mathrm{mid}}} & \underbrace{1-2,}_{o^{\mathrm{mid}}}
\end{array}
$$

where we let $m^{\mathrm{mid}} := \gamma n - \hat{w} - 2z_1^{\mathrm{mid}} - 2z_2^{\mathrm{mid}}$. The number below the corresponding representation denotes how often we expect this representation to appear among all representations of $-1, 0$ and 1 coordinates. Therefore note that as required the total number of 1 and -1 entries, i.e., the sum over the number of the corresponding row, adds up to $\hat{w}/2$ and the number of 0 entries to $\gamma n - \hat{w}$. After we have specified how often the respective events occur, we can directly derive the number of representations as

$$R_2 = \binom{\gamma n - \hat{w}}{m^{\mathrm{mid}}, z_1^{\mathrm{mid}}, z_1^{\mathrm{mid}}, z_2^{\mathrm{mid}}, z_2^{\mathrm{mid}}} \binom{\hat{w}/2}{\hat{w}/4 - o^{\mathrm{mid}}, \hat{w}/4 - o^{\mathrm{mid}}, o^{\mathrm{mid}}, o^{\mathrm{mid}}}^2,$$

where the first factor counts the possibilities to represent 0s and the second those to represent ± 1s. Now a simple counting argument yields the previously omitted number of coordinates equal to ± 1s and ± 2s in the mid level domains as[5]

$$n_1^{\mathrm{mid}} = z_1^{\mathrm{mid}} + \hat{w}/4 - o^{\mathrm{mid}} + o^{\mathrm{mid}} = \hat{w}/4 + z_1^{\mathrm{mid}} \quad \text{and} \quad n_2^{\mathrm{mid}} = z_2^{\mathrm{mid}} + o^{\mathrm{mid}},$$

where $z_1^{\mathrm{mid}}, z_2^{\mathrm{mid}}$ and o^{mid} are subject to optimization. Note that for $\gamma = \beta = 1$ we obtain as a special case the necessary representation formula for the REP-2 instantiation of May, which we omitted previously (see Sect. 3).

Next let us determine the number of representations of any element from the mid-level domains $\mathcal{D}_i$ as sum of elements from the function domains $\mathcal{T}_i$. Therefore

---

[5] We have to count the appearances of 1 (resp. 2) entries on the left (or right) of the possible representations given in Eq. (12).

let us again specify the number of representations, which is similar to before, but we additionally get multiple possibilities to represent 2 and -2 entries

$$
\begin{array}{cccccc}
0: & \underbrace{0+0}_{m}, & \underbrace{1-1}_{z_1}, & \underbrace{-1+1}_{z_1}, & \underbrace{2-2}_{z_2}, & \underbrace{-2+2}_{z_2}, \\[2mm]
1: & \underbrace{1+0}_{\frac{n_1^{\mathrm{mid}}}{2}-o}, & \underbrace{0+1}_{\frac{n_1^{\mathrm{mid}}}{2}-o}, & \underbrace{2-1}_{o}, & \underbrace{-1+2}_{o}, \\[2mm]
-1: & \underbrace{-1+0}_{\frac{n_1^{\mathrm{mid}}}{2}-o}, & \underbrace{0-1}_{\frac{n_1^{\mathrm{mid}}}{2}-o}, & \underbrace{-2+1}_{o}, & \underbrace{1-2}_{o}, \\[2mm]
2: & \underbrace{2+0}_{\frac{n_2^{\mathrm{mid}}-t}{2}}, & \underbrace{0+2}_{\frac{n_2^{\mathrm{mid}}-t}{2}}, & \underbrace{1+1}_{t}, \\[2mm]
-2: & \underbrace{-2+0}_{\frac{n_2^{\mathrm{mid}}-t}{2}}, & \underbrace{0-2}_{\frac{n_2^{\mathrm{mid}}-t}{2}}, & \underbrace{-1-1}_{t},
\end{array}
$$

where $m := \gamma n - 2(n_1^{\mathrm{mid}} + n_2^{\mathrm{mid}} + z_1 + z_2)$, and again z_1, z_2, o and t denote optimization parameters for the number of zeros, ones and twos represented via the respective combinations. Observe that again the number of total represented 1s (resp. -1s) add to n_1^{mid}, the number of 2s (resp. -2s) to n_2^{mid} and the number of 0s to $\gamma n - 2(n_1^{\mathrm{mid}} + n_2^{\mathrm{mid}})$ as required for mid-level elements. From here we can derive the number of representations as

$$
R_1 = \binom{\gamma n - 2(n_1^{\mathrm{mid}} + n_2^{\mathrm{mid}})}{m, z_1, z_1, z_2, z_2} \binom{n_1^{\mathrm{mid}}}{\frac{n_1^{\mathrm{mid}}}{2} - o, \frac{n_1^{\mathrm{mid}}}{2} - o, o, o}^2 \binom{n_2^{\mathrm{mid}}}{\frac{n_2^{\mathrm{mid}}-t}{2}, \frac{n_2^{\mathrm{mid}}-t}{2}, t}^2 ,
$$

where the first term counts the representations of 0, the second those of ± 1 and the last those of ± 2 coordinates. As before, a counting argument yields the necessary number of ± 1 and ± 2 coordinates in the function domains as

$$
n_1 = z_1 + \frac{n_1^{\mathrm{mid}}}{2} - o + o + t = z_1 + t + \frac{n_1^{\mathrm{mid}}}{2} \quad \text{and} \quad n_2 = z_2 + o + \frac{n_2^{\mathrm{mid}} - t}{2}.
$$

Now that we determined the number of representations R_1 and R_2 we obtain the running time $T_{\text{NESTED-2}^*}$ of this instantiation using Eq. (11). In our numerical optimization of the running time we optimize over the choice of $\tilde{z}_1, \tilde{z}_2, \tilde{o}, \tilde{t}, \tilde{z}_1^{\mathrm{mid}}, \tilde{z}_2^{\mathrm{mid}}, \tilde{o}^{\mathrm{mid}}, \tilde{t}^{\mathrm{mid}}, \gamma$ and β, where for integer optimization parameters χ we let $\chi = \tilde{\chi} n$ with $\chi \in [0, 1]$.

We illustrate the optimized runtime exponents of our NESTED-1* and NESTED-2* instantiations in comparison to our previous NESTED-1$^+$ instantiation in Fig. 10 on the left. We observe improvements especially for high weights. However, we also obtain improvements for smaller weights. In the same figure on the right, we illustrate the exponent difference between NESTED-1* and NESTED-1$^+$ as well as between NESTED-1* and NESTED-2*. For NESTED-1* we observe improvements starting from $w/n \geq 0.44$, which marks the point where

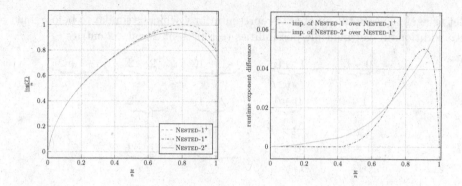

Fig. 10. On the left: Runtime exponents of Nested-1$^+$, Nested-1* and Nested-2*. On the right: Improvement in the runtime exponent $(\log T_A - \log T_B)/n$ of $B = $ Nested-1* over $A = $ Nested-1$^+$ (dash dotted line) and the improvement of $B = $ Nested-2* over $A = $ Nested-1* (solid line).

we have $\gamma < 1$. Since the improvement of Nested-1* stems entirely from using the permutation to shift more weight to the disjoint part of size $(1 - \gamma)n$, we expect no improvement as long as $\gamma = 1$. We also observe that for $w/n = 1$ both instantiations Nested-1$^+$ and Nested-1* converge to the same running time, resulting in a difference of zero. On the other hand, Nested-2* obtains further improvements over Nested-1* for all choices of the weight w, with higher gains towards larger values of w. The gain in this case stems entirely from adding the ± 2 to the representations and is therefore not bound to parameterizations with $\gamma < 1$.

4.4 An Improvement for Uniform Secrets

We conclude this section by outlining a (small) improvement for a weight close to $w/n = 2/3$, i.e. around the weight of uniform ternary secrets. The idea is to apply an initial permutation to redistribute the weight on $(\mathbf{e}, \mathbf{s})$, similar to Information Set Decoding (ISD) techniques [35]. Therefore we rewrite the LWE identity $\mathbf{As} = \mathbf{b} + \mathbf{e}$ as

$$(\mathbf{I} \mid \mathbf{A})(-\mathbf{e}, \mathbf{s}) = \mathbf{b},$$

where $\mathbf{I}$ is the $n \times n$ identity matrix. Now applying a permutation to the columns of $(\mathbf{I} \mid \mathbf{A})$ yields

$$(\mathbf{I} \mid \mathbf{A})\mathbf{P}\big(\mathbf{P}^{-1}(-\mathbf{e}, \mathbf{s})\big) = \mathbf{H}(-\mathbf{e}', \mathbf{s}') = \mathbf{b},$$

where $(-\mathbf{e}', \mathbf{s}') := \mathbf{P}^{-1}(-\mathbf{e}, \mathbf{s})$. Further multiplying both sides of the equation with an invertible matrix $\mathbf{Q}$, such that $\mathbf{QH} = (\mathbf{I} \mid \mathbf{A}')$ and defining $\mathbf{b}' := \mathbf{Qb}$ yields $\mathbf{A}'\mathbf{s}' = \mathbf{b}' + \mathbf{e}'$.

Now, assume that the permutation distributes a balanced weight of $w - p$ on $\mathbf{s}'$ and accordingly a balanced weight of $2n/3 + p$ on $\mathbf{e}'$, since $\mathbf{e}$ is usually a uniform ternary vector. Then we expect Algorithm 2 to perform faster on the reduced weight instance $(\mathbf{A}', \mathbf{b}')$ than on the initial instance $(\mathbf{A}, \mathbf{b})$ as its running time (compare to Eq. (11)) depends only on the weight of $\mathbf{s}$ but not on the weight of $\mathbf{e}$. On the downside we need to reapply the algorithm $P = \dfrac{\binom{2n}{\frac{n}{3}+\frac{w}{2},\frac{n}{3}+\frac{w}{2},\cdot}}{\binom{n}{\frac{w-p}{2},\frac{w-p}{2},\cdot}\binom{n}{\frac{n}{3}+\frac{p}{2},\frac{n}{3}+\frac{p}{2},\cdot}}$ times on random permutations of the instance to expect the weight to be distributed as desired for one of the instances. The running time is then given as $P \cdot T_{w-p}$, where T_{w-p} is the same as T in Eq. (11) but for $w - p$ instead of w. In the uniform secret case of $w/n = 2/3$ this yields a (slight) improvement from $2^{0.93n}$ down-to $2^{0.926n}$ for our NESTED-2* instantiation. Note that if w is small the secret $\mathbf{s}'$ after the permutation is expected to have weight $w' > w$, which is why we do not obtain improvements in this regime.

5   Complexity of Solving Ternary LWE Without Memory

Eventually, let us give a concluding comparison between the best instantiations of the basic collision search by van Vredendaal (V-V) and May (REP-2) and our best NESTED-2* instantiation of the nested collision search approach. We illustrate the runtime exponents of all these algorithms on the left of Fig. 11. Observe that our NESTED-2* algorithm yields the best running time for all choices of the weight w. Moreover the improvement in the exponent compared to the minimum of V-V and REP-2 reaches as high as 0.2 for a weight of $w = 0.81n$. While the most interesting weights are usually smaller than that, note that we also obtain significant improvements for all cryptographically relevant weights. For instance for a weight of $w = 0.667n$, which models the uniform secret case we obtain a significant improvement by a factor larger than $2^{0.13n}$. Table 1 shows the runtime exponent of all three methods for various weights used in schemes belonging to the NTRU-family. The exponent improvement of our NESTED-2* for all weights w/n compared to the best previous approach is illustrated on the right of Fig. 11. As comparison the graphic shows the runtime improvement of May over van Vredendaal. Note that for $w \geq 0.82$ May does not obtain any improvement over van Vredendaal.

Table 1. Runtime exponents for nested collision search (including improvement from Sect. 4.4) in comparison to conventional collision search approaches.

w/n	V-V	REP-2	NESTED-2*
0.300	0.8860	0.7716	**0.6482**
0.375	0.9971	0.8573	**0.7272**
0.441	1.0732	0.9172	**0.7928**
0.500	1.1250	0.9620	**0.8425**
0.621	1.1837	1.0376	**0.9140**
0.668	1.1887	1.0632	**0.9262**

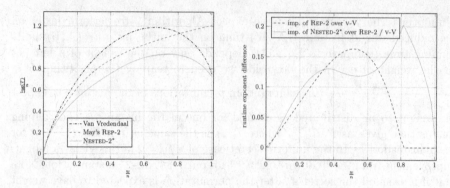

Fig. 11. On the left: Runtime exponents of van Vredendaal's, May's and our nested approach. Improvement close to uniform case (Sect. 4.4) illustrated as orange dotted line. On the right: Improvement in the runtime exponent of May's REP-2 over van Vredendaal (dashed line) and of NESTED-2* over the minimum of van Vredendaal's and May's algorithms (solid line). (Color figure online)

6   Extending Results to Kyber and Dilithium

In the following, we extend our results as well as the results from May and van Vredendaal to the cases of Kyber and Dilithium, which also rely on the hardness of LWE with small max norm keys. We recall that this extension requires the heuristic assumption that the introduced structure does not affect our analysis.

More precisely, Kyber uses keys sampled from a centered binomial distribution $\mathcal{B}(\eta)$ with parameter $\eta \in \{2, 3\}$, resulting in keys $s \in \{-\eta, \ldots, \eta\}$. Dilithium keys have coordinates uniformly distributed over $\{\pm 2, \pm 1, 0\}$, which we denote by $\mathcal{U}(2)$, implying keys $s \in \{-2, \ldots, 2\}$.

Table 2. Runtime exponents for nested collision instantiations and conventional collision search approaches with different key distributions.

Key-Dist.	v-V	REP-3	NESTED-3*
$\mathcal{U}(1)$	1.1888	1.0625	**0.9297**
$\mathcal{U}(2)$	1.7415	1.4601	**1.2815**
$\mathcal{U}(3)$	1.9698	1.7323	**1.5049**
$\mathcal{B}(1)$	1.1250	0.9620	**0.8427**
$\mathcal{B}(2)$	1.5230	1.2118	**1.0404**
$\mathcal{B}(3)$	1.7501	1.3585	**1.1838**

We give in Table 2 the runtime exponents on Kyber and Dilithium key distributions of Algorithm 1 using the van-Vredendaal instantiations (v-V) as well as using REP-3 representations, i.e., we represent the solution $s = s_1 + s_2$ with

$s_i \in \{\pm 3, \pm 2, \pm 1, 0\}$. Additionally, we state the runtime exponent of our nested collision search, Algorithm 2, using a NESTED-3* instantiation, which is the same as NESTED-2*, but extending function domains by ± 3. We also provide data for the $\mathcal{U}(1), \mathcal{U}(3)$ and $\mathcal{B}(1)$ distributions to indicate the scaling.

Additionally we provide in Table 3 the running time exponent c in dependence on the search space, i.e., the running time is of the form $T = \mathcal{D}^c$ with $\mathcal{D}$ the size of the search space. We observe that for both distributions the attacks become more efficient for increasing η, indicated by the decreasing value of c. This is related to the representation method, which overcompensates the increase in domain size by the increasing number of representations. Note that this indicates that with respect to combinatorial approaches increasing η will not result in significantly increased security.

Our attacks are especially efficient on the centered binomial distributions used in Kyber, where they reach almost the meet-in-the-middle exponent $c = 0.5$. However, for Dilithium like distributions ($\mathcal{U}(2)$) we also obtain a notable improvement down to a constant of $c = 0.552$. For the full details of the analysis we refer the reader to the full version of this article [16].

Table 3. Runtime exponents $c = \log_{\mathcal{D}} T$ for nested collision instantiations and conventional collision search approaches with different key distributions in dependence on the search space size $\mathcal{D}$.

Key-Dist.	v-V	REP-3	NESTED-3*
$\mathcal{U}(1)$	0.75	0.6704	**0.5866**
$\mathcal{U}(2)$	0.75	0.6289	**0.5519**
$\mathcal{U}(3)$	0.75	0.6171	**0.5361**
$\mathcal{B}(1)$	0.75	0.6414	**0.5619**
$\mathcal{B}(2)$	0.75	0.5968	**0.5124**
$\mathcal{B}(3)$	0.75	0.5832	**0.5074**

7 Time-Memory Trade-Off Using PCS

So far, all our attacks can be instantiated with a polynomial amount of memory. However, in a realistic attack scenario even low memory devices such as FPGAs or GPUs still have a small amount of memory available. In the following we show how to apply the time-memory trade-off technique known as Parallel Collision Search (PCS) [38] to our construction to further speed up our algorithms by the use of small but exponential amounts of memory.

Theorem 1 (Parallel Collision Search, [38]). *Let $f_1, f_2 : S \to S$ be two independent random functions. Then Parallel Collision Search finds M collisions between f_1 and f_2 using on expectation $\tilde{\mathcal{O}}\left((M \cdot |S|)^{1/2}\right)$ function evaluations and $\tilde{\mathcal{O}}(M)$ units of memory.*

Recall that, to succeed Algorithm 2 has to find multiple collisions between g_1 and g_2, namely on expectation $C := (q_1 q_2 q_3)^{-1}$ many (compare to Eq. (9)). So far, those collisions are found by iterative applications of the collision search technique. We now use the PCS technique to find M collisions at once by increasing the memory usage of the algorithm to $\tilde{\mathcal{O}}(M)$.

However, such a straightforward application of the PCS technique is not sufficient to achieve meaningful trade-offs for reasonable amounts of memory. This is because the amount of needed collisions C is an upper bound for the maximum memory that can be spend and usually C is quite small for optimal instantiations. In order to obtain instantiations leveraging more memory, we adapt the time complexity to incorporate the PCS speedup and perform a numerical re-optimization of the running time. This allows for a choice of instantiations with larger C that in turn enables to fully leverage the available memory. However, once C becomes maximal no further speedups by increasing the memory are possible. Table 4 provides a comparison of the running time using polynomial memory and the running time using the maximal amount of memory that can be leveraged.

Table 4. Runtime and memory exponents for time-memory trade-offs in comparison to polynomial memory algorithm NESTED-2*.

w/n	time at poly. memory	best time	required memory
0.300	0.6482	0.6204	0.06
0.375	0.7272	0.6974	0.07
0.441	0.7928	0.7569	0.09
0.500	0.8425	0.8017	0.11
0.621	0.9140	0.8669	0.15
0.668	0.9262	0.8824	0.17

Note that there also exist instantiations for any memory smaller than the maximal memory given in the table. We provide the full trade-off curves in the full version of this work [16].

References

1. Adj, G., Cervantes-Vázquez, D., Chi-Domínguez, J.J., Menezes, A., Rodríguez-Henríquez, F.: On the cost of computing isogenies between supersingular elliptic curves. In: Cid, C., Jacobson Jr., M.J. (eds.) SAC 2018. LNCS, vol. 11349, pp. 322–343. Springer, Heidelberg (2019). https://doi.org/10.1007/978-3-030-10970-7_15
2. Albrecht, M.R., Bai, S., Ducas, L.: A subfield lattice attack on overstretched NTRU assumptions. In: Robshaw, M., Katz, J. (eds.) CRYPTO 2016. LNCS, vol. 9814, pp. 153–178. Springer, Heidelberg (2016). https://doi.org/10.1007/978-3-662-53018-4_6

3. Albrecht, M.R., Bai, S., Fouque, P.-A., Kirchner, P., Stehlé, D., Wen, W.: Faster enumeration-based lattice reduction: root hermite factor $k^{1/(2k)}$ Time $k^{k/8+o(k)}$. In: Micciancio, D., Ristenpart, T. (eds.) CRYPTO 2020, Part II. LNCS, vol. 12171, pp. 186–212. Springer, Cham (2020). https://doi.org/10.1007/978-3-030-56880-1_7

4. Becker, A., Coron, J.-S., Joux, A.: Improved generic algorithms for hard knapsacks. In: Paterson, K.G. (ed.) EUROCRYPT 2011. LNCS, vol. 6632, pp. 364–385. Springer, Heidelberg (2011). https://doi.org/10.1007/978-3-642-20465-4_21

5. Bellini, E., et al.: Parallel isogeny path finding with limited memory. In: Isobe, T., Sarkar, S. (eds.) INDOCRYPT 2022. LNCS, vol. 13774, pp. 294–316. Springer, Cham (2023). https://doi.org/10.1007/978-3-031-22912-1_13

6. Bernstein, D.J., Chuengsatiansup, C., Lange, T., van Vredendaal, C.: NTRU prime: reducing attack surface at low cost. In: Adams, C., Camenisch, J. (eds.) SAC 2017. LNCS, vol. 10719, pp. 235–260. Springer, Cham (2018). https://doi.org/10.1007/978-3-319-72565-9_12

7. Bi, L., Lu, X., Luo, J., Wang, K.: Hybrid dual and meet-LWE attack. In: Nguyen, K., Yang, G., Guo, F., Susilo, W. (eds.) ACISP 2022. LNCS, vol. 13494, pp. 168–188. Springer, Cham (2022). https://doi.org/10.1007/978-3-031-22301-3_9

8. Bonnetain, X., Bricout, R., Schrottenloher, A., Shen, Y.: Improved classical and quantum algorithms for subset-sum. In: Moriai, S., Wang, H. (eds.) ASIACRYPT 2020, Part II. LNCS, vol. 12492, pp. 633–666. Springer, Cham (2020). https://doi.org/10.1007/978-3-030-64834-3_22

9. Bos, J., et al.: Crystals-kyber: a CCA-secure module-lattice-based KEM. In: 2018 IEEE European Symposium on Security and Privacy (EuroS&P), pp. 353–367. IEEE (2018)

10. Bos, J.W., Kaihara, M.E., Kleinjung, T., Lenstra, A.K., Montgomery, P.L.: Solving a 112-bit prime elliptic curve discrete logarithm problem on game consoles using sloppy reduction. Int. J. Appl. Cryptogr. $2(3)$, 212–228 (2012)

11. Bricout, R., Chailloux, A., Debris-Alazard, T., Lequesne, M.: Ternary syndrome decoding with large weight. In: Paterson, K.G., Stebila, D. (eds.) SAC 2019. LNCS, vol. 11959, pp. 437–466. Springer, Cham (2020). https://doi.org/10.1007/978-3-030-38471-5_18

12. Delaplace, C., Esser, A., May, A.: Improved low-memory subset sum and LPN algorithms via multiple collisions. In: Albrecht, M. (ed.) IMACC 2019. LNCS, vol. 11929, pp. 178–199. Springer, Cham (2019). https://doi.org/10.1007/978-3-030-35199-1_9

13. Dinur, I., Dunkelman, O., Keller, N., Shamir, A.: Memory-efficient algorithms for finding needles in haystacks. In: Robshaw, M., Katz, J. (eds.) CRYPTO 2016, Part II. LNCS, vol. 9815, pp. 185–206. Springer, Heidelberg (2016). https://doi.org/10.1007/978-3-662-53008-5_7

14. Ducas, L., Durmus, A., Lepoint, T., Lyubashevsky, V.: Lattice signatures and bimodal gaussians. In: Canetti, R., Garay, J.A. (eds.) CRYPTO 2013, Part I. LNCS, vol. 8042, pp. 40–56. Springer, Heidelberg (2013). https://doi.org/10.1007/978-3-642-40041-4_3

15. Ducas, L., Stevens, M., van Woerden, W.P.J.: Advanced lattice sieving on GPUs, with tensor cores. In: Canteaut, A., Standaert, F.X. (eds.) EUROCRYPT 2021, Part II. LNCS, vol. 12697, pp. 249–279. Springer, Heidelberg (2021). https://doi.org/10.1007/978-3-030-77886-6_9

16. Esser, A., Girme, R., Mukherjee, A., Sarkar, S.: Memory-efficient attacks on small LWE keys. Cryptology ePrint Archive, Report 2023/243 (2023). https://eprint.iacr.org/2023/243

17. Esser, A., May, A.: Low weight discrete logarithm and subset sum in $2^{0.65n}$ with polynomial memory. In: Canteaut, A., Ishai, Y. (eds.) EUROCRYPT 2020, Part III. LNCS, vol. 12107, pp. 94–122. Springer, Cham (2020). https://doi.org/10.1007/978-3-030-45727-3_4

18. Esser, A., May, A., Zweydinger, F.: McEliece needs a break - solving McEliece-1284 and quasi-cyclic-2918 with modern ISD. In: Dunkelman, O., Dziembowski, S. (eds.) EUROCRYPT 2022, Part III. LNCS, vol. 13277, pp. 433–457. Springer, Heidelberg (2022). https://doi.org/10.1007/978-3-031-07082-2_16

19. Esser, A., Zweydinger, F.: New time-memory trade-offs for subset sum - improving ISD in theory and practice. In: Hazay, C., Stam, M. (eds.) EUROCRYPT 2023, Part V. LNCS, vol. 14008, pp. 360–390. Springer, Cham (2023). https://doi.org/10.1007/978-3-031-30589-4_13

20. Gama, N., Nguyen, P.Q., Regev, O.: Lattice enumeration using extreme pruning. In: Gilbert, H. (ed.) EUROCRYPT 2010. LNCS, vol. 6110, pp. 257–278. Springer, Heidelberg (2010). https://doi.org/10.1007/978-3-642-13190-5_13

21. Gentry, C.: Fully homomorphic encryption using ideal lattices. In: Mitzenmacher, M. (ed.) 41st ACM STOC, pp. 169–178. ACM Press (2009). https://doi.org/10.1145/1536414.1536440

22. Glaser, T., May, A.: How to enumerate LWE keys as narrow as in Kyber/dilithium. Cryptology ePrint Archive, Report 2022/1337 (2022). https://eprint.iacr.org/2022/1337

23. Güneysu, T., Lyubashevsky, V., Pöppelmann, T.: Practical lattice-based cryptography: a signature scheme for embedded systems. In: Prouff, E., Schaumont, P. (eds.) CHES 2012. LNCS, vol. 7428, pp. 530–547. Springer, Heidelberg (2012). https://doi.org/10.1007/978-3-642-33027-8_31

24. Hhan, M., Kim, J., Lee, C., Son, Y.: How to meet ternary LWE keys on Babai's nearest plane. Cryptology ePrint Archive (2022)

25. Hoffstein, J., Pipher, J., Silverman, J.H.: NTRU: a ring-based public key cryptosystem. In: Buhler, J.P. (ed.) ANTS 1998. LNCS, vol. 1423, pp. 267–288. Springer, Heidelberg (1998). https://doi.org/10.1007/BFb0054868

26. Howgrave-Graham, N.: A hybrid lattice-reduction and meet-in-the-middle attack against NTRU. In: Menezes, A. (ed.) CRYPTO 2007. LNCS, vol. 4622, pp. 150–169. Springer, Heidelberg (2007). https://doi.org/10.1007/978-3-540-74143-5_9

27. Howgrave-Graham, N., Joux, A.: New generic algorithms for hard knapsacks. In: Gilbert, H. (ed.) EUROCRYPT 2010. LNCS, vol. 6110, pp. 235–256. Springer, Heidelberg (2010). https://doi.org/10.1007/978-3-642-13190-5_12

28. Hülsing, A., Rijneveld, J., Schanck, J.M., Schwabe, P.: High-speed key encapsulation from NTRU. In: Fischer, W., Homma, N. (eds.) CHES 2017. LNCS, vol. 10529, pp. 232–252. Springer, Heidelberg (2017). https://doi.org/10.1007/978-3-319-66787-4_12

29. Lyubashevsky, V.: Lattice signatures without trapdoors. In: Pointcheval, D., Johansson, T. (eds.) EUROCRYPT 2012. LNCS, vol. 7237, pp. 738–755. Springer, Heidelberg (2012). https://doi.org/10.1007/978-3-642-29011-4_43

30. Lyubashevsky, V., Peikert, C., Regev, O.: On ideal lattices and learning with errors over rings. In: Gilbert, H. (ed.) EUROCRYPT 2010. LNCS, vol. 6110, pp. 1–23. Springer, Heidelberg (2010). https://doi.org/10.1007/978-3-642-13190-5_1

31. May, A.: How to meet ternary LWE keys. In: Malkin, T., Peikert, C. (eds.) CRYPTO 2021, Part II. LNCS, vol. 12826, pp. 701–731. Springer, Cham (2021). https://doi.org/10.1007/978-3-030-84245-1_24

32. Nguyen, D.H., Nguyen, T.T., Duong, T.N., Pham, P.H.: Cryptanalysis of MD5 on GPU cluster. In: Proceedings of International Conference on Information Security and Artificial Intelligence, vol. 2, pp. 910–914 (2010)

33. Niederhagen, R., Ning, K.-C., Yang, B.-Y.: Implementing Joux-Vitse's crossbred algorithm for solving $\mathcal{MQ}$ systems over $\mathbb{F}_2$ on GPUs. In: Lange, T., Steinwandt, R. (eds.) PQCrypto 2018. LNCS, vol. 10786, pp. 121–141. Springer, Cham (2018). https://doi.org/10.1007/978-3-319-79063-3_6

34. Peikert, C.: Public-key cryptosystems from the worst-case shortest vector problem: extended abstract. In: Mitzenmacher, M. (ed.) 41st ACM STOC, pp. 333–342. ACM Press (2009). https://doi.org/10.1145/1536414.1536461

35. Prange, E.: The use of information sets in decoding cyclic codes. IRE Trans. Inf. Theory **8**(5), 5–9 (1962)

36. Regev, O.: On lattices, learning with errors, random linear codes, and cryptography. In: Gabow, H.N., Fagin, R. (eds.) 37th ACM STOC, pp. 84–93. ACM Press (2005). https://doi.org/10.1145/1060590.1060603

37. Stehlé, D., Steinfeld, R., Tanaka, K., Xagawa, K.: Efficient public key encryption based on ideal lattices. In: Matsui, M. (ed.) ASIACRYPT 2009. LNCS, vol. 5912, pp. 617–635. Springer, Heidelberg (2009). https://doi.org/10.1007/978-3-642-10366-7_36

38. van Oorschot, P.C., Wiener, M.J.: Parallel collision search with cryptanalytic applications. J. Cryptol. **12**(1), 1–28 (1999). https://doi.org/10.1007/PL00003816

39. van Vredendaal, C.: Reduced memory meet-in-the-middle attack against the NTRU private key. LMS J. Comput. Math. **19**(A), 43–57 (2016). https://doi.org/10.1112/S1461157016000206

Too Many Hints – When LLL Breaks LWE

Alexander May[(✉)] and Julian Nowakowski

Ruhr-University Bochum, Bochum, Germany
{alex.may,julian.nowakowski}@rub.de

Abstract. All modern lattice-based schemes build on variants of the LWE problem. Information leakage of the LWE secret $\mathbf{s} \in \mathbb{Z}_q^n$ is usually modeled via so-called hints, i.e., inner products of $\mathbf{s}$ with some known vector.

At Crypto'20, Dachman-Soled, Ducas, Gong and Rossi (DDGR) defined among other so-called *perfect hints* and *modular hints*. The trail-blazing DDGR framework allows to integrate and combine hints successively into lattices, and estimates the resulting LWE security loss.

We introduce a new methodology to integrate and combine an arbitrary number of perfect and modular in a single stroke. As opposed to DDGR's, our methodology is significantly more efficient in constructing lattice bases, and thus easily allows for a large number of hints up to cryptographic dimensions – a regime that is currently impractical in DDGR's implementation. The efficiency of our method defines a large LWE parameter regime, in which we can fully carry out attacks faster than DDGR can solely estimate them.

The benefits of our approach allow us to practically determine which number of hints is sufficient to efficiently break LWE-based lattice schemes in practice. E.g., for mod-q hints, i.e., modular hints defined over $\mathbb{Z}_q$, we reconstruct KYBER-512 secret keys via LLL reduction (only!) with an amount of 449 hints.

Our results for perfect hints significantly improve over these numbers, requiring for LWE dimension n roughly $n/2$ perfect hints. E.g., we reconstruct via LLL reduction KYBER-512 keys with merely 234 perfect hints. If we resort to stronger lattice reduction techniques like BKZ, we need even fewer hints.

For mod-q hints our method is extremely efficient, e.g., taking total time for constructing our lattice bases and secret key recovery via LLL of around 20 mins for dimension 512. For perfect hints in dimension 512, we require around 3 h.

Our results demonstrate that especially perfect hints are powerful in practice, and stress the necessity to properly protect lattice schemes against leakage.

Keyword: LWE with Hints, Partial Key Exposure, PQC Standards

1 Introduction

History of Lattice Schemes. Basing the (post-quantum) security of cryptographic schemes on the hardness of lattice problems has been a big success

© International Association for Cryptologic Research 2023
J. Guo and R. Steinfeld (Eds.): ASIACRYPT 2023, LNCS 14441, pp. 106–137, 2023.
https://doi.org/10.1007/978-981-99-8730-6_4

story in the last 25 years, resulting in the recent NIST standardization of KYBER [BDK+18], DILITHIUM [DKL+18] and FALCON [FHK+18]. Moreover, Google [KMS22] currently chooses to secure its internal communication with NTRU [HPS98].

As a historical curiosity, back in the 80 s and early 90 s lattices were mainly considered a powerful cryptanalysis tool [JS98]. After the invention of the famous Lenstra-Lenstra-Lovász (LLL) lattice reduction algorithm [LLL82], many cryptosystems have been broken disastrously via lattice reduction. E.g., knapsack-based cryptosystems [Odl90], which can be seen as an early predecessor of modern lattice schemes, were successfully attacked via lattices [CLOS91].

This led to a common belief that lattice reduction behaves much better than theoretically predicted, and not few cryptographers thought that finding short lattice vectors is feasible in general. This misunderstanding came from the design of knapsack/lattice schemes in too small dimension, for which lattices do not reveal their hardness.

The situation changed with Ajtai's [Ajt96] NP hardness proof of the shortest vector problem, and the construction of the Ajtai-Dwork cryptosystem [AD97] with its cryptographically desirable worst- to average-case reduction.

While Ajtai-Dwork focussed on the hardness guarantees of lattice-based crypto, the invention of the NTRU cryptosystem of Hoffstein, Pipher and Silverman [HPS98] with its compact lattice bases as public keys was a cornerstone for the practicality of lattice schemes.

Back on the provable security path, the introduction of the Learning with Errors (LWE) problem together with Regev's encryption scheme [Reg05] paved the way to amazingly versatile lattice constructions in all areas of cryptography. Eventually, a combination of the strong LWE security guarantees with the practicality of the NTRU cryptosystem was achieved via formulating the Ring-LWE [SSTX09,LPR10,PRS17] and Module-LWE [BGV14,LS15] variants.

LWE in Practice. In summer 2022, NIST announced the standardization of KYBER [BDK+18] as a lattice-based encryption/key encapsulation mechanism, and DILITHIUM [DKL+18] and FALCON [FHK+18] as lattice-based signature schemes. KYBER can be considered a highly-optimized version of Regev encryption [Reg05], based on Module-LWE. KYBER encryption comes in a package, called CRYSTALS, with a corresponding signature scheme DILITHIUM [DKL+18], also based on Module-LWE. The signature scheme FALCON [FHK+18] is based on an NTRU-type security assumption.

Motivation of Hints. Given the importance of side-channel leakage in real-world cryptography, NIST especially focused before its standardization decision on vetting lattice candidates against secret key leakage.

An LWE public key $(\mathbf{A}, \mathbf{b}, q) \in \mathbb{Z}_q^{n \times m} \times \mathbb{Z}_q^m \times \mathbb{N}$ satisfies the LWE relation $\mathbf{sA} + \mathbf{e} \equiv \mathbf{b} \bmod q$ for some small-norm secret $\mathbf{s} \in \mathbb{Z}_q^n$, and some error $\mathbf{e} \in \mathbb{Z}_q^m$. NTRU can be considered a special case with $\mathbf{b} = \mathbf{0}^m$.

LWE-based encryption schemes like Regev [Reg05] and Kyber [BDK+18] only store the secret $\mathbf{s}$, but not the error $\mathbf{e}$. Decryption of a ciphertext $\mathbf{c} \in \mathbb{Z}_q^n$ is realized via computing the inner product $\langle \mathbf{c}, \mathbf{s} \rangle$. This computation may leak information about $\mathbf{s}$.

LWE/NTRU-based signature schemes like DILITHIUM [DKL+18] and FALCON [FHK+18] usually store both $(\mathbf{s}, \mathbf{e})$ as secret key. DILITHIUM computes for a salted hash $\mathbf{h} := H(\mathbf{m}, \cdot)$ of message $\mathbf{m}$ both inner products $\langle \mathbf{h}, \mathbf{s} \rangle$ and $\langle \mathbf{h}, \mathbf{e} \rangle$. FALCON computes for a salted hash $\mathbf{h} = H(\mathbf{m}, \cdot)$ a polynomial ring product $\mathbf{h} \cdot \mathbf{s} \in \mathbb{Z}_q[X]/(X^n + 1)$, and later a ring product involving $(\mathbf{s}, \mathbf{e})$. As a conclusion, all these computations may either leak information on $\mathbf{s}$ or $\mathbf{e}$ alone, or on $(\mathbf{s}, \mathbf{e})$ together.

In order to model the effect of such a secret key leakage, Dachman-Soled, Ducas, Gong, and Rossi [DDGR20] proposed a general lattice framework that quantifies the LWE security loss when revealing a so-called hint $(\mathbf{v}, \mathbf{w}, \ell) \in \mathbb{Z}_q^n \times \mathbb{Z}_q^m \times \mathbb{Z}$ satisfying

$$\langle (\mathbf{v}, \mathbf{w}), (\mathbf{s}, \mathbf{e}) \rangle = \ell. \tag{1}$$

The inner product computation of Eq. (1) is usually performed in $\mathbb{Z}_q$, which we call a *mod-q hint*. However, the authors of [DDGR20] also point out that fast NTT-based schemes like KYBER, DILITHIUM and FALCON usually postpone the reduction modulo q to the end of the computation for efficiency reasons. Thus, a side-channel may as well leak the value of ℓ in Eq. (1) before mod q reduction, a so-called *perfect hint*.

The framework of [DDGR20] is more generally applicable, also allowing for *modular hints* other than mod-q hints, and for so-called *approximate hints*. In this work, we solely focus on perfect and modular hints, since they are especially simple, and allow for tremendous speedups in practice. Additionally, we study mod-q hints in more detail, as we consider them practically highly relevant for cryptographic systems with mod-q arithmetic. It remains an interesting open problem to provide similar speedups for the technically more involved approximate hints in the DDGR-framework.

As opposed to DDGR, our approach addresses hints for the secret $\mathbf{s}$ only, i.e., hints $(\mathbf{v}, \ell)$ with $\langle \mathbf{v}, \mathbf{s} \rangle = \ell$. We show that (at least) for mod-q hints this is no limitation, and actually provides benefits. Additionally, for perfect hints and general modular hints (i.e., not necessarily mod-q hints), this significantly simplifies the analysis of the resulting lattice bases.

Too Many Hints. Any mod-q hint $(\mathbf{v}, \ell)$ can be considered an error-free LWE sample. If we obtain n hints $(\mathbf{v}_1, \ell_1), \ldots, (\mathbf{v}_n, \ell_n)$ with linearly independent $\mathbf{v}_i$, then we can solve for $\mathbf{s}$ via Gaussian elimination, even without $\mathbf{A}$. Therefore, clearly an amount of n (linearly independent) mod-q hints is sufficient to reach a *too many hints* regime, in which we can attack LWE in polynomial time. Since perfect hints can be reduced modulo q, the upper bound of n also trivially holds for perfect hints.

Our goal in this work is to explore and expand the *too many hints* regime as far as possible by determining the minimal number of hints that is required to break LWE and its various cryptographic instances in practice, efficiently. This includes the regime where we break LWE in polynomial time using LLL reduction only, as well as the regime where breaking LWE is still feasible in practice with BKZ lattice reduction. In such a hint regime where BKZ reduction is feasible, our algorithm yields practical LWE attacks, as opposed to the implementation of the DDGR framework, in which the lattice construction (and therefore the whole attack) is currently infeasible.

While [DDGR20] provides pioneering work on LWE hints and their effects, the DDGR framework currently fails to let us explore the *too many hints* regime in a satisfactory way. First, the implementation of DDGR includes hints successively in a computationally intensive manner via the dual lattice, which in practice does not allow us for integrating a number of hints in the order of n. Second, since we cannot even construct the desired lattice bases, we especially cannot test lattice reduction on real-world instances of lattice schemes.

Our Results. Our new approach resolves these issues, and provides us with real-world data on standardized schemes, rather than security estimates.

Idea of Our Method. In comparison to DDGR, our method is less lattice-centric and more LWE-centric. That is, whereas DDGR starts with a basis, which is successively transformed by each hint, we first process all hints, and then integrate them into a lattice basis.

From the trivial upper bound n argument for the *too many hints* regime we already see that every mod-q hint reduces the subspace of all possible $\mathbf{s}$ by one dimension. Thus, one can view mod-q hints as a dimension reduction method, as it was, e.g., used in the recent analysis of NTRU in the more restricted attack setting of secret key bit leakage [EMVW22]. Hence, we expect that k mod-q hints leave us with the hardness of an $(n-k)$-dimensional LWE problem.

Since, e.g., LWE with KYBER-like parameters is solvable with LLL reduction in dimension around $n = 63$, we would expect that $512 - 63 = 449$ modular hints are sufficient for extracting KYBER-512 secret keys. We show that this is indeed the case.

Efficiency of Lattice Basis Construction. For mod-q hints we propose a simple, and extremely efficient linear algebra approach that in the presence of k hints reduces the LWE dimension from n to $n - k$. Even in cryptographic dimensions, our lattice basis construction takes only a matter of seconds.

For perfect hints our lattice basis construction is technically more involved. We first construct a matrix solely involving our hints, then use LLL for dimension reduction, and eventually integrate the reduced hints together with the LWE samples into a lattice basis. This construction is still efficient, but significantly slower than our mod-q hint method. Lattice basis construction takes, e.g., 3 h for LWE dimension $n = 512$, and up to one week for $n = 1024$.

The case of general *modular hints* is (essentially) reduced to the case of *perfect hints*, making their lattice basis construction as efficient as in the perfect hint case.

Our lattice basis construction methodology does not only allow to integrate different types of hints separately, but also to freely combine them.

Quality of Lattice Basis. It goes without saying, that a construction method for a lattice basis that incorporates hints should be efficient. But of even larger importance is the quality of the resulting basis, meaning from a cryptanalyst's perspective that the information provided by the hints has been fully exploited, and the resulting lattice requires reduction methods as weak as possible to reveal the LWE secret.

We thoroughly analyze the characteristics of our constructed lattices, in terms of the three main criteria lattice dimension, lattice determinant, and length of the desired secret short vector. Our analysis shows that the quality of our lattice bases for all types of hints is identical to the quality achievable with the DDGR framework.

Our Experimental Results. A rough outline of our experiments is provided in Table 1.

Table 1. Minimal amount k of mod-q/perfect hints required for solving instances with LLL. Time includes both lattice basis construction and LLL reduction.

	KYBER 512	FALCON 512	NTRU-HRSS 701	KYBER 768	DILITHIUM 1024
mod-q	449 (88%)	452 (88%)	622 (89%)	702 (91%)	876 (85%)
Time	20 mins	20 mins	45 mins	35 mins	10 h
perfect	234 (46%)	233 (46%)	332 (47%)	390 (51%)	463 (45%)
Time	3 h	3 h	11 h	1 day	7 days

In the case of mod-q hints, we require for LWE dimension n roughly $k \approx 0.9n$ hints too reach the *too many hints* regime, in which we can solve via LLL reduction, see Table 1. Recall that our mod-q approach directly constructs an LWE problem in dimension $n - k \approx 0.1n$.

Notice that for KYBER-512, FALCON-512, and KYBER-768 we have $60 \leq n - k \leq 66$. NTRU-HRRS allows for larger LWE dimension $n - k = 79$, since it has larger q and smaller secret vector norm. As one would expect, Dilithium's very large q enables LLL-only attacks for the largest LWE dimension $n - k = 148$.

We would like to stress that Table 1 only provides the number of hints, for which we can solve via simple LLL reduction. E.g. we also solved KYBER-512 instances with 440 mod-q hints with stronger BKZ reduction of block-size 3 in less than an hour. Thus, Table 1 basically provides the number of hints for which we obtain minimal attack time. The attack time in the mod-q scenario is almost exclusively spend on LLL reduction, since our lattice basis construction can be performed in a matter of seconds.

In the case of perfect hints, we require for LWE dimension n roughly $k \approx n/2$ hints. We find such a small number of hints quite remarkable!

Interestingly, in contrast to the mod-q setting, run time in the perfect hint setting is almost exclusively spend on lattice basis construction. Recall that our construction process first uses the hints only, uses LLL reduction for dimension reduction, and eventually integrates the LWE samples. It seems that LLL reduction of the hints only already yields an overall well-reduced lattice basis. Hence, after our lattice basis construction step we could almost always directly read off the desired secret lattice vector, and therefore solve LWE.

Our Software. We provide a highly efficient open-source Python implementation of our framework. The source code is available together with an extensive documentation at

https://github.com/juliannowakowski/lwe_with_hints .

At the heart of our implementation lies the class `LWELattice`, which allows to easily construct lattice bases for attacking LWE – with or without hints. The class `LWELattice` also provides an implementation of the (progressive) BKZ algorithm, based on the fpylll library [dt21]. Our implementation also ships with key generation algorithms for KYBER, FALCON, NTRU-HPS, NTRU-HRSS and DILITHIUM, as well as for KYBER-like and FALCON-like toy instances in small dimensions.

Lattice Attacks Go Practice. Classical public-key schemes like RSA encryption and DSA signatures have experienced extensive studies on hint vulnerabilities, starting with the seminal works of Boneh and Venkatesan [BV96] and Coppersmith [Cop97]. This led to critical security issues in real world application like [HDWH12]. We see our work as a step towards making hint vulnerabilities also practical in the lattice world.

Organisation of the Paper. In Sect. 2, we provide some background on lattices and LWE. Section 3 introduces our highly efficient LWE transformation for mod-q hints. Section 4 is devoted to our technically more involved lattice basis construction for perfect hints. In Sect. 5, we show how to integrate general modular hints in the aforementioned lattice basis construction. Section 6 provides a runtime comparison of our method with DDGR, and demonstrates how significant we improve in efficiency. Our experiments are presented in Sect. 7.

2   Preliminaries

2.1   Linear Algebra

Vectors are denoted by lower-case bold vectors, matrices are denoted by upper-case bold vectors. We use row notation for vectors and write $\mathbf{B} = [\mathbf{b}_1, \ldots, \mathbf{b}_n]$

for a matrix $\mathbf{B}$ with rows $\mathbf{b}_i$. To denote a matrix $\mathbf{B}$ with columns $\mathbf{b}_i^T$, where $(\cdot)^T$ denotes the transpose, we write $\mathbf{B} = (\mathbf{b}_1^T | \ldots | \mathbf{b}_n^T)$. The i-th vector of the standard basis of $\mathbb{R}^n$ is denoted by $\mathbf{e}_i$, e.g., $\mathbf{e}_1 = (1, 0, \ldots, 0)$. The n-dimensional identity matrix is denoted by $\mathbf{I}_n$, all-zero $(n \times m)$-matrices are denoted by $\mathbf{0}_{n \times m}$, and the n-dimensional all-zero vector is denoted by $\mathbf{0}^n$. If the dimensions are clear from the context, we drop the indices from $\mathbf{0}_{n \times m}$ and $\mathbf{0}^n$. The Euclidean norm and the Euclidean inner product are denoted by $\| \cdot \|$ and $\langle \cdot, \cdot \rangle$, respectively.

Lemma 2.1. *Let $\mathbf{v} = (v_1, \ldots, v_n) \in \mathbb{R}^n$ be a vector, whose coordinates are i.i.d. random variables with zero mean and standard deviation $\sigma < \infty$. Then it holds that*

$$\mathbb{E}[\|\mathbf{v}\|] \leq \sigma \sqrt{n}.$$

Asymptotically, the upper bound is sharp, i.e.,

$$\mathbb{E}[\|\mathbf{v}\|] \sim \sigma \sqrt{n}$$

as $n \to \infty$.

A proof for Lemma 2.1 is given in the full version of the paper [MN23].

For $\mathbf{v} \in \mathbb{R}^n$, we denote by $\mathbf{v}^\perp$ the subspace orthogonal to $\mathbf{v}$. More generally, for a linear subspace $U \subseteq \mathbb{R}^n$, we denote by $U^\perp$ the orthogonal complement of U. The orthogonal projection of $\mathbf{v}$ onto U is denoted by $\pi_U(\mathbf{v})$.

2.2   Lattices

For a matrix $\mathbf{B} = [\mathbf{b}_1, \ldots, \mathbf{b}_n] \in \mathbb{Q}^{n \times m}$, we denote by

$$\mathcal{L}(\mathbf{B}) := \mathbb{Z}^n \cdot \mathbf{B} = \{\alpha_1 \mathbf{b}_1 + \ldots + \alpha_n \mathbf{b}_n \mid \alpha_i \in \mathbb{Z}\}$$

the lattice generated by the rows of $\mathbf{B}$.[1] If the rows of $\mathbf{B}$ are linearly independent, we call $\mathbf{B}$ a *basis matrix* of $\mathcal{L}(\mathbf{B})$. Two bases $\mathbf{B}_1, \mathbf{B}_2 \in \mathbb{R}^{n \times m}$ generate the same lattice if and only if there exists a unimodular matrix $\mathbf{U} \in \mathbb{Z}^{n \times n}$ such that $\mathbf{B}_1 = \mathbf{U} \cdot \mathbf{B}_2$. The number of rows in any basis matrix of some lattice Λ is called the *dimension* of Λ and denoted by $\dim \Lambda$. Equivalently, the dimension of Λ is defined as the dimension of the linear subspace $\mathrm{span}_{\mathbb{R}}(\Lambda)$. A lattice with quadratic basis matrix is called a *full-rank* lattice.

The *determinant* of a lattice Λ with basis matrix $\mathbf{B}$ is defined as

$$\det \Lambda := \sqrt{\det(\mathbf{B}\mathbf{B}^T)}.$$

Notice that the determinant does not depend on the choice of basis. The *i-th successive minimum* of Λ is defined as

$$\lambda_i(\Lambda) := \min\{r > 0 \mid \Lambda \text{ contains } i \text{ linearly independent vectors of length} \leq r\}.$$

A lattice vector $\mathbf{v} \in \Lambda$ of length $\|\mathbf{v}\| = \lambda_1(\Lambda)$ is called a *shortest vector* of Λ.

---

[1] We restrict ourselves to rational matrices, because for irrational $\mathbf{B}$ with linearly dependent rows, the resulting set $\mathcal{L}(\mathbf{B})$ might not be a lattice.

Heuristic 2.2 (Gaussian Heuristic). *Let Λ be an n-dimensional lattice. The Gaussian heuristic predicts that $\lambda_1(\Lambda)$ equals*

$$\mathrm{gh}(\Lambda) := \sqrt{\frac{n}{2\pi e}}\, \det(\Lambda)^{1/n}.$$

A set of linearly independent lattice vectors $\{\mathbf{v}_1, \ldots, \mathbf{v}_k\} \subset \Lambda$ is called *primitive* (with respect to Λ), if it can be extended to a basis of Λ. Equivalently, the set $\{\mathbf{v}_1, \ldots, \mathbf{v}_k\}$ is called primitive, if $\Lambda \cap \mathrm{span}_{\mathbb{R}}(\{\mathbf{v}_1, \ldots, \mathbf{v}_k\}) = \mathcal{L}(\mathbf{v}_1, \ldots, \mathbf{v}_k)$.

For instance, $\{2\mathbf{e}_1, \ldots, 2\mathbf{e}_n\} \subset \mathbb{Z}^n$ is not primitive with respect to $\mathbb{Z}^n$, since $\mathbb{Z}^n \cap \mathrm{span}_{\mathbb{R}}(\{2\mathbf{e}_1, \ldots, 2\mathbf{e}_n\}) = \mathbb{Z}^n$, but $\mathcal{L}(2\mathbf{e}_1, \ldots, 2\mathbf{e}_n) = 2\mathbb{Z}^n$.

Lemma 2.3. *Let $\mathbf{V} = [\mathbf{v}_1, \ldots, \mathbf{v}_k] \in \mathbb{Z}^{k \times n}$. The set $\{\mathbf{v}_1, \ldots, \mathbf{v}_k\} \subset \mathbb{Z}^n$ is primitive with respect to $\mathbb{Z}^n$ if and only if $\mathcal{L}(\mathbf{V}^T) = \mathbb{Z}^k$.*

A proof for Lemma 2.3 is given in the full version of the paper [MN23].

Lemma 2.4 (Adapted from [MRW11, Proposition 1]). *Let $1 \leq k < n$ be integers. Let $\mathbf{B} \in \mathbb{Z}^{n \times k}$ be a matrix, whose entries are independent and uniformly distributed over $\{-B, \ldots, B-1\}$ for some $B \in \mathbb{N}$. Then it holds that*

$$\Pr[\mathcal{L}(\mathbf{B}) = \mathbb{Z}^k] > (1 - 2^{2+k-n}) + o(1),$$

as $B \to \infty$.

A proof for Lemma 2.4 is given in the full version of the paper [MN23].

The *dual* of a lattice Λ is defined as

$$\Lambda^* := \{\mathbf{w} \in \mathrm{span}_{\mathbb{R}}(\Lambda) \mid \forall \mathbf{v} \in \Lambda : \langle \mathbf{w}, \mathbf{v} \rangle \equiv 0 \mod 1\}.$$

For every lattice Λ it holds that $(\Lambda^*)^* = \Lambda$. If $\Lambda \neq \{\mathbf{0}\}$, then it holds that

$$\det(\Lambda) \cdot \det(\Lambda^*) = 1. \tag{2}$$

The integer lattice $\mathbb{Z}^n$ is self-dual, i.e., $(\mathbb{Z}^n)^* = \mathbb{Z}^n$.

Lemma 2.5 ([Mar13, Proposition 1.3.4]). *Let $\Lambda \subset \mathbb{R}^n$ be a full-rank lattice and let $U \subseteq \mathbb{R}^n$ be a linear subspace. Then it holds that $\Lambda \cap U = (\pi_U(\Lambda^*))^*$.*

Lemma 2.6 ([Mar13, Proposition 1.2.9]). *Let $\Lambda \subset \mathbb{R}^n$ be a full-rank lattice and let $U \subset \mathbb{R}^n$ be a d-dimensional linear subspace with $0 < d < n$, such that $\Lambda \cap U$ is a d-dimensional lattice. Then it holds that*

$$\det(\pi_{U^\perp}(\Lambda)) = \frac{\det \Lambda}{\det(\Lambda \cap U)}.$$

2.3 LWE

Definition 2.7 (LWE). *Let n, m and q be positive integers, and let χ be a distribution over $\mathbb{Z}$. The* LWE *problem or more precisely the* LWE *problem with short secrets for parameters (n, m, q, χ) is defined as follows: Given*

- *a uniformly random matrix $\mathbf{A} \in \mathbb{Z}_q^{n \times m}$, and*
- *a vector $\mathbf{b} \equiv \mathbf{sA} + \mathbf{e} \mod q$, where $\mathbf{s} \leftarrow \chi^n$, $\mathbf{e} \leftarrow \chi^m$,*

find $\mathbf{s} \in \mathbb{Z}_q^n$. The vector $\mathbf{s}$ is called the secret, $\mathbf{e}$ *is called the* error. *The tuple $(\mathbf{A}, \mathbf{b}, q)$ is called an* LWE *instance. A tuple $(\mathbf{a}_i^T, b_i)$, where $\mathbf{a}_i^T$ is the i-th column of $\mathbf{A}$ and $b_i = \langle \mathbf{a}_i, \mathbf{s} \rangle + e_i$ is the i-th coordinate of $\mathbf{b}$, is called an* LWE *sample.*

We note that in Regev's original definition of LWE [Reg05], the coordinates of the secret and the error do not follow the same distribution. Most practical LWE-based schemes, however, use the *short secret* variant from Definition 2.7. We further note that for efficiency purposes most practical LWE-based schemes do not sample the matrix $\mathbf{A}$ uniformly at random, but instead use $\mathbf{A}$'s, which can be stored more compactly. Most importantly, in so-called *Ring-LWE* and *Module-LWE* variants one encodes ring-/module structure into $\mathbf{A}$. This allows to store $\mathbf{A}$ with only $k \cdot n$ elements from $\mathbb{Z}_q$, where $k \ll n$ is a small integer, typically $1 \le k < 10$. The *NTRU problem* [HPS98] can be considered as a special variant of (Ring-)LWE, where the vector $\mathbf{b}$ is fixed to $\mathbf{0}$.

An overview of parameters used in practice is given in Table 2.

Table 2. Parameters of practical LWE-based schemes.

Scheme	n	m	q	$\sigma \approx \frac{\mathbb{E}[\|(\mathbf{e},\mathbf{s})\|]}{\sqrt{m+n}}$	Variant
Kyber-512	512	512	3329	1.22	Module-LWE
Kyber-768	768	768	3329	1.00	Module-LWE
Kyber-1024	1024	1024	3329	1.00	Module-LWE
Dilithium-1024	1024	1024	8380417	1.41	Module-LWE
Dilithium-1280	1280	1536	8380417	2.58	Module-LWE
Dilithium-1792	1792	2048	8380417	1.41	Module-LWE
Falcon-512	512	512	12289	4.05	NTRU
Falcon-1024	1024	1024	12289	2.87	NTRU
NTRU-HPS-509	509	509	2048	0.76	NTRU
NTRU-HPS-677	677	677	2048	0.72	NTRU
NTRU-HPS-821	677	677	4096	0.80	NTRU
NTRU-HRSS	701	701	8192	0.99	NTRU

Remark 2.8 For Kyber and Dilithium we calculated the standard deviation of the coordinates of $(\mathbf{e}, \mathbf{s})$, and then used Lemma 2.1 to approximate $\frac{\mathbb{E}[\|(\mathbf{e},\mathbf{s})\|]}{\sqrt{m+n}}$

in Table 2. For NTRU, we could not apply Lemma 2.1, because NTRU-HRSS and NTRU-HPS keys do not meet the requirements of the lemma. Instead, we determined the value of $\mathbb{E}[\|(\mathbf{e}, \mathbf{s})\|]$ experimentally by calculating the average over 100 random keys each. FALCON keys, on the other hand, follow a discrete Gaussian distribution with standard deviation $\sigma = 1.17\sqrt{\frac{q}{m+n}}$, allowing us to compute $\mathbb{E}[\|(\mathbf{e}, \mathbf{s})\|] = 1.17\sqrt{q}$ exactly.

2.4   The Primal Lattice Reduction Attack

Definition 2.9 (LWE Lattice). *For an LWE instance* $(\mathbf{A}, \mathbf{b}, q)$, *where* $\mathbf{A} \in \mathbb{Z}^{n \times m}$, *we define the corresponding LWE lattice* Λ^{LWE} *as the lattice generated by the rows of the following basis matrix*

$$\mathbf{B}^{\mathsf{LWE}} := \begin{pmatrix} q\mathbf{I}_m & \mathbf{0} & \mathbf{0} \\ \mathbf{A} & \mathbf{I}_n & \mathbf{0} \\ \mathbf{b} & \mathbf{0} & 1 \end{pmatrix}. \tag{3}$$

Equivalently, Λ^{LWE} *is defined as*

$$\Lambda^{\mathsf{LWE}} := \Big\{ (\mathbf{x}, \mathbf{y}, t) \in \mathbb{Z}^m \times \mathbb{Z}^n \times \mathbb{Z} \mid \mathbf{x} \equiv \mathbf{yA} + t\mathbf{b} \mod q \Big\}.$$

One can easily verify that the LWE lattice contains the vector

$$\mathbf{t} := (-\mathbf{e}, \mathbf{s}, -1) \in \Lambda^{\mathsf{LWE}}. \tag{4}$$

Since the coordinates of $\mathbf{s}$ and $\mathbf{e}$ follow in practice a distribution with zero mean and small standard deviation σ, we have by Lemma 2.1

$$\mathbb{E}[\|(\mathbf{e}, \mathbf{s})\|] \leq \sigma\sqrt{m + n}.$$

For typical parameters (see Table 2), the expected norm of $\mathbf{t}$ is therefore significantly shorter than what the Gaussian heuristic $\mathrm{gh}(\Lambda^{\mathsf{LWE}})$ predicts for $\lambda_1(\Lambda^{\mathsf{LWE}})$. Accordingly, $\mathbf{t}$ is likely a shortest vector of Λ^{LWE}.

The *primal lattice reduction attack* solves the LWE problem by running the BKZ algorithm [Sch87] on $\mathbf{B}^{\mathsf{LWE}}$ to search for a shortest vector of Λ^{LWE}.

Complexity. The complexity of the primal lattice reduction attack is usually measured in the *Core-SVP* model, as introduced in [ADPS16]. In this model, one only estimates the so-called *BKZ-blocksize* at which BKZ will successfully recover $\mathbf{t}$ from Λ^{LWE}. The blocksize is the most important parameter for the runtime of BKZ. Running the algorithm with blocksize β takes time at least

$$2^{0.292\beta + o(\beta)}.$$

Worth noting, for $\beta = 2$ the BKZ algorithm is (essentially) identical to the famous LLL algorithm [LLL82].

Estimating the exact required blocksize is still an active area of research. The current state of the art is heavily based on heuristics and experimental observations. We refer the reader to the survey of Albrecht and Ducas [AD21] for a nice overview. The *Leaky-LWE estimator* from [DDGR20] currently provides the most accurate estimates for the required blocksize.

For our purposes, it suffices to know that the complexity of BKZ for finding a shortest vector $\mathbf{v}$ in a lattice Λ mainly depends on the following two parameters:

1. the lattice dimension $\dim \Lambda$,
2. the so-called *gap* $\frac{\|\mathbf{v}\|}{\mathrm{gh}(\Lambda)}$.

The smaller the above two parameters get, the smaller is the necessary blocksize for BKZ to recover $\mathbf{v}$ from Λ, i.e., BKZ performs the better, the smaller the dimension and the length of $\mathbf{v}$ get, and the larger the determinant of Λ gets.

The Embedding Factor. In the typical setting, where both secret and error follow a distribution with zero mean and (known) standard deviation σ, one can slightly improve the lattice basis $\mathbf{B}^{\mathsf{LWE}}$ by replacing the so-called *embedding factor*, i.e., the 1 in the bottom right of $\mathbf{B}^{\mathsf{LWE}}$, by σ. (This slightly decreases the gap of Λ^{LWE}.) Additionally, if the distribution has a non-zero mean $\mu \neq 0$, then the vectors $\mathbf{b}$ and $\mathbf{0}$ in the last row of $\mathbf{B}^{\mathsf{LWE}}$ should be replaced by $\mathbf{b} - \boldsymbol{\mu}^m$ and $\boldsymbol{\mu}^n$, respectively, where $\boldsymbol{\mu}^i := (\mu, \ldots, \mu) \in \mathbb{Z}^i$.

2.5   Ignoring LWE Samples

By removing columns from the LWE matrix $\mathbf{A}$ and accordingly updating the lattice basis $\mathbf{B}^{\mathsf{LWE}}$, we can easily decrease the dimension of Λ^{LWE}, while still keeping the secret $\mathbf{s}$ in the lattice. In the literature, this technique is commonly known as *ignoring LWE samples*.

For typical parameters, the current estimators suggest that applying this technique decreases the required blocksize for the primal attack. For instance, for KYBER-768, the leaky LWE estimator suggests that ignoring 70 samples minimizes the required blocksize.

However, as discussed in [DDGR20, Remark 30], it is not the case that (manually) ignoring samples actually decreases the required blocksize in practice. In fact, when adding too many samples, the estimators simply start to overestimate the required blocksize, but the actual blocksize necessary in practice will not increase. (See Fig. 1 for an illustration of this phenomenon.)

This is caused by the fact that the estimators currently do not capture the phenomenon that BKZ can ignore unnecessary samples *on its own*. (See again [DDGR20, Remark 30] for an explanation.) For simplicity, one can therefore always use all available LWE samples, i.e., keep $\mathbf{A}$ unchanged, and let BKZ perform the optimization on its own.

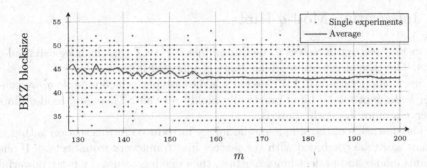

Fig. 1. Required blocksize for the primal attack on 32 random KYBER-like LWE instances with $n = 128$, $q = 3329$, $\|(\mathbf{e}, \mathbf{s})\| \approx 1.22 \cdot \sqrt{m+n}$ and varying $m \in \{128, \ldots, 200\}$. For all $m \geq 157$ we require an average blocksize of roughly 43.

2.6 LWE Hints

In this section we recall the definition of *LWE hints*, as first introduced by Dachman-Soled, Ducas, Gong and Rossi (DDGR) in [DDGR20].

Definition 2.10 (LWE Hints). *Let* $\mathbf{s} \in \mathbb{Z}_q^n$ *be an LWE secret. We define the following* LWE hints *for* $\mathbf{s}$.

1. *A tuple* $\overline{\mathbf{v}} = (\mathbf{v}, \ell) \in \mathbb{Z}^n \times \mathbb{Z}$ *with*

$$\langle \mathbf{v}, \mathbf{s} \rangle = \ell$$

   is called a perfect hint.
2. *A tuple* $\overline{\mathbf{v}} = (\mathbf{v}, \ell, m) \in \mathbb{Z}^n \times \mathbb{Z} \times \mathbb{N}$ *with*

$$\langle \mathbf{v}, \mathbf{s} \rangle \equiv \ell \mod m$$

   is called a modular hint. *If* $m = q$, *we call* $\overline{\mathbf{v}}$ *a* mod-q hint.

As discussed in the introduction, we slightly deviate from the original definition in the DDGR framework.

First, the DDGR framework defines hints more generally for both LWE error and secret. However, we restrict ourselves to *secret-only* hints. Second, DDGR also define a noisy variant of perfect hints, called *approximate hints*. It is an open problem to adapt our framework for this type of hints. Third, DDGR define a fourth type of hints, called *short vector hints*. However, short vector hints are of a very different nature than perfect, modular and approximate hints. In particular, as noted in [DDGR20, Section 4.5], these are not expected to be obtained via side channels, but rather *by design*. For integrating approximate and short vector hints we do not propose any new techniques.

3   Integrating Mod-q Hints

Let us first restrict ourselves to modular hints $\bar{\mathbf{v}} = (\mathbf{v}, \ell, q)$, which we call mod-$q$ hints. The case of general modular hints is analyzed in Sect. 5.

Since all operations in LWE-based schemes are performed modulo q, we consider leakage of mod-q hints practically highly relevant. Therefore, mod-q hints deserve a more in-depth analysis.

The downside of the simple methodology introduced in this section is that it cannot easily be combined with the perfect hint framework from Sects. 4. If one obtains mod-q and perfect hints *together*, then one has to use the more powerful general modular hint approach from Sect. 5.

Secret-Only Hints. Recall that in our work we use *secret-only* hints $(\mathbf{v}, \ell, q)$ satisfying $\langle \mathbf{v}, \mathbf{s} \rangle \equiv \ell \bmod q$. In contrast, [DDGR20] uses *secret-error* hints $(\mathbf{v}, \mathbf{w}, \ell, q)$ satisfying $\langle (\mathbf{v}, \mathbf{w}), (\mathbf{s}, \mathbf{e}) \rangle \equiv \ell' \bmod q$. In the full version of the paper [MN23], we show that the more general secret-error hints form in the mod-q case equivalence classes with the following two properties.

(1) Each equivalence class contains exactly one representative with $\mathbf{w} = \mathbf{0}$, i.e., a secret-only hint.
(2) Integrating more than one hint from the same equivalence class does not improve the resulting lattice basis.

By Property (1), we may work in the mod-q setting without loss of generality with secret-only hints. By Property (2), it is also advised to exclude secret-error hints in the mod-q setting for avoiding useless hints.

Transforming LWE. Suppose we are given mod-q hints $\bar{\mathbf{v}}_i = (\mathbf{v}_i, \ell_i, q)$, $i = 1, \ldots, k$ for some LWE instance $(\mathbf{A}, \mathbf{b}, q) \in \mathbb{Z}_q^{n \times m} \times \mathbb{Z}_q^m \times \mathbb{N}$ with n-dimensional secret $\mathbf{s} = (s_1, \ldots, s_n) \in \mathbb{Z}_q^n$ and error $\mathbf{e} \in \mathbb{Z}_q^m$. Then we construct via linear algebra an LWE instance $(\hat{\mathbf{A}}, \hat{\mathbf{b}}, q) \in \mathbb{Z}_q^{(n-k) \times m} \times \mathbb{Z}_q^m \times \mathbb{N}$ with

– $(n-k)$-dimensional secret $\hat{\mathbf{s}} = (s_{k+1}, \ldots, s_n)$,
– and the same error $\mathbf{e} \in \mathbb{Z}_q^m$.

In particular, we decrease the dimension by k, while leaving the number of samples m unchanged, thereby increasing the sample/dimension ratio from m/n to $m/(n-k)$. Other works that addressed mod-q hints to reduce the LWE-dimension either addressed the restrictive case of standard unit vectors (that directly provide coordinates of $\mathbf{s}$ and therefore also can be considered as perfect hints) [EMVW22], or transformed into a large norm secret [WWX22], unsuited for lattice reduction.

In lattice language, our mod-q hint transformation of the LWE instance improves the primal lattice reduction attack from Sect. 2.4 by

(1) decreasing the dimension of Λ^{LWE} by k,

(2) decreasing the length of the secret vector $\mathbf{t}$ from Eq. (4),

(3) while preserving the determinant of Λ^{LWE}.

Remark 3.1. As in the DDGR framework, we assume throughout this work that our hints $\overline{\mathbf{v}}_1, \ldots, \overline{\mathbf{v}}_k$ are linearly independent. In particular, we assume $k \leq n$. We would like to stress that linear independence is a very natural restriction. If there was a framework that could improve the primal lattice reduction attack via linearly *dependent* hints, then LWE would not be hard, since after guessing one initial perfect/modular hint an attacker can easily generate arbitrarily many linearly dependent hints.

3.1 Mod-q Hints Provide LWE Dimension Reduction

Throughout this section, we assume that q is prime, which is true for all LWE-based schemes addressed in this work, only NTRU uses a power-of-two q. At the end of the section, we discuss in Remark 3.4 the small necessary adaptation for NTRU.

Let us begin by defining some useful matrix notation.

Definition 3.2 (Hint Matrix). *Let* $\overline{\mathbf{v}}_i = (\mathbf{v}_i, \ell_i) \in \mathbb{Z}^n \times \mathbb{Z}$, *where* $i = 1, \ldots, k$. *We define the corresponding* hint matrix *as*

$$\mathsf{Hint}(\overline{\mathbf{v}}_1, \ldots, \overline{\mathbf{v}}_k) := \begin{pmatrix} | & & | \\ \mathbf{v}_1^T & \cdots & \mathbf{v}_k^T \\ | & & | \\ \hline \ell_1 & \cdots & \ell_k \end{pmatrix} = \left(\frac{V}{\ell} \right) \in \mathbb{Z}_q^{(n+1) \times k}. \tag{5}$$

Idea of Dimension Reduction. The hint matrix from Definition 3.2 satisfies

$$(\mathbf{s}, -1) \cdot \left(\frac{V}{\ell} \right) \equiv \mathbf{0}^k \bmod q. \tag{6}$$

Since the hint vectors $\mathbf{v}_1, \ldots, \mathbf{v}_k$ are linearly independent, there exists a full rank $k \times k$ submatrix of $\mathbf{V}$. For ease of notation, we assume that the first k rows of $\mathbf{V}$ form a full rank matrix $\mathbf{V}_1$. This can always be achieved by row permutation of $\mathbf{V}$, where $\mathbf{s}$ has to be permuted accordingly.

Let $\mathbf{V}_1^{-1}$ be the inverse of $\mathbf{V}_1$ in $\mathbb{F}_q^{k \times k}$. Multiplying Eq. (6) by $\mathbf{V}_1^{-1}$ gives

$$(\mathbf{s}, -1) \cdot \left(\frac{\mathbf{I}_k}{\frac{\mathbf{V}_2 \mathbf{V}_1^{-1}}{\ell \mathbf{V}_1^{-1}}} \right) \equiv (\mathbf{s}, -1) \cdot \left(\frac{\mathbf{V}}{\ell} \right) \cdot \mathbf{V}_1^{-1} \equiv \mathbf{0}^k \bmod q. \tag{7}$$

Let $(\mathbf{A}, \mathbf{b}, q) \in \mathbb{Z}_q^{n \times m} \times \mathbb{Z}_q^m \times \mathbb{N}$ be an LWE instance with secret $\mathbf{s}$ and error $\mathbf{e}$. Write

$$\mathbf{A} = \left(\frac{\mathbf{A}_1}{\mathbf{A}_2} \right) \text{ with } \mathbf{A}_1 \in \mathbb{Z}_q^{k \times m}, \mathbf{A}_2 \in \mathbb{Z}_q^{(n-k) \times m}.$$

Then

$$(\mathbf{s}, -1) \cdot \left(\begin{array}{c|c} \mathbf{I}_k & \mathbf{A}_1 \\ \hline \mathbf{V}_2 \mathbf{V}_1^{-1} & \mathbf{A}_2 \\ \hline \boldsymbol{\ell} \mathbf{V}_1^{-1} & \mathbf{b} \end{array} \right) \equiv (\mathbf{0}^k, -\mathbf{e}) \bmod q.$$

Using column operations, we now use the identity matrix $\mathbf{I}_k$ to eliminate $\mathbf{A}_1$, i.e., we eliminate the first k rows of $\mathbf{A}$. Notice that since our k modular hints are error-free, this operation *does not increase* the error vector $\mathbf{e}$. We obtain

$$(\mathbf{s}, -1) \cdot \left(\begin{array}{c|c} \mathbf{I}_k & \mathbf{0} \\ \hline \mathbf{V}_2 \mathbf{V}_1^{-1} & \hat{\mathbf{A}} \\ \hline \boldsymbol{\ell} \mathbf{V}_1^{-1} & \hat{\mathbf{b}} \end{array} \right) \equiv (\mathbf{0}^k, -\mathbf{e}) \bmod q.$$

Eventually, $(\hat{\mathbf{A}}, \hat{\mathbf{b}}, q)$ is our new LWE instance with the $(n - k)$-dimensional secret $\hat{\mathbf{s}} = (s_{k+1}, \ldots, s_n)$. Thus, we used our k mod-q hints to eliminate the first k coordinates of $\mathbf{s}$.

Reconstruction of s. Our transformation of $\mathbf{s}$ to $\hat{\mathbf{s}}$ eliminates the first k coordinates $(s_1, \ldots, s_k)$. By Eq. (7) we have

$$(s_1, \ldots, s_k) \equiv -\hat{\mathbf{s}} \mathbf{V}_2 \mathbf{V}_1^{-1} + \boldsymbol{\ell} \mathbf{V}_1^{-1} \bmod q,$$

which allows us to easily reconstruct the remaining k coordinates when given $\hat{\mathbf{s}}$.

The following theorem details all required linear algebra transformations in our LWE dimension reduction.

Theorem 3.3. *Let* $(\mathbf{A}, \mathbf{b}, q) \in \mathbb{Z}_q^{n \times m} \times \mathbb{Z}_q^m \times \mathbb{N}$ *be an LWE instance with n-dimensional secret* $\mathbf{s} = (s_1, \ldots, s_n) \in \mathbb{Z}_q^n$ *and error* $\mathbf{e} \in \mathbb{Z}_q^m$. *Let* $\bar{\mathbf{v}}_1, \ldots, \bar{\mathbf{v}}_k$ *be mod-q hints with hint matrix* $\mathsf{Hint}(\bar{\mathbf{v}}_1, \ldots, \bar{\mathbf{v}}_k) = [\mathbf{V}, \boldsymbol{\ell}] \in \mathbb{Z}_q^{(n+1) \times k}$. *Let us denote* $\mathbf{A} = [\mathbf{A}_1, \mathbf{A}_2], \mathbf{V} = [\mathbf{V}_1, \mathbf{V}_2]$ *with* $\mathbf{A}_1 \in \mathbb{Z}_q^{k \times m}, \mathbf{V}_1 \in \mathbb{Z}_q^{k \times k}$. *Then* $(\hat{\mathbf{A}}, \hat{\mathbf{b}}, q) \in \mathbb{Z}_q^{(n-k) \times m} \times \mathbb{Z}_q^m \times \mathbb{N}$ *with*

$$\hat{\mathbf{A}} \equiv \mathbf{A}_2 - \mathbf{V}_2 \mathbf{V}_1^{-1} \mathbf{A}_1 \bmod q,$$
$$\hat{\mathbf{b}} \equiv \mathbf{b} - \boldsymbol{\ell} \mathbf{V}_1^{-1} \mathbf{A}_1 \bmod q$$

is an LWE instance with secret $\hat{\mathbf{s}} = (s_{k+1}, \ldots, s_n) \in \mathbb{Z}_q^{n-k}$ *and error* $\mathbf{e} \in \mathbb{Z}_q^m$.

Proof. Let $\mathbf{s} = (\mathbf{s}_1, \mathbf{s}_2)$ with $\mathbf{s}_2 = \hat{\mathbf{s}} \in \mathbb{Z}_q^{n-k}$. We have to show that $\hat{\mathbf{s}} \hat{\mathbf{A}} \equiv \hat{\mathbf{b}} - \mathbf{e} \bmod q$. Using the definition of $\hat{\mathbf{A}}$ we obtain

$$\hat{\mathbf{s}} \hat{\mathbf{A}} \equiv \mathbf{s}_2 \mathbf{A}_2 - \mathbf{s}_2 \mathbf{V}_2 \mathbf{V}_1^{-1} \mathbf{A}_1 \bmod q.$$

By Eq. (7) we have $\mathbf{s} \mathbf{V} \mathbf{V}_1^{-1} \equiv \boldsymbol{\ell} \mathbf{V}_1^{-1}$. Since also $\mathbf{s} \mathbf{V} \mathbf{V}_1^{-1} \equiv \mathbf{s}_1 + \mathbf{s}_2 \mathbf{V}_2 \mathbf{V}_1^{-1}$, we obtain $\mathbf{s}_2 \mathbf{V}_2 \mathbf{V}_1^{-1} \equiv \boldsymbol{\ell} \mathbf{V}_1^{-1} - \mathbf{s}_1$. This implies

$$\hat{\mathbf{s}} \hat{\mathbf{A}} \equiv \mathbf{s}_2 \mathbf{A}_2 - (\boldsymbol{\ell} \mathbf{V}_1^{-1} - \mathbf{s}_1) \mathbf{A}_1 \equiv \mathbf{s}_1 \mathbf{A}_1 + \mathbf{s}_2 \mathbf{A}_2 - \boldsymbol{\ell} \mathbf{V}_1^{-1} \mathbf{A}_1 \bmod q$$

$$\equiv \mathbf{s} \mathbf{A} + \hat{\mathbf{b}} - \mathbf{b} \equiv \hat{\mathbf{b}} - \mathbf{e} \bmod q.$$

$\square$

Remark 3.4. For the NTRU case with power-of-two q, we require that some $k \times k$ submatrix $\mathbf{V}_1$ of $\mathbf{V}$ is invertible over $\mathbb{F}_2$, which implies invertibility over $\mathbb{Z}_q$. For $k \ll n$ this happens with overwhelming probability.

4 Integrating Perfect Hints

Suppose we are given k perfect hints $\overline{\mathbf{v}}_i = (\mathbf{v}_i, \ell_i) \in \mathbb{Z}^n \times \mathbb{Z}$, $i = 1, \ldots, k$. In this section, we introduce our new approach for incorporating perfect hints, that improves the primal lattice reduction attack by

(1) decreasing the dimension of the LWE lattice Λ^{LWE} by k (Sect. 4.1),
(2) increasing its determinant by a factor $\det \mathcal{L}(\overline{\mathbf{v}}_1, \ldots, \overline{\mathbf{v}}_k)$ (Sect. 4.2), while
(3) preserving the length of the secret vector $\mathbf{t}$ from Eq. (4) (Sect. 4.1).

Additionally, we show that the effect of the integration of perfect hints is the exact same as in the original DDGR framework (Sect. 4.2). However, in contrast to DDGR's approach, our novel and simplified view allows for a highly efficient implementation (Sect. 4.3). We provide a run time comparison with DDGR in Sect. 6.

4.1 Decreasing the Dimension of Λ^{LWE}, While Preserving $\|\mathbf{t}\|$

Embedding Hints into Λ^{LWE}. Let us first *embed* the perfect hints into our lattice basis. Let $(\mathbf{A}, \mathbf{b}, q) \in \mathbb{Z}_q^{n \times m} \times \mathbb{Z}_q^m \times \mathbb{N}$ be an LWE instance with secret $\mathbf{s} \in \mathbb{Z}_q^n$. The main idea behind our new approach is to view the perfect hints

$$\ell_i = \langle \mathbf{v}_i, \mathbf{s} \rangle$$

as *error-free* LWE samples *without* reduction modulo q. A very natural approach for embedding the perfect hints into our lattice is then to construct a hint matrix $\mathbf{H} = \mathsf{Hint}(\overline{\mathbf{v}}_1, \ldots, \overline{\mathbf{v}}_k) = (\mathbf{V}, \boldsymbol{\ell})$ (Definition 3.2) and to generalize the definition of the LWE lattice Λ^{LWE} (Definition 2.9) as follows.

Definition 4.1 (Hint Lattice). *Let $(\mathbf{A}, \mathbf{b}, q)$ be an LWE instance, where $\mathbf{A} \in \mathbb{Z}^{n \times m}$, and let $\mathbf{H} = (\mathbf{V}, \boldsymbol{\ell}) \in \mathbb{Z}^{(n+1) \times k}$ be a hint matrix. The corresponding hint lattice $\Lambda_{\mathbf{H}}^{\mathsf{LWE}}$ is defined as the lattice generated by the following matrix:*

$$\mathbf{B}_{\mathbf{H}}^{\mathsf{LWE}} := \begin{pmatrix} q\mathbf{I}_m & \mathbf{0} & \mathbf{0} & \mathbf{0} \\ \mathbf{A} & \mathbf{V} & \mathbf{I}_n & \mathbf{0} \\ \mathbf{b} & \boldsymbol{\ell} & \mathbf{0} & 1 \end{pmatrix} \in \mathbb{Z}^{(m+n+1) \times (m+k+n+1)}. \tag{8}$$

Notice that we did not change the lattice dimension yet: Even though the hint lattice $\Lambda_{\mathbf{H}}^{\mathsf{LWE}}$ lies in the larger vector space $\mathbb{R}^{m+k+n+1}$ (as opposed to Λ^{LWE} lying in $\mathbb{R}^{m+n+1}$), the dimension of the lattice remains

$$\dim \Lambda_{\mathbf{H}}^{\mathsf{LWE}} = \dim \Lambda^{\mathsf{LWE}} = m + n + 1.$$

Decreasing Dimension of $\Lambda_{\mathbf{H}}^{\mathsf{LWE}}$. By definition of the hint matrix $\mathbf{H} = (\mathbf{V}, \ell)$, the LWE secret $\mathbf{s}$ satisfies

$$(\mathbf{s}, -1) \cdot \left(\frac{\mathbf{V}}{\ell} \right) = \left(\langle \mathbf{v}_1, \mathbf{s} \rangle - \ell_1, \ldots, \langle \mathbf{v}_k, \mathbf{s} \rangle - \ell_k \right) = \mathbf{0}^k.$$

From that, it easily follows that the hint lattice $\Lambda_{\mathbf{H}}^{\mathsf{LWE}}$ contains the short vector

$$\mathbf{t}_{\mathbf{H}} := (-\mathbf{e}, \mathbf{0}^k, \mathbf{s}, -1),$$

which has the same length as the original secret vector $\mathbf{t}$, defined in Eq. (4).

To reduce the dimension of our lattice by k, we now simply use the fact that the coordinates of $\mathbf{t}_{\mathbf{H}}$ at positions $m + 1$ to $m + k$ are zero. Instead of searching for $\mathbf{t}_{\mathbf{H}}$ in $\Lambda_{\mathbf{H}}^{\mathsf{LWE}}$, we simply search in the $(m + n + 1 - k)$-dimensional[2] sublattice $\Lambda_{\mathbf{H},k}^{\mathsf{LWE}} \subset \Lambda_{\mathbf{H}}^{\mathsf{LWE}}$ as defined below:

$$\Lambda_{\mathbf{H},k}^{\mathsf{LWE}} := \left\{ (v_1, \ldots, v_{n+m+k+1}) \in \Lambda_{\mathbf{H}}^{\mathsf{LWE}} \mid v_{m+1} = \ldots = v_{m+k} = 0 \right\}$$
$$= \Lambda_{\mathbf{H}}^{\mathsf{LWE}} \cap \mathbf{e}_{m+1}^{\perp} \cap \ldots \cap \mathbf{e}_{m+k}^{\perp}.$$

4.2   Perfect Hints Increase $\det \Lambda^{\mathsf{LWE}}$ by $\det \mathcal{L}(\overline{\mathbf{v}}_1, \ldots, \overline{\mathbf{v}}_k)$

To integrate k perfect hints $\overline{\mathbf{v}}_1, \ldots, \overline{\mathbf{v}}_k$, DDGR suggest to intersect the LWE lattice Λ^{LWE} with the subspace orthogonal to all $\overline{\mathbf{v}}_i$'s, i.e., to work with the lattice

$$\Lambda_{\overline{\mathbf{v}}_1, \ldots, \overline{\mathbf{v}}_k}^{\mathsf{DDGR}} := \Lambda^{\mathsf{LWE}} \cap (\mathbf{0}^m, \overline{\mathbf{v}}_1)^{\perp} \cap \ldots \cap (\mathbf{0}^m, \overline{\mathbf{v}}_k)^{\perp}.$$

As shown by DDGR, this reduces the dimension of the lattice by k and increases the determinant by a factor of roughly $\|\overline{\mathbf{v}}_1\| \cdot \ldots \cdot \|\overline{\mathbf{v}}_k\|$.[3]

At first glance, the DDGR approach may seem complementary to our approach, where we first construct the hint lattice $\Lambda_{\mathbf{H}}^{\mathsf{LWE}}$ (lying in a different vector space than $\Lambda_{\overline{\mathbf{v}}_1, \ldots, \overline{\mathbf{v}}_k}^{\mathsf{DDGR}}$) and then intersect it with the subspace orthogonal to the standard basis vectors $\mathbf{e}_{m+1}, \ldots, \mathbf{e}_{m+k}$.

While we already showed that our approach also reduces the lattice dimension by k, it is not so obvious, how the determinant of our lattice $\Lambda_{\mathbf{H},k}^{\mathsf{LWE}}$ compares with that of $\Lambda_{\overline{\mathbf{v}}_1, \ldots, \overline{\mathbf{v}}_k}^{\mathsf{DDGR}}$. In particular, it is unclear whether one lattice performs better than the other.

Interestingly, our Theorem 4.2 below shows, however, that our new lattice has the exact same determinant as DDGR's. In fact, Theorem 4.2 even shows something slightly stronger: The lattices $\Lambda_{\overline{\mathbf{v}}_1, \ldots, \overline{\mathbf{v}}_k}^{\mathsf{DDGR}}$ and $\Lambda_{\mathbf{H},k}^{\mathsf{LWE}}$ are *isometric*, i.e., there is an isomorphism between them, that preserves their geometries. Hence,

---

[2] Here we require the hints to be linearly independent. More generally, we have $\dim \Lambda_{\mathbf{H},k}^{\mathsf{LWE}} = n + m + 1 - \mathrm{rank}_{\mathbb{R}}(\mathbf{H})$.

[3] The DDGR estimate is correct under some primitivity condition (see [DDGR20, Section 4.1]) and the assumption that the hints are not too far from orthogonal (see [DDGR20, Remark 25]).

the lattices $\Lambda^{\mathsf{DDGR}}_{\overline{\mathbf{v}}_1,\ldots,\overline{\mathbf{v}}_k}$ and $\Lambda^{\mathsf{LWE}}_{\mathbf{H},k}$ have the exact same *quality* from a cryptanalytic perspective.

More importantly, we show in Theorem 4.3 that our restriction to secret-only hints allows us to precisely estimate the determinant. We prove under a mild assumption that the determinant increases exactly by a factor of $\det \mathcal{L}(\overline{\mathbf{v}}_1,\ldots,\overline{\mathbf{v}}_k)$, as opposed to DDGR's rough estimation of $\|\overline{\mathbf{v}}_1\| \cdot \ldots \cdot \|\overline{\mathbf{v}}_k\|$.

Theorem 4.2. *Let $\overline{\mathbf{v}}_1,\ldots,\overline{\mathbf{v}}_k$ be perfect hints with hint matrix $\mathbf{H} = \mathsf{Hint}(\overline{\mathbf{v}}_1,\ldots,\overline{\mathbf{v}}_k)$. There exists an isometry from the hint sublattice $\Lambda^{\mathsf{LWE}}_{\mathbf{H},k}$ to $\Lambda^{\mathsf{DDGR}}_{\overline{\mathbf{v}}_1,\ldots,\overline{\mathbf{v}}_k}$. In particular,*

$$\dim \Lambda^{\mathsf{LWE}}_{\mathbf{H},k} = \dim \Lambda^{\mathsf{DDGR}}_{\overline{\mathbf{v}}_1,\ldots,\overline{\mathbf{v}}_k}, \text{ and}$$
$$\det \Lambda^{\mathsf{LWE}}_{\mathbf{H},k} = \det \Lambda^{\mathsf{DDGR}}_{\overline{\mathbf{v}}_1,\ldots,\overline{\mathbf{v}}_k}.$$

Proof. Let $\mathbf{u} = (\mathbf{u}_1, \mathbf{u}_2) \in \mathbb{Z}^m \times \mathbb{Z}^{n+1}$ and let

$$\mathbf{x} := \mathbf{u} \cdot \mathbf{B}^{\mathsf{LWE}} \in \Lambda^{\mathsf{LWE}},$$
$$\mathbf{y} := \mathbf{u} \cdot \mathbf{B}^{\mathsf{LWE}}_{\mathbf{H}} \in \Lambda^{\mathsf{LWE}}_{\mathbf{H}},$$

where $\mathbf{B}^{\mathsf{LWE}}$ and $\mathbf{B}^{\mathsf{LWE}}_{\mathbf{H}}$ are defined as in Eqs. (3) and (8), respectively. From the shapes of $\mathbf{B}^{\mathsf{LWE}}$ and $\mathbf{B}^{\mathsf{LWE}}_{\mathbf{H}}$ it easily follows that

$$\mathbf{x} = (\mathbf{w}, \mathbf{u}_2), \tag{9}$$
$$\mathbf{y} = (\mathbf{w}, \mathbf{u}_2 \cdot \mathbf{H}, \mathbf{u}_2), \tag{10}$$

for some $\mathbf{w} \in \mathbb{Z}^m$. Comparing the definitions of $\Lambda^{\mathsf{DDGR}}_{\overline{\mathbf{v}}_1,\ldots,\overline{\mathbf{v}}_k}$ and $\Lambda^{\mathsf{LWE}}_{\mathbf{H},k}$ with Eqs. (9) and (10), we obtain the following chain of equivalences:

$$\mathbf{x} \in \Lambda^{\mathsf{DDGR}} \iff \langle \mathbf{u}_2, \overline{\mathbf{v}}_i \rangle = 0, \text{ for all } i = 1,\ldots,k$$
$$\iff \mathbf{u}_2 \cdot \mathbf{H} = \mathbf{0}^k$$
$$\iff \mathbf{y} \in \Lambda^{\mathsf{LWE}}_{\mathbf{H},k}.$$

This, in turn, implies that

$$\varphi : \Lambda^{\mathsf{DDGR}}_{\overline{\mathbf{v}}_1,\ldots,\overline{\mathbf{v}}_k} \to \Lambda^{\mathsf{LWE}}_{\mathbf{H},k}, (x_1,\ldots,x_{m+n+1}) \mapsto (x_1,\ldots,x_m, \mathbf{0}^k, x_{m+1},\ldots,x_{m+n+1})$$

is an isometry, which proves the theorem. □

Theorem 4.3. *Let $\overline{\mathbf{v}}_1,\ldots,\overline{\mathbf{v}}_k$ be (secret-only) perfect hints with hint matrix $\mathbf{H} = \mathsf{Hint}(\overline{\mathbf{v}}_1,\ldots,\overline{\mathbf{v}}_k)$. Suppose $\mathcal{L}(\mathbf{H}) = \mathbb{Z}^k$. Then it holds that*

$$\det \Lambda^{\mathsf{LWE}}_{\mathbf{H},k} = \det \Lambda^{\mathsf{DDGR}}_{\overline{\mathbf{v}}_1,\ldots,\overline{\mathbf{v}}_k} = \det \Lambda^{\mathsf{LWE}} \cdot \det \mathcal{L}(\overline{\mathbf{v}}_1,\ldots,\overline{\mathbf{v}}_k).$$

Proof. The proof uses the technique from [DDGR20, Lemma 12]. Let $U := \overline{\mathbf{v}}_1^{\perp} \cap \ldots \cap \overline{\mathbf{v}}_k^{\perp}$. From the shape of the basis matrix $\mathbf{B}^{\mathsf{LWE}}$ (see Eq. (3)), it easily follows that[4]

$$\det \Lambda^{\mathsf{DDGR}}_{\overline{\mathbf{v}}_1,\ldots,\overline{\mathbf{v}}_k} = q^m \cdot \det(\mathbb{Z}^{n+1} \cap U) = \det(\Lambda^{\mathsf{LWE}}) \cdot \det(\mathbb{Z}^{n+1} \cap U). \tag{11}$$

---

[4] Equation (11) would become false, if we would allow secret-error hints.

Using Lemma 2.5 and the fact that $\mathbb{Z}^{n+1}$ is self-dual, we obtain

$$\mathbb{Z}^{n+1} \cap U = (\pi_U(\mathbb{Z}^{n+1}))^*,$$

which together with Eq. (2) and Lemma 2.6 gives

$$\det(\mathbb{Z}^{n+1} \cap U) = \frac{1}{\det(\pi_U(\mathbb{Z}^{n+1}))} = \frac{\det(\mathbb{Z}^{n+1} \cap U^\perp)}{\det(\mathbb{Z}^{n+1})} = \det(\mathbb{Z}^{n+1} \cap U^\perp). \quad (12)$$

By assumption, the rows of $\mathbf{H}$ span the integer lattice $\mathbb{Z}^k$. Together with Lemma 2.3 and the definition of $\mathbf{H}$ (Definition 3.2) this implies that $\{\overline{\mathbf{v}}_1, \ldots, \overline{\mathbf{v}}_k\}$ is primitive with respect to $\mathbb{Z}^{n+1}$, and thus

$$\mathbb{Z}^{n+1} \cap U^\perp = \mathbb{Z}^{n+1} \cap \operatorname{span}_{\mathbb{R}}(\overline{\mathbf{v}}_1, \ldots, \overline{\mathbf{v}}_k) = \mathcal{L}(\overline{\mathbf{v}}_1, \ldots, \overline{\mathbf{v}}_k). \quad (13)$$

Combining Eqs. (11), (12) and (13), we obtain

$$\det \Lambda^{\mathsf{DDGR}}_{\overline{\mathbf{v}}_1, \ldots, \overline{\mathbf{v}}_k} = \det(\Lambda^{\mathsf{LWE}}) \cdot \det \mathcal{L}(\overline{\mathbf{v}}_1, \ldots, \overline{\mathbf{v}}_k),$$

which together with Theorem 4.2 proves the theorem. $\qquad\square$

The Condition $\mathcal{L}(\mathbf{H}) = \mathbb{Z}^k$. Theorem 4.3 requires the hint matrix $\mathbf{H}$ to generate the integer lattice $\mathbb{Z}^k$. In practice, we can expect that $\mathbf{H}$ behaves like a random matrix. If k is significantly smaller than n, then Lemma 2.4 shows that $\mathcal{L}(\mathbf{H}) = \mathbb{Z}^k$ holds with very high probability. Hence, we expect that Theorem 4.3 typically applies in practice.

In the case of a single perfect hint, i.e., $k = 1$, the condition $\mathcal{L}(\mathbf{H}) = \mathbb{Z}^k$ simply requires that the greatest common divisor of the entries of $\overline{\mathbf{v}}_1$ equals 1. From the shape of the basis matrix $\mathbf{B}^{\mathsf{LWE}}$ (Eq. (3)), it is easy to see that for a secret only hint this is equivalent to requiring that $\overline{\mathbf{v}}_1$ is primitive with respect to the dual $(\Lambda^{\mathsf{LWE}})^*$. Hence, for the case of $k = 1$, our new Theorem 4.3 boils down to DDGR's original result.

Corollary 4.4 ([DDGR20, Lemma 12]). *Let $\overline{\mathbf{v}}_1$ be a (secret-only) perfect hint with hint matrix $\mathbf{H} = \mathsf{Hint}(\overline{\mathbf{v}}_1)$. Suppose $\overline{\mathbf{v}}_1$ is primitive with respect to the dual lattice $(\Lambda^{\mathsf{LWE}})^*$. Then it holds that*

$$\det \Lambda^{\mathsf{LWE}}_{\mathbf{H},1} = \Lambda^{\mathsf{DDGR}}_{\overline{\mathbf{v}}_1} = \det \Lambda^{\mathsf{LWE}} \cdot \det \mathcal{L}(\overline{\mathbf{v}}_1) = \det \Lambda^{\mathsf{LWE}} \cdot \|\overline{\mathbf{v}}_1\|.$$

4.3 Computing a Basis for $\Lambda^{\mathsf{LWE}}_{\mathbf{H},k}$

To be able to search for the secret vector $\mathbf{t}_{\mathbf{H}}$ in the sublattice $\Lambda^{\mathsf{LWE}}_{\mathbf{H},k} \subset \Lambda^{\mathsf{LWE}}_{\mathbf{H}}$, we of course first have to compute a basis for $\Lambda^{\mathsf{LWE}}_{\mathbf{H},k}$. To this end, we introduce our new algorithm CONSTRUCT-SUBLATTICE (Algorithm 1). The runtime of CONSTRUCT-SUBLATTICE is dominated by one call to LLL in dimension $n+1$, and by multiplying two matrices in dimensions $(n+1) \times (n+1)$ and $(n+1) \times m$ – making the algorithm highly practical.

Algorithm 1: CONSTRUCT-SUBLATTICE

Input: An LWE instance $(\mathbf{A}, \mathbf{b}, q)$, where $\mathbf{A} \in \mathbb{Z}^{n \times m}$, a hint matrix
$\mathbf{H} := \mathsf{Hint}((\overline{\mathbf{v}}_1, \ldots, \overline{\mathbf{v}}_k)) \in \mathbb{Z}^{(n+1) \times k}$, and a scaling parameter $c > 0$.
Output: A basis of $\Lambda_{\mathbf{H},k}^{\mathsf{LWE}}$ or FAIL.

1 Multiply the first k columns of $\mathbf{H}$ by $\lceil 2^{\frac{n}{2}} \cdot c \rceil$. Denote the resulting matrix by $\widetilde{\mathbf{H}}$.

2 Run the LLL algorithm on $(\widetilde{\mathbf{H}} \mid \mathbf{I}_{n+1})$ to obtain a reduced basis
$\mathbf{H}_{\mathsf{LLL}} \in \mathbb{Z}^{(n+1) \times (n+k+1)}$ and a unimodular matrix $\mathbf{U} \in \mathbb{Z}^{(n+1) \times (n+1)}$, such that

$$\mathbf{H}_{\mathsf{LLL}} = \mathbf{U} \cdot (\widetilde{\mathbf{H}} \mid \mathbf{I}_{n+1}).$$

3 **if** the upper-left $(n+1-k) \times k$ block of $\mathbf{H}_{\mathsf{LLL}}$ is non-zero **then**
4 | **Return** FAIL.
5 **else**
6 | Compute a matrix $\widetilde{\mathbf{A}}$ as follows:

$$\widetilde{\mathbf{A}} := \mathbf{U} \cdot \begin{pmatrix} \mathbf{A} \\ \mathbf{b} \end{pmatrix}.$$

7 | Construct the following matrix:

$$\mathbf{B} := \begin{pmatrix} q\mathbf{I}_m & \mathbf{0} \\ \widetilde{\mathbf{A}} & \mathbf{H}_{\mathsf{LLL}} \end{pmatrix} \in \mathbb{Z}^{(m+n+1) \times (m+k+n+1)}.$$

8 | Delete the last k rows of $\mathbf{B}$.
9 | **Return** the resulting matrix.

The main idea behind our algorithm is to appropriately scale the basis matrix $\mathbf{B}_{\mathbf{H}}^{\mathsf{LWE}}$ of $\Lambda_{\mathbf{H}}^{\mathsf{LWE}}$ by some *scaling parameter* c, such that LLL can only find lattice vectors in $\Lambda_{\mathbf{H}}^{\mathsf{LWE}}$, which have zeros in the coordinates $m+1$ to $m+k$. Additionally, we exploit the fact that the q-vectors (i.e., the first m rows of $\mathbf{B}_{\mathbf{H}}^{\mathsf{LWE}}$, as defined in Eq. (5)) already belong to the sublattice $\Lambda_{\mathbf{H},k}^{\mathsf{LWE}}$.

In Theorem 4.5 below, we prove a rigorous – yet impractical – bound on the scaling parameter, for which CONSTRUCT-SUBLATTICE provably returns a basis for $\Lambda_{\mathbf{H},k}^{\mathsf{LWE}}$. Building on the theorem, we then derive a heuristic bound on the scaling parameter, that works well in practice.

Theorem 4.5. *Let* $\mathbf{H} := \mathsf{Hint}(\overline{\mathbf{v}}_1, \ldots, \overline{\mathbf{v}}_k)$ *be a hint matrix. Let* $U := \mathbf{e}_1^{\perp} \cap \ldots \cap \mathbf{e}_m^{\perp} \subset \mathbb{R}^{m+k+n+1}$ *be the subspace orthogonal to the first m standard basis vectors. If we call* CONSTRUCT-SUBLATTICE *with scaling parameter* $c \geq \lambda_{n+1-k}(\pi_U(\Lambda_{\mathbf{H},k}^{\mathsf{LWE}}))$, *then the algorithm outputs a basis of* $\Lambda_{\mathbf{H},k}^{\mathsf{LWE}}$.

Proof. Let us first show that on input $c \geq \lambda_{n+1-k}(\pi_U(\Lambda_{\mathbf{H},k}^{\mathsf{LWE}}))$, the algorithm does not output FAIL. Let $c' := \lceil 2^{\frac{n}{2}} \cdot c \rceil$. By construction, every row $\mathbf{h}_i$ of $\mathbf{H}_{\mathsf{LLL}}$ is of the form

$$\mathbf{h}_i = (c' \cdot h_{i,1}, \ldots, c' \cdot h_{i,k}, h_{i,k+1}, \ldots, h_{i,n+k+1}). \tag{14}$$

Since $\mathbf{H}_{LLL}$ is LLL-reduced, it holds that

$$\|\mathbf{h}_i\| \leq 2^{\frac{n}{2}} \cdot \lambda_i(\mathcal{L}(\tilde{\mathbf{H}})), \tag{15}$$

see [LLL82, Proposition 1.12].

From the shape of the basis matrix $\mathbf{B}_{\mathbf{H}}^{LWE}$ (Eq. (8)) and the definition of $\Lambda_{\mathbf{H},k}^{LWE}$, it easily follows that the $(n+1-k)$-dimensional lattice $\pi_U(\Lambda_{\mathbf{H},k}^{LWE})$ is (isometric to) a sublattice of $\mathcal{L}(\tilde{\mathbf{H}})$. Together with Eq. (15), this yields

$$\|\mathbf{h}_i\| \leq 2^{\frac{n}{2}} \cdot \lambda_i(\pi_U(\Lambda_{\mathbf{H},k}^{LWE})) \leq 2^{\frac{n}{2}} \cdot \lambda_{n+1-k}(\pi_U(\Lambda_{\mathbf{H},k}^{LWE})) \leq c', \tag{16}$$

for every $i = 1, \ldots, n+1-k$.

Since by Eq. (14), the first k coordinates of $\mathbf{h}_i$ are multiples of c', Eq. (16) implies that these coordinates are, in fact, equal to zero. In particular, the upper-left $(n+1-k) \times k$ block of $\mathbf{H}_{LLL}$ is non-zero. Hence, the algorithm does not output FAIL.

It remains to show that the matrix returned in Step 9 indeed is a basis matrix for $\Lambda_{\mathbf{H},k}^{LWE}$. Let $\mathbf{U}$ be the unimodular matrix produced by Step 2. One can easily verify that the matrix $\mathbf{B}$, produced by Step 7 of the algorithm, is given by

$$\mathbf{B} = \begin{pmatrix} \mathbf{I}_m & \mathbf{0} \\ \mathbf{0} & \mathbf{U} \end{pmatrix} \cdot \mathbf{B}_{\mathbf{H}}^{LWE} \cdot \begin{pmatrix} \mathbf{I}_m & \mathbf{0} & \mathbf{0} \\ \mathbf{0} & c'\mathbf{I}_k & \mathbf{0} \\ \mathbf{0} & \mathbf{0} & \mathbf{I}_{n+1} \end{pmatrix}.$$

The matrix $\mathbf{B}$ is thus obtained by scaling the columns $m+1$ to $m+k$ of a basis matrix of $\Lambda_{\mathbf{H}}^{LWE}$ by c'. Since by construction the first $m+n+1-k$ rows are zero in the columns $m+1$ to $m+k$, this shows that the matrix returned in Step 9 is a basis for $\Lambda_{\mathbf{H},k}^{LWE}$, as required. □

To use CONSTRUCT-SUBLATTICE in practice, Theorem 4.5 shows that we need to efficiently compute an upper bound c on the $(n+1-k)$-th successive minimum of $\pi_U(\Lambda_{\mathbf{H},k}^{LWE})$. Unfortunately, we can not hope to rigorously prove any useful upper bound on $\lambda_{n+1-k}(\pi_U(\Lambda_{\mathbf{H},k}^{LWE}))$.[5] However, we may heuristically assume that

$$\lambda_1 \approx \lambda_2 \approx \ldots \approx \lambda_{n+1-k}$$

and then use the Gaussian heuristic[6]

$$gh(\pi_U(\Lambda_{\mathbf{H},k}^{LWE})) = \sqrt{\frac{n+m+1-k}{2\pi e}} \cdot (\det \pi_U(\Lambda_{\mathbf{H},k}^{LWE}))^{1/(n+m+1-k)}$$

$$= \sqrt{\frac{n+m+1-k}{2\pi e}} \cdot \left(\frac{\det \Lambda_{\mathbf{H},k}^{LWE}}{q^m} \right)^{1/(n+m+1-k)} \tag{17}$$

---

[5] E.g., we cannot hope to upper bound $\lambda_{n+1-k}(\pi_U(\Lambda_{\mathbf{H},k}^{LWE}))$ in terms of the determinant of the lattice, since it is easy to construct examples, where λ_2 is arbitrarily large, while the determinant is small.

[6] Equation (17) easily follows from the shape of $\mathbf{B}_{\mathbf{H}}^{LWE}$ (see Eq. (8)).

as an upper bound on $\lambda_{n+1-k}(\pi_U(\Lambda_{\mathbf{H},k}^{\mathsf{LWE}}))$. Making the additional assumption that $\mathcal{L}(\mathbf{H}) = \mathbb{Z}^k$ (which is justified by Lemma 2.4), we obtain by Theorem 4.3

$$\det \Lambda_{\mathbf{H},k}^{\mathsf{LWE}} = \det \Lambda^{\mathsf{LWE}} \cdot \det \mathcal{L}(\overline{\mathbf{v}}_1, \ldots, \overline{\mathbf{v}}_k) = q^m \cdot \det \mathcal{L}(\overline{\mathbf{v}}_1, \ldots, \overline{\mathbf{v}}_k),$$

which then yields the following heuristic:

Heuristic 4.6. *Let* $\mathbf{H} := \mathsf{Hint}(\overline{\mathbf{v}}_1, \ldots, \overline{\mathbf{v}}_k)$ *be a hint matrix. If we call* CONSTRUCT-SUBLATTICE *with scaling parameter*

$$c = \sqrt{\frac{n+m+1-k}{2\pi e}} \cdot \det \mathcal{L}(\overline{\mathbf{v}}_1, \ldots, \overline{\mathbf{v}}_k)^{1/(n+m+1-k)},$$

then the algorithm outputs a basis of $\Lambda_{\mathbf{H},k}^{\mathsf{LWE}}$.

We experimentally confirm correctness of Heuristic 4.6 in Sect. 7.

Remark 4.7. Instead of LLL-reducing $(\widetilde{\mathbf{H}} \mid \mathbf{I}_{n+1})$ in Step 2 of the algorithm, we could first reduce only $\widetilde{\mathbf{H}}$, and after that apply the corresponding transformation matrix to the $(n+1)$-dimensional identity matrix. (Similarly, as we do with $[\mathbf{A}, \mathbf{b}]$ in Step 6.) However, using $(\widetilde{\mathbf{H}} \mid \mathbf{I}_{n+1})$ has the benefit that the identity matrix forces LLL to take *small* linear combinations of the rows of $\widetilde{\mathbf{H}}$. In particular, it increases the probability of LLL taking the particularly small linear combination $(\mathbf{s}, -1)$ to create a zero in the first k coordinates. Whenever this happens, we can immediately read off the LWE secret from the basis. As we show in Sect. 7, in the regime of *too many hints*, this frequently occurs in practice.

Remark 4.8. More generally, given any lattice $\Lambda \subset \mathbb{R}^d$ and a collection of standard basis vectors $\{\mathbf{e}_i\}_{i \in I}$, $I \subseteq \{1, \ldots, d\}$, the ideas behind CONSTRUCT-SUBLATTICE can easily be adapted to efficiently compute a basis of $\Lambda \cap (\bigcap_{i \in I} \mathbf{e}_i^\perp)$.

5   Integrating Modular Hints

Suppose we are given k modular hints $\overline{\mathbf{v}}_i = (\mathbf{v}_i, \ell_i, m_i) \in \mathbb{Z}^n \times \mathbb{Z} \times \mathbb{N}$, for $i = 1, \ldots, k$. Our new algorithm for incorporating modular hints improves the primal lattice reduction attack by

(1) increasing the determinant of Λ^{LWE} by a factor of $\prod_{i=1}^k m_i$,
(2) while leaving dimension of the lattice,
(3) and norm of the secret vector $\mathbf{t}$ from Eq. (4) unchanged.

As in the perfect hint case, the effect of the integration of modular hints is thus the exact same as in the DDGR framework. However, since our approach uses our algorithm CONSTRUCT-SUBLATTICE (Algorithm 1) from Sect. 4.3, it is significantly more efficient than DDGR's. Yet, it is slightly less efficient than our approach for mod-q hints from Sect. 3, which requires only elementary linear algebra.

As we discuss in Sect. 5.2, an advantage of our general modular hint approach over our mod-q approach is, however, that it allows to easily combine *modular* hints with *perfect* hints, and to integrate both types of hints very efficiently in one stroke. We give a more in-depth comparison with the approach from Sect. 3 in Sect. 5.3.

5.1   Increasing det Λ^{LWE}, While Preserving dim Λ^{LWE} and $\|\mathbf{t}\|$

Let $(\mathbf{A}, \mathbf{b}, q) \in \mathbb{Z}_q^{n \times m} \times \mathbb{Z}_q^m \times \mathbb{N}$ be an LWE instance with secret $\mathbf{s} \in \mathbb{Z}_q^n$, and let $\overline{\mathbf{v}}_i = (\mathbf{v}_i, \ell_i, m_i) \in \mathbb{Z}^n \times \mathbb{Z} \times \mathbb{N}$ be modular hints such that

$$\langle \mathbf{v}_i, \mathbf{s} \rangle \equiv \ell_i \mod m_i, \tag{18}$$

for $i = 1, \ldots, k$.

Our main idea from Sect. 4 for integrating *perfect* hints is to view our hints as error-free LWE samples without reduction modulo q. For *modular hints* we now follow a very similar approach: We simply view the hints as error-free LWE samples with reduction modulo m_i. Apart from some minor modifications, our approach for modular hints then boils down to the perfect hint setting.

Embedding Hints Into Λ^{LWE}. Let $\overline{\mathbf{v}}_i' := (\mathbf{v}_i, \ell_i)$. Similarly as in Sect. 4, we start by defining a hint matrix $\mathbf{H} = \mathsf{Hint}(\overline{\mathbf{v}}_1', \ldots, \overline{\mathbf{v}}_k') = (\mathbf{V}, \boldsymbol{\ell}) \in \mathbb{Z}^{(n+1) \times k}$ (Definition 3.2). However, instead of using $\mathbf{H}$ to directly construct the hint lattice $\Lambda_{\mathbf{H}}^{\mathsf{LWE}}$ from Definition 4.1 (as we would in the perfect hint setting), we first define an additional matrix

$$\mathbf{M} := \begin{pmatrix} m_1 & & \\ & \ddots & \\ & & m_k \end{pmatrix} \in \mathbb{Z}^{k \times k}. \tag{19}$$

Then, closely following the definition of the hint lattice $\Lambda_{\mathbf{H},k}^{\mathsf{LWE}}$, we define the following matrix

$$\mathbf{B}_{\mathbf{M},\mathbf{H}}^{\mathsf{LWE}} := \begin{pmatrix} q\mathbf{I}_m & \mathbf{0} & \mathbf{0} & \mathbf{0} \\ \mathbf{0} & \mathbf{M} & \mathbf{0} & \mathbf{0} \\ \mathbf{A} & \mathbf{V} & \mathbf{I}_n & \mathbf{0} \\ \mathbf{b} & \boldsymbol{\ell} & \mathbf{0} & 1 \end{pmatrix} \in \mathbb{Z}^{(m+k+n+1) \times (m+k+n+1)}. \tag{20}$$

Notice that $\mathbf{B}_{\mathbf{M},\mathbf{H}}^{\mathsf{LWE}}$ naturally extends the definition of the original basis matrix $\mathbf{B}^{\mathsf{LWE}}$ from Eq. (3). Indeed, the columns $m+1$ to $m+k$ of $\mathbf{B}_{\mathbf{M},\mathbf{H}}^{\mathsf{LWE}}$ simply correspond to additional LWE samples, defined over $\mathbb{Z}_{m_i}$, instead of $\mathbb{Z}_q$.

Increased Determinant. Let $\Lambda_{\mathbf{M},\mathbf{H}}^{\mathsf{LWE}} := \mathcal{L}(\mathbf{B}_{\mathbf{M},\mathbf{H}}^{\mathsf{LWE}})$. Since $\mathbf{B}_{\mathbf{M},\mathbf{H}}^{\mathsf{LWE}}$ is triangular and $\mathbf{M}$ is diagonal, we have

$$\det \Lambda_{\mathbf{M},\mathbf{H}}^{\mathsf{LWE}} = q^m \cdot \det \mathbf{M} = q^m \cdot \prod_{i=1}^{k} m_i = \det \Lambda^{\mathsf{LWE}} \cdot \prod_{i=1}^{k} m_i.$$

Hence, we already increased the determinant of Λ^{LWE} by the desired factor.

Notice that the increase in determinant, though, comes at the cost of increasing the lattice dimension by k.[7] However, as we show below, the techniques,

---

[7] This is in contrast to the perfect hint setting, where embedding the hints does not increase the lattice dimension.

that allow us to *decrease* the lattice dimension in the perfect hint setting to $n + m + 1 - k$, now allow us to *preserve* our lattice dimension of $n + m + 1$ in the modular hint setting.

Preserving dimΛ^{LWE}. Lifting Eq. (18) to the integers, we obtain

$$\langle \mathbf{v}_i, \mathbf{s} \rangle = \ell_i - r_i m_i,$$

for some *unknown* $r_i \in \mathbb{Z}$. Let $\mathbf{r} := (r_1, \ldots, r_k)$. By construction, it then holds that

$$(\mathbf{r}, \mathbf{s}, -1) \cdot \begin{pmatrix} \mathbf{M} \\ \overline{\mathbf{V}} \\ \boldsymbol{\ell} \end{pmatrix} = \left(r_1 m_1 + \langle \mathbf{v}_1, \mathbf{s} \rangle - \ell_1, \ldots, r_k m_k + \langle \mathbf{v}_k, \mathbf{s} \rangle - \ell_k \right) = \mathbf{0}^k.$$

Hence, by Eq. (20), $\Lambda_{\mathbf{M},\mathbf{H}}^{\mathsf{LWE}}$ contains the short vector

$$\mathbf{t_H} := (-\mathbf{e}, \mathbf{0}^k, \mathbf{s}, -1),$$

which has the same length as the original secret vector $\mathbf{t}$, defined in Eq. (4).

Completely analogous to the perfect hint setting, we now simply suggest to search for $\mathbf{t_H}$ in the following $(m + n + 1)$-dimensional sublattice of $\Lambda_{\mathbf{M},\mathbf{H}}^{\mathsf{LWE}}$:

$$\begin{aligned} \Lambda_{\mathbf{M},\mathbf{H},k}^{\mathsf{LWE}} &:= \left\{ (v_1, \ldots, v_{n+m+k+1}) \in \Lambda_{\mathbf{M},\mathbf{H}}^{\mathsf{LWE}} \mid v_{m+1} = \ldots = v_{m+k} = 0 \right\} \\ &= \Lambda_{\mathbf{M},\mathbf{H}}^{\mathsf{LWE}} \cap \mathbf{e}_{m+1}^{\perp} \cap \ldots \cap \mathbf{e}_{m+k}^{\perp}, \end{aligned}$$

which has the same dimension as the original lattice Λ^{LWE}.

Making again the assumption that our hint matrix $\mathbf{H}$ behaves like a random matrix (as we already did in Sect. 4.2), Lemma 2.4 then suggests that with high probability $\mathbf{H}$ generates the integer lattice $\mathbb{Z}^k$. In that case, the sublattice $\Lambda_{\mathbf{M},\mathbf{H},k}^{\mathsf{LWE}}$ also has the required determinant, as we show in the following theorem.

Theorem 5.1. *Suppose $\mathcal{L}(\mathbf{H}) = \mathbb{Z}^k$. Then it holds that*

$$\det \Lambda_{\mathbf{M},\mathbf{H},k}^{\mathsf{LWE}} = \det \Lambda_{\mathbf{M},\mathbf{H}}^{\mathsf{LWE}} = \det \Lambda^{\mathsf{LWE}} \cdot \prod_{i=1}^{k} m_i.$$

Proof. Let $U := \mathbf{e}_{m+1}^{\perp} \cap \ldots \cap \mathbf{e}_{m+k}^{\perp}$. By Lemma 2.6, we obtain

$$\det(\Lambda_{\mathbf{M},\mathbf{H},k}^{\mathsf{LWE}}) = \det(\Lambda_{\mathbf{M},\mathbf{H}}^{\mathsf{LWE}} \cap U) = \frac{\det(\Lambda_{\mathbf{M},\mathbf{H}}^{\mathsf{LWE}})}{\det(\pi_{U^{\perp}}(\Lambda_{\mathbf{M},\mathbf{H}}^{\mathsf{LWE}}))}. \tag{21}$$

For any subset $A \subseteq \mathbb{R}^k$, let $A^{\sim} := \{0\}^m \times A \times \{0\}^{n+1} \subset \mathbb{R}^{m+k+n+1}$. Looking at the shape of the basis matrix $\mathbf{B}_{\mathbf{M},\mathbf{H}}^{\mathsf{LWE}}$ in Eq. (20) and using $U^{\perp} = (\mathbb{R}^k)^{\sim}$, it easily follows that

$$\pi_{U^{\perp}}(\Lambda_{\mathbf{M},\mathbf{H}}^{\mathsf{LWE}}) = \mathcal{L}([\mathbf{M},\mathbf{H}])^{\sim} \supseteq \mathcal{L}(\mathbf{H})^{\sim} = (\mathbb{Z}^k)^{\sim}.$$

Together with $\pi_{U^\perp}(\Lambda_{\mathbf{M,H}}^{\mathsf{LWE}}) \subseteq (\mathbb{Z}^k)^\sim$, this yields $\pi_{U^\perp}(\Lambda_{\mathbf{M,H}}^{\mathsf{LWE}}) = (\mathbb{Z}^k)^\sim$, and thus

$$\det(\pi_{U^\perp}(\Lambda_{\mathbf{M,H}}^{\mathsf{LWE}})) = 1. \tag{22}$$

Plugging in Eq. (22) into Eq. (21), the theorem follows.   □

We note that (as in the previous sections) we require our hints $\overline{\mathbf{v}}_i'$ to be linearly independent, see also Remark 3.1. If the hints were linearly dependent, we would have $\mathcal{L}(\mathbf{H}) \subsetneq \mathbb{Z}^k$, in which case Theorem 5.1 no longer applies, and we would have $\det \Lambda_{\mathbf{M,H},k}^{\mathsf{LWE}} < \det \Lambda_{\mathbf{M,H}}^{\mathsf{LWE}}$.

Efficiently Computing a Basis for $\Lambda_{\mathbf{M,H},k}^{\mathsf{LWE}}$. As discussed above, our new lattice $\Lambda_{\mathbf{M,H},k}^{\mathsf{LWE}}$ has the exact same quality as the original lattice of DDGR. However, since our lattice $\Lambda_{\mathbf{M,H},k}^{\mathsf{LWE}}$ is obtained by intersecting $\Lambda_{\mathbf{M,H}}^{\mathsf{LWE}}$ with standard basis vectors, we can compute a basis for our lattice much more efficiently than DDGR, by simply using our algorithm CONSTRUCT-SUBLATTICE (Algorithm 1), as discussed in Remark 4.8.

5.2   Combining Modular and Perfect Hints

In a scenario, where we are given both *modular* hints $\overline{\mathbf{v}}_i = (\mathbf{v}_i, \ell_i, m_i)$, for $i = 1, \dots, k$, as well as *perfect* hints $\overline{\mathbf{w}}_i = (\mathbf{w}_i, \ell_i)$, for $i = k+1, \dots, k+\ell$, our approach has the additional advantage that we can easily integrate all hints in one stroke. To this end, we simply construct a second hint matrix $\mathbf{H}' := \mathsf{Hint}(\overline{\mathbf{w}}_{k+1}, \dots, \overline{\mathbf{w}}_{k+\ell}) = (\mathbf{W}, \boldsymbol{\ell}')$, along with the following lattice basis

$$\begin{pmatrix} q\mathbf{I}_m & \mathbf{0} & \mathbf{0} & \mathbf{0} & \mathbf{0} \\ \mathbf{0} & \mathbf{M} & \mathbf{0} & \mathbf{0} & \mathbf{0} \\ \mathbf{A} & \mathbf{V} & \mathbf{W} & \mathbf{I}_n & \mathbf{0} \\ \mathbf{b} & \boldsymbol{\ell} & \boldsymbol{\ell}' & \mathbf{0} & 1 \end{pmatrix},$$

and then search for the LWE secret in the sublattice, that has zeros in the columns $m+1$ to $m+k+\ell$.

5.3   Comparison with Section 3

In our simple linear algebra approach from Sect. 3 for integrating k mod-q hints, the hints eliminate k coordinates of the secret vector $\mathbf{t}$, and decrease the dimension of Λ^{LWE} by k, while leaving the determinant unchanged. At first glance, this seems complementary to our more involved approach from Sect. 5.1, where $\|\mathbf{t}\|$ and dimension remain unchanged, while the determinant grows by a factor q^k.

Notice that after increasing the determinant by q^k we may ignore, however, up to k LWE samples, as explained in Sect. 2.5. Since every ignored LWE sample decreases the dimension of the lattice by one, eliminates one coordinate of $\mathbf{t}$, and decreases the determinant by a factor q, our more involved approach thus

(1) eliminates i coordinates of $\mathbf{t}$,

(2) decreases the dimension of Λ^{LWE} by i,

(3) and increases the determinant by q^{k-i},

for some freely choosable parameter $0 \leq i \leq k$. As discussed in Sect. 2.5, the BKZ algorithm can optimize the value of i on its own.

As one expects, this additional degree of freedom makes the more involved approach from Sect. 5.1 slightly better than the approach from Sect. 3, in the sense that it requires slightly smaller BKZ blocksizes to recover the secret. Worth noting, in the regime of *too many hints*, where mere basis construction dominates the runtime, the approach from Sect. 3 is, however, still preferable.

Clocktime in minutes

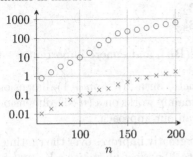

Clocktime in minutes

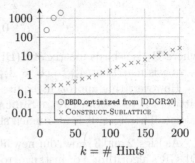

Fig. 2. Required runtime for integrating $n/2$ random perfect hints into n-dimensional random KYBER-like LWE instances with $m = n$, $q = 3329$ and $\|(\mathbf{e}, \mathbf{s})\| \approx 1.22 \cdot \sqrt{m+n}$.

Fig. 3. Required runtime for integrating k random perfect hints into random KYBER-512 instances.

6 Runtime Comparison with DDGR

Instead of using CONSTRUCT-SUBLATTICE for constructing a basis for $\Lambda_{\mathbf{H},k}^{\mathsf{LWE}} \subset \Lambda_{\mathbf{H}}^{\mathsf{LWE}}$ (or $\Lambda_{\mathbf{M},\mathbf{H},k}^{\mathsf{LWE}} \subset \Lambda_{\mathbf{M},\mathbf{H}}^{\mathsf{LWE}}$), we could also use the following slight modification of [DDGR20] for integrating perfect hints. Using the algorithm from [DDGR20, Section 4.1] for computing a *lattice slice*, we first compute a basis for $\Lambda_1 := \Lambda_{\mathbf{H},k}^{\mathsf{LWE}} \cap \mathbf{e}_{m+1}^{\perp}$, and then iteratively compute bases for $\Lambda_i := \Lambda_{i-1} \cap \mathbf{e}_{m+i}^{\perp}$, with $i = 2, \ldots, k$, until we obtain a basis for Λ_k. Since

$$\Lambda_{\mathbf{H},k}^{\mathsf{LWE}} = \Lambda_{\mathbf{H}}^{\mathsf{LWE}} \cap \mathbf{e}_{m+1}^{\perp} \cap \ldots \cap \mathbf{e}_{m+k}^{\perp} = \Lambda_k,$$

we obtain a basis for $\Lambda_{\mathbf{H},k}^{\mathsf{LWE}}$.

While this approach runs in polynomial time, it is unfortunately too slow in practice, because it is sequential. This is, in fact, precisely the issue that renders DDGR's implementation impractical in cryptographic dimensions.

Another Inferior Approach. As another alternative to compute a basis for $\Lambda_{\mathbf{H},k}^{\mathsf{LWE}}$, we could also use the following standard approach for computing the intersection of two lattices. Let $d := m+k+n+1$, define $U := \mathbf{e}_{m+1}^{\perp} \cap \ldots \cap \mathbf{e}_{m+k}^{\perp} \subset \mathbb{R}^d$, and let $\mathbf{B}_U \in \mathbb{Z}^{(d-k)\times d}$ be a basis matrix for the linear subspace U. (For instance, $\mathbf{B}_U$ may be obtained by taking the identity matrix $\mathbf{I}_d$, and removing the $(m+1)$-th to $(m+k)$-th rows.) We construct the following lattice basis

$$\begin{pmatrix} \mathbf{B}_\mathbf{H}^{\mathsf{LWE}} & \mathbf{B}_\mathbf{H}^{\mathsf{LWE}} \\ \mathbf{B}_U & \mathbf{0} \end{pmatrix} \in \mathbb{Z}^{(2d-2k)\times 2d},$$

and compute its Hermite normal form (HNF). By a simple dimension counting argument, it is easy to see that the HNF then has the following shape

$$\left(\begin{array}{c|c} \mathbf{B}_1 & \mathbf{B}_2 \\ \hline \mathbf{0}_{d-k\times d} & \mathbf{B}_3 \end{array} \right),$$

where $\mathbf{B}_1$ is a basis matrix of $\mathcal{L}(\mathbf{B}_\mathbf{H}^{\mathsf{LWE}}) + \mathcal{L}(\mathbf{B}_U)$, and – more importantly – $\mathbf{B}_3$ is a basis matrix of $\Lambda_\mathbf{H}^{\mathsf{LWE}} \cap U = \Lambda_{\mathbf{H},k}^{\mathsf{LWE}}$.

However, this approach requires arithmetic on a $2(n+m+1)$-dimensional lattice, whereas CONSTRUCT-SUBLATTICE mainly works on a $(n+1)$-dimensional lattice. Therefore, it is also much slower than our approach.

As Figs. 2 and 3 show, our new algorithm greatly improves over the runtime of DDGR's algorithm. For instance, to integrate 30 perfect hints into a KYBER-512 instance, the DDGR algorithm requires more than 31 h, whereas ours requires less than 20 s.[8]

7   Experimental Results

We provide experimental data for our implementation of the mod-q hint approach as described Sect. 3, and the implementation of CONSTRUCT-SUBLATTICE (Algorithm 1) from our perfect hint approach from Sect. 4.

Setup. In our experiments, we took hints $\overline{\mathbf{v}}_i = (\mathbf{v}_i, \ell_i)$, respectively $\overline{\mathbf{v}}_i = (\mathbf{v}_i, \ell_i, q)$, where $\mathbf{v}_i$ is drawn uniformly at random from $\{0, \ldots, q\}^n$. In the mod-q hint setting, we generated 16 random keys per scheme. In the perfect hint setting, we generated 32 random keys per scheme (with the exception of DILITHIUM, where we used only 16 keys.)

Worth noting, we did not implement CONSTRUCT-SUBLATTICE exactly as in the pseudocode from Algorithm 1, but added a minor tweak: Instead of directly LLL-reducing the matrix $(\widetilde{\mathbf{H}} \mid \mathbf{I}_{n+1})$ (see Step 2 of the algorithm), we first removed for every perfect hint one column from the $(n+1)$-dimensional identity matrix. (In other words, we projected the lattice $\Lambda_{\mathbf{H},k}^{\mathsf{LWE}}$ against some more standard basis vectors.) Curiously, we observed that this slightly worsens the gap of

---

[8] We ran both the DDGR algorithm and CONSTRUCT-SUBLATTICE in Sage9.7, using the latest patch to speed up fpylll, see https://github.com/fplll/fpylll/pull/239.

the lattice (the dimension remains unchanged), but BKZ finds the LWE secret at slightly smaller blocksizes. Additionally, this decreases the practical runtime of LLL, since the lattice lies in a smaller vector space. We leave it as an interesting open question to further study this BKZ behavior.

Hardware. We performed all our experiments on an AMD EPYC 7763 with 1 TB of RAM, as well as on an AMD EPYC 7742 with 2 TB of RAM. Each EPYC is equipped with 128 physical cores that with parallelization give 256 threads. We used the high number of cores only to run multiple experiments in parallel, but we did *not* use parallelism do speed up any single experiment.

Results. Our results are depicted in Figs. 4, 5, 6, 7, 8, 9, 10, 11, 12 and 13. In the mod-q setting, BKZ blocksize 2 denotes LLL reduction. We see, e.g., that for KYBER-512 with $k \geq 449$ all instances could be solved via LLL, determining our *too many hints* regime. In the perfect hint setting, we denote by blocksize 0 that after running CONSTRUCT-SUBLATTICE we could already directly read off our secret vector, without further reduction of the resulting hint lattice $\Lambda_{\mathbf{H},k}^{\mathsf{LWE}}$. We see, e.g., that we are in the *too many hints* regime for perfect hints for KYBER-512 with $k \geq 233$.

We choose a different format for displaying our DILITHIUM perfect hint results, because we were unable to run the BKZ algorithm on the hint lattice $\Lambda_{\mathbf{H},k}^{\mathsf{LWE}}$ for DILITHIUM, since we always encountered the infamous `infinite loop in babai` error. Nevertheless, we still provide the data points, at which we could already read off the LWE secret from the output of CONSTRUCT-SUBLATTICE.

As expected, Heuristic 4.6 was valid in every experiment.

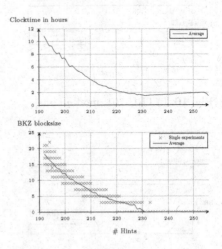

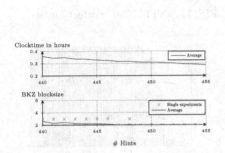

Fig. 4. [KYBER-512, mod-q hints]   **Fig. 5.** [KYBER-512, perfect hints]

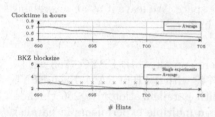

Fig. 6. [KYBER-768, mod-q hints]

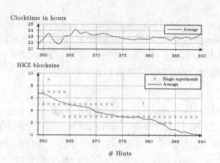

Fig. 7. [KYBER-768, perfect hints]

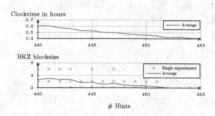

Fig. 8. [FALCON-512, mod-q hints]

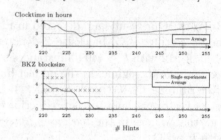

Fig. 9. [FALCON-512, perfect hints]

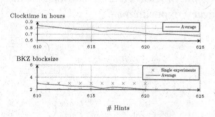

Fig. 10. [NTRU-701, mod-q hints]

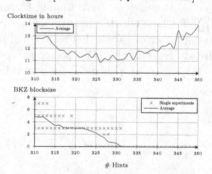

Fig. 11. [NTRU-701, perfect hints]

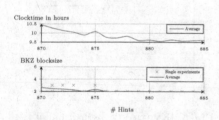

Fig. 12. [DILITHIUM-1024, mod-q hints]

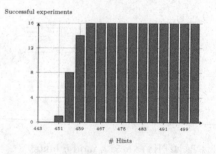

Fig. 13. [DILITHIUM-1024, perfect hints]

Acknowledgements. We are grateful to Carl Richard Theodor Schneider and Martin R. Albrecht for help with and bug-fixing in fpylll. We thank the anonymous reviewers for their detailed comments, that helped to improve our work.

Both authors are funded by the Deutsche Forschungsgemeinschaft (DFG, German Research Foundation) - grant 465120249. Alexander May is additionally supported by grant 390781972.

References

[AD97] Ajtai, M., Dwork, C.: A public-key cryptosystem with worst-case/average-case equivalence. In: 29th Annual ACM Symposium on Theory of Computing, pp. 284–293. ACM Press (1997)

[AD21] Albrecht, M.R., Ducas, L.: Lattice Attacks on NTRU and LWE: a history of refinements, pp. 15–40 (2021)

[ADPS16] Alkim, E., Ducas, L., Pöppelmann, T., Schwabe, P.: Post-quantum key exchange - A new hope. In: Holz, T., Savage, S. (eds.) USENIX Security 2016: 25th USENIX Security Symposium, pp. 327–343. USENIX Association (2016)

[Ajt96] Ajtai, M.: Generating hard instances of lattice problems (extended abstract). In: 28th Annual ACM Symposium on Theory of Computing, pp. 99–108. ACM Press (1996)

[BDK+18] Bos, J., et al.: CRYSTALS-Kyber: a CCA-secure module-lattice-based KEM. In: 2018 IEEE European Symposium on Security and Privacy (EuroS&P), pp. 353–367. IEEE (2018)

[BGV14] Brakerski, Z., Gentry, C., Vaikuntanathan, V.: (Leveled) fully homomorphic encryption without bootstrapping. ACM Trans. Comput. Theory (TOCT) **6**(3), 1–36 (2014)

[BV96] Boneh, D., Venkatesan, R.: Hardness of computing the most significant bits of secret keys in Diffie-Hellman and related schemes. In: Koblitz, N. (ed.) CRYPTO 1996. LNCS, vol. 1109, pp. 129–142. Springer, Heidelberg (1996). https://doi.org/10.1007/3-540-68697-5_11

[CLOS91] Coster, M.J., LaMacchia, B.A., Odlyzko, A.M., Schnorr, C.P.: An improved low-density subset sum algorithm. In: Davies, D.W. (ed.) EUROCRYPT 1991. LNCS, vol. 547, pp. 54–67. Springer, Heidelberg (1991). https://doi.org/10.1007/3-540-46416-6_4

[Cop97] Coppersmith, D.: Small solutions to polynomial equations, and low exponent RSA vulnerabilities. J. Cryptol. **10**(4), 233–260 (1997)

[DDGR20] Dachman-Soled, Dana, Ducas, Léo., Gong, Huijing, Rossi, Mélissa.: LWE with side information: attacks and concrete security estimation. In: Micciancio, Daniele, Ristenpart, Thomas (eds.) CRYPTO 2020. Part II. LNCS, vol. 12171, pp. 329–358. Springer, Cham (2020). https://doi.org/10.1007/978-3-030-56880-1_12

[DKL+18] Ducas, L., et al.: Crystals-dilithium: a lattice-based digital signature scheme. In: IACR Transactions on Cryptographic Hardware and Embedded Systems, pp. 238–268 (2018)

[dt21] The FPLLL development team. fpyLLL, a Python wraper for the fpLLL lattice reduction library, Version: 0.5.7 (2021). https://github.com/fplll/fpylll

[EMVW22] Esser, A., May, A., Verbel, J.A., Wen, W.: Partial key exposure attacks on BIKE, rainbow and NTRU. In: Dodis, Y., Shrimpton, T. (eds.) CRYPTO 2022. Part III. LNCS, vol. 13509, pp. 346–375. Springer, Heidelberg (2022). https://doi.org/10.1007/978-3-031-15982-4_12

[FHK+18] Fouque, P.A., et al.: Falcon: fast-Fourier lattice-based compact signatures over NTRU. Submission NIST's Post-quantum Crypt. Stand. Process **36**(5), 1–75 (2018)

[HDWH12] Heninger, N., Durumeric, Z., Wustrow, E., Halderman, J.A.: Mining your PS and QS: detection of widespread weak keys in network devices. In: Presented as part of the 21st {USENIX} Security Symposium ({USENIX} Security 12), pp. 205–220 (2012)

[HPS98] Hoffstein, J., Pipher, J., Silverman, J.H.: NTRU: a ring-based public key cryptosystem. In: Buhler, J.P. (ed.) ANTS 1998. LNCS, vol. 1423, pp. 267–288. Springer, Heidelberg (1998). https://doi.org/10.1007/BFb0054868

[JS98] Joux, A., Stern, J.: Lattice reduction: a toolbox for the cryptanalyst. J. Cryptol. **11**, 161–185 (1998)

[KMS22] Kölbl, S., Misoczki, R., Schmieg, S.: Securing tomorrow today: why Google now protects its internal communications from quantum threats (2022). https://cloud.google.com/blog/products/identity-security/why-google-now-uses-post-quantum-cryptography-for-internal-comms?hl=en

[LLL82] Lenstra, A.K., Lenstra, H.W., Lovász, L.: Factoring polynomials with rational coefficients. Math. Ann. **261**, 515–534 (1982)

[LPR10] Lyubashevsky, V., Peikert, C., Regev, O.: On ideal lattices and learning with errors over rings. In: Gilbert, H. (ed.) EUROCRYPT 2010. LNCS, vol. 6110, pp. 1–23. Springer, Heidelberg (2010). https://doi.org/10.1007/978-3-642-13190-5_1

[LS15] Langlois, A., Stehlé, D.: Worst-case to average-case reductions for module lattices. Des. Codes Cryptogr. **75**(3), 565–599 (2015)

[Mar13] Martinet, J.: Perfect Lattices in Euclidean Spaces, vol. 327. Springer, Heidelberg (2013). https://doi.org/10.1007/978-3-662-05167-2

[MN23] May, A., Nowakowski, J.: Too many hints - when LLL breaks LWE. Cryptology ePrint Archive, Paper 2023/777 (20230. https://eprint.iacr.org/2023/777

[MRW11] Maze, G., Rosenthal, J., Wagner, U.: Natural density of rectangular unimodular integer matrices. Linear Algebra Appl. **434**(5), 1319–1324 (2011)

[Odl90] Odlyzko, A.M.: The rise and fall of knapsack cryptosystems. Cryptol. Comput. Number Theory **42**(2) (1990)

[PRS17] Peikert, C., Regev, O., Stephens-Davidowitz, N.: Pseudorandomness of ring-LWE for any ring and modulus. In: Hatami, H., McKenzie, P., King, V. (eds.) Proceedings of the 49th Annual ACM SIGACT Symposium on Theory of Computing, STOC 2017, Montreal, QC, Canada, 19–23 June 2017 (2017)

[Reg05] Regev, O.: On lattices, learning with errors, random linear codes, and cryptography. In: Gabow, H.N., Fagin, R. (eds.) 37th Annual ACM Symposium on Theory of Computing, pp. 84–93. ACM Press (2005)

[Sch87] Schnorr, C.-P.: A hierarchy of polynomial time lattice basis reduction algorithms. Theor. Comput. Sci. **53**, 201–224 (1987)

[SSTX09] Stehlé, D., Steinfeld, R., Tanaka, K., Xagawa, K.: Efficient public key encryption based on ideal lattices. In: Matsui, M. (ed.) ASIACRYPT 2009. LNCS, vol. 5912, pp. 617–635. Springer, Heidelberg (2009). https://doi.org/10.1007/978-3-642-10366-7_36

[WWX22] Wu, H., Wang, X., Xu, G.: Reducing an LWE instance by modular hints and its applications to primal attack, dual attack and BKW attack. Cryptology ePrint Archive, Paper 2022/1404 (2022). https://eprint.iacr.org/2022/1404

We are on the Same Side. Alternative Sieving Strategies for the Number Field Sieve

Charles Bouillaguet[1]([⊠]) [iD], Ambroise Fleury[2], Pierre-Alain Fouque[3] [iD], and Paul Kirchner[3]

[1] Sorbonne Université, CNRS, LIP6, 75005 Paris, France
charles.bouillaguet@lip6.fr
[2] Université Paris-Saclay, CEA, List, 91120 Palaiseau, France
ambroise.fleury@cea.fr
[3] Univ Rennes, CNRS, IRISA, Rennes, France
{pierre-alain.fouque,paul.kirchner}@irisa.fr

Abstract. The Number Field Sieve (NFS) is the state-of-the art algorithm for integer factoring, and sieving is a crucial step in the NFS. It is a very time-consuming operation, whose goal is to collect many relations. The ultimate goal is to generate random smooth integers mod N with their prime decomposition, where smooth is defined on the rational and algebraic sides according to two prime factor bases.

In modern factorization tool, such as Cado-NFS, sieving is split into different stages depending on the size of the primes, but defining good parameters for all stages is based on heuristic and practical arguments. At the beginning, candidates are sieved by small primes on both sides, and if they pass the test, they continue to the next stages with bigger primes, up to the final one where we factor the remaining part using the ECM algorithm. On the one hand, first stages are fast but many false relations pass them, and we spend a lot of time with useless relations. On the other hand final stages are more time demanding but outputs less relations. It is not easy to evaluate the performance of the best strategy on the overall sieving step since it depends on the distribution of numbers that results at each stage.

In this article, we try to examine different sieving strategies to speed up this step since many improvements have been done on all other steps of the NFS. Based on the relations collected during the RSA-250 factorization and all parameters, we try to study different strategies to better understand this step. Many strategies have been defined since the discovery of NFS, and we provide here an experimental evaluation.

1 Introduction

The RSA cryptosystem was one of the first primitives of public-key cryptography to be invented. It still plays a dominant role in the computer security ecosystem, even though post-quantum alternatives are gaining traction. Together with the

J. Guo and R. Steinfeld (Eds.): ASIACRYPT 2023, LNCS 14441, pp. 138–166, 2023.
https://doi.org/10.1007/978-981-99-8730-6_5

Diffie-Hellman key exchange protocol, it is related to hard number theoretic questions such as integer factorization, which thus underpin most of modern cryptography, both now and in the years to come.

The major cryptanalytic tool to assess the hardness of integer factoring, and therefore the security of RSA-based cryptography, is the Number Field Sieve algorithm (NFS). While the asymptotic complexity of this algorithm is well-known, it is often difficult to estimate the time and resources that are needed to factor an integer. As such, all regulatory bodies recommend that people either avoid RSA entirely, or prefer large RSA key sizes for safety, *e.g.* at least 2048 bits until 2030, and at least 3072 bits after this date. In environments where computing power is plentiful, this recommendation is most often followed. Yet, we do rely on cryptography that uses smaller key sizes. The first author's credit card has a 1152-bit RSA public key which is valid until 2026. In some European countries (including France), the complete certification chain credit cards hinges on the security of 1408-bit RSA. This is well below recommended key sizes, but also well above the latest published academic record (829 bits [6]).

The regular publication of computational records [6,14] enables the cryptographic community and the greater public to gain a better understanding of the actual security level offered by the RSA cryptosystem. For this purpose, high-quality implementations of the NFS algorithm are required. The most recent record, the factorization of a 250-digit RSA challenge key, was done using Cado-NFS [20]. It is an open-source software, whose source code is publicly available.

The most time-consuming step of a large factorization using the NFS is the collection of many *relations*: in the recent RSA-250 record, it required 2450 core-years, which is 90% of the total computation time. A "relation" in the NFS is a pair of small integers (a, b) such that the evaluations of two homogeneous polynomials $F_0(a, b)$ and $F_1(a, b)$ are sufficiently smooth. $F_0(a, b)$ is often called the "rational norm" and $F_1(a, b)$ is the "algebraic norm".

Collecting relations can be done using many algorithms; among these, *sieving* is one of the most efficient. Cado-NFS uses a highly optimized sieve. It follows that improving sieving algorithms would have a practical impact on the performance of integer factoring algorithms, and in turn on the security of RSA.

The "batch smooth part" algorithm of Bernstein [4] was also used with practical success in the recent record [6]. It was used in combination with sieving: sieving happened on the algebraic side, while Bernstein's algorithm was used on the surviving (a, b) pairs on the rational side.

In this paper, we explore the idea of combining sieving and batch smooth part extraction *on the same side*. Our guiding principle is that sieving small primes is costly because they "hit" more often than large ones. We explore the possibility of not sieving primes less than, say about 100000, and instead recover the missing small factors using Bernstein's algorithm.

Our contribution is two-fold. First, we describe statistical properties of the relations collected during the factorization of RSA-250. While it was widely assumed that a prime factor p occurs in a "random" relation with probability $1/p$, we observe (and justify theoretically) that p occur with probability $1/p^\alpha$

for some $\alpha < 1$ that we characterize. We also propose an empirical model of the number of relations found per special-q, which enables us to reason about alternative relation collection strategies; in particular, we are able to assess the actual effectiveness of a relation collection algorithm that finds less relations but faster. These might need to sieve more special-q, with diminishing returns.

Second, we implemented the combination of sieving and batch smooth part extraction described above inside Cado-NFS, thanks to its open-source nature. Exploiting the availability of the relations collected during the record factorization of RSA-250, we carefully selected parameters to obtain an alternative relation collection procedure that finds 90% of all relations found by the "original" Cado-NFS implementation, using only 80% of the time. Combined with the previous reasoning about, we expect that this procedure will have to process 16% more special-q to collect as many relations as Cado-NFS did during the factorization of RSA-250. As such, we expect our implementation to yield a $\approx 5\%$ speedup over the whole factorization of a 250-digit integer.

This paper is organized as follows: in Sect. 2, we describe Bernstein's batch smooth part algorithm. In Sect. 3, we give some background on the NFS and some implementation aspects of Cado-NFS that enable us to control the size of the integers $F_1(a, b)$ (the "algebraic norms") that are sieved. In Sect. 4 we describe the relation collection algorithm of Cado-NFS in more details. In Sect. 5, we present a statistical analysis of the relations collected during the factorization of RSA-250. In Sect. 6, we discuss the combination of sieving and batch smoothness detection on the same side, and we present practical results in Sect. 7.

All experiments described in this paper were conducted on a cluster of identical nodes equipped with two Intel Xeon Gold 6130 CPUs.

2   Bernstein's Batch Smooth Part Algorithm

Given a set of integers $N = \{n_1, \dots, n_k\}$ and a set of prime numbers P, Bernstein's batch smooth part algorithm [4] finds simultaneously for each integer in N the product of its prime factors that are in P. When P contains all the primes up to a given bound, this extracts the *smooth part* of these integers. Its time complexity is $\mathcal{O}\left(b \log^{2+o(1)} b\right)$, b being the total number of bits in N and P.

This algorithm uses product and remainder trees (see [9, pp. 325–384] for more details). A product tree is a binary tree used to compute the product of many integers. Its leaves are labelled with the input integers while each internal node is labelled with the product of the labels of its children. The computation thus proceeds from the bottom up. The root is therefore labelled with the product of all the leaves. This structure enables the faster computation of $x_1 x_2 \dots x_n$ as often multiplies integers of similar sizes.

A remainder tree is a tree built upon a product tree to compute $z \bmod n_i$ efficiently, for a given z and a large set of n_i's. First compute the product tree of the n_i's. Then the computation proceeds from the top down as shown in Fig. 1. The root initially receives z; when an internal node receives a value x, it reduces

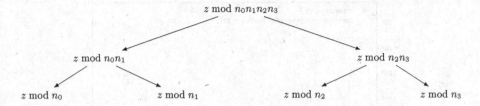

Fig. 1. Remainder tree as used in Cado-NFS

it modulo its label and sends the result to its children. The leaf labelled by n_i then outputs $z \bmod n_i$.

Bernstein later proposed "scaled remainder trees" [5] that trade divisions for multiplications, thus saving a constant factor. This variant is implemented and used in Cado-NFS. In our experiments, the scaled version is always faster than the simple version, when both are implemented using the GMP.

The batch smooth part algorithm works as follows, for a set of integers $N = \{n_1, \ldots, n_k\}$ and a set of prime numbers $P = \{p_1, \ldots, p_\ell\}$:

1. Using a product tree, compute $z \leftarrow p_1 \times \cdots \times p_\ell$
2. Using a remainder tree, compute $r_i \leftarrow z \bmod n_i$ (for all $1 \le i \le k$)
3. For $1 \le i \le k$, do:
   (a) Set $s_i \leftarrow 1$
   (b) Set $g \leftarrow \gcd(r_i, n_i)$
   (c) If $g = 1$, then s_i is the smooth part of n_i
   (d) Otherwise, set $s_i \leftarrow s_i \times g$ and $n_i \leftarrow n_i/g$, then return to step 3b

The computation of the smooth part of a huge number of integers N can be done by invoking the algorithm multiple times with small chunks of N. Because the first operation in the remainder tree algorithm is the computation of $z \bmod \prod_{i=1}^{k} n_i$, it would be a waste of resources to have z much smaller than the product of the n_i's. It is more efficient to split N in batches of about $0.5 \log_2 z$ bits, and to process them separately, keeping only z across all iterations.

Some performance measurements (using the implementation in Cado-NFS) are shown in Fig. 1.

3 The Number Field Sieve

The Number Field Sieve (NFS) is the state-of-the-art algorithm for integer factoring, discrete logarithm modulo p as well as in medium and large characteristics finite fields. Completely describing the NFS is out of the scope of this article; the interested reader can consult the books [8, 13, 16] or the recent computational record [6].

The full algorithm consists of several steps executed in sequence: polynomial selection, sieving, filtering, linear algebra and square root. Each of this step can be performed by a variety of sub-algorithms. Because we are mostly concerned

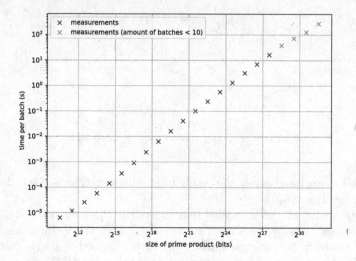

Fig. 2. Performance of batch smooth part algorithm of [4]. The implementation is taken from Cado-NFS. This shows the time needed to process $n/2$ bits with a prime product of n bits

with sieving strategies, we only very briefly describe the global mathematical setup and we will not discuss other steps beyond the strict necessary. We also focus on the case of integer factoring.

3.1 Mathematical Background

We briefly present some mathematical background below; for more details about number fields, the reader may refer to [17].

Let $f = f_d x^d + \cdots + f_1 x + f_0$ denote a polynomial with integer coefficients, of degree d, irreducible over $\mathbb{Q}$, and let α be a complex root of f (*i.e.* $f(\alpha) = 0$). We denote by $F(x, y) = f(x/y)y^d$ the "homogenized version" of f. We work inside the number field $K := \mathbb{Q}(\alpha)$ defined by f. Any element $A \in \mathbb{Q}(\alpha)$ can be represented as $A = P(\alpha)$ for some polynomial P with rational coefficients.

A complex number is an *algebraic integer* if it is the root of a *monic* polynomial (leading coefficient 1) with integer coefficients. The set R of all algebraic integers contained in K forms the *ring of integers* of K (equivalently, the maximal order of K). In general, α is not an algebraic integer unless f is monic, *i.e.* $f_d = 1$. However, $\hat{\alpha} = f_d \cdot \alpha$ is always an algebraic integer because $\hat{f}(x) = F(x, f_d)/f_d = x^d + f_{d-1}x^{d-1} + f_{d-2}f_d x^{d-2} + \ldots + f_0 f_d^{d-1}$ is a monic polynomial with integer coefficients and $\hat{f}(\hat{\alpha}) = f_d^{d-1} f(\alpha) = 0$.

The ring of integers R is often strictly larger than $\mathbb{Z}[\hat{\alpha}]$. In addition, it is well-known that R is usually not a unique factorization domain, which means that elements do not always have a unique factorization as a product of other irreducible elements. However R is a *Dedekind domain*: any ideal of R factors uniquely as a product of prime ideals of R. This property is not necessarily true in $\mathbb{Z}[\hat{\alpha}]$, but we have a good enough substitute (see [8, Proposition 5.4] for details).

The *norm* of $u \in K$, denoted by $N(u)$, is the product of all its conjugates in $\mathbb{Q}$. Concretely, if $u = P(\alpha)$, then $N(u) = (1/f_d)^{\deg P}\mathrm{Res}(f, P)$—because the resultant is the product of the evaluations of P at all the complex roots of f. In general, $N(u) \in \mathbb{Q}$ and when u is an algebraic integer, then $N(u)$ is an integer. In the special case where $u = a + \alpha b$ with $a, b \in \mathbb{Z}$, then $N(f_d u) = f_d^{-1} \cdot F(a, b)$.

For a non-zero ideal I of $\mathbb{Z}[\hat{\alpha}]$, denote by $\|I\|$ the "norm" of I, namely the cardinality of the quotient ring $\mathbb{Z}[\hat{\alpha}]/I$, which is always finite. For any two ideals I and J of $\mathbb{Z}[\hat{\alpha}]$, we have $\|IJ\| = \|I\| \times \|J\|$; it follows that I is a prime ideal of $\mathbb{Z}[\hat{\alpha}]$ whenever $\|I\|$ is a prime integer. For a principal ideal spanned by $u \in \mathbb{Z}[\hat{\alpha}]$, we have $\|\langle u \rangle\| = |N(u)|$. It follows that if $u \in \mathbb{Z}[\hat{\alpha}]$ and the principal ideal spanned by u is factored as a product of ideals: $\langle u \rangle = I_1 \ldots I_k$, then we have a factorization of $N(u)$ over $\mathbb{Z}$: $N(u) = \|I_1\| \times \cdots \times \|I_k\|$. In this case, finding the factorization of $\langle u \rangle$ can be done by factoring the integer $N(u)$; from its prime factors, the prime ideals that appear in the factorization of $\langle u \rangle$ over $\mathbb{Z}[\hat{\alpha}]$ can usually be found relatively easily.

If I is a *prime* ideal[1] of $\mathbb{Z}[\hat{\alpha}]$, then $I \cap \mathbb{Z}$ is also a prime ideal of $\mathbb{Z}$. As such, I contains a unique prime number p (I "lies over" p). When I is prime, the quotient $\mathbb{Z}[\hat{\alpha}]/I$ is a finite integral domain, hence a finite field, and therefore $\|I\| = p^k$ for some k (the *inertial degree* of I).

Suppose that p does not divide f_d. Under this assumption, we describe the prime ideals contained in $\mathbb{Z}[\hat{\alpha}]$ of inertial degree one that lie over p. These ideals are of the form $\langle p, \hat{\alpha} - r \rangle$ where $f(r) \equiv 0 \bmod p$. Here is why: suppose that I is such an ideal; then because $\mathbb{Z}[\hat{\alpha}]/I \simeq \mathbb{Z}_p$ and $\hat{\alpha}$ is a root of $\hat{f}$, the canonical ring homomorphism $\mathbb{Z}[\hat{\alpha}] \to \mathbb{Z}[\hat{\alpha}]/I$ sends $\hat{\alpha}$ to a root r of $\hat{f}$ modulo p (it follows that there are prime ideals that lie over p only when $\hat{f}$ has roots modulo p, and therefore when f does). Hence, a prime ideal gives rise to a pair (p, r) with $f(r) \equiv 0 \bmod p$. Conversely, consider such a pair (p, r) and consider the ring homomorphism $\mathbb{Z}[\hat{\alpha}] \to \mathbb{Z}_p$ that sends $\hat{\alpha}$ to r and p to 0. Its kernel is an ideal of $\mathbb{Z}[\hat{\alpha}]$ of norm p, therefore it is a prime ideal of inertial degree one. These prime ideals can be fully described by a pair of integers (p, r).

In the context of NFS, we are interested in the factorization of ideals $\langle a - b\alpha \rangle$ when $a, b \in \mathbb{Z}$ are coprime. It turns our that only prime ideals of inertial degree 1 can appear in the factorization (see [8] for a proof). When f is monic, testing if $\langle p, \alpha - r \rangle$ divides $\langle a - b\alpha \rangle$ amounts to testing if the latter is contained in the former, and this comes down to checking if $a - b\alpha$ can be written as an integer linear combination of p and $\alpha - r$. In turn, this is equivalent to $a \equiv br \bmod p$.

The theory of the NFS is often presented in the simpler situation where f is monic. In practice this is not the case: there is a performance incentive to choose a non-monic polynomial f. Indeed, this gives more freedom in the choice of f and enables the use of polynomials with smaller coefficients, which is beneficial. The main mathematical hurdle is that α is not an algebraic integer in that case.

---

[1] Recall that $I \neq \mathbb{Z}[\hat{\alpha}]$ is prime iff $rs \in I$ implies that $r \in I$ or $s \in I$ for any $r, s \in \mathbb{Z}[\hat{\alpha}]$—in particular, a product of ideals is not prime.

The principal ideals $\langle a - b\alpha \rangle$ are therefore *fractional ideals*, *i.e.* they can be written as $u^{-1}I$ where u is an algebraic integer and I is an ideal of R. Indeed, $\langle a - b\alpha \rangle = f_d^{-1}I$ with $I = \langle f_d a - b(f_d \alpha) \rangle$, and this is a (usual) ideal of R. More precisely, I is an ideal of $\mathbb{Z}[\hat{\alpha}]$.

Montgomery introduced a clever way of dealing with the fact that α is not an algebraic integer [18]. Let $J = \{x \in R : x\alpha \in R\}$. It is easy to check that J is an ideal of R. Because $f_d \alpha \in R$, then $f_d \in J$; in addition, a complete set of generators of J is always available. In fact, $J \times \langle 1, \alpha \rangle = R$ and $\|J\| = f_d$. The point is that $J \times \langle a - b\alpha \rangle$ is an ideal of R; Its norm is precisely $\mathrm{Res}(a - bx, f) = F(a, b)$. In addition, $J \times \langle p, r - \alpha \rangle$ is a prime ideal of norm exactly p.

Up to minor details, we can multiply all ideals by J when f is not monic and work in $\mathbb{Z}[\hat{\alpha}]$ instead of $\mathbb{Z}[\alpha]$. In both cases, the norm of $\langle a - b\alpha \rangle$ (or $J \times \langle a - b\alpha \rangle$ when f is not monic) is exactly $\mathrm{Res}(a - bx, f)$, and the norm of $\langle p, \alpha - r \rangle$ (or $J \times \langle p, \alpha - r \rangle$) is exactly p.

3.2   Overview of the Algorithm

In order to factor an integer N, the first thing to do is to find two irreducible polynomials $f_0(X)$ and $f_1(X)$ in $\mathbb{Z}[x]$ with a common root m modulo N. These two polynomials define two algebraic number fields $\mathbb{Q}(\alpha_i)$, with $f_i(\alpha_i) = 0$. This leads to the commutative diagram shown in Fig. 3.

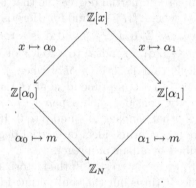

Fig. 3. The mathematical setup of NFS.

Finding two polynomials with a common root modulo a composite N of unknown factorization is difficult in general, and therefore $f_0(X)$ is usually only of degree one. It follows that $\mathbb{Z}[\alpha_0]$ is in fact a subring of $\mathbb{Q}$. This leads to a commonly used terminology that distinguishes the "rational side" (f_0) and the "algebraic side" (f_1).

The main idea, and the most time-consuming operation in the NFS, consists in finding *relations*. A relation is a pair (a, b) of coprime and preferably small integers, such that the two principal ideals $\langle a - b\alpha_i \rangle \in \mathbb{Z}[\alpha_i]$ completely factor as a product of prime ideals of small norm contained in some predetermined finite sets $\mathcal{F}_0$ and $\mathcal{F}_1$. This presentation implicitly assumes that $f_1(X)$ is monic; see the discussion above for the complications when it is not the case.

The intuitive idea is then to multiply a subset of these relations to obtain a square in $\mathbb{Z}$ on the rational side and a square in $\mathbb{Z}[\alpha_1]$ on the algebraic side. Then, walking down the commutative diagram, we "transfer" these to $\mathbb{Z}_N$ in order to obtain a congruence of squares modulo N. Then, given $a^2 \equiv b^2 \bmod N$, we find that there is some integer k such that $(a-b)(a+b) = kN$, so that if $a \neq \pm b$, then the greatest common divisor of $a+b$ and N will be a divisor of N.

For a pair (a,b) to yield an actual relation, the above conditions mean that $a - mb$ factors over primes less than a given bound (on the rational side) and that the principal ideal $\langle a - \alpha_1 b \rangle$ factors over prime ideals, necessarily of inertial degree 1, of norm less than a given bound (on the algebraic side). As explained above, these ideals are described by pairs (p,r) where $f_1(r) \equiv 0 \bmod p$. Concretely, this means that the integer $F_1(a,b)$ has to split into a set of precomputed primes integers less than the chosen bound—this holds true even when f is not monic.

In the next subsections, we give enough background to control the size of the integers $F_1(a,b)$ that are sieved for smoothness. These integers are often called the "norms".

3.3 Polynomial Selection

For the factorization of RSA-250, the following polynomials were chosen:

$f_0 = 18511296881863829288191 3X - 32565717159340474386643557747343303 86901$

$f_1 = 86130508464000X^6 - 815835130764290488377337814383769841229 61112000$

$\quad - 66689953322631501408X^5 - 17216144295387401200117600348293857920 19395X$

$\quad - 52733221034966333966198X^4 - 31136272536132022651269074205506483 26X^2$

$\quad + 46262124564021437136744523465879X^3$

It can be observed that the coefficients of f_1 approximately form a geometric progression of reason $s = 354109.861$; s is the *skewness* of the polynomial. If $f(X) = \sum_{i=0}^{d} f_i X^i$, write $\|f\|_1 = \sum |f_i|$ the ℓ_1-*norm* of f (also for multivariate polynomials) and write:

$$F_1'(X,Y) = \frac{1}{f_d} F_1(X,Y/s)$$
$$\approx X^6 - 2.19X^5Y - 0.0049X^4Y^2 + 12.1X^3Y^3$$
$$- 2.3X^2Y^4 - 3.59XY^5 - 0.48Y^6$$

It follows that if $|a| \leq x$ and $|bs| \leq x$, then $|F_1(a,b)| = f_d|F_1'(a,bs)| \leq f_d x^6 \|F_1'\|_1$. In the case of RSA-250, $\|F_1'\|_1 \approx 21.66$, so we get an upper-bound of $|F_1(a,b)| \leq 2^{50.73}x^6$.

3.4   Relation Collection

The goal of the relation collection step is to collect a large number of (a, b) pairs such that both "norms" $F_0(a, b)$ and $F_1(a, b)$ are sufficiently smooth. Several strategies can be used (and combined) for this purpose, but current implementations of the NFS all rely on a form of *sieving*. The interested reader will find an introduction and many details about sieving in general in [13].

From a high-level perspective, the process works as follows (for side i):

1. Initialize a large array S representing many (a, b) pairs.
2. For all ideals $\mathfrak{p}$ in the *factor base*, *mark* all locations in S where $\mathfrak{p} \mid \langle a - b\alpha_i \rangle$.
3. Discard (as probably non-smooth) all pairs with cofactor larger than a threshold T.
4. Finish factoring the remaining cofactors and check if they are B-smooth.

Concretely, the large array stores the (log of the) "norm" associated to the ideal $\langle a - b\alpha_i \rangle$, which is the result of the evaluation of $F_i(a, b)$. On the rational side, the factor base is composed of all prime integers less than some bound. On the algebraic side, the factor base is composed of all prime ideals (of inertial degree 1) described by pairs (p, r) with p a prime integer less than some other bound and $f_1(r) \equiv 0 \bmod p$. The locations where $\mathfrak{p}$ divides $\langle a - b\alpha_i \rangle$ are those where $a \equiv br \bmod p$. Marking the ideal amounts to subtracting the log of p from the log of $F_1(a, b)$. After all primes have been sieved, the large array contains the log of the norms of the cofactors.

Implementing this procedure requires choosing the range of sieved primes and the threshold T. A simple option consists in sieving all prime (and prime powers) up to B, which makes the fourth step ("cofactorization") trivial. In practice, it is usually more efficient to sieve only a subset of those primes. Cado-NFS sieves all primes up some bound (denoted as lim_i for side i), which is less than the final smoothness bound 2^{lpb_i} (lpb stands for large prime bound), and uses the elliptic curve method in the cofactorization step. Primes that are in $[\text{lim}_i, 2^{\text{lpb}_i}]$ are called "large primes".

Implementing this strategy is a matter of trade-offs. If the threshold T is too low, many potential relations will be discarded by the filter (false negatives). If T is too high, many non-smooth numbers will proceed to the cofactorization step (false positives) and increase its cost.

Sieving more primes makes this filter more "precise" (reduce both false rates), but obviously makes sieving more expensive. Choosing these parameters is a non-trivial balancing act.

It is possible to either sieve on both side to identify (a, b) pairs where both norms are smooth (this requires choosing two sets of parameters), or to sieve on one side and process the "surviving" (a, b) pairs using an other strategy for the other side. In particular, because algebraic norms are larger than their rational counterparts, the proportion of pairs where $F_1(a, b)$ is sufficiently smooth may potentially be small. The number of surviving pairs after sieving on the algebraic side may therefore be small enough that checking the smoothness of $F_0(a, b)$ using the product tree algorithm (for the survivors only) gets faster than sieving again all (a, b) pairs on the rational side. Both strategies were used during the factorization of RSA-250. In the sequel, we focus on sieving and assume that sieving happens on both sides.

Lattice Sieving. Cado-NFS uses the technique of *lattice sieving* or *special-q sieving* [19]. The idea consists in picking a particular prime ideal q with description (p, r)—it will be "special"—and restricting our attention to (a, b) pairs such that q divides $\langle a - b\alpha_1 \rangle$. We then know in advance that $F_1(a, b)$ is a multiple of p, and this reduces the problem to testing if $F_1(a, b)/p$ is smooth. Because this is a smaller number, it is a bit more likely.

Relation collection can then work by allocating a large array that holds A pairs, filling it with (a, b) such that the special-q divides the principal ideal on the algebraic side and detecting all actual relations in the array. The process can then be repeated for all special-q ideals of norm inside a specific interval, the "special-q" range. In the factorization of RSA-250, this was the interval [1G; 12G].

For each special-q described by (p, r), the set all of (a, b) pairs such that $a - br \equiv 0 \bmod p$, or, in other terms, such that $a - br = kp$ for $k \in \mathbb{Z}$, forms a Euclidean lattice. More precisely, we have:

$$(a, bs) = (b, k) \begin{pmatrix} r & s \\ p & 0 \end{pmatrix}$$

where s is the skewness of f_1. Let $V = ps$ the module of the determinant of the basis matrix; in this case, it is also the volume of the lattice. This shows that the larger the special-q, the farthest apart are the corresponding (a, b) pairs.

Using Lagrange reduction, a reduced basis of this lattice can be computed in quadratic time. This yields two integer vectors $\mathbf{u} = (a_0, b_0)$ and $\mathbf{v} = (a_1, b_1)$ such that $\|\mathbf{u}\| \leq \|\mathbf{v}\|$ and $\|\mathbf{u}\| \cdot \|\mathbf{v}\| \leq \sqrt{4/3}V$. A *sieving area* A is chosen depending on the available amount of memory ($A = 2^{33}$ for RSA-250). A total of A pairs (a, b) are sieved, with

$$(a, bs) = i \cdot \mathbf{u} + j \cdot \mathbf{v} \qquad \text{where} \qquad |i| \leq \frac{I}{2}, \quad 0 \leq j \leq J \quad \text{and} \quad IJ = A.$$

Choice of Sieve Regions. The bounds I and J can be chosen so as to minimize the maximum norm of F_1 over the corresponding parallelogram. It follows from the properties of Lagrange-reduction that $\|\mathbf{u}\|^2 \leq \sqrt{4/3}V$, and therefore both a_0 and b_0 are less than $B := (4/3)^{1/4}\sqrt{V}$ in absolute value. Next, write $t = B/\max(|a_1|, |b_1|)$ so that

$$|a_1| \cdot t \leq B \qquad \text{and} \qquad |b_1| \cdot t \leq B.$$

t is a measure of how "thin" the sieved parallelogram is, because $t = \Theta\left(\sqrt{\|\mathbf{u}\|/\|\mathbf{v}\|}\right)$. In general, the ratio $\|\mathbf{u}\|/\|\mathbf{v}\|$ could be as low as $1/V$, with $\mathbf{u} = (1, 0)$ and $\mathbf{v} = (0, V)$. However, this is quite unlikely if the input basis is "sufficiently random". Let $\mathbf{v}^* = \mathbf{v} - \mu\mathbf{u}$ with $\mu = \mathbf{uv}/\|\mathbf{u}\|^2$; $\mathbf{v}^*$ is the orthogonal projection of $\mathbf{v}$ onto the orthogonal of $\mathbf{u}$. Define γ as $\|\mathbf{u}\|/\|\mathbf{v}^*\|$. It is shown in [21] that $\Pr[\gamma \leq x]$ tends to $3x/\pi$ for "random" inputs. Because $\|\mathbf{v}^*\| \leq \|\mathbf{v}\|$, it follows that $\|\mathbf{u}\|/\|\mathbf{v}\| \leq \gamma$. As a consequence, the probability to obtain a seriously unbalanced basis is small.

In any case, very thin sieve regions are unfavorable for a variety of reasons, and special-q's are discarded if t is too small (say less than $1/100$). It follows that, concretely, t is lower-bounded by some constant.

Finally, observe that

$$|a| = |ia_0 + ja_1| \leq \frac{I}{2}a_0 + Ja_1 \leq B\left(\frac{I}{2} + J/t\right),$$

$$|bs| = |ib_0 + jb_1| \leq \frac{I}{2}b_0 + Jb_1 \leq B\left(\frac{I}{2} + J/t\right).$$

It remains to choose I and J such that $I/2 + J/t$ is minimal under the constraint that $IJ = A$. It is not difficult to see that the optimal choice is $I = \sqrt{2A/t}$. In that case we have that both $|a|$ and $|bs|$ are less than $2\sqrt{Aps/(t\sqrt{3})}$. This choice of I and J thus guarantees that $|F_1(a,b)|$ is less than $f_d 2^6 A^3 p^3 s^3 t^{-3} \sqrt{3}^{-3} \|F_1'\|_1$ over the sieved region.

Plugging in the numerical constants of the RSA-250 factorization yields an upper-bound of about $2^{208}p^3$, assuming $t \approx 1$. Example of sieved zones are shown in Fig. 4.

Random (a, b) Pairs Processed by Cado-NFS.

For our purpose, we need to observe statistical properties of the norms of "random" (a, b) pairs processed during a factorization. Assuming that $F_1(a, b)$ behaves like a random number is not reasonable, at least because $F_1(a, b) \equiv 0 \bmod 6$ in RSA-250 for the chosen polynomial.

However, it is possible to accumulate a realistic sample using the following simple-minded procedure:

1. Pick a random special-q (in the full range used in the factorization)
2. Compute the sieve region as discussed above.
3. Pick a random (a, b) pair that would have been sieved with this special-q
4. Compute the "norms", i.e. $F_0(a, b)$ and $F_1(a, b)$.

We accumulated a bit more than 100M samples using this procedure, mostly to observe empirically the smoothness properties of the norms "under real-life conditions".

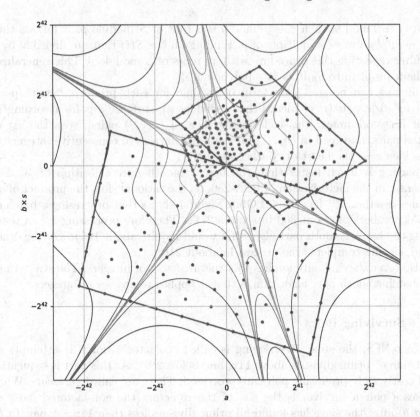

Fig. 4. Sieved regions for $q = 1G$ (red), $q = 4G$ (green), $q = 12G$ (blue). The level sets of $|F_1(a, bs)|$ are shown in black. From outer to inner, they correspond to the following sizes (in bits): 300, 294, 288, 282, 274 and 268). (Color figure online)

4 Relation Collection in Cado-NFS

In this section, we give a succinct description of the algorithm implemented in Cado-NFS. Its goal is to find pairs (a, b) such that both $F_0(a, b)$ and $F_1(a, b)$ are sufficiently smooth. The smoothness bound on the rational side is 2^{lpb_0}, and it is 2^{lpb_1} on the algebraic side (lpb stands for "large prime bound"). In RSA-250, $\mathrm{lpb}_0 = 36$ and $\mathrm{lpb}_1 = 37$.

The global process follows the outline given in Sect. 3.4 and uses special-q sieving. Given a large collection of pairs (a, b), the *sieve* finds "small" prime divisors of $F_i(a, b)$ up to some bounds. In Cado-NFS, the smoothness bounds used by the sieve are called lim_0 (on the rational side) and lim_1 (on the algebraic side). In the factorization of RSA-250, their values are: $\mathrm{lim}_0 = \mathrm{lim}_1 = 2^{31}$.

Factoring with a sieve is akin to finding primes with the sieve of Eratosthenes. It is a very efficient method and works best on large sets of numbers. However, sieving requires the target set of integers to have a specific structure. In particular, given a polynomial $S \in \mathbb{Z}[X]$, it is easy to sieve $S(0), S(1), S(2), \dots$. Indeed, if $S(n) \equiv 0 \bmod p$, then $r \leftarrow n \bmod p$ is a root of S modulo p. It follows that $S(r + kp)$ is always a multiple of p. Finding all the $S(i)$ that are divisible by p requires repeating this procedure with all roots of S modulo p. This generalizes without problem to multivariate polynomials.

Sieving can be seen as a form of sorting: for each prime p, "emit" pairs $(r + kp, p)$ [a pair (n, p) means that p divides n]; sort these pairs according to their first coordinate [this collects together all $(n, \ldots)$ pairs]; scan the list of sorted pairs, and read in $(n, \ldots)$ all the prime factors of consecutive integers n. This idea is at the heart of "bucket sieving" [1].

Sieving is much faster than the batch smooth part algorithm of [4]. For instance, in the factorization of RSA-250, on the rational side, the product of all primes less than 2^{31} has size 3.1 Gbit. Figure 1 shows that processing a batch of $\approx$ 5M numbers of about 300 bits takes 271 s. Therefore processing 2^{33} of them using the batch smooth part algorithm would require about 125 h. On the other hand, sieving completes the process in about 216 s.

However, sieving only applies to structured sets of integers. The strength of the batch smooth part algorithm is that it applies to any set of integers.

4.1 Surviving Pairs

In Cado-NFS, the step after sieving is called "cofactorization". It attempts to find "large" prime divisors above $\texttt{lim}_i$ and below $2^{\texttt{lpb}_i}$. As this part is sequential and costly, only promising pairs are processed. There are called *survivors*. What makes a pair a survivor is the size of the *cofactor* (the non-factored part) of $F_i(a, b)$ after the sieve has found all prime divisors less than $\texttt{lim}_i$. A pair (a, b) "survives" if the size the cofactors on both sides are less than $2^{\texttt{mfb}_i}$. As discussed above, choosing $\texttt{lim}_i$ and $\texttt{mfb}_i$ is a matter of compromises. The goal of the sieve is to discard a huge proportion of (a, b) pairs without removing too many would-be relations.

Sieving is thus done as follows:

1. **Sieve** norms on both algebraic and rational sides.
2. Keep only promising pairs (= survivors).
3. Find tiny factors with trial division on both sides.
4. Filter survivors once more.
5. Send them to cofactoring.

Product tree factoring is preferred on the rational side for large special-q's. Indeed, as opposed to sieving, product tree (batch) factoring doesn't need its inputs to follow any sequence and can thus be used directly on surviving pairs in any order. This makes it possible to filter promising pairs right after sieving on the algebraic side, effectively swapping sieving the entire rational side with batch factoring a small subset of these pairs. A second filter is then applied after batch factoring. Sieving is thus done as follows:

1. **Sieve** norms on the algebraic side.
2. Keep only promising pairs (= survivors).
3. Find tiny factors with trial division in survivors on the algebraic side.

4. Filter survivors once more.
5. **Batch factor** survivors on the rational side.
6. Filter survivors once more.
7. Send them to cofactoring.

4.2 Different Sieves

Inside Cado-NFS sieving, different techniques are used depending on the side and targeted ideals. An overview of these are shown on Table 1.

Small primes, that is primes in $[2, 2^I]$, are sieved using the *small sieve* (the parameter I is the same as the sieving region bound introduced in Sect. 3.4). The small sieve is done in two passes. The first one is approximate, a base L is first picked in order for all values of $log_L norm_i(a, b)$ for all pairs (a, b) to fit in $[0, 255]$. Logs of norms are then rounded to the nearest integer so they fit in an 8-bit integer. This approximation is then sieved by primes from the factor base. Newly found factors are not written next to norms they divide—or their logarithmic approximation—. Instead, every small prime is reduced through log_L to an 8-bit integer as well. This integer is then subtracted to all norms they are a factor of. The approximate information gathered on the first pass is enough to pick survivors. Following this, a second pass, lossless, is done on all small primes but tiny ones. Primes sieved are registered only as factors if ticking a survivor. Tiny factors are found after all sieving is done with trial division.

Primes above 2^I are sieved using a bucket sieving technique, similar to a bucket sort, with one pass for medium-sized (below bkthresh1) and two for larger ones. As opposed to the small sieve, this is lossless.

Table 1. Repartition of sieving algorithms

Factor base range	$[2, 2^I]$	$[2^I,\text{bkthresh1}]$	$[\text{bkthresh1},\text{lim}]$
Sieving algorithm	Small sieve	1-level bucket sieve	2-level bucket sieve

5 Relations Collected During the Factorisation of RSA-250

During the factorization of RSA-250, 8.4G relations were produced in total and were kept after the factorization was completed. We were kindly provided access to this dataset, hereafter denoted as "RSA-250 relations".

The relations are stored in gzipped text files totaling 786 GB (1.5 TB uncompressed), in a straightforward format. Analyzing this dataset enables us to simulate various algorithmic strategies and choose parameters for the proposed improvement without having to run costly exploratory experiments. This process also uncovered minor discrepancies between the actual data and what is announced on the web page of the record[2].

[2] https://gitlab.inria.fr/cado-nfs/records/-/tree/master/rsa250.

This section describes simple statistics about the relations. As a foreword, parsing 780 GB of compressed text data is an interesting "big-data" engineering problem. The relations are spread over many gzipped files. While we could have used off-the-shelf MapReduce-style solutions [11] such as Apache Hadoop or Apache Spark [22] for this purpose, we found it easier to write a collection of multi-threaded C programs that parse the relations and accumulate various statistics. A single file is processed by a single thread—this is imposed by the sequential nature of access to the content gzipped files. This programs reads from the network file system at 370 MB/s and parses about 3.8M relations per second using 32 cores. The whole dataset is then processed in about 40 min.

The special-q range is split in two: the "small" ones (less than 4G) and the "large" ones (greater than 4G), with different algorithmic strategies and different parameters on both ranges. Table 2 shows basic information about the collected relations.

Table 2. Basic statistics about the RSA-250 relations.

	small	large
special-q range	[1G; 4G)	[4G; 12G)
# relations	3.9G	4.5G
Algorithm for the rational side	Sieve	Product tree
Avg. Rational norms (bits), stdev	151.8 ± 2.0	152.6 ± 2.0
Algebraic norms (bits)	283 ± 8.6	288 ± 8.4
$\mathtt{mfb}_1$	111	74

The relation-collection process is controlled by several parameters described in Sect. 4. The most important for our purposes are lim (largest sieved prime), lpb (large prime bound—size of the largest prime allowed in a relation) and mfb (size of the largest residue after sieving). These parameters usually have different values on both sides, and mfb changes over the special-q range. These values can be found on the web page of the record and are summarized in Table 3. The choices of lpb and mfb allow for two large primes on the rational side and three large primes on the algebraic side (this may include the special-q).

Table 3. Parameters used to collect the RSA-250 relations.

Side	0 (rational)	1 (algebraic)
lim	2^{31}	2^{31}
lpb	36	37
mfb	72	111 (small q) or 74 (large q)

It follows that in a collected relation:

- The rational norm (≈ 152 bits) is 2^{36}-smooth, and contains a relatively large part of size $\approx 152 - 72 = 80$ bits which is 2^{31}-smooth.

- The algebraic norm ($\approx$ 285 bits) is 2^{37}-smooth. Over the large special-q range, it contains a relatively large part of size at least $285 - 32 - 74 = 179$ bits which is 2^{31}-smooth.

This is another indication that the norms in the collected relations are *not* uniformly random B-smooth integers. It must be noted in addition that in the "small" special-q range, half of the special-q fall into the range of sieved primes.

5.1   Frequency of Primes

While this is not directly related to our primary objective (improving sieving strategies), we take the opportunity to discuss an interesting phenomenon about the collected relations. Earlier works about structured Gaussian elimination applied to integer factoring (including notably [2,7]), assume that the prime factor p occur with probability $1/p$ in the collected relations, as it would in random integers.

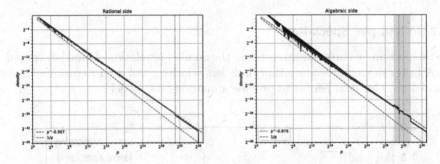

Fig. 5. Density of primes in the RSA-250 relations (log-log scale). The vertical dotted blue line marks the largest sieved prime. The special-q range [1G; 12G) appears in pink. (Color figure online)

The distribution of primes in the RSA-250 relations can be observed in Fig. 5. It is clearly visible that p occurs with frequency $1/p^\alpha$ with $\alpha < 1$. This phenomenon is not surprising; intuitively, smooth numbers should have more small factors than random integers. This can be quantified as follows. Let $\Psi(x, y)$ denote the number of y-smooth integers less than x. Take a y-smooth integers less than x which is a multiple of p; divide it by p; this yields a y-smooth number less than x/p (this is in fact a bijection). It follows that the number of such integers is exactly $\Psi(x/p, y)$.

The probability that a random y-smooth number less than x is divisible by p is therefore $\Psi(x/p, y)/\Psi(x, y)$. Tenenbaum and Hildebrand have shown in 1986 [12, Theorem 3] that $\Psi(cx, y)/\Psi(x, y) \approx c^\alpha$ with $c \leq y$ and α is the unique positive solution of

$$\sum_{p \leq y} \frac{\log p}{p^\alpha - 1} = \log x.$$

It follows that:

$$\frac{\Psi(x/p, y)}{\Psi(x, y)} \approx \frac{1}{p^\alpha}.$$

Because of the "classical" Mertens-like asymptotic evaluation $\sum_{p \le x} (\log p)/(p - 1) = \log x - \gamma + o(1)$ when $x \to +\infty$, the value of α is necessarily less than 1 ($\gamma = 0.56...$ denotes the Euler-Mascheroni constant).

It is shown in [12] that $\alpha = \frac{\log(1 + y/\log x)}{\log y} \left(1 + \mathcal{O}\left(\frac{\log\log y}{\log y}\right)\right)$. This is quite consistent with Fig. 5. When y is large compared to $\log x$, this can be simplified to $\alpha \approx 1 - \log u/(\log y)$, where u is defined as usual as $u := \log x / \log y$, or even to $\alpha \approx 1 - (\log\log x)/(\log y)$. See [10] for more details.

Beyond statistics properties of smooth numbers, the particular algorithm used to collect relations also has visible effects: sieved primes appear more frequently than large primes (slight drop on the right of the dashed vertical blue line). Special-q's appear with a frequency boost because lattice sieving favors relations that contain them. This highlights again that the RSA-250 relations are not uniformly random smooth numbers.

5.2 Yield per Special-q

In this section, we turn our attention to the number of relations found per special-q. A faster sieving procedure that finds less relations will need to examine more special-q's. Our goal here is to provide a quantitative model.

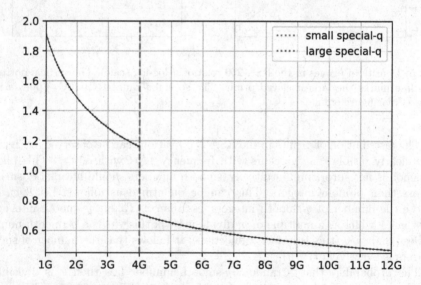

Fig. 6. Density of relations per special-q.

Table 2 shows that the yield is higher for small special-q's: the average "density" of relations is 1.3 for small special-q *versus* 0.56 for large special-q—this means that over a range $[a, b)$ of small special-q's, the average number of relations found is $1.3(b - a)$. Note that this numbers do not account for duplicate relations; the proportion of duplicates is expected to be higher for small special-q's. In total, 70% of these relations are unique.

The sieving parameters are different for small and large special-q's, and this is sufficient to explains a large drop in yield at the transition between the two ranges. However, the number of relations found per special-q decreases with q. Figure 6 shows this well-known phenomenon more precisely. Two causes may account for this.

Firstly, because a special-q contains a prime integer, their density is about $1/\log q$ thanks to the prime number theorem. This means that the density of primes is about 4.5% at for $q = 4G$, and it drops to 4.30% at the end of the special-q range ($q = 12G$). Even if the number of relations found per special-q were strictly constant, the rarefaction of primes would accounts for a 5% drop in the "density" of relations over the large special-q range.

Secondly, as argued in Sect. 3.4, the algebraic norms are less than $\approx 2^{208}p^3$ in the sieved zones, however since the special-q can be taken out, we are left with numbers of size less than $\approx 2^{208}p^2$. It seems plausible that the number of relations collected per special-q is correlated with the probability that integers of this size are 2^{37}-smooth.

The proportion of y-smooth integers between x and $x + dx$ is given by

$$\frac{\Psi(x + dx, y) - \Psi(x, y)}{dx} = \rho(u) + \mathcal{O}\left(\frac{1}{\log x}\right)$$

where $u = (\log x)/(\log y)$ and ρ is the Dickman function—see [15] for details. Let $R(q)$ denote the "density" of relations at this value of q (this is what Fig. 6 shows). Our initial assumption was that $R(q)$ would be correlated with $f(q) = 1/\log(q) \cdot \rho((208 + 2\log_2 q)/37)$. One standard way of visually asserting the quality of this model is to plot the "residues" $R(q)/f(q)$. Figure 7 (left) shows that $R(q)$ decreases faster than this simple model predicts.

However, tinkering a bit shows that a slightly more general model is sufficient. Define $f_\alpha(q) = 1/\log(q) \cdot \rho((208 + \alpha \log_2 q)/37)$; then over the small special-q range, $R(q)$ is about 297M times $f_{2.419245}(q)$ whereas over the large special-q it is about 255M times $f_{2.53737}(q)$. Figure 7 (right) shows that the residues are flat. The values of α given above have been found by dichotomy search with the objective of minimizing the absolute value of the slope of a linear regression performed on $R(q)/f_\alpha(q)$. This model seems empirically good; however we have no explanation as to why values of α greater than 2 (and less than 3) provide a better fit.

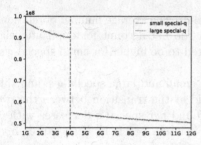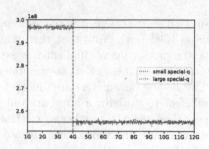

Fig. 7. Residues of potential models of the yield per special-q. Left: $R(q)/f_2(q)$. Right $R(q)/f_{2.419245}(q)$ (small) and $R(q)/f_{2.53737}(q)$ (large).

In any case, this yields a good model of the yield per special-q (it is shown in black in Fig. 6). The multiplicative constants (297M and 255M) accounts for the sieving area, the fact that pairs where a and b are not coprime are discarded, the fact that there is a large 2^{31}-smooth part, etc. With $y = 2^{37}$ and p in $[10^9; 10^{1000}]$, we have $7 \le u \le 8$, where u is again $\log p / \log y$. In this range, $\rho(u)$ can be approximated to good accuracy by a power series. Set $x \leftarrow 2u - 15$ and:

$$10^7 \rho(u) \approx 1.7178674920 - 2.8335703447x + 2.3000577581x^2 - 1.2233613236x^3$$
$$+ 0.47877283118x^4 - 0.14657423350x^5 + 0.036375058464x^6 + \dots$$

If one is willing to commit to these estimates, then they can be used to predict the number of relations that would have been obtained over a larger range of special-q's:

$$\#\text{relations} = 3.9G + \int_{4G}^{q_{\max}} f_{2.53737}(q)dq \tag{1}$$

This can easily be estimated using a generic numerical integration algorithm. Over the range of small special-q, this model overestimates the number of relations found by 8%. However, the quality of the fit over the large special-q range is amazingly good: (1) predicts the actual number of collected relations when $4G \le q \le 12G$ with relative error 0.027%.

This has interesting consequences. For instance, assume that an alternative relation collection procedure runs faster but produces (say) only 50% of the relations compared to the current one; further assume that this proportion remain constant for all special-q's. The above reasoning enables us to venture the following prediction: recovering as many relations will require sieving special-q's up to $\approx 34.5G$. Taking into account the density of primes, the new procedure has to sieve about 2.75× more special-q's. As such, it breaks even if it is at least 2.75× faster than the original. In the same way, a procedure that keeps 85% of the relations will need to sieve almost 3.3G extra special-q's, i.e. do $\approx 26\%$ extra work.

6   Combining Sieving and the Batch Smooth Part Algorithm on the Same Side

During the factorization of RSA-250, sieving and the batch smooth part algorithm described in Sect. 2 were both used—on different sides. In this section, we explore the possibility of using both on the same side. To the best of our knowledge, this has not been tested in practice.

This idea is however not new. In 2002, Bernstein [3] suggested the following strategy:

> Sieve all primes p up through, say, B; throw away the n's whose unfactored part is uncomfortably large; then apply some other method to the n's that remain.

"Some other method" could reasonably be understood as the batch smooth factor algorithm and presented in the very same manuscript, and the faster batch smooth part version described in [4]. The suggestion here is to sieve *only small primes*. A potential advantage is that it would enable the use of a smaller sieve area, thus reducing memory consumption, and/or improving memory locality.

Another option would be to *skip small primes entirely*. Again this is not a new idea; it seems that it was already part of the folklore in 1993:

> Furthermore, one often does not sieve with the small primes below a certain small prime bound [...] [16]

Indeed, small primes have more "hits" and require more time than large ones.

Prime ideals below 2^I—small sieved ones—are of particular interest to speed up the sieving process. Indeed, our intuition is that comparatively more time is spent on small primes to retrieve fewer factor bits than sieving larger primes. In addition, finding the remaining small factors after sieving larger ones would be efficient as their size would be small. That is to say, sieving is more efficient on large primes while batch factoring is more efficient on small ones as it benefits from a smaller factor base.

To discuss these two ideas, we split sieved primes (below lim_i) in two subsets: extra-small primes that are below a certain bound 2^B and medium primes that are above.

1. **Sieve** using either extra-small or medium primes on both sides
2. Keep only promising pairs (= survivors) that have small enough cofactors
3. Use the **Batch smooth part** algorithm on survivors to find extra-small factors on side 1
4. Filter survivors once more on side 1 (discard those with cofactor size greater than mfb_1 bits)
5. Use the **Batch smooth part** algorithm again on survivors to find extra-small factors on side 0
6. Filter survivors again on side 0 (discard those with cofactor size greater than mfb_0 bits)

7. Send survivors to the cofactoring step

We introduce new parameters for intermediate bounds, mfbb0 and mfbb1. After sieving one of the subsets of primes on both sides, a pair (a, b) is considered a survivor in step 2 if the cofactor on side i has less than mfbb_i bits.

6.1 Sieving only Extra-Small Primes

In this section, we try to evaluate the idea of sieving only extra-small primes. This enables the use of a smaller sieve area, which may have some benefits.

We now show that using a "large-ish" sieve region of size $A = 2^{33}$ as was done in the factorization of RSA-250 is indeed not a good strategy. Sieving primes up to 2^{31} with sieve area 2^{33} requires 213 s using a single-thread. Extracting the 2^{31}-smooth part of a single batch of size ≈ 1.5 Gbit requires 270 s. This is the size of about 15M cofactors of size, say, 100 bits. Therefore, rejecting pairs with "uncomfortably large" cofactors should only allow a fraction 0.1746% of all pairs to survive, otherwise applying the batch smooth part algorithm will be slower than sieving altogether. Note that this is a very conservative stance: even a lower proportion could make the combination of sieving + batch smoothness detection slower than just sieving.

For each value of the bound B that delimits the extra-small primes from the medium ones, we exhaustively try all pairs of thresholds mfbb_0 and mfbb_1. For each combination of $(B, \text{mfbb}_0, \text{mfbb}_1)$, we estimate the proportion of pairs that would survive until after step 2 of the procedure above and enter the batch smooth part algorithm. This estimation is done using our collection of "random" pairs from Sect. 3.4. If this proportion is larger than the threshold given above, we reject the set of parameters. Among all valid parameters set, we find the one that preserves the maximum number of relations found during the factorization of RSA-250—this is estimated thanks to the RSA-250 dataset. The result is shown in Table 4.

Looking at Table 4, we are tempted to conclude that the procedure will not be practical. Unless 2^B gets quite close to the actual limit of 2^{31}, the test in step 2 is not precise enough to simultaneously keep the actual relations and discard sufficiently many unpromising (a, b) pairs. Therefore, restricting sieving to a small set of extra-small primes seems bound to discard a significant fraction of potential relations. In turn, as discussed in Sect. 5.2, it seems difficult to be able to break even with pure sieving.

This does not mean that the overall strategy is doomed. In particular, the above reasoning does not rule out the possibility that it could be competitive when used with a *smaller* sieve area. Here, the argument was that if the sieve area is large, then the proportion of pairs that survive the test must be small otherwise their number will overwhelm the batch smoothness detection algorithm. Reducing the sieve area will reduce the number of surviving pairs, and may alleviate this problem.

However, we believe that we have shown that this specific strategy *requires* very different parameters than those used in the factorization of RSA-250. This, in turn, is not surprising.

Table 4. "Optimal" parameters for sieving only extra-small primes with a sieve area of 2^{33}. The fourth column shows the proportion of RSA-250 relations that would survive the process. The fifth column shows the proportion of pairs that survive step 2. The last row of the table describes what was actually done in the factorization of RSA-250.

B	$\mathtt{mfbb_0}$	$\mathtt{mfbb_1}$	% surviving rel.	% surviving pairs
8	123	266	0.5	0.17
9	121	258	0.8	0.17
10	119	253	1.1	0.17
11	115	255	1.6	0.17
12	113	250	2.2	0.17
13	114	239	2.9	0.17
14	112	236	4.0	0.17
15	113	228	5.2	0.17
16	115	220	6.9	0.17
17	118	212	9.2	0.17
18	117	209	12.3	0.17
19	115	207	15.8	0.17
20	113	205	19.1	0.17
21	99	216	25.9	0.17
22	96	215	33.5	0.17
23	96	210	39.8	0.17
24	100	201	48.5	0.17
25	101	195	61.8	0.17
26	99	193	72.3	0.17
27	99	189	76.7	0.17
28	123	168	82.5	0.17
29	103	177	92.6	0.17
30	103	172	98.4	0.17
31	99	155	100.0	0.11

6.2 The Other Way Around: Do Not Sieve Extra-Small Primes

We now turn our attention to the opposite strategy: sieving only the medium primes, on both sides. Extra-small ones are found in a second step using the batch smooth part algorithm. The intuition is that step 1 is the most efficient part of sieving. It gives us a lot of information to decide if a pair is in a good position to be a relation while being very fast. It allows us to remove a good amount of pairs in step 2 before looking for small factors in steps 3 and 5 using the batch smooth part algorithm.

This is bound to be less precise compared to "pure" sieving as it starts filtering pairs earlier, after fewer prime factors have been treated. Ideally, this loss of precision would not lead to too many useless survivors (false positives) nor lost relations (false negatives). The challenge is to find parameters that would make the alternative faster while limiting the loss of relations compared to the original implementation of Cado-NFS.

We essentially had a dual approach: we imposed a proportion of RSA-250 relations that must survive the whole procedure. For each value of the bound B that delimits extra-small primes (not sieved) and medium primes, we exhaustively try all pairs of thresholds $\mathtt{mfbb_0}$ and $\mathtt{mfbb_1}$. For each combination of $(B, \mathtt{mfbb_0}, \mathtt{mfbb_1})$, we estimate the fraction of RSA-250 relations that would be found. If this proportion is too low, we discard the parameters. Note that if $(\mathtt{mfbb_0}, \mathtt{mfbb_1})$ is valid, then so does $(\mathtt{mfbb_0} + u, \mathtt{mfbb_1} + v)$. Among all valid parameter sets, we single out the ones that minimize the proportion of surviving pairs at the end of step 2. The results can be seen in Fig. 8.

In light of the discussion in Sect. 5.2, we focus on high proportions of preserved RSA-250 relations. In addition, one particularly relevant choice of B is $B = 17$, as it means that the "small sieve" can be completely disabled (only bucket sieving remains). Reasonable parameters set are shown in Table 5.

7   Experiments and Practical Results

We implemented the strategy discussed in Sect. 6.2 inside Cado-NFS. This has been a non-trivial programming effort, as this required modifying a complex program made of 29K lines of C++ code spread over nearly 50 files.

The modifications we performed can be summarized as follows:

- We altered the piece of code that holds the factor base for sieving to remove primes less than 2^B, where B is a new command-line parameter. We also inserted there a precomputation of the product of extra-small prime factors.
- The sieve area is divided into "sieve regions" of size about 64 KB. We altered the piece of code that fully processes a sieve region. The original searches "survivors" (cofactor of less than $\mathtt{mfb_i}$ bits) after sieving and launches an asynchronous cofactorization task for each surviving pair. We inserted a modified survivor detection procedure using the new $\mathtt{mfbb_i}$ parameters; the extra-small primes factors of survivors are recovered by the batch smooth part algorithm; then pairs are fed back to the preexisting mechanism.

Our implementation is not particularly well optimised. In particular, because we operate inside a single sieve region, we may or may not have enough survivors to completely fill one batch. Regardless of its performance, the sheer availability of our implementation enabled us to empirically validate the results of the simulations presented in Fig. 8 and in Table 5.

Actual performance results are shown in Figs. 9 and 10. With $B = 17$ (*i.e.* disabling the small sieve entirely), our code manages to get faster than the original Cado-NFS implementation, while targeting 85% or 90% of the RSA-250 relations. The figures strongly suggest that $B = 17$ is the optimal choice.

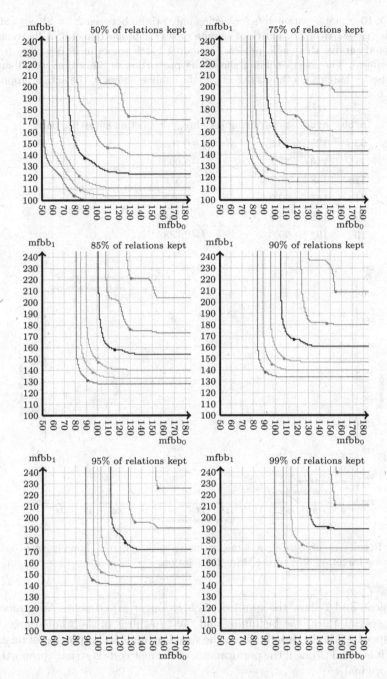

Fig. 8. Possible choices of mfbb$_0$ and mfbb$_1$ that preserve the given fraction of RSA-250 relations. Sieving all primes between 2^i and 2^{31} with $i = 10$ (red), $i = 12$ (green), $i = 14$ (orange), $i = 17$ (black), $i = 20$ (cyan) and $i = 24$ (olive). The big dot shows the values that minimize the proportion of pairs that survive step 2. (Color figure online)

Table 5. Reasonable parameters for sieving only primes between $2^B = 2^{17}$ and $\text{lim}_i = 2^{31}$ with a sieve area of 2^{33}. The third column shows the proportion of RSA-250 relations that would survive the whole process (including batch smoothness detection to find small primes). The fourth column shows the proportion of pairs that would survive step 2, before batch smoothness detection (the column shows x, the actual proportion is 10^x).

mfbb$_0$	mfbb$_1$	% surviving rel.	$\log_{10}$ proportion surviving pairs
93	135	50.3	-6.165
115	146	75.1	-5.063
116	158	85.0	-4.556
117	167	90.0	-4.233
125	178	95.0	-3.568
136	192	99.0	-2.788

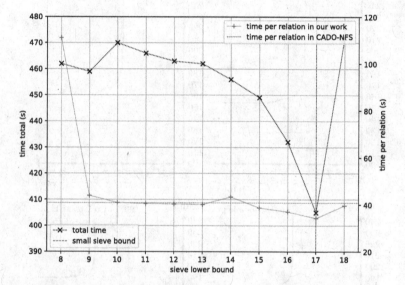

Fig. 9. Results of processing a large special-q with different bounds with optimal parameters targeting 85% of the RSA-250 relations

Tables 6 and 7 show the result of slightly longer experiments. We processed several special-q near the beginning and the two-thirds of the whole range. The "local speedup" is the ratio between the speed-up and the proportion of relations found (it is equal to one if the performance of the new code is strictly proportional to the original).

The observed speed-up may seem modest; we nevertheless consider it a significant achievement in view of the fact that Cado-NFS is a complex, highly optimized piece of code that holds the current computational record.

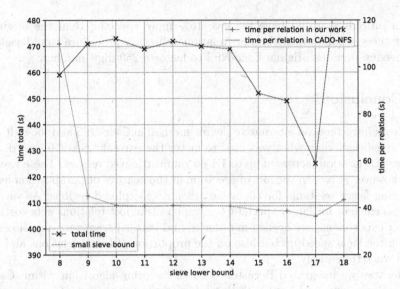

Fig. 10. Results of processing a large special-q with different bounds with optimal parameters targeting 90% of the RSA-250 relations

Table 6. Results when processing 34 special-q's in the range [8204724066, 8204725068].

B	mfbb$_0$	mfbb$_1$	# relations found	× original	Time (s)	× original	local speed-up
Original Cado-NFS			390	–	8619	–	–
17	89	137	232	0.59	6589	0.76	0.78
17	108	143	328	0.84	6691	0.78	1.08
17	111	147	347	0.89	6940	0.81	1.10
17	114	152	361	0.93	7292	0.85	1.09
17	116	158	367	0.94	7450	0.86	1.09
17	117	167	371	0.95	8088	0.94	1.01

Table 7. Results when processing 25 special-q's in the range [2500000000, 2500000500].

B	mfbb$_0$	mfbb$_1$	# relations found	× original	Time (s)	× original	local speed-up
Original Cado-NFS			674	–	6942	–	–
17	114	152	519	0.77	5242	0.76	1.02
17	116	158	561	0.83	5442	0.78	1.06
17	117	167	606	0.90	5684	0.82	1.10
17	125	178	646	0.96	7558	1.01	0.88
17	148	191	667	0.99	20077	2.89	0.34

Tables 6 and 7 hints at the possibility of collecting 90% of the relations found by the "original" Cado-NFS, in roughly 82% of the time. Assume that this is feasible over the whole special-q range. According to the estimate given in Sect. 5.2, such a procedure would have to sieve 16% more special-q than the original. Under these assumptions, the new relation collection procedure would yield a 5% speedup over the original Cado-NFS to factor a 250-digit number.

8 Conclusion

This work introduces an alternative sieving method in Cado-NFS and shows it can be more efficient than what was used to factor the current RSA-250 record. We achieve acceleration factors of up to 1.1 on sampled sieved regions. These results come however at a cost: the loss of precision at the heart of our proposition leads to finding fewer relations for the same amount of explored regions. As sieving gets less efficient for larger special-q's, compensating lost relations gets costlier. Further experiments are needed in order to find better parameters, focusing not only on the local speed-up but also on the proportion of found relations and the added work they imply.

The way we integrated Bernstein's batch factoring algorithm within Cado-NFS sieving might not be optimal. Batch factoring happens twice for each sieved region, once on each side. It is more efficient to fill one batch. In our implementation, this is however usually not the case on the first side (algebraic) and far from it on the second side (rational) as most norms are discarded between both steps. Dissociating batch factoring from sieved regions might then lead to further acceleration.

We showed experiments on the bound B separating sieved primes and those in batch factoring. We have yet to try experimenting different bounds for each side (B_0 and B_1) although it appears disabling entirely the small sieve for both sides, as we did, is the straightforward approach.

Finally, data collected during RSA-250 allowed us to draw early conclusions to pick optimal parameters such as mfbb0 and mfbb1 for each targeted proportion of relations. This brings us closer to an answer to the question "would the RSA-250 record have been beaten quicker using our alternative?". Exploring parameters for yet-to-be factored sized numbers would bring an answer to the more interesting one "will the next RSA record be faster with it?".

Acknowledgments. We are indebted to Régis de la Bretèche for pointing us to the results that are the basis of Sect. 5.1. We also thank the authors of [6] for giving us access to the relations collected during the factorization of RSA-250, as well as answering our many questions.

We acknowledge financial support from the French Agence Nationale de la Recherche under projects "GORILLA" (ANR-20-CE39-0002) and "KLEPTOMA-NIAC" (ANR-21-CE39-0008-02).

Experiments presented in this paper were carried out using the Grid'5000 testbed, supported by a scientific interest group hosted by Inria and including CNRS, RENATER and several Universities as well as other organizations (see https://www.grid5000.fr).

References

1. Aoki, K., Ueda, H.: Sieving using bucket sort. In: Lee, P.J. (ed.) Advances in Cryptology - ASIACRYPT 2004, 10th International Conference on the Theory and Application of Cryptology and Information Security, Jeju Island, Korea, 5–9 December 2004, Proceedings. LNCS, vol. 3329, pp. 92–102. Springer, Cham (2004). https://doi.org/10.1007/978-3-540-30539-2_8

2. Bender, E.A., Canfield, E.: An approximate probabilistic model for structured Gaussian elimination. J. Algorithms **31**(2), 271–290 (1999). https://doi.org/10.1006/jagm.1999.1008

3. Bernstein, D.J.: How to find small factors of integers, September 2002. https://cr.yp.to/papers.html#sf, (Apparenly) unpublished manuscript

4. Bernstein, D.J.: How to find smooth parts of integers, May 2004. https://cr.yp.to/papers.html#smoothparts, unpublished manuscript

5. Bernstein, D.J.: Scaled remainder trees, August 2004. https://cr.yp.to/papers.html#scaledmod, unpublished manuscript

6. Boudot, F., Gaudry, P., Guillevic, A., Heninger, N., Thomé, E., Zimmermann, P.: Comparing the difficulty of factorization and discrete logarithm: a 240-digit experiment. In: Micciancio, D., Ristenpart, T. (eds.) Advances in Cryptology - CRYPTO 2020–40th Annual International Cryptology Conference, CRYPTO 2020, Santa Barbara, CA, USA, 17–21 August 2020, Proceedings, Part II. LNCS, vol. 12171, pp. 62–91. Springer, Cham (2020). https://doi.org/10.1007/978-3-030-56880-1_3

7. Bouillaguet, C., Zimmermann, P.: Parallel structured Gaussian elimination for the number field sieve. Math. Cryptol. **0**(1), 22–39 (2021). https://journals.flvc.org/mathcryptology/article/view/126033

8. Buhler, J.P., Lenstra, H.W., Pomerance, C.: Factoring integers with the number field sieve. In: Lenstra, A.K., Lenstra, H.W. (eds.) The development of the number field sieve. LNM, vol. 1554, pp. 50–94. Springer, Heidelberg (1993). https://doi.org/10.1007/BFb0091539

9. Buhler, J., Stevenhagen, P.: Algorithmic Number Theory: Lattices, Number Fields, Curves and Cryptography. Mathematical Sciences Research Institute Publications, Cambridge University Press (2011)

10. De La Bretèche, R., Tenenbaum, G.: Propriétés statistiques des entiers friables. Ramanujan J. **9**, 139–202 (2005). https://doi.org/10.1007/s11139-005-0832-6

11. Dean, J., Ghemawat, S.: MapReduce: simplified data processing on large clusters. Commun. ACM **51**(1), 107–113 (2008). https://doi.org/10.1145/1327452.1327492

12. Hildebrand, A., Tenenbaum, G.: On integers free of large prime factors. Trans. Am. Math. Soc. **296** (1986). https://doi.org/10.2307/2000573

13. Joux, A.: Algorithmic Cryptanalysis. CRC Press, Boca Raton (2009)

14. Kleinjung, T., et al.: Factorization of a 768-bit RSA modulus. In: Rabin, T. (ed.) Advances in Cryptology - CRYPTO 2010, 30th Annual Cryptology Conference, Santa Barbara, CA, USA, 15–19 August 2010, Proceedings. LNCS, vol. 6223, pp. 333–350. Springer, Cham (2010). https://doi.org/10.1007/978-3-642-14623-7_18, https://doi.org/10.1007/978-3-642-14623-7

15. Kruppa, A.: Speeding up integer multiplication and factorization. Theses, Université Henri Poincaré - Nancy 1, January 2010. https://theses.hal.science/tel-01748662

16. Lenstra, A.K., Lenstra, H.W., Manasse, M.S., Pollard, J.M.: The number field sieve. In: Lenstra, A.K., Lenstra, H.W. (eds.) The Development of the Number Field Sieve, pp. 11–42. Springer, Heidelberg (1993)

17. Marcus, D.: Number Fields. Universitext, Springer, New York (2012). https://doi.org/10.1007/978-1-4684-9356-6
18. Montgomery, P.L.: Square roots of products of algebraic numbers. In: Gautschi, W. (ed.) Mathematics of Computation 1943–1993: A Half-Century of Computational Mathematics, pp. 567–571. American Mathematical Society, Providence (1994)
19. Pollard, J.M.: The lattice sieve. In: Lenstra, A.K., Lenstra, H.W. (eds.) The development of the number field sieve. LNM, vol. 1554, pp. 43–49. Springer, Heidelberg (1993). https://doi.org/10.1007/BFb0091538
20. The CADO-NFS Development Team: CADO-NFS, an implementation of the number field sieve algorithm (2017). https://gitlab.inria.fr/cado-nfs/cado-nfs, release 2.3.0
21. Vallée, B., Vera, A.: Probabilistic analyses of lattice reduction algorithms. In: Nguyen, P.Q., Vallée, B. (eds.) The LLL Algorithm - Survey and Applications, pp. 71–143. Information Security and Cryptography. Springer, Cham (2010). https://doi.org/10.1007/978-3-642-02295-1_3
22. Zaharia, M., et al.: Apache spark: a unified engine for big data processing. Commun. ACM **59**(11), 56–65 (2016). https://doi.org/10.1145/2934664

Exploiting the Symmetry of $\mathbb{Z}^n$: Randomization and the Automorphism Problem

Kaijie Jiang[1], Anyu Wang[1,5,6(✉)], Hengyi Luo[2,3], Guoxiao Liu[4], Yang Yu[1,5,6], and Xiaoyun Wang[1,5,6,7,8]

[1] Institute for Advanced Study, BNRist, Tsinghua University, Beijing, China
jkj21@mails.tsinghua.edu.cn,
{anyuwang,yu-yang,xiaoyunwang}@tsinghua.edu.cn
[2] Key Laboratory of Mathematics Mechanization, Academy of Mathematics and Systems Science, Chinese Academy of Sciences, Beijing, China
luohengyi23@mails.ucas.ac.cn
[3] School of Mathematical Sciences, University of Chinese Academy of Sciences, Beijing, China
[4] Institute for Network Sciences and Cyberspace, Tsinghua University, Beijing, China
lgx22@mails.tsinghua.edu.cn
[5] Zhongguancun Laboratory, Beijing, China
[6] National Financial Cryptography Research Center, Beijing, China
[7] Shandong Institute of Blockchain, Jinan, China
[8] Key Laboratory of Cryptologic Technology and Information Security (Ministry of Education), School of Cyber Science and Technology, Shandong University, Qingdao, China

Abstract. $\mathbb{Z}^n$ is one of the simplest types of lattices, but the computational problems on its rotations, such as $\mathbb{Z}$SVP and $\mathbb{Z}$LIP, have been of great interest in cryptography. Recent advances have been made in building cryptographic primitives based on these problems, as well as in developing new algorithms for solving them. However, the theoretical complexity of $\mathbb{Z}$SVP and $\mathbb{Z}$LIP are still not well understood.

In this work, we study the problems on rotations of $\mathbb{Z}^n$ by exploiting the symmetry property. We introduce a randomization framework that can be roughly viewed as 'applying random automorphisms' to the output of an oracle, without accessing the automorphism group. Using this framework, we obtain new reduction results for rotations of $\mathbb{Z}^n$. First, we present a reduction from $\mathbb{Z}$LIP to $\mathbb{Z}$SCVP. Here $\mathbb{Z}$SCVP is the problem of finding the shortest characteristic vectors, which is a special case of CVP where the target vector is a deep hole of the lattice. Moreover, we prove a reduction from $\mathbb{Z}$SVP to γ-$\mathbb{Z}$SVP for any constant $\gamma = O(1)$ in the same dimension, which implies that $\mathbb{Z}$SVP is as hard as its approximate version for any constant approximation factor. Second, we investigate the problem of finding a nontrivial automorphism for a given lattice, which is called LAP. Specifically, we use the randomization framework to show that $\mathbb{Z}$LAP is as hard as $\mathbb{Z}$LIP. We note that our result can be viewed as a $\mathbb{Z}^n$-analogue of Lenstra and Silverberg's result in [JoC2017], but with

© International Association for Cryptologic Research 2023
J. Guo and R. Steinfeld (Eds.): ASIACRYPT 2023, LNCS 14441, pp. 167–200, 2023.
https://doi.org/10.1007/978-981-99-8730-6_6

a different assumption: they assume the G-lattice structure, while we assume the access to an oracle that outputs a nontrivial automorphism.

Keywords: Lattice automorphism · Randomized reduction · $\mathbb{Z}$LIP · Gradient descent · Characteristic vectors of the unimodular lattice

1   Introduction

Lattices are fundamental mathematical concept that represent discrete additive subgroups of $\mathbb{R}^m$. A lattice is usually defined by a set of n linearly independent basis vectors $\mathbf{b}_1, \mathbf{b}_2, \ldots, \mathbf{b}_n \in \mathbb{R}^m$, such that any point in the lattice can be expressed as an integer linear combination of the basis vectors. Lattices offer a rich geometric structure that can be used to define various computationally hard problems. Two of the famous problems are the *Shortest Vector Problem* (SVP), which involves finding the shortest non-zero vector in a given lattice, and the *Closest Vector Problem* (CVP), which involves finding the lattice point closest to a given target point. Both of these problems are known to be NP-hard, and their theoretical complexity and solving algorithms have been extensively studied [1,5, 8,10]. In recent decades, lattices have played a crucial role in cryptography, with numerous cryptographic schemes being constructed based on the lattice-related computationally hard problems [45].

In addition to SVP and CVP, there are also other important lattice-related problems that have gained considerable attention. One such problem is the *Lattice Isomorphism Problem* (LIP). Two lattices $\mathcal{L}_1$ and $\mathcal{L}_2$ are said to be isomorphic if there exists an orthogonal transformation that maps $\mathcal{L}_1$ to $\mathcal{L}_2$. The LIP is to find such an orthogonal transformation given the lattice bases of $\mathcal{L}_1$ and $\mathcal{L}_2$. Research on the LIP dates back to the 1990s, with the development of algorithms for solving low-dimensional LIP [46]. Then a subsequent work studies the asymptotic complexity of LIP and proves that LIP is at least as hard as the *Graph Isomorphism Problem* (GIP) [50]. In [28], Haviv and Regev propose an $n^{O(n)}$-time algorithm for the general LIP, which remains the fastest known algorithm for solving LIP. There are also works that study LIP from different perspectives. Sikirić et al. [21] demonstrate that with access to an SVP oracle, an LIP instance can be converted to a GIP instance. Although GIP has a quasi-polynomial time algorithm as shown in [7], the worst-case number of shortest vectors may be exponential, which can lead to a potentially exponential-sized graph in [21]. Recently, Ducas and Gibbons have adapted the notion of the hull of a code and showed that it could be used to launch geometric attacks on certain special lattices [17]. Another line of research focuses on constructing cryptographic schemes based on the LIP. The proposed schemes include public-key encryption, signature, key encapsulation mechanism, and identification [9,18,19]. Notably, the security of some of these schemes relies on a special case of the LIP, i.e., the $\mathbb{Z}$LIP.

The $\mathbb{Z}$LIP involves finding an orthogonal transformation that maps $\mathbb{Z}^n$ to $\mathcal{L}$, provided that $\mathcal{L}$ is isomorphic to $\mathbb{Z}^n$. Initially, the $\mathbb{Z}$LIP is studied for cryptanalysis purposes of GGH [26] and NTRUSign [30]. In [25], Gentry and Szydlo extract the secret key of NTRUSign by solving an special form of the $\mathbb{Z}$LIP, i.e., solving a structured $\mathbf{U}$ from its Gram matrix $\mathbf{G} = \mathbf{U}^\top \mathbf{U}$ up to a signed permutation. Then Nguyen and Regev propose an alternative method for GGH by tackling a learning a parallelepiped problem using gradient descent [43]. Additionally, an in-depth analysis of the algorithm proposed by Gentry and Szydlo is provided in [32,33]. For the theoretic complexity of $\mathbb{Z}$LIP, Szydlo [53] provides a reduction from search $\mathbb{Z}$LIP to decision LIP, and results from [31] suggest that $\mathbb{Z}$LIP is in co-NP. On the other hand, solving algorithms and experiments for $\mathbb{Z}$LIP are proposed in [11,23]. Recent progress has also been made in [20], where Ducas provides a reduction from n-dimensional $\mathbb{Z}$LIP to $\frac{n}{2}$-dimensional SVP. Plugging in the fastest known algorithm for SVP from [2], it results in a $2^{n/2}$-time algorithm for $\mathbb{Z}$LIP. In addition, Bennett et al. [9] provide a reduction from $\mathbb{Z}$SVP to $O(1)$-uSVP, which leads a $2^{n/2}$ time algorithm for $\mathbb{Z}$SVP. Due to the well-known reduction from $\mathbb{Z}$LIP to $\mathbb{Z}$SVP, the results of [9] imply a reduction from $\mathbb{Z}$LIP to $O(1)$-uSVP and a $2^{n/2}$-time algorithm for $\mathbb{Z}$LIP.

1.1 Our Results and Techniques

The basis observation of this work is that $\mathbb{Z}^n$ (and its rotations) possesses a remarkable degree of symmetry. For a lattice $\mathcal{L}$ isomorphic to $\mathbb{Z}^n$, the automorphism group $\mathrm{Aut}(\mathcal{L})$ is isomorphic to the signed permutation group $\mathcal{S}_n^{\pm}$ (see Sect. 2), which is known to be the largest possible for any lattice in $\mathbb{R}^n$ when $n > 10$.[1] Leveraging this powerful property of symmetry, we delve into the $\mathbb{Z}$LIP and focus on two key questions, i.e.,

Q1: *Can the symmetry be used to assist in the solving or the reduction of the computational problems associated with $\mathbb{Z}^n$?*

Q2: *Is it feasible to efficiently obtain a nontrivial automorphism for a lattice isomorphic to $\mathbb{Z}^n$?*

Centered on these two questions, we present the following results.

A Randomization Framework. To address the first question, we provide a *randomization framework*, which can be roughly viewed as 'applying random automorphisms' in $\mathrm{Aut}(\mathcal{L})$ to the output of an oracle, without knowing the specific elements in $\mathrm{Aut}(\mathcal{L})$. The framework utilizes the fact the $\mathrm{Aut}(\mathcal{L})$ is a subgroup of the orthogonal group $O_n(\mathbb{R})$, and the latter can be efficiently sampled uniformly at random.[2] The following toy example illustrates how the randomization framework operates.

---

[1] In fact, the signed permutation group $\mathcal{S}_n^{\pm}$ is the largest possible automorphism group among all lattices in $\mathbb{R}^n$, with the exception of dimensions $n = 2, 4, 6, 7, 8, 9, 10$ [44].

[2] Strictly speaking, we can efficiently generate matrices in $O_n(\mathbb{R})$ distributed with Haar measure. We refer to Sect. 3 for a detailed discussion.

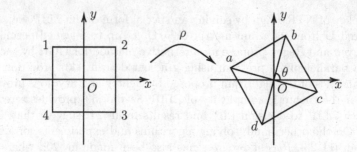

Denote the square on the left-hand side as $\Box_0$, and define $G = \mathbb{R}/(2\pi\mathbb{Z})$. Consider the action of G on $\Box_0$ as rotations, i.e., $\rho(\Box_0) = \Box_\rho, \forall \rho \in G$, where $\Box_\rho$ is the rotation of $\Box_0$ around the origin O by ρ. In terms of rotations, the automorphism group of $\Box_0$ can be expressed as $\mathrm{Aut}(\Box_0) = \frac{\pi}{2}\mathbb{Z}_4$, which is a subgroup of $G = \mathbb{R}/(2\pi\mathbb{Z})$. We assume there is an oracle $\mathcal{O}$ that takes as input any $\Box_\rho$ and outputs an arbitrary vertex of $\Box_\rho$. The oracle does not know the specific rotation ρ and the correspondence of the vertices between $\Box_0$ and $\Box_\rho$. Next, we show how the randomization framework can obtain random vertices of $\Box_0$ without accessing $\mathrm{Aut}(\Box_0)$. Specifically, the randomization framework 1) generates a $\rho \in G$ uniformly at random; 2) invokes the oracle $\mathcal{O}$ with input $\rho(\Box_0) = \Box_\rho$ and obtains an arbitrary vertex of $\Box_\rho$; 3) applies ρ^{-1} to the obtained vertex and outputs a vertex of $\Box_0$. Using the randomness of ρ, it can be proved that the obtained vertex is uniformly distributed with respect to the action of $\mathrm{Aut}(\Box_0)$ (see Appendix A).

The randomization framework for lattices generalizes the above example. Specifically, given a lattice $\mathcal{L}$ and an oracle defined for any rotations of $\mathcal{L}$, the framework randomizes the oracle's output such that the resulting samples follow a distribution that is invariant under the action of $\mathrm{Aut}(\mathcal{L})$. Another challenge should be addressed by the randomization framework is how to 'conceal' the information of the random orthogonal matrix from the oracle's input. This is achieved by using the method introduced in [9,19,28], which samples a basis via a discrete Gaussian distribution.

New Reduction Results for $\mathbb{Z}$LIP. The randomization framework enables us to derive new reduction results for $\mathbb{Z}$LIP or $\mathbb{Z}$SVP.

Theorem 1.1. *There is an efficient randomized reduction from $\mathbb{Z}$LIP to $\mathbb{Z}$SCVP.*

In Theorem 1.1, we introduce a new problem, $\mathbb{Z}$SCVP, which requires finding the shortest characteristic vector of a given lattice $\mathcal{L} \cong \mathbb{Z}^n$. We note that the set of characteristic vectors forms a coset $\mathbf{w} + 2\mathcal{L}$, and a characteristic vector can be efficiently computed for a given basis (see Lemma 2.6). Thus $\mathbb{Z}$SCVP can be viewed as a CVP in the lattice $2\mathcal{L}$. Previous studies on $\mathbb{Z}$LIP mainly focused on reductions to SVP or its variants [9,18,20]. To the best of our knowledge, Theorem 1.1 is the first direct reduction from $\mathbb{Z}$LIP to CVP. Moreover, $\mathbb{Z}$SCVP is a very special case of CVP, where the target vector is a deep hole in the lattice $2\mathcal{L}$.

We believe this is a non-trivial observation that could facilitate further research on $\mathbb{Z}$LIP, as finding or verifying a deep hole for a lattice is generally hard [27].

The proof of Theorem 1.1 relies on the fact that $\text{Aut}(\mathcal{L})$ acts transitively on the set of shortest characteristic vectors. This allows us to sample uniformly from this set using the randomization framework. Then we can show that with polynomial many samples, we can efficiently find the shortest vectors of $\mathcal{L}$ by using the gradient descent method adopted in [43].

Theorem 1.2. *For any constant* $\gamma = O(1)$, *there is an efficient randomized reduction from* $\mathbb{Z}SVP$ *to* γ-$\mathbb{Z}SVP$ *in the same dimension.*

Theorem 1.2 shows that $\mathbb{Z}$SVP is as hard as its approximate version for any constant approximation factor. Plugging the best known algorithm for $O(1)$-SVP in [6, 39] gives a $2^{0.802n}$-time algorithm for $\mathbb{Z}$SVP. However, γ-$\mathbb{Z}$SVP is a special case of γ-SVP, so a more efficient algorithm for $\mathbb{Z}$SVP might exist if we can exploit its special structure, which can be an open problem for future research.

The proof of Theorem 1.2 relies on an analysis of the orbits of the vectors in $\mathcal{L} \cap \gamma \mathcal{B}_2^n$ under the action of $\text{Aut}(\mathcal{L})$. We show that we can sample uniformly from one orbit using the randomization framework. The shortest vectors can then be obtained by doing pairwise subtraction on a polynomial number of vectors in the same orbit.

The Lattice Automorphism Problem. To answer the second question, we introduce a new problem, $\mathbb{Z}$LAP, which requires finding a nontrivial automorphism in $\text{Aut}(\mathcal{L})$. Our main result is the following reduction.

Theorem 1.3. *There is an efficient randomized reduction from* $\mathbb{Z}LIP$ *to* $\mathbb{Z}LAP$.

According to Theorem 1.3, it has $\mathbb{Z}\text{LIP} \leq \mathbb{Z}\text{LAP}$. On the other hand, a simple deduction gives $\mathbb{Z}\text{LAP} \leq \mathbb{Z}\text{LIP}$ by using Lemma 2.8. Therefore, we can conclude that $\mathbb{Z}\text{LAP} = \mathbb{Z}\text{LIP}$ with respect to the randomized reduction.

The key idea to prove Theorem 1.3 is still to use the randomization framework to sample automorphisms for a lattice $\mathcal{L} \cong \mathbb{Z}^n$, such that they are uniformly distributed with respect to the conjugate action of $\text{Aut}(\mathcal{L})$. However, the number of conjugacy classes of $\text{Aut}(\mathcal{L})$ is exponential in n, which makes direct application of the randomization framework inefficient. To overcome this, we devise a preprocessing method and a two-level randomization technique, which effectively transform the automorphisms into some specific conjugacy classes, while maintaining the uniformity. Then our problem turns to how to use these random automorphisms to recover the shortest vectors of $\mathcal{L}$. To solve this problem, we consider the distribution of $\langle \mathbf{x}, \phi\mathbf{x} \rangle$ for a random automorphism ϕ uniformly distributed over a conjugacy class and a fixed $\mathbf{x} \in \mathbb{R}^n$. This distribution captures the geometric information of the automorphisms, and we show that the shortest vectors of $\mathcal{L}$ can be recovered from this distribution using the gradient descent method.

Additionally, we can use the hardness of $\mathbb{Z}$LAP to link $\mathbb{Z}$LIP with the hidden subgroup problem (HSP) on $GL_n(\mathbb{Z})$. To see this, let $\mathcal{L}$ be a lattice with a basis $\mathbf{B}$. Then $\mathrm{Aut}(\mathcal{L})$ is isomorphic to the stabilizer group $\mathrm{Stab}(\mathbf{G})$, where $\mathbf{G} = \mathbf{B}^\top\mathbf{B}$. Hence, LAP of $\mathcal{L}$ is equivalent to finding a nontrivial element in $\mathrm{Stab}(\mathbf{G})$ (see Lemma 2.9). Since $\mathrm{Stab}(\mathbf{G})$ is a subgroup of $GL_n(\mathbb{Z})$, we can formulate a corresponding HSP on $GL_n(\mathbb{Z})$. By Theorem 1.3, we eventually obtain the following result. The only previous relation between lattice problems and HSP that we are aware of is due to Regev [47], who shows that HSP on the dihedral group is harder than $\sqrt{n}$-uSVP.

Corollary 1.1. *There exists an efficient randomized reduction from $\mathbb{Z}$LIP to a variant of HSP on $GL_n(\mathbb{Z})$.*

1.2   Related Works

Reduction from $\mathbb{Z}$SVP to Approximate SVP. In [9], Bennet et al. present a reduction from $\mathbb{Z}$SVP to γ-uSVP for any constant $\gamma = O(1)$ using lattice sparsification techniques [34,51]. They also propose a simple projection-based reduction from $\mathbb{Z}$SVP to $\sqrt{2}$-SVP, and suggest that this result may be extended to a more general case. Our result in Theorem 1.2 provides a different perspective on the reduction from $\mathbb{Z}$SVP to approximate SVP, and includes the $\sqrt{2}$-SVP result in [9] as a special case.

Graph Automorphism Problem (GAP). The GAP, which requires to find a generating set of the automorphism group of a given graph,[3] is a well-studied problem that has a close connection to the GIP. It is known that GAP and GIP are computationally equivalent [40]. Our result shows that $\mathbb{Z}$LIP and $\mathbb{Z}$LAP are also equivalent in the sense of randomized reduction. For general lattices, we further prove that LAP $\leq$ LIP (Corollary 4.2), while the reverse direction remains open.

LIP for G-Lattices. In [33], Lenstra and Silverberg investigate the isomorphism problem between a G-lattice and $\mathbb{Z}\langle G\rangle = \mathbb{Z}[G]/(u+1)$, where G is a finite abelian group containing an element u of order 2. A G-lattice is defined as a lattice $\mathcal{L}$ equipped with a homomorphism $f : G \to \mathrm{Aut}(\mathcal{L})$ such that $f(u) = -1$. The authors propose a deterministic polynomial time algorithm for solving the isomorphism problem between a G-lattice and $\mathbb{Z}\langle G\rangle$. Our results on LAP can be viewed as a $\mathbb{Z}^n$-analogue of Lenstra and Silverberg's result, but there are two key differences. Firstly, Lenstra and Silverberg's algorithm assumes the G-lattice structure, whereas in our reduction we assume access to an oracle that returns an arbitrary nontrivial automorphism. Secondly, they focus on deterministic algorithms, where we employ a randomization framework that produces randomized reductions.

---

[3] This differs slightly from our definition of LAP, which only asks to find a nontrivial automorphism. We remark that for $\mathbb{Z}$LAP, finding a nontrivial automorphism and finding a generating set of the automorphism group are equivalent by Theorem 1.3.

1.3   Outline

The rest of the paper is organized as follows. Section 2 provides basic definitions and preliminaries. In Sect. 3, we present the randomization framework and use it to prove Theorem 1.1 and Theorem 1.2, along with some corollaries. In Sect. 4, we show the proof of Theorem 1.3 and some corollaries. Section 5 concludes the paper.

2   Preliminary

2.1   Notations

- Matrices and column vectors are denoted by bold letters, such as $\mathbf{A}$ and $\mathbf{a}$. For a matrix $\mathbf{A} = (\mathbf{a}_1, \dots, \mathbf{a}_n)$ we denote its Gram-Schmidt orthogonalisation by $\tilde{\mathbf{A}} = (\tilde{\mathbf{a}}_1, \dots, \tilde{\mathbf{a}}_n)$. The Euclidean norm of $\mathbf{a} \in \mathbb{R}^n$ is denoted by $\|\mathbf{a}\|$. The transpose of $\mathbf{A}$ is denoted by $\mathbf{A}^\top$, and $(\mathbf{A}^{-1})^\top$ is abbreviated as $\mathbf{A}^{-\top}$.
- Let $[n] = \{1, 2, \dots, n\}$ for a positive integer n. The size of a finite set A is denoted by $|A|$. For $a, b \in \mathbb{Z}$, $a \mid b$ means that b is divisible by a.
- Let $GL_n(\mathbb{R})$ and $GL_n(\mathbb{Z})$ be the general linear group of rank n over $\mathbb{R}$ and $\mathbb{Z}$ respectively. We use $O_n(\mathbb{R})$ to represent the group of orthogonal matrices $\mathbf{O} \in GL_n(\mathbb{R})$ such that $\mathbf{O}^\top \mathbf{O} = \mathbf{I}_n$, where $\mathbf{I}_n$ is the identity matrix.
- For a matrix $\mathbf{B} \in GL_n(\mathbb{R})$, we denote $\mathcal{L}(\mathbf{B})$ as the lattice generated by $\mathbf{B}$. We denote the standard basis of $\mathbb{Z}^n$ as $\{\mathbf{e}_i\}_{i \in [n]}$. We use $\mathcal{L}_1 \cong \mathcal{L}_2$ to represent that two lattices $\mathcal{L}_1$ and $\mathcal{L}_2$ are isomorphic.
- We denote the group of permutation matrices of size $n \times n$ as $\mathcal{S}_n$, and denote the group of signed permutation matrices of size $n \times n$ as $\mathcal{S}_n^{\pm}$, where a signed permutation matrix is a type of generalized permutation matrix, where the nonzero entries are ± 1. We use $\mathbf{P}_n$ to represent the permutation matrix $\left(\begin{smallmatrix} 0 & 1 \\ \mathbf{I}_{n-1} & 0 \end{smallmatrix} \right)$. For two groups G and H, we use $H \leq G$ to represent H is a subgroup of G.

2.2   Lattice and Related

A lattice $\mathcal{L}$ of rank n and dimension m is a set of points in $\mathbb{R}^m$ that can be expressed as integer combinations of n linearly independent basis vectors $\mathbf{b}_1, \dots, \mathbf{b}_n$. Denote $\mathbf{B} = (\mathbf{b}_1, \dots, \mathbf{b}_n)$ as the basis of the lattice $\mathcal{L}$, and then $\mathcal{L} = \{\mathbf{B}\mathbf{z} : \mathbf{z} \in \mathbb{Z}^n\}$. In the rest of this paper, we will consider only full-rank lattices, where $m = n$ and $\mathbf{B} \in GL_n(\mathbb{R})$. The dual lattice of $\mathcal{L}$ is defined as $\mathcal{L}^* \overset{\text{def}}{=} \{\mathbf{u} \in \mathbb{R}^n : \langle \mathbf{u}, \mathbf{v} \rangle \in \mathbb{Z} \text{ for all } \mathbf{v} \in \mathcal{L}\}$, and the dual basis of a lattice basis $\mathbf{B}$ is defined as $\mathbf{B}^* = \mathbf{B}^{-\top}$. Let $\lambda_i(\mathcal{L})$ denote the i-th successive minimum of the lattice $\mathcal{L}$, and let $bl(\mathcal{L})$ denote the minimum value of $\max_{i \in [n]} \|\mathbf{b}_i\|$ taken over all bases of $\mathcal{L}$. It is known that $\lambda_n(\mathcal{L}) \leq bl(\mathcal{L}) \leq \frac{\sqrt{n}}{2} \lambda_n(\mathcal{L})$ [13].

For the lattice $\mathbb{Z}^n$, a bound on the number of integer points contained in a ball of radius r centered at the origin is established in [48].

Lemma 2.1 [48]. *Suppose r satisfies $1 \le r \le \sqrt{n}$ and $r^2 \in \mathbb{Z}$, then it has*

$$\left(2n/r^2\right)^{r^2} \le \left|\mathbb{Z}^n \cap r\mathcal{B}_2^n\right| \le \left(2e^3 n/r^2\right)^{r^2}, \tag{1}$$

where $\mathcal{B}_2^n$ is the closed Euclidean unit ball. Then for $r = O(1)$, it has $\left|\mathbb{Z}^n \cap r\mathcal{B}_2^n\right| \le n^{O(1)}$.

Lattice Problems. In addition to SVP and CVP, the following approximate lattice problem is also involved in our reduction.

Definition 2.1 (γ-SVP). *Given a basis $\mathbf{B}$ of a lattice $\mathcal{L}$ as input, the γ-SVP is to find a nonzero short vector in $\mathcal{L}$ of length at most $\gamma\lambda_1(\mathcal{L})$. If $\mathcal{L} \cong \mathbb{Z}^n$, we call this problem γ-$\mathbb{Z}$SVP.*

γ-SVP has been extensively studied in the literature, see, e.g., [3,4,6,39,54]. The lemma below states the best-known result for γ-SVP with $\gamma = O(1)$.

Lemma 2.2 [39]. *For every constant $\epsilon > 0$, there exists a constant $\gamma = \gamma(\epsilon) \ge 1$ depending only on ϵ such that there is a randomized algorithm that solves γ-SVP on lattices of dimension n in $2^{(0.802+\epsilon)n}poly(n)$ time.*

Gaussian Measure Over Lattices. Let $\rho_s(\boldsymbol{y}) = \exp\left(-\pi\|\boldsymbol{y}\|^2/s^2\right), \boldsymbol{y} \in \mathbb{R}^n$, to be the Gaussian function centered at origin with parameter s, then the discrete Gaussian distribution with parameter s on a lattice $\mathcal{L}$ of rank n defined by

$$\mathcal{D}_{\mathcal{L},s}(\boldsymbol{y}) = \rho_s(\boldsymbol{y})/\rho_s(\mathcal{L}), \boldsymbol{y} \in \mathcal{L}. \tag{2}$$

For a set $A \subseteq \mathcal{L}$, we denote $\rho_s(A) = \sum_{\boldsymbol{x} \in A} \rho_s(\boldsymbol{x})$. The following results will be used in our reduction.

Lemma 2.3 [28]. *Let $\mathcal{L}$ be a lattice of dimension n with $det(\mathcal{L}) \ge 1$. Then for any $s \ge bl(\mathcal{L})$, the probability that a set of $\left(n^2 + n(n + 20\log\log(s\sqrt{n}))\right)$ $\log(s\sqrt{n})$ vectors chosen independently according to $\mathcal{D}_{\mathcal{L},s}$ does not generate $\mathcal{L}$ is $2^{-\Omega(n)}$.*

In [24], Gentry et al. present an efficient approach that produces a sample distribution that is statistically close to the $\mathcal{D}_{\mathcal{L},s}$ for sufficiently large parameter s. Furthermore, Brakerski et al. provide an algorithm that samples exactly according to $\mathcal{D}_{\mathcal{L},s}$ [12].

Lemma 2.4 [12]. *Suppose $\mathcal{L}$ is a lattice of dimension n with a basis $\mathbf{B}$. Then there exists an efficient algorithm **SampleD** which inputs $\mathbf{B}$ and outputs a vector from $\mathcal{D}_{\mathcal{L},s}$ for any $s \ge \sqrt{\ln(2n+4)/\pi} \cdot \max_i \left\|\tilde{\boldsymbol{b}}_i\right\|$.*

Lemma 2.5 (Chernoff-Hoeffding Bound [29]**).** *Let $X_1, \ldots, X_M \in [0,1]$ be independent and identically distributed random variables. Then for $s > 0$ it has*

$$\Pr\left[\left|M \cdot \mathbb{E}\left[X_i\right] - \sum X_i\right| \ge sM\right] \le 2e^{-Ms^2/10}. \tag{3}$$

2.3 Characteristic Vector of Unimodular Lattices

A lattice $\mathcal{L}$ is said to be unimodular if $\mathcal{L} = \mathcal{L}^*$. Equivalently, the Gram matrix of $\mathbf{B}$ is unimodular, i.e., $\mathbf{B}^\top \mathbf{B} \in GL_n(\mathbb{Z})$, where $\mathbf{B} \in GL_n(\mathbb{R})$ is a basis of $\mathcal{L}$. Clearly, any rotation of $\mathbb{Z}^n$ is unimodular. However, a lattice being unimodular does not necessarily imply that it is isomorphic to $\mathbb{Z}^n$, e.g., the unimodular lattice E_8 is not isomorphic to $\mathbb{Z}^8$.

Definition 2.2 (Characteristic Vector). *Suppose $\mathcal{L}$ is a unimodular lattice. A vector $\mathbf{w} \in \mathcal{L}$ is called a characteristic vector of $\mathcal{L}$ if it has $\langle \mathbf{w}, \mathbf{v} \rangle \equiv \langle \mathbf{v}, \mathbf{v} \rangle$ mod 2 for all $\mathbf{v} \in \mathcal{L}$.*

We denote the set of characteristic vectors as $\chi(\mathcal{L})$. For any unimodular lattice $\mathcal{L}$, the following properties hold for the characteristic vector, and their proofs can be found in [41] and Appendix B.

Lemma 2.6. *Assume $\mathbf{B} = (\mathbf{b}_1, ..., \mathbf{b}_n)$ is a basis of a unimodular lattice $\mathcal{L}$ and $\mathbf{B}^{-\top} = (\mathbf{d}_1, ..., \mathbf{d}_n)$, then it has:*

1) $\mathbf{w} = \sum_{i=1}^n \|\mathbf{d}_i\|^2 \mathbf{b}_i$ *is a characteristic vector of $\mathcal{L}$.*
2) $\chi(\mathcal{L}) = \mathbf{w} + 2\mathcal{L}$ *for any characteristic vector $\mathbf{w} \in \chi(\mathcal{L})$.*
3) $\mathbf{w} \in \mathcal{L}$ *is a characteristic vector if and only if $\langle \mathbf{w}, \mathbf{b}_i \rangle \equiv \langle \mathbf{b}_i, \mathbf{b}_i \rangle$ mod 2 for $i \in [n]$.*

Lemma 2.6 indicates that for a given basis $\mathbf{B}$, we can efficiently compute a characteristic vector of $\mathcal{L}$, as well as efficiently verify whether a given vector is a characteristic vector. For a lattice $\mathcal{L}$ that is isomorphic to $\mathbb{Z}^n$, the characteristic vector has the following more particular properties.

Lemma 2.7. *Suppose $\mathcal{L} \cong \mathbb{Z}^n$. Assume $\mathbf{B} = \mathbf{OU}$ is a basis of $\mathcal{L}$, where $\mathbf{O} \in O_n(\mathbb{R})$ and $\mathbf{U} \in GL_n(\mathbb{Z}^n)$. Then it has:*

1) $\chi(\mathcal{L}) = \{\mathbf{Oz} : \mathbf{z} \in \mathbb{Z}^n$ *such that $\mathbf{z}_i \equiv 1$ mod $2, \forall i \in [n]\}$.*
2) The shortest characteristic vectors are exactly $\{\mathbf{Oz} : \mathbf{z}_i = \pm 1, \forall i \in [n]\}$.

The problem of finding the shortest characteristic vector plays a crucial role in our reduction. We note that this problem is equivalent to the CVP in the lattice $2\mathcal{L}$, with the target point being any characteristic vector $\mathbf{w} \in \chi(\mathcal{L})$.

Definition 2.3 (Shortest Characteristic Vector Problem (SCVP)). *Given a basis $\mathbf{B} \in GL_n(\mathbb{R})$ of a unimodular lattice $\mathcal{L}$ as input, SCVP is to find a shortest characteristic vector $\mathbf{w} \in \chi(\mathcal{L})$. In particular, if $\mathcal{L} \cong \mathbb{Z}^n$, we call this problem $\mathbb{Z}$SCVP.*

2.4   Lattice Isomorphism and Automorphism

Two n-dimensional lattices $\mathcal{L}_1$ and $\mathcal{L}_2$ are said to be isomorphic if there exists an orthogonal matrix $\mathbf{O} \in \mathcal{O}_n(\mathbb{R})$ such that $\mathcal{L}_2 = \{\mathbf{Ov} : \mathbf{v} \in \mathcal{L}_1\}$. The automorphism group $\mathrm{Aut}(\mathcal{L})$ of an n-dimensional lattice $\mathcal{L}$ consists of all orthogonal matrices that preserve $\mathcal{L}$, i.e.,

$$\mathrm{Aut}(\mathcal{L}) = \{\mathbf{O} \in \mathcal{O}_n(\mathbb{R}) : \mathbf{Ov} \in \mathcal{L} \text{ for all } \mathbf{v} \in \mathcal{L}\}. \tag{4}$$

It is clear that $\mathrm{Aut}(\mathcal{L})$ contains the automorphisms $\pm\mathbf{I}_n$, which are called *trivial automorphisms* of $\mathcal{L}$.

Lemma 2.8 *For any two isomorphic lattices $\mathcal{L}_1$ and $\mathcal{L}_2$, it has:*

1) $\mathrm{Aut}(\mathcal{L}_1) \cong \mathrm{Aut}(\mathcal{L}_2)$. *For any $\mathbf{O} \in \mathcal{O}_n(\mathbb{R})$ such that $\mathcal{L}_2 = \mathbf{O}\mathcal{L}_1$, the map ϕ defined by $\phi(\mathbf{O}_1) = \mathbf{O}\mathbf{O}_1\mathbf{O}^{-1}, \forall \mathbf{O}_1 \in \mathrm{Aut}(\mathcal{L}_1)$, is an isomorphism from $\mathrm{Aut}(\mathcal{L}_1)$ to $\mathrm{Aut}(\mathcal{L}_2)$.*
2) *There is a one-to-one correspondence between $\mathrm{Aut}(\mathcal{L}_1)$ and the set all isomorphisms between $\mathcal{L}_1$ and $\mathcal{L}_2$. For any $\mathbf{O} \in \mathcal{O}_n(\mathbb{R})$ such that $\mathcal{L}_2 = \mathbf{O}\mathcal{L}_1$, the map ψ defined by $\psi(\mathbf{O}_1) = \mathbf{O}\mathbf{O}_1, \forall \mathbf{O}_1 \in \mathrm{Aut}(\mathcal{L}_1)$, is a bijection between $\mathrm{Aut}(\mathcal{L}_1)$ and the isomorphisms from $\mathcal{L}_1$ to $\mathcal{L}_2$.*

For a lattice $\mathcal{L}$ with a basis $\mathbf{B}$, $\mathrm{Aut}(\mathcal{L})$ is closely related to the stabilizer of $\mathbf{G} = \mathbf{B}^\top\mathbf{B}$. Particularly, for a positive definite $n \times n$ matrix $\mathbf{G}$, the stabilizer of $\mathbf{G}$ is a finite group defined by $\mathrm{Stab}(\mathbf{G}) = \{\mathbf{U} \in \mathrm{GL}_n(\mathbb{Z}) : \mathbf{U}^\top\mathbf{G}\mathbf{U} = \mathbf{G}\}$.

Lemma 2.9 *Let $\mathcal{L}$ be a lattice with a basis $\mathbf{B}$. Then it has $\mathrm{Stab}(\mathbf{B}^\top\mathbf{B}) \cong \mathrm{Aut}(\mathcal{L})$, and the map ϕ defined by $\phi(\mathbf{U}) = \mathbf{B}\mathbf{U}\mathbf{B}^{-1}, \forall \mathbf{U} \in \mathrm{Stab}(\mathbf{B}^\top\mathbf{B})$, is an isomorphism from $\mathrm{Stab}(\mathbf{B}^\top\mathbf{B})$ to $\mathrm{Aut}(\mathcal{L})$.*

Proof. For any $\mathbf{U} \in \mathrm{Stab}(\mathbf{B}^\top\mathbf{B})$, it has $(\phi(\mathbf{U}))^\top(\phi(\mathbf{U})) = \mathbf{B}^{-\top}\mathbf{U}^\top(\mathbf{B}^\top\mathbf{B})\mathbf{U}\mathbf{B}^{-1}$ $= \mathbf{I}_n$ and $\phi(\mathbf{U})\mathbf{B} = \mathbf{B}\mathbf{U}$. Thus it has $\phi(\mathbf{U}) \in \mathrm{Aut}(\mathcal{L})$. On the other hand, for any $\mathbf{O} \in \mathrm{Aut}(\mathcal{L})$, there exists a $\mathbf{U}' \in \mathrm{GL}_n(\mathbb{Z})$ such that $\mathbf{O}\mathbf{B} = \mathbf{B}\mathbf{U}'$. Thus $\mathbf{B}^{-1}\mathbf{O}\mathbf{B} \in \mathrm{GL}_n(\mathbb{Z})$ and it can be easily verified that $\phi^{-1}(\mathbf{O}) \in \mathrm{Stab}(\mathbf{B}^\top\mathbf{B})$. Besides, it is clear that ϕ defines a homomorphism, which completes the proof. □

A natural problem related to lattice automorphism is how to find a nontrivial automorphism for a given lattice $\mathcal{L}$, which is defined as follows.

Definition 2.4 (Lattice Automorphism Problem (LAP)). *Given a basis $\mathbf{B}$ of a lattice $\mathcal{L}$, such that $\mathrm{Aut}(\mathcal{L}) \neq \{\pm\mathbf{I}_n\}$. The LAP is to find an automorphism $\mathbf{O} \in \mathrm{Aut}(\mathcal{L})$ such that $\mathbf{O} \neq \pm\mathbf{I}_n$. In particular, If $\mathcal{L} \cong \mathbb{Z}^n$, we call this problem $\mathbb{Z}LAP$.*

Automorphisms of Rotations of $\mathbb{Z}^n$. It is known that $\mathrm{Aut}(\mathbb{Z}^n) = \mathcal{S}_n^\pm$. Then for any $\mathcal{L} \cong \mathbb{Z}^n$, it has $\mathrm{Aut}(\mathcal{L}) \cong \mathcal{S}_n^\pm$. Specifically, from Lemma 2.8 it has $\mathrm{Aut}(\mathcal{L}) = \mathbf{O}\mathcal{S}_n^\pm\mathbf{O}^{-1}$ for any isomorphism $\mathbf{O}$ such that $\mathcal{L} = \mathbf{O}\mathbb{Z}^n$. Besides, suppose $\mathbf{w} \in \chi(\mathcal{L})$ is a shortest characteristic vector of $\mathcal{L}$, then the set of shortest characteristic vectors of $\mathcal{L}$ can be expressed as $\{\mathbf{Ow} : \mathbf{O} \in \mathrm{Aut}(\mathcal{L})\}$.

Besides, it is worth noting that finding a shortest vector of $\mathcal{L} \cong \mathbb{Z}^n$ directly yields a non-trivial automorphism of $\mathcal{L}$. Assume that we have a shortest vector $\mathbf{v} \in \mathcal{L}$. Let $\mathcal{L}' = \pi_{\mathrm{span}(\mathbf{v})^\perp}(\mathcal{L}) \cong \mathbb{Z}^{n-1}$, then $\mathcal{L} = \mathbf{v}\mathbb{Z} \oplus \mathcal{L}'$. From this, we can easily construct an $\mathbf{O} \in O_n(\mathbb{R})$ such that $\mathbf{O}\mathbf{v} = -\mathbf{v}$ and $\mathbf{O}\mathbf{x} = \mathbf{x}$ for all $\mathbf{x} \in \mathcal{L}'$. Thus $\mathbf{O} \in \mathrm{Aut}(\mathcal{L})$ and $\mathbf{O} \neq \pm\mathbf{I}_n$.

3 Randomized Reduction Framework for Rotations of $\mathbb{Z}^n$

This section demonstrates how the randomization framework can be used to obtain specific reductions for rotations in $\mathbb{Z}^n$. In Sect. 3.1, we explain the randomization framework and discuss how it can be used to get a reduction from $\mathbb{Z}$LIP to $\mathbb{Z}$SCVP. Then we prove the reduction from $\mathbb{Z}$SVP to γ-$\mathbb{Z}$SVP in Sect. 3.2. Additionally, Sect. 3.3 presents some other interesting results that can be obtained using the randomization framework.

3.1 A Reduction from $\mathbb{Z}$LIP to $\mathbb{Z}$SCVP

Suppose that $\mathcal{L} \cong \mathbb{Z}^n$ and $\mathbf{B}$ is a basis of $\mathcal{L}$. Given a $\mathbb{Z}$SCVP oracle $\mathcal{O}$, which takes a lattice basis $\mathbf{B}$ as input and returns a shortest characteristic vector in $\chi(\mathcal{L})$. We first show that the randomization framework enables us to sample uniformly and independently from the set of shortest characteristic vectors of $\mathcal{L}$. We then prove that, with a polynomial number of such samples, we can effectively recover the shortest vectors in $\mathcal{L}$ and thus solve the $\mathbb{Z}$LIP.

The Randomization Step. To begin with, we establish the following lemma, which states we can efficiently sample a basis according to some distribution, such that the distribution is invariant under the action of $\mathrm{Aut}(\mathcal{L})$ on the input. The primary technique used in this lemma is to sample a basis via a discrete Gaussian distribution over $\mathcal{L}$, which has been commonly utilized in existing lattice literature. e.g., [9,14,19,28].

Lemma 3.1. *There is an efficient algorithm that takes as input a basis* $\mathbf{B}$ *for a lattice* $\mathcal{L}$ *and outputs a basis according to a distribution* $\mathcal{A}(\mathbf{B})$, *such that the distribution* $\mathcal{A}(\mathbf{B})$ *is identical to* $\mathcal{A}(\mathbf{OB})$ *for any* $\mathbf{O} \in \mathrm{Aut}(\mathcal{L})$.

Proof. We assume that $\det(\mathcal{L}) = 1$. If this is not the case, we can consider $\mathcal{L}/\det(\mathcal{L})^{\frac{1}{n}}$ instead of $\mathcal{L}$. To start with, we apply LLL algorithm to $\mathbf{B}$ and obtain a reduced basis $\mathbf{B}' = [\mathbf{b}'_1, \ldots, \mathbf{b}'_n]$ of $\mathcal{L}$ such that $\|\mathbf{b}'_i\| \leq 2^{n/2}$. Then using Lemma 2.4, we can efficiently sample $p(n)$ vectors $\mathbf{v}_1, \ldots, \mathbf{v}_{p(n)}$ according $\mathcal{D}_{\mathcal{L},s}$, where $s = 2^n$ and $p(n)$ is the number of vectors required in Lemma 2.3. We note that the vectors $\mathbf{v}_1, \ldots, \mathbf{v}_{p(n)}$ generate $\mathcal{L}$ with overwhelming probability by Lemma 2.3. Finally, we run LLL algorithm on $\mathbf{v}_1, \ldots, \mathbf{v}_{p(n)}$ to get a basis $\mathbf{B}_1$ of $\mathcal{L}$ and output it. Observe that applying $\mathrm{Aut}(\mathcal{L})$ to the input basis has no effect on the distribution $\mathcal{D}_{\mathcal{L},s}$, and thus has no effect on the output distribution $\mathcal{A}(\mathbf{B})$. $\qquad \square$

An intuitive explanation of Lemma 3.1 is that the input basis is 'concealed' within the output basis. This is a crucial point in our randomization framework.

Proposition 3.1 (Randomization). *Given a $\mathbb{Z}SCVP$ oracle $\mathcal{O}$, which takes a lattice basis $\tilde{\mathbf{B}}$ as input, subject to the condition that $\mathcal{L}(\tilde{\mathbf{B}}) \cong \mathbb{Z}^n$, and returns a shortest characteristic vector in $\chi(\mathcal{L}(\tilde{\mathbf{B}}))$. Then for a lattice $\mathcal{L} \cong \mathbb{Z}^n$, we can sample uniformly and independently from the set of shortest characteristic vectors of $\mathcal{L}$.*

Proof. Let $\mathbf{B}$ be a basis of the lattice $\mathcal{L}$. To start with, we sample an orthogonal matrix $\mathbf{O}_1$ from $O_n(\mathbb{R})$ uniformly at random. Here the term "uniform" refers to the *Haar measure*, which ensures that the distribution of the matrix remains unchanged when multiplied by any orthogonal matrix [15]. Please refer to the discussion following this proof for the sampling method. Using Lemma 3.1 we can obtain a basis $\mathbf{B}_1 \leftarrow \mathcal{A}(\mathbf{O}_1\mathbf{B})$ of the lattice $\mathcal{L}_1 = \mathbf{O}_1\mathcal{L}$. Then we call the $\mathbb{Z}SCVP$ oracle $\mathcal{O}$, taking $\mathbf{B}_1$ as input to obtain a shortest characteristic vector $\mathbf{w}_1 \in \chi(\mathcal{L}_1)$. Finally, we compute $\mathbf{O}_1^{-1}\mathbf{w}_1 \in \chi(\mathcal{L})$.

We claim that $\mathbf{O}_1^{-1}\mathbf{w}_1$ is uniformly distributed in the set of shortest characteristic vectors of $\mathcal{L}$. In other words, the probability

$$\Pr_{\mathbf{O}_1 \leftarrow O_n(\mathbb{R}); \mathbf{B}_1 \leftarrow \mathcal{A}(\mathbf{O}_1\mathbf{B})}[\mathbf{O}_1^{-1}\mathcal{O}(\mathbf{B}_1) = \mathbf{w}] \tag{5}$$

is identical for any shortest characteristic vector $\mathbf{w} \in \chi(\mathcal{L})$. Note that the set of shortest characteristic vectors of $\mathcal{L}$ can be written as $\{\mathbf{O}\mathbf{w} : \mathbf{O} \in \mathrm{Aut}(\mathcal{L})\}$. Then it suffices to show that $\Pr[\mathbf{O}_1^{-1}\mathcal{O}(\mathbf{B}_1) = \mathbf{w}] = \Pr[\mathbf{O}_1^{-1}\mathcal{O}(\mathbf{B}_1) = \mathbf{O}\mathbf{w}]$ for any $\mathbf{O} \in \mathrm{Aut}(\mathcal{L})$. Note that

$$\begin{aligned}
&\Pr_{\mathbf{O}_1 \leftarrow O_n(\mathbb{R}); \mathbf{B}_1 \leftarrow \mathcal{A}(\mathbf{O}_1\mathbf{B})}[\mathbf{O}_1^{-1}\mathcal{O}(\mathbf{B}_1) = \mathbf{O}\mathbf{w}] \\
&= \Pr_{\mathbf{O}_1 \leftarrow O_n(\mathbb{R}); \mathbf{B}_1 \leftarrow \mathcal{A}(\mathbf{O}_1\mathbf{B})}[(\mathbf{O}_1\mathbf{O})^{-1}\mathcal{O}(\mathbf{B}_1) = \mathbf{w}] \\
&= \Pr_{(\mathbf{O}_1\mathbf{O}) \leftarrow O_n(\mathbb{R}); \mathbf{B}_1 \leftarrow \mathcal{A}(\mathbf{O}_1\mathbf{B})}[(\mathbf{O}_1\mathbf{O})^{-1}\mathcal{O}(\mathbf{B}_1) = \mathbf{w}] \\
&= \Pr_{(\mathbf{O}_1\mathbf{O}) \leftarrow O_n(\mathbb{R}); \mathbf{B}_1 \leftarrow \mathcal{A}(\mathbf{O}_1\mathbf{O}\mathbf{B})}[(\mathbf{O}_1\mathbf{O})^{-1}\mathcal{O}(\mathbf{B}_1) = \mathbf{w}] \\
&= \Pr_{\mathbf{O}_1 \leftarrow O_n(\mathbb{R}); \mathbf{B}_1 \leftarrow \mathcal{A}(\mathbf{O}_1\mathbf{B})}[\mathbf{O}_1^{-1}\mathcal{O}(\mathbf{B}_1) = \mathbf{w}].
\end{aligned}$$

The second equality follows from the property of Haar measure. The third equality can be deduced from the fact that $\mathbf{O}_1\mathbf{O}\mathbf{B} = (\mathbf{O}_1\mathbf{O}\mathbf{O}_1^{-1})\mathbf{O}_1\mathbf{B}$ and $\mathbf{O}_1\mathbf{O}\mathbf{O}_1^{-1} \in \mathrm{Aut}(\mathcal{L}_1)$ using Lemma 3.1. The last equality is simply a substitution of the variable. Thus $\mathbf{O}_1^{-1}\mathbf{w}_1$ is uniformly distributed in the set of shortest characteristic vectors of $\mathcal{L}$.

To establish the independence of $\mathbf{O}_1^{-1}\mathbf{w}_1$ for each trial, we can consider the joint distribution by leveraging the above method and taking into account that the choice of $\mathbf{O}_1$ is independent. See the full version of the paper for a proof. $\square$

To carry out the randomization framework, it is necessary to generate a uniformly distributed random orthogonal matrix, i.e., with respect to the Haar measure. Random orthogonal matrices are important in various fields, such as multivariate analysis, directional statistics, and physical systems modeling. There have been numerous studies on efficiently generating random orthogonal matrices. One method is to perform a QR decomposition on a matrix whose entries are independently drawn from a standard normal distribution, with the resulting orthogonal matrix distributed according to the Haar measure [42]. Another approach involves constructing a Householder reflection from a uniformly distributed unit vector of dimension n, and then applying it to an $(n-1) \times (n-1)$ uniformly distributed orthogonal matrix [16,52].

Remark 1. It appears that we need to tackle the precision issue in our approach because matrices over $\mathbb{R}$ are involved. Precision is a subtle issue for LIP because orthogonal matrices often involve irrational numbers that cannot be represented exactly. This issue has been explored in the literature on lattices, such as [9, 28]. In our paper, we follow their approach of ignoring the precision issue and focus on the core aspects of reduction. We note that the precision issue is not a critical concern in our reduction. As demonstrated in the recovery step, it is possible to efficiently reconstruct the shortest vectors from their approximations. Furthermore, the connection between the automorphism group and the stabilizer group, as described in Lemma 2.9, allows us to transform our reductions using the Gram matrix (as adopted in [18,19,21]). For a detailed discussion, please see the full version of the paper.

The Recovery Step. In this step, we demonstrate how to recover the shortest vectors in $\mathcal{L}$ from a polynomial number of shortest characteristic vectors in $\chi(\mathcal{L})$ obtained in the previous step. Essentially, our task is to solve the following problem.

Problem 3.1. *Given a basis* **B** *of a lattice* $\mathcal{L} \cong \mathbb{Z}^n$, *and* $\mathbf{w}_1, \mathbf{w}_2, \ldots, \mathbf{w}_{poly(n)} \in \chi(\mathcal{L})$ *that are drawn uniformly and independently from the set of shortest characteristic vectors of* $\mathcal{L}$. *The goal is to find the shortest vectors of* $\mathcal{L}$.

Suppose that $\{\mathbf{v}_1, \ldots, \mathbf{v}_n\}$ is a set of n linearly independent shortest vectors of $\mathcal{L}$, and denote $\mathbf{O} = (\mathbf{v}_1, \ldots, \mathbf{v}_n) \in O_n(\mathbb{R})$. Then by Lemma 2.7, the set of shortest characteristic vectors of $\mathcal{L}$ can be expressed as $\{z_1 \mathbf{v}_1 + \cdots + z_n \mathbf{v}_n : z_i = \pm 1, \forall i \in [n]\}$. Define the function

$$M_k(\mathbf{x}) = \mathbb{E}[\langle \mathbf{w}, \mathbf{x} \rangle^k], x \in \mathbb{R}^n, \tag{6}$$

where $k \in \mathbb{Z}^+$, and $\mathbf{w}$ is uniformly distributed over the set of shortest characteristic vectors of $\mathcal{L}$. From Chernoff-Hoeffding bound, we can effectively approximate $M_k(\mathbf{x})$ by making use of a polynomials number of shortest characteristic vector as provided in Problem 3.1. As the set of shortest characteristic vectors is symmetric around the origin, it has $M_k(\mathbf{x}) = 0$ for any odd k. On the other hand, a straightforward calculation shows that

$$M_4(\mathbf{x}) = 3 \|\mathbf{x}\|^4 - 2 \sum_{i=1}^{n} \langle \mathbf{v}_i, \mathbf{x} \rangle^4 \tag{7}$$

Next, we focus on the $\mathbf{x}$ that is on the unit sphere and define

$$f(\mathbf{x}) = -\frac{1}{2}(M_4(\mathbf{x}) - 3) = \sum_{i=1}^{n} \langle \mathbf{v}_i, \mathbf{x} \rangle^4. \tag{8}$$

Then the following lemma is clear.

Lemma 3.2. *The global maximum of $f(\mathbf{x})$ over the unit sphere is attained at $\{\pm \mathbf{v}_1, \ldots, \pm \mathbf{v}_n\}$, which is exactly the set of shortest vectors of $\mathcal{L}$.*

Lemma 3.2 allows us to convert Problem 3.1 into the problem of maximizing $f(\mathbf{x})$ over the unit sphere. One widely-used approach to solve this problem is via gradient descent as that adopted in [43]. Taking into account the approximation error of $M_k(x)$, we present Algorithm 1 as a solution to Problem 3.1, as well as an analysis of the algorithm in Proposition 3.2.

Algorithm 1: Solve Problem 3.1 via Gradient Descent.

Require: A polynomial number of samples uniformly distributed over the shortest characteristic vectors of a lattice $\mathcal{L} \cong \mathbb{Z}^n$

Ensure: An approximation a shortest vector of $\mathcal{L}$

1: Choose $\mathbf{x}$ uniformly at random from the unit sphere of $\mathbb{R}^n$
2: Compute an approximation of the gradient $\nabla f(\mathbf{x})$
3: $\mathbf{x}_{new} \leftarrow \nabla f(\mathbf{x})$
4: $\mathbf{x}_{new} \leftarrow \mathbf{x}_{new} / \|\mathbf{x}_{new}\|$
5: Compute the approximations of $f(\mathbf{x}_{new})$ and $f(\mathbf{x})$
6: **if** $f(\mathbf{x}_{new}) \leq f(\mathbf{x})$ **then**
7:     **return** $\mathbf{x}$
8: **else**
9:     Replace $\mathbf{x}$ by $\mathbf{x}_{new}$ and go to step 2
10: **end if**

In step 2 of Algorithm 1, we need to approximate the gradient $\nabla f(x)$, which can be done via two methods. The first method involves using the equations $\nabla M_4(\mathbf{x}) = \mathbb{E}[\nabla(\langle \mathbf{w}, \mathbf{x} \rangle^4)] = 4\mathbb{E}[\langle \mathbf{w}, \mathbf{x} \rangle^3 \mathbf{w}]$, and $\nabla f(\mathbf{x}) = -\frac{1}{2}(\nabla M_4(\mathbf{x}) - 12\mathbf{x})$. Alternatively, the second method involves approximating $f(\mathbf{x} + t\mathbf{y}) = \sum_{i=1}^{n} \langle \mathbf{v}_i, \mathbf{x} + t\mathbf{y} \rangle^4$ for $0 \leq t \leq 4$, and then computing $\sum_{i=1}^{n} \langle \mathbf{v}_i, \mathbf{x} \rangle^k \langle \mathbf{v}_i, \mathbf{y} \rangle^{4-k}, 0 \leq k \leq 4$, using linear algebra. Specifically, by setting $k = 3$, we get $\sum_{i=1}^{n} \langle \mathbf{v}_i, \mathbf{x} \rangle^3 \langle \mathbf{v}_i, \mathbf{y} \rangle = \langle \sum_{i=1}^{n} \langle \mathbf{v}_i, \mathbf{x} \rangle^3 \mathbf{v}_i, \mathbf{y} \rangle$, and by letting $\mathbf{y}$ run over the standard basis $\mathbf{e}_i$, $i \in [n]$, we can obtain an approximation of $\nabla f(\mathbf{x}) = 4\sum_{i=1}^{n} \langle \mathbf{v}_i, \mathbf{x} \rangle^3 \mathbf{v}_i$.

Proposition 3.2. *Suppose that $\mathcal{L} \cong \mathbb{Z}^n$. For any $c_0 > 0$, there exists a constant $c_1 > 0$ such that Algorithm 1 inputs n^{c_1} samples that are independently and uniformly distributed over the shortest characteristic vectors of $\mathcal{L}$, and outputs a vector $\mathbf{x}$ such that $\|\mathbf{x} - \mathbf{v}\| \leq n^{-c_0}$ for some shortest vector $\mathbf{v} \in \mathcal{L}$, with $O(\log \log n)$ descent steps and a constant probability. Moreover, $O(n \log n)$ calls to Algorithm 1 will find all shortest vectors of $\mathcal{L}$ with an overwhelming probability.*

Proof. We start by ignoring the approximation error and analyzing Algorithm 1. In this proof, we use the coordinate representation of vectors under the orthogonal basis $\{\mathbf{v}_i\}_{1 \leq i \leq n}$, i.e., $\mathbf{x} = (x_1, \ldots, x_n) \in \mathbb{R}^n$, where $x_i = \langle \mathbf{x}, \mathbf{v}_i \rangle$. Then by

$$\nabla f(\mathbf{x}) = 4 \sum_{i=1}^{n} \langle \mathbf{v}_i, \mathbf{x} \rangle^3 \mathbf{v}_i, \tag{9}$$

we can deduce that a single iteration transforms the the vector $\mathbf{x} = (x_1, \ldots, x_n)$ into $\alpha \cdot (x_1^3, \ldots, x_n^3)$ for some normalization factor α. Thus after r iterations, a vector $(x_1, \ldots, x_n)$ becomes a vector $\alpha \cdot (x_1^{3^r}, \ldots, x_n^{3^r})$ for some normalization factor α. We note that the original vector $(x_1, \ldots, x_n)$ is uniformly sampled from the unit sphere. It can be proved that with some constant probability, there exits a $k \in [n]$ such that $|x_k| \geq (1 + \Omega(1/\log n))|x_i|, \forall i \neq k$ [43]. For such a vector, $r = O(\log \log n)$ iterations are enough to increase this gap to more than $n^{\log n}$, which means that we have one coordinate very close to ± 1, and all others are at most $n^{-\log n}$ in absolute value.

Next, we take into account the approximation error. By Chernoff-Hoeffding bound, for any $c > 0$, there exits a c_1 such that with overwhelming probability all gradients in $r < poly(n)$ iterations have errors at most n^{-c} in the Euclidean norm. In one iteration, let $\mathbf{x} = (x_1, \ldots, x_n)$ be such that $|x_k| \geq (1 + \Omega(1/\log n))|x_i|, \forall i \neq k$. Then clearly $|x_k| > n^{-1/2}$ since $\|\mathbf{x}\| = 1$. Let $(y_1, \ldots, y_n) = \nabla f(\mathbf{x})$ and hence $|y_k| = 4|x_k|^3 > n^{-2}$.

Let $(\tilde{y}_1, \ldots, \tilde{y}_n)$ be an approximation of $\nabla f(\mathbf{x})$. By our assumption on the approximation $\nabla f(\mathbf{x})$, for each i, we have $|\tilde{y}_i - y_i| \leq n^{-c}$. Then, for any $i \neq k$, we have

$$\frac{|\tilde{y}_k|}{|\tilde{y}_i|} \geq \frac{|y_k| - n^{-c}}{|y_i| + n^{-c}} \geq \frac{|y_k|(1 - n^{-(c-2)})}{|y_i| + n^{-c}}. \tag{10}$$

Hence, if $|y_i| > n^{-(c-1)}$, then $\frac{|\tilde{y}_k|}{|\tilde{y}_i|}$ is at least $(1 - O(1/n))(x_k/x_i)^3$. Otherwise, $\frac{|\tilde{y}_k|}{|\tilde{y}_i|}$ is at least $\Omega(n^{c-3})$. After $r = O(\log \log n)$ steps, the gap x_k/x_i becomes $\Omega(n^{c-3})$. Therefore, for any $c_0 > 0$, we can choose c appropriately such that the Euclidean distance between the output vector and one of $\pm \mathbf{v}_i$'s is less than n^{-c_0}.

Finally, from the Coupon Collector's problem, $O(n \log n)$ calls to Algorithm 1 will find all shortest vectors of $\mathcal{L}$ with overwhelming probability. $\square$

Given approximations of the shortest vectors of $\mathcal{L}$ as in Proposition 3.1, there is an effective way to recover the exact shortest vectors $\{\mathbf{v}_i\}_{1 \leq i \leq n}$ from its approximations $\{\tilde{\mathbf{v}}_i\}_{1 \leq i \leq n}$ using a set of n linearly independent shortest characteristic vectors. Specifically, let $\mathbf{W} = \{\mathbf{w}_1, \ldots, \mathbf{w}_n\}$ be a set of n linearly independent shortest characteristic vectors, where $\mathbf{w}_i = z_{i1}\mathbf{v}_1 + \ldots + z_{in}\mathbf{v}_n$ and $z_{ij} = \pm 1$, and suppose $\tilde{\mathbf{v}}_i = \mathbf{v}_i + \epsilon_i$ such that $\|\epsilon_i\| \leq n^{-c}$. Observe that $\langle \mathbf{w}_i, \tilde{\mathbf{v}}_j \rangle = z_{ij} + \sum_{l=1}^{n} z_{il}\langle \mathbf{v}_l, \epsilon_j \rangle$, and $\langle \mathbf{v}_l, \epsilon_j \rangle \leq \|\mathbf{v}_l\| \cdot \|\epsilon_j\| \leq n^{-c}$. It follows that $|\langle \mathbf{w}_i, \tilde{\mathbf{v}}_j \rangle - z_{ij}| \leq n^{-(c-1)} < \frac{1}{2}$ for $c > 2, n > 2$. Thus z_{ij} can be recovered by just taking $\text{sign}(\langle \mathbf{w}_i, \tilde{\mathbf{v}}_j \rangle)$, and $\{\mathbf{v}_i\}_{1 \leq i \leq n}$ can be exactly recovered consequently.

Proof of the Reduction. By combining the above two steps, we can conclude the following reduction.

Theorem 3.1. *There is an efficient randomized reduction from* $\mathbb{Z}LIP$ *to* $\mathbb{Z}SCVP$.

Proof. The theorem is a direct result of Proposition 3.1 and Proposition 3.2. □

For a unimodular lattice $\mathcal{L}$, it has $\chi(\mathcal{L}) = \mathbf{w} + 2\mathcal{L}$ for any characteristic vector $\mathbf{w} \in \chi(\mathcal{L})$ according to Lemma 2.6. Therefore, SCVP can be considered as a CVP in the lattice $2\mathcal{L}$, with the target vector being $\mathbf{w}$. Furthermore, for $\mathcal{L} \cong \mathbb{Z}^n$, the $\mathbb{Z}SCVP$ is a very special case of CVP. Lemma 2.6 tells us the target $\mathbf{w}$ is completely dependent on the given basis and Lemma 2.7 tells us that the distance between $\mathbf{w}$ and $2\mathcal{L}$ is $\sqrt{n}$, and the deep holes of $2\mathcal{L}$ are exactly $\chi(\mathcal{L})$. Therefore, the $\mathbb{Z}SCVP$ can be viewed as a CVP in the lattice $2\mathcal{L}$, with a deep hole as the target vector. We believe this is a non-trivial observation that could aid in further study of $\mathbb{Z}LIP$, as it is known that calculating or verifying a deep hole for a lattice is a difficult problem in general [27].

3.2 A Reduction from $\mathbb{Z}SVP$ to γ-$\mathbb{Z}SVP$

The randomization framework can be readily adapted to other oracles for rotations of $\mathbb{Z}^n$. In this subsection, we explore the approximate $\mathbb{Z}SVP$ and establish the following reduction.

Theorem 3.2. *There is an efficient randomized reduction from* $\mathbb{Z}SVP$ *to* γ-$\mathbb{Z}SVP$ *for any constant* $\gamma = O(1)$.

Proof. Suppose that $\mathcal{L} \cong \mathbb{Z}^n$. Denote $A = \mathcal{L} \cap \gamma\mathcal{B}_2^n$, then by Lemma 2.1 it has $|A| = |\mathbb{Z}^n \cap \gamma\mathcal{B}_2^n| \leq n^c$ for some constant c. Consider the action of $\mathrm{Aut}(\mathcal{L})$ on A. Write $A = \cup_{\mathbf{v} \in \bar{A}} A_{\mathbf{v}}$ to be the disjoint union of distinct orbits, where $A_{\mathbf{v}} = \{\mathbf{O}\mathbf{v} : \mathbf{O} \in \mathrm{Aut}(\mathcal{L})\}$ and $\bar{A}$ is a set of representative vectors with respect to the action of $\mathrm{Aut}(\mathcal{L})$ on A.

Using the randomization framework, we can invoke the γ-$\mathbb{Z}SVP$ oracle $m = poly(n)$ times, with $m > n^c$, yielding a vector set $X = \{\mathbf{x}_1, \ldots, \mathbf{x}_m\} \subseteq A$. Then through a deduction similar to Proposition 3.1, it can be shown that, if $X \cap A_{\mathbf{v}}$ is nonempty, the vectors in $X \cap A_{\mathbf{v}}$ are independently and uniformly distributed over $A_{\mathbf{v}}$. Since $m > n^c \geq |\bar{A}|$, there must exist two $\mathbf{x}_i$ and $\mathbf{x}_j$ fall in a same orbit $A_{\mathbf{v}}$. We claim that the probability that $\mathbf{x}_i - \mathbf{x}_j$ is a multiple of a shortest vector of $\mathcal{L}$, (i.e., $\frac{\mathbf{x}_i - \mathbf{x}_j}{\|\mathbf{x}_i - \mathbf{x}_j\|}$ is a shortest vector), is at least $1/|A_{\mathbf{v}}| \geq 1/n^c$. To prove the claim, suppose that $\mathbf{v}_1, \ldots, \mathbf{v}_n$ are n linearly independent shortest vectors of $\mathcal{L}$, and write $\mathbf{x}_i = x_{i,1}\mathbf{v}_1 + \cdots + x_{i,n}\mathbf{v}_n$. Without loss of generality, we assume $x_{i,1} \neq 0$. It is evident that $x_{i,1}(-\mathbf{v}_1) + x_{i,2}\mathbf{v}_2 + \cdots + x_{i,n}\mathbf{v}_n \in A_{\mathbf{v}}$. Moreover, with probability $1/|A_{\mathbf{v}}|$, it has $\mathbf{x}_j = x_{i,1}(-\mathbf{v}_1) + x_{i,2}\mathbf{v}_2 + \cdots + x_{i,n}\mathbf{v}_n$ for a randomly chosen $\mathbf{x}_j$ from $A_{\mathbf{v}}$. Thus $\mathbf{x}_i - \mathbf{x}_j = 2x_{i,1}\mathbf{v}_1$, which is a multiple of the shortest vector $\mathbf{v}_1$.

Then we compute $\mathbf{x}_i - \mathbf{x}_j$ for all $i, j \in [m]$, and check if it is a multiple of a shortest vector. This step requires at most m^2 checks. Finally, repeating the whole process $O(n^{c+1})$ times, we can get a shortest vector in $\mathcal{L}$ with an overwhelming probability. $\qquad\qquad\qquad\qquad\qquad\qquad\qquad\qquad\qquad\qquad\qquad\qquad$ $\square$

Using the fastest known algorithm for $O(1)$-SVP as stated in Lemma 2.2, we can obtain a $2^{0.802n}$-time algorithm for the $\mathbb{Z}$SVP. It is worth noting that γ-$\mathbb{Z}$SVP is a special case of γ-SVP, so there is potential for a better algorithm for the $\mathbb{Z}$SVP problem if we can develop a more specialized algorithm for γ-$\mathbb{Z}$SVP. However, further research is needed to establish such an algorithm.

The approach used in Theorem 3.2 can be extended to handle general values of γ, but the resulting reduction may not have a guaranteed polynomial-time complexity. Specifically, denote $\ell(\gamma, n) = |\bar{A}|$ and $\xi(\gamma, n) = \max_{\mathbf{v} \in \bar{A}} |A_{\mathbf{v}}|$. Let $T_{\mathbb{Z}SVP}(\gamma, n)$ be the run time of an algorithm for γ-$\mathbb{Z}$SVP on lattices of dimension n.

Corollary 3.1. *There is a randomized algorithm that solves $\mathbb{Z}$SVP on lattices of dimension n in $\xi(\gamma, n) \cdot (\ell(\gamma, n) \cdot T_{\mathbb{Z}SVP}(\gamma, n) + \ell(\gamma, n)^2) \cdot poly(n)$ time.*

3.3 Other Corollaries from the Randomization Framework

Another advantage of the randomization framework is the suitability for using fixed-dimensional oracles, which makes it useful for fixed-dimensional reduction. As a simple example, we demonstrate how to use the randomization framework to establish a reduction from $\mathbb{Z}$LIP to $\mathbb{Z}$SVP for a fixed dimension in the following corollary. Note that without the fixed dimension restriction, a reduction from $\mathbb{Z}$LIP to $\mathbb{Z}$SVP can be established by employing the projecting method [9]. Specifically, suppose that $\mathcal{L} \cong \mathbb{Z}^n$. We call an n-dimensional $\mathbb{Z}$SVP oracle to obtain a shortest vector $\mathbf{v}_1 \in \mathcal{L}$, from which we can efficiently obtain a basis for the $(n-1)$-dimensional sublattice $\mathcal{L}_1 \subseteq \mathcal{L}$ that is orthogonal to $\mathbf{v}_1$. Then we call an $(n-1)$-dimensional $\mathbb{Z}$SVP oracle to obtain a shortest vector in $\mathcal{L}_1$, and then we recursively find n linearly independent shortest vectors of $\mathcal{L}$.

Corollary 3.2. *There is an efficient randomized reduction from $\mathbb{Z}$LIP to $\mathbb{Z}$SVP in the same dimension.*

Proof. Suppose that $\mathcal{L} \cong \mathbb{Z}^n$. Note that $\text{Aut}(\mathcal{L})$ acts transitively on the set of shortest vectors of $\mathcal{L}$. By invoking the $\mathbb{Z}$SVP oracle with the randomization framework, we can obtain vectors that are independently and uniformly distributed over the set of shortest vectors of $\mathcal{L}$. Then we just need to sample $O(n \log n)$ shortest vectors to get a set of linearly independent ones, e.g., $\{\mathbf{v}_1, \ldots, \mathbf{v}_n\}$. This gives the matrix $\mathbf{O} = (\mathbf{v}_1, \ldots, \mathbf{v}_n) \in O_n(\mathbb{R})$ which is an isomorphism from $\mathcal{L}$ to $\mathbb{Z}^n$. $\qquad\qquad\qquad\qquad\qquad\qquad$ $\square$

It is worth noting that, like Corollary 3.1, the reductions in Theorem 3.1 and Theorem 3.2 can also be modified to fixed-dimensional reductions. Another simple application of the randomization framework is demonstrated by the following result.

Corollary 3.3. *In the sense of randomized reduction, the $(n-1)$-dimensional $\mathbb{Z}SVP$ is easier than the n-dimensional $\mathbb{Z}SVP$.*

Proof. Suppose that $\mathcal{L} \cong \mathbb{Z}^{n-1}$. We first embed $\mathcal{L}$ into an n-dimensional lattice $\mathcal{L}_1 \cong \mathbb{Z}^n$ by adding $\mathbf{e}_n$ to the basis of $\mathcal{L}$. Then we invoke the n-dimensional $\mathbb{Z}SVP$ oracle using the randomization framework to obtain vectors that are independently and uniformly distributed over the set of shortest vectors of $\mathcal{L}_1$. The probability of such a vector falling into $\mathcal{L}$ is $1 - \frac{1}{n}$. By invoking the n-dimensional $\mathbb{Z}SVP$ oracle $O(\log n)$ times, we can obtain a shortest vector in $\mathcal{L}(\mathbf{B})$ with an overwhelming probability.   □

4   A Reduction from $\mathbb{Z}LIP$ to $\mathbb{Z}LAP$

This section focuses on the $\mathbb{Z}LAP$, which involves finding a nontrivial automorphism in $\mathrm{Aut}(\mathcal{L})$ for a given lattice $\mathcal{L} \cong \mathbb{Z}^n$ (Definition 2.4). Although the effect of 'applying random automorphisms' to the output of an oracle can be achieved via the randomization framework, the $\mathbb{Z}LAP$ still seems difficult. In fact, we can prove that the $\mathbb{Z}LAP$ is as hard as $\mathbb{Z}LIP$. Note that $\mathbb{Z}LAP \leq \mathbb{Z}LIP$ follows directly from Lemma 2.8. Therefore, in this section, we focus on the reduction from $\mathbb{Z}LIP$ to $\mathbb{Z}LAP$, which is achieved in two steps. The first step shows how to efficiently sample automorphisms independently and uniformly from a special conjugacy class by invoking the $\mathbb{Z}LAP$ oracle using the randomization framework (Sect. 4.1). The second step demonstrates how to use these automorphisms to recover the shortest vectors (Sect. 4.2). Besides, in Sect. 4.3 we introduce other results related to $\mathbb{Z}LAP$.

4.1   Random Sample from a Conjugacy Class

To begin with, we give a brief introduction to the conjugation of the automorphism group $\mathrm{Aut}(\mathcal{L})$ for any lattice $\mathcal{L} \cong \mathbb{Z}^n$. For convenience, lowercase Greek letters such as ϕ are used to represent automorphisms in $\mathrm{Aut}(\mathcal{L})$ throughout this section. In $\mathrm{Aut}(\mathcal{L})$, two automorphisms ϕ_1 and ϕ_2 are conjugate if there exists an automorphism $\phi \in \mathrm{Aut}(\mathcal{L})$ such that $\phi_1 = \phi\phi_2\phi^{-1}$, which is denoted by $\phi_1 \sim \phi_2$. Conjugation is an equivalence relation that divides $\mathrm{Aut}(\mathcal{L})$ into disjoint conjugacy classes, which are denoted by $\mathfrak{C}_\phi = \{\phi_1 \in \mathrm{Aut}(\mathcal{L}) : \phi_1 \sim \phi\}$. For two lattices $\mathcal{L}_1 \cong \mathcal{L}_2$, from Lemma 2.8 it has $\mathrm{Aut}(\mathcal{L}_1) \cong \mathrm{Aut}(\mathcal{L}_2)$. This implies that the isomorphisms between $\mathcal{L}_1$ and $\mathcal{L}_2$ induce a canonical bijection between the conjugacy classes of $\mathcal{L}_1$ and those of $\mathcal{L}_2$, i.e., $\tau : \mathfrak{C}_\phi \to \mathfrak{C}_{\mathbf{O}\phi\mathbf{O}^{-1}}$ for any $\phi \in \mathrm{Aut}(\mathcal{L}_1)$ and any $\mathbf{O} \in O_n(\mathbb{R})$ such that $\mathcal{L}_2 = \mathbf{O}\mathcal{L}_1$. Thus by an abuse of notation, we also use $\phi_1 \sim \phi_2$ to represent $\tau(\mathfrak{C}_{\phi_1}) = \mathfrak{C}_{\phi_2}$ for any $\phi_1 \in \mathrm{Aut}(\mathcal{L}_1)$ and $\phi_2 \in \mathrm{Aut}(\mathcal{L}_2)$.

For the lattice $\mathbb{Z}^n$, it has $\mathrm{Aut}(\mathbb{Z}^n) = S_n^\pm$ and we are particularly interested in the conjugacy classes defined by the following types of matrices in $S_n^\pm$.

– $\mathbf{T}_{i,j,k} = \mathrm{diag}\{\left(\begin{smallmatrix} 0 & 1 \\ 1 & 0 \end{smallmatrix}\right), \ldots, \left(\begin{smallmatrix} 0 & 1 \\ 1 & 0 \end{smallmatrix}\right), -\mathbf{I}_i, \mathbf{I}_j\}$, where there are k $\left(\begin{smallmatrix} 0 & 1 \\ 1 & 0 \end{smallmatrix}\right)$'s on the diagonal such that $2k + i + j = n$ and $i, j < n$.

- $\mathbf{T}_{p,k} = \mathrm{diag}\{\mathbf{P}_p, \dots, \mathbf{P}_p, \mathbf{I}_{n-pk}\}$, where there are k $\mathbf{P}_p$'s on the diagonal and $p > 2$ is an odd prime number. We remind that $\mathbf{P}_p = \left(\begin{smallmatrix} 0 & 1 \\ \mathbf{I}_{p-1} & 0 \end{smallmatrix} \right)$.
- $\mathbf{T}_n = \mathrm{diag}\{\left(\begin{smallmatrix} 0 & -1 \\ 1 & 0 \end{smallmatrix} \right), \dots, \left(\begin{smallmatrix} 0 & -1 \\ 1 & 0 \end{smallmatrix} \right)\}$, where n is even.

The aim of this subsection is to prove the following statement, which claims that we can efficiently sample automorphisms from one conjugacy class.

Proposition 4.1. *Assume that n is odd and the lattice $\mathcal{L} \cong \mathbb{Z}^n$. Given a $\mathbb{Z}LAP$ oracle $\mathcal{O}$ for dimension n. Then there exists i, j, k such that we efficiently obtain $poly(n)$ samples $\phi_1, \phi_2, \dots, \phi_{poly(n)} \in Aut(\mathcal{L})$ that are independently and uniformly distributed over the conjugacy class $\{\phi \in Aut(\mathcal{L}) | \phi \sim \mathbf{T}_{i,j,k}\}$.*

The main approach for proving the proposition is still utilizing the randomization framework to generate samples uniformly distributed over each conjugacy class. However, due to the total number of conjugacy classes being exponential in n, we can not effectively sample from one class as that in Theorem 3.2. To address this, we modify the randomization procedure by preprocessing the outputs of the oracle to ensure that the resulting automorphisms belong to one of the conjugacy classes corresponding to $\mathbf{T}_{i,j,k}$, $\mathbf{T}_{p,k}$ or $\mathbf{T}_n$. The number of these types of conjugacy classes is a polynomial of n, allowing for efficient sampling from one conjugacy class.

Preprocessing and Randomization. Firstly, we give an efficient preprocessing algorithm that transforms the output of the oracle into specific conjugacy classes.

Lemma 4.1 (Preprocessing). *Suppose that $\mathcal{L} \cong \mathbb{Z}^n$. Then there exists an efficient algorithm $\mathcal{P}$ that takes a nontrivial automorphism $\phi \in Aut(\mathcal{L})$ as input and returns an automorphism $\mathcal{P}(\phi) \in Aut(\mathcal{L})$ falling into one of the conjugacy classes corresponding to $\mathbf{T}_{i,j,k}$, $\mathbf{T}_{p,k}$, or $\mathbf{T}_n$. Additionally, it can be efficiently identified which conjugacy class $\mathcal{P}(\phi)$ belongs to.*

Proof. The algorithm begins by computing $\mathrm{ord}(\phi) := \min\{i \in \mathbb{Z}^+ : \phi^i = \mathbf{I}_n\}$. It is clear that $\mathrm{ord}(\phi) \mid |S_n^{\pm}|$. We note that $\mathrm{ord}(\phi)$ can be computed in a polynomial time of n, which is proved in Lemma 4.2. In the following, the algorithm processes ϕ according to its order.

(1) $\mathrm{ord}(\phi)$ is odd. Let p be the smallest odd prime factor of $\mathrm{ord}(\phi)$.[4] Then the algorithm outputs $\mathcal{P}(\phi) = \phi^{\mathrm{ord}(\phi)/p}$. It can be deduced that $\mathcal{P}(\phi) \sim \mathbf{T}_{p,k}$, where $k = (n-d)/(p-1)$ and d is the dimension of the eigenspace associated with the eigenvalue 1 of $\mathcal{P}(\phi)$. The proof is given in Lemma 4.3.
(2) $\mathrm{ord}(\phi)$ is even and $\phi^{\mathrm{ord}(\phi)/2} = -\mathbf{I}_n$. If $4 \nmid \mathrm{ord}(\phi)$, it can be deduced that $\mathrm{ord}(-\phi) = \mathrm{ord}(\phi)/2$ is odd. Thus, we can preprocess ϕ by multiplying it with $-\mathbf{I}_n$, which transforms it into the case of (1). If $4 \mid \mathrm{ord}(\phi)$, then the algorithm outputs $\mathcal{P}(\phi) = \phi^{\mathrm{ord}(\phi)/4}$, and it can be deduced that $\mathcal{P}(\phi) \sim \mathbf{T}_n$. The proof is given in Lemma 4.3.

---

[4] Note that $\mathrm{ord}(\phi) \mid |S_n^{\pm}|$, then each prime divisor of $\mathrm{ord}(\phi)$ is no more than n. Therefore p can be computed efficiently.

(3) ord(ϕ) is even and $\phi^{\text{ord}(\phi)/2} \neq -\mathbf{I}_n$. The algorithm outputs $\mathcal{P}(\phi) = \phi^{\text{ord}(\phi)/2}$. Let V_1 be the eigenspace associated with the eigenvalue 1 of $\mathcal{P}(\phi)$, and let d be the dimension of V_1. Define $\mathcal{L}_1 = V_1 \cap \mathcal{L}$. It can be deduced that $\mathcal{P}(\phi) \sim \mathbf{T}_{n-d-k,d-k,k}$, where $k = \log_2(\det(\mathcal{L}_1)^2)$. The proof is given in Lemma 4.3. □

Lemma 4.2. *Suppose that $\mathcal{L} \cong \mathbb{Z}^n$. Then there is an efficient algorithm that takes any $\phi \in \text{Aut}(\mathcal{L})$ as input and computes ord(ϕ).*

Proof. Suppose that $\lambda_\phi(x) \in \mathbb{Z}[x]$ is the characteristic polynomial of ϕ. Then $\lambda_\phi(x)$ can be factorized into the product of integer irreducible polynomials using LLL algorithm [38]. Since the eigenvalues of ϕ are roots of unity, it follows that these irreducible polynomials are cyclotomic polynomials of degrees no more than n. Next, we turn to determine the order of these cyclotomic polynomials. For a cyclotomic polynomial $\Phi_m(x)$ of order m, its degree is the Euler's totient function $\varphi(m)$. It is known that $\varphi(m) \geq \sqrt{m/2}$, then the orders of these cyclotomic polynomials are no more than $2n^2$, and thus can be efficiently determined. Finally, ord(ϕ) is computed by just taking the least common multiple of the orders of these cyclotomic polynomials. □

Lemma 4.3. *Suppose that $\psi \in S_n^{\pm}$. Let V_1 be the eigenspace associated with the eigenvalue 1 of ψ, $d = dim(V_1)$, and let $\mathcal{L}_1 = V_1 \cap \mathbb{Z}^n$. Then*

- *If ord(ψ) = p for a odd prime p, it has $\psi \sim \mathbf{T}_{p,k}$, where $k = (n-d)/(p-1)$.*
- *If ord(ψ) = 4 and $\psi^2 = -\mathbf{I}_n$, it has $\psi \sim \mathbf{T}_n$.*
- *If ord(ψ) = 2 and $\psi \neq -\mathbf{I}_n$, it has $\psi \sim \mathbf{T}_{n-d-k,d-k,k}$ for $det(\mathcal{L}_1) > 1$, where $k = \log_2(det(\mathcal{L}_1)^2)$.*

Proof. As ψ is a signed permutation, we focus on the action of ψ on the set of vectors $E = \{\pm\mathbf{e}_1, \ldots, \pm\mathbf{e}_n\}$.

If ord(ψ) = p for a odd prime p. For any $\mathbf{e}_i \in E$, it has either $\psi\mathbf{e}_i = \mathbf{e}_i$ or the vectors $\mathbf{e}_i, \psi\mathbf{e}_i, \ldots, \psi^{p-1}\mathbf{e}_i \in E$ are linearly independent. Thus $\psi \sim \mathbf{T}_{p,k}$. It follows that $d = \dim(V_1) = k + (n - pk)$, i.e., $k = (n-d)/(p-1)$.

If ord(ψ) = 4 and $\psi^2 = -\mathbf{I}_n$. For any $\mathbf{e}_i \in E$, there is a $\mathbf{v} \in E$ such that $\mathbf{v} \neq \pm\mathbf{e}_i$ and $\psi\mathbf{e}_i = \mathbf{v}, \psi\mathbf{v} = -\mathbf{e}_i$. It follows that $\psi \sim \mathbf{T}_n$.

If ord(ψ) = 2 and $\psi \neq -\mathbf{I}_n$. Then the vectors in E can be divided into three categories. The first catergry consists of the $\mathbf{v} \in E$ such that $\psi\mathbf{v} = \mathbf{v}$, and the second catergry consists of the $\mathbf{v} \in E$ such that $\psi\mathbf{v} = -\mathbf{v}$. The third catergry contains all $\mathbf{u}, \mathbf{v} \in E$ such that $\mathbf{u} \neq \mathbf{v}$, $\psi\mathbf{u} = \mathbf{v}$ and $\psi\mathbf{v} = \mathbf{u}$. It follows that $\psi \sim \mathbf{T}_{i,j,k}$. Since $\psi \neq \pm\mathbf{I}_n$, it has $i, j < n$. Moreover, observe that for $\mathbf{T}_{i,j,k}$, a basis of V_1 is $\{\mathbf{e}_1+\mathbf{e}_2, \mathbf{e}_3+\mathbf{e}_4, \ldots, \mathbf{e}_{2k-1}+\mathbf{e}_{2k}\} \cup \{\mathbf{e}_{n-j+1}, \ldots, \mathbf{e}_n\}$. Thus $d = k+j$ and $\det(\mathcal{L}_1) = 2^{\frac{k}{2}}$, which implies that $k = \log_2(\det(\mathcal{L}_1)^2)$, $i = n - d - k$ and $j = d - k$. □

Next, we integrate the randomization framework (Proposition 3.1) and the preprocessing technique (Lemma 4.1) to establish the following proposition.

Lemma 4.4 (Randomization). *Given a $\mathbb{Z}LAP$ oracle $\mathcal{O}$, which takes a lattice basis $\tilde{\mathbf{B}}$ as input, subject to the condition that $\mathcal{L}(\tilde{\mathbf{B}}) \cong \mathbb{Z}^n$, and returns a nontrivial automorphism in $\mathrm{Aut}(\mathcal{L}(\tilde{\mathbf{B}}))$. Then for a lattice $\mathcal{L} \cong \mathbb{Z}^n$, we can efficiently sample automorphisms in $\mathrm{Aut}(\mathcal{L})$ such that they are uniformly and independently distributed in each of the conjugacy classes corresponding to $\mathbf{T}_{i,j,k}$, $\mathbf{T}_{p,k}$, or $\mathbf{T}_n$.*

Proof. Let $\mathbf{B}$ be a basis of $\mathcal{L}$. Similar to Proposition 3.1, we sample an orthogonal matrix $\mathbf{O}_1$ from $O_n(\mathbb{R})$ uniformly at random, and obtain a basis $\mathbf{B}_1 \leftarrow \mathcal{A}(\mathbf{O}_1\mathbf{B})$ of the lattice $\mathcal{L}_1 = \mathbf{O}_1\mathcal{L}$. Then we call the $\mathbb{Z}LAP$ oracle, taking $\mathbf{B}_1$ as input to obtain a nontrivial automorphism $\phi_1 \in \mathrm{Aut}(\mathcal{L}_1)$. Applying the preprocessing technique in Lemma 4.1 to ϕ_1, we obtain an automorphism $\psi_1 \in \mathrm{Aut}(\mathcal{L}_1)$ in one of the conjugacy classes corresponding to $\mathbf{T}_{i,j,k}$, $\mathbf{T}_{p,k}$, or $\mathbf{T}_n$. Finally, we compute $\mathbf{O}_1^{-1}\psi_1\mathbf{O}_1 \in \mathrm{Aut}(\mathcal{L})$.

Next we prove that for any conjugacy class $\mathfrak{C}_{\phi_0}$, $\phi_0 \in \mathrm{Aut}(\mathcal{L})$, the probability

$$\mathrm{Pr}_{\mathbf{O}_1 \leftarrow O_n(\mathbb{R}); \mathbf{B}_1 \leftarrow \mathcal{A}(\mathbf{O}_1\mathbf{B})}[\mathbf{O}_1^{-1}\psi_1\mathbf{O}_1 = \phi] \tag{11}$$

is identical for each $\phi \in \mathfrak{C}_{\phi_0}$. Note that for each $\phi' \in \mathrm{Aut}(\mathcal{L})$, it has

$$\mathrm{Pr}_{\mathbf{O}_1 \leftarrow O_n(\mathbb{R}); \mathbf{B}_1 \leftarrow \mathcal{A}(\mathbf{O}_1\mathbf{B})}[\mathbf{O}_1^{-1}\psi_1\mathbf{O}_1 = \phi'\phi\phi'^{-1}]$$
$$= \mathrm{Pr}_{(\mathbf{O}_1\phi') \leftarrow O_n(\mathbb{R}); \mathbf{B}_1 \leftarrow \mathcal{A}(\mathbf{O}_1\mathbf{B})}[(\mathbf{O}_1\phi')^{-1}\psi_1(\mathbf{O}_1\phi') = \phi]$$
$$= \mathrm{Pr}_{\mathbf{O}_1 \leftarrow O_n(\mathbb{R}); \mathbf{B}_1 \leftarrow \mathcal{A}(\mathbf{O}_1\mathbf{B})}[\mathbf{O}_1^{-1}\psi_1\mathbf{O}_1 = \phi].$$

Moreover, it is clear that $\mathbf{O}_1^{-1}\psi_1\mathbf{O}_1$ is in one of the conjugacy classes corresponding to $\mathbf{T}_{i,j,k}$, $\mathbf{T}_{p,k}$, or $\mathbf{T}_n$, which proves the uniformity. The independence of each trial follows from the same reason as in Proposition 3.1. $\square$

Conversion to a Special Conjugacy Class. Observe that the total number of conjugacy classes corresponding to $\mathbf{T}_{i,j,k}$, $\mathbf{T}_{p,k}$ and $\mathbf{T}_n$ is $O(n^2)$. Then by Lemma 4.1 and Lemma 4.4, we can efficiently sample $poly(n)$ automorphisms in $\mathrm{Aut}(\mathcal{L})$ such that they are independently and uniformly distributed in a conjugacy class corresponding to one of the $\mathbf{T}_{i,j,k}$, $\mathbf{T}_{p,k}$ and $\mathbf{T}_n$. In order to ease the analysis of the shortest vector recovery, we further introduce a technique that transforms the automorphisms into a conjugacy class that corresponds to $\mathbf{T}_{i,j,k}$. For the sake of simplicity, we will focus on the case where n is odd, which excludes $\mathbf{T}_n$. To begin with, we establish the following lemma.

Lemma 4.5. *Assume that n is odd and $\mathcal{L} \cong \mathbb{Z}^n$. Let $\phi \in \mathrm{Aut}(\mathcal{L})$ be an automorphism such that $\phi \sim \mathbf{T}_{p,k}$, and let ϕ_1 be an automorphism that is uniformly distributed over $\mathfrak{C}_\phi$. Then the probability that $2 \mid \mathrm{ord}(\phi_1\phi)$ and $(\phi_1\phi)^{\mathrm{ord}(\phi_1\phi)/2} \neq -\mathbf{I}_n$ is at least $1/n^4$.*

Proof. Suppose $\mathbf{O} \in O_n(\mathbb{R})$ is an isomorphism from $\mathbb{Z}^n$ to $\mathcal{L}$ such that $\phi = \mathbf{O}\mathbf{T}_{p,k}\mathbf{O}^{-1}$. Then we can express ϕ_1 as $\mathbf{O}\mathbf{S}\mathbf{T}_{p,k}\mathbf{S}^{-1}\mathbf{O}^{-1}$, where $\mathbf{S}$ is uniformly distributed over $S_n^\pm$. Therefore $\phi_1\phi = \mathbf{O}\mathbf{S}\mathbf{T}_{p,k}\mathbf{S}^{-1}\mathbf{T}_{p,k}\mathbf{O}^{-1}$. In the following, we analyze the probability that $\mathbf{S}\mathbf{T}_{p,k}\mathbf{S}^{-1}\mathbf{T}_{p,k}$ contains a 2-cycle. There are two cases.

(1) $p > 3$ or $k \geq 2$. In this case there exist four distinct integers $i_1, i_2, i_3, i_4 \in [n]$ such that $\mathbf{T}_{p,k}\mathbf{e}_{i_1} = \mathbf{e}_{i_2}$ and $\mathbf{T}_{p,k}\mathbf{e}_{i_3} = \mathbf{e}_{i_4}$. We are interested in the probability that $\mathbf{ST}_{p,k}\mathbf{S}^{-1}\mathbf{T}_{p,k}\mathbf{e}_{i_1} = \mathbf{e}_{i_3}$ and $\mathbf{ST}_{p,k}\mathbf{S}^{-1}\mathbf{T}_{p,k}\mathbf{e}_{i_3} = \mathbf{e}_{i_1}$, i.e., (i_1, i_3) is a 2-cycle with respect to the action of $\mathbf{ST}_{p,k}\mathbf{S}^{-1}\mathbf{T}_{p,k}$. Note that the above conditions can be written as $\mathbf{T}_{p,k}(\mathbf{S}^{-1}\mathbf{e}_{i_2}) = \mathbf{S}^{-1}\mathbf{e}_{i_3}$ and $\mathbf{T}_{p,k}(\mathbf{S}^{-1}\mathbf{e}_{i_4}) = \mathbf{S}^{-1}\mathbf{e}_{i_1}$. Since $\mathbf{S}$ is uniformly distributed over $S_n^{\pm}$, it can be deduced that the probability is as least $\frac{1}{4} \cdot \frac{kp(kp-3)}{n^4} \geq \frac{1}{n^4}$.

(2) $p = 3, k = 1$. In this case we are interested on the probability that $(1,2)$ is a 2-cycle with respect to the action of $\mathbf{ST}_{p,k}\mathbf{S}^{-1}\mathbf{T}_{p,k}$, i.e., $\mathbf{ST}_{p,k}\mathbf{S}^{-1}\mathbf{T}_{p,k}\mathbf{e}_1 = \mathbf{e}_2$ and $\mathbf{ST}_{p,k}\mathbf{S}^{-1}\mathbf{T}_{p,k}\mathbf{e}_2 = \mathbf{e}_1$. The conditions can be written as $\mathbf{T}_{p,k}(\mathbf{S}^{-1}\mathbf{e}_2) = \mathbf{S}^{-1}\mathbf{e}_2$ and $\mathbf{T}_{p,k}(\mathbf{S}^{-1}\mathbf{e}_3) = \mathbf{S}^{-1}\mathbf{e}_1$. It can be deduced that the probability is at least $\frac{n-pk}{n} \cdot \frac{1}{2} \cdot \frac{pk}{n^2} > \frac{1}{n^4}$.

Observe that $\mathbf{ST}_{p,k}\mathbf{S}^{-1}\mathbf{T}_{p,k}$ contains a 2-cycle implies that $2 \mid \mathrm{ord}(\phi_1\phi)$ and $(\phi_1\phi)^{\mathrm{ord}(\phi_1\phi)/2} \neq -\mathbf{I}_n$. Therefore we can conclude the lemma. □

In the rest of this subsection, we give the proof of Proposition 4.1. Particularly, we present a two-level randomization technique for generating automorphisms that are uniformly and independently distributed over a conjugacy class associated with $\mathbf{T}_{i,j,k}$.

medskip*Proof of* Proposition 4.1. To begin with, we randomly select $\mathbf{O}_1 \in O_n(\mathbb{R})$ and create the lattice $\mathcal{L}_1 = \mathbf{O}_1\mathcal{L}$ (first-level randomization). Using Lemma 4.4, we can efficiently obtain $poly(n)$ samples in $\phi_1, \ldots, \phi_{poly(n)} \in \mathrm{Aut}(\mathcal{L}_1)$ that are uniformly and independently distributed in one of the conjugacy classes corresponding to $\mathbf{T}_{i,j,k}$ or $\mathbf{T}_{p,k}$ (second-level randomization). Note that we exclude $\mathbf{T}_n$ since n is odd. There are two cases.

(1) These $poly(n)$ samples are in a conjugacy class corresponding to $\mathbf{T}_{i,j,k}$. We just apply $\mathbf{O}_1^{-1}\phi_i\mathbf{O}_1$ and obtain $poly(n)$ samples in $\mathrm{Aut}(\mathcal{L})$.

(2) These $poly(n)$ samples are in a conjugacy class corresponding to $\mathbf{T}_{p,k}$. Using Lemma 4.5, we can show that, with a probability of at least $1/n^4$, the automorphisms $\phi_2\phi_1, \phi_3\phi_1 \ldots, \phi_{poly(n)}\phi_1 \in \mathrm{Aut}(\mathcal{L}_1)$ satisfy the conditions $2 \mid \mathrm{ord}(\phi_i\phi)$ and $(\phi_1\phi)^{\mathrm{ord}(\phi_i\phi)/2} \neq -\mathbf{I}_n$. By properly defining $poly(n)$, we can obtain such an automorphism $\phi_i\phi$ with overwhelming probability. We can then apply the preprocessing procedure (Lemma 4.1) to $\phi_i\phi$ to get an automorphism in a conjugacy class corresponding to $\mathbf{T}_{i,j,k}$, resulting in a desired random automorphism in $\mathrm{Aut}(\mathcal{L})$.

Then Proposition 4.1 can be proved by repeating the above procedure polynomial times. □

4.2   Recover the Shortest Vectors

Using Proposition 4.1, a reduction from $\mathbb{Z}$LIP to $\mathbb{Z}$LAP can be established by solving the following problem, which can be viewed as an analogue of Problem 3.1.

Problem 4.1. *Given a basis* $\mathbf{B}$ *of a lattice* $\mathcal{L} \cong \mathbb{Z}^n$, *and a set of automorphisms* $\phi_1, \phi_2, \ldots, \phi_{poly(n)} \in \mathrm{Aut}(\mathcal{L})$ *that are drawn uniformly and independently from a conjugacy class* $\mathfrak{C}_{\phi_0}$, *where* $\phi_0 \sim \mathbf{T}_{k_1,k_2,l}$ *and* k_1, k_2, l *are fixed. The goal is to find the shortest vectors of* $\mathcal{L}$.

Define the function

$$g_k(\mathbf{x}) = \mathbb{E}[\langle \phi \mathbf{x}, \mathbf{x} \rangle^k], \mathbf{x} \in \mathbb{R}^n, \tag{12}$$

where $k \in \mathbb{Z}^+$ and ϕ is uniformly distributed over $\mathfrak{C}_{\phi_0}$. Similar to the deduction in Sect. 3, for any $x \in \mathbb{R}^n$, $g_k(\mathbf{x})$ can be effectively approximated by using the given samples in $\mathfrak{C}_{\phi_0}$ due to Chernoff bound. Suppose $\{\mathbf{v}_1, \ldots, \mathbf{v}_n\}$ is a set of independent shortest vectors of $\mathcal{L}$. Then any $\mathbf{x} \in \mathbb{R}^n$ can be expressed as a linear combination $\mathbf{x} = x_1 \mathbf{v}_1 + \cdots + x_n \mathbf{v}_n$, i.e., $x_i = \langle \mathbf{x}, \mathbf{v}_i \rangle$ for $1 \leq i \leq n$. Then the following lemma can be derived.

Lemma 4.6. *For* $k = 1, 2$, *it has*

$$g_1(\mathbf{x}) = \frac{k_2 - k_1}{n} \sum_{i=1}^{n} x_i^2 = \frac{k_2 - k_1}{n} \|\mathbf{x}\|^2$$

$$g_2(\mathbf{x}) = \frac{n^2 - 2nl - (k_1 - k_2)^2 - 4l}{n(n-1)} \sum_{i=1}^{n} x_i^4 + \frac{6l + (k_1 - k_2)^2 - n}{n(n-1)} (\sum_{i=1}^{n} x_i^2)^2$$

Proof. We refer the proof to Appendix C. $\qquad\qquad\qquad\qquad\qquad\qquad\qquad\square$

On the other hand, note that

$$\nabla \mathbb{E}[\langle \phi \mathbf{x}, \mathbf{x} \rangle^2] = \mathbb{E}[\nabla \langle \phi \mathbf{x}, \mathbf{x} \rangle^2] = 2\mathbb{E}[\langle \phi \mathbf{x}, \mathbf{x} \rangle \cdot (\phi + \phi^\top)\mathbf{x}]. \tag{13}$$

Thus the gradient

$$\nabla g_2(\mathbf{x}) = 4 \sum_{i=1}^{n} (\frac{n^2 - 2nl - (k_1 - k_2)^2 - 4l}{n(n-1)} x_i^3 + \frac{6l + (k_1 - k_2)^2 - n}{n(n-1)} x_i \|\mathbf{x}\|^2) \mathbf{v}_i$$

can be effectively approximated by using the given samples in $\mathfrak{C}_{\phi_0}$.

Observe that n is odd and $n = k_1 + k_2 + 2l$, it follows that the coefficient $n^2 - 2nl - (k_1 - k_2)^2 - 4l = 4k_1 k_2 + 2l(k_1 + k_2 - 2) \neq 0$. Again we can use the gradient descent to solve Problem 4.1. Specifically, we assume that $\mathbf{x}$ is on the unit sphere, and define

$$f_2(\mathbf{x}) = (g_2(\mathbf{x}) - \frac{6l + (k_1 - k_2)^2 - n}{n(n-1)}) / \frac{n^2 - 2nl - (k_1 - k_2)^2 - 4l}{n(n-1)} = \sum_{i=1}^{n} \langle \mathbf{v}_i, \mathbf{x} \rangle^4.$$

Then $\nabla f_2(\mathbf{x}) = 4 \sum_{i=1}^{n} \langle \mathbf{v}_i, \mathbf{x} \rangle^3 \mathbf{v}_i$ can be computed from $\nabla g_2(x)$[5], and clearly the global maximum of $f_2(\mathbf{x})$ over the unit sphere is attained at $\{\pm \mathbf{v}_1, \ldots, \pm \mathbf{v}_n\}$. Taking into account the approximation error, we present Algorithm 2 as a solution to Problem 4.1, and an analysis of the algorithm in Proposition 4.2.

---

[5] The second method described in Sect. 3 can also be used to approximate the gradient $\nabla g_2(\mathbf{x})$.

Algorithm 2: Solve Problem 4.1 via Gradient Descent

Require: A polynomial number of samples in $\mathrm{Aut}(\mathcal{L})$ that are uniformly and independently distributed over the conjugacy class $\mathfrak{C}_{\phi_0}$, where k_1, k_2, l are fixed and $\phi_0 \sim \mathbf{T}_{k_1, k_2, l}$

Ensure: An approximation a shortest vector of $\mathcal{L}$

1: Choose $\mathbf{x}$ uniformly at random from the unit sphere of $\mathbb{R}^n$
2: Compute an approximation of the gradient $\nabla f_2(\mathbf{x})$
3: $\mathbf{x}_{new} \leftarrow \nabla f_2(\mathbf{x})$
4: $\mathbf{x}_{new} \leftarrow \mathbf{x}_{new} / \|\mathbf{x}_{new}\|$
5: Compute the approximations of $f_2(\mathbf{x}_{new})$ and $f_2(\mathbf{x})$
6: **if** $f_2(\mathbf{x}_{new}) \leq f_2(\mathbf{x})$ **then**
7:     **return** $\mathbf{x}$
8: **else**
9:     Replace $\mathbf{x}$ by $\mathbf{x}_{new}$ and go to step 2
10: **end if**

Proposition 4.2. *Suppose that n is odd and $\mathcal{L} \cong \mathbb{Z}^n$. For any $c_0 > 0$, there exists a constant $c_1 > 0$ such that Algorithm 2 inputs n^{c_1} samples that are independently and uniformly distributed over a conjugacy class $\mathfrak{C}_{\phi_0}$, where k_1, k_2, l are fixed and $\phi_0 \sim \mathbf{T}_{k_1, k_2, l}$. And Algorithm 2 outputs a vector $\mathbf{x}$ such that $\|\mathbf{x} - \mathbf{v}\| \leq n^{-c_0}$ for some shortest vector $\mathbf{v} \in \mathcal{L}$, with $O(\log \log n)$ descent steps and a constant probability. Moreover, $O(n \log n)$ calls to Algorithm 2 will find all shortest vectors of $\mathcal{L}$ with an overwhelming probability.*

Proof. The proof is similar to that of Proposition 3.2 and is omitted here.   □

Similar to Proposition 3.2, we can also recover the exact shortest vectors through good enough approximations of the shortest vectors of $\mathcal{L}$ by using a set of random automorphisms. The details can be found in Appendix D.

Combining Proposition 4.1 and Proposition 4.2, we can prove our main result in this section.

Theorem 4.1. *There is an efficient randomized reduction from $\mathbb{Z}LIP$ to $\mathbb{Z}LAP$.*

Proof. If the dimension n is odd, then the theorem follows directly from Proposition 4.1 and Proposition 4.2. For even n, we utilize Corollary 3.3 to convert the $\mathbb{Z}LIP$ into an $n + 1$ dimensional problem, which we can then solve using the same approach.   □

Remark 2. It is worth mentioning that all reductions in this paper are dimension-preserving, except for Theorem 4.1. In Theorem 4.1, the condition that n is odd (required in Proposition 4.1 and Proposition 4.2) is primarily for ease of analysis and is not a fundamental requirement. We believe that for even n, similar results can be obtained through a more complex deduction process. However, we do not provide a detailed analysis in this paper and leave it as future work.

4.3   Related Corollaries of Lattice Automorphisms

To begin with, we show that the lattice automorphisms can be linked with the hidden subgroup problem (HSP) on $GL_n(\mathbb{Z})$. HSP is a fundamental problem in quantum computation that encompasses a variety of problems, including factoring, discrete logarithm [49], principal ideal [22], graph isomorphism [35], and unique shortest vector problem [47]. It is of great importance in the theory of quantum computing as virtually all known quantum algorithms that run super-polynomially faster than classical algorithms solve special cases of the HSP on abelian groups such as those presented in [22,49], while the other problems correspond to non-abelian groups. As far as we know, prior to this paper, there were no known applications of the HSP on $GL_n(\mathbb{Z})$.

Definition 4.1 (HSP). *Given a group G, a subgroup $H \leq G$, and a set X. Let $f : G \to X$ be a function that hides H, i.e., $\forall g_1, g_2 \in G$, $f(g_1) = f(g_2) \Leftrightarrow g_1 H = g_2 H$. The HSP is to find a generating set of H given the function f as an oracle.*

Typically G and X are required to be finite, allowing for a well-defined problem size and efficient solution strategies. Nevertheless, for certain special infinite groups G and sets X, well-defined problems can still be formulated and solved efficiently [36,37]. Additionally, the case where G is a continuous group is also addressed in [22].

Corollary 4.1. *There is an efficient randomized reduction from $\mathbb{Z}$LIP to a variant of HSP on $GL_n(\mathbb{Z})$.*

Proof. Given a basis $\mathbf{B}$ of lattice $\mathcal{L} \cong \mathbb{Z}^n$. Let $G = X = GL_n(\mathbb{Z})$ and $H = \mathrm{Stab}(\mathbf{B}^\top \mathbf{B}) \leq G$. Define $f : G \to X$ such that $f(\mathbf{U}) = \mathbf{U}^\top \mathbf{B}^\top \mathbf{B} \mathbf{U}, \forall \mathbf{U} \in GL_n(\mathbb{Z})$. Then clearly f can be computed efficiently, and f hides H. By Lemma 2.9 there is a direct connection between $H = \mathrm{Stab}(\mathbf{B}^\top \mathbf{B})$ and $\mathrm{Aut}(\mathcal{L})$, and thus the statement follows directly from Theorem 4.1. $\qquad\square$

Another natural question is whether the randomization framework can be applied in the reduction of general lattices. The following conclusions demonstrate that it is still applicable to specific problems. However, we believe that the randomization framework is better suited to lattices with high symmetry, i.e., those with a large automorphism group.

Corollary 4.2. *There is an efficient randomized reduction from LAP to LIP in the same dimension.*

Proof. Let $\mathcal{L}$ be an n dimensional lattice with a basis $\mathbf{B}$. To begin with, we choose a random $\mathbf{O}_1 \in O_n(\mathbb{R})$. Using Lemma 3.1, we can obtain a basis $\mathbf{B}_1 \leftarrow \mathcal{A}(\mathbf{O}_1 \mathbf{B})$. Then we call the LIP oracle $\mathcal{O}$ with input $\mathbf{B}$ and $\mathbf{B}_1$, and get an isomorphism $\mathbf{O} = \mathcal{O}(\mathbf{B}, \mathbf{B}_1)$ from $\mathcal{L}$ to $\mathcal{L}_1$. For any $\phi, \phi_0 \in \mathrm{Aut}(\mathcal{L})$, it can be deduced that

$$\mathrm{Pr}_{\mathbf{O}_1 \leftarrow O_n(\mathbb{R}); \mathbf{B}_1 \leftarrow \mathcal{A}(\mathbf{O}_1 \mathbf{B})}[\mathbf{O}_1^{-1} \mathcal{O}(\mathbf{B}, \mathbf{B}_1) = \phi \phi_0]$$
$$= \mathrm{Pr}_{\mathbf{O}_1 \phi \leftarrow O_n(\mathbb{R}); \mathbf{B}_1 \leftarrow \mathcal{A}(\mathbf{O}_1 \phi \mathbf{B})}[(\mathbf{O}_1 \phi)^{-1} \mathcal{O}(\mathbf{B}, \mathbf{B}_1) = \phi_0]$$
$$= \mathrm{Pr}_{\mathbf{O}_1 \leftarrow O_n(\mathbb{R}); \mathbf{B}_1 \leftarrow \mathcal{A}(\mathbf{O}_1 \mathbf{B})}[\mathbf{O}_1^{-1} \mathcal{O}(\mathbf{B}, \mathbf{B}_1) = \phi_0],$$

which implies that $\mathbf{O}_1^{-1} \mathcal{O}(\mathbf{B}, \mathbf{B}_1)$ is uniformly distributed in $\mathrm{Aut}(\mathcal{L})$. Thus if $\mathrm{Aut}(\mathcal{L}) \neq \{\pm \mathbf{I}_n\}$, we can efficiently obtain a nontrivial automorphism from $\mathrm{Aut}(\mathcal{L})$ with an overwhelming probability by repeating the above process $O(n)$ times. $\qquad\square$

5   Conclusion

We present a randomization framework for lattices that randomizes the output of an oracle in such a way that the resulting samples conform to a distribution that is invariant under the action of the automorphism group. Using this framework, we derive three randomized reductions related to the rotation of $\mathbb{Z}^n$: $\mathbb{Z}$LIP to $\mathbb{Z}$SCVP, $\mathbb{Z}$SVP to $O(1)$-$\mathbb{Z}$SVP, and $\mathbb{Z}$LIP to $\mathbb{Z}$LAP. These results offer new insights into the study of rotations of $\mathbb{Z}^n$, and we believe they will pave the way for further research into $\mathbb{Z}$LIP and $\mathbb{Z}$SVP.

Acknowledgments. We thank the anonymous reviewers from ASIACRYPT 2023 for the valuable comments. We thank Yilei Chen, Ji Luo, Shihe Ma and Shuoxun Xu for helpful conversations. This work is supported by the National Key R&D Program of China (2018YFA0704701, 2020YFA0309705), Shandong Key Research and Development Program (2020ZLYS09), the Major Scientific and Technological Innovation Project of Shandong, China (2019JZZY010133), the Major Program of Guangdong Basic and Applied Research (2019B030302008), the Mathematical Tianyuan Fund of the National Natural Science Foundation of China (12226006) and the National Natural Science Foundation of China (62102216) and Tsinghua University Dushi Program.

Appendix A   Proof of the Toy Example

With respect to the oracle $\mathcal{O}$, the rotated square is determined by the angle θ between the line connecting its vertex on the first quadrant to the origin O and the positive direction of the x-axis. Denoted the rotated square by $\square_\theta, \theta \in [0, \frac{\pi}{2})$. Note we can regard θ as functional of ρ, and write $\theta[\rho] = \theta[\rho + \frac{\pi}{2}]$. We'll show that,

$$\mathrm{Pr}_{\rho \leftarrow G}[\rho^{-1} \mathcal{O}(\square_{\theta[\rho]}) = i] = \frac{1}{4}, \ \forall i \in \mathbb{Z}/4\mathbb{Z}.$$

Proof. For any $i \in \mathbb{Z}/4\mathbb{Z}$, $\mathrm{Pr}_{\rho \leftarrow G}[\rho^{-1}\mathcal{O}(\square_{\theta[\rho]}) = i]$ is a functional about ρ which is a distribution on $G = \mathbb{R}/2\pi\mathbb{Z}$. Then we have

$$\mathrm{Pr}_{\rho \leftarrow G}[\rho^{-1}\mathcal{O}(\square_{\theta[\rho]}) = i] = \mathrm{Pr}_{\rho \leftarrow G}[\mathcal{O}(\square_{\theta[\rho]}) = \rho(i)]$$
$$= \mathrm{Pr}_{\rho + \frac{\pi}{2} \leftarrow G}[\mathcal{O}(\square_{\theta[\rho + \frac{\pi}{2}]}) = (\rho + \frac{\pi}{2})(i)]$$
$$= \mathrm{Pr}_{\rho + \frac{\pi}{2} \leftarrow G}[\mathcal{O}(\square_{\theta[\rho]}) = \rho(i+1)]$$
$$= \mathrm{Pr}_{\rho \leftarrow G}[\mathcal{O}(\square_{\theta[\rho]}) = \rho(i+1)].$$

This means $\forall i \in \mathbb{Z}/4\mathbb{Z}$, $\mathrm{Pr}_{\rho \leftarrow G}[\rho^{-1}\mathcal{O}(\square_{\theta[\rho]}) = i] = \frac{1}{4}$. $\qquad\square$

Appendix B   Proof of the Property of the Characteristic Vectors

Lemma 2.6. *Assume* $\mathbf{B} = (\mathbf{b}_1, ..., \mathbf{b}_n)$ *is a basis of* $\mathcal{L}$ *and* $\mathbf{B}^{-\top} = (\mathbf{d}_1, ..., \mathbf{d}_n)$, *then it has:*

1) $\mathbf{w} = \sum_{i=1}^n \|\mathbf{d}_i\|^2 \mathbf{b}_i$ *is a characteristic vector of* $\mathcal{L}$.
2) $\chi(\mathcal{L}) = \mathbf{w} + 2\mathcal{L}$ *for any characteristic vector* $\mathbf{w} \in \chi(\mathcal{L})$.
3) $\mathbf{w}$ *is a characteristic vector if and only if* $\langle \mathbf{w}, \mathbf{b}_i \rangle \equiv \langle \mathbf{b}_i, \mathbf{b}_i \rangle \mod 2$ *for* $i \in [n]$.

Proof. 1) Let $\mathbf{v} = \sum_{i=1}^n v_i \mathbf{d}_i \in \mathcal{L}(\mathbf{B})$, then $\langle \mathbf{w}, \mathbf{v} \rangle = \langle \sum_{i=1}^n \|\mathbf{d}_i\|^2 \mathbf{b}_i, \sum_{i=1}^n v_i \mathbf{d}_i \rangle$ $= \sum_{i=1}^n v_i \|\mathbf{d}_i\|^2 \equiv \sum_{i=1}^n v_i^2 \|\mathbf{d}_i\|^2 \equiv \langle \mathbf{v}, \mathbf{v} \rangle \mod 2$, we used $v_i \equiv v_i^2 \mod 2$. Thus $\mathbf{w}$ is a characteristic vector.

2) Assume $\mathbf{w}$ is a characteristic vector of $\mathcal{L}$, then for any $\mathbf{x} \in \mathcal{L}$, $\mathbf{w} + 2\mathbf{x}$ is also a characteristic vector of $\mathcal{L}$, because $\langle \mathbf{w} + 2\mathbf{x}, \mathbf{v} \rangle = \langle \mathbf{w}, \mathbf{v} \rangle + 2\langle \mathbf{x}, \mathbf{v} \rangle \equiv \langle \mathbf{w}, \mathbf{v} \rangle \equiv \langle \mathbf{v}, \mathbf{v} \rangle \mod 2$. On the other hand, if $\mathbf{w}' = \sum_{i=1}^n a_i \mathbf{b}_i \in \chi(\mathcal{L})$, then $a_i = \langle \mathbf{w}', \mathbf{d}_i \rangle \equiv \langle \mathbf{d}_i, \mathbf{d}_i \rangle = \|\mathbf{d}_i\|^2 \mod 2$, thus for any $i \in [n]$, $a_i \equiv \|\mathbf{d}_i\|^2 \mod 2$ and we know $\mathbf{w} = \sum_{i=1}^n \|\mathbf{d}_i\|^2 \mathbf{b}_i \in \chi(\mathcal{L})$, thus $\mathbf{w}' = \mathbf{w} + 2\mathcal{L}$. Thus $\chi(\mathcal{L})$ is a coset of $\mathbf{w} + 2\mathcal{L}$, where $\mathbf{w}$ is any element in $\chi(\mathcal{L})$.

3) Obviously, if $\mathbf{w} \in \chi(\mathcal{L})$, $\forall i \in [n]$, $\langle \mathbf{w}, \mathbf{b}_i \rangle \equiv \langle \mathbf{b}_i, \mathbf{b}_i \rangle \mod 2$. On the other hand, if $\mathbf{w} \in \mathcal{L}$ satisfying $\forall i \in [n]$, $\langle \mathbf{w}, \mathbf{b}_i \rangle \equiv \langle \mathbf{b}_i, \mathbf{b}_i \rangle \mod 2$. Then for any $\mathbf{v} = \sum_{i=1}^n v_i \mathbf{b}_i \in \mathcal{L}$, without loss of generality, assume $v_i \equiv 1 \mod 2$ for $1 \le i \le k$, and $v_i \equiv 0 \mod 2$ for $k + 1 \le i \le n$. Thus we have $\langle \mathbf{w}, \mathbf{v} \rangle \equiv \langle \mathbf{w}, \mathbf{b}_1 + ... + \mathbf{b}_k \rangle \equiv \sum_{i=1}^k \langle \mathbf{w}, \mathbf{b}_i \rangle \equiv \sum_{i=1}^k \langle \mathbf{b}_i, \mathbf{b}_i \rangle \equiv \langle \mathbf{v}, \mathbf{v} \rangle \mod 2$. $\qquad\square$

Lemma 2.7. *Suppose* $\mathcal{L} \cong \mathbb{Z}^n$. *Assume* $\mathbf{B} = \mathbf{OU}$ *is a basis of* $\mathcal{L}$, *where* $\mathbf{O} \in O_n(\mathbb{R})$ *and* $\mathbf{U} \in GL_n(\mathbb{Z}^n)$. *Then it has:*

1) $\chi(\mathcal{L}) = \{\mathbf{Oz} : \mathbf{z} \in \mathbb{Z}^n \text{ such that } \mathbf{z}_i \equiv 1 \mod 2, \forall i \in [n]\}$.
2) *The shortest characteristic vectors are exactly* $\{\mathbf{Oz} : \mathbf{z}_i = \pm 1, \forall i \in [n]\}$.

Proof. 1) Let $\mathbf{O} = (\mathbf{v}_1, ..., \mathbf{v}_n)$ and $\mathbf{w} = \mathbf{B}(\mathbf{U}^{-1}\mathbf{z}) = \mathbf{Oz}$, where $\mathbf{z} \in \mathbb{Z}^n$ is the vector that $\forall i \in [n]$, $z_i = 1$. Note that $\mathcal{L} = \mathbf{O} \cdot \mathbb{Z}^n$. Thus assume $\mathbf{v} = \sum_{i=1}^n a_i \mathbf{v}_i$, then $\langle \mathbf{w}, \mathbf{v} \rangle = \sum_{i=1}^n a_i z_i \equiv \sum_{i=1}^n a_i^2 = \langle \mathbf{v}, \mathbf{v} \rangle \mod 2$, where we used $a_i^2 \equiv a_i \mod 2$ and $z_i \equiv 1 \mod 2$. Thus $\mathbf{w} \in \chi(\mathcal{L})$, so $\chi(\mathcal{L}) = \{\mathbf{Oz} : \mathbf{z} \in \mathbb{Z}^n \text{ such that } \mathbf{z}_i \equiv 1 \mod 2, \forall i \in [n]\}$.

2) Note that $\mathbf{O}$ is an orthogonal matrix, thus the shortest characteristic vectors are $\{\mathbf{Oz} : \mathbf{z}_i = \pm 1, \forall i \in [n]\}$ by 1). $\qquad\square$

Appendix C   Proof of Lemma 4.6

Proof. Let $\mathcal{D}$ be the set of $n \times n$ diagonal matrices whose diagonal entries are ± 1. Then $\mathcal{D}$ forms a subgroup of $\mathcal{S}_n^{\pm}$, and $\mathcal{S}_n^{\pm}$ is the semidirect product of $\mathcal{D}$ and $\mathcal{S}_n$.[6] For $\phi_0 \in \mathrm{Aut}(\mathcal{L})$ and $\phi_0 \sim \mathbf{T}_{k_1,k_2,l}$, let $\mathbf{O} \in \mathcal{O}_n(\mathbb{R})$ such that $\mathcal{L} = \mathbf{O}\mathbb{Z}^n$, then it has $\mathfrak{C}_{\phi_0} = \{\mathbf{O}\mathbf{T}\mathbf{T}_{k_1,k_2,l}\mathbf{T}^{-1}\mathbf{O}^{-1} : \mathbf{T} \in \mathcal{S}_n^{\pm}\}$. Denote $\mathbf{y} = \mathbf{O}^{-1}\mathbf{x} = (x_1, \cdots, x_n)$.[7]

For $k = 1$, it has

$$
\begin{aligned}
g_1(\mathbf{x}) = \mathbb{E}[\langle \phi \mathbf{x}, \mathbf{x} \rangle] &= \frac{1}{|\mathcal{S}_n^{\pm}|} \sum_{\mathbf{T} \in \mathcal{S}_n^{\pm}} \langle \mathbf{O}\mathbf{T}\mathbf{T}_{k_1,k_2,l}\mathbf{T}^{-1}\mathbf{O}^{-1}\mathbf{x}, \mathbf{x} \rangle \\
&= \frac{1}{|\mathcal{S}_n^{\pm}|} \sum_{\mathbf{P} \in \mathcal{S}_n} \sum_{\mathbf{D} \in \mathcal{D}} \langle \mathbf{O}\mathbf{P}\mathbf{D}\mathbf{T}_{k_1,k_2,l}\mathbf{D}^{-1}\mathbf{P}^{-1}\mathbf{O}^{-1}\mathbf{x}, \mathbf{x} \rangle \\
&= \frac{1}{|\mathcal{S}_n^{\pm}|} \sum_{\mathbf{P} \in \mathcal{S}_n} \sum_{\mathbf{D} \in \mathcal{D}} \langle \mathbf{D}\mathbf{T}_{k_1,k_2,l}\mathbf{D}^{-1}\mathbf{P}^{-1}\mathbf{O}^{-1}\mathbf{x}, \mathbf{P}^{-1}\mathbf{O}^{-1}\mathbf{x} \rangle \\
&= \frac{1}{|\mathcal{S}_n^{\pm}|} \sum_{\mathbf{P} \in \mathcal{S}_n} \sum_{\mathbf{D} \in \mathcal{D}} \langle \mathbf{D}\mathbf{T}_{k_1,k_2,l}\mathbf{D}^{-1}\mathbf{P}^{-1}\mathbf{y}, \mathbf{P}^{-1}\mathbf{y} \rangle.
\end{aligned}
$$

Denote $\mathbf{W}_{k_1,k_2,l} = \mathrm{diag}\{\mathbf{0}_{2l}, -\mathbf{I}_{k_1}, \mathbf{I}_{k_2}\}$, where $\mathbf{0}_{2l}$ is the $2l \times 2l$ zero matrix. Then it has $\sum_{\mathbf{D} \in \mathcal{D}} \mathbf{D}\mathbf{T}_{k_1,k_2,l}\mathbf{D}^{-1} = |\mathcal{D}| \cdot \mathbf{W}_{k_1,k_2,l}$, and thus

$$
\begin{aligned}
g_1(\mathbf{x}) &= \frac{|\mathcal{D}|}{|\mathcal{S}_n^{\pm}|} \sum_{\mathbf{P} \in \mathcal{S}_n} \langle \mathbf{W}_{k_1,k_2,l}\mathbf{P}^{-1}\mathbf{y}, \mathbf{P}^{-1}\mathbf{y} \rangle \\
&= \frac{1}{|\mathcal{S}_n|} \sum_{\mathbf{P} \in \mathcal{S}_n} (-(x_{\mathbf{P}(2l+1)}^2 + \cdots + x_{\mathbf{P}(2l+k_1)}^2) + (x_{\mathbf{P}(2l+k_1+1)}^2 + \cdots + x_{\mathbf{P}(n)}^2)) \\
&= \frac{-k_1 + k_2}{n}(x_1^2 + \cdots + x_n^2) = \frac{k_2 - k_1}{n}\|\mathbf{x}\|^2,
\end{aligned}
$$

where $\mathbf{P}(i)$ represents the row number of the '1' in $\mathbf{P}$'s i-th column.

For $k = 2$, it has

$$
\begin{aligned}
g_2(\mathbf{x}) &= \frac{1}{|\mathcal{S}_n^{\pm}|} \sum_{\mathbf{T} \in \mathcal{S}_n^{\pm}} \langle \mathbf{O}\mathbf{T}\mathbf{T}_{k_1,k_2,l}\mathbf{T}^{-1}\mathbf{O}^{-1}\mathbf{x}, \mathbf{x} \rangle^2 \\
&= \frac{1}{|\mathcal{S}_n^{\pm}|} \sum_{\mathbf{P} \in \mathcal{S}_n} \sum_{\mathbf{D} \in \mathcal{D}} \langle \mathbf{D}\mathbf{T}_{k_1,k_2,l}\mathbf{D}^{-1}\mathbf{P}^{-1}\mathbf{O}^{-1}\mathbf{x}, \mathbf{P}^{-1}\mathbf{O}^{-1}\mathbf{x} \rangle^2 \\
&= \frac{1}{|\mathcal{S}_n^{\pm}|} \sum_{\mathbf{P} \in \mathcal{S}_n} \sum_{\mathbf{D} \in \mathcal{D}} \langle \mathbf{D}\mathbf{T}_{k_1,k_2,l}\mathbf{D}^{-1}\mathbf{P}^{-1}\mathbf{y}, \mathbf{P}^{-1}\mathbf{y} \rangle^2.
\end{aligned}
$$

---

[6] 'Semidirect product' means that $\mathcal{S}_n^{\pm} = \mathcal{D}\mathcal{S}_n$, $\mathcal{D} \cap \mathcal{S}_n = \{\mathbf{I}_n\}$ and $\mathcal{D}$ is a normal subgroup of $\mathcal{S}_n^{\pm}$. This implies that for any $\mathbf{T} \in \mathcal{S}_n^{\pm}$, there exist unique $\mathbf{D} \in \mathcal{D}$ and $\mathbf{P} \in \mathcal{S}_n$ such that $\mathbf{T} = \mathbf{P}\mathbf{D}$.

[7] This is consistent with the notation $x_i \stackrel{.}{=} \langle \mathbf{x}, \mathbf{v}_i \rangle$ in Sect. 4.2.

For fixed $\mathbf{P} \in \mathcal{S}_n$ and $\mathbf{D} \in \mathcal{D}$, denote $\mathbf{z} = \mathbf{P}^{-1}y = (z_1, \cdots, z_n)$ and $\mathbf{D} = \mathbf{D}^{-1} = \text{diag}\{d_1, \cdots, d_n\}$, where $d_i = \pm 1$. Then it has

$$\mathbf{DT}_{k_1,k_2,l}\mathbf{D}^{-1}\mathbf{z} = (d_1 d_2 z_2, d_1 d_2 z_1, \ldots, d_{2l-1} d_{2l} z_{2l}, d_{2l-1} d_{2l} z_{2l-1},$$
$$- z_{2l+1}, \ldots, -z_{2l+k_1}, z_{2l+k_1+1}, \ldots, z_n),$$

and $\langle \mathbf{DT}_{k_1,k_2,l}\mathbf{D}^{-1}\mathbf{z}, \mathbf{z} \rangle = \sum_{i=1}^{l} 2 d_{2i-1} d_{2i} z_{2i-1} z_{2i} - \sum_{i=2l+1}^{2l+k_1} z_i^2 + \sum_{i=2l+k_1+1}^{n} z_i^2$.
It follows that

$$\sum_{\mathbf{D} \in \mathcal{D}} \langle \mathbf{DT}_{k_1,k_2,l}\mathbf{D}^{-1}\mathbf{z}, \mathbf{z} \rangle^2 = |\mathcal{D}| \left(4 \sum_{i=1}^{l} z_{2i-1}^2 z_{2i}^2 + \sum_{i=2l+1}^{n} z_i^4 + \sum_{2l+1 \leq i,j \leq 2l+k_1} z_i^2 z_j^2 \right.$$

$$\left. -2 \sum_{\substack{2l+1 \leq i \leq 2l+k_1 \\ 2l+k_1+1 \leq j \leq n}} z_i^2 z_j^2 + \sum_{2l+k_1+1 \leq i,j \leq n} z_i^2 z_j^2 \right).$$

Observe that $z_i = x_{\mathbf{P}(i)}$ for $1 \leq i \leq n$, then it can be deduced that

$$g_2(\mathbf{x}) = \frac{1}{|\mathcal{S}_n^{\pm}|} \sum_{\mathbf{P} \in \mathcal{S}_n} \sum_{\mathbf{D} \in \mathcal{D}} \langle \mathbf{DT}_{k_1,k_2,l}\mathbf{D}^{-1}\mathbf{z}, \mathbf{z} \rangle^2$$

$$= \frac{4l + k_1(k_1-1) - 2k_1 k_2 + k_2(k_2-1)}{n(n-1)} \sum_{1 \leq i,j \leq n} x_i^2 x_j^2 + \frac{(n-2l)}{n} \sum_{1 \leq i \leq n} x_i^4$$

$$= \frac{6l + (k_1-k_2)^2 - n}{n(n-1)} \sum_{1 \leq i,j \leq n} x_i^2 x_j^2 + \frac{(n-2l)}{n} \sum_{1 \leq i \leq n} x_i^4$$

$$= \frac{n^2 - 2nl - (k_1-k_2)^2 - 4l}{n(n-1)} \sum_{i=1}^{n} x_i^4 + \frac{6l + (k_1-k_2)^2 - n}{n(n-1)} (\sum_{i=1}^{n} x_i^2)^2.$$

$\square$

Appendix D   Recover the Exact Shortest Vectors in Proposition 4.2

In this appendix, we demonstrate how to recover the exact shortest vectors by using good enough approximations of the shortest vectors of $\mathcal{L}$ and automorphisms of $\text{Aut}(\mathcal{L})$, thereby completing Proposition 4.2. In fact, this can be reduced to the following problem.

Problem D.1. *Suppose n is odd. Given a basis $\mathbf{B}$ of a lattice $\mathcal{L} \cong \mathbb{Z}^n$, a polynomial number of automorphisms $\phi_1, \phi_2, \ldots, \phi_{p(n)} \in \text{Aut}(\mathcal{L})$ that are drawn uniformly and independently from a conjugacy class $\mathfrak{C}_{\phi_0}$, where $\phi_0 \sim \mathbf{T}_{k_1,k_2,l}$ and k_1, k_2, l are fixed, and an approximation of a set of independent shortest vectors $\mathbf{v}_i$, i.e., $\{\tilde{\mathbf{v}}_1, \ldots, \tilde{\mathbf{v}}_n\}$ such that $\tilde{\mathbf{v}}_i = \mathbf{v}_i + \epsilon_i$ and $\|\epsilon_i\| \leq n^{-c}$. The goal is to find the shortest vectors of $\mathcal{L}$, i.e., $\mathbf{V} = \{\mathbf{v}_1, \ldots, \mathbf{v}_n\}$.*

Note that for any $\phi \in \mathfrak{C}_{\phi_0}$, it has $\phi = \mathbf{V}\mathbf{S}\mathbf{V}^{-1}$, where $\mathbf{S} \in \mathcal{S}_n^{\pm}$ and $\mathbf{S} \sim \mathbf{T}_{k_1,k_2,l}$ (i.e., $\exists \mathbf{T} \in \mathcal{S}_n^{\pm}$ such that $\mathbf{S} = \mathbf{T}\mathbf{T}_{k_1,k_2,l}\mathbf{T}^{-1}$), and ϕ acts on the set of shortest vectors $\{\pm\mathbf{v}_1, \ldots, \pm\mathbf{v}_n\}$. Then for $1 \le i, j \le n$, it has $\|\phi\mathbf{v}_i \pm \mathbf{v}_j\| = 0$ or 2 and

$$\left| \|\phi\tilde{\mathbf{v}}_i \pm \tilde{\mathbf{v}}_j\| - \|\phi\mathbf{v}_i \pm \mathbf{v}_j\| \right| \le \|\phi\boldsymbol{\epsilon}_i \pm \boldsymbol{\epsilon}_j\| \le 2n^{-c}. \tag{14}$$

Thus, for any given $\phi \in \mathfrak{C}_{\phi_0}$, we can decide whether $\|\phi\mathbf{v}_i \pm \mathbf{v}_j\| = 0$, and thus exactly recover the corresponding matrix $\mathbf{S} \in \mathcal{S}_n^{\pm}$.

Next, we demonstrate that, for the given automorphisms $\phi_1, \phi_2, \ldots, \phi_{p(n)} \in \mathfrak{C}_{\phi_0}$ and the corresponding matrices $\mathbf{S}_i \in \mathcal{S}_n^{\pm}, 1 \le i \le p(n)$, such that $\phi_i = \mathbf{V}\mathbf{S}_i\mathbf{V}^{-1}$, we can efficiently recover $\mathbf{V}$. For $\phi, \mathbf{S} \in \mathbb{R}^{n \times n}$, define $K(\phi, \mathbf{S}) := \{\mathbf{X} \in \mathbb{R}^{n \times n} : \mathbf{X}\mathbf{S}\mathbf{X}^{-1} = \phi\}$. Then clearly, $K(\phi, \mathbf{S})$ is an $\mathbb{R}$-linear space, and $\mathbf{V} \in K(\phi_i, \mathbf{S}_i)$. Moreover,

$$\begin{aligned}
K(\phi_i, \mathbf{S}_i) &= \{\mathbf{X} : \mathbf{X}\mathbf{S}_i\mathbf{X}^{-1} = \mathbf{V}\mathbf{S}_i\mathbf{V}^{-1}\} \\
&= \{\mathbf{X} : (\mathbf{V}^{-1}\mathbf{X})\mathbf{S}_i(\mathbf{V}^{-1}\mathbf{X})^{-1} = \mathbf{S}_i\} \\
&= \{\mathbf{V}\mathbf{X} : \mathbf{X}\mathbf{S}_i\mathbf{X}^{-1} = \mathbf{S}_i\} \\
&= \mathbf{V} \cdot \{\mathbf{X} : \mathbf{X}\mathbf{S}_i\mathbf{X}^{-1} = \mathbf{S}_i\} \\
&= \mathbf{V} \cdot K(\mathbf{S}_i, \mathbf{S}_i).
\end{aligned}$$

Therefore, $\mathbf{V} \in \mathbf{V} \cdot \bigcap_{i=1}^{p(n)} K(\mathbf{S}_i, \mathbf{S}_i)$. Note that $K(\mathbf{S}_i, \mathbf{S}_i)$ is a subgroup of $\mathcal{S}_n^{\pm}$. Let $\mathbf{T}_i \in \mathcal{S}_n^{\pm}$ such that $\mathbf{S}_i = \mathbf{T}_i\mathbf{T}_{k_1,k_2,l}\mathbf{T}_i^{-1}$. Then it has

$$\begin{aligned}
K(\mathbf{S}_i, \mathbf{S}_i) &= \{\mathbf{X} : \mathbf{X}\mathbf{S}_i\mathbf{X}^{-1} = \mathbf{S}_i\} \\
&= \{\mathbf{X} : \mathbf{X}\mathbf{T}_i\mathbf{T}_{k_1,k_2,l}\mathbf{T}_i^{-1}\mathbf{X}^{-1} = \mathbf{T}_i\mathbf{T}_{k_1,k_2,l}\mathbf{T}_i^{-1}\} \\
&= \{\mathbf{X} : (\mathbf{T}_i^{-1}\mathbf{X}\mathbf{T}_i)\mathbf{T}_{k_1,k_2,l}(\mathbf{T}_i^{-1}\mathbf{X}\mathbf{T}_i)^{-1} = \mathbf{T}_{k_1,k_2,l}\} \\
&= \mathbf{T}_i K(\mathbf{T}_{k_1,k_2,l}, \mathbf{T}_{k_1,k_2,l})\mathbf{T}_i^{-1}.
\end{aligned}$$

Since ϕ_i is drawn uniformly from the conjugacy class $\mathfrak{C}_{\phi_0}$, then $\mathbf{S}_i$ is distributed uniformly in the conjugacy class $\mathfrak{C}_{\mathbf{T}_{k_1,k_2,l}}$. Then from the group action perspective, the coset $\mathbf{T}_i K(\mathbf{T}_{k_1,k_2,l}, \mathbf{T}_{k_1,k_2,l})$ is distributed uniformly in the left cosets of $\mathbf{T}_{k_1,k_2,l}$ in $\mathcal{S}_n^{\pm}$. Equivalently, $K(\mathbf{S}_i, \mathbf{S}_i) = \mathbf{T}_i K(\mathbf{T}_{k_1,k_2,l}, \mathbf{T}_{k_1,k_2,l})\mathbf{T}_i^{-1}$ can be viewed as a random subgroup of $\mathcal{S}_n^{\pm}$ such that $\mathbf{T}_i$ is drawn uniformly at random from $\mathcal{S}_n^{\pm}$. There are two cases for $\mathbf{T}_{k_1,k_2,l}$.

Case 1. $l = 0$. In this case, it has $k_1, k_2 > 0$, and thus there exists $1 \le a \ne b \le n$ such that $\mathbf{T}_{k_1,k_2,l}\mathbf{e}_a = \mathbf{e}_a$ and $\mathbf{T}_{k_1,k_2,l}\mathbf{e}_b = -\mathbf{e}_b$ (we recall that $\{\mathbf{e}_a\}_{a \in [n]}$ is the standard basis). Thus, for an $\mathbf{X} \in K(\mathbf{T}_{k_1,k_2,l}, \mathbf{T}_{k_1,k_2,l})$, we have $\mathbf{e}_a^\top \mathbf{X}\mathbf{e}_b = -\mathbf{e}_a^\top \mathbf{X}\mathbf{T}_{k_1,k_2,l}\mathbf{e}_b = -\mathbf{e}_a^\top \mathbf{T}_{k_1,k_2,l}\mathbf{X}\mathbf{e}_b = -\mathbf{e}_a^\top \mathbf{X}\mathbf{e}_b$, i.e., $\mathbf{e}_a^\top \mathbf{X}\mathbf{e}_b = 0$. Similarly, it can be deduced that $\mathbf{e}_b^\top \mathbf{X}\mathbf{e}_a = 0$.

Therefore, for any $\mathbf{Y} \in K(\mathbf{S}_i, \mathbf{S}_i)$, we have $\mathbf{T}_i^\top \mathbf{Y}\mathbf{T}_i \in K(\mathbf{T}_{k_1,k_2,l}, \mathbf{T}_{k_1,k_2,l})$. It follows that $(\mathbf{T}_i\mathbf{e}_a)^\top \mathbf{Y}(\mathbf{T}_i\mathbf{e}_b) = (\mathbf{T}_i\mathbf{e}_b)^\top \mathbf{Y}(\mathbf{T}_i\mathbf{e}_a) = 0$. Note that $\mathbf{T}_i$ can be viewed as drawn uniformly at random from $\mathcal{S}_n^{\pm}$, and $\mathcal{S}_n^{\pm}$ acts transitively on all the pairs $\{(\pm\mathbf{e}_a, \pm\mathbf{e}_b) : 1 \le a \ne b \le n\}$. Thus, for a sufficiently large polynomial $p(n)$, it has $\mathbf{e}_a^\top \mathbf{Y}\mathbf{e}_b = \mathbf{e}_b^\top \mathbf{Y}\mathbf{e}_a = 0$ for all $1 \le a \ne b \le n$ and $\mathbf{Y} \in$

$\bigcap_{i=1}^{p(n)} K(\mathbf{S}_i, \mathbf{S}_i)$. In other words, $\bigcap_{i=1}^{p(n)} K(\mathbf{S}_i, \mathbf{S}_i)$ consists of all diagonal matrices in $\mathbb{R}^{n \times n}$, i.e., $\bigcap_{i=1}^{p(n)} K(\phi_i, \mathbf{S}_i) = \{\mathbf{V} \cdot \mathrm{diag}\{d_1, \ldots, d_n\} : d_i \in \mathbb{R}\}$. Then $\mathbf{V}$ can be reconstructed by first computing an $\mathbb{R}$-linear basis of the space $\bigcap_{i=1}^{p(n)} K(\phi_i, \mathbf{S}_i)$ and then recovering each $\pm \mathbf{v}_i$ via vector normalization.

Case 2: $l \neq 0$. In this case, it has $k_1 \neq 0$ (or $k_2 \neq 0$). Thus we have $\mathbf{T}_{k_1,k_2,l}\mathbf{e}_1 = \mathbf{e}_2$, $\mathbf{T}_{k_1,k_2,l}\mathbf{e}_2 = \mathbf{e}_1$, and there exists $3 \leq j \leq n$ such that $\mathbf{T}_{k_1,k_2,l}\mathbf{e}_j = -\mathbf{e}_j$ (or $\mathbf{T}_{k_1,k_2,l}\mathbf{e}_j = \mathbf{e}_j$ if $k_2 \neq 0$). Then, by a similar deduction as in Case 1, we have $\mathbf{e}_1^\top \mathbf{X}\mathbf{e}_1 = \mathbf{e}_2^\top \mathbf{X}\mathbf{e}_2$, $\mathbf{e}_1^\top \mathbf{X}\mathbf{e}_2 = \mathbf{e}_2^\top \mathbf{X}\mathbf{e}_1$, and $\mathbf{e}_1^\top \mathbf{X}\mathbf{e}_j = -\mathbf{e}_2^\top \mathbf{X}\mathbf{e}_j$ (or $\mathbf{e}_1^\top \mathbf{X}\mathbf{e}_j = \mathbf{e}_2^\top \mathbf{X}\mathbf{e}_j$ if $k_2 \neq 0$) for all $j \in [n]$ and $\mathbf{X} \in K(\mathbf{T}_{k_1,k_2,l}, \mathbf{T}_{k_1,k_2,l})$.

Again, due to the transitivity of the action of $\mathcal{S}_n^\pm$ on $\{(\pm\mathbf{e}_a, \pm\mathbf{e}_b, \pm\mathbf{e}_c)\}$, we can deduce that for a large enough polynomial $p(n)$, it has $\mathbf{e}_a^\top \mathbf{Y}\mathbf{e}_a = \mathbf{e}_b^\top \mathbf{Y}\mathbf{e}_b$, $\mathbf{e}_a^\top \mathbf{Y}\mathbf{e}_b = \mathbf{e}_b^\top \mathbf{Y}\mathbf{e}_a$, and $\mathbf{e}_a^\top \mathbf{Y}\mathbf{e}_c = -\mathbf{e}_b^\top \mathbf{Y}\mathbf{e}_c$, $\mathbf{e}_a^\top \mathbf{Y}\mathbf{e}_c = \mathbf{e}_b^\top \mathbf{Y}\mathbf{e}_c$ for all $1 \leq a \neq b \neq c \leq n$ and $\mathbf{Y} \in \bigcap_{i=1}^{p(n)} K(\mathbf{S}_i, \mathbf{S}_i)$. In other words, $\bigcap_{i=1}^{p(n)} K(\mathbf{S}_i, \mathbf{S}_i) = \{h\mathbf{I}_n : h \in \mathbb{R}\}$. Then $\mathbf{V}$ can be reconstructed by first computing a nonzero matrix in $\bigcap_{i=1}^{p(n)} K(\phi_i, \mathbf{S}_i)$ and then performing normalization.

References

1. Aggarwal, D., Bennett, H., Golovnev, A., Stephens-Davidowitz, N.: Fine-grained hardness of CVP(P) - everything that we can prove (and nothing else). In: Marx, D. (ed.) Proceedings of the 2021 ACM-SIAM Symposium on Discrete Algorithms, SODA 2021, Virtual Conference, 10–13 January 2021, pp. 1816–1835. SIAM (2021). https://doi.org/10.1137/1.9781611976465.109

2. Aggarwal, D., Dadush, D., Regev, O., Stephens-Davidowitz, N.: Solving the shortest vector problem in 2^n time using discrete gaussian sampling: extended abstract. In: Servedio, R.A., Rubinfeld, R. (eds.) Proceedings of the Forty-Seventh Annual ACM on Symposium on Theory of Computing (STOC 2015), Portland, 14–17 June 2015, pp. 733–742. ACM (2015). https://doi.org/10.1145/2746539.2746606

3. Aggarwal, D., Li, J., Nguyen, P.Q., Stephens-Davidowitz, N.: Slide reduction, revisited—filling the gaps in SVP approximation. In: Micciancio, D., Ristenpart, T. (eds.) CRYPTO 2020. LNCS, vol. 12171, pp. 274–295. Springer, Cham (2020). https://doi.org/10.1007/978-3-030-56880-1_10

4. Aggarwal, D., Li, Z., Stephens-Davidowitz, N.: A $2^{n/2}$-time algorithm for $\sqrt{n}$-SVP and $\sqrt{n}$-hermite SVP, and an improved time-approximation tradeoff for (H)SVP. In: Canteaut, A., Standaert, F.-X. (eds.) EUROCRYPT 2021. LNCS, vol. 12696, pp. 467–497. Springer, Cham (2021). https://doi.org/10.1007/978-3-030-77870-5_17

5. Aggarwal, D., Stephens-Davidowitz, N.: Just take the average! an embarrassingly simple 2^n-time algorithm for SVP (and CVP). In: Seidel, R. (ed.) 1st Symposium on Simplicity in Algorithms, SOSA 2018, 7–10 January 2018, New Orleans. OASIcs, vol. 61, pp. 12:1–12:19. Schloss Dagstuhl - Leibniz-Zentrum für Informatik (2018). https://doi.org/10.4230/OASIcs.SOSA.2018.12

6. Aggarwal, D., Ursu, B., Vaudenay, S.: Faster sieving algorithm for approximate SVP with constant approximation factors. Cryptology ePrint Archive (2019)

7. Babai, L.: Graph isomorphism in quasipolynomial time [extended abstract]. In: Wichs, D., Mansour, Y. (eds.) Proceedings of the 48th Annual ACM SIGACT Symposium on Theory of Computing (STOC 2016) Cambridge, 18–21 June 2016, pp. 684–697. ACM (2016). https://doi.org/10.1145/2897518.2897542

198 K. Jiang et al.

8. Bennett, H.: The complexity of the shortest vector problem. Electron. Colloquium Comput. Complex. TR22-170 (2022). https://eccc.weizmann.ac.il/report/2022/170
9. Bennett, H., Ganju, A., Peetathawatchai, P., Stephens-Davidowitz, N.: Just how hard are rotations of Z^n? algorithms and cryptography with the simplest lattice. IACR Cryptol. ePrint Arch., p. 1548 (2021). https://eprint.iacr.org/2021/1548
10. Bennett, H., Golovnev, A., Stephens-Davidowitz, N.: On the quantitative hardness of CVP. In: Umans, C. (ed.) 58th IEEE Annual Symposium on Foundations of Computer Science (FOCS 2017), Berkeley, 15–17 October 2017, pp. 13–24. IEEE Computer Society (2017). https://doi.org/10.1109/FOCS.2017.11
11. Blanks, T.L., Miller, S.D.: Generating cryptographically-strong random lattice bases and recognizing rotations of $\mathbb{Z}^n$. In: Cheon, J.H., Tillich, J.-P. (eds.) PQCrypto 2021 2021. LNCS, vol. 12841, pp. 319–338. Springer, Cham (2021). https://doi.org/10.1007/978-3-030-81293-5_17
12. Brakerski, Z., Langlois, A., Peikert, C., Regev, O., Stehlé, D.: Classical hardness of learning with errors. In: Boneh, D., Roughgarden, T., Feigenbaum, J. (eds.) Symposium on Theory of Computing Conference (STOC 2013), Palo Alto, 1–4 June 2013, pp. 575–584. ACM (2013). https://doi.org/10.1145/2488608.2488680
13. Cai, J., Nerurkar, A.: An improved worst-case to average-case connection for lattice problems. In: 38th Annual Symposium on Foundations of Computer Science (FOCS 1997), Miami Beach, 19–22 October 1997, pp. 468–477. IEEE Computer Society (1997). https://doi.org/10.1109/SFCS.1997.646135
14. Cash, D., Hofheinz, D., Kiltz, E., Peikert, C.: Bonsai trees, or how to delegate a lattice basis. In: Gilbert, H. (ed.) EUROCRYPT 2010. LNCS, vol. 6110, pp. 523–552. Springer, Heidelberg (2010). https://doi.org/10.1007/978-3-642-13190-5_27
15. Collins, B., Śniady, P.: Integration with respect to the haar measure on unitary, orthogonal and symplectic group. Commun. Math. Phys. **264**(3), 773–795 (2006)
16. Diaconis, P., Shahshahani, M.: The subgroup algorithm for generating uniform random variables. Probab. Eng. Inf. Sci. **1**(1), 15–32 (1987)
17. Ducas, L., Gibbons, S.: Hull attacks on the lattice isomorphism problem. IACR Cryptol. ePrint Arch., p. 194 (2023). https://eprint.iacr.org/2023/194
18. Ducas, L., Postlethwaite, E.W., Pulles, L.N., van Woerden, W.P.J.: Hawk: module LIP makes lattice signatures fast, compact and simple. In: Agrawal, S., Lin, D. (eds.) ASIACRYPT 2022. LNCS, vol. 13794, pp. 65–94. Springer, Cham (2022). https://doi.org/10.1007/978-3-031-22972-5_3
19. Ducas, L., van Woerden, W.P.J.: On the lattice isomorphism problem, quadratic forms, remarkable lattices, and cryptography. In: Dunkelman, O., Dziembowski, S. (eds.) EUROCRYPT 2022. LNCS, vol. 13277, pp. 643–673. Springer, Cham (2022). https://doi.org/10.1007/978-3-031-07082-2_23
20. Ducas, L.: Provable lattice reduction of Z^n with blocksize $n/2$. Cryptology ePrint Archive, Paper 2023/447 (2023). https://eprint.iacr.org/2023/447
21. Dutour Sikirić, M., Haensch, A., Voight, J., van Woerden, W.P.: A canonical form for positive definite matrices. Open Book Ser. **4**(1), 179–195 (2020)
22. Eisenträger, K., Hallgren, S., Kitaev, A.Y., Song, F.: A quantum algorithm for computing the unit group of an arbitrary degree number field. In: Shmoys, D.B. (ed.) Symposium on Theory of Computing, STOC 2014, New York, 31 May–03 June 2014, pp. 293–302. ACM (2014). https://doi.org/10.1145/2591796.2591860
23. Geißler, K., Smart, N.P.: Computing the $M = U\,U^t$ integer matrix decomposition. In: Paterson, K.G. (ed.) Cryptography and Coding. LNCS, vol. 2898, pp. 223–233. Springer, Heidelberg (2003). https://doi.org/10.1007/978-3-540-40974-8_18

24. Gentry, C., Peikert, C., Vaikuntanathan, V.: Trapdoors for hard lattices and new cryptographic constructions. In: Dwork, C. (ed.) Proceedings of the 40th Annual ACM Symposium on Theory of Computing, Victoria, 17–20 May 2008, pp. 197–206. ACM (2008). https://doi.org/10.1145/1374376.1374407

25. Gentry, C., Szydlo, M.: Cryptanalysis of the revised NTRU signature scheme. In: Knudsen, L.R. (ed.) EUROCRYPT 2002. LNCS, vol. 2332, pp. 299–320. Springer, Heidelberg (2002). https://doi.org/10.1007/3-540-46035-7_20

26. Goldreich, O., Goldwasser, S., Halevi, S.: Public-key cryptosystems from lattice reduction problems. In: Jr., B.S.K. (ed.) CRYPTO 1997. LNCS, vol. 1294, pp. 112–131. Springer, Heidelberg (1997). https://doi.org/10.1007/BFb0052231

27. Haviv, I., Regev, O.: Hardness of the covering radius problem on lattices. Chic. J. Theor. Comput. Sci. (2012). https://cjtcs.cs.uchicago.edu/articles/2012/4/contents.html

28. Haviv, I., Regev, O.: On the lattice isomorphism problem. In: Chekuri, C. (ed.) Proceedings of the Twenty-Fifth Annual ACM-SIAM Symposium on Discrete Algorithms (SODA 2014), Portland, 5–7 January 2014, pp. 391–404. SIAM (2014). https://doi.org/10.1137/1.9781611973402.29

29. Hoeffding, W.: Probability inequalities for sums of bounded random variables. In: The Collected Works of Wassily Hoeffding, pp. 409–426 (1994)

30. Hoffstein, J., Howgrave-Graham, N., Pipher, J., Silverman, J.H., Whyte, W.: NTRUSign: digital signatures using the NTRU lattice. In: Joye, M. (ed.) CT-RSA 2003. LNCS, vol. 2612, pp. 122–140. Springer, Heidelberg (2003). https://doi.org/10.1007/3-540-36563-X_9

31. Hunkenschröder, C.: Deciding whether a lattice has an orthonormal basis is in co-np. arXiv preprint arXiv:1910.03838 (2019)

32. Lenstra, H.W., Jr., Silverberg, A.: Revisiting the gentry-szydlo algorithm. In: Garay, J.A., Gennaro, R. (eds.) CRYPTO 2014. LNCS, vol. 8616, pp. 280–296. Springer, Heidelberg (2014). https://doi.org/10.1007/978-3-662-44371-2_16

33. Lenstra, H.W., Jr., Silverberg, A.: Lattices with symmetry. J. Cryptol. **30**(3), 760–804 (2017). https://doi.org/10.1007/s00145-016-9235-7

34. Khot, S.: Hardness of approximating the shortest vector problem in lattices. In: Proceedings of the 45th Symposium on Foundations of Computer Science (FOCS 2004), October 17–19 2004, Rome, pp. 126–135. IEEE Computer Society (2004). https://doi.org/10.1109/FOCS.2004.31

35. Köbler, J., Schöning, U., Torán, J.: The graph isomorphism problem: its structural complexity. Prog. Theor. Comput. Sci., Birkhäuser/Springer (1993). https://doi.org/10.1007/978-1-4612-0333-9

36. Kuperberg, G.: The hidden subgroup problem for infinite groups (2020). https://simons.berkeley.edu/sites/default/files/docs/21261/berkeley.pdf

37. Kuperberg, G.: The hidden subgroup problem for $\mathbb{Z}^k$ for infinite-index subgroups (2022). https://simons.berkeley.edu/sites/default/files/docs/21261/berkeley.pdf

38. Lenstra, A.K., Lenstra, H.W., Lovász, L.: Factoring polynomials with rational coefficients. Math. Annalen **261**, 515–534 (1982)

39. Liu, M., Wang, X., Xu, G., Zheng, X.: Shortest lattice vectors in the presence of gaps. Cryptology ePrint Archive (2011)

40. Luks, E.M.: Permutation groups and polynomial-time computation. In: Finkelstein, L., Kantor, W.M. (eds.) Groups and Computation, Proceedings of a DIMACS Workshop, New Brunswick, 7–10 October 1991. DIMACS Series in Discrete Mathematics and Theoretical Computer Science, vol. 11, pp. 139–175. DIMACS/AMS (1991). https://doi.org/10.1090/dimacs/011/11

41. Martinet, J.: Perfect Lattices in Euclidean Spaces, vol. 327. Springer, Heidelberg (2013). https://doi.org/10.1007/978-3-662-05167-2
42. Mezzadri, F.: How to generate random matrices from the classical compact groups. arXiv preprint arXiv:math-ph/0609050 (2006)
43. Nguyen, P.Q., Regev, O.: Learning a parallelepiped: cryptanalysis of GGH and NTRU signatures. In: Vaudenay, S. (ed.) EUROCRYPT 2006. LNCS, vol. 4004, pp. 271–288. Springer, Heidelberg (2006). https://doi.org/10.1007/11761679_17
44. Elkies, N.D.: Intro to SPLAG (2002). https://people.math.harvard.edu/~elkies/M55a.02/lattice.html
45. Peikert, C.: A decade of lattice cryptography. Found. Trends Theor. Comput. Sci. 10(4), 283–424 (2016). https://doi.org/10.1561/0400000074
46. Plesken, W., Souvignier, B.: Computing isometries of lattices. J. Symb. Comput. 24(3–4), 327–334 (1997)
47. Regev, O.: Quantum computation and lattice problems. In: Proceedings of the 43rd Symposium on Foundations of Computer Science (FOCS 2002), 16–19 November 2002, Vancouver, pp. 520–529. IEEE Computer Society (2002). https://doi.org/10.1109/SFCS.2002.1181976
48. Regev, O., Stephens-Davidowitz, N.: A reverse minkowski theorem. In: Hatami, H., McKenzie, P., King, V. (eds.) Proceedings of the 49th Annual ACM SIGACT Symposium on Theory of Computing (STOC 2017), Montreal, 19–23 June 2017, pp. 941–953. ACM (2017). https://doi.org/10.1145/3055399.3055434
49. Shor, P.W.: Algorithms for quantum computation: discrete logarithms and factoring. In: 35th Annual Symposium on Foundations of Computer Science, Santa Fe, 20–22 November 1994, pp. 124–134. IEEE Computer Society (1994). https://doi.org/10.1109/SFCS.1994.365700
50. Sikiric, M.D., Schürmann, A., Vallentin, F.: Complexity and algorithms for computing voronoi cells of lattices. Math. Comput. 78(267), 1713–1731 (2009). https://doi.org/10.1090/S0025-5718-09-02224-8
51. Stephens-Davidowitz, N.: Search-to-decision reductions for lattice problems with approximation factors (slightly) greater than one. In: Jansen, K., Mathieu, C., Rolim, J.D.P., Umans, C. (eds.) Approximation, Randomization, and Combinatorial Optimization. Algorithms and Techniques, APPROX/RANDOM 2016, 7–9 September 2016, Paris. LIPIcs, vol. 60, pp. 19:1–19:18. Schloss Dagstuhl - Leibniz-Zentrum für Informatik (2016). https://doi.org/10.4230/LIPIcs.APPROX-RANDOM.2016.19
52. Stewart, G.W.: The efficient generation of random orthogonal matrices with an application to condition estimators. SIAM J. Numer. Anal. 17(3), 403–409 (1980)
53. Szydlo, M.: Hypercubic lattice reduction and analysis of GGH and NTRU signatures. In: Biham, E. (ed.) EUROCRYPT 2003. LNCS, vol. 2656, pp. 433–448. Springer, Heidelberg (2003). https://doi.org/10.1007/3-540-39200-9_27
54. Wei, W., Liu, M., Wang, X.: Finding shortest lattice vectors in the presence of gaps. In: Nyberg, K. (ed.) CT-RSA 2015. LNCS, vol. 9048, pp. 239–257. Springer, Cham (2015). https://doi.org/10.1007/978-3-319-16715-2_13

Side-Channels

SCA-LDPC: A Code-Based Framework for Key-Recovery Side-Channel Attacks on Post-quantum Encryption Schemes

Qian Guo[1] , Denis Nabokov[1](✉) , Alexander Nilsson[1,2] ,
and Thomas Johansson[1]

[1] Department of Electrical and Information Technology, Lund University, Lund,
Sweden
{qian.guo,denis.nabokov,alexander.nilsson,thomas.johansson}@eit.lth.se
[2] Advenica AB, Malmö, Sweden

Abstract. Whereas theoretical attacks on standardized cryptographic primitives rarely lead to actual practical attacks, the situation is different for side-channel attacks. Improvements in the performance of side-channel attacks are of utmost importance.

In this paper, we propose a framework to be used in key-recovery side-channel attacks on CCA-secure post-quantum encryption schemes. The basic idea is to construct chosen ciphertext queries to a plaintext checking oracle that collects information on a set of secret variables in a single query. Then a large number of such queries is considered, each related to a different set of secret variables, and they are modeled as a low-density parity-check code (LDPC code). Secret variables are finally determined through efficient iterative decoding methods, such as belief propagation, using soft information. The utilization of LDPC codes offers efficient decoding, source coding, and error correction benefits. It has been demonstrated that this approach provides significant improvements compared to previous work by reducing the required number of queries, such as the number of traces in a power attack.

The framework is demonstrated and implemented in two different cases. On one hand, we attack implementations of HQC in a timing attack, lowering the number of required traces considerably compared to attacks in previous work. On the other hand, we describe and implement a full attack on a masked implementation of Kyber using power analysis. Using the ChipWhisperer evaluation platform, our real-world attacks recover the long-term secret key of a first-order masked implementation of Kyber-768 with an average of only 12 power traces.

Keywords: Lattice-based cryptography · code-based cryptography · side-channel attacks · NIST post-quantum cryptography standardization · low-density parity-check codes

© International Association for Cryptologic Research 2023
J. Guo and R. Steinfeld (Eds.): ASIACRYPT 2023, LNCS 14441, pp. 203–236, 2023.
https://doi.org/10.1007/978-981-99-8730-6_7

1   Introduction

NIST [1] is running a standardization process (referred to as the NIST PQ project) for post-quantum public-key cryptographic algorithms (PQC schemes), which are supposed to be secure even against attacks from quantum computers. This is not the case for most public-key algorithms in use today [43]. The project started in 2017 and just recently the first choices for standardization were announced. The project is ongoing and round 4 will involve a further examination of additional schemes. All of the schemes in the NIST PQ project are based on a variety of hard problems that are believed to be intractable for quantum computers, and many of them can be categorized as either Public-key Encryption (PKE) or Key Encapsulation Mechanisms (KEMs). These PKE/KEM schemes are based on either the Learning with Errors (LWE) problem as introduced by Regev [37] in 2005 or on code-based problems, initiated in [28].

Two such schemes will be considered in this paper. One is CRYSTALS-Kyber [41], selected by NIST as the candidate for standardization for KEMs. The security of Kyber is based on the Module LWE problem and has strong confidence in its theoretical security, while also offering a good performance. The other scheme is HQC [2], a code-based round 4 candidate. Other code-based round 4 candidates are BIKE [4] and Classic McEliece [3]. NIST has stated that one of the schemes HQC or BIKE may be standardized.

LWE- or code-based PKE/KEMs are usually built to be secure against chosen plaintext attacks (IND-CPA secure) and then transformed to be secure against adaptive chosen ciphertext attacks (IND-CCA secure) by applying some CCA conversion method, such as the Fujisaki-Okamoto (FO) transform. The FO transform involves a re-encryption after decryption, which enables the detection of invalid ciphertexts and correspondingly return failure. Invalid chosen ciphertexts that are not proper encryptions of a message will almost always be rejected by the decryption/decapsulation.

Side-Channel Attacks (SCA) were introduced by Kocher [27] and are a separate area of research today. For PQC schemes, it is a major concern and NIST also in the later rounds encouraged more research on the security of PQC schemes against side-channel cryptanalysis. In relation to this, there has been great research interest in developing new side-channel attacks on all relevant NIST candidates as well as studying efficient side-channel protection techniques.

There are many different approaches to SCA on PQC schemes. Following previous work, we may roughly classify attacks into two main categories. The first category includes attacks that require either a single trace or at least only a few traces to perform key recovery or message recovery and targets very precise leakages in an implementation. The second category includes attacks of a more generic type, exploiting arbitrary leakages in the implementation of the algorithm, but typically requiring the collection of many traces in the attack phase. These more generic attacks are modeled by instantiating a side-channel oracle for chosen ciphertexts. The oracle is explained in more detail in the following.

1.1   Related Works

Key-recovery chosen-ciphertext side-channel attacks (KR-CCA-SCA) are attacks where the adversary recovers the secret key in the scheme by using chosen ciphertext calls to the decryption or decapsulation algorithm and getting measurement data from some side-channel.

KR-CCA-SCA attacks on PQC encryption schemes are a well-established research field, as evidenced by numerous publications [9,14,16–18,22,29,34, 36,40,42,47]. These attacks can be classified depending on where the information leakages are detected. The first type of KR-CCA-SCAs [16,18,36] exploits leakages from the two added procedures, the re-encryption and ciphertext comparison, of the FO transform, since these two components in the FO transform depend on the decrypted message vector. There are also KR-CCA-SCAs [14,17,22,29,40] that exploit side-channel leakages from the CPA-secure decryption, where parts of the decryption procedure will directly use the secret key.

In [35], Ravi et al. classified side-channel-assisted CCA attacks on lattice-based KEMs into three main categories, plaintext-checking (PC) oracle based attacks [9,36], decryption-failure (DF) oracle based attacks [18], and full-domain (FD) oracle based attacks [29,47]. The classification depends on what kind of answer the oracle gives. In a DF oracle, the oracle answer is simply whether the chosen ciphertext decodes/decrypts to a valid message or not. On the other hand, a PC oracle and an FD oracle require message recovery before key recovery can take place. In a PC oracle, the response of the oracle is whether the chosen ciphertext results in a specific given message upon decryption. In an FD Oracle, the oracle returns the full message that has been decrypted. As a result, in a PC oracle based attack, it is possible to recover a maximum of one bit of secret information from a single side-channel measurement; however, if the message is of m-bit length (where m is 256 for Kyber), it is possible to recover m bits of secret information with an FD oracle based attack.

Recently, Tanaka et al. in [44] and Rajendran et al. in [33] have independently proposed a new type of oracle called multi-values PC oracle. This oracle can extract 8–12 bits of information from a single decapsulation oracle call through multi-class classification. The multi-values PC oracle can be considered as a compromise between the PC oracle and the FD oracle, although it is still much less efficient than the latter.

For general PQC schemes, Ueno et al. [45] have shown that all round-3 NIST KEM candidates except for Classic McEliece are vulnerable to KR-CCA-SCAs. However, it was later established in [40] that the attack detailed in [45] is only applicable to earlier versions of the HQC proposal and not to the recent Reed-Muller-Reed-Solomon (RMRS) version. Schamberger et al. in [40] and Goy et al. in [14] very recently proposed new power side-channel attacks on the RMRS version of the HQC scheme, but their attack only applied to power analysis with leakages from the CPA decryption. In [16] a generic PC oracle based attack on the RMRS version of the HQC scheme has been proposed, presented in the format of timing attacks.

One central problem in KR-CCA-SCAs is *identifying a generic approach to optimize the selection of chosen ciphertexts, in order to efficiently extract secret keys from various types of oracles.* The main obstacles arise from two primary sources: (1) the inaccuracies that may occur in the construction of oracles and (2) the non-uniform distribution from which secret symbols are generated. To overcome these challenges, one may need to incorporate concepts from coding theory, particularly in the areas of source coding and error correction. Several early research efforts are made to address these challenges, as documented in [29, 32, 42]. But the existing solutions are limited in scope, either because they are restricted to a specific oracle or because they are applicable only to particular types of side-channel leakages. Finally, there is ample room for improvement in terms of attack efficiency.

1.2   Contributions

In this paper, we propose a framework named SCA-LDPC to improve the key-recovery side-channel attacks on CCA-secure PQC encryption schemes. The basic idea is to construct chosen ciphertext queries to an oracle that collects information on a set of secret variables in a single query. Then a large number of such queries are considered, each related to a different set of secret variables, and they are modeled as a low-density parity-check code (LDPC code). The secret variables are then determined through efficient iterative decoding methods, such as belief propagation (BP), using soft information.

New Concepts. The concept of designing chosen-ciphertexts to gather side-channel information in a linear parity check is novel. This approach has the potential to provide both source coding and error correction simultaneously. The reason for this is that the combination of multiple secret entries is typically more closely aligned with the uniform distribution, which allows for more effective extraction of information from a single side-channel measurement. This effect echoes the concept of source coding in information theory, leading us to term it as the *source coding gain* throughout the paper. This gain can result in a substantial improvement for proposals with extremely low entropy secret symbols, as demonstrated for HQC, as well as a noticeable improvement for lattice-based schemes. The error correction gain is realized through the utilization of linear parity checks, which enable the utilization of correctly recovered coefficients to rectify incorrect decisions. The implementation of these linear checks in the form of an LDPC code was selected due to its efficient decoding capabilities and its well-known near-optimal performance from an information-theoretical perspective.

The new framework has significantly transformed the design philosophy of prior methods for source coding and error correction, as documented in [29,32,42]. The previously proposed methods aimed to achieve full key recovery with higher accuracy by introducing additional measurements for each individual secret symbol, thereby increasing the success rate of symbol recovery. The new framework, however, proposes a novel approach by allowing for fewer measurements on the secret symbols, leading to a higher level of symbol-level errors, which are subsequently corrected by the specially designed LDPC codes through inter-symbol parity checks.

We emphasize that the framework is generic in nature and can be applied to both code-based and lattice-based schemes, across adaptive and non-adaptive attack models, and in a multitude of side-channel leakage scenarios, including timing, cache-timing, power, and electromagnetic leakages. To demonstrate the applicability of the framework, we have instantiated it in two relevant applications: an adaptive timing attack on an HQC implementation with PC oracles, and a non-adaptive power attack on a Kyber implementation with FD oracles. The choice of Kyber and HQC as the primary targets was motivated by their significance, with Kyber being selected as the primary KEM/PKE algorithm for standardization by NIST and HQC still being considered for standardization at the end of round-4. In the full version of the paper [20], we extend our discussions to include the methods of attacking Saber and FrodoKEM to further enhance the generality of the framework.

New Results. We list the contributions of the paper in the following.

- We introduce a code design method in designing capacity-approaching LDPC /QC-LDPC codes over binary and non-binary alphabets. Our method establishes a relationship between oracle calls and parity checks in the LDPC code, leading to substantial improvements over previous methods in both noiseless and noisy real-world scenarios. The prior improvement is primarily attributed to source coding, while the latter improvement is the result of a combination of source coding and error correction.
- We simulate the performance with different noise levels and characterize the performance of the new approach through a simulation method. The simulated gains are substantial. For example, when the oracle accuracy is 100%, as is the case for the key misuse oracle or an oracle constructed from highly reliable side-channels such as cache-timing leaks on an Intel-SGX platform [25], we can recover the secret key of hqc-128 with approximately 9,000 traces in the PC oracle. Using the same oracle setting as the ideal oracle in [16], we have achieved an improvement factor of 86.6, as we only need about 10,000 traces, compared to the 866,000 traces reported in [16]. This significant improvement is due to the fact that the HQC secret entries are sampled from a distribution with extremely low entropy and the previously known methods (e.g., in [16]) ignore the potential source coding gain. In the scenario of perfect FD oracles, the number of traces required to recover Kyber-768 is only 7, which meets the Shannon lower bound.
- We perform actual attacks on two target algorithms, Kyber and HQC, in real-world scenarios. The results of our study demonstrate a close alignment, or even an improvement, of the real attack performance when compared to the simulation results. The first attack is a full power analysis on a masked implementation of Kyber-768. The attack was carried out using the Chip-Whisperer framework on the open-source mkm4 library in [23] with the profiling and attack phases performed on two distinct boards, both equipped with

ARM-Cortex-M4 CPUs. In the real-world scenario, we obtained FD oracles with varying accuracy levels based on their positions. The average accuracy was estimated to be approximately 95%. The full secret key was success-fully recovered with an average of 12 traces. In comparison, the simulation required roughly 17 traces for the same oracle accuracy. The better perfor-mance in the real-world scenario can be attributed to the availability of soft information and the possibility of some secret symbols having a high accuracy since they are related to a high-accuracy oracle, which in turn helps in the correct decoding of other positions through the parity checks of the specially designed LDPC codes.

The second attack is a full timing attack simulation on HQC, validated with a real-world timing oracle. The real-life attack performance highly depends on the targeted platform. On our laptop with an Intel Core i5 CPU, we can achieve full key recovery against hqc-128 with 2^{18} decapsulation calls.

– The software for attack and simulation is made open-source[1].

It is important to note that, in accordance with previous research, our app-roach focuses on recovering the entire secret vector through side-channel leak-ages. The sample complexity can be reduced by performing additional post-processing procedures, such as information set decoding and lattice reduction [8], to recover a portion of the secret entries. The specific reduction in the number of traces depends on the permissible amount of computation for post-processing.

Comparison with Previous Studies in [29,32,42]. In [32], Qin et al. presented an efficient PC oracle based attack on lattice-based schemes by adaptively choosing a new ciphertext for decryption based on the side-channel information obtained from previous power/electromagnetic measurements. Their approach is similar to the well-known Huffman coding method and can result in a source coding gain. Shen et al. in [42] further extended this work by proposing a detection coding method to identify incorrectly recovered positions and to send additional measurements for those secret positions. Note that these studies are limited to PC oracle based attacks on lattice-based schemes and operate in adaptive mode, resulting in a more restrictive attack model and lower efficiency compared to other attacks based on more powerful oracles. For example, when the oracle accuracy is 95%, it was reported in [42] that 3874 traces are required to attack the Kyber-512 scheme; in contrast, the new attack based on the FD oracle presented in this paper only requires 12 traces in a real attack (or 17 traces in simulation) to attack the Kyber-768 scheme. Furthermore, from a viewpoint of information theory, LDPC codes are attractive due to their near-optimal performance. As a result, they are expected to provide improved performance in scenarios where the oracle accuracy is low, compared to the detection codes proposed in [42].

A relevant study [29] has proposed the extended Hamming coding method to enhance the FD oracle based power attack on the masked Saber, a round-3 NIST PQ KEM candidate, in the non-adaptive attack model. However, this approach does not provide any source coding gain and its error correction is

---

[1] https://github.com/atneit/SCA-LDPC.

limited to an inner-symbol style, resulting in a lack of inter-symbol connections and a less potent error correction mechanism. A more detailed comparison of our work with [29] can be found in Sect. 6.3.

Differences from SASCA. The new framework connects to soft-analytic side-channel attacks (SASCAs) proposed by Veyrat-Charvillon et al. in [46] since both employ iterative decoding. A coding-theoretical treatment on SASCA is presented in [15]. SASCA has been employed for attacking lattice-based scenarios by exploiting leakages from the number-theoretical transform (NTT) of secret polynomials (e.g., in [22,31]).

While both attacks use iterative coding, the new SCA-LDPC attack differs from SASCA in several ways. First, the applicability of SASCA extends to both symmetric and asymmetric cryptography; in contrast, the SCA-LDPC attacks fall into the category of PC oracle (and its variants) based KR-CCA-SCAs for lattice-based and code-based systems, presenting unique advantages for these types of systems. Our SCA-LDPC framework employs oracles, thereby being capable of utilizing various types of leakages, including those related to timing that are seldom explored in SASCA. SASCA, mainly used to extract information from physical leakages, can offer an alternative means for generating oracles in contrast to the template attack or the machine learning approaches. The second primary distinction is that SASCA builds its code using pre-existing connections formed by the intrinsic structure of the cipher or implementation, whereas SCA-LDPC provides the attacker with greater flexibility in choosing ciphertexts to create new parity check variables and establish new connections, ultimately constructing a linear code with near-optimal decoding efficiency.

Relations to Concurrent and Subsequent Works. The new SCA-LDPC framework is generic in the investigation of side-channel security for post-quantum PKE/KEMs. Given the current relevance of this subject, numerous concurrent and subsequent studies are emerging, such as [5,10,25]. We detail the connections between these works in the full version of the paper [20].

1.3 Organization

The remaining parts of the paper are organized as follows. In Sect. 2, we present the necessary background information. In Sect. 3, we present a general description of the new attacking framework. We apply the new attack ideas towards Kyber and HQC, in Sect. 4 and Sect. 5, respectively. Then, we present the extensive computer simulation results and real-world attacks in Sect. 6. We finally conclude the paper and present future directions in Sect. 7.

2 Preliminaries

We present the necessary background in this section. We first provide the employed notations and terminology in coding theory, followed by a description of the two KEM candidates, Kyber and HQC. Finally, we conclude this section by outlining the threat model.

2.1   Notations and Coding Terminology

Notation. For a finite set $\mathcal{I}$, the symbol $\#\{\mathcal{I}\}$ denotes the number of elements in $\mathcal{I}$. Let $\mathbb{F}_q$ be the finite field of size q, $\lceil x \rfloor$ the rounding function, and $\mathcal{H}$, $\mathcal{G}$, and $\mathcal{K}$ three cryptographic hash functions. Let $\mathcal{R}_q$ be a polynomial ring $\mathbb{F}_q[x]/(x^{256}+1)$. The central binomial distribution B_μ outputs $\sum_{i=1}^{\mu}(a_i - b_i)$, where a_i and b_i are independently and uniformly randomly sampled from $\{0,1\}$. The Bernoulli distribution Ber_η defines a random variable from $\{0,1\}$, which is 1 with probability η and 0 otherwise. The notation $\mathbf{a} \xleftarrow{\$} \mathsf{U}$ denotes that the entries in $\mathbf{a}$ are randomly sampled from the distribution U, where $\mathbf{a}$ is a vector or polynomial. For a set $\mathcal{I}$, $\mathbf{a} \xleftarrow{\$} \mathcal{I}$ means that the entries in $\mathbf{a}$ are uniformly sampled from the set $\mathcal{I}$ at random. For a vector or polynomial $\mathbf{a}$, $\mathbf{a}[i]$ refers to the coefficient of $\mathbf{a}$ at the index i. The Shannon's binary entropy function of a random variable X is defined as $H(X) = -\sum_{x \in \mathcal{X}} \mathbf{Pr}\,[X = x] \log_2 \mathbf{Pr}\,[X = x]$.

Linear Codes. The Hamming weight of a vector $\mathbf{x}$ is its number of non-zero elements, denoted by $w_\mathrm{H}(\mathbf{x})$. We define an $[n, k, d]_q$ linear code $\mathcal{C}$ as a linear subspace over $\mathbb{F}_q$ of length n, dimension k, and minimum distance d. Here minimum distance is defined as the minimum Hamming weight of its non-zero elements. Since a linear code $\mathcal{C}$ is a subspace, we can define it as the image of a matrix $\mathbf{G}$, called a *generator matrix*. We can also define the code $\mathcal{C}$ as the kernel of a matrix $\mathbf{H} \in \mathbb{F}_q^{(n-k) \times n}$. Here $\mathbf{H}$ is called a parity-check matrix of $\mathcal{C}$.

LDPC Codes. Low-density parity-check (LDPC) codes are linear codes with a sparse parity-check matrix first introduced in [13]. LDPC codes can be considered sparse graph codes because they can be decoded efficiently using iterative decoding (such as belief propagation [30]) on the *Tanner graph*, a bipartite graph with edges corresponding to non-zero elements in the parity-check matrix $\mathbf{H}$.

Concatenated Codes. Forney [11] in 1965 firstly proposed the concatenated code construction approach of combining two simple codes called an *inner code* and an *outer code*, respectively, to achieve good error-correcting capability with reasonable decoding complexity. Let the inner code $\mathcal{C}_{in} : \mathcal{A}^k \rightarrow \mathcal{A}^n$, the outer code $\mathcal{C}_{out} : \mathcal{B}^K \rightarrow \mathcal{B}^N$, and $\#\{\mathcal{B}\} = \#\{\mathcal{A}\}^k$. The concatenated code is a code $\mathcal{C}_{con} : \mathcal{A}^{kK} \rightarrow \mathcal{A}^{nN}$. The key of the concatenated code construction method is that the decoding can be done sequentially by passing first the inner code decoder and then the outer code decoder. Typically in the inner code decoding, one can use a maximum-likelihood decoding approach, while the outer code allows efficient decoding in polynomial time (e.g. by employing an LDPC code).

2.2   Kyber

Kyber [41], the KEM version of the Cryptographic Suite for Algebraic Lattices (CRYSTALS), is based on the module Learning with Errors (MLWE) problem and has been solicited as the KEM/PKE standard in the NIST PQ project.

Table 1. Parameter sets for Kyber [41]

	n_{mod}	d	q	μ_1	μ_2	(d_u, d_v)
Kyber-512	256	2	3329	3	2	(10,4)
Kyber-768	256	3	3329	2	2	(10,4)
Kyber-1024	256	4	3329	2	2	(11,5)

Kyber achieves the IND-CCA security through a tweaked Fujisaki-Okamoto transform [12] transforming an IND-CPA-secure PKE KYBER.CPAPKE to an IND-CCA-secure KEM KYBER.CCAKEM. The description algorithms of KYBER.CPAPKE and KYBER.CCAKEM can be found in [41]. We include a simplified description of these functions in the full version of paper [20].

In the following, we define the compression function and the decompression function, i.e., $\mathbf{Comp}_q(x, d)$ and $\mathbf{Decomp}_q(x, d)$, respectively.

Definition 1. *The Compression function is defined as:* $\mathbb{Z}_q \rightarrow \mathbb{Z}_{2^d}$

$$\mathbf{Comp}_q(x, d) = \left\lceil \frac{2^d}{q} \cdot x \right\rfloor \pmod{2^d}. \tag{1}$$

Definition 2. *The Decompression function is defined as:* $\mathbb{Z}_{2^d} \rightarrow \mathbb{Z}_q$

$$\mathbf{Decomp}_q(x, d) = \left\lceil \frac{q}{2^d} \cdot x \right\rfloor. \tag{2}$$

The compression and decompression function can be done coefficient-wise if the input is a polynomial or a vector of polynomials $\mathbf{x} \in \mathcal{R}_q^d$. The procedure KDF($\cdot$) denotes a key-derivation function.

The security parameter sets for the three versions of Kyber, Kyber-512, Kyber-768, and Kyber-1024 are shown in Table 1. In Kyber q is a prime 3329. Let $\mathbf{H}_0$ be a *negacyclic* matrix from a vector $\mathbf{h}_0$, i.e. the first row is $\mathbf{h}_0$, subsequent rows are cyclically shifted, when the value is moved from the last column to the first one, it is multiplied by -1. Let d denote the rank of the module, set to be 2, 3, and 4, respectively, for Kyber-512, Kyber-768, and Kyber-1024. When sampling from central binomial distribution B_μ, Kyber also has two parameters (μ_1, μ_2), set to be $(3, 2)$ for Kyber-512 and $(2, 2)$ for Kyber-768 and Kyber-1024.

2.3   HQC

HQC (Hamming Quasi-Cyclic) [2] is one of the main code-based IND-CCA-secure KEMs in the NIST PQ project, which has advanced to the fourth round. Its security is based on the hardness of decoding a random quasi-cyclic code in the Hamming metric. In HQC, the base field is $\mathbb{F}_2$ and $\mathcal{R}_2$ denotes the polynomial ring $\mathbb{F}_2[x]/(x^n - 1)$. The multiplication of two polynomials $\mathbf{u}, \mathbf{v} \in \mathcal{R}_2$ can be represented as a vector and a *circulant matrix*, induced from a vector in $\mathbb{F}_2^n$. Given $\mathbf{y} = (y_1, y_2, \ldots, y_n) \in \mathbb{F}_2^n$, its corresponding circulant matrix is defined as

$$
\mathbf{rot}(\mathbf{y}) = \begin{pmatrix} y_1 & y_n & \cdots & y_2 \\ y_2 & y_1 & \cdots & y_3 \\ \vdots & \vdots & \ddots & \vdots \\ y_n & y_{n-1} & \cdots & y_1 \end{pmatrix}.
$$

We can write the multiplication of $\mathbf{uv}$ as $\mathbf{u} \cdot \mathbf{rot}(\mathbf{v})^{\mathrm{T}}$ or $\mathbf{v} \cdot \mathbf{rot}(\mathbf{u})^{\mathrm{T}}$. The transpose of the circulant matrix is the counterpart of the negacyclic matrix.

The detailed description of the IND-CPA-secure PKE version of HQC and the IND-CCA-secure KEM version can be found in the HQC reference document [2]. We list them in the full version of paper [20]. The procedure $\mathsf{KeyGen}(\cdot)$ randomly generates two private vectors $\mathbf{x}, \mathbf{y} \in \mathcal{R}_2$ with a low Hamming weight w as the private key. It also generates a random public vector $\mathbf{h} \in \mathcal{R}_2$, computes $\mathbf{s} = \mathbf{x} + \mathbf{h} \cdot \mathbf{y}$, and returns $(\mathbf{h}, \mathbf{s})$ as the public key. The scheme employs a linear code $\mathcal{C}$ with a generator matrix $\mathbf{G}$ and generates noise $\mathbf{e}, \mathbf{r}_1, \mathbf{r}_2 \in \mathcal{R}_2$ with low Hamming weight in the encryption. The encryption function computes $\mathbf{u} = \mathbf{r}_1 + \mathbf{h} \cdot \mathbf{r}_2$ and $\mathbf{v} = \mathbf{mG} + \mathbf{s} \cdot \mathbf{r}_2 + \mathbf{e}$ and returns $(\mathbf{u}, \mathbf{v})$ as the ciphertext. In decryption, the secret vector $\mathbf{y}$ is an input and it computes

$$
\mathbf{v} - \mathbf{u} \cdot \mathbf{y} = \mathbf{mG} + \underbrace{\mathbf{s} \cdot \mathbf{r}_2 - \mathbf{u} \cdot \mathbf{y} + \mathbf{e}}_{\hat{\mathbf{e}}}. \tag{3}
$$

Since $w_{\mathrm{H}}(\hat{\mathbf{e}})$ is small, the decryption function inputs $\mathbf{v} - \mathbf{u} \cdot \mathbf{y}$ to the decoder of $\mathcal{C}$ and can succeed with high probability.

The parameter sets of HQC are shown in Table 2. In the recent version published in June 2021, HQC employs a concatenation of outer $[n_1, k_1, n_1 - k_1 + 1]_{256}$ Reed-Solomon (RS) codes and inner duplicated Reed-Muller (RM) codes built from the first-order $[128, 8, 64]_2$ Reed-Muller code. The encoding procedure first encodes a message $\mathbf{m} \in \mathbb{F}_2^{8k_1}$ to a codeword $\hat{\mathbf{m}} \in \mathbb{F}_{2^8}^{n_1}$ of the employed shortened Reed-Solomon codes. It then maps each byte of $\hat{\mathbf{m}}$ to a codeword of the first-order RM and repeats the RM codeword for 3 or 5 times depending on the security level to obtain a duplicated RM codeword in $\mathbb{F}_2^{n_2}$. In summary, we employ a linear code $\mathbf{mG} \in \mathbb{F}_2^{n_1 n_2}$. The HQC proposal makes all computations in the ambient space $\mathbb{F}_2^n$ and truncates the remaining $n - n_1 n_2$ useless bits.

The IND-CCA security of the KEM version of HQC is achieved by the Hofheinz-Hövelmanns-Kiltz (HHK) transform [24].

2.4 Threat Model

We consider a side-channel-assisted chosen-ciphertext attack on a KEM's decapsulation algorithm, where the attacker selects ciphertexts and observes specific side-channel data, such as timing [18], cache-timing [25], or power/electromagnetic leakages [36], from the targeted device, which can be a high-end CPU, low-end CPU (e.g., ARM cortex-M4), or hardware device.

Table 2. The HQC parameter sets [2]. The inner code is the duplicated Reed-Muller code defined by the first-order $[128, 8, 64]_2$ Reed-Muller code.

Instance	RS-S			Duplicated RM						
	n_1	k_1	d_{RS}	Mult	n_2	d_{RM}	$n_1 n_2$	n	ω	$\omega_r = \omega_e$
hqc-128	46	16	31	3	384	192	17 664	17 669	66	75
hqc-192	56	24	33	5	640	320	35 840	35 851	100	114
hqc-256	90	32	49	5	640	320	57 600	57 637	131	149

Specifically, we assume that a communication party Alice is using her device for key establishment. An adversary called Mallory sends selected ciphertexts to Alice to recover Alice's long-term secret key. Alice runs the decapsulation algorithm and Mallory will fail if the used KEM algorithm is IND-CCA secure. However, the designed side-channel-assisted CCAs can make the attack successful after a few such attempts, using the observed side-channel leakages.

This side-channel-assisted CCA attack model is well-established – it is stated in [45] that all the NIST round-3 KEM candidates except for Classic McEliece are vulnerable to such attacks exploring leakages from FO transform. The basic idea is to construct a PC oracle outputting whether $\mathbf{Dec}(c') \overset{?}{=} m$, where c' is the chosen ciphertext and m is a message vector.

Finally, the attacker recovers the long-term secret keys based on the output of the PC oracle. Since the PC oracle is generally built from measurements of side-channel leakages, it cannot be 100% correct, in practice. We denote the accuracy of the constructed PC oracle ρ, i.e., the oracle outputs the right decision with probability ρ and the wrong one with probability $1 - \rho$.

Note that we are discussing general methods for near-optimal CCA SCAs. This new coding-theoretical approach for reduced sample (trace) complexity can be applied in various side-channel attacks on various platforms, while the starting oracle accuracy ρ can be different. A PC oracle with 100% correctness ($\rho = 1$) can also be connected to a key misuse attack model, as described in [32].

Profiled Power/EM Attacks. Specific to power/EM attacks, we mainly consider a profiled setting that the adversary has a similar but different device to perform training activities. Though the adversary has no access to the secret key in the targeted device, the secret key in the training device can be freely set. We can also apply the new idea to non-profiled attacks that can build the required abstract oracles online, but the sample complexity analysis will be different.

Comparison with the Adaptive Model in Power/EM Attacks. The studies [32, 33, 42] proposed efficient adaptive KR-CCA-SCAs on lattice-based proposals. This attack model allows the adversary to select a new chosen ciphertext based on information obtained from previous power/EM traces, which can be employed for source coding on secret coefficients. This approach can result in reduced sample complexity close to the lower Huffman or Shannon bounds. However, this attack model is strong for many practical (say IoT) applications since the adversary needs to have good connections with the device measuring the power/EM leakages and good computation capability to instantly process the obtained traces. We highlight that our new SCA-LDPC attack framework eliminates the requirement and offers source coding gain in a non-adaptive attack model.

3   The SCA-LDPC Attack Framework

This section presents a new idea of incorporating LDPC codes and soft information to design chosen ciphertexts and improve previously established KR-CCA-SCAs for CCA-secure post-quantum Key Encapsulation Mechanisms (KEMs) and encryption schemes. We propose a novel technique to extract, from a single side-channel measurement, information regarding a low-weight parity check of the secret coefficients, as opposed to information regarding a single coefficient in previous methods. The sparse system is then solved using iterative decoding methods, such as belief propagation. This new approach enables the attainment of both source coding benefits and error correction advantages. This is due to the combination of several secret coefficients, which leads to a more uniform extraction of information from a single trace. Additionally, the correct recovery of coefficients facilitates the correction of erroneous decisions through spare parity-check relations. The adoption of this new method significantly reduces the number of necessary side-channel measurements. We call the new attack strategy a framework as it is generic and can be applied to both code-based and lattice-based schemes, in a multitude of side-channel leakage scenarios including timing, cache-timing, power, and electromagnetic leakages.

We start this section by assuming the availability of a well-designed LDPC code with specific dimensions and proceed to explain its utilization for improved side-channel information extraction. We then in Sect. 3.2 present a simple method for constructing such linear codes, the effectiveness of which will be demonstrated through experiments in Sect. 6. In addition, we broaden the framework by introducing a concatenated construction, where the LDPC codes are utilized as the outer code. This construction is particularly efficient for lattice-based schemes that feature a large alphabet size or for scenarios where the accuracy of the oracle constructed from side-channel measurements is limited.

3.1   New Attack Idea

Given a good linear code with a sparse parity-check matrix $\mathbf{H}_{r \times n}$, there are $k = n - r$ secret positions to recover. In lattice-based and code-based KEM proposals, the value k is usually divided into b blocks, each of which has the size of k/b. We add the constraint that $\mathbf{H}$ should have the form of

$$\mathbf{H} = \left[\mathbf{H}_{r \times k} | -\mathbf{I}_{r \times r} \right].$$

Our goal is to recover the first k secret entries s_i. One parity-check equation, i.e., one row in the parity-check matrix $\mathbf{H}$, will introduce one check variable c_i for

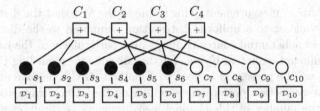

Fig. 1. The Tanner graph explanation.

$i \in \{k+1, \ldots, k+r\}$. We can rewrite each parity-check equation as $c_i = \sum_{j \in \mathcal{I}} s_j$ and the size of $\#\{\mathcal{I}\}$ is small since the matrix $\mathbf{H}$ is of low density.

The secret entries s_i are typically generated according to a certain secret distribution. For example, in the lattice-based scheme Kyber, the secret entries are generated from the central binomial distribution B_μ; in the code-based scheme HQC, the secret vector is very sparse and each secret entry can be viewed as a Bernoulli variable Ber_η, where η is a small positive number. The secret distribution can be utilized as the prior information for s_i. Moreover, additional information can be obtained through the implementation of side-channel measurements of s_i, which subsequently updates the relevant distribution. This approach is particularly beneficial in lattice-based scenarios. We then design new ciphertexts to obtain side-channel leakages of sparse linear combination c_i of s_j for $j \in \mathcal{I}$. The side channel information could reveal an empirical probability of c_i. The problem of recovering all s_i for $i \in \{1, \ldots, k\}$ is transformed into a coding problem through a noisy discrete channel. Note that the design method for ciphertexts that can reveal partial information of c_i, is unique to each proposed scheme and differs between lattice-based and code-based schemes. This ciphertext design is one main technical challenge in the proposed attack framework.

Explanation. The attack idea is illustrated in Fig. 1. We assume that six secret coefficients or variables s_i for $1 \le i \le 6$ need to be recovered. For each s_i, we can use the a priori distribution (e.g., in the HQC case), or we have more traces or oracle calls to get a better knowledge of its distribution (e.g., in the Kyber case). We show 4 parity checks in this example, and each check connects to a new variable v_i. From side-channel measurements or oracle calls, we got additional information about these variables. Thus, we could assign the corresponding distribution to these variables and build a Tanner graph as in Fig. 1. With this sparse bipartite Tanner graph, we perform iterative decoding to recover the desired secret coefficients s_i for $1 \le i \le 6$.

The Gain of Using LDPC Codes. It is essential to select a sparse graph code that facilitates efficient decoding and renders the key recovery procedure computationally feasible. Therefore, it is natural to examine LDPC codes that have favorable characteristics from an information-theoretic point of view. We introduce the variables c_i, which are sparse linear combinations of the secret coefficients s_j, thereby facilitating a more efficient extraction of information from a single side-channel measurement. This is due to the fact that the distribution of c_i is typically closer to a uniform distribution compared to the distribution of s_i, resulting in substantial source coding gains, particularly in the case of HQC and to a significant extent in Kyber. Further discussions regarding these source coding gains will be presented in Sect. 6. Finally, LDPC codes can offer close to optimal error correction performance, rendering the attack framework efficient in terms of the number of side-channel measurements required, even when the oracle constructed from side-channel leakages is highly inaccurate.

Example 1 (The source coding gain for hqc-128*).* In hqc-128, the length of $\mathbf{y}$ is $n = 17669$ and the Hamming weight of $\mathbf{y}$ is $w_H(\mathbf{y}) = 66$. Hence, we can approximate each position of $\mathbf{y}$ as a Bernoulli distribution Ber_η, where $\eta \approx 0.0037$. Assume that we have a perfect oracle to inform us of the value of one position from one oracle call. If we try to recover a bit in $\mathbf{y}$ by one oracle call, with Shannon's binary entropy function, the obtained information is bounded by 0.0352 bit. If we xor 50 i.i.d. secret positions (as we did later in Sect. 6) and try to recover the new random bit from one oracle call, then we can instead obtain 0.6255 bit of information. Thus, from an information-theoretical perspective, the new framework is much more advantageous.

The Ciphertext Selection. If PC oracle variants can be developed to directly reveal information about a single secret symbol (see [45] for example), the framework can be utilized to extract information about linear combinations of multiple symbols. Therefore, the new attack framework can be applied to enhancing attacks on LWE/LWR-based schemes, NTRU-based schemes, and HQC-like schemes.

In the case of LWE/LWR-based schemes and HQC-like schemes, the ciphertexts are made up of two components, one of which is directly multiplied by the secret key in decryption. Prior attack strategies select a single non-zero position in this component (a matrix or a vector) to extract information about a single secret symbol. We could instead select a small number of non-zero positions to recover information about linear combinations. The specific implementations for NTRU-based schemes are more intricate, necessitating further research.

3.2 Code Generation

It has been demonstrated in previous research [39] that random sparse linear codes exhibit superior decoding performance and specific classes of Low-Density Parity-Check (LDPC) codes, such as [38], can attain error-correction capabilities that approach the Shannon capacity. In this work, we present a straightforward code construction method that has shown remarkable results in our experiments.

We first borrow the concept of distance spectrum from [19].

Definition 3 (Distance Spectrum [19]). *For a binary vector* $\mathbf{h} \in \mathbb{F}_2^{n_o}$, *we define its distance spectrum* $D(\mathbf{h})$ *as*

$$D(\mathbf{h}) = \{d : 1 \leq d \leq \lfloor n_0/2 \rfloor, d \text{ classified as existing in } \mathbf{h}\},$$

where "existing in **h**" *means there are two ones in* **h** *with distance d or* $(n_0 - d)$
*inbetween. A distance d can appear many times in the distance spectrum of a
given bit pattern* **h**. *We call this number the multiplicity of d.*

In our new attack, we first generate QC-LDPC codes with mb blocks of the
parity-check matrix

$$\mathbf{H}_{\text{ini}} = \begin{bmatrix} \mathbf{H}_{11} & \cdots & \mathbf{H}_{1b} \\ \vdots & \ddots & \vdots \\ \mathbf{H}_{m1} & \cdots & \mathbf{H}_{mb} \end{bmatrix},$$

where $\mathbf{H}_{ij}$ is the circulant matrix (or the negacyclic matrix in the q-ary case)
generated from a binary vector $\mathbf{h}_{ij}$ for $1 \le i \le m, 1 \le j \le b$ with a low Hamming
weight. We generate the vectors $\mathbf{h}_{ij}$ randomly with the constraint that only
distances of multiplicity 1 are allowed in its distance spectrum. This can be
done with high probability since the constructed LDPC codes are sparse. The
key point in the design is that a length-4 cycle occurs in the associated Tanner
graph if the multiplicity of a distance in the distance spectrum is larger than 2.
By avoiding such patterns in a block, we can avoid many length-4 cycles; such
attempts can improve the decoding performance as short cycles can substantially
hurt the decoding performance [39].

We select r rows of $\mathbf{H}_{\text{ini}}$ (randomly or according to certain rules) to form a
sub-matrix $\mathbf{H}'$ and append $-\mathbf{I}_{r \times r}$, where $\mathbf{I}_{r \times r}$ is the identity matrix. Thus, the
parity-check matrix of the final generated code is

$$\mathbf{H} = \begin{bmatrix} \mathbf{H}'_{r \times n_0 b} | -\mathbf{I}_{r \times r} \end{bmatrix} \tag{4}$$

Concatenated Code Construction. The LDPC codes generated from the above
simple approach can serve as the outer code in the concatenated construction.
The inner code can be any linear code such as a repetition code, the extended
Hamming codes, and a further concatenation of the extended Hamming codes
and repetition codes in [29]. Moreover, we can include a soft-input-soft-output
decoder (e.g., in [26]) to utilize the soft-information. Note that in the soft-
decoding procedure (e.g., the BP algorithm) of the outer code, only a distribution
of each secret coefficient random variable is required; we could thus employ a
code with an efficient maximum likelihood decoding procedure as the inner code
allowing an efficient calculation of the soft output of the coefficient distribution.

In summary, such concatenated code construction enhances decoding capability and also balances decoding complexity, as the decoding of both outer and
inner codes is efficient. This construction is particularly effective for lattice-based
proposals or when the side-channel oracle exhibits a low level of accuracy.

4   Application to Kyber

In this section, we outline the details of how the new SCA-LDPC framework
can be applied to Kyber. The attack is more effective for Kyber if we have
side-channel leakages for both s_i and c_j. We demonstrate how to obtain these
leakages, construct inner codes for them, and apply the outer LDPC decoder.

4.1   Basic Key Recovery Attack

In the following, we explain the basic attack to obtain side-channel information about secret coefficients s_i. We focus on Kyber-768 mostly because the new protected implementation [23] that we target supports only this set of parameters. For Kyber-768, the secret key is $\mathbf{s} = (\mathbf{s}_0, \mathbf{s}_1, \mathbf{s}_2)$, a ciphertext is a pair $(\mathbf{u}', \mathbf{v}')$. To decrypt a ciphertext, one computes $\mathbf{m} = \mathbf{Comp}_q(\mathbf{v} - \mathbf{s}^\mathsf{T}\mathbf{u}, 1)$, where $\mathbf{u} = \mathbf{Decomp}_q(\mathbf{u}', d_u) = (\mathbf{u}_0, \mathbf{u}_1, \mathbf{u}_2)$, $\mathbf{v} = \mathbf{Decomp}_q(\mathbf{v}', d_v)$. The common practice [36] is to choose a ciphertext that leads to $\mathbf{m} = (0, 0, \ldots, 0)$ or $\mathbf{m} = (1, 0, \ldots, 0)$. In other words, all bits of the message are fixed to 0 except the first one. This can be done, for example, by setting $\mathbf{u}_0 = (k_u, 0, \ldots, 0)$, $\mathbf{u}_1 = \mathbf{u}_2 = \mathbf{0}$ and $\mathbf{v} = (k_v, 0, \ldots, 0)$, where k_u, k_v are some numbers modulo q. In this case, the message bits are subject to the following equation.

$$\mathbf{m}[i] = \begin{cases} \mathbf{Comp}_q(k_v - k_u \cdot \mathbf{s}_0[0], 1), & i = 0 \\ \mathbf{Comp}_q(k_u \cdot \mathbf{s}_0[i], 1), & i \geq 1 \end{cases} \tag{5}$$

By choosing appropriate values for k_u and k_v, it is possible to force $\mathbf{m}[i]$ to always be zero for $i \geq 1$, while the value of $\mathbf{m}[0]$ depends on the first secret coefficient $\mathbf{s}_0[0]$. Since secret coefficients for Kyber-768 are taken from the range $[-2, \ldots, 2]$, some of the coefficients are encoded as 0, while others are encoded as 1. We can use several such ciphertexts with (possibly) different k_v and/or k_u to get an inner code of longer length. This way, using an oracle that distinguishes message $(1, 0, \ldots, 0)$ from $(0, 0, \ldots, 0)$, the attacker can get the distribution of a secret coefficient closer to the real value the more ciphertexts he uses.

There are restrictions for the values k_u and k_v: (1) these values are taken from the image of $\mathbf{Decomp}_q$; (2) k_u is chosen in a way such that $\mathbf{Comp}_q(k_u \cdot s, 1) = 0$ for any secret coefficient s (follows from Eq. (5)). Thus, one cannot use any code; even though it is possible to encode each secret coefficient with only $\lceil \log_2(5) \rceil = 3$ bits, for any fixed in-advance combination of 3 ciphertexts one cannot fully determine an arbitrary secret coefficient even with perfect oracle.

One way to solve this problem [42] is to choose ciphertexts adaptively based on the output of the oracle, but we take a different approach. Consider an FD oracle based attack, i.e., assume that we have a set of oracles $(\mathcal{O}_i)_{i \in (0..n-1)}$, where n is the length of the message. Given a ciphertext, the oracle $\mathcal{O}_i$ says if $\mathbf{m}[i] = 1$ or not. Essentially, the attacker calls all of these oracles at once, giving them the same ciphertext, this way he can get information about the whole message to be decrypted, the scenario is the same as in [29]. The attacker can create a ciphertext in the following way, set $\mathbf{u}_0 = (k_u, 0, \ldots, 0)$, $\mathbf{u}_1 = \mathbf{u}_2 = \mathbf{0}$, and $\mathbf{v} = (k_v, k_v, \ldots, k_v)$, then

$$\mathbf{m}[i] = \mathbf{Comp}_q(k_v - k_u \cdot \mathbf{s}_0[i], 1), \tag{6}$$

i.e., i^{th} bit of the message depends on $\mathbf{s}_0[i]$. Thus, from one ciphertext the information about the block of 256 coefficients $\mathbf{s}_0$ can be obtained. Since there is no more restriction on $\mathbf{m}[i] = 0$ for $i \geq 1$, the amount of possible inner codes increases greatly. Table 3 shows an inner code from three ciphertexts built from

Table 3. Example of an inner code for the secret coefficients. Each value from the range $[-2, \ldots, 2]$ is encoded with 3 bits (columns of the table), therefore, the secret coefficient could be fully determined with just 3 oracle calls given that the oracle is perfect.

(k'_u, k'_v)	Secret coefficient				
	-2	-1	0	1	2
$(630, 14)$	0	1	0	1	1
$(706, 6)$	0	0	1	1	0
$(706, 10)$	0	1	1	0	0

(k'_u, k'_v) pairs, this code can be used to fully determine 256 secret coefficients with perfect oracles. Note that to create an actual ciphertext $(\mathbf{u}', \mathbf{v}')$ we need a pair (k'_u, k'_v) that maps to (k_u, k_v) with coefficient-wise function $\mathbf{Decomp}_q$. The next block of secret coefficients $\mathbf{s}_1$ can be retrieved by setting $\mathbf{u}_0 = \mathbf{0}$, $\mathbf{u}_1 = (k_u, 0, \ldots, 0)$, $\mathbf{u}_2 = \mathbf{0}$ and so on. Note that the attacker could choose different values in $\mathbf{v}$, this way different encodings can be used for different message bits (although all those encodings should have the same k_u) and this potentially opens up the possibility of the adaptive attack. However, such an attack is more complicated since the set of allowed encodings given the fixed k_u is quite limited, and the attacker has to choose the same k_u for all 256 coefficients. We leave it as a potential follow-up work and focus on the situation where for all message bits there is a fixed in-advance encoding to be used.

The common approach in the literature is to use just an inner code for secret coefficients (without outer code) that makes the probability of getting the wrong coefficient to be very small (with real imperfect oracles), such that the probability to get all secret coefficients correctly is close to 1. In our approach, however, we use a shorter inner code that is not sufficient by itself, for example in our real attack from Sect. 6.1 we encode each secret coefficient with only 2 bits and encode the values -2 and 2 the same way, i.e., with only inner code it is impossible to differentiate between these values.

How to Choose Inner Code. For the fixed in-advance code length ℓ we want to create an inner code C_ℓ that maximizes the information we get from the oracles with accuracy ρ. We solve this problem by considering the entropy of secret coefficients. Initially, each of them is distributed according to B_μ, whose entropy is $H(\mathsf{B}_\mu) \approx 2.03$, for $\mu = 2$. Each value $s \in \mathsf{B}_\mu$ is encoded as $C_\ell(s)$ – a binary string of length ℓ. Given an output string $\mathbf{y}$ of length ℓ from an oracle (note that $\mathbf{y}$ can be different from every $C_\ell(s)$, $s \in \mathsf{B}_\mu$), consider the probability $\mathbf{Pr}\,[\mathsf{B}_\mu = s \mid \mathbf{y}]$ for each $s \in \mathsf{B}_\mu$. As an example from Table 3, $\mathbf{Pr}\,[\mathsf{B}_\mu = 0 \mid 011] = 1$ for the perfect oracle, but it is less than 1 for an oracle with $\rho < 1$ since we could have reached this $\mathbf{y}$ from another coefficient.

To avoid ambiguity, we denote $\mathbf{y}_\rho$ as the output of the oracle with the accuracy ρ. The conditional distribution $\mathsf{B}_\mu | \mathbf{y}_\rho$ can be naturally defined as $\mathbf{Pr}\,[(\mathsf{B}_\mu | \mathbf{y}_\rho) = s] = \mathbf{Pr}\,[\mathsf{B}_\mu = s | \mathbf{y}_\rho]$. Now, the difference between the entropy values $H(\mathsf{B}_\mu) - H(\mathsf{B}_\mu | \mathbf{y}_\rho)$ shows how much information the output $\mathbf{y}_\rho$ gives. To assess how good the code is, we can compute the expectation of this information as

$$I(C_\ell) = \sum_{\mathbf{y}_\rho \in \{0,1\}^\ell} (H(\mathsf{B}_\mu) - H(\mathsf{B}_\mu | \mathbf{y}_\rho)) \cdot \mathbf{Pr}\,[Y = \mathbf{y}_\rho],$$

where Y is a random variable that describes the output of an oracle with accuracy ρ on a random secret coefficient. The probability of the specific oracle's output is computed as follows.

$$\mathbf{Pr}\,[Y = \mathbf{y}_\rho] = \sum_{x \in \mathrm{supp}(\mathsf{B}_\mu)} \rho^{d(\mathbf{y}_\rho, C_\ell(x))} (1 - \rho)^{\ell - d(\mathbf{y}_\rho, C_\ell(x))} \mathbf{Pr}\,[\mathsf{B}_\mu = x],$$

where $d(\cdot, \cdot)$ is the Hamming distance. To decode a received word $\mathbf{y}_\rho$, one computes conditional probability $\mathsf{B}_\mu | \mathbf{y}_\rho$ of secret coefficient, i.e. we use maximum-likelihood decoding approach.

4.2   Improving the Attack Using LDPC

The basic attack allows us to compute the conditional distribution for each secret coefficient using the inner code. Now, following our framework, we create an outer LDPC code. For it to work, we also need a way to get information about parity checks c_i. Let us describe how to create a ciphertext corresponding to a parity check. Consider an example: Let $\mathbf{u}_1, \mathbf{u}_2$ and $\mathbf{v}$ be as above, but $\mathbf{u}_0 = k_u + k_u x^2$, then

$$\mathbf{s}^\mathsf{T}\mathbf{u} = k_u \left((\mathbf{s}_0[0] - \mathbf{s}_0[n-2]) + (\mathbf{s}_0[1] - \mathbf{s}_0[n-1])x + (\mathbf{s}_0[2] + \mathbf{s}_0[0])x^2 + \ldots \right).$$

Looking at the first message bit

$$\mathbf{m}[0] = \mathbf{Comp}_q(k_v - k_u \cdot (\mathbf{s}_0[0] - \mathbf{s}_0[n-2]), 1)$$

and comparing it to Eq. (6), one can recover $c_0 \leftarrow \mathbf{s}_0[0] - \mathbf{s}_0[n-2]$ using a similar approach as in recovering $\mathbf{s}_0[0]$ with $\mathcal{O}_0$. However, c_0 lies in the range $[-4, \ldots, 4]$, therefore the recovery process is more complicated. However, we still use several different ciphertexts to get an inner code for the check variables. In other words, there are two inner codes: one for secret coefficients, and another one for check variables. Each of them helps us to compute conditional distributions, which we use with outer LDPC code.

Now, let us represent c_0 as a vector $\mathbf{h}_0$ with values from $\{-1, 0, 1\}$ such that $c_0 = \mathbf{h}_0^\mathsf{T}(\mathbf{s}_0[0], \ldots, \mathbf{s}_0[n-1])$. In general, if $\mathbf{u}_0 = k_u \cdot \sum_{j=1}^{w} x^{i_j}$, then $\mathbf{h}_0$ is a vector with w nonzero entries at the positions $(-i_j) \bmod n$, where the entry is 1 if and only if $i_j = 0$. Let $\mathbf{H}_0$ be a negacyclic matrix of the vector $\mathbf{h}_0$. With this ciphertext, the ith message bit is connected to the ith row of $\mathbf{H}_0(\mathbf{s}_0[0], \ldots, \mathbf{s}_0[n-1])^\mathsf{T}$. Note that, unlike in Sect. 3.1, c_i is the sum of secret coefficients, possibly multiplied by -1. However, this does not significantly affect the result since from the distribution of the coefficient it is trivial to obtain the distribution of the negative coefficient and vice versa. Thus, we still call c_i the sum of secret coefficients.

Let $\mathbf{u}_r = k_u \cdot \sum_{j=1}^{w} x_j^{i_j^{(r)}}$, $r \in \{0,1,2\}$. Ciphertext $(\mathbf{u}, \mathbf{v})$ with the help of oracles $\mathcal{O}_i$ reveals information about 256 parity checks. The parity-check matrix of the outer LDPC code in this case is of the form

$$\mathbf{H}_{ini} = \begin{bmatrix} \mathbf{H}_0 | \mathbf{H}_1 | \mathbf{H}_2 \end{bmatrix},$$

where $\mathbf{H}_j$ is the negacyclic matrix obtained from the vector connecting c_0 and $\mathbf{s}_j$. Due to the FD oracle, parity checks $c_1, \ldots, c_{n-1}$ must be negacyclic shifts of c_0. We only demonstrated the parity-check matrix for the outer LDPC code consisting of block of 256 checks, but there could be several such blocks. Note that in general, the polynomials $\mathbf{u}_r$ do not have to use the same w.

There are three main ways to increase the success probability of the attack.

1. Increase the length of the inner code for the secret coefficients. Querying oracles as in Sect. 4.1 leads to a more accurate distribution for each coefficient.
2. Similarly, increase the length of the inner code for the check variables, i.e., fix the indexes $i_j^{(r)}$ and use different (k_u, k_v).
3. Increase the number of check blocks. The resulting parity-check matrix of the LDPC code $\mathbf{H}_{ini}$ consists of $3 \times m$ blocks of negacyclic matrices, where m is the number of "unique" parity checks $c_0, c_n, c_{2n}, \ldots$

Creating the best inner code for the check variables that maximizes the amount of information is a challenging task. An educated guess would be the most accurate way to describe our approach to tackling this problem.

5 Application to HQC

In this section, we describe the detailed attack on HQC. $\mathcal{O}_{\text{HQC}}$ denotes a general side-channel-based PC oracle for HQC, referenced prior-art assumes timing leakage, but this is not required. We treat a key-misuse oracle as a chosen-ciphertext side-channel oracle with 100% oracle accuracy.

5.1 Key-Recovery Attack with $\mathcal{O}_{\text{HQC}}$

In [16] the authors presented a plaintext checking (PC) oracle based on timing information due to the use of rejection sampling. In this section, we describe how the PC attack works and then explain how we can improve it by using our new SCA-LDPC framework, which is based on coding theory.

Currently, HQC makes use of so-called rejection sampling in the CPA secure encryption function [2,16]. The rejection sampling algorithm is used to construct random vectors with a specific Hamming weight ω. It works by random sampling of bit positions in the vector, and if some positions are sampled twice, they are rejected. Straight-forwardly implemented, this algorithm leaks timing information due to the inherently random number of rejections that occur. The HQC implementations tested in [16] leak timing information mainly through the use of so-called "seedexpander" calls. The output of the seedexpander function is deterministic pseudo-randomness given by an eXtendable Output Function (XOF). The rejection sampling algorithm uses the seedexpander function to generate relatively large blocks of randomness, at a time. The timing distribution, therefore, is highly dependent on the number of seedexpander calls needed. The minimum number of seedexpander calls occurs when there are no rejections in the rejection sampling algorithm. In practice, we classify timing measurements based on the number of *additional* seedexpander calls. They are each related to one of the four[2] distributions S_0, S_1, S_2, S_3, listed in increasing order of rarity.

Prior to the publication of the referenced work, it was believed that this randomness was only dependent on values known to the attacker, in this case, the plaintext $\mathbf{m}$. The assumption then was that constant time implementation was not needed for the rejection sampling algorithm. Certainly, it was shown in [16] that this assumption is problematic. Although $\mathbf{m}$ is indeed known to the attacker, the result of the implicitly carried out comparison $\mathbf{m}' \overset{?}{=} \mathbf{m}$ is not. Here $\mathbf{m}' = \mathrm{decode}(\mathbf{c} + \mathbf{e}')$ and $\mathbf{e}'$ is a extra noise supplied by the attacker.

The authors showed a key-recovery attack where, by using the timing information due to rejection sampling, knowledge of $\mathbf{m}' \overset{?}{=} \mathbf{m}$ is leaked. The attack required 866,000 so-called "idealized oracle" ($\mathcal{O}_{\mathrm{HQC}}^{\mathrm{ideal}}$) queries for the 128-bit security setting. The idealized oracle assumes a noise-free environment where a single timing measurement is sufficient to determine the membership of S_j (where $j = 3$ in [16]). Unfortunately, this is not sufficient for a 100% correct oracle, due to reasons explained in the following paragraph.

What follows is a high-level summary of the referenced attack; A plaintext $\mathbf{m}$ is selected according to some criteria useful for the distinguisher. In the case of timing leakage, the distinguishing property is such that the selected $\mathbf{m}$ results in the timing distribution S_3, since it is the one most easily distinguished. The probability of for any random $\mathbf{m}'$, where $\mathbf{m}' \neq \mathbf{m}$, resulting in the same S_3 timing distribution is low (0.58% per [16]). In other words, $\mathbf{m}' \overset{?}{=} \mathbf{m}$ can be distinguished with a high, yet-not-complete, advantage.

A ciphertext $\mathbf{c}' = (\mathbf{u}, \mathbf{v})$ is crafted in the next step such that $\mathbf{r_1}$ is $1 \in \mathcal{R}$ and $\mathbf{r_2}$ and $\mathbf{e}$ is $0 \in \mathcal{R}$. By Eq. (3) this results in

$$\mathbf{v} - \mathbf{u} \cdot \mathbf{y} = \mathbf{m}G + \mathbf{s} \cdot \mathbf{r_2} + \mathbf{e} - (\mathbf{r_1} + \mathbf{h} \cdot \mathbf{r_2}) \cdot \mathbf{y} = \mathbf{m}G - \mathbf{r_1} \cdot \mathbf{y} = \mathbf{m}G - \mathbf{y} \quad (7)$$

which makes $\mathbf{y}$ the only remaining error for the decoder to correct. Note too that by knowledge of $-\mathbf{y} = \mathbf{y}$ it is a simple computation to find the rest of the private key, since $\mathbf{x} = \mathbf{s} - \mathbf{h} \cdot \mathbf{y}$. Calculating $\mathbf{x}$ is quite unnecessary, however, since it is not used in decapsulation.

Plainly, this crafted ciphertext is invalid and will be rejected in the ciphertext comparison step of the decapsulation. However, a valid ciphertext is not required

---

[2] Strictly, there is no upper bound, but the practical benefit of finding a value for $S_{\geq 4}$ is not worth the exponential effort required [16].

due to the timing leakage in the XOF via the non-constant time rejection sampling algorithm. The reencryption step immediately preceding the comparison derives the values of r_1, r_2 and e from the XOF seeded by m. The single bit information $m' \stackrel{?}{=} m$ leaks prior to the ciphertext comparison step.

Hall et al. proposed in [21] a way to recover y; An additional error vector e' is added to c'. e' is of just sufficient weight to cause a decoding failure (i.e. $m' \neq m$ is leaked). The basic attack then simply iterates through each bit $0 \leq i \leq N$ of e' not already flipped to find those positions that if flipped would result in a decoding success. If this is the case for any value of i this indicates that the bit was already flipped in y in the ciphertext.

However, this technique alone is not sufficient to provide decisions on all bits in the ciphertext. The reason is twofold. First, unflipping a bit in the error pattern given to the RMRS decoder does not guarantee a decoding success, and secondly due to the possibility that both m' and m result in the timing distribution S_3, even though $m' \neq m$. This is modeled by $\mathcal{O}_{HQC}^{ideal}$, the idealized oracle from [16], which though noise-free, is not 100% correct.

The first problem is solved by using many different error patterns e'. The second was solved by majority voting, i.e. by gathering three or more decisions for every bit. Both of these solutions drive up the number of required oracle calls, even in the ideal timing leakage setting. For the 128-bit security level, this number adds up to 866,000 oracle calls [16].

5.2 New Improved Attack Using LDPC Codes

What follows is a description of the new attack listed in Fig. 2, a PC oracle $\mathcal{O}_{HQC}$ is assumed. Like in the original attack [16] we select a plaintext with good side-channel detection properties (in the original case this is a timing property).

The next step is to construct a $N \times N$ regular cyclic LDPC parity-check matrix H_{ini} without cycles of length 4, with a good decoding performance. H_{ini} has a row-weight of W. This construction is detailed in Sect. 3.2, with $(m = 1, b = 1)$. The first row of H_{ini} is the vector h_{ini}.

We craft a special ciphertext c' where $r_2 = 0, e = 0$ and $r_1 = h_{ini}$. Similarly to the case given by Eq. (7) above, this results in

$$v - u \cdot y = \ldots = mG - r_1 \cdot y = mG - h_{ini}y \qquad (8)$$

which makes the added noise that the decoder has to correct equal to $h_{ini}y$. In other words, each bit position i in c' correspond to the result of a parity-check equation over y, given by $h_{ini} >> i$ (cyclic shift by i steps) due to the cyclic nature of our LDPC code.

The Reed-Muller (RM) and Reed-Solomon (RS) concatenated (RMRS) decoder, used in HQC, can be attacked in two stages. First we select $(d_{RS} - 1)/2$ outer RM blocks (each RM block decodes to one RS symbol) to flip in c' (by XOR with e'). This results in a state where if one more block is flipped it will result in a decoding error in the RS decoder. A decoding failure such as that

Input: $\mathcal{O}_{\mathrm{HQC}}$, public key
Output: $\mathbf{y}$

1: Select plaintext $\mathbf{m}$ ▷ *With good side channel distinguishing properties*
2: Generate sparse vector $\mathbf{h}_{\mathrm{ini}}$ ▷ *According to Section 3.2*
3: Construct $\mathbf{H}_{\mathrm{ini}}$ ▷ *From $\mathbf{h}_{ini}$ by cyclic shifts*
4: Craft $\mathbf{c}'$ with $\mathbf{r_2} = 0, \mathbf{e} = 0$ and $\mathbf{r_1} = \mathbf{h}_{\mathrm{ini}}$
5: $\mu \leftarrow 0^N$ ▷ *Initialize message*
6: **loop**
7:    $\mathbf{e}' \leftarrow 0^N$,
8:    $\mathcal{B}' \leftarrow$ random subset of size $(d_{RS} - 1)/2$ from $\{0, \ldots, n_1 - 1\}$
9:    **for each** $B' \in \mathcal{B}'$ **do**   ▷ *Flip $(d_{RS} - 1)/2$ RM-blocks*
10:      Flip block B' in $\mathbf{e}'$
11:   **end for**
12:   $B \overset{\$}{\leftarrow} \{0, \ldots, n_1\} \setminus \mathcal{B}'$ ▷ *Select a random unflipped block*
13:   $\mathcal{I}^B \leftarrow \{Bn_2, \ldots, B(n_2 + 1) - 1\}$
14:   $\mathcal{I}_{\mathbf{e}'}^B, \mathcal{I}_0^B, \mathcal{I}_1^B, \leftarrow \emptyset, \emptyset, \emptyset,$
15:   **while** $\mathcal{O}_{\mathrm{HQC}}^{0=\mathrm{repeat}}(\mathbf{c}' + \mathbf{e}')$ **do** ▷ *Find an initial error pattern for block B*
16:      $\mathcal{I}_{\mathbf{e}'}^B \leftarrow \mathcal{I}_{\mathbf{e}'}^B \cup \{i\}$, where $i \overset{\$}{\leftarrow} \mathcal{I}^B$
17:      $\mathbf{e}'[i] \leftarrow 1$
18:   **end while**
19:   **for each** $i \in \mathcal{I}_{\mathbf{e}'}^B$ **do**   ▷ *Minimize the error pattern*
20:      $\mathbf{e}'[i] \leftarrow 0$ ▷ *Unflip bit in error pattern*
21:      **if** $\mathcal{O}_{\mathrm{HQC}}^{1=\mathrm{repeat}}(\mathbf{c}' + \mathbf{e}')$ **then**
22:         $\mathcal{I}_0^B \leftarrow \mathcal{I}_0^B \cup \{i\}$ ▷ *Satisfied parity check, add i to $\mathcal{I}_0^B$*
23:         $\mathbf{e}'[i] \leftarrow 1$ ▷ *Restore bit in error pattern*
24:      **end if**
25:   **end for**
26:   **for each** $i \in \left(\mathcal{I}^B \setminus \mathcal{I}_{\mathbf{e}'}^B\right)$ **do**   ▷ *Find unsatisfied parity checks*
27:      **if** $\mathcal{O}_{\mathrm{HQC}}(\mathbf{c}' + \mathbf{e}')$ **then**
28:         $\mathcal{I}_1^B \leftarrow \mathcal{I}_1^B \cup \{i\}$ ▷ *If found, store in $\mathcal{I}_1^B$*
29:      **end if**
30:   **end for**
31:   Select rows $i \in (\mathcal{I}_0^B \cup \mathcal{I}_1^B)$ from $\mathbf{H}_{\mathrm{ini}}$ and add to $\mathbf{H}'$
32:   Construct $\mathbf{H} = [\mathbf{H}'|\mathbf{I}]$
33:   $\mu \leftarrow \mu \mid 0^{\#\{\mathcal{I}_0^B\}} \mid 1^{\#\{\mathcal{I}_1^B\}}$
34:   $\mathbf{y} \leftarrow \mathrm{Decode}_{\mathbf{H}}(\mu)[0..n]$ ▷ *Decoder returns the error vector*
35:   **if** $\mathbf{y}$ correct **then**   ▷ *Try to decrypt a valid message*
36:      **return** $\mathbf{y}$
37:   **end if**
38: **end loop**

Fig. 2. HQC new attack algorithm. $\mathcal{O}_{\mathrm{HQC}}^{0=\mathrm{repeat}}$ denotes a PC oracle which is repeated as necessary (determined by empirical study) to achieve better than nominal error rate in the case of decoding failure; decoding successes are never repeated. $\mathcal{O}_{\mathrm{HQC}}^{1=\mathrm{repeat}}$ works in a similar but opposite fashion.

would be detected by $\mathcal{O}_{\text{HQC}}$. We randomly select another block which we denote B.

The next stage is to find which bits $\mathcal{I}_{\mathbf{e}'}^{B}$ to flip in the block B that results in a decoding failure. We do this by flipping bits $i \in \mathcal{I}_{\mathbf{e}'}^{B}$ such that $\mathbf{e}'[i] = 1$ in block B until a RM decoding failure occurs. This propagates as a failure symbol to the RS decoder which is already on the brink of being overwhelmed. This results in a state where $\mathbf{c}' + \mathbf{e}'$ fails to decode due to too much additional noise in the block B partition of $\mathbf{e}'$.

An Aside on Oracle Accuracy. The LDPC code helps with recovery from bad oracle decisions. However, the stateful nature of the new algorithm can cause certain poor oracle decisions to propagate and result in the algorithm ending up in a bad state. Such errors occur naturally more often for less accurate oracles. We compensate for these effects by introducing extra confirmation calls to those oracle decisions which are most sensitive. These are denoted in Fig. 2 by $\mathcal{O}_{\text{HQC}}^{r=\text{repeat}}$, where $r \in \{0,1\}$ indicates which Oracle outputs are repeated for confirmation. $\mathcal{O}_{\text{HQC}}^{0=\text{repeat}}$ means decoding failures are confirmed but decoding successes are not. The number of repeated oracle calls is determined by empirical study.

After finding an error pattern resulting in decoding failure, the next step is to reduce the number of flipped bits, in block B. The goal is to find the minimal pattern that still results in a decoding failure. We do this by unflipping each of the flipped bits $i \in \mathcal{I}_{\mathbf{e}'}^{B}$ in block B. This results in one of two cases:

1. If we get a decoding success we record it in $\mathcal{I}_{0}^{B}$ for later use, undo the flip and then move on to select another bit $i \in \mathcal{I}_{\mathbf{e}'}^{B}$.
2. If we still get a decoding failure we try again with another flipped bit $i \in \mathcal{I}_{\mathbf{e}'}^{B}$.

Once we have run out of flipped bits in $\mathcal{I}_{\mathbf{e}'}^{B}$ to check, we have achieved a minimal bit pattern in $\mathcal{I}_{0}^{B}$ for block B that results in decoding failure. That is, the set $\mathcal{I}_{0}^{B}$ contains those bits that result in a decoding success if any are unflipped. Conversely, when flipped, they have been unambiguously shown to increase the noise for the RMRS decoder. All bits in $\mathcal{I}_{0}^{B}$ can therefore reliably be assumed to correspond to a satisfied parity check. So, for each bit $i \in \mathcal{I}_{0}^{B}$ we construct[3] our sub matrix $\mathbf{H}'$ by the selection of row i of $\mathbf{H}_{\text{ini}}$.

Working from the minimal decoding failure pattern ($\mathbf{e}'[i] = 1 \forall i \in \mathcal{I}_{0}^{B}$ and $\mathbf{e}'[i] = 0 \forall i \notin \mathcal{I}_{0}^{B}$) for RM block B we can now flip bits that so far have been left untouched ($i \notin \mathcal{I}_{\mathbf{e}'}^{B}$), one at a time. For each flip, if it results in a decoding success, then we record it in $\mathcal{I}_{1}^{B}$. Such a bit must mean that by flipping it we reduce the noise that the RMRS decoder has to handle. Therefore, this bit can be reliably assumed to correspond to an unsatisfied parity-check equation, or a '1' in the vector $\mathbf{h}_{\text{ini}}\mathbf{y}$. When all bits have been tested we extend our sub matrix $\mathbf{H}'$ by the selection of all rows $i \in \mathcal{I}_{1}^{B}$ of $\mathbf{H}_{\text{ini}}$.

At this time in the algorithm, r number of parity-check equations have been collected in $\mathbf{H}'$. The remaining step is to construct parity-check matrix $\mathbf{H} = [\mathbf{H}'_{r \times n} | \mathbf{I}_{r \times r}]$ and a message vector

---

[3] or extend if this is not the first selected block/iteration of the algorithm.

$$\mu = \left[\mathbf{0}^n | \mathbf{0}^{\#\{\mathcal{I}_0^{B^0}\}} | \mathbf{1}^{\#\{\mathcal{I}_1^{B^0}\}} \dots | \mathbf{0}^{\#\{\mathcal{I}_0^{B^t}\}} | \mathbf{1}^{\#\{\mathcal{I}_1^{B^t}\}} \right] \tag{9}$$

in such a way that we have n zeroes, each representing an unknown bit-value of $\mathbf{y}$ to be recovered. The message is appended by the following redundancies: a single 0 for each satisfied parity-check equation hitherto selected ($i \in \mathcal{I}_0^B$) and a 1 for each unsatisfied parity check ($i \in \mathcal{I}_1^B$). We do this for all t blocks B that have so far been selected.

We try to decode the message μ and recover $\mathbf{y}$ from the first n bits. We use $\mathbf{H}$ as input and a suitable decoder such as sum-product or the min-sum approximation.

If the decoding is not successful we unflip all bits in block B and unflip all other blocks. Then we restart the algorithm (using the same ciphertext) and select another block. The old $\mathcal{I}_0^B$ and $\mathcal{I}_1^B$ are saved and re-used in the next decoding attempt. We continue until successful.

In some cases (for less accurate oracles) one might still fail to decode even after all outer RM blocks have been exhausted. In such cases, one can simply save μ and $\mathbf{H}'$ and continue extending them by restarting the algorithm.

6 Experiments

In this section, we show the results of simulations and real-world experiments for Kyber and HQC.

6.1 Masked Kyber

Software Simulations. We introduce software simulations, where we fix the accuracy ρ of each oracle $\mathcal{O}_i$ to be the same.

The attack improves as the weight of the rows in the parity matrix increases. However, the decoding time increases exponentially with it. In the course of experiments, we found that the value $w = 2$ works best, i.e., the parity-check matrix consists of negacyclic matrices with row weight 2. For Kyber-768, this means that each check variable is the sum of 6 secret coefficients.

The three main parameters of the attack are m_0, m_1 and m_2, where m_0 and m_2 are the lengths of the inner code for the secret coefficients and the check variables, resp., m_1 is the number of blocks of check variables. Recall that Kyber-768 has 3 blocks of 256 secret coefficients, and we assume that from one power trace we get information about all 256 message bits. This means that we need $3m_0$ and $m_1 \cdot m_2$ traces to get the distributions for secret coefficients and check variables, respectively. The interested reader is referred to the full version of the paper [20] for the actual codes used in the simulation and in the real attack.

We evaluate our methodology against the majority voting technique, a conceptually simple coding approach that can be considered as a repetition code. Majority voting is a typical approach to ensure that a single secret coefficient can be recovered with high accuracy. This approach has been selected as the baseline attack method due to its relevance as the most frequently used coding

Table 4. Comparison with the majority voting for full-key recovery. t is the number of votes cast, values in the brackets are m_0, m_1 and m_2, resp.

$\rho = 0.995$	Number of traces	Average number of errors
Majority Voting ($t = 3$)	27 (ref)	0.21/768
Our Method $(2, 1, 4)$	10 (-63%)	0.37/768
$\rho = 0.95$	Number of traces	Average number of errors
Majority Voting ($t = 7$)	63 (ref)	0.47/768
Our Method $(3, 4, 2)$	17 (-73%)	0.16/768
$\rho = 0.9$	Number of traces	Average number of errors
Majority Voting ($t = 11$)	99 (ref)	0.67/768
Our Method $(4, 3, 4)$	24 (-75.8%)	0.46/768

scheme for attacking Kyber in previous literature (e.g., in [42]). For majority voting, we choose the code as in Table 3 and use t votes, i.e., the actual code is repeated t times. We run 1000 tests and compute the average number of wrong secret coefficients, the attack is considered successful if this number is less than 1. For our approach, we choose m_0, m_1, and m_2 such that the total number of traces is minimized and the average number of errors is close to majority voting. We run 100 tests, and all tests are done with randomly generated secret keys. The results for a wide range of accuracy levels are shown in Table 4.

Real-World Experiments. We conduct our experiments in the ChipWhisperer toolkit, including the ChipWhisperer-Lite board, the CW308 UFO board, and the CW308T-STM32F4 target board with a 32-bit ARM Cortex-M4 CPU. We target the mkm4 library[4] in [23] implementing a first-order masked version of Kyber. The library is compiled using the -O3 optimization level, which is typically harder to attack [29,42]. The target board is run at 24 MHz, and the traces are sampled at 24 MHz.

We attacked the function masked_poly_tomsg in the first draft of the work and it was the first power analysis attack on an open-source masked implementation of Kyber, as far as we know. Then we switched to the function masked_poly_frommsg similarly to [10]. With this approach, real oracles from side-channel leakages have better accuracy, leading to a lower amount of traces.

The function masked_poly_frommsg (shown in Fig. 3) maps each masked polynomial coefficient to a corresponding message bit during decapsulation. In one loop the function works on the message bits XORed with random bits; on the other loop it works with these random bits themselves. Obtaining a power trace for these two loops allows us to retrieve information about all message bits and implement the FD oracles $\mathcal{O}_i$.

The attack scenario is the same as in [29]. First, there is the profiling stage during which, using the profiling device D_1, we collect 100,000 power traces of

---

[4] https://github.com/masked-kyber-m4/mkm4.

```
masked_poly_frommsg(uint16_t poly[2][256], uint8_t msg[2][32])
 1: ... /* initialization */
 2: for i = 0 to 31 do
 3:    for j = 0 to 7 do
 4:       mask = -((msg[0][i] >> j) & 1)
 5:       poly[0][8*i+j] += mask & ((KYBER_Q+1)/2)
 6:    end for
 7: end for
 8: for i = 0 to 31 do
 9:    for j = 0 to 7 do
10:       mask = -((msg[1][i] >> j) & 1)
11:       poly[1][8*i+j] += mask & ((KYBER_Q+1)/2)
12:    end for
13: end for
14: ...
```

Fig. 3. The attacked function in KYBER.CPAPKE.Enc() (from [23])

Table 5. Accuracy of recovering particular bit for models. Device D_1 is the profiling device, and D_2 is the device to be attacked.

Device	ρ_0	ρ_1	ρ_2	ρ_3	ρ_4	ρ_5	ρ_6	ρ_7
D_1	0.9651	0.9986	0.9985	0.9985	0.9992	0.9995	1.0000	1.0000
D_2	0.9390	0.9811	0.9923	0.9023	0.9654	0.8940	0.9404	0.9873

the function masked_poly_frommsg. It is done by generating a random message which is encrypted using the device's public key, the resulting ciphertext is passed to the measured by the ChipWhisperer decapsulation function. Each byte of the message is computed in the same way, and the power traces corresponding to each byte are similar. Thus, we can train only 8 neural network models, one for each bit of the byte. Models are trained for up to 100 epochs. The interested reader is referred to the full version of the paper [20] for the architecture of the model.

Each of the 8 models simulates the 32 oracles $\mathcal{O}_{i+8j}$, $j = 0, \ldots, 31$, with some accuracy ρ_i. The oracle behaves like a binary symmetric channel with success probability ρ_i, but the model provides soft values, which can be treated as the probabilities of output being 1 or 0 from the model's perspective. Thus, the real-world attack is more powerful since there is more information we can work with.

After the profiling stage, there is the attacking stage. The assumption is that the attacker has access for a (relatively) short period of time to a similar device D_2. After collecting power traces for decapsulation on chosen ciphertexts, the attacker's goal is to recover the key using the trained models. The Table 5 shows the accuracy ρ_i of recovering i^{th} bit for devices D_1 and D_2.

Table 6. Real-world attack results on the first-order masked Kyber-768. We performed 100 runs of the attack with a random secret key for each run.

	Number of traces	Average number of errors
Majority Voting ($t = 11$)	99	0.34/768
Our Method $(2,2,3)$	12	0.82/768

The experimental results (shown in Table 6) with the average oracle accuracy of 0.9502 are better than the simulation results with an accuracy of 0.95. There are two reasons for this: (1) real models provide soft values, making the attack more powerful; (2) In the simulation, the accuracy of each bit is the same, but for our LDPC approach, it is more beneficial for some bits to be more reliable than others.

On the other hand, the success of majority voting approach depends on the worst bit position. In other words, in the real world majority voting works worse since the bottleneck is the worst bit. The real attack with accuracy from Table 5 uses $t = 11$ votes, i.e. in total we need 99 traces (instead of 63 as in Table 4). In this case, our framework uses 86% fewer traces.

6.2 HQC

In order to test the new attack strategy against HQC it is advantageous to make as close to an apples-to-apples comparison as possible against the results of [16]. To this end, we model the PC oracle as follows; The success probability for an oracle query is determined by ρ_0 and ρ_1, which are the probabilities of correctly classifying decoding failures and decoding successes, respectively. For the case of the ideal HQC timing oracle used in [16] these values are listed in Table 7 and correspond to $\rho_0 = \rho_f$ and $\rho_1 = \rho_s$. We label the ideal oracle $\mathcal{O}_{\text{HQC}}^{\text{ideal}}$.

Table 7. Ideal HQC timing oracle, $\mathcal{O}_{\text{HQC}}^{\text{ideal}}$, as modelled with ρ_f and ρ_s.

Real	Reported as	
	decoding failure	decoding success
decoding failure	$\rho_f = 0.9942$	$1 - \rho_f = 0.0058$
decoding success	$1 - \rho_s = 0$	$\rho_s = 1.0$

Simulating real-world attacks with noisy measurements can be done by selecting other values of ρ_0 and ρ_1. For simplicity, we introduce ρ as a single representative value of PC oracle accuracy, where $\rho = \rho_0 = \rho_1$. We label the corresponding oracle $\mathcal{O}_{\text{HQC}}^{\rho}$.

By empirical study we have selected a row weight of $W = 50$ in the constructed LDPC code (for hqc-128). This is close to the upper limit of our code generation algorithm. Using a bigger W would occasionally require a more advanced algorithm with backtracking of the random walk. Regardless, the decoding appears to suffer in reliability for values $W > 50$. Smaller values of W require more parity checks and thus make the attack slower.

Some interesting ρ values, corresponding to real attacks, are $\{1.0, 0.995, 0.95, 0.9\}$. In Fig. 4 we show the results of simulations using the various oracle models we have described so far. The results for $\mathcal{O}_{HQC}^{ideal}$ indicate an 86.6 times improvement over the original attack [16].

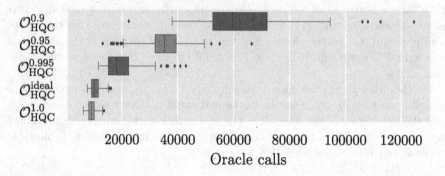

Fig. 4. Experiment for hqc-128. The median number of oracle calls for successful key recovery, are 59500, 35250, 18000, 10000, and 9000 respectively for the listed oracles. For each oracle model, 100 key-recovery simulations ran to completion.

We have validated our attack by running a real timing oracle on a Ubuntu 20.04 LTS laptop with Intel Core i5-7200@2.50GHz. Measurement noise was reduced by turning of hyper-threading and by running in recovery mode. We used 2^{18} measurements to generate a profile, first of a decoding success and again of a decoding failure. Measuring 8 decapsulations resulted in an oracle accuracy of $\rho_{\mathcal{O}_{HQC}^{real}} = 0.951$ as determined by 1000 trials. The simulated results for $\mathcal{O}_{HQC}^{0.95}$ indicate a real-life key recovery attack of hqc-128 can be done by measuring $2^3 \times 35250 \approx 2^{18}$ decapsulation calls.

6.3 Discussions

In this section, we present discussions on the performance of the new SCA-LDPC framework, including its information-theoretical advantages and limitations. Furthermore, we compare the SCA-LDPC framework with the inner-symbol error correction method proposed in [29] and highlight the advantages of the former.

A Non-rigorous Information Theoretical Bound. Assuming that a single side-channel measurement provides a certain amount of information (denoted by I bits), and considering the fact that there are k secret symbols that are independently generated from a distribution with entropy E bits, it is possible to calculate a lower bound for the number of measurements required. This can be accomplished by dividing $k \cdot E$ by I. Estimation of I can be performed by considering each recovered message bit as a Bernoulli variable, with a specified probability ρ_i of being correct. It is noteworthy that the value of ρ_i may vary for different secret positions. This information-theoretical estimation is approximate in nature. It is subject to limitations arising from the simplicity of the Bernoulli model. Additionally, near-optimal source coding and channel coding are required to match the derived lower bound. Notwithstanding these limitations, the estimation suggests the possibility of improvement, though the extent of such improvement may be constrained.

The aforementioned lower bound is equivalent to the well-known Shannon source coding bound when the accuracy of the oracle is 100%, which can be used to characterize the source coding gain. The results obtained from the FD oracle based attack on the scheme Kyber-768 exactly meet the lower bound of 7 traces. Conversely, for the PC oracle based attack on hqc-128, 1324 parity checks were required, a factor of 2.1 times the lower bound of 628 checks.

It has been observed that the difference between the simulated results and the lower bound increases as the oracle accuracy decreases. For example, in the case of the PC oracle based attack on hqc-128, when the oracle accuracy drops to 0.95, the ratio of the simulated parity checks to the lower bound increases to approximately 2.7, as calculated by 2396/880. For the FD oracle based real-world attack on Kyber-768, based on the message recovery accuracy data presented in the second row of Table 5, the lower bound was determined to be 9, which is slightly lower than the 12 traces utilized in the actual attack.

Limitations. Despite the remarkable reduction of necessary side-channel measurements, a gap remains between actual performance and our non-rigorous information-theoretical lower bound. This gap may be attributed to the requirement of an extremely long codeword, potentially in the range of tens of millions of bits, for the LDPC codes to approach optimality. Additionally, it may be a result of the simplicity and inadequacy of our current code-construction method. More sophisticated LDPC code construction techniques could further reduce the required number of measurements.

Our Method vs. Inner-Symbol Error Correction. The new SCA-LDPC framework utilizes a system of sparse parity checks to interconnect all the secret symbols. As a result, accurately determined symbols can be utilized to rectify incorrectly determined symbols, categorizing this method as inter-symbol error correction. On the other hand, the method presented in [29] falls under the category of inner-symbol error correction, as the utilization of extended Hamming codes increases the possibility of recovering individual secret symbols, which all must be recovered independently.

Both methods can be applied to the FD oracle based attack on lattice-based schemes in a non-adaptive attack model. However, the inner-symbol error correction method presented in [29] offers no source coding gain and has inferior error correction capabilities. For instance, it is demonstrated in [29] that for a platform with an average message bit recovery rate of 0.972, 216 traces, or 9×24, are required to recover the long-term secret key of a masked Saber implementation. We utilize the detailed message bit recovery rates recorded in Table 20 of [29] to calculate the corresponding lower bound, which is determined to be 10 traces. This demonstrates a significant gap of 21.6 between the actual performance in a real-world scenario and the calculated lower bound. While there is no guarantee that the non-rigorous lower bound will always be attainable, the small ratio of 1.33, or 12/9, for our SCA-LDPC attack on Kyber, illustrates the superior efficiency of our method in terms of the required number of traces.

The substantial improvement of the new SCA-LDPC framework can be attributed to various factors, such as the utilization of soft information in the real-world attack that we conducted. The dominant reason is that all the secret symbols are interconnected and correlated, and redundant symbols are introduced, allowing for the effective handling of a significant number of symbol-level errors. On the contrary, in the inner-symbol error correction method, all the symbols (e.g., 768 symbols in the Saber case) are independent and needs to be successfully recovered, thus precluding the tolerance of any symbol-level errors. Last, in a real-world attack scenario, several secret positions typically have a higher chance of containing errors, which can be effectively corrected through the inter-symbol approach, but may prove to be a bottleneck for the inner-symbol method where all symbols must be correctly identified independently.

7   Concluding Remarks and Future Work

From coding theory, we have presented a generic framework for key-recovery side-channel attacks on CCA-secure post-quantum encryption/KEM schemes. Our design philosophy is to employ randomly generated LDPC codes with efficient decoding to connect secret coefficients, which introduces additional benefits of source coding and error correction. We presented simulation results and real-world experiments on the main lattice-based KEM Kyber and the code-based KEM HQC. The new attack framework can significantly improve the state-of-the-art in terms of the required number of side-channel measurements. Our improvement has great practical impact. For instance, in real-world attack scenarios against a masked Kyber implementation, we require just 12% of the traces compared to the majority voting method. As our simulation results indicate that the gain would increase as the oracle accuracy decreases, this significant reduction could feasibly turn a previously impractical attack into a practical one. Also, we have a remarkable gain in the HQC timing attack instance. An explanation for our substantial improvements is that LDPC codes are considered to have near-optimal performance from an information-theoretic standpoint.

The sample complexity of the new attack framework can be improved further by (i) employing a more advanced code-construction method with improved decoding performance or by (ii) heavy post-processing such as lattice-reduction or information-set decoding. An intriguing area of study is to utilize sophisticated coding-theoretical methods [39], such as density evolution or EXIT charts, to carry out efficient and precise security assessments against proposed attacks.

While the new attack framework is general, the specific attack instances can vary due to the diversity of schemes, oracle types, and leakages. We note that schemes selected as new standards such as Kyber should be given primary consideration for investigation. From a research standpoint, it would be engaging to explore the framework's precise implementation and performance in NTRU [7] and NTRU prime [6]. Additionally, future research could explore whether this framework could be extended to target Classic McEliece and BIKE.

Last, the new attack framework shows the need for countermeasures such as constant-time implementations or higher-order masked implementations. As noted in [45], masked hardware exhibits much higher security compared to masked software when considering PC oracle-based side-channel attacks. As our simulations indicate that the gain of the new attack framework increases with less accurate oracles, it would be fascinating to examine the exact improvements in this attack scenario. Furthermore, it would also be worthwhile to investigate whether SASCA could deliver more accurate PC oracles than a deep learning-based approach in this context.

Acknowledgement. We thank F.X. Standaert for his helpful comments. This work was supported by the Swedish Research Council (grant numbers 2019-04166 and 2021-04602); the Swedish Civil Contingencies Agency (grant number 2020-11632); the Swedish Foundation for Strategic Research (Grant No. RIT17-0005); and the Wallenberg AI, Autonomous Systems and Software Program (WASP) funded by the Knut and Alice Wallenberg Foundation. The computations and simulations were partly enabled by resources provided by LUNARC.

References

1. Nist post-quantum cryptography standardization. https://csrc.nist.gov/Projects/Post-Quantum-Cryptography/Post-Quantum-Cryptography-Standardization, (Accessed 24 Sep 2018)
2. Aguilar Melchor, C., et al.: HQC. Tech. rep., National Institute of Standards and Technology (2020). https://csrc.nist.gov/projects/post-quantum-cryptography/round-3-submissions
3. Albrecht, M.R., et al.: Classic McEliece. Tech. rep., National Institute of Standards and Technology (2020). https://csrc.nist.gov/projects/post-quantum-cryptography/round-3-submissions
4. Aragon, N., et al.: BIKE. Tech. rep., National Institute of Standards and Technology (2020), available at https://csrc.nist.gov/projects/post-quantum-cryptography/round-3-submissions
5. Backlund, L., Ngo, K., Gärtner, J., Dubrova, E.: Secret key recovery attacks on masked and shuffled implementations of crystals-kyber and saber. Cryptology ePrint Archive, Paper 2022/1692 (2022). https://eprint.iacr.org/2022/1692
6. Bernstein, D.J., et al.: NTRU Prime. Tech. rep., National Institute of Standards and Technology (2020). https://csrc.nist.gov/projects/post-quantum-cryptography/round-3-submissions
7. Chen, C., et al.: NTRU. Tech. rep., National Institute of Standards and Technology (2020), available at https://csrc.nist.gov/projects/post-quantum-cryptography/round-3-submissions

8. Dachman-Soled, D., Ducas, L., Gong, H., Rossi, M.: LWE with side information: attacks and concrete security estimation. In: Micciancio, D., Ristenpart, T. (eds.) CRYPTO 2020. LNCS, vol. 12171, pp. 329–358. Springer, Cham (2020). https://doi.org/10.1007/978-3-030-56880-1_12
9. D'Anvers, J.P., Tiepelt, M., Vercauteren, F., Verbauwhede, I.: Timing attacks on error correcting codes in post-quantum schemes. In: Proceedings of ACM Workshop on Theory of Implementation Security Workshop, TIS 2019, pp. 2–9. Association for Computing Machinery, New York (2019). https://doi.org/10.1145/3338467.3358948, https://doi.org/10.1145/3338467.3358948
10. Dubrova, E., Ngo, K., Gärtner, J., Wang, R.: Breaking a fifth-order masked implementation of crystals-kyber by copy-paste. In: Proceedings of the 10th ACM Asia Public-Key Cryptography Workshop, APKC 2023, pp. 10–20. Association for Computing Machinery, New York (2023). https://doi.org/10.1145/3591866.3593072
11. Forney, G.D.: Concatenated codes. Technical Report 440. MIT (1965)
12. Fujisaki, E., Okamoto, T.: Secure integration of asymmetric and symmetric encryption schemes. In: Wiener, M. (ed.) CRYPTO 1999. LNCS, vol. 1666, pp. 537–554. Springer, Heidelberg (1999). https://doi.org/10.1007/3-540-48405-1_34
13. Gallager, R.: Low-density parity-check codes. IRE Trans. Inform. Theory 8(1), 21–28 (1962)
14. Goy, G., Loiseau, A., Gaborit, P.: A new key recovery side-channel attack on hqc with chosen ciphertext. In: Cheon, J.H., Johansson, T. (eds.) Post-Quantum Cryptography, pp. 353–371. Springer International Publishing, Cham (2022). https://doi.org/10.1007/978-3-031-17234-2_17
15. Guo, Q., Grosso, V., Standaert, F.X., Bronchain, O.: Modeling soft analytical side-channel attacks from a coding theory viewpoint. IACR TCHES 2020(4), 209–238 (2020). https://doi.org/10.13154/tches.v2020.i4.209-238, https://tches.iacr.org/index.php/TCHES/article/view/8682
16. Guo, Q., Hlauschek, C., Johansson, T., Lahr, N., Nilsson, A., Schröder, R.L.: Don't reject this: Key-recovery timing attacks due to rejection-sampling in HQC and BIKE. IACR Trans. Cryptogr. Hardw. Embed. Syst. 2022(3), 223–263 (2022). https://doi.org/10.46586/tches.v2022.i3.223-263
17. Guo, Q., Johansson, A., Johansson, T.: A key-recovery side-channel attack on classic mceliece implementations. IACR Trans. Cryptogr. Hardw. Embed. Syst. 2022(4), 800–827 (2022). https://doi.org/10.46586/tches.v2022.i4.800-827
18. Guo, Q., Johansson, T., Nilsson, A.: A key-recovery timing attack on post-quantum primitives using the fujisaki-okamoto transformation and its application on FrodoKEM. In: Micciancio, D., Ristenpart, T. (eds.) CRYPTO 2020. LNCS, vol. 12171, pp. 359–386. Springer, Cham (2020). https://doi.org/10.1007/978-3-030-56880-1_13
19. Guo, Q., Johansson, T., Stankovski, P.: A key recovery attack on MDPC with CCA security using decoding errors. In: Cheon, J.H., Takagi, T. (eds.) ASIACRYPT 2016. LNCS, vol. 10031, pp. 789–815. Springer, Heidelberg (2016). https://doi.org/10.1007/978-3-662-53887-6_29
20. Guo, Q., Nabokov, D., Nilsson, A., Johansson, T.: Sca-ldpc: a code-based framework for key-recovery side-channel attacks on post-quantum encryption schemes. Cryptology ePrint Archive, Paper 2023/294 (2023). https://eprint.iacr.org/2023/294
21. Hall, C., Goldberg, I., Schneier, B.: Reaction attacks against several public-key cryptosystem. In: Varadharajan, V., Mu, Y. (eds.) ICICS 1999. LNCS, vol. 1726, pp. 2–12. Springer, Heidelberg (1999). https://doi.org/10.1007/978-3-540-47942-0_2

22. Hamburg, M., et al.: Chosen ciphertext k-trace attacks on masked CCA2 secure kyber. IACR TCHES **2021**(4), 88–113 (2021). https://doi.org/10.46586/tches. v2021.i4.88-113, https://tches.iacr.org/index.php/TCHES/article/view/9061

23. Heinz, D., Kannwischer, M.J., Land, G., Pöppelmann, T., Schwabe, P., Sprenkels, D.: First-order masked kyber on arm cortex-m4. Cryptology ePrint Archive, Paper 2022/058 (2022). https://eprint.iacr.org/2022/058

24. Hofheinz, D., Hövelmanns, K., Kiltz, E.: A modular analysis of the Fujisaki-Okamoto transformation. In: Kalai, Y., Reyzin, L. (eds.) TCC 2017. LNCS, vol. 10677, pp. 341–371. Springer, Cham (2017). https://doi.org/10.1007/978-3-319-70500-2_12

25. Huang, S., Sim, R.Q., Chuengsatiansup, C., Guo, Q., Johansson, T.: Cache-timing attack against hqc. Cryptology ePrint Archive, Paper 2023/102 (2023). https://eprint.iacr.org/2023/102

26. Johansson, T., Zigangirov, K.S.: A simple one-sweep algorithm for optimal APP symbol decoding of linear block codes. IEEE Trans. Inf. Theory **44**(7), 3124–3129 (1998). https://doi.org/10.1109/18.737541

27. Kocher, P.C.: Timing attacks on implementations of Diffie-Hellman, RSA, DSS, and other systems. In: Koblitz, N. (ed.) CRYPTO 1996. LNCS, vol. 1109, pp. 104–113. Springer, Heidelberg (1996). https://doi.org/10.1007/3-540-68697-5_9

28. McEliece, R.J.: A public-key cryptosystem based on algebraic coding theory. DSN Progress Report **42–44**, 114–116 (1978)

29. Ngo, K., Dubrova, E., Guo, Q., Johansson, T.: A side-channel attack on a masked IND-CCA secure saber KEM implementation. IACR TCHES **2021**(4), 676–707 (2021). https://doi.org/10.46586/tches.v2021.i4.676-707, https://tches.iacr.org/index.php/TCHES/article/view/9079

30. Pearl, J.: Reverend bayes on inference engines: A distributed hierarchical approach. In: AAAI (1982)

31. Primas, R., Pessl, P., Mangard, S.: Single-trace side-channel attacks on masked lattice-based encryption. In: Fischer, W., Homma, N. (eds.) CHES 2017. LNCS, vol. 10529, pp. 513–533. Springer, Cham (2017). https://doi.org/10.1007/978-3-319-66787-4_25

32. Qin, Y., Cheng, C., Zhang, X., Pan, Y., Hu, L., Ding, J.: A systematic approach and analysis of key mismatch attacks on lattice-based NIST candidate KEMs. In: Tibouchi, M., Wang, H. (eds.) ASIACRYPT 2021. LNCS, vol. 13093, pp. 92–121. Springer, Cham (2021). https://doi.org/10.1007/978-3-030-92068-5_4

33. Rajendran, G., Ravi, P., D'Anvers, J.P., Bhasin, S., Chattopadhyay, A.: Pushing the limits of generic side-channel attacks on lwe-based kems - parallel pc oracle attacks on kyber kem and beyond. Cryptology ePrint Archive, Paper 2022/931 (2022). https://eprint.iacr.org/2022/931

34. Ravi, P., Ezerman, M.F., Bhasin, S., Chattopadhyay, A., Roy, S.S.: Will you cross the threshold for me? generic side-channel assisted chosen-ciphertext attacks on ntru-based kems. IACR Trans. Cryptogr. Hardw. Embed. Syst. **2022**(1), 722–761 (2022). https://doi.org/10.46586/tches.v2022.i1.722-761

35. Ravi, P., Roy, S.S.: Side-channel analysis of lattice-based pqc candidates. https://csrc.nist.gov/CSRC/media/Projects/post-quantum-cryptography/documents/round-3/seminars/mar-2021-ravi-sujoy-presentation.pdf, (Accessed 29 Sep 2022)

36. Ravi, P., Roy, S.S., Chattopadhyay, A., Bhasin, S.: Generic side-channel attacks on CCA-secure lattice-based PKE and KEMs. IACR TCHES **2020**(3), 307–335 (2020). https://doi.org/10.13154/tches.v2020.i3.307-335, https://tches.iacr.org/index.php/TCHES/article/view/8592

37. Regev, O.: On lattices, learning with errors, random linear codes, and cryptography. In: Gabow, H.N., Fagin, R. (eds.) 37th ACM STOC, pp. 84–93. ACM Press (2005). https://doi.org/10.1145/1060590.1060603
38. Richardson, T., Shokrollahi, M., Urbanke, R.: Design of capacity-approaching irregular low-density parity-check codes. IEEE Trans. Inf. Theory **47**(2), 619–637 (2001). https://doi.org/10.1109/18.910578
39. Richardson, T., Urbanke, R.: Modern Coding Theory. Cambridge University Press, USA (2008)
40. Schamberger, T., Holzbaur, L., Renner, J., Wachter-Zeh, A., Sigl, G.: A power side-channel attack on the reed-muller reed-solomon version of the hqc cryptosystem. Cryptology ePrint Archive, Paper 2022/724 (2022). https://eprint.iacr.org/2022/724
41. Schwabe, P., et al.: CRYSTALS-KYBER. Tech. rep., National Institute of Standards and Technology (2020), available at https://csrc.nist.gov/projects/post-quantum-cryptography/round-3-submissions
42. Shen, M., Cheng, C., Zhang, X., Guo, Q., Jiang, T.: Find the bad apples: an efficient method for perfect key recovery under imperfect SCA oracles - A case study of Kyber. IACR Trans. Cryptogr. Hardw. Embed. Syst. **2023**(1), 89–112 (2023). https://doi.org/10.46586/tches.v2023.i1.89-112, https://doi.org/10.46586/tches.v2023.i1.89-112
43. Shor, P.W.: Algorithms for quantum computation: discrete logarithms and factoring. In: 35th FOCS, pp. 124–134. IEEE Computer Society Press (1994). https://doi.org/10.1109/SFCS.1994.365700
44. Tanaka, Y., Ueno, R., Xagawa, K., Ito, A., Takahashi, J., Homma, N.: Multiple-valued plaintext-checking side-channel attacks on post-quantum kems. Cryptology ePrint Archive, Paper 2022/940 (2022). https://eprint.iacr.org/2022/940
45. Ueno, R., Xagawa, K., Tanaka, Y., Ito, A., Takahashi, J., Homma, N.: Curse of re-encryption: A generic power/em analysis on post-quantum kems. IACR Trans. Cryptogr. Hardw. Embed. Syst. **2022**(1), 296–322 (2022). https://doi.org/10.46586/tches.v2022.i1.296-322
46. Veyrat-Charvillon, N., Gérard, B., Standaert, F.-X.: Soft analytical side-channel attacks. In: Sarkar, P., Iwata, T. (eds.) ASIACRYPT 2014. LNCS, vol. 8873, pp. 282–296. Springer, Heidelberg (2014). https://doi.org/10.1007/978-3-662-45611-8_15
47. Xu, Z., Pemberton, O., Roy, S.S., Oswald, D., Yao, W., Zheng, Z.: Magnifying side-channel leakage of lattice-based cryptosystems with chosen ciphertexts: the case study of kyber. IEEE Trans. Comput. **71**(9), 2163–2176 (2022). https://doi.org/10.1109/TC.2021.3122997

Exploiting Algebraic Structures in Probing Security

Maxime Plançon[1,2(✉)]

[1] IBM Research Europe, Zurich, Switzerland
mpl@zurich.ibm.com
[2] ETH Zurich, Zurich, Switzerland

Abstract. The so-called ω-encoding, introduced by Goudarzi, Joux and Rivain (Asiacrypt 2018), generalizes the commonly used arithmetic encoding. By using the additionnal structure of this encoding, they proposed a masked multiplication gadget (GJR) with quasilinear (randomness and operations) complexity. A follow-up contribution by Goudarzi, Prest, Rivain and Vergnaud in this line of research appeared in TCHES 2021. The authors revisited the aforementioned multiplication gadget (GPRV), and brought the IOS security notion for refresh gadgets to allow secure composition between probing secure gadgets.

In this paper, we propose a follow up on GPRV, that is, a region-probing secure arithmetic circuit masked compiler. Our contribution stems from a single Lemma, linking algebra and probing security for a wide class of circuits, further taking advantage of the algebraic structure of ω-encoding, and the extension field structure of the underlying field $\mathbb{F}$ that was so far left unexploited. On the theoretical side, we propose a security notion for ω_d-masked circuits which we call Reducible-To-Independent-K-linear (RTIK). When the number of shares d is less than or equal to the degree k of $\mathbb{F}$, RTIK circuits achieve region-probing security. Moreover, RTIK circuits may be composed naively and remain RTIK. We also propose a weaker version of IOS, which we call KIOS, for refresh gadgets. This notion allows to compose RTIK circuits with a randomness/security tradeoff compared to the naive composition.

To substantiate our new definitions, we also provide examples of competitively efficient gadgets verifying the latter weaker security notions. Explicitly, we give 1) two refresh gadgets that use $d - 1$ random field elements to refresh a length d encoding, both of which are KIOS but not IOS, and 2) a multiplication gadget with bilinear multiplication complexity $d^{\log 3}$ and uses d fresh random elements per run. Our compiler outperforms ISW asymptotically, but for our security proofs to hold, we do require that the number of shares d is less than or equal to the degree of $\mathbb{F}$ as an extension, so that there is sufficient structure to exploit.

Keywords: Masking · RTIK · Refresh Gadget · Multiplication Gadget

Part of this work was done during an internship at PQShield in collaboration and under the supervision of Thomas Prest.

© International Association for Cryptologic Research 2023
J. Guo and R. Steinfeld (Eds.): ASIACRYPT 2023, LNCS 14441, pp. 237–267, 2023.
https://doi.org/10.1007/978-981-99-8730-6_8

1 Introduction

Since their introduction in the late 90's by Kocher [KJJ99, Koc96], side-channel attacks have proven to be a major threat to cryptography. While cryptanalysis can evaluate the black-box security of cryptographic protocols, their security can be totally compromised by physical attacks. In a nutshell, side-channel attacks refer to any attack taking advantage of the implementation of a cryptographic protocol, rather than only the public parameters and public communications. If a hardware device is manipulating carelessly a secret value, many observable signals (such as its temperature, power consumption, electromagnetic field, etc) are likely to leak secret information, and might even lead to a full-key recovery. These practical security flaws call for a solid non-ad hoc response.

Of all the side-channel adversary models such as the noisy leakage model [PR13, DDF14, DFS15] or the random probing model [ADF16], arguably the easiest to deal with is the so called (threshold) t-probing model [ISW03]. A t-probing adversary may choose adaptively and learn any t intermediate values of the circuit. While t-probing security reduces to the more realistic models, the reductions are somewhat loose and depend more on the ratio t divided by the size of the circuit than t itself.

Masking is a countermeasure that provably prevents recovering information when the adversary is snooping on the circuit. Informally, masking uses secret-sharing techniques to provide probing security to a circuit. A sensitive intermediate value x of the cryptographic protocol is encoded into a vector of d shares $(x_0, \ldots, x_{d-1})$. While the knowledge of all d shares allows to recover the secret it encodes, masking requires that any $d-1$ shares are independent of the secret value x. Any partial knowledge of the shares is therefore made useless in masking schemes, so as to provide t-probing security for $t < d$. The operations (additions, negations and multiplications for arithmetic circuits) then have to be performed *securely* in the encoded domain, so as to never manipulate secret variables directly. Each operation (or gate) of the circuit is transformed into a secure counterpart (or gadget), that takes as input encodings of the secrets, and outputs an encoding of the evaluation of the corresponding operation. Usually, masking schemes admit a coordinate-wise secure addition, leaving the multiplication the most challenging operation to perform securely in the encoded domain.

Replacing every gate with probing secure gadgets unfortunately does not imply probing security for the whole circuit [BCPZ16, CPRR13], and extra efforts have to be put into composition security. Composition of gadgets is a line of research that has received a lot of attention, and is still an active field of research [ADF16, CS20, BCPZ16, GPRV21, BBD+16].

The first masked multiplication for any number of shares was introduced in 2003 in [ISW03], and several variants achieving different trade-offs have been proposed [RP10, BBP+16, BBP+17]. The encoding used by ISW is the so called arithmetic masking (originally for boolean masking, but the arithmetic masking translation remains secure [RP10]), where the shares $\mathbf{x} = (x_1, \ldots, x_d)$ of some field element $x \in \mathbb{F}$ are such that $x_1 + \cdots + x_d = x$. Another way to interpret arithmetic masking is to say that the shares are the coefficients of a polynomial such that its evaluation in 1 is the secret. From a high level, the multiplication of two sharings $\mathbf{a}, \mathbf{b}$ of two secrets a, b in ISW computes the coefficients of the polynomial $\mathbf{c} = \mathbf{ab}$ and rearranges the coefficients so as to have $\mathbf{c}$ of the same length d as $\mathbf{a}$ and $\mathbf{b}$. This polynomial multiplication is performed following the schoolbook multiplication algorithm mixed up with some randomness for security. This yields a·multiplication gadget running in $O(d^2)$ time with $O(d^2)$ randomness. The paper [GJR18], started a line of research towards constructing multiplication gadgets based on the Fast Fourier Transform. GJR uses a different type of encoding called ω-encoding, where $\mathbf{a}$'s evaluation is taken in some field element ω rather than 1. Arithmetic masking seems to be incompatible with the FFT since $a_1 + \cdots + a_d$ is an intermediate value of the FFT algorithm, which the adversary may therefore probe, and immediately break the masking scheme. There was a flaw in the original security proof of the GJR multiplication gadget, which was patched later in [GPRV21] and named GJR+. While GJR is a theoretical breakthrough, its range of application excludes AES for example. The security relies on the random choice of ω, hence for reaching a reasonable level of security, GJR+ requires an underlying field of exponential size in the security parameter, which limits its practical applications. The follow-up paper [GPRV21] proposed a security proof for GJR+ for fields of smaller sizes. This security proof relies on a non-standard ad-hoc assumption. This assumption, roughly speaking assumes that the computation of the FFT and inverse FFT of a polynomial are both probing secure. While one can check this hypothesis by exhaustive search, the computation becomes very costly as d increases. The authors raise the open problem to build a strong theoretical foundation for replacing their assumption with a full proof.

The randomness complexity of a compiler (meaning the transformation of a circuit that replaces operation gates with secure masked gadgets) is of major importance. The predilection physical support for masked implementation is embedded systems, where randomness is expensive to produce. In this consideration, one of the goals in the field of masking is to achieve notions of security using as little randomness as possible. The authors of [GPRV21] give a generic composition Theorem that only requires t-probing security for the operation gadgets, and mask refreshing (they give such refresh algorithm verifying the desired Input-Output-Separation property) in between any two gadgets. This theorem ensures that the obtained compiler achieves the r-region-probing-security notion. Informally, region probing security means that the circuit can be split into independent regions, in which the side-channel adversary may probe a fixed ratio of the intermediate values yet learns no information on the secrets. The authors prove that a variant of the refresh gadget from [BCPZ16] achieves the IOS property and only requires $\frac{d \log d}{2}$ random field elements.

1.1   Results and Technical Overview

From a high level, this paper is a retake on the circuit compiler from [GPRV21], and proposes a region-probing secure masked compiler for arithmetic circuits over extension fields. The contributions of this paper are listed in 4 categories:

1. Revisiting probing security from a probabilistic angle.
2. Introduction of new security notions tailored for circuits over extension fields: for operation gadgets (RTIK) and for refresh gadgets (RTK, KIOS)
3. Composition Theorems for RTIK gadgets and KIOS refresh gadgets, and security reductions from the latter notions to region-probing security.
4. Examples of competitively efficient multiplication gadgets and refresh gadgets achieving the aforementioned notions, constituting our masked compiler.

We detail separately each of these items in the following.

From Game-Based Definitions to Probabilistic Definitions. The usual definition of t-probing security involves the existence of a simulator able to simulate the distribution of given wires with only partial knowledge of the secret. This simulation-based definition is inherited from the idea that a t-probing side-channel adversary plays a t-probing security game, in which the adversary learns some information on the wires W of the circuit C, then wins if he guesses right the decoding of the sharings. The simulation argument implies that the side-channel information yields no advantage. While simulators can be suitable tools for proving probing security, they do not seem to be a good fit with our techniques. We propose to take a different path and redefine probing security as the statistical independence of the leakage and the secrets. While this idea is nothing new, we believe that the formal definitions from Subsect. 3.1 can be of independent interest. In particular, we formally define the intuitive idea that a given set of probes Q contains more information than some other set of probes P. This syntax enables "game hop"-based proof strategy. Informally, we let the adversary pick the initial set of probes P of his choice, then instead of proving some independence relation between P and the secrets directly, we reduce, via successive elementary game hops, the set of probes P to a set of probes Q that at least preserves the information of the adversary. At the end of this reduction from P to Q, the latter set of probes Q is such that our techniques apply and we manage to prove the independence of Q and the secrets, which in turn implies independence between P and the secrets.

Bridging Algebra and Probing Security. We consider a circuit C over a finite field $\mathbb{F}$. We remind that our goal in this paper is to exploit the underlying field extension structure of $\mathbb{F}$, thus for the sake of clarity, we assume that $\mathbb{F} = \mathbb{F}_{p^k}$ is the finite field with p^k elements where p is a prime and $k \geq 2$. An even more concrete example is taking $\mathbb{F}$ to be the AES field $\mathbb{F}_{2^8}$. We deal with polynomial encodings, which is a special case of linear sharings where our decoding vector is chosen to be $\boldsymbol{\omega}_d = (1, \omega, \ldots, \omega^{d-1})$, for some field element $\omega \in \mathbb{F}$. In other words, an $\boldsymbol{\omega}_d$-encoding $\mathbf{x} \in \mathbb{F}^d$ of some element x is such that

$$\boldsymbol{\omega}_d^T \mathbf{x} = \sum_{i=0}^{d-1} x_i \omega^i = x.$$

The bridge relating the structure of $\mathbb{F}$ and probing security is the single Lemma 2. Consider that our circuit C takes as input an $\boldsymbol{\omega}_d$-encoding $\mathbf{x}$. In a nutshell, Lemma 2 says that under the conditions that

1. The number of shares is at most the degree of the extension: $d \leq k$
2. The intermediate values that the adversary can probe in $\mathcal{C}$ are of the form $\mathbf{p}^T \mathbf{x}$ with $\mathbf{p} \in \mathbb{F}_p^d$,

then there exists a choice of ω for which $\mathcal{C}$ is $d-1$-probing secure. This choice of ω is actually any ω of algebraic degree greater than or equal to d over $\mathbb{F}_p$. The geometry of this Lemma makes it intuitively more permissive than the usual definitions for t-probing, r-region-probing, (strong) non-interference and probe-isolating-non-interference. Indeed, the latter definitions (in probabilistic terms) require roughly speaking that the probes are independent of at least one coordinate of each sharings. The former on the other hand implies security regardless of the direction of the affine subspace in which the encoding lies, provided that the latter subspace is directed by the kernel of a matrix over the subfield, and that its dimension is at least 1.

By following the rules for modifying the set of probes of the adversary, we can relax condition 2.: our circuit $\mathcal{C}$ is also $d-1$-probing secure if for all sets P of $d-1$ probes (that does not necessarily verify 2.), we can find a set of $d-1$ probes Q that contain at least as much information as P, but Q does verify 2.

The RTIK security notion (which stands for Reducible-To-Independent-K-Linear) for ω_d-masked circuits over extension fields roughly encompasses the circuits that fulfill the requirements of the above. The requirements for a circuit to be RTIK are slightly more general: the subfield K that contains the coefficients of the probes may be bigger than the prime field of $\mathbb{F}$, and the circuit $\mathcal{C}$ may take several encodings as input. In that case, we simply require that there exists some mutually independent encodings $(\mathbf{x}_1, \ldots, \mathbf{x}_n)$ and sets of probes $(Q_1, \ldots, Q_n)$ such that each Q_i is K-linear in $\mathbf{x}_i$. Notice that some of these encodings may not be inputs neither outputs of $\mathcal{C}$.

Since by construction, RTIK circuits over extension fields fall into the requirements of the core Lemma, it follows that RTIK circuits are $d-1$-probing secure. Actually, RTIK circuits are secure in the stronger r-region-probing model, where the adversary may place some number of probes in several different subcircuits. We note that similarly as the Probe-Isolating-Non-Interfering security notion [CS20], (all known) RTIK gadgets can be composed directly without refresh, in which case the composition of RTIK circuits remains RTIK, which in turn is r-region probing secure for some ratio r. We also mention that in terms of implementation, RTIK circuits seem rather stable, since as long as the wires are of the right K-linear form, the order of the operations does not affect security.

Although RTIK circuits may be composed directly and remain region-probing secure, the size of the probing regions of the composite circuits may increase and hence reduce the probing ratio, thus reduce the overall security of the implementation. To mitigate this loss of security, we introduce a security notion for refresh gadgets inspired by the Input-Output Separative (IOS) property. We briefly recall the idea behind the IOS property. Consider an IOS refresh gadget R and two encodings $\mathbf{x}$ and $\mathbf{y}$ with $\mathbf{y} = R(\mathbf{x})$. Let us also assume that $\mathbf{x}$ is an output of some gadget G_1, and $\mathbf{y}$ is an input of some gadget G_2. We now let the t-probing adversary pick and learn t intermediate variables in either G_1, R, or G_2. In this setting, the IOS property claims that any probe inside of the refresh gadget can be "moved" to a probe on a coordinate of $\mathbf{x}$ and/or a probe on a coordinate of $\mathbf{y}$. The probes on $\mathbf{x}$ are then considered as probes in G_1, the probes on $\mathbf{y}$ are then considered as probes on G_2, and R itself is no more probed by the adversary. This reduces the security of the composition of the two gadgets G_1, G_2 to the individual security of each of the two gadgets. The security notion α-KIOS that we define is identical to the IOS property, except the probes on $\mathbf{x}$ and $\mathbf{y}$ do not have to be coordinates, but any K-linear function of those inputs.[1] Executing the same reduction as the one explained above for IOS refresh gadgets, one ends up with K-linear probes on $\mathbf{x}, \mathbf{y}$, which in turn fall into the requirements of our core Lemma. Applying a KIOS refresh to an encoding in between two RTIK circuits creates a new region at the cost of using random elements.

KIOS Refresh Gadgets Using $d - 1$ Randomness for Length d Input Encoding. To substantiate the KIOS notion, we give examples of KIOS refresh gadgets. Notice that 1-KIOS is strictly weaker than IOS, and therefore any IOS refresh is an example of 1-KIOS refresh, including the one from [GPRV21](Actually, we prove the IOS property for a mild generalization of this algorithm) which uses $\frac{d \log d}{2}$ random elements. We also give an example of a 2-KIOS refresh gadget that is not IOS. This gadget is obtained by simply adding coordinate-wise an encoding of 0, obtained by running the algorithm PolyGenZero presented in Algorithm 4, which uses $d - 1$ random field elements. We highlight that for security, we need the algebraic degree of ω over K to be greater than d, and for PolyGenZero to be correct, we also need the algebraic degree of ω over K to be less than d. In other words, we need ω to have algebraic degree exactly d over K, and such choice of ω is only possible when d divides $[\mathbb{F} : K]$. The intuition on the construction of this 2-KIOS gadget is detailed in Sect. 5.2.

We give a second example of KIOS refresh, which also uses $d - 1$ random elements, and is 1-KIOS. The counterpart for this improvement is that it is slightly bigger than the previous one as a circuit. The intuition behind this algorithm is derived from the RTIK multiplication gadget Algorithm 8. In a nutshell, the idea is to sample a uniformly random vector $\mathbf{r}$, then multiply it using Karatsuba's algorithm with some fixed polynomial $\mathbf{u}$. Provided that the only common factor of $\mathbf{u}$ and the minimal polynomial of ω is $X - \omega$ (which again requires $\deg_K(\omega) = d$), this algorithm generates $\boldsymbol{\omega}_d$-encodings of 0, which we can add coordinate-wise to obtain a 1-KIOS refresh gadget.

A Tight Compression Algorithm. The masked multiplication of two order d encodings should remain an order d encoding, but the computation of the polynomial product of two polynomials $\mathbf{a}, \mathbf{b}$ of degree $d - 1$ yields a polynomial

---

[1] We also add a coefficient α to its definition, which upper bounds the ratio of K-linear probes on $\mathbf{x}, \mathbf{y}$ after the reduction and the count of initial probes in the KIOS gadget.

$\mathbf{z}$ of degree $2d - 1$. The compression algorithm proposed in [GJR18, GPRV21] entails a loss of a factor 2 on the number of tolerated probes in the (region) probing security of the multiplication gadget. We define a folding algorithm that achieves the conversion of order $2d - 1$ encoding into order d encoding, and such that each of its intermediate values are K-linear. As a consequence, it can be composed without refresh and without tightness loss at the end of a multiplication gadget. Nonetheless, our folding algorithm is a bigger circuit (we left as an interesting open question estimating the count of operations in this algorithm depending on ω and K) than the compression algorithm from [GJR18, GPRV21], which mildly decreases the tolerated probing rate of the adversary.

Multiplication Gadgets with Subquadratic Randomness and Multiplications.[2] The multiplication gadget GJR+ [GPRV21] has two security proofs, depending on the size of $\mathbb{F}$ (and to some extent d). When $|\mathbb{F}| \geq 2^\lambda$ for some security parameter λ a statistical argument based on the random choice of ω implies security in the random-probing model. When $|\mathbb{F}|$ is too small, the authors rely on a non-standard ad-hoc assumption that the circuit computing the FFT and its inverse are t-probing secure. Due to combinatorial explosion, it is only possible to test the assumption for small values of d, thus leaving a hole in the shape of the RTIK notion. Our first multiplication gadget is a generalization of GJR+, where one can use *any* evaluation-interpolation polynomial multiplication algorithm (not only the FFT), and turn it into a multiplication gadget. The regimes in which we can prove that [GPRV21]'s assumption hold is restricted to the tuples $(\mathbb{F}, d)$ such that $d \leq [\mathbb{F} : K]$. The subfield K for which the RTIK property holds is the smallest subfield that contains the coefficients of both evaluation and interpolation. Hence for maximizing the upper bound on d, one should choose the multiplication algorithm so that K is as small as possible, which is a first hint towards switching to Karatsuba's multiplication.

We also propose an optimized version of a multiplication gadget based on Karatsuba's algorithm. This Algorithm 8 uses d random field elements per run (which is most likely close to optimal), but does $d^{\log 3}$ bilinear multiplications. It verifies the RTIK property, thus it is composable without extra refreshing.[3] The intuition behind the optimizations is detailed in Sect. 6. We compare the performances of our optimized multiplication gadget with a few existing constructions in Fig. 1. We highlight that Algorithm 8 and ISW are the only multiplication gadgets that can be securely composed without extra refreshing. In terms of bilinear multiplication, Algorithm 8 is worse than GJR+ and Belaïd bil [BBP+17], but better than Belaïd rand [BBP+17] and ISW. In terms of randomness, Algorithm 8 is close to optimal with d random elements, only beaten by Belaïd rand by one random element. Further details on this comparison can be found in the full

---

[2] Please note that while we discuss about the asymptotic behaviour of the performances of our multiplication gadgets, their security only falls into our framework for bounded order of masking d, for a fixed $\mathbb{F}$.

[3] This multiplication gadget actually behaves as a KIOS refresh with regards to region-probing secure composition. It introduces d random elements to increment the number of regions when composed with other circuits.

version, including estimates of the probing ratio of the gadgets, where Algorithm 8 is also competitive.

	ISW	Belaïd bil	Belaïd rand	GJR+	Algorithm 8
Bilinear mul	d^2	$2d-1$	d^2	$2d$	$d^{\log 3}$
Randomness	$\frac{d(d-1)}{2}$	$2(d-1)^2 + \frac{(d-1)(d-2)}{2}$	$d-1$	$d\log(2d)$	d
t-threshold	$d-1$	$d-1$	$d-1$	$d/2-1$	$d-1$
Composable	YES	NO	NO	NO	YES

Fig. 1. Comparison table of multiplication gadgets for a number of shares d. ISW [ISW03] for arithmetic encodings, Belaid rand [BBP+17] Alg. 5, Belaid bil [BBP+17] Alg. 4, and GJR+ [GPRV21]). The composable row answers the question: "Is naive composition of this multiplication gadget secure ?"

1.2   Limitations and Open Questions

Lack of Concreteness. Our contribution mostly stands on the theoretical side. While we give performance comparisons in the full version and make a toy implementation in sage available, the concrete evaluation of the algorithms developed in this paper would deserve a thorough investigation, that is left for future work. Determining if masking an actual cryptographic algorithm using our techniques can be more efficient than state-of-the-art masked implementation is another interesting open question.

Range of Applications. An extension field $\mathbb{F}/K$ of degree k is proven secure with our techniques up to $d = k$ shares. For example, in the AES field $\mathbb{F}_{256}$, we have $k = 8$, thus our masked compiler tolerates a number of shares d up to 8, with extra efficiency for $d|k$, i.e $d \in \{2, 4, 8\}$. The real world masked implementation are for the most part within this range, but it seems to be an interesting open question to lift the upper bound, especially for the extension field of lower degree, that have insufficient algebraic structure for our techniques to apply. An example where this restriction is virtually absent is in the NTRUprime field [BCLV17]. This field is chosen as $\mathbb{F}_{p^q}$, where both q and p are primes, and q is a few hundreds. Gadget expansion [AIS18, BCP+20, BRTV21, BRT21], which is, waving hands, aiming at boosting the security by repeating the masked compilation several times instead of just one, is an interesting direction which we leave for future work.

Masking Lattice-Based Cryptography. We believe that part of the techniques and algorithms proposed in this paper may apply to the usual power-of-two cyclotomic ring structure underlying lattice-based cryptography. It is also an interesting open question to know to what extent our constructions survive in the ring setting. Since the standardization of several lattice-based schemes, especially Kyber, constructing efficient equality-testing gadgets [DVBV22, CGMZ21, BC22] has received a lot of attention and the contributions of this paper may provide a different angle towards constructing efficient equality-test gadgets.

Formal Verification of Implementations. Maskverif [BBC+18, BBC+19] is a tool that, roughly speaking, when fed an implementation and an adversary model returns the level of security achieved by the input implementation against the given adversary model. The RTIK property seems like a nice property for automated testing, and appears to be more resilient against glitches (due to the fact that the order in which a computation is made is irrelevant, as long as the wires are K-linear) thus it is also an interesting open question to construct a verification tool for implementations.

Remark 1. The proofs of Lemmas, Propositions and Theorems that are missing from the body of the paper can be found in the appendix, sorted by Sections in increasing order.

2 Background

2.1 Notations

Algebra. Throughout the paper, $\mathbb{F}$ denotes a field and $K \subset \mathbb{F}$ a subfield of $\mathbb{F}$. We write $\mathbb{F}_q$ the finite field with q elements. Field elements are written in lower-case letters, vectors are written in bold lower-case letters and matrices are written in bold upper-case letters. Unless stated otherwise, vectors are column vectors, and for a vector $\mathbf{x}$, we denote $\mathbf{x}^T$ its transpose. We write $\odot$ the component-wise product of two vectors. We write $\mathbb{F}_d[X]$ the set of polynomials in X of degree at most d that have coefficients in $\mathbb{F}$. To ease the readability, we identify a polynomial to its list of coefficients, and use either notations interchangeably. An element $\mathbf{a} \in \mathbb{F}^d$ can be treated as an element of $\mathbb{F}_{d-1}[X]$ depending on context, e.g by writing $\mathbf{a}(\omega)$ the evaluation of the polynomial whose coefficients list is $\mathbf{a}$ in a field element ω, or multiplying two polynomials $\mathbf{ab}$ while keeping the vector notation. We write $\pi_K(\omega)$ the minimal polynomial of ω over K, and we write $\deg_K(\omega)$ the degree of $\pi_K(\omega)$. The notation $[n]$ shall denote the set $\{1, \ldots, n\}$.

Distributions. For a distribution D, we do not have notation conventions whether the support of D is a scalar or a vector, but rather rely on context. For random variables X, Y, we write $X \perp Y$ when X is independent of Y. For a random variable X and a set A in the domain of X, we use the standard notation $X(A) = \sum_{a \in A} X(a)$. We write $(X|Y)$ the conditional probability of X given Y. To ease the notations, we write $(X|Y, Z) = (X|(Y, Z))$.

Circuits. A circuit is a directed acyclic graph whose vertices are operations, and each edge is an intermediate value, intermediate variable or wire. We shall call internal randomness of a circuit the list $\boldsymbol{\rho}$ of the elements sampled by random gates in the circuit. This way, every intermediate value of the circuit is a deterministic function of its input and the internal randomness of the circuit. For a set of intermediate values $P = (p_1, \ldots, p_n)$ of a circuit with input χ and internal randomness ρ, we write $P(\chi, \rho) = (p_1(\chi, \rho), \ldots p_n(\chi, \rho))$. When ρ is not in the argument of P, we shall write $P(\chi)$ the random variable $P(\chi, \rho)$ for a uniformly random ρ. We assume throughout the paper that the secret information manipulated by a circuit is a deterministic function of its input and internal randomness. For a circuit $\mathcal{C}$, we usually write $\mathcal{W}$ its set of wires, and we shall write $|\mathcal{W}|$ the number of intermediate variables of $\mathcal{C}$.

2.2   Masking

Encodings. For a vector $\mathbf{v} \in (\mathbb{F} \backslash \{0\})^d$, a $\mathbf{v}$-linear sharing of an element $x \in \mathbb{F}$ is a vector $\mathbf{x}$ satisfying $\mathbf{v}^T \mathbf{x} = x$. Arithmetic masking is a particular case of $\mathbf{v}$-linear sharing, where $\mathbf{v} = (1 \ \ldots \ 1)$. For ω an element of $\mathbb{F}$, we let $\boldsymbol{\omega}_d = (\omega^i)_{0 \leq i \leq d-1}$. We say that a vector $\mathbf{x} \in \mathbb{F}^d$ is an $\boldsymbol{\omega}_d$-encoding of a field element $x \in \mathbb{F}$ when $\boldsymbol{\omega}_d^T \mathbf{x} = x$ (or equivalently $\mathbf{x}(\omega) = x$), which is also a particular case of linear sharing. For $x \in \mathbb{F}$, the set of $\mathbf{v}$-encodings of x is $H_x^{\mathbf{v}} = \{\mathbf{x} \in \mathbb{F}^d, \ \mathbf{v}^T \mathbf{x} = x\}$ and can be seen both as an affine hyperplane (with the convention $H_0^{\mathbf{v}} = H^{\mathbf{v}}$). We shall omit the superscript $\mathbf{v}$ when it is clear from context, and we notice that $H_x^{\boldsymbol{\omega}_d}$ can also be seen as the set of degree d polynomials $\mathbf{x}$ such that $\mathbf{x}(\omega) = x$. We define $\mathcal{U}_{\mathbf{v}}(x)$ to be the uniform distribution over $H_x^{\mathbf{v}}$, and extend it coordinate-wise when applied on multiple entries. We say that $(\mathbf{x}_1, \ldots, \mathbf{x}_n)$ are mutually independent $\boldsymbol{\omega}_d$-encodings when for all $x_1, \ldots, x_n$, the distributions $(\mathbf{x}_1 | \boldsymbol{\omega}_d^T \mathbf{x}_1 = x_1), \ldots, (\mathbf{x}_n | \boldsymbol{\omega}_d^T \mathbf{x}_n = x_n)$ are mutually independent.

We call an addition gadget (respectively a multiplication gadget) with respect to $\boldsymbol{\omega}_d$-encodings a circuit that takes as input two $\boldsymbol{\omega}_d$-encodings $\mathbf{a}, \mathbf{b}$ and returns an $\boldsymbol{\omega}_d$-encoding of $\boldsymbol{\omega}_d^T \mathbf{a} + \boldsymbol{\omega}_d^T \mathbf{b}$ (respectively $\boldsymbol{\omega}_d^T \mathbf{a} \cdot \boldsymbol{\omega}_d^T \mathbf{b}$). A correct refresh gadget with respect to $\boldsymbol{\omega}_d$-encodings is a circuit that takes as input an $\boldsymbol{\omega}_d$-encoding and returns an $\boldsymbol{\omega}_d$-encoding of the same secret. In general, for a gate g in a circuit $\mathcal{C}$, we say that G is a correct $\boldsymbol{\omega}_d$-encoding gadget for g when G takes as input $\boldsymbol{\omega}_d$-encodings of the sensitive inputs of g, and returns $\boldsymbol{\omega}_d$-encodings of the sensitive outputs of g.

Security Properties. We define the threshold-probing security game, region-probing security game, the simulation-based Input-Output Separation property for refresh gadgets and the associated composition theorem.

Definition 1 (*t*-probing security game). *Let $n, t \geq 1$, $\mathcal{C}$ be a circuit and $\mathcal{W}$ be its set of intermediate variables. Let χ be the distribution of the input in of $\mathcal{C}$ and $x_1, \ldots, x_n$ be secret random variables following a distribution ϕ. A t-probing adversary $\mathcal{A}$ on $(\mathcal{C}, \chi, \phi)$ plays the following game:*

1. *The challenger samples the input in from χ*
2. *$\mathcal{A}$ chooses a set of probes $P \subset \mathcal{W}$ with $|P| \leq t$*
3. *The challenger runs $\mathcal{C}(\text{in})$ and sends $P(\text{in})$ to $\mathcal{A}$*
4. *$\mathcal{A}$ returns $(y_1, \ldots, y_n)$. He wins if $(y_1, \ldots, y_n) = (x_1, \ldots, x_n)$.*

A circuit $\mathcal{C}$ for which there is no unbounded adversary $\mathcal{A}$, playing the t-probing security game with respect to secrets $x_1, \ldots, x_n$, that has an advantage against an adversary who skips steps 1) and 2) is called t-probing secure. In the context of masking, the input distribution χ of $\mathcal{C}$ contains uniform encodings of the secret inputs, and the decoding of these are the secrets of this circuit that the adversary attempts to guess after probing.

Definition 2 (r-region probing security game). *Let $n \geq 1$, $0 < r < 1$, $\mathcal{C}$ be a circuit with input random variable **in** following a distribution χ and $x_1, \ldots, x_n$ be secret random variables following a distribution ϕ. Let $\mathcal{C}_1, \ldots, \mathcal{C}_m$ be subcircuits of $\mathcal{C}$ such that $(\mathcal{C}_1, \ldots, \mathcal{C}_m)$ is a disjoint covering of $\mathcal{C}$, $\mathcal{W}_1, \ldots, \mathcal{W}_m$ be the respective sets of intermediate variables of each subcircuit. A r-region probing adversary against $(\mathcal{C}, \chi, \phi)$ with regions $\mathcal{C}_1, \ldots, \mathcal{C}_m$ plays the following game :*

1. *The challenger samples the input **in** from χ*
2. *$\mathcal{A}$ chooses m sets of probes $(P_i \subset \mathcal{W}_i)_{i \leq m}$ with $|P_i| \leq \lceil r|\mathcal{W}_i| \rceil$*
3. *The challenger runs $\mathcal{C}(\chi)$ and sends $(P_i(\chi))_{i \leq m}$ to $\mathcal{A}$*
4. *$\mathcal{A}$ returns $(y_1, \ldots, y_n)$. He wins if $(y_1, \ldots, y_n) = (x_1, \ldots, x_n)$.*

With identical input distribution χ and secrets to hide, any t-probing secure circuit $\mathcal{C}$ is trivially $t/|\mathcal{C}|$-region probing secure. Conversely, if a circuit is r-region probing secure with $m = 1$, it is $\lfloor r|\mathcal{C}| \rfloor$-probing secure. When χ and ϕ are clear from context, we simply say that $\mathcal{C}$ is t-probing secure, and similarly for region-probing security. For saving space and improving the readability, we omit the input of the probes when it is clear from context and write P instead of $P(\mathbf{in})$.

Definition 3 (t-input-output separation). *Let $\mathbf{v} \in (\mathbb{F} \backslash \{0\})^d$. A refresh gadget G^R is called t-input-output separative when for any $\mathbf{x}, \mathbf{y}$ with $\mathbf{y} = G^R(\mathbf{x})$, we have that $\mathbf{y}$ follows $\mathcal{U}(\mathbf{v}^T \mathbf{x})$ and for any set of intermediate values $\mathcal{W}$ with $|\mathcal{W}| \leq t$, we have that there exists a two-stage simulator $\mathcal{S}_{G^R, \mathcal{W}} = (\mathcal{S}_{G^R, \mathcal{W}}^1, \mathcal{S}_{G^R, \mathcal{W}}^2)$ with the following properties.*

1. *The first one $\mathcal{S}_{G^R, \mathcal{W}}^1$ returns two sets of indices $\mathcal{I}, \mathcal{J} \subset [d]$ such that $|\mathcal{I}|, |\mathcal{J}| \leq |\mathcal{W}|$.*
2. *The second one $\mathcal{S}_{G^R, \mathcal{W}}^2$, ran on input $\mathbf{x}_{|\mathcal{I}}, \mathbf{y}_{|\mathcal{J}}$, returns an output identically distributed as $\mathcal{W}(\mathbf{x}, \mathbf{r})$, where $\mathbf{r}$ is the internal randomness of G^R, $\mathbf{x}_{|\mathcal{I}}$ is $\mathbf{x}$ restricted to the coordinates that appear in $\mathcal{I}$ and similarly for $\mathbf{y}_{|\mathcal{J}}$.*

The following composition Theorem claims that if a circuit $\mathcal{C}$ is split into t-probing secure subcircuits separated by t-IOS refresh gadgets, then the whole circuit is r-region probing secure for some ratio r. The statement of the Theorem deals with so-called standard masked compilers of arithmetic circuits, but similar proof techniques could aim for a more general claim involving non-arithmetic gadgets.

Theorem 1 (Composition Theorem, adapted from Theorem 1 [GPRV21]). *Let $\mathcal{C}$ be an arithmetic circuit. If G^+ is a t^+-probing secure addition gadget, $G^\times$ is a $t^\times$-probing secure multiplication gadget and G^R is a t^R-IOS* *refresh gadget, then the circuit* $\widehat{\mathcal{C}}$ *taking as input an encoding of the input of* $\mathcal{C}$ *obtained by replacing addition gates with* G^+, *multiplication gates by* $G^\times$ *and applying a refresh gadget* G^R *to any input of an operation gadget is* r-*region probing secure, with*

$$r = \max_{t \le t^R} \min \left(\frac{t^+ - 3t}{|G^+|}, \frac{t^\times - 3t}{|G^\times|}, \frac{t}{|G^R|} \right).$$

3   Probabilistic Approach to Probing Security

In this section, we make our first step towards bridging probing security and algebra, which boils down to redefining from a probabilistic perspective the usual definitions of probing security, region-probing security and the IOS composition property. While the usual simulation-based definitions have their advantages, the probabilistic versions of the latter properties are a much better fit with our techniques. All the results, definitions and propositions in this section are stated for linear sharings (**v**-encodings for any $\mathbf{v} \in (\mathbb{F}\backslash\{0\})^d$).

3.1   Redefining Probing Security Through Sets of Probes and Distribution of Secrets

The t-probing security game, as defined in Definition 1, is usually translated as the simulatability of the leakage. In this subsection, we redefine t-probing security (as well as r-region probing security) in a formalism that relies on distributions rather than simulation. From a high level, one can think of these probabilistic definitions as simply cutting the middle-man, where the middle-man is the simulator. Indeed, in a simulation-based proof, one has to define the simulator for any given set of probed wires (and maybe modify the probes of the adversary before doing so), and then justify that this simulator is actually giving samples of the right distribution. By relying directly on the distribution argument, we focus on proving that the leakage distribution is independent of the secrets, which in our mind highlights the key arguments of the proof and arguably makes it shorter.

We start off with a binary relation written $\le$ on sets of probes, from which we derive that various elementary operations on sets of probes at least preserve the information learnt by the adversary.

Definition 4 (Partial order of probe sets). *Let* P, Q *be two sets of probes on a circuit* $\mathcal{C}$, *taking as input a random variable* **in** *following a distribution* χ *and manipulating secret random variables* $x_1, \ldots, x_n$ *following a distribution* ϕ. *We say that* Q *contains more information than* P, *and we write* $P \le Q$, *when*

$$((x_1, \ldots, x_n)|(P(\mathbf{in}), Q(\mathbf{in}))) = ((x_1, \ldots, x_n)|Q(\mathbf{in})).$$

When $P \leq Q$, intuitively, all the sensitive information on the input **in** of $\mathcal{C}$ carried by P is also carried by Q. The binary relation $\leq$ verifies reflexivity and transitivity, but not antisymmetry. Since antisymmetry is irrelevant for our purposes, we chose to write this binary relation as a partial order relation. The point of this binary relation is to provide a formal justification for modifying the set of probes that the adversary initially chooses in the probing security games. By using a few allowed elementary operations one after another, we are able to reduce any initial set of probes to another set of probes that has a shape that fits our techniques in the following sections.

We now provide an illustration of elementary operations on a set of probes P_1. The obtained sets P_2, P_3 are such that $P_3 \geq P_2 \geq P_1$, thus $P_3 \geq P_1$. Consider some circuit $\mathcal{C}$ that takes as input two arithmetic encodings $(x_0, x_1), (y_0, y_1)$. The secrets manipulated by the circuit are $x = x_0 + x_1$ and $y = y_0 + y_1$. Consider that a 3-probing adversary choses the set of probes $P_1 = (2x_0, y_0, x_0 + y_0)$. The first operation that we can do on this set of probes while preserving the information it contains is to remove the constant factor 2: with $P_2 = (x_0, y_0, x_0 + y_0)$, we have $P_2 \geq P_1$. Second, we can remove the redundancy : if the adversary learns x_0 and y_0, he might as well compute $x_0 + y_0$ himself. With $P_3 = (x_0, y_0)$, we have $P_3 \geq P_2$. Adding extra relations to a set of probes also yields that it contains more information. For instance if $Q_1 = (x_0 + y_0)$, then $Q_2 = (x_0, y_0)$ is such that $Q_2 \geq Q_1$. Examples of proofs that rely on an increasing sequence of sets of probes can be found in the proofs of Propositions 5 and 6 and Theorems 5 and 6.

We now proceed to define t-probing security and r-region probing security for masked circuit from a probabilistic perspective.

Definition 5 (t-probing security of linear-masked circuits, convenient version). *Let* $\mathbf{v} \in (\mathbb{F}\backslash\{0\})^d$, $\mathcal{C}$ *be a circuit taking as input* $\mathbf{v}$*-encodings* $\mathbf{x}_1, \ldots, \mathbf{x}_n$ *and* $\mathcal{W}$ *be the set of intermediate variables of* $\mathcal{C}$*. Then* $\mathcal{C}$ *is t-probing secure when* $\forall P \subset \mathcal{W}$ *with* $|P| \leq t$*, we have*

$$(\mathbf{v}^T \mathbf{x}_1, \ldots, \mathbf{v}^T \mathbf{x}_n) \perp P(\mathbf{x}_1, \ldots, \mathbf{x}_n).$$

Definition 6 (r-region-probing security of linear-masked circuits, convenient version). *Let* $\mathbf{v} \in (\mathbb{F}\backslash\{0\})^d$, $0 < r < 1$, $\mathcal{C}$ *be a circuit,* $\mathcal{C}_1, \ldots, \mathcal{C}_m$ *be subcircuits of* $\mathcal{C}$ *such that* $(\mathcal{C}_1, \ldots, \mathcal{C}_m)$ *is a disjoint covering of* $\mathcal{C}$*,* $\mathcal{W}_1, \ldots, \mathcal{W}_m$ *be the induced sets of intermediate variables of the subcircuits. We let* $\mathbf{x}_1, \ldots \mathbf{x}_n$ *be the input* $\mathbf{v}$*-encodings of* $\mathcal{C}$*. Then* $\mathcal{C}$ *is r-region-probing secure when* $\forall P = (P_1, \ldots, P_m) \subset \mathcal{W}_1 \times \cdots \times \mathcal{W}_m$*, with* $P_i \subset \mathcal{W}_i$ *and* $|P_i| \leq \lceil r|\mathcal{C}_i| \rceil$*, we have*

$$(\mathbf{v}^T \mathbf{x}_1, \ldots, \mathbf{v}^T \mathbf{x}_n) \perp P(\mathbf{x}_1, \ldots, \mathbf{x}_n).$$

In both definitions, the information learnt by the adversary (i.e $P(\mathbf{x}_1, \ldots, \mathbf{x}_n)$) is therefore independent of the secrets hidden in the circuit (i.e each sensitive entry $x_i = \mathbf{v}^T \mathbf{x}_i$). Since there is information-theoretically no information learnt by the adversary by probing, if a masked circuit verifies one of the definitions above, it also verifies the corresponding usual game-based definition. The following Proposition links the relation $\leq$ to region probing security.

Proposition 1. *Let* $\mathbf{v} \in (\mathbb{F}\backslash\{0\})^d$, $0 < r < 1$, $\mathcal{C}$ *be a circuit taking as input* $\mathbf{v}$*-encodings* $\mathbf{x}_1, \ldots, \mathbf{x}_n$. *Assume that there exists a set of disjoint subcircuits* $\mathcal{C}_1, \ldots, \mathcal{C}_m$ *covering* $\mathcal{C}$, *inducing sets of intermediate variables* $(\mathcal{W}_1, \ldots, \mathcal{W}_m)$, *such that for all set of probes* $P = (P_1, \ldots, P_m)$ *with* $|P_i| \leq \lceil r|\mathcal{W}_i| \rceil$ *for all* $i \leq m$, *there exists a set of probes* $Q = (Q_1, \ldots, Q_m)$ *such that*

1. $\forall\, i \leq m,\ P_i \leq Q_i$
2. $(\mathbf{v}^T\mathbf{x}_1, \ldots, \mathbf{v}^T\mathbf{x}_n) \perp Q(\mathbf{x}_1, \ldots, \mathbf{x}_n)$.

Then $\mathcal{C}$ *is* r*-region probing secure.*

Using the correspondence between t-probing security and r-region probing security with $m = 1$, the Proposition above then implies that if for any set P of t probes on a circuit $\mathcal{C}$, there exists a set Q with $P \leq Q$ and Q is independent of the secrets, then the latter circuit is $\mathcal{C}$ is t-probing secure.

3.2 Revisiting Input-Output-Separation: Refreshing ω_d-encodings and Composition of Gadgets

For our own technical purposes (e.g. the proof of Theorem 5) and for exposing the close relation between KIOS Definition 11 and IOS Definition 3, we redefine the Input-Output Separation property introduced in [GPRV21]. The property Reducible-To-Coordinates (RTC) for generators of $\mathbf{v}$-encodings of 0 is closely connected to the ℓ-free property defined in the proof of Theorem 2 from [GPRV21] (from which the authors deduce the IOS property), thus we redefine the IOS property based on this RTC property. We prove that our new definition encompasses the original one, and give explicitly the template to build an IOS refresh gadget Algorithms 2 and 4 from an RTC generator of encodings of 0.

Definition 7. *(Reducible-To-Coordinates)* *Let* $\mathbf{v} \in (\mathbb{F}\backslash\{0\})^d$, t *be an integer and* R *be a gadget taking as input a dimension* d, *and returning a uniform* $\mathbf{v}$*-encoding* $\mathbf{r}$ *of 0. We say that* R *is Reducible-To-Coordinates (RTC) when the distribution of* $\mathbf{r}$ *is uniform conditioned on* $\mathbf{v}^T\mathbf{r} = 0$ *and for every set of* t *probes* P *on* R, *there exists two sets of probes* Q_1, Q_2 *such that*

1. $|Q_1| \leq t$
2. $(Q_1, Q_2) \geq P$
3. *Every probe in* Q_1 *is a coordinate of* $\mathbf{r}$
4. *The distributions* Q_2 *and* $(\mathbf{r}|Q_1)$ *are independent*

Notice that in the definition above, the binary relation $\leq$ is taken with respect to the secret $r_0, \ldots, r_{d-1}$, i.e all the coordinates of the fresh vector $\mathbf{r}$, where for t-probing security of masked circuits we take the secrets to be the decoding of the masked inputs.

Proposition 2. *Algorithm 1 is RTC with* $\mathbf{v} = (1, \ldots, 1)$.

Algorithm 1. ArithGenZero, adapted from Appendix C [BCPZ16]

Require: Masking order d
Ensure: $\mathbf{t} \in \mathbb{F}^d$ such that $\sum r_i = 0$

1: **if** $d = 1$ **then**
2:     **return** 0
3: **end if**
4: **if** $d = 2$ **then**
5:     $r \leftarrow \mathbb{F}$
6:     **return** $(-r, r)$
7: **end if**
8: $(r_0, \ldots, r_{\lfloor d/2 \rfloor - 1}) = \text{ArithGenZero}(\lfloor d/2 \rfloor)$
9: $(r_{\lfloor d/2 \rfloor}, \ldots, r_{d-1}) = \text{ArithGenZero}(\lceil d/2 \rceil)$
10: **for** $i = 0$ to $\lfloor d/2 \rfloor - 1$ **do**
11:     $s_i \leftarrow \mathbb{F}$
12:     $t_i = r_i + s_i$
13:     $t_{\lfloor d/2 \rfloor + i} = r_{\lfloor d/2 \rfloor + i} - s_i$
14: **end for**
15: **if** d is odd **then**
16:     $t_{d-1} = r_{d-1}$
17: **end if**
18: **return** t

The Proposition above is a mild generalization of Theorem 2 from [GPRV21]. They prove that the refresh gadget obtained by adding coordinate-wise an encoding of 0 generated using ArithGenZero is IOS when d is a power-of-two. We adapt their result from IOS to RTC, and extend it to any $d \geq 1$ by considering the refresh gadget from Appendix C [BCPZ16].

Definition 8. *(Input-Output Separative) Let $\mathbf{v} \in (\mathbb{F} \backslash \{0\})^d$, t be an integer and G be a gadget taking as input a $\mathbf{v}$-encoding $\mathbf{x}$, and returning an encoding $\mathbf{y}$ of the same secret as $\mathbf{x}$. We say that G is t-IOS when the distribution of $\mathbf{y}$ is uniform conditioned on $\mathbf{v}^T \mathbf{y} = \mathbf{v}^T \mathbf{x}$ and for every set of t probes P on G, there exists three sets of probes Q_x, Q_y, Q_2 such that*

1. *$|Q_x| \leq t$, $|Q_y| \leq t$*
2. *$(Q_x, Q_y, Q_2) \geq P$*
3. *Every probe in Q_x is a coordinate of $\mathbf{x}$ and every probe in Q_y is a coordinate of $\mathbf{y}$*
4. *The distributions Q_2 and $((\mathbf{x}, \mathbf{y})|(Q_x, Q_y))$ are independent*

Proposition 3. *Let $\mathbf{v} \in (\mathbb{F} \backslash \{0\})^d$, t be an integer and G be a gadget taking as input a $\mathbf{v}$-encoding $\mathbf{x}$, and returning an encoding $\mathbf{y}$ of the same secret as $\mathbf{x}$. If G is t-IOS according to Definition 8, then it is also t-IOS according to Definition 3 and vice-versa.*

Algorithm 2. RTC generator to IOS refresh template

Require: Masking order d, $\mathbf{v} \in (\mathbb{F} \backslash \{0\})^d$, RTC generator of arithmetic encodings of
    0 R, $\mathbf{v}$-encoding $\mathbf{x}$
Ensure: $\mathbf{y} \in \mathbb{F}^d$ such that $\mathbf{v}^T \mathbf{y} = \mathbf{v}^T \mathbf{x}$

1: $\mathbf{r} = R(d)$
2: **for** $i = 0$ to $d - 1$ **do**
3:      $s_i = v_i^{-1} r_i$
4: **end for**
5: $\mathbf{y} = \mathbf{x} + \mathbf{s}$
6: **return** $\mathbf{y}$

Proposition 4. *If R is an RTC generator of arithmetic encodings of 0, then the refresh gadget obtained by instantiating Algorithm 2 with R is an IOS refresh gadget for $\mathbf{v}$-encodings.*

4 Algebraic Approach in Probing Security for Extension Fields

In this section, we focus on the setting where $\mathbb{F}$ is an extension field over some subfield K. We only consider a specific type of encoding, which is $\boldsymbol{\omega}_d$-encoding, where $\boldsymbol{\omega}_d = (1, \omega, \omega^2, \dots, \omega^{d-1})$ is the vector with all the first d powers of some fixed field element $\omega \in \mathbb{F}$. Unless specified otherwise, ω is chosen so that its algebraic degree over the subfield K is at least the number of shares, in order to apply the core Lemmas from Sect. 4.1. We remind the reader that the notions detailed in this section exploit the algebraic structure of $\mathbb{F}$, and for our techniques to apply, the number of shares d cannot exceed $[\mathbb{F} : K]$.

In the first subsection, we state the core Lemmas that make the connection between the extension field structure of $\mathbb{F}/K$ and probing security. In the second subsection, we introduce the RTIK security notion for circuits (a priori of any size between operation gadget to a full cryptographic algorithm implementation) that in turn implies region-probing security. In the last subsection, we show that RTIK circuits admit nice composition properties without refresh. We finally show that refreshing the encodings in between two RTIK circuits gives more security at the cost of randomness, and that the refresh gadget is still secure with a slightly weaker notion KIOS than the IOS notion.

4.1 Probing Security of K-Linear Circuits

This subsection contains two technical results Lemmas 1 and 2 that are building blocks for proving t-probing security of $\boldsymbol{\omega}_d$-masked circuits.

From a high level, the first Lemma 1 claims that when $\deg_K(\omega) \geq d$, the vector $\boldsymbol{\omega}_d$ is never in the span of $\ell < d$ vectors over K, where K is a subfield of $\mathbb{F}$. The intuition of the connection between this statement and probing security is as follows: This statement says, roughly speaking, that the probes are linearly independent of the decoding operation, and this statement is in turn used to prove the probabilistic independence between probes and secret in Lemma 2.

To illustrate the correspondance between K-linear circuits and threshold-probing security, consider a t-probing adversary against some circuit $\mathcal{C}$, taking as input a uniform ω_d-encoding of the secret. We assume that the adversary has no prior knowledge on the secret $a = \omega_d^T \mathbf{a}$ manipulated by $\mathcal{C}$, hence from the adversary's perspective, before probing, $\mathbf{a}$ is distributed uniformly over $\mathbb{F}^d$. Now, say we can force every intermediate value of our circuit $\mathcal{C}$ to be K-linear in $\mathbf{a}$. Then, when the adversary probes $t < d$ linearly independent inner products of the encoding $\mathbf{a}$, he receives some values $\mathbf{v} \in \mathbb{F}^t$ of the form $\mathbf{v} = \mathbf{Pa}$ where $\mathbf{P} \in K^{t \times d}$. The probability that the secret is some $a' \in \mathbb{F}$, from the adversary's perspective, is then proportional to the number of solutions to the equations $\mathbf{v} = \mathbf{Pa}$ and $\omega_d^T \mathbf{a} = a'$. When $\deg_K(\omega) \geq d$ is satisfied, Lemma 1 tells us that $\omega_d \notin \operatorname{Span} \mathbf{P}^T$, from which follows that the set of solutions to the latter equations is an affine subspace of dimension $d - t - 1$, of cardinality $|\mathbb{F}|^{d-t-1}$ no matter what $a' \in \mathbb{F}$ is. In other words, the secret in the adversary's view is distributed uniformly random, therefore the adversary did not learn anything by probing, which is t-probing security.

We prove (in a slightly more general fashion) the result sketched above in Lemma 2. This Lemma is central in our framework: every security notion introduced in the next subsection relates to it. The convenient form of Lemma 2 makes it likely to find other applications in constructing efficient masked gadgets.

Lemma 1. *Let $\mathbb{F}$ be a finite field, K be a subfield of $\mathbb{F}$, $\mathbf{P} \in K^{t \times d}$ such that* rank $\mathbf{P} = t$ *and* $\omega \in \mathbb{F}$. *If* $\deg_K(\omega) \geq d$ *and* $t < d$, *then*

$$\operatorname{rank} \begin{bmatrix} \mathbf{P} \\ \omega_d^T \end{bmatrix} = t + 1.$$

Proof. Let us assume for one moment that rank $\begin{bmatrix} \mathbf{P} \\ \omega_d^T \end{bmatrix} = t$, i.e $\omega_d \in \operatorname{Span} \mathbf{P}^T$. This means that there exists t coefficients $\lambda_i \in \mathbb{F}^t$ such that $\mathbf{P}^T \lambda = \omega_d$. Now, since $t < d$, there exists vectors $\mathbf{p}_{t+1}, \ldots, \mathbf{p}_d$ with coefficients in K that complete $\mathbf{P}$ into an invertible matrix. We let $\mathbf{Q}$ be its inverse, and we write $\mathbf{q}$ the last row of $\mathbf{Q}$. We have

$$\left[\mathbf{P}^T | \mathbf{p}_{t+1} | \cdots | \mathbf{p}_d \right] \begin{bmatrix} \lambda \\ 0 \\ \vdots \\ 0 \end{bmatrix} = \omega_d$$

$$\begin{bmatrix} \lambda \\ 0 \\ \vdots \\ 0 \end{bmatrix} = \mathbf{Q} \omega_d.$$

Taking the last row in the last equality, we get $\mathbf{q}^T \omega_d = 0$, and due to the invertibility of $\mathbf{Q}$, $\mathbf{q} \neq \mathbf{0}$. In other words, the polynomial with coefficients $\mathbf{q}$ cancels ω and has degree at most $d-1$, which is a contradiction with $\deg_K(\omega) \geq d$, and the claim follows.

Lemma 2. *Let d be an order of masking, $\mathcal{C}$ be a circuit taking as input a uniform ω_d-encoding $\mathbf{x}$ with $\omega \in \mathbb{F}$. If all the intermediate variables p of $\mathcal{C}$ are of the form $p(\mathbf{x}) = \mathbf{p}^T \mathbf{x}$ for some vector $\mathbf{p} \in K^d$, then $\mathcal{C}$ is $d-1$-probing secure.*

Proof. Let $\mathcal{A}$ be a $d-1$-probing adversary against $\mathcal{C}$, probing a set P of intermediate values of $\mathcal{C}$. Let ϕ be the distribution of the secret input x, inducing by uniformity a distribution $\bar{\phi}(\mathbf{x}) = \frac{1}{|\mathbb{F}|^{d-1}}\phi(\omega^T \mathbf{x})$. There exists a matrix $\mathbf{P} \in K^{(d-1)\times d}$ such that $P(\mathbf{x}) = \mathbf{P}\mathbf{x}$. We assume without loss of generality that $\mathbf{P}$ is full-rank, otherwise some rows of $\mathbf{P}$ are redundant and the matrix $\mathbf{P}'$ obtained by removing redundancy defines a set of probes $P' \geq P$, and is full-rank. For $x \in \mathbb{F}, \mathbf{v} \in \mathbb{F}^{d-1}$, we have

$$\mathbb{P}(\omega_d^T \mathbf{x} = x \cap P(\mathbf{x}) = \mathbf{v}) = \mathbb{P}(\omega_d^T \mathbf{x} = x \cap \mathbf{P}\mathbf{x} = \mathbf{v}) \tag{1}$$

$$= \bar{\phi}\left(\ker \begin{bmatrix} \mathbf{P} \\ \omega_d^T \end{bmatrix} + \mathbf{x}^*\right) \tag{2}$$

$$= \bar{\phi}(\mathbf{x}^*) = \frac{1}{|\mathbb{F}|^{d-1}}\phi(x) \tag{3}$$

$$= \mathbb{P}(P(\mathbf{x}) = \mathbf{v})) \cdot \mathbb{P}(\omega_d^T \mathbf{x} = x), \tag{4}$$

where Eq. (1) is the hypothesis of the Lemma, Eq. (2) holds for some solution $\mathbf{x}^*$ to the equation $\begin{bmatrix} \mathbf{P} \\ \omega_d^T \end{bmatrix} \mathbf{x}^* = \begin{bmatrix} \mathbf{v} \\ x \end{bmatrix}$, Equation (3) follows from Lemma 1 which implies that the matrix $\begin{bmatrix} \mathbf{P} \\ \omega_d^T \end{bmatrix}$ is of rank d, therefore its kernel is 0, and Eq. (4) holds because $\mathbb{P}(P(\mathbf{x}) = \mathbf{v}) = \mathbb{P}(\mathbf{x} \in \ker \mathbf{P} + \mathbf{x}') = \frac{1}{|\mathbb{F}|^{d-1}}\sum_{y \in \mathbb{F}}\phi(y) = \frac{1}{|\mathbb{F}|^{d-1}}$, where $\mathbf{x}'$ is an offset vector solution to $P(\mathbf{x}') = \mathbf{v}$. Since we have $\mathbb{P}(P(\mathbf{x}) = \mathbf{v}) = |\mathbb{F}|^{-(d-1)}$ and $\phi(x) = \mathbb{P}(\omega_d^T \mathbf{x} = x)$, we conclude independence.

4.2 Weaker Condition for Region-Probing Security in Extension Fields

In this section, we extend the results of the above subsection to circuits manipulating several ω_d-encodings. Namely, we introduce the RTIK security notion and show that RTIK circuits are region-probing secure. Rephrasing (and simplifying) the RTIK property: an ω_d-masked circuit $\mathcal{C}$ is said RTIK when any set of probes P can be reduced to a set of probes Q in which every probe is K-linear in a single ω_d-masked encoding.

Definition 9 (Reducible-To-Independent-K-Linear (RTIK)). *Let C be a circuit over a finite field $\mathbb{F}$, K be a subfield of $\mathbb{F}$, $\mathcal{W}$ be the set of wires of C and $(\mathbf{x}_1, \ldots, \mathbf{x}_n)$ be mutually independent ω_d-encodings. We say that C is RTIK w.r.t $(\mathbf{x}_1, \ldots, \mathbf{x}_n)$ when for all set of probes $P \subset \mathcal{W}$, there exists a set of probes $Q = (Q_1, \ldots, Q_n) \subset \mathcal{W}$ such that the following holds:*

1. *$Q \geq P$*
2. *$\forall i \in [n], \ |Q_i| \leq |P|$*
3. *For all $i \in [n]$, every probe in Q_i is a linear function of $\mathbf{x}_i$ over K.*

Theorem 2 (Security of RTIK circuits.). *Let n, d be integers, C be a circuit over a finite field $\mathbb{F}$, K be a subfield of $\mathbb{F}$, $\mathcal{W}$ be the set of wires of C, $\omega \in \mathbb{F}$ be a field element such that $\deg_K(\omega) \geq d$ and $(\mathbf{x}_1, \ldots, \mathbf{x}_n)$ be mutually independent ω_d-encodings.*

If C is RTIK with respect to $(\mathbf{x}_1, \ldots, \mathbf{x}_n)$, then there exists a number $m \geq n$, a ratio r, and m regions $(C_1, \ldots, C_m)$ such that C is r-region-probing secure with respect to $(C_1, \ldots, C_m)$. The probing ratio r is given by

$$
\min_{i \in [n]} \left(\frac{d-1}{\displaystyle\sum_{\substack{I \subset [n] \\ s.t\ i \in I}} |\mathcal{W}_I|} \right),
$$

$\mathcal{W}_I$ and the subcircuits $C_1, \ldots, C_m$ are explicited in the proof.

Regions and Probing Ratio. Our proof of Theorem 2 is tight for two reasons. First, it is tight in the sense that any ratio r greater than the one defined in the proof leads to an attack in the region-probing model. Second, it is tight in the sense that there exists an RTIK circuit C (wrt encodings $\mathbf{x}_1, \ldots, \mathbf{x}_n$) such that the ratio r satisfies $r|C| = n(d-1)$, which is optimal. The latter justifies an improvement upon the direct reduction from the threshold probing model.

4.3 Composition Notions for RTIK Circuits

We first show that some RTIK gadgets with a nice additionnal feature can be composed naively and still enjoy region-probing security.

Theorem 3. *Let C be a circuit over a finite field $\mathbb{F}$, and K be a subfield of $\mathbb{F}$. If C can be split into two disjoint subcircuits C_1, C_2 such that*

1. *C_1 is RTIK with respect to encodings $(\mathbf{x}_1^1, \ldots, \mathbf{x}_n^1)$*
2. *C_2 is RTIK with respect to encodings $(\mathbf{x}_1^2, \ldots, \mathbf{x}_m^2)$*
3. *The intersection of the input encodings of C_2 and the output encodings of C_1 is contained in both $(\mathbf{x}_1^1, \ldots, \mathbf{x}_n^1)$ and $(\mathbf{x}_1^2, \ldots, \mathbf{x}_m^2)$,*

then C is RTIK.

On the Extra Condition for Naive Composition of RTIK Circuits.
The condition 2. from the Theorem above asks, roughly speaking, that when
evaluating C_2 on (part of) the output of C_1, the encodings that are passed on
from C_1 to C_2 are part of those vectors that define the RTIK property for both
circuits. In practice, we are not aware of any combination of useful circuits that
do not verify the aforementioned property. In all generality, we were not able
to prove that this condition is always verified, but all our gadgets, as well as
all coordinate-wise gadgets do verify the condition, and any circuit composed of
our gadgets also verifies this condition.

Composition of More Than Two Gadgets. As one would expect, it is
possible to prove that the composition of several gadgets which enjoy the nice
extra composability feature is RTIK. Indeed, by induction, one can step by step
prove using Theorem 3 that the successive compositions are indeed RTIK, as the
property propagates with no slack from two circuits to their composition. The
fact that there is no slack is ensured by 2. from Definition 9. While it is possible
to construct gadgets that verify 1. 2. and 4. as well as $|Q_i| \leq \alpha|P|$ for some
slack factor α (e.g. the NaiveFold algorithm defined in Sect. 5.1), we decide not
to introduce this extra notation as the slack factor of a compound circuit grows
exponentially with the number of subcircuits, and thus leads to rather inefficient
constructions.

Why Refreshing a Secure Circuit? Again, the probing ratio r is given by
the minimum over i of the individual $\frac{d-1}{\sum |W_I|}$, where I is a subset of indices
containing i, and W_I is the set of wires mapped to $|I|$ probes, each on a single
encoding $\mathbf{x}_j, j \in I$. When one of the subcircuits

$$\bigcup_{\substack{I \subset [n] \\ i \in I}} W_I,$$

is particularly large compared to the others, it may be beneficial to break it
down into smaller independent subcircuits so as to increase the security of the
compound circuit. This act of splitting a circuit into subcircuits can be done
using an IOS refresh on the encodings, but the weaker notion of KIOS, more
adapted to our RTIK circuits, is also suited. This notion is very similar to the
IOS notion, thus we follow a similar path towards defining it.

Definition 10. *(Reducible-To-K-Linear) Let $\omega \in \mathbb{F}$ and K be a subfield of $\mathbb{F}$.
Consider a gadget R taking as input a dimension d and returning an ω_d-encoding
$\mathbf{r}$ of 0. Let $\alpha > 0$ be the slack factor of R. We say that R is α-Reducible-To-K-
Linear (RTK) when the output distribution of R is a uniform ω_d-sharing of 0,
and for any set of independent probes P on R with $|P| = t < d$, there exists sets
of probes Q_1, Q_2 such that*

1) $|Q_1| \leq \alpha t$.
2) $(Q_1, Q_2) \geq P$

3) Every probe in Q_1 is K-linear in **r**.
4) The distributions Q_2 and $(\mathbf{r}|Q_1)$ are independent.

Notice that with this definition, if R is RTC with respect to $\boldsymbol{\omega}_d$, then R is 1-RTK. We now define the security notion achieved by the $\boldsymbol{\omega}_d$-encoding refresh gadget obtained by adding coordinate-wise a fresh $\boldsymbol{\omega}_d$-encoding of 0 to the input. The intuition why the KIOS security notion for refresh gadget brings composition security is similar to the one for IOS refresh gadgets. If we have $\mathbf{y} = \mathbf{r} + \mathbf{x}$, where $\mathbf{x}$ is some input $\boldsymbol{\omega}_d$-encoding and $\mathbf{r}$ is generated using an α-RTK generator of encodings of 0, then we can reduce the probes in the α-RTK to K-linear probes on $\mathbf{r}$, given by some matrix $\mathbf{P}$. In the next reduction step, we give to the adversary $\mathbf{Px}$ and $\mathbf{Py}$, which are still both K-linear. We can then remove the probes on $\mathbf{r}$ as they are redundant, and that way we achieve separation between $\mathbf{x}$ and $\mathbf{y}$.

Definition 11. ((K-Input-Output Separative)). *Let $\omega \in \mathbb{F}$, K be a subfield of $\mathbb{F}$, $\alpha > 0$ and G be a gadget taking as input an $\boldsymbol{\omega}_d$-encoding $\mathbf{x}$, and returning an $\boldsymbol{\omega}_d$-encoding $\mathbf{y}$ of the same secret as $\mathbf{x}$. We say that G is K-Input-Output Separative (KIOS) when the distribution of $\mathbf{y}$ is uniform conditioned on $\mathbf{y}(\omega) = \mathbf{x}(\omega)$ and for every set of t probes P on G, there exists three sets of probes Q_x, Q_y, Q_2 such that*

*1. $|Q_x| \leq \alpha t, |Q_y| \leq \alpha t$
2. $(Q_x, Q_y, Q_2) \leq P$
3. Every probe in Q_x is K-linear in $\mathbf{x}$, and every probe in Q_y is K-linear in $\mathbf{y}$
4. The distributions Q_2 and $((\mathbf{x}, \mathbf{y})|(Q_x, Q_y))$ are independent*

We finally state in the Theorem below that placing a KIOS refresh in between RTIK circuits achieves region-probing security as well. The idea behind this composition Theorem is very similar to the intuition detailed in [GPRV21] on IOS composition. The basic idea is that when C_2 takes as input the output of some circuit C_1, one applies a KIOS refresh gadget on each input encoding of C_2. In the reduction, using the KIOS property, the leakage of the refresh is transferred to K-linear probes on C_1 and C_2. The leakage from the two subcircuits are then independent, and from the RTIK property, those leakages are K-linear, and Lemma 2 yields the region probing security.

Randomness/Security Tradeoffs of Refreshing. As stated throughout the subsection, using KIOS refresh gadgets on the encodings increases the amount of encodings $(\mathbf{x}_1, \ldots, \mathbf{x}_n)$ in the RTIK definition, which in turn increases the number of subcircuits in the region-probing security of the latter circuit, and eventually increases the region-probing ratio r. One has to keep in mind that refreshing the shares of an encoding is costly in terms of randomness (and slightly increases the total number of wires in the circuit), thus one has to carefully optimize the amount of refreshing in a circuit to reach the desired security level. Notice that we assume that we use a KIOS refresh gadget in the statement of the KIOS composition Theorem with slack factor 1. Indeed, when the slack factor of the KIOS refresh is 1, then the resulting circuit is RTIK, but when the slack factor $\alpha > 1$, the resulting circuit is not RTIK as it does not verify the property

3. of the RTIK definition, but it does verify the other ones 1. 2. and 4. When $\alpha > 1$, the resulting circuit remains r-region probing secure, but the number of tolerated probes per region is divided by α.

Theorem 4. (KIOS Composition Theorem). *Let $\mathcal{C}$ be a circuit over a finite field $\mathbb{F}$, and K be a subfield of $\mathbb{F}$. If there exists two disjoint RTIK subcircuits $\mathcal{C}_1, \mathcal{C}_2$ of $\mathcal{C}$ such that $\mathcal{C}$ is the composition of $\mathcal{C}_1$ and $\mathcal{C}_2$, then the circuit $\widehat{\mathcal{C}}$ obtained by applying a 1-KIOS refresh to the outputs of $\mathcal{C}_1$ that are inputs of $\mathcal{C}_2$ is RTIK.*

5   Miscellaneous RTIK and KIOS Gadgets

This section contains two ω_d-encodings building-block algorithms for constructing a masked compiler. Both algorithms rely on an additional restriction on d and $\deg_K(\omega)$: For security in our framework of RTIK gadgets, we need $d \leq \deg_K(\omega)$ and for correctness of the gadgets presented in this section, we also need $d \geq \deg_K(\omega)$. In other words, we need ω to be of degree *exactly* d. A classical result in algebra tells us that such a choice of ω is only possible when d is a factor of $[F : K]$. The reason why we add the restriction $d \geq \deg_K(\omega)$ for correctness is that we will exploit the minimal polynomial ω, which we write π_ω throughout the section, in ways that are detailed in the subsections below.

5.1   Folding Gadget

This subsection is dedicated to a folding gadget that exploits the algebraic structure brought by ω_d-encodings. Folding gadgets are those that on input some ω_{d_1}-encoding $\mathbf{x}$ return an ω_{d_2}-encoding $\mathbf{y}$ of the same secret, where $d_1 \geq d_2$. Since we only need $(d_1, d_2) = (2d - 1, d)$, we shall particularize to these specific values in the following, but our construction extends to $d_1 \geq 2d - 1$. We first recall the so-called NaiveFold algorithm, as used in [GJR18, GPRV21]. This folding algorithm does not require any extra condition to be correct, but entails a factor two loss in probe tolerance.

Algorithm 3. NaiveFold

Require: ω_{2d-1}-encoding $\mathbf{x}$
Ensure: $\mathbf{y} \in \mathbb{F}^d$ such that $\mathbf{x}^T \omega_{2d-1} = \mathbf{y}^T \omega_d$

1: **for** $i = 0$ to $d - 2$ **do**
2:     $y_i = x_i + \omega^d x_{d+i}$
3: **end for**
4: $y_{d-1} = x_{d-1}$
5: **return** $\mathbf{y}$

As stated above, one problem with this compression is that in the current state-of-the-art methods for proving probing security, when the adversary probes some $x_i + \omega^d x_{d+i}$, we have to give away both x_i and x_{d+i}. This entails a slack factor of 2 that doubles the number of probes of the adversary, hence in the end halves the number of probes tolerated in the region. Evaluating our folding matrix is an RTIK circuit (in particular it has no slack factor), but it may also contain more wires than the NaiveFold algorithm, thus the gain in probing ratio is slightly fewer than a factor 2. We also remark that the NaiveFold algorithm computes the reduction modulo $(X^d - \omega^d)$, while the folding matrix computes the reduction modulo π_ω.

The intuition of the construction is as follows: we define a full-rank folding matrix $\mathbf{F} \in K^{d \times (2d-1)}$, with coefficients in the subfield K, and mapping the ω_{2d-1}-encodings of some $x \in \mathbb{F}$ to the ω_d-encodings of this same x. This way, the computation of $\mathbf{y} = \mathbf{F}\mathbf{x}$ is K-linear and the folding circuit is RTIK. The existence of this matrix is only guaranteed when $\deg_K(\omega) \geq d$, therefore, so we can also use Lemma 2, we actually need the equality.

We now proceed to describe how to construct such a matrix, for a given ω and d. Suppose $\deg_K(\omega) = d$. Then, the minimal polynomial π_ω of ω over K has degree d, therefore $\pi = \omega^d - \pi_\omega$ is of degree $d-1$ and is such that $\pi(\omega) = \omega^d$. In general, any ω^{d+i} for $0 \leq i \leq d - 2$ is a polynomial in ω with coefficients in K and degree $\leq d - 1$. Let us therefore write π_i the column vector of coefficients of the i-th polynomial, for example $\pi_0 = \pi$. One can check that the matrix

$$\mathbf{F} = [\mathbf{I}_d \ \pi_0 \ \pi_1 \ \dots \ \pi_{d-2}]$$

satisfies the equation $\mathbf{F}^T \omega_d = \omega_{2d-1}$. This implies that $\omega_{2d-1}^T \mathbf{x} = \omega_d^T \mathbf{F} \mathbf{x} = \omega_d^T \mathbf{y}$.

Optimizing the Choice of ω. We emphasize on the fact that one should choose ω so as to minimize the count of operations in the folding process, to in turn minimize the ratio of tolerated probes per gate in the region. The element ω has to be chosen from a fixed field $\mathbb{F}$, among the elements of given degree d over some fixed subfield K and it seems hard to make a general statement about the sparsity of the matrix $\mathbf{F}$. Nonetheless, in very specific cases, $\mathbf{F}$ can be very sparse. For example, if $K = \mathbb{F}_p$, and $d + 1$ is a prime, one can chose ω to be a primitive $d + 1$-th root of unity. This way, the minimal polynomial of ω is $1 + X + \cdots + X^d$, and $\omega^{d+1} = 1$. Then, for any $0 \leq d - 3$, we have $\omega^{d+1+i} = \omega^i$ and $\omega^d = -\sum_{i=0}^{d-1} \omega^i$. In this particular setting, the computation of $\mathbf{y} = \mathbf{F}\mathbf{x}$ takes approximately $3d$ wires.

5.2 Refresh Gadgets

In this subsection, we describe a 2-RTK generator of ω_d-encodings of 0 that only uses $d - 1$ random field elements, as well as a 1-RTK generator of ω_d-encodings of 0 that uses $d - 1$ random field elements. While the second one seems strictly better than the first one, it also contains more gates, and thus depending on the use-case and the metric to be optimized, the first one may yield a better efficiency. We may recall that we are using the minimal polynomial π_ω of ω, which can only be made possible if $d\,|\,[\mathbb{F}:K]$.

2-RTK Algorithm. For the first construction, we require, on top of the condition $d\,|\,[\mathbb{F}:K]$, that the greatest common divisor of $\omega^d - \pi_\omega$ and $X^d - \omega^d$ is $X - \omega$. The intuition how Algorithm 4 works is as follows. First, the algorithm samples a uniformly random vector $\mathbf{x} \in \mathbb{F}^{d-1}$. Next, we compute $\mathbf{s} = \pi_\omega \mathbf{x}$, and we obtain a polynomial $\mathbf{s}$ of degree $d + d - 2$. The algorithm then returns $\mathbf{r}$ as the naive fold of $\mathbf{s}$ as described in the subsection above. The correctness is verified by construction: the evaluation of $\mathbf{r}$ in ω is 0 since π_ω divides $\mathbf{s}$ and the evaluation in ω is invariant through the naive fold. Remember that as explained in the previous section, the algorithm that takes as input an ω_d-encoding $\mathbf{x}$ and returns $\mathbf{y} = \mathbf{x} + \mathbf{r}$ where $\mathbf{r}$ is generated by such an α-RTK generator of encodings of 0 is α-KIOS.

Algorithm 4. PolyGenZero

Require: Masking order d with $d = \deg_K(\omega)$
Ensure: $\mathbf{r} \in \mathbb{F}^d$ such that $\mathbf{r}^T \omega_d = 0$

1: $\mathbf{x} \leftarrow \mathbb{F}^{d-1}$
2: $\mathbf{s} = \pi_\omega \mathbf{x}$
3: $\mathbf{r} = \mathsf{NaiveFold}(\mathbf{s})$
4: return $\mathbf{r}$

Proposition 5. *If* $\deg_K(\omega) = d$ *and the greatest common divisor of* π_ω *and* $X^d - \omega^d$ *is* $X - \omega$, *then* PolyGenZero *is 2-RTK.*

1-RTK Algorithm. The second RTK algorithm that we detail here is very similar to the refreshing procedure of Algorithm 8 that cuts the bilinear dependencies of our optimized RTIK multiplication gadget. We detail the instantiation of this RTK algorithm with Karatsuba's multiplication. More details on the associated evaluation matrix $\mathbf{M}_1$ and interpolation matrix $\mathbf{M}_2$ can be found in the full version of the paper. We start off by fixing a polynomial $\mathbf{u} \in \mathbb{F}^d$ with the following properties:

$$\text{The Karatsuba evaluation } \mathbf{u}' = \mathbf{M}_1 \mathbf{u} \text{ has all non-zero entries} \qquad (5)$$

$$\text{The greatest common divisor of } \mathbf{u}(X) \text{ and } \pi_\omega(X) \text{ is } X - \omega. \qquad (6)$$

We store the fix evaluation vector $\mathbf{u}'$. Then, Algorithm 5 samples a uniformly random polynomial $\mathbf{r} \in \mathbb{F}^d$, which therefore encodes a uniformly random value. We compute its Karatsuba evaluation of $\mathbf{r}' = \mathbf{M}_1 \mathbf{r}$, and multiply this vector with $\mathbf{u}'$ coordinate-wise to obtain $\mathbf{x}' = \mathbf{r}' \odot \mathbf{u}'$. Finally, we return $\mathbf{s} = \mathbf{F}\mathbf{M}_2 \mathbf{x}'$, which is the folding of the Karatsuba's interpolation of $\mathbf{x}'$.

Proposition 6. *If* $\deg_K(\omega) = d$ *and the vector* $\mathbf{u} \in \mathbb{F}^d$ *is such that Eqs.* (5) *and* (6) *hold, then Algorithm 5 is a 1-RTK generator of* ω_d-*encodings of* 0.

Algorithm 5. KaratsubaRTK

Require: Masking order d with $d = \deg_K(\omega)$
Ensure: $\mathbf{s} \in \mathbb{F}^d$ such that $\mathbf{s}^T \omega_d = 0$

1: $\mathbf{r} \leftarrow \mathbb{F}^{d-1}$
2: $\mathbf{r}' = \mathbf{M}_1 \mathbf{r}$
3: $\mathbf{x}' = \mathbf{r}' \odot \mathbf{u}'$
4: $\mathbf{s} = \mathbf{FM}_2(\mathbf{x}')$
5: return $\mathbf{s}$

5.3 Square Gadget in Characteristic 2

In this subsection, we show that the usual square gadget in characteristic 2 is RTIK. The typical example of use of this gadget is to compute the inverse of an element of $\mathbb{F}_{256}$ in the AES S-box as a subalgorithm of the square-and-multiply computation of the 255-th power. The RTIK security of this gadget falls into the wider class of coordinate-wise gadgets.

The algorithm works as follows: since we are working in characteristic 2, we have the classical identity that for any $x, y \in \mathbb{F}$, $(x + y)^2 = x^2 + y^2$. We apply this identity to the decryption of the encoding $\mathbf{x}$:

$$\left(\sum_{i=0}^{d-1} x_i \omega^i \right)^2 = \sum_{i=0}^{d-1} x_i^2 \omega^{2i}.$$

In other words, to compute and encoding $\mathbf{y}$ of the square of $\mathbf{x}^T \omega_d$, we can square each coordinate of $\mathbf{x}$, and multiply the result coordinate-wise with the vector $\mathbf{w} = (\omega^{-i})_{0 \le i \le d-1}$. Correctness follows from the latter identity, and since all the operations are coordinate-wise, this gadget is RTIK.

Algorithm 6. SquareGadget

Require: Encoding $\mathbf{x} \in \mathbb{F}^d$ of length d
Ensure: $\mathbf{y} \in \mathbb{F}^d$ such that $\mathbf{y}^T \omega_d = (\mathbf{x}^T \omega_d)^2$

1: $\mathbf{z} = \mathbf{x}^2$ ▷ Coordinate-wise operation
2: $\mathbf{y} = \mathbf{z} \odot \mathbf{w}$
3: return $\mathbf{y}$

---

6   Subquadratic Multiplication Gadgets

In this section, we show that the FFT-based multiplication gadget from GPRV [GPRV21] can be proven secure in the region-probing model - provided that there is sufficient structure in $\mathbb{F}$ for the targeted number of shares. The framework that we prove secure in the first subsection is actually a generalization of

GPRV, where the evaluation-interpolation polynomial multiplication algorithm used does not have to be the FFT, but *any* evaluation-interpolation-based multiplication gadget. There is a counterpart for using a polynomial multiplication with low bilinear multiplication complexity: roughly speaking, the fewer bilinear multiplications, the lower the upper bound on the available number of shares. In the second subsection, we detail an optimized version of the previous construction based on Karatsuba's multiplication. This masked multiplication gadget is RTIK (thus in the proper setting, it is region-probing secure) and performs competitively well (see the full version for detailed comparison with existing gadgets.) The mutliplication gadgets presented in this section verify the extra composability condition from Theorem 3.

6.1 (Re)Revisited Quasilinear Masked Multiplication: Region-Probing Security Proof for GPRV

In this subsection, we show that (almost) any polynomial multiplication algorithm can be turned into a masked multiplication gadget. More precisely, the polynomial multiplication gadgets that fit our transformation ˆare those algorithms that are based on evaluation-interpolation. This definition encompasses Karatsuba's algorithm, all Toom-Cook variants (which contains Karatsuba) and the FFT. The FFT instantiation of this transformation is GPRV's multiplication.

Definition 12. (Evaluation-Interpolation-Based Polynomial Multiplication Algorithms). *Let $\mathcal{M}$ be an algorithm taking as input two polynomials of degree $d - 1$ that returns the product of the two inputs and K a subfield of $\mathbb{F}$. We say that $\mathcal{M}$ is a K-Interpolation-Multiplication algorithm (K-IM for short) when there exists matrices $\mathbf{M}_1, \mathbf{M}_2$ with coefficients in K such that for any $(\mathbf{a}, \mathbf{b}) \in \mathbb{F}_{d-1}[X]^2$, we have $\mathcal{M}(a, b) = \mathbf{M}_2 \cdot (\mathbf{M}_1 \mathbf{a} \odot \mathbf{M}_1 \mathbf{b})$.*

The architecture of our transformation applied to the FFT follows the blueprint from [GPRV21], whose security relies on the assumption that the circuits computing the evaluation and interpolation of the FFT are t-probing secure for some t. The assumption can be tested by exhausting the subsets of probes for a given size among the circuits, which is only possible for small number of shares. Our gadgets on the other hand are proven RTIK, which in turn yields region-probing security through Lemma 1. Our gadgets are thus theoretically sound, since they rely on no assumption, but rather a condition relating the multiplication algorithm $\mathcal{M}$, the order of masking d and to some extent the size of $\mathbb{F}$ (we need $d \leq \log |\mathbb{F}|$). This condition is $d \leq k$ where $k = [\mathbb{F} : K]$, in order to apply Lemma 1. To be specific, K is defined as the subfield such that $\mathcal{M}$ is a K-IM, as defined in Definition 12. In other words, K is the smallest subfield of $\mathbb{F}$ such that the evaluation and interpolation operations induced by $\mathcal{M}$ are K-linear.

Intuition of the Transformation. The transformation of a suitable multiplication algorithm $\mathcal{M}$ taking as input two polynomials $\mathbf{a}, \mathbf{b}$ into a secure multiplication gadget works as follows. Since $\mathcal{M}$ can be split into two phases, namely evaluation and interpolation, our gadget $\widehat{\mathcal{M}}$ starts by computing the evaluation of both polynomial entries $\mathbf{a}' = \mathbf{M}_1\mathbf{a}$ and $\mathbf{b}' = \mathbf{M}_1\mathbf{b}$. Then, $\widehat{\mathcal{M}}$ computes the evaluation $\mathbf{x}' = \mathbf{a}' \odot \mathbf{b}'$ of the product $\mathbf{ab}$ by multiplying coordinate-wise their evaluations. Before proceeding to interpolation, we need to cut the bilinear dependencies between $\mathbf{a}, \mathbf{b}$, which is done using the IOS refresh template Algorithm 2, with a suitably chosen $\mathbf{v}$ (that depends on the interpolation of $\mathcal{M}$) and ArithGenZero Algorithm 1. $\widehat{\mathcal{M}}$ now computes the interpolation of the refreshed encoding $\mathbf{y}'$, which yields the $2d - 1$ coefficients of a polynomial $\mathbf{z}$ encoding $\mathbf{ab}$. Notice that if $\mathbf{a}(\omega) = a$, $\mathbf{b}(\omega) = b$, we want to find a polynomial $\mathbf{c}$ that encodes ab, for the same ω and masking order d. To this end, we multiply $\mathbf{z}$ with the folding matrix $\mathbf{F}$ so $\mathbf{c} = \mathbf{Fz}$ has degree $d - 1$, and $\mathbf{c}(\omega) = \mathbf{z}(\omega) = \mathbf{a}(\omega)\mathbf{b}(\omega) = ab$, and the algorithm finally returns this $\mathbf{c}$. The construction of the matrix $\mathbf{F}$ is detailed in Sect. 5.1.[4]

Intuition of the Security Proof. By definition of K, all the wires in the evaluation and interpolation subcircuits are K-linear. When the adversary probes an $x_i = a'_i b'_i$, the reduction gives him both factors a'_i, b'_i, which we recall are K-linear functions of $\mathbf{a}, \mathbf{b}$. The effect of the refresh is to create a third independent encoding $\mathbf{c}$ (the output of the gadget), together with a third probing region in which the probes are reducible to K-linear functions of $\mathbf{c}$. Notice that since the length of $\mathbf{x}$ is $T(d)$ (the multiplication complexity of $\mathcal{M}$), the cost of this refresh in randomness is $T(d)\log T(d)/2$. When the folding matrix $\mathbf{F}$ does not exist, one can use the NaiveFold algorithm instead. Probes in the NaiveFold of the form $(z_i + \omega^d z_{d+i})$ are reduced to (z_i, z_{d+i}), doubling the total number of probes of the adversary in the circuit.

Algorithm 7. Multiplication gadget $\widehat{\mathcal{M}}(\mathbf{a}, \mathbf{b})$. The algorithm $\mathcal{R}$ on line 4 is Algorithm 2 instantiated with ArithGenZero

Require: A K-IM $\mathcal{M}$ with matrices $\mathbf{M}_1, \mathbf{M}_2$, folding matrix $\mathbf{F}$ (see Subsection 5.1) and two input encodings $\mathbf{a}, \mathbf{b} \in \mathbb{F}^d$
Ensure: $\mathbf{c} \in \mathbb{F}^d$ such that $\boldsymbol{\omega}_d^T \mathbf{a} \cdot \boldsymbol{\omega}_d^T \mathbf{b} = \boldsymbol{\omega}_d^T \mathbf{c}$

1: $\mathbf{a}' = \mathbf{M}_1\mathbf{a}$	▷ Evaluation of $\mathbf{a}$
2: $\mathbf{b}' = \mathbf{M}_1\mathbf{b}$	▷ Evaluation of $\mathbf{b}$
3: $\mathbf{x}' = \mathbf{a}' \odot \mathbf{b}'$	▷ Component-wise multiplication of evaluations
4: $\mathbf{y}' = \mathcal{R}(\mathbf{x}', \mathbf{M}_2^T \boldsymbol{\omega}_{2d-1})$	▷ Refresh
5: $\mathbf{z} = \mathbf{M}_2\mathbf{y}'$	▷ Interpolation of the product
6: $\mathbf{c} = \mathbf{Fz}$	▷ Folding
7: return $\mathbf{c}$	

---

[4] We assume that the folding matrix exists i.e $d|[\mathbb{F} : K]$. If this condition is not verified, one can still use the NaiveFold at the cost of roughly halving the tolerated probing ratio.

Theorem 5. *Let d be an order of masking, K be a subfield of $\mathbb{F}$, $\mathcal{M}$ be a K-IM and $\omega \in \mathbb{F}$ such that $\deg_K(\omega) = d$. Then, the instantiation of Algorithm 7 with $\mathcal{M}$ is a correct RTIK multiplication gadget.*

6.2   Efficient Karatsuba-Based Multiplication Gadget

In this subsection, we detail an optimized version of the GPRV-type transformation from the previous subsection. The optimizations come from various technical improvements detailed below. We assume in the description of Algorithm 8 that d is a divisor of k, where k is the degree of $\mathbb{F}$ over its prime field. This assumption allows us to work with the degree d minimal polynomial π of ω over K, hence use the folding matrix Sect. 5.1.

Choice of Karatsuba's Multiplication. Choosing particularly Karatuba's multiplication benefits our algorithm in several ways. Firstly, Karatsuba's algorithm offers a trade-off between the size of the circuit and the number of bilinear multiplications that is advantageous for degrees relevant to masking in practice (e.g. between 2 and a few dozens). Second, the subfield K associated to Karatsuba's algorithm is $\mathbb{F}$'s prime field, which maximizes the degree k of $\mathbb{F}/K$. Remind that in our framework, the maximum number of probes per region is $k - 1$. Finally, Karatsuba's algorithm verifies a crucial property for the randomness optimization detailed below.

Linear Randomness. The transformation presented in Sect. 6.1 yields a multiplication gadget running in the same time $O(T(d))$ as $\mathcal{M}$, and requiring $O(T(d) \log T(d))$ random field elements. The randomness cost of the multiplication comes solely from the use of ArithGenZero on the evaluation vector of the product. Intuitively, it may seem expensive to spend $T(d) \log T(d)/2$ random field elements on refreshing an encoding that masks the product of the two inputs. The encoding $\mathbf{x}'$ to be refreshed is even compressed into the ω_d-encoding $\mathbf{c}$, thus a single ω_d-encoding of 0 is enough entropy to mask $\mathbf{x}'$. To refresh $\mathbf{x}'$ into $\mathbf{y}'$, we compute $\mathbf{x}' = \mathbf{y}' + \mathbf{r}' \odot \mathbf{u}'$ as follows. We sample a completely uniform ω_d-encoding $\mathbf{r}$ from $\mathbb{F}^d$, and compute its Karatsuba's evaluation $\mathbf{r}' = \mathbf{M}_1\mathbf{r}$. We then multiply this vector $\mathbf{r}'$ coordinate-wise with a fixed vector $\mathbf{u}'$ and add this vector to $\mathbf{x}'$ to obtain $\mathbf{y}'$. This vector $\mathbf{u}'$ is the Karatsuba's evaluation of some fixed polynomial $\mathbf{u}$ satisfying the following two properties.

1. We require that $\mathbf{u}$ is such that its evaluation $\mathbf{u}'$ has all non-zero coefficients. This condition allows us to swap the probes of the form r_i' for probes of the form $r_i' u_i'$.
2. We require that the GCD of $\mathbf{u}(X)$ and $\pi(X)$ is $X - \omega$. The first consequence of the latter condition is that $\mathbf{u}(\omega) = 0$, thus $\mathbf{r}\mathbf{u}(\omega) = 0$ from which we deduce the correctness of the gadget. The second consequence of this condition is that the reduction modulo (π) of the polynomial $\mathbf{r}\mathbf{u}$ is therefore a uniformly random encoding of 0, from which we conclude the mutual independence of $\mathbf{a}, \mathbf{b}, \mathbf{c}$.

Special Variant for $d = 2$. We mention that a variant of Algorithm 8, where $\mathbf{r}$ is sampled with an RTC generator of encodings of 0 such as ArithGenZero and $\mathbf{u}$ only has to be such that $\mathbf{u}'$ has all non-zero entries. This variant is also RTIK and uses $\frac{d \log d}{2}$ random elements. While $\frac{d \log d}{2}$ means more random elements than the d random elements needed for Algorithm 8 whenever $d \geq 3$, for $d = 2$, this variant uses only one random element versus two for Algorithm 8.

Algorithm 8. Multiplication gadget karaopti$(\mathbf{a}, \mathbf{b})$

Require: $\mathbf{a}, \mathbf{b} \in \mathbb{F}^d$ independent encodings
Ensure: $\mathbf{c} \in \mathbb{F}^d$ such that $\omega_d^T \mathbf{a} \cdot \omega_d^T \mathbf{b} = \omega_d^T \mathbf{c}$

1: $\mathbf{a}' = \mathbf{M}_1 \mathbf{a}$	▷ Evaluation of $\mathbf{a}$
2: $\mathbf{b}' = \mathbf{M}_1 \mathbf{b}$	▷ Evaluation of $\mathbf{b}$
3: $\mathbf{x}' = \mathbf{a}' \odot \mathbf{b}'$	▷ Share-wise multiplication
4: $\mathbf{r} \leftarrow \mathbb{F}^d$	▷ Fresh uniform encoding
5: $\mathbf{r}' = \mathbf{M}_1 \mathbf{r}$	
6: $\mathbf{s}' = \mathbf{r}' \odot \mathbf{u}'$	
7: $\mathbf{y}' = \mathbf{x}' + \mathbf{s}'$	▷ Refresh
8: $\mathbf{z} = \mathbf{M}_2 \mathbf{y}'$	▷ Interpolation of the product
9: $\mathbf{c} = \mathbf{F}\mathbf{z}$	▷ Folding
10: return $\mathbf{c}$	

Theorem 6. *Let $\mathbb{F}$ be a finite field of degree k over its prime field K, $\omega \in \mathbb{F}$ be a fixed element of $\mathbb{F}$, π be the minimal polynomial of ω over K, d be the number of shares and $\mathbf{u} \in \mathbb{F}^d$ a fixed polynomial. Let $\mathbf{M}_1, \mathbf{M}_2$ be the evaluation and interpolation matrices of Karatsuba's multiplication. We assume that the two entries $\mathbf{a}, \mathbf{b}$ are mutually independent encodings.*

If we have the following three properties:

1. $\deg_K(\omega) = d$
2. $gcd(\mathbf{u}(X), \pi(X)) = X - \omega$
3. $\mathbf{M}_1 \mathbf{u} = \mathbf{u}'$ has all non-zero coefficients

then karaopti *is a correct RTIK multiplication gadget with respect to* $\mathbf{a}, \mathbf{b}, \mathbf{c}$.

References

[ADF16] Andrychowicz, M., Dziembowski, S., Faust, S.: Circuit compilers with $O(1/\log(n))$ leakage rate. In: Fischlin, M., Coron, J.-S. (eds.) EURO-CRYPT 2016. LNCS, vol. 9666, pp. 586–615. Springer, Heidelberg (2016). https://doi.org/10.1007/978-3-662-49896-5_21

[AIS18] Ananth, P., Ishai, Y., Sahai, A.: Private circuits: a modular approach. In: Shacham, H., Boldyreva, A. (eds.) CRYPTO 2018. LNCS, vol. 10993, pp. 427–455. Springer, Cham (2018). https://doi.org/10.1007/978-3-319-96878-0_15

[BBC+18] Barthe, G., Belaïd, S., Cassiers, G., Fouque, P.-A., Grégoire, B., Standaert, F.-X.: maskverif: Automated analysis of software and hardware higher-order masked implementations. Cryptology ePrint Archive (2018)

[BBC+19] Barthe, G., Belaïd, S., Cassiers, G., Fouque, P.-A., Grégoire, B., Standaert, F.-X.: maskVerif: automated verification of higher-order masking in presence of physical defaults. In: Sako, K., Schneider, S., Ryan, P.Y.A. (eds.) ESORICS 2019. LNCS, vol. 11735, pp. 300–318, Springer, Cham (2019). https://doi.org/10.1007/978-3-030-29959-0_15

[BBD+16] Barthe, G., et al.: Strong non-interference and type-directed higher-order masking. In: Proceedings of the 2016 ACM SIGSAC Conference on Computer and Communications Security, pp. 116–129 (2016)

[BBP+16] Belaïd, S., Benhamouda, F., Passelègue, A., Prouff, E., Thillard, A., Vergnaud, D.: Randomness complexity of private circuits for multiplication. In: Fischlin, M., Coron, J.-S. (eds.) EUROCRYPT 2016. LNCS, vol. 9666, pp. 616–648. Springer, Heidelberg (2016). https://doi.org/10.1007/978-3-662-49896-5_22

[BBP+17] Belaïd, S., Benhamouda, F., Passelègue, A., Prouff, E., Thillard, A., Vergnaud, D.: Private multiplication over finite fields. In: Katz, J., Shacham, H. (eds.) CRYPTO 2017. LNCS, vol. 10403, pp. 397–426. Springer, Cham (2017). https://doi.org/10.1007/978-3-319-63697-9_14

[BC22] Bronchain, O., Cassiers, G.: Bitslicing arithmetic/boolean masking conversions for fun and profit with application to lattice-based KEMs. Cryptology ePrint Archive (2022)

[BCLV17] Bernstein, D.J., Chuengsatiansup, C., Lange, T., van Vredendaal, C.: NTRU prime: reducing attack surface at low cost. In: Adams, C., Camenisch, J. (eds.) SAC 2017. LNCS, vol. 10719, pp. 235–260. Springer, Cham (2018). https://doi.org/10.1007/978-3-319-72565-9_12

[BCP+20] Belaïd, S., Coron, J.-S., Prouff, E., Rivain, M., Taleb, A:R.: Random probing security: verification, composition, expansion and new constructions. In: Micciancio, D., Ristenpart, T. (eds.) CRYPTO 2020. LNCS, vol. 12170, pp. 339–368. Springer, Cham (2020). https://doi.org/10.1007/978-3-030-56784-2_12

[BCPZ16] Battistello, A., Coron, J.-S., Prouff, E., Zeitoun, R.: Horizontal side-channel attacks and countermeasures on the ISW masking scheme. In: Gierlichs, B., Poschmann, A.Y. (eds.) CHES 2016. LNCS, vol. 9813, pp. 23–39. Springer, Heidelberg (2016). https://doi.org/10.1007/978-3-662-53140-2_2

[BRT21] Belaïd, S., Rivain, M., Taleb, A.R.: On the power of expansion: more efficient constructions in the random probing model. In: Canteaut, A., Standaert, F.-X. (eds.) EUROCRYPT 2021. LNCS, vol. 12697, pp. 313–343. Springer, Cham (2021). https://doi.org/10.1007/978-3-030-77886-6_11

[BRTV21] Belaïd, S., Rivain, M., Taleb, A.R., Vergnaud, D.: Dynamic random probing expansion with quasi linear asymptotic complexity. In: Tibouchi, M., Wang, H. (eds.) ASIACRYPT 2021. LNCS, vol. 13091, pp. 157–188. Springer, Cham (2021). https://doi.org/10.1007/978-3-030-92075-3_6

[CGMZ21] Coron, J.-S., Gérard, F., Montoya, S., Zeitoun, R.: High-order polynomial comparison and masking lattice-based encryption. Cryptology ePrint Archive (2021)

[CPRR13] Coron, J.-S., Prouff, E., Rivain, M., Roche, T.: Higher-order side channel security and mask refreshing. In: Moriai, S. (ed.) FSE 2013. LNCS, vol. 8424, pp. 410–424. Springer, Heidelberg (2014). https://doi.org/10.1007/978-3-662-43933-3_21

[CS20] Cassiers, G., Standaert, F.-X.: Trivially and efficiently composing masked gadgets with probe isolating non-interference. IEEE Trans. Inf. Forensics Secur. **15**, 2542–2555 (2020)

[DDF14] Duc, A., Dziembowski, S., Faust, S.: Unifying leakage models: from probing attacks to noisy leakage. In: Nguyen, P.Q., Oswald, E. (eds.) EUROCRYPT 2014. LNCS, vol. 8441, pp. 423–440. Springer, Heidelberg (2014). https://doi.org/10.1007/978-3-642-55220-5_24

[DFS15] Dziembowski, S., Faust, S., Skorski, M.: Noisy leakage revisited. In: Oswald, E., Fischlin, M. (eds.) EUROCRYPT 2015. LNCS, vol. 9057, pp. 159–188. Springer, Heidelberg (2015). https://doi.org/10.1007/978-3-662-46803-6_6

[DVBV22] D'Anvers, J.-P., Van Beirendonck, M., Verbauwhede., I.: Revisiting higher-order masked comparison for lattice-based cryptography: algorithms and bit-sliced implementations. Cryptology ePrint Archive (2022)

[GJR18] Goudarzi, D., Joux, A., Rivain, M.: How to securely compute with noisy leakage in quasilinear complexity. In: Peyrin, T., Galbraith, S. (eds.) ASIACRYPT 2018. LNCS, vol. 11273, pp. 547–574. Springer, Cham (2018). https://doi.org/10.1007/978-3-030-03329-3_19

[GPRV21] Goudarzi, D., Prest, T., Rivain, M., Vergnaud, D.: Probing security through input-output separation and revisited quasilinear masking. IACR Trans. Cryptograph. Hardw. Embed. Syst. 599–640 (2021)

[ISW03] Ishai, Y., Sahai, A., Wagner, D.: Private circuits: securing hardware against probing attacks. In: Boneh, D. (ed.) CRYPTO 2003. LNCS, vol. 2729, pp. 463–481. Springer, Heidelberg (2003). https://doi.org/10.1007/978-3-540-45146-4_27

[KJJ99] Kocher, P., Jaffe, J., Jun, B.: Differential power analysis. In: Wiener, M. (ed.) CRYPTO 1999. LNCS, vol. 1666, pp. 388–397. Springer, Heidelberg (1999). https://doi.org/10.1007/3-540-48405-1_25

[Koc96] Kocher, P.C.: Timing attacks on implementations of Diffie-Hellman, RSA, DSS, and other systems. In: Koblitz, N. (ed.) CRYPTO 1996. LNCS, vol. 1109, pp. 104–113. Springer, Heidelberg (1996). https://doi.org/10.1007/3-540-68697-5_9

[PR13] Prouff, E., Rivain, M.: Masking against side-channel attacks: a formal security proof. In: Johansson, T., Nguyen, P.Q. (eds.) EUROCRYPT 2013. LNCS, vol. 7881, pp. 142–159. Springer, Heidelberg (2013). https://doi.org/10.1007/978-3-642-38348-9_9

[RP10] Rivain, M., Prouff, E.: Provably secure higher-order masking of AES. In: Mangard, S., Standaert, F.-X. (eds.) CHES 2010. LNCS, vol. 6225, pp. 413–427. Springer, Heidelberg (2010). https://doi.org/10.1007/978-3-642-15031-9_28

Practically Efficient Private Set Intersection from Trusted Hardware with Side-Channels

Felix Dörre, Jeremias Mechler$^{(\boxtimes)}$, and Jörn Müller-Quade

KASTEL Security Research Labs, Karlsruhe Institute of Technology, Karlsruhe, Germany
{felix.doerre,jeremias.mechler,joern.mueller-quade}@kit.edu

Abstract. Private set intersection (PSI) is one of the most important privacy-enhancing technologies with applications such as malware and spam detection, recognition of child pornography, contact discovery, or, more recently, contact tracing. In this paper, we investigate how PSI can be constructed and implemented simply and practically efficient. To this end, a natural possibility is the use of trusted execution environments (TEEs), which are commonly used in place of a trusted third party due to their presumed security guarantees. However, this trust is often not warranted: Today's TEEs like Intel SGX suffer from a number of side-channels that allow the host to learn secrets of a TEE, unless countermeasures are taken. Furthermore, due to the high complexity and closed-source nature, it cannot be ruled out that a TEE is passively corrupted, *i.e.* leaks secrets to the manufacturer or a government agency such as the NSA. When constructing a protocol using TEEs, such (potential) vulnerabilities need to be accounted for. Otherwise, all security may be lost.

We propose a protocol for two-party PSI whose security holds in a setting where TEEs cannot be fully trusted, *e.g.* due to the existence of side-channels. In particular, we deal with the possibilities that i) the TEE is completely transparent for the host, except for very simple secure cryptographic operations or ii) that it leaks *all* secrets to a third party, *e.g.* the manufacturer. Even in this challenging setting, our protocol is not only very fast, but also conceptually simple, which is an important feature as more complex protocols tend to be implemented with subtle security faults.

To formally capture this setting, we define variants of the ideal functionality for TEEs due to Pass *et al.* (EUROCRYPT 2017). Using these functionalities, we prove our protocol's security, which holds under universal composition. To illustrate the usefulness of our model, we sketch other possible applications like (randomized) oblivious transfer or private computation of the Hamming distance.

Our PSI implementation, which uses Intel SGX as TEE, computes the intersection between two sets with 2^{24} 128-bit elements in 7.3 s. This makes our protocol the fastest PSI protocol to date with respect to single-threaded performance.

Keywords: private set intersection · universal composability · trusted execution environments

© International Association for Cryptologic Research 2023
J. Guo and R. Steinfeld (Eds.): ASIACRYPT 2023, LNCS 14441, pp. 268–301, 2023.
https://doi.org/10.1007/978-981-99-8730-6_9

1   Introduction

Private set intersection (PSI) allows mutually distrusting parties $P_1, \ldots, P_n$ with input sets $S_1, \ldots, S_n$ to compute the intersection $S = S_1 \cap \cdots \cap S_n$ such that a dishonest party does not learn anything about another party's set that it cannot compute from its own input and the intersection S.

PSI can be used for a number of problems, making it an important privacy-enhancing technology:

- malware [45,46] or spam [23] detection, where a server holds a list of signatures against which a client wants to check an email or an executable,
- recognition of child pornography, for example on mobile devices or on cloud storage, either by direct comparison or through perceptual hashing [30],
- contact discovery for messenger services [33],
- COVID contact tracing [21] or
- learning if secret agents have been arrested [3].

In many of these cases, it is not only suffices, but highly desirable for privacy reasons if only *one* party learns the intersection result. This natural variant, called one-sided PSI [42], has been widely considered in the literature (*e.g.* [3, 22,26,40–42]).

Security Notions for PSI. For a long time, the security of PSI protocols has mainly been considered for the case of passive corruptions in a stand-alone setting, *i.e.* for *semi-honest* adversaries that adhere to the protocol description and without the presence of other protocol executions. While this setting allows (relatively) efficient protocols, the offered security is often insufficient: In real life, one or more of the protocol parties may behave maliciously with the intent of gaining information about another party's secrets. Thus, it is very important that PSI protocols are secure even against *malicious* adversaries. Most recent works like [40,41] have both a semi-honest and a malicious variant with the malicious variant being a bit slower as it has to perform additional consistency checks.

Typically, protocols are seldom executed in isolation. When PSI is used for contact discovery by a messenger on a smartphone, other apps are executed in the background and may also execute cryptographic protocols, *e.g.* the establishment of TLS sessions. These other cryptographic protocols should not affect the security of the PSI, and vice versa.

In order for security to hold in such a setting, an appropriate security notion that is closed under general concurrent composition, *i.e.* holds in the presence of *arbitrary* other protocols that are executed concurrently, is necessary. This is fulfilled by Universally Composable (UC) security [10].

Composable Security. UC security is based on the simulation paradigm where the "real-world" execution of a protocol π is compared to the "ideal-world" execution of an ideal functionality $\mathcal{F}$, which acts as a trusted third party performing the desired task by definition. For every real-world adversary $\mathcal{A}$ in the execution with π, the existence of a corresponding ideal-world adversary $\mathcal{S}$ interacting with

F. Dörre et al.

$\mathcal{F}$, called the simulator, must be proven. Both executions must be indistinguishable for an interactive distinguisher $\mathcal{Z}$, called the environment. The environment (adaptively) chooses the parties' inputs and may communicate with the adversary freely throughout the execution. If $\mathcal{Z}$ cannot distinguish between the real and the ideal execution, then all properties of the ideal execution, which is secure by definition, carry over to the real execution. In contrast to stand-alone security notions, this strong security notion is harder to achieve.

In order to achieve UC security, several prerequisites have to be met:

1. A trusted setup such as a common reference string, a public key infrastructure or a random oracle is necessary [12,13].
2. The simulator has to be able to *extract* the inputs of a corrupted party.

For a large class of setups such as a common reference string or a public-key infrastructure, a protocol's communication complexity is lower-bounded by the size of a party's input (implicit in [36]). Unlike in protocols with stand-alone security, we thus cannot hope to *compress* the set elements by simply (locally) applying a cryptographic hash function, as this would prevent extraction.

Use of Random Oracles in Previous Protocols. In order to circumvent this extractability problem and still allow compression, many protocols for composable PSI (*e.g.* [22,40–42]) resort to the use of *random oracles*, which can be thought of as idealized hash functions. As they provide input awareness, extraction and thus composable security becomes possible.

However, all security may be lost when the random oracle is instantiated by *e.g.* a cryptographic hash function [14,15]. Thus, there usually is a large gap between the security proof and the actual security provided by the modified protocol used in the implementation. Moreover, security proofs may use properties such as *code-correlation robustness* (*e.g.* in [22,40]) provided by the random oracle, which also may not be fulfilled by its instantiation.

Additional and more subtle problems may arise during protocol composition, as several protocol instances may implicitly *share state* via a common hash function[1] that is used to instantiate the random oracle, possibly allowing malleability attacks. This also holds for *global* random oracles [9,16], unless special care to obtain the session ID or hash key is taken. Thus, the gap between the protocol with security proof and the implemented protocol may be even larger.

Hardware Assumptions as Alternatives. In order to close the gap between the protocol under analysis and the protocol to be implemented while still achieving high performance, in particular with network communication complexity that is independent of the elements' size, we investigate how hardware assumptions can be leveraged to achieve composable PSI.

---

[1] While this can be prevented in principle by using appropriate building blocks (*e.g.* by obtaining an independent key for the hash function using a coin-toss build from a non-malleable commitment scheme), we are not aware that this is done in practice.

Trusted execution environments (TEEs), which have been available for several years on mainstream CPUs, promise the secure execution of user-supplied programs in isolation from the host system at near native speed. In particular, some modern TEEs have a feature called *remote attestation*, which enables a third party to obtain evidence about the code running inside a TEE. This is sufficient to establish a cryptographic secret with the TEE. Using this secret, private inputs can be passed into the TEE for further processing. Due to the isolation properties of the TEE, secrets are assumed to be protected even if the computer hosting the TEE is compromised.

With such strong assumptions, one-sided PSI for two parties seems trivial: Both parties perform remote attestation with the TEE, thereby verifying that it runs the expected code and establishing a secure channel. Via this secure channel, they send their private inputs. After the TEE has received the inputs and computed the intersection, one party obtains the output. However, it can be shown that *any* protocol with only one TEE cannot satisfy UC security [7,39] for many tasks, including PSI, highlighting the technical challenges in achieving such a strong security notion.

Reducing Trust. Leaving this fact aside, the simple PSI protocol suffers from several problems. First of all, the run-time of the program executed inside the TEE may depend on a party's secret input: If one input is $\{0\}$, the computation might take one second. If it is $\{1\}$, it might take one minute. This inherent timing side-channel, which can be easily observed from the outside by waiting for the result, is not mitigated by TEEs.

Even if the run-time of the program in question is not subject to such gross timing side-channels, the TEE usually needs to be trusted completely, which may not be warranted:

- TEEs such as Intel SGX may not protect against even more subtle side-channels resulting *e.g.* from memory access patterns by design [19], possibly requiring expensive techniques such as oblivious RAM (ORAM) [1,24] to mitigate them.
- They repeatedly suffered from a number of vulnerabilities exposing additional side-channels, allowing the party hosting the TEE to learn all its secrets and even impersonate a TEE [37,38,43,48].

Even when ignoring *vulnerabilities*, side-channels that exist by design could render the above protocol completely insecure, as the party hosting the TEE could be able to learn all the inputs of the other party. Thus, measures against side-channels have to be included into the protocol design.

Transparent enclaves, introduced by [47], (also in [39]) consider this setting. Transparent enclaves are able to securely perform remote attestation, but otherwise have no secrets whatsoever with respect to their respective host, thereby capturing all possible side-channels. Interestingly, such transparent enclaves still allow for the efficient realization of cryptographic building blocks like commitment schemes or zero-knowledge proof systems [39,47]. This is because the transparent TEE only sees secrets belonging to its owner (and attestation secrets also remain secure, preventing a corrupted party to impersonate a TEE). For the same reason, transparent enclaves can be used as efficient passive-security-to-active-security compilers.

In line with the model of [39, 47], we consider an intermediate setting between fully trusted and fully transparent TEEs. In particular, we assume that very simple cryptographic building blocks like key exchange or secret-key encryption schemes are also implemented side-channel-free, just like the signature scheme in [39] used for remote attestation. Otherwise, the enclaves are again completely transparent. We believe that such an intermediate model is well-motivated as

- it can be plausibly realized (see Sect. 3.4 for a discussion) in practice,
- provides a natural framework for the design and analysis of protocols using cryptography (or possibly other operations on sensitive data) in a setting where side-channels may be present and
- if even the proposed simple operations cannot be performed securely, it may be plausible to assume that remote attestation is also impossible.

We call such a TEE *almost-transparent*.

Additionally, we consider the setting of "passively corrupted" or "semi-honest" TEEs where *all* TEEs leak *all* secrets (to a third party that does not participate in the protocol execution as a party), *e.g.* to the manufacturer or some government agency. In the case of Intel SGX, such fears are particularly plausible due to the use of an Intel attestation service [29] or the out-of-band communication supported by many chipsets [31]. A similar model has been proposed before [32].

Interestingly, even such a weak assumption enables to construct a protocol for one-sided PSI that is practically efficient and features a low asymptotic communication complexity.

In order to formally capture the proposed variants, we adapt the global ideal functionality for TEEs of [39]. Given the fact that *e.g.* Intel SGX instances share state via common attestation keys, it is crucial that this shared state is also captured in the model. Here, this is achieved by using a *global* functionality that can be used by multiple protocols, faithfully capturing subtleties that may arise from such shared state. Using our adapted functionalities, we can prove the security of our protocol in the UC framework [10, 12], using the "Universal Composability with Global Subroutines" (UCGS) [4] formalism to capture global ideal functionalities within UC.

In contrast to protocols using random oracles, we believe that the structural gap between the protocol under analysis and the protocol to be implemented is much smaller in our case as our model faithfully captures the expected security guarantees of TEEs without fully trusting them.

Looking ahead, we will demonstrate the usefulness of our model by proposing protocols for additional interesting tasks like oblivious transfer or computing the Hamming distance.

In the following, we give an informal description of our construction for PSI.

1.1 The PSI Protocol in a Nutshell

In our protocol for two-party one-sided PSI, we assume that both protocol parties P_1 and P_2 each have access to a TEE. Intuitively, we use the TEEs to

1. implement a "query-once" oracle for the party P_1 that receives the output and to
2. enforce honest behavior of the party P_2 that does not receive the intersection, but can compute arbitrary hashes (without having any hashes of P_1 to compare against).

Using their TEEs together with local computations, P_1 and P_2 both create hashes of their encrypted inputs (in order to improve communication efficiency), with P_2 eventually sending its hashes to P_1, which can then compute the intersection.

The interaction with the TEEs is done in a way such that the TEEs neither learn the parties' inputs nor the intersection's size.

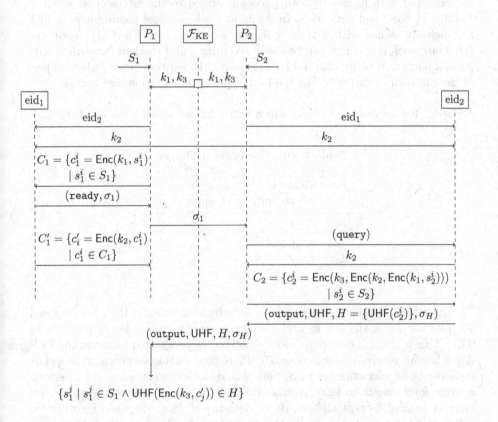

Fig. 1. Overview of the messages exchanged in our PSI protocol (simplified).

Protocol Description. An overview of the messages exchanged is given in Fig. 1. Initially, P_1 and P_2 exchange two keys k_1 and k_3 through the ideal functionality for key exchange $\mathcal{F}_{\mathrm{KE}}$. They use k_1 to deterministically encrypt their sets S_1 resp. S_2. P_1 then sends the resulting set of ciphertexts C_1 to its TEE, which encrypts these ciphertexts deterministically with another key k_2 that it has exchanged with the TEE of P_2, resulting in C_1'. This key k_2 can be obtained by P_2 from its TEE, but not by P_1. P_2 encrypts its ciphertexts of S_2 under k_1 iteratively also under k_2 and k_3, resulting in the set C_2. The ciphertexts in C_2, each for one element in S_2, are sorted lexicographically (to later hide the "position" of elements in the intersection) and then sent to P_2's TEE (via P_2). P_2's TEE samples a universal hash function UHF, evaluates UHF on the ciphertexts, resulting in the set H and returns UHF and H to P_2, which forwards the (signed) hashes to P_1. After having obtained the hashes H, P_1 queries its TEE to obtain C_1'. Using k_3, P_1 also encrypts the ciphertexts in C_1' with k_3, applies UHF and compares its own hashes with the hashes obtained from P_2 in H. Each element in S_1 that is associated with hashes of both parties is added to the intersection result S. Finally, P_1 sorts and outputs S. In our model, all messages coming from a TEE are digitally signed with a trusted master key and include a TEE's code and ID. Thus, such signatures can be easily recognized and checked for authenticity. Also, a party can verify that a TEE is running the expected code, which is part of the protocol description. For the formal protocol definition, see Sect. 4.

Security. For an overview about which entity knows which keys, see Table 1.

Table 1. Overview of the used keys.

Key	Known to			
	P_1	P_2	TEE of P_1	TEE of P_2
k_1	✓	✓	–	–
k_2	–	✓	✓	✓
k_3	✓	✓	–	–

The intuition behind the protocol's security is as follows: If P_1 is corrupted, P_1 does not know the key k_2 and can create ciphertexts under k_2 only via its TEE. This is possible only once, as specified by the program running on the TEE. After having received hashes from P_2, P_1 is thus unable to create appropriate ciphertexts for elements not in S_1 that would, for example, allow it to perform a brute-force search to learn inputs of S_2 not in the intersection. At the same time, it cannot decrypt ciphertexts of elements of P_2 (even when ignoring the information lost due to the application of the hash function). As the hashes result from lexicographically sorted ciphertexts, a malicious P_1 with partial knowledge of P_2's input cannot learn anything about P_2's inputs not in the intersection from the order of the transmitted hashes. (If we omitted the sorting, a party P_1 with input $\{2\}$ could distinguish between inputs $\{1,2\}$ and $\{2,3\}$ of P_2 by observing if the first or the second hash matches.) With respect to simulation-based security, we note that the protocol does not continue unless P_1 sends its ciphertexts C_1 to the TEE. The simulator can observe this and decrypt the ciphertexts with k_1.

Conversely, if P_2 is corrupted, privacy trivially follows from the fact that P_2 does not see input-dependent messages from P_1. Extractability of a corrupted P_2's input follows from a similar argument like in the case of a corrupted P_1, together with the fact that the hash function is evaluated by the TEE, preventing P_2 from cheating after the extraction.

If P_1 and P_2 are honest, but both TEEs are passively corrupted in the sense that they leak *all* information (including randomness of local cryptographic operations) to a third party, we observe the following: All private inputs of P_1 to its TEE are encrypted with k_1, which the TEE does not know. The private inputs of P_2 are iteratively encrypted using keys k_1, k_2 and k_3, where k_3 is unknown to the TEEs. Thus, jointly corrupted TEEs may learn the size of each party's input, but nothing else about them. Also, the intersection's size remains hidden.

In any case, the program running on the TEEs is deterministic and does not operate on secrets, with the exception of simple cryptographic assumptions, which we assume to be secure, and, in particular, free of side channels. As a consequence, side channels (which we assume do not affect these cryptographic operations) do not affect the security of our protocol.

For the formal security proof, see the full version.

Implementation and Evaluation. We implemented our protocol with Intel SGX enclaves using a single AES operation on 128-bit blocks as deterministic encryption. For the universal hash function, we selected xxhash with a randomly chosen seed. We used the SGX remote attestation functionality to ensure that the expected enclave code is running. To verify the remote attestation, the Intel Attestation Service needs to be contacted and returns a signed confirmation of the validity of the attestation data.

We evaluated the runtime of the protocol for different input set sizes. With respect to the runtime, we distinguish between a constant input-independent *setup phase* and an input-dependent *online phase*, whose runtime is linear in the number of input elements. Computing the intersection of two sets with 2^{24} 128-bit elements takes 7.3 s, of which the setup phase, including communication with the Intel Attestation Service, takes 2.0 s.

1.2 Our Contribution

We present a new approach for composable private set intersection, namely the use of trusted execution environments (TEEs). This approach comes with a number of benefits, namely

- very simple protocols, facilitating an easy analysis and implementation,

- high practical performance and asymptotic complexity, with a single-threaded performance that is better than the best known protocol for (composable and maliciously secure) PSI and
- meaningful security guarantees, as the assumptions for the TEEs are comparatively weak. Moreover, there is no large gap between the protocol under analysis and the protocol to be implemented. With random oracles, which are usually used by the most efficient protocols, such a large gap exists.

In more detail, the network communication complexity of our protocol is in $\Theta(\text{poly}(\kappa) + |S_2| \cdot \lambda)$, where λ is the statistical security parameter and $|S_2|$ the cardinality of P_2's set. In particular, it is independent of the set elements' size. The run-time complexity of our protocol is in $O(\text{poly}(\kappa, \lambda, \ell)) \cdot (|S_1| + |S_2|)$, where ℓ is an upper bound for the set elements' size. Concretely, without having the implementation explicitly optimized for bandwidth, we measure 135MByte on sets of 2^{24} elements, which is roughly 64.1 bits per element, outperforming [41] at 300 bits per element for the same setting.

We achieve this performance by using TEEs, which are a powerful tool to guarantee the correct and secure execution of a computation. In our protocol, we use them i) to *locally* extract a corrupted party's input, allowing the network communication to be compressed and ii) to force honest behavior without having to rely on *e.g.* zero-knowledge proofs.

A main advantage of our approach is that we do not require full trust in the security of the used TEEs. Our main requirement is the correct attestation of an execution, together with the existence of secure implementations for very simple cryptographic building blocks like key exchange, deterministic encryption and signature schemes, including secure handling of the keys.

Under these assumptions, our protocol can deal with the following cases:

- The TEE leaks all secrets to the host, except for locally performed simple cryptographic operations. This captures a setting where side channels for the general execution exist, but a limited set of operations can still be performed securely, *e.g.* because they have been implemented in a way that addresses platform-specific side-channels.
- The TEE leaks all secrets to the vendor or another party not participating in the protocol execution, including secrets of locally performed cryptographic operations. Intuitively, this captures the setting of a manufacturer or a government agency introducing backdoors to TEEs. (We call such enclaves *semi-honest* or *passively corrupted*.)

To the best of our knowledge, we are the first to consider TEEs with a realistic security model for the task of PSI. In any case, we can protect the private inputs of honest parties P_1 and P_2 from the TEEs. Surprisingly, we can also protect the size of the intersection from passively corrupted TEEs, which is not guaranteed by naïve constructions using TEEs or some server-aided PSI protocols.

Our main technical tool consists of a deterministic secret-key encryption scheme to hide a party's inputs from the TEEs and the other party, while still allowing efficient comparisons on ciphertexts. Using an appropriate operation mode, a deterministic encryption scheme can be constructed very efficiently using an arbitrary block cipher such as AES. In particular, this allows fast implementations when accelerated AES is available, *e.g.* via the widely-available AES-NI instruction set [25].

To reduce the communication complexity, we employ universal hashing. A key insight is that this hashing must be performed by the TEE in order to allow extraction.

In order to formally capture the properties of semi-honest or almost-transparent TEEs, we extend the model of [39]. Using this extended functionality, we prove the security of our protocol in the UC framework [4,10].

To demonstrate the efficiency of our approach, we also provide an implementation of our protocol using Intel SGX [19] as TEEs.

1.3 Related Work

Private set intersection has been intensively studied during the previous decades, considering different aspects such as optimizing intersections between two parties versus considering arbitrary many parties, having a server that does not collude with the parties aide in the computation versus only having the parties take part or semi-honest versus malicious security.

We focus the examination of existing PSI protocols on three other publications as they consider a similar setting compared to our work, are fairly recent and highly efficient.

[40] introduces a new data structure called PaXoS (a probe-and-XOR of strings) from which the authors build a PSI protocol. The protocol has both a semi-honest and a malicious variant with only a small performance difference. [22] generalizes the idea of encoding one input set into a data structure, and improves the failure probability of such an encoding. The authors use amplification techniques to ensure a low failure probability while simultaneously improving the runtime by 20–40%.

[41] further drastically improves the OKVS (oblivious key value store) constructions by using VOLE (vector oblivious linear evaluation) as the main primitive. Using similar techniques as the other protocols, this work also has a semi-honest and malicious variant with only a relatively small performance difference.

In order to achieve composable security and not resorting to random oracles, we assume trusted hardware that may have side-channels or be corrupted semi-honestly as a compromise between having no trusted hardware at all and performing the whole computation blindly trusting the hardware. Such a use case for trusted hardware was also considered by [32]. In their work, the authors use SGX enclaves to generate correlated randomness like randomized oblivious transfer tuples to use in generic stand-alone multi-party computation protocols. Their security model assumes trusted hardware, like an independent server in server-aided computation, that can only be corrupted independently of the parties that execute the protocol. If the trusted hardware in [32] is passively corrupted, the setting is comparable to our model of *semi-honest enclaves* (see

Sect. 3.3).However, our achieved security notion is stronger, featuring universal composability.

1.4 Insecurity of Previous Implementations

When giving a simulation-based proof of security, the simulator must be able to faithfully simulate the execution by what it learns from the ideal functionality. Often, protocols are given in pseudocode only, using mathematical abstractions such as sets for the protocol parties' inputs. When implementing the protocol, these abstractions have to be instantiated using data structures, *e.g.* by lists or arrays for variables that are typed as sets in the pseudocode.

A problem arises when these data structures have a different semantic. In lists or arrays, elements are ordered, whereas sets may be unordered. This may lead to subtle problems such as the implementation allowing to distinguish if an *honest* party's input is $\{1, 2\}$ versus $\{2, 3\}$, even if the intersection is $\{2\}$ in both cases, due to the position of the matching element. If UC security is considered, this is a problem, as the simulator only learns the intersection $\{2\}$, while the environment knows the input $\{1, 2\}$ resp. $\{2, 3\}$.

Two implementations [40,41] exhibit this problem, allowing to learn something about the input of the party that does not learn the intersection, because the used data structures are ordered. Due to the use of (unordered) sets in the protocol description, this is not accounted for in the proof. As the simulator is not given this leakage, the simulators stated (implicitly) in [40,41] cannot correctly simulate in presence of this leakage. While the proof of security is arguably sound, a *different and insecure* protocol is implemented. While even more severe, this problem due to implementing a different protocol than the analyzed one is similar to the one that exists when random oracles are replaced by hash functions (see *Use of Random Oracles in Previous Protocols* in Sect. 1).

In order to fix the vulnerability, we propose the implementation to be modified to hide the order of the input, *e.g.* by (pseudo)randomly permuting it or possibly by sorting the hashes or ciphertexts of the input, which also leads to a (pseudo)random permutation. Unfortunately, the price to pay for this solution is a decrease in efficiency, as sorting and permuting are computationally expensive.

We believe that this issue highlights a general problem with respect to the usability of cryptographic protocols: Many important assumptions are implicit (and thus overlooked later on, *e.g.* for the implementation), and today's protocols are increasingly complex in order to achieve the best performance or security guarantees, making their security hard to analyze.

1.5 Outline

After the preliminaries in Sect. 2, we present our models for semi-trusted TEEs in Sect. 3. Using these ideal functionalities, we give our construction for efficient one-sided two-party private set intersection in Sect. 4. Then, we present our implementation and evaluate its performance in Sect. 5. Finally, we present

further applications of our model in Sect. 6. The security proof and a short introduction to UC security can be found in the full version.

2   Preliminaries

2.1   Notation

For a probabilistic algorithm X, let $x \leftarrow X(a)$ denote the output of X on input
a. For a set S, let $s \xleftarrow{\$} S$ denote that s is chosen uniformly at random from S.
$\kappa \in \mathbb{N}$ denotes a (computational) security parameter, $\lambda \in \mathbb{N}$ a statistical one. For
a hybrid H_i, let out_i denote its output.

2.2   Building Blocks and Security Notions

Deterministic Secret-Key Encryption. In our protocol, we use deterministic stateless secret-key encryption schemes (SKE). It is well known that such encryption
schemes cannot fulfill the established notion of indistinguishability under chosen
plaintext attack (IND-CPA) security: Upon sending challenges (m_0, m_1) and
receiving a ciphertext c, the adversary can determine if c is associated with m_0
or m_1 by simply querying its encryption oracle on m_0 or m_1 and comparing the
result with c.

By restricting such queries, IND-CPA security can be meaningfully relaxed
for the deterministic and stateless setting. Instead of using the "find-then-guess"
variant of IND-CPA as in the example above, we propose a notion based on
the "left-or-right" (LoR) variant of IND-CPA security [6] (also in [8]), which
is often more convenient in reductions and equivalent to the find-then-guess
variant. In LoR-CPA, the adversary is not given a single challenge ciphertext c,
but interacts with a LoR oracle that can be queried multiple times on ciphertext
pairs (m_0^i, m_1^i). Depending on the choice bit b, the adversary always receives
encryptions of m_b^i.

Definition 1 (det-LoR-CPA Security for SKE).   *Let* $\mathsf{SKE}_{\mathsf{detCPA}} =$
$(\mathsf{Gen}, \mathsf{Enc}, \mathsf{Dec})$ *be a deterministic SKE scheme and let* $\mathrm{Exp}_{\mathcal{A},\mathsf{SKE}_{\mathsf{detCPA}}}^{\mathsf{det\text{-}LoR\text{-}CPA}}(\kappa, z)$
denote the output of the following experiment:

Experiment $\mathrm{Exp}_{\mathcal{A},\mathsf{SKE}_{\mathsf{detCPA}}}^{\mathsf{det\text{-}LoR\text{-}CPA}}(\kappa, z)$:

1. *Define* $\mathcal{O}_{\mathsf{Enc}}(k, b, m_0, m_1)$ *as* $\mathsf{Enc}(k, m_b)$.
2. $k \leftarrow \mathsf{Gen}(1^\kappa)$
3. $b \xleftarrow{\$} \{0, 1\}$
4. $b' \leftarrow \mathcal{A}(1^\kappa, z)^{\mathcal{O}_{\mathsf{Enc}}(k, b, \cdot, \cdot)}$
5. *Return 1 if* $b = b'$ *and 0 otherwise.*

We *say that* $\mathsf{SKE}_{\mathsf{detCPA}}$ *is* deterministic left-or-right-secure under chosen-
plaintext attack (det-LoR-CPA-secure) *if for every legal PPT adversary* $\mathcal{A}$, *there*

exists a negligible function negl *such that for all* $\kappa \in \mathbb{N}$ *and all* $z \in \{0,1\}^*$, *it holds that* $\mathrm{Adv}^{\text{det-LoR-CPA}}_{\mathcal{A},\mathsf{SKE}_{\text{detCPA}}} := |\mathrm{Pr}[\mathrm{Exp}^{\text{det-LoR-CPA}}_{\mathcal{A},\mathsf{SKE}_{\text{detCPA}}}(\kappa, z) = 1] - \frac{1}{2}| \leq \text{negl}(\kappa)$.

Let $\mathcal{Q}$ *be the set of queries sent by* $\mathcal{A}$ *to* $\mathcal{O}_{\mathsf{Enc}}$. *An adversary* $\mathcal{A}$ *is legal if it holds that*

- $|m_0^i| = |m_1^i|$ *for all* $(m_0^i, m_1^i) \in \mathcal{Q}$ *and*
- $m_0^i = m_0^j \iff m_1^i = m_1^j$ *for all* i, j *in* $\{1, \ldots, |\mathcal{Q}|\}$.

Looking ahead to our construction, we only reduce to the security of ciphertexts created by honest parties. Thus, the adversary has no (implicit) access to an encryption oracle. As such, the restrictions in Definition 1 for the adversary are natural in the considered setting and do not require additional assumptions about the adversary.

Key Exchange. Key exchange allows parties to exchange a secret key in the presence of an adversary. In the following, we re-state the definition of universally composable key exchange from [17]. This definition can be satisfied by a variant of the well-known Diffie-Hellman key exchange [20] if authenticated communication is available [17].

Definition 2 (Ideal Functionality $\mathcal{F}_{\mathrm{KE}}$ (adapted from [17])). $\mathcal{F}_{\mathrm{KE}}$ *proceeds as follows, running on security parameter* κ, *with parties* $P_1, \ldots, P_n$ *and an adversary* $\mathcal{S}$.

Upon receiving an input (**Establish-session**, $sid, P_i, P_j, role$) *from some party* P_i, *record the tuple* $(sid, P_i, P_j, role)$ *and send this tuple to the adversary. In addition, if there already is a recorded tuple* $(sid, P_j, P_i, role')$ *(either with* $role' \neq role$ *or* $role = role'$) *then proceed as follows:*

1. *If both* P_i *and* P_j *are uncorrupted then choose* $k \xleftarrow{\$} \{0,1\}^\kappa$ *and make a private delayed output* (**key**, sid, k) *to* P_i *and* P_j.
2. *If either* P_i *or* P_j *is corrupted, then send a message* (**Choose-value**, sid, P_i, P_j) *to the adversary; receive a value* k *from the adversary, make outputs* (**key**, sid, k) *to* P_i *and* P_j *and halt.*

Universal Hash Functions. Universal hash functions (UHFs) [18] allow the compression of elements with a bounded collision probability. In contrast to cryptographic hash functions, collision resistance is only guaranteed if the UHF is chosen *after* the elements to be hashed. However, UHFs exist unconditionally, *i.e.* no complexity assumptions are required.

Definition 3 (Universal Hash Function). *We say that a family of hash functions* $H_\lambda = \{h : X_\lambda \to Y_\lambda\}$ *is* universal *if for all* $x_1, x_2 \in X_\lambda$ *such that* $x_1 \neq x_2$, *it holds that* $\mathrm{Pr}[h(x_1) = h(x_2) \mid h \leftarrow H_\lambda] \leq 1/|Y_\lambda|$, *where the probability is over the choice of* h.

We usually consider Y to depend on a *statistical security parameter* λ instead of a computational security parameter κ.

3   Transparent Enclaves with Secure Operations

A *secure enclave* or *trusted execution environment* (TEE) a is a part of a system isolated from any interference of other parts of the platform (*e.g.* by the operating system or other applications running on the same system), promising the secure execution of arbitrary user-defined programs.

Remote Attestation. The real power of enclaves comes in the form of so-called *remote attestation*, which can be used to attest for another system that a specific output was computed by an enclave running a specific program. Intuitively, a remote attestation can be viewed as a signature of an enclave's output together with the enclave's program code using a secret key that is only available to the enclave. Often, *e.g.* in the case of Intel SGX, the verification key for such a signature would be globally known and shared between all protocols using enclaves, and as such a remote attestation would be verifiable by anyone.

Remote attestation can be used together with a key exchange to establish a secure channel into an enclave: The enclave performs one side of the key exchange and outputs the result with an attestation. The client verifies the attestation and completes the key exchange. The attestation confirms to the client that the other side of the key exchange was executed by an enclave running the specified program, and, if the enclave program does not leak the secret, no one outside will have access to the exchanged key. Additionally, the client can embed a verification key into the enclave's program and sign their part of the key exchange to ensure that the enclave will only accept input from them. After the key exchange has finished, the client can then send its inputs, encrypted with the exchanged key using *e.g.* an IND-CCA-secure encryption scheme, to the enclave.

Computing Arbitrary Functionalities. TEEs with remote attestation seem to solve secure computation problems very efficiently: The parties agree on a functionality and a system that they will trust to run the enclave. Every party providing input will perform a key exchange with the enclave and send their input as described above. Having all parties embed a verification key into the enclave's program prevents the entity managing the trusted hardware to mix up the parties' inputs or swap them with their own. The enclave will perform the desired computation and uses the same secure channels to send each party their output.[2]

Side-Channels and Vulnerabilities. However, trusting the enclave completely with the inputs might not be desirable: First of all, today's enclaves like Intel SGX may have side-channels by design, *e.g.* in the form of allowing the observation of memory access patterns, which may depend on secrets stored inside the enclave.

---

[2] Depending on the model considered, this approach may not yield provable security for technical reasons. For example the model of [39] provably requires *two* TEEs for any two-party functionality. However, as this is outside the scope of our paper, we will not further discuss it and refer the interested reader to [39].

Furthermore, the enclave might be subject to vulnerabilities. For Intel SGX, there was a series of (now patched) attacks on enclaves that range from extracting an enclave's inner state, injecting computation faults into an enclave's program or even extracting the attestation key. This allows an attacker to forge attestations and thereby break the security of enclaves completely. Therefore, protocols should require as little trust as possible.

Formal Models. Given their usefulness, TEEs have seen wide application in cryptography, with several formal models existing (*e.g.* [5,32,39,47]). As we are interested in universal composability, we focus on the work of [39].

Often having one verification key for the remote attestation for many enclaves, *e.g.* as in the case of Intel SGX, a natural choice is to model TEEs in a framework like the Generalized Universal Composability (GUC) framework [12], which is the framework used by [39]. Following a recent result [4], global ideal functionalities can also be captured within the standard UC framework, which has been done for the ideal functionality of [39] in [7].

The ideal functionality of [39], called $\mathcal{G}_{att}$, models TEEs without any kind of side-channels. $\mathcal{G}_{att}$ uses a common signing key pair for signing remote attestations, where everyone can obtain the verification key. Further, $\mathcal{G}_{att}$ is parameterized with a list of parties that may *install* enclaves with arbitrary programs, called the registry. Once the installation has been performed, the installing party receives a handle for the corresponding enclave instance. A second interface of the ideal functionality allows parties to resume the execution of their own enclaves by providing input and obtain the program's output together with a signature on the session identifier, the enclave handle, the program's code and the program's output. This signature models remote attestation.

Unfortunately, the ideal functionality $\mathcal{G}_{att}$ is very optimistic in the sense that it considers the TEE to be completely trusted and does not model *any* side-channels—neither those inherent in the program that is to be executed, nor those present *e.g.* in Intel SGX due to memory access patterns.

To alleviate this, [39] also propose a variant of $\mathcal{G}_{att}$ to model so-called *transparent enclaves*, first introduced by [47]. For transparent enclaves, it is assumed that the attestation of the enclave system is secure (*i.e.* there will only be attestations of correct enclave outputs with the program that produces them), but that, at the same time, the enclave's owner has access to all of the enclave's randomness. In such a model, performing a key exchange with the enclave is useless, as the enclave owner would learn the secret key and could subsequently decrypt ciphertexts containing secret inputs. Here, leaking the randomness seems to capture many, if not all, side-channels.

Interestingly, transparent enclaves are still useful, as they can be used as very efficient passive-security-to-active-security compilers. In particular, very efficient protocols for commitments and zero-knowledge proofs are presented in [39].

A More Realistic Model. Given that Intel SGX's remote attestation is (in part) performed by a so-called *quoting enclave* provisioned by Intel that has access to the attestation key, but is not fundamentally different from any other enclave running on that system [19], transparent enclaves seem to be overly pessimistic. Of course, Intel has spent significant effort in hardening the code of the attestation enclave *e.g.* by using side-channel-free algorithms or placing memory barriers after security checks to prevent speculative execution, but the same argument might hold for careful implementations of cryptographic primitives offered by the trusted cryptographic library provided by the Intel SGX SDK, which can be used by any user-defined enclave program.

This observation suggests that there is a practically motivated and natural middle ground between fully trusted enclaves and transparent enclaves where additional cryptographic operations are possible in a secure way, whereas the rest of the execution is subject to side-channels (unless countermeasures are taken).

To this end, we extend the ideal functionality for transparent enclaves to additionally allow secure key exchange and symmetric encryption, in total analogy to the digital signatures in [39]. This choice is motivated by what operations are assumed to secure for Intel SGX, given appropriate side-channel-free implementations. However, we stress that this list is not final. Indeed, we envision further variants of our ideal functionality depending on which cryptographic primitives are needed and can plausibly be implemented in a secure way.

Adding these additional secure operations comes, however, with a caveat: Only leaking the enclave's randomness does no longer lead to a meaningful model. In the original model, transparent enclaves could not keep a secret from the host because the host could extract the key exchange by learning the randomness. In our model, key exchange between enclaves is possible. Consider the following protocol between parties P_1 and P_2 with enclaves E_1 and E_2 respectively:

1. E_1 and E_2 exchange a key k in a side-channel-free manner.
2. P_1 sends its secret x to its enclave E_1.
3. E_1 encrypts x using k in a side-channel-free manner to the ciphertext c and sends c to E_2 (via P_1 and P_2).
4. E_2 decrypts c to x using k in a side-channel-free manner and evaluates a *deterministic* function f that is affected by side-channels, *e.g.* in the form of memory access patterns, on x and halts without output.

Clearly, P_2 should learn x in the above example. In the original model for transparent enclaves, this would be the case as P_2 would learn k via the leaked randomness, could decrypt c and obtain x. If not for this leakage, P_2 could not learn x, as the computation of f is deterministic, leading to no leakage according to the model.

In order to address this problem, we augment our ideal functionality to not only leak randomness, but also i) the enclave memory as well as ii) the output of secure operations, *e.g.* released keys. This leads again to a meaningful model.

By explicitly distinguishing between secure operations and a side-channel-affected general execution, the requirements of an implementation become explicit.

3.1   Ideal Functionality with Secure Operations

We start with a definition of *secure* TEEs, *i.e.* TEEs without side-channels or
leakage. This definition is based on the definition of [39] (with a fix from [7]),
with the following differences:

1. In the original definition, the functionality is parameterized with a list of
   parties reg (the registry) able to install programs. Intuitively, this captures
   that only a subset of the protocol parties may have a TEE. In particular, the
   adversary (resp. simulator) is unable to install a program if all parties in the
   registry are honest. This leads to technical problems (see [39] for details). We
   have chosen to allow *all* parties *and* the adversary to create TEEs by removing
   reg. We believe that this is plausible in our practice-oriented setting due to
   the wide availability of TEEs such as Intel SGX.
2. We introduce a number of *secure enclave operations*, allowing to *e.g.* exchange
   keys between two enclaves or to perform deterministic encryption. While such
   secure enclave operations are not necessary if the TEEs are fully trusted, they
   are useful if we assume side-channels during the execution of enclave programs
   (see Definitions 5 and 6). Note that in the original definition of transparent
   enclaves [47], the signature scheme used for the attestation signatures is also
   modeled to keep its security. If this were not the case, all security guarantees
   would be lost as an adversary could completely impersonate a TEE.

Definition 4 (Ideal Functionality $\mathcal{G}_{att}[\mathsf{Sig}, \mathsf{SKE}, \kappa]$).
// initialization:
On initialize: $(\mathrm{mpk}, \mathrm{msk}) \leftarrow \mathsf{Sig.Gen}(1^\kappa), T = \emptyset, \ S = \emptyset.$

// public query interface
On receive* getpk *from some P: Send* mpk *to P.*

Secure enclave operations

On receive* $(\mathbf{kex}, \mathrm{eid}_2)$ *from a TEE with EID* eid_1:

- *Sample* $k \xleftarrow{\$} \{0,1\}^\kappa$ *and* hdl $\xleftarrow{\$} \{0,1\}^\kappa$.
- *For* $i \in \{1,2\}$, *send* $(\mathbf{key\text{-}exchange}, \mathrm{eid}_1, \mathrm{eid}_2, \mathrm{eid}_i)$ *to the adversary. Upon
  confirmation, set* $S[\mathrm{eid}_i, \mathsf{hdl}] = k$ *and output* $(\mathrm{eid}_1, \mathrm{eid}_2, \mathsf{hdl})$ *to the TEE with*
  eid_i.

On receive* $(\mathbf{ske.gen})$ *from a TEE with EID* eid:

- *Let* $k \leftarrow \mathsf{SKE.Gen}(1^\kappa)$.
- *Sample a random handle* hdl $\xleftarrow{\$} \{0,1\}^\kappa$, *set* $S[\mathrm{eid}, \mathsf{hdl}] = k$ *and return* hdl.

On receive* $(\mathbf{ske.enc}, \mathsf{hdl}, m)$ *from a TEE with EID* eid:

- *If there is no entry* $S[\mathrm{eid}, \mathsf{hdl}]$, *abort. Otherwise, return*
  $\mathsf{SKE.Enc}(S[\mathrm{eid}, \mathsf{hdl}], m)$.

*On receive** (ske.dec, hdl, c) *from a TEE with EID* eid:

- *If there is no entry* S[eid, hdl], *abort. Otherwise, return*
  SKE.Dec(S[eid, hdl], c).

*On receive** (release-key, hdl) *from a TEE with EID* eid:

- *If there is no entry* S[eid, hdl], *abort. Otherwise, return* S[eid, hdl].

Normal enclave operations

// *local interface — install an enclave:*
*On receive** (install, idx, prog) *from some ITI* μ *where* μ *is either a protocol party or the adversary:*

- *If P is honest, assert* idx = sid.
- *Generate nonce* eid $\xleftarrow{\$}$ $\{0,1\}^\kappa$, *store* T[eid, μ] = (idx, prog, $\mathbf{0}$), *send* eid *to* μ.

//*local interface — resume an enclave*
*On receive** (resume, eid, inp) *from some ITI where* μ *is either a protocol party or the adversary:*

- *Let* (idx, prog, mem) = T[eid, μ], *abort if not found.*
- *Let* (outp, mem') = prog(inp, mem), *update* [eid, μ] = (idx, prog, mem').
- *Let* σ = Sig.Sign(msk, (idx, eid, prog, outp)) *and send* (outp, σ) *to* μ.

Remark 1. For the sake of an easier description, the key exchange between enclaves is modeled in an ideal way similar to Definition 2. Alternatively, we could have incorporated an explicit protocol such as the signed Diffie-Hellman key exchange.

Remark 2. Sometimes, we need to be able to iteratively perform secure enclave operations without leaking intermediate results. For example, we might want to encrypt a message m under a key with handle hdl and then encrypt the resulting ciphertext with a key with a different handle hdl' in a way that the ciphertext resulting from the encryption with hdl is not leaked.

To this end, we can naturally augment the secure enclave operations to optionally return handles only and to accept them as inputs instead of real messages. The release-key operation could be generalized to work on arbitrary handles. However, for the sake of better readability, we have chosen to not to include these additional modes of operation in the formal description of the model and our protocols.

Following this basic definition, we define two variants of TEEs that capture side-channels resp. semi-honest TEEs leaking all secrets to the adversary.

3.2   Almost-Transparent Enclaves

We now consider a variant of the functionality in Definition 4 where all normal enclave operations are affected by side-channels. Per the discussions above, it is insufficient to only leak the used randomness in the setting we consider. Instead, we also leak the pre-computation memory. Using this information, the computation can be fully reproduced, including its timing (which is not modeled), inputs and outputs as well as memory access patterns.

Definition 5. (Almost-transparent Enclave $\hat{\mathcal{G}}_{att}$). $\hat{\mathcal{G}}_{att}$ *is defined identically to* $\mathcal{G}_{att}$, *except that besides outputting the pair* (outp, σ) *to the caller upon the* resume *entry point, it also leaks to the caller*

- *all random bits internally generated during the computation,*
- *the enclave memory* mem *pre-execution and*
- *the output of secure operations.*

Note that this definition, adapted from [39], does not include randomness or memory used by secure enclave operations or the randomness used to generate the signing key.

3.3   Semi-honest Enclaves

Apart from side-channels that leak information to a TEE's host, we are also interested in the setting where the TEE is passively corrupted and leaks all information about the computation. In contrast to the leakage due to side-channels, this leakage could be to a third party not participating in the protocol execution, *e.g.* the manufacturer or a government agency. The fear of such leakage is plausible because many of today's TEE implementations are very complex, closed-source and could possibly interact with other hardware building blocks, *e.g.* the network interface, without knowledge of the operating system (OS). On Intel systems, out-of-band network communication is often supported by the chipset [31]. This adversarial model has been previously considered in [32], albeit in a much simpler model without composability.

Definition 6 (Semi-honest Enclave $\tilde{\mathcal{G}}_{att}$). $\tilde{\mathcal{G}}_{att}$ *is defined identically to* $\mathcal{G}_{att}$, *except that for each activation, a tuple* (inp, outp, r) *is stored, where* inp *denotes the functionality's input,* outp *the output (if applicable,* $\perp$ *otherwise) and* r *the randomness used during the activation, including secure operations. The adversary may retrieve all previously stored and new tuples by sending a special message* leak *to* $\tilde{\mathcal{G}}_{att}$.

In contrast to transparent enclaves, semi-honest enclaves leak *all* inputs, outputs and randomness, including enclave operations and the randomness used for the signature key generation.

With semi-honest enclaves, one cannot simply execute a passively secure protocol fully inside the TEEs anymore and hope to achieve meaningful security.

Looking ahead, we find that our construction for PSI is secure even in the presence of semi-honest TEEs, as long as no protocol party is corrupted. This captures a setting where the TEE leaks everything to *e.g.* the manufacturer or a government agency, but does not cooperate with the parties using the TEEs.

3.4   Possible Realizations of Our Model

Our model of TEEs with secure and side-channel-free cryptographic operations is motivated by a number of existing systems:

- Enclaves that are free of side-channels are trivially able to perform cryptographic operations in a secure manner, given appropriate implementations.
- Intel SGX needs to perform a number of cryptographic operations in a secure manner for attestation [19]. In particular, this includes i) message authentication codes (MACs) and ii) digital signatures. Also, the trusted cryptographic library distributed by Intel as part of the SGX SDK contains implementations of i) key exchange and ii) secret-key encryption. Given the prevalence of SGX vulnerabilities, realizing secure enclave programs is indeed a difficult task. However, there are "best practices" provided by Intel [28]. Additionally using memory barriers, constant-time code and data-oblivious implementations may be helpful to avoid side-channel leakage.

  We also note that one needs to consider the adversarial model of the used TEE. For example, advanced attacks using fault injection or power attacks may (or may not) invalidate the adversarial model altogether, rendering the assumption (that certain operations can be performed securely) wrong. In the case of SGX, mitigations for vulnerabilities covered by the adversarial model are available and are checkable via remote attestation.
- Intel SGX could also be combined with different technologies for trusted execution, *e.g.* Intel Trusted Execution Technology (TXT), to perform cryptographic operations. Intel TXT has previously been used to securely perform cryptographic operations [34].
- Many mobile devices that feature enclaves such as ARM TrustZone have dedicated secure hardware for cryptographic operations, *e.g.* recent Apple iPhones [2] or Google Pixel smartphones [35].
- Some IBM systems have a feature called *IBM Secure Execution* [27], which provides Linux-based secure enclaves. These could be combined with a dedicated hardware security module (HSM), which are also available from IBM.
- Secure enclaves are also supported by the open-source instruction set RISC-V [44]. If necessary, this instruction set could possibly be extended to be able to perform basic cryptographic operations in hardware.

4   One-Sided Private Set Intersection

Before describing our protocol, we state the ideal functionality we realize. $\mathcal{F}_{\mathrm{oPSI}}$, the ideal functionality for one-sided PSI, takes inputs S_1 and S_2 from P_1 resp.

P_2 and computes the intersection $S = S_1 \cap S_2$, which is lexicographically sorted and returned to P_1. The lexicographical sorting is employed in order to avoid ambiguity and the introduction of leakage of the private inputs depending on the result's sorting. See Sect. 1.4 for examples in previous protocols.

Definition 7 (Ideal Functionality $\mathcal{F}_{\text{oPSI}}$). *Parameterized by a security parameter κ and two parties P_1 and P_2. The input of each party consists of a set with elements from $\{0,1\}^\kappa$.*

- *On input* (input, sid, S_1) *from P_1, store S_1 and send* (input$_1$, sid, $|S_1|$) *to the adversary.*
- *On input* (input, sid, S_2) *from P_2, store S_2 and send* (input$_2$, sid, $|S_2|$) *to the adversary.*
- *When having received input from both parties, compute the intersection $S = S_1 \cap S_2$ and sort S lexicographically. Also, send* (size, sid, $|S|$) *to the adversary.*
- *Generate a private delayed output* (result, sid, S) *for P_1.*

Remark 3. In Definition 7, the adversary always learns $|S_1|$, $|S_2|$ and $|S|$, regardless of which parties are corrupted. More fine-grained leakage can be modeled (and realized by our protocol) at the cost of a more complex description of $\mathcal{F}_{\text{oPSI}}$.

Remark 4. In $\mathcal{F}_{\text{oPSI}}$, only the party P_1 obtains the intersection result. If the considered universe U is small enough (*e.g.* when U consists of telephone numbers), a malicious party P_1 could use the whole universe U as its input and would then learn the input of P_2. Under notions of PSI where both parties learn the output, this could possibly be detected heuristically by P_2 after it has learned the result. In the case of one-sided PSI, this is not possible.

If protection against such an attack strategy is necessary, $\mathcal{F}_{\text{oPSI}}$ can be easily modified in a number of ways to *e.g.* i) limit the input size of either or both parties, ii) tell P_2 the size of P_1's input or to iii) only output the result to P_1 if a certain threshold for the intersection's size is met or kept.

Looking ahead, our construction could be easily adapted to the first two points while retaining its security properties. For the last point, an easy modification is possible that would, however, allow the TEEs to learn the intersection's size, which we currently prevent.

We now present our construction π_{oPSI}. We assume the existence of authenticated communication and consider adversaries that statically corrupt protocol parties, *i.e.* at the very beginning of the execution.

The protocol description is split into three parts: The actual protocol executed by P_1 and P_2, together with the programs executed by each party's TEE.

Construction 1 (Protocol π_{oPSI}). *Let* Sig *be a signature scheme and* SKE$_{\text{detCPA}}$ *a deterministic secret-key encryption scheme. Let $\kappa \in \mathbb{N}$ be a security parameter. Let $\mathcal{G}_{att} = \mathcal{G}_{att}[\text{Sig}, \text{SKE}_{\text{detCPA}}, \kappa]$.*

Program prog$_1$ *of P_1's enclave:*

1. *Receive* $(\mathsf{mpk}, \mathsf{eid}_1, \mathsf{eid}_2, \mathsf{prog}_2)$ *as first input.*
2. *Execute* $(\textbf{key-exchange}, \mathsf{eid}_2)$. *Eventually, receive a message* $(\mathsf{eid}_1', \mathsf{eid}_2', \mathsf{hdl})$. *Store* hdl *if* $\mathsf{eid}_1' = \mathsf{eid}_1$ *and* $\mathsf{eid}_2' = \mathsf{eid}_2$.
3. *On input* $(\textbf{input}, sid, C_1)$:
   - *Set* $C_1' = \{c_i' \mid c_i' = \mathsf{ske.enc}(\mathsf{hdl}, c_i), c_i \in C_1\}$.
   - *Output* $(\textbf{ready}, sid)$.
   - *Upon the next activation, output* (sid, C_1').
4. *Ignore all further messages.*

Program prog_2 *of* P_2's *enclave:*

1. *Receive* $(\mathsf{mpk}, \mathsf{eid}_1, \mathsf{eid}_2, \mathsf{prog}_2)$ *as first input.*
2. *Eventually receive a message* $(\mathsf{eid}_1', \mathsf{eid}_2', \mathsf{hdl})$. *Store* hdl *if* $\mathsf{eid}_1' = \mathsf{eid}_1$ *and* $\mathsf{eid}_2' = \mathsf{eid}_2$.
3. *On input* $(\textbf{query}, sid)$, *execute* $(\textbf{release-key}, \mathsf{hdl})$ *to obtain* k_2 *and output* $(\textbf{key}, sid, k_2)$.
4. *On input* $(\textbf{input}, sid, C_2, \lambda)$, *sample a UHF* UHF *from the set of UHFs with domain* $\{0,1\}^{\mathsf{poly}(\kappa)}$, *codomain* $\{0,1\}^{\lambda}$ *and super-polynomial image size in* λ *where* $\mathsf{poly}(\kappa)$ *is a polynomial denoting the length of the ciphertexts to be hashed. Compute* $H = \{h_i \mid h_i = \mathsf{UHF}(c_i), c_i \in C_2\}$ *and output* $(\textbf{output}, sid, \mathsf{UHF}, H)$.
5. *Ignore all further messages.*

Protocol:
If activated without the initial input, a party yields the execution until the input is received.

1. *Each party* P_i *(eventually) receives input* $(\textbf{input}, sid, S_i)$ *and is parameterized with a security parameter* κ *and a statistical security parameter* λ.
2. P_1 *and* P_2 *each send* $(\textbf{getpk})$ *to* $\mathcal{G}_{att}$ *to obtain the master public key* mpk.
3. P_1 *and* P_2 *call* $\mathcal{F}_{KE}$ *twice, using SIDs* $sid\|1$ *and* $sid\|2$ *(with* P_1 *acting as initiator) to obtain keys* k_1, k_3.
4. P_1 *sends* $(\textbf{install}, sid, \mathsf{prog}_1)$ *to* $\mathcal{G}_{att}$, *where* prog_1 *is the program for* P_1's *enclave in Construction 1. It obtains* eid_1 *as answer and sends* eid_1 *to* P_2.
5. *Similarly,* P_2 *installs an enclave with program* prog_2, *obtains* eid_2 *and sends it to* P_1.
6. P_1 *sends* $(\mathsf{mpk}, \mathsf{eid}_1, \mathsf{eid}_2, \mathsf{prog}_2)$ *to its TEE with EID* eid_1 *via* $\mathcal{G}_{att}$. *Conversely,* P_2 *sends* $(\mathsf{mpk}, \mathsf{eid}_1, \mathsf{eid}_2, \mathsf{prog}_1)$ *to its TEE with EID* eid_2.
7. *Let* $S_1 = \{s_1^1, \ldots, s_1^{n_1}\}$. *For* $i = 1, \ldots, n_1$, *let* $c_1^i = \mathsf{SKE}_{\mathsf{detCPA}}.\mathsf{Enc}(k_1, s_1^i)$. P_1 *sends* $C_1 = \{c_1^1, \ldots c_1^{n_1}\}$ *to the TEE with EID* eid_1 *and receives* $(\textbf{ready}, \sigma_1)$ *as answer, which it forwards to* P_2.
8. *On receiving* $(\textbf{ready}, \sigma_1)$ *from* P_1, P_2 *verifies the signature* σ_1 *and sends, upon successful verification,* $(\textbf{query})$ *to its TEE with EID* eid_2 *to obtain* k_2. *Let* $S_2 = \{s_2^1, \ldots, s_2^{n_2}\}$. *Then,* P_2 *computes* $c_2^i = \mathsf{SKE}_{\mathsf{detCPA}}.\mathsf{Enc}(k_3, \mathsf{SKE}_{\mathsf{detCPA}}.\mathsf{Enc}(k_2, \mathsf{SKE}_{\mathsf{detCPA}}.\mathsf{Enc}(k_1, s_2^i)))$ *for* $i = 1, \ldots, n_2$, *sorts* $C_2 = \{c_2^1, \ldots, c_2^{n_2}\}$ *lexicographically and sends it, together with the statistical security parameter* λ, *to the TEE with* eid_2. *It receives* $(\textbf{output}, sid, \mathsf{UHF}, H, \sigma_H)$, *which it forwards to* P_1.

9. On receiving $(\text{output}, sid, \mathsf{UHF}, H, \sigma_H)$, P_1 verifies the signature σ_H. Upon successful verification, it verifies that H is consistent with λ, it queries its TEE with EID eid_1 to obtain C_1'. Then, it computes $S = \{s_1^j \mid s_1^j \in S_1 \land \mathsf{UHF}(\mathsf{SKE}_{\mathsf{detCPA}}.\mathsf{Enc}(k_3, c_j')) \in H, c_j' \in C_1'\}$, sorts S lexicographically and outputs (result, sid, S).

In order to prove the security of our protocol, it is crucial that the environment is not able to access $\mathcal{G}_{att}$ (and its variants) arbitrarily. In particular, the environment may access $\mathcal{G}_{att}$ only with identities of 1. corrupted parties (and thus through the adversary) or 2. (honest) parties with a session ID that does not belong to an actual session in the execution. The first criterion is necessary to achieve a meaningful security notion, while the last criterion prevents the environment from accessing $\mathcal{G}_{att}$ with identities belonging to the *test session* or *challenge session*. This is in line with what is assumed by prior work, in particular in [7,39] For a discussion on the formalism, see [4,11].

We formally define the following *identity bound* ξ.

Definition 8 (Identity Bound). *Let* $\text{eid} = (\mu, sid\|pid)$ *be an extended identity. Then,* $\xi(\text{eid}) = 1$ *if and only if*

– *the party with extended ID* eid *is corrupted or*
– *sid is not the session ID of an ITI existing in the current execution.*

With this definition at hand, we are ready to state our main theorem.

Theorem 1. *Let* $\hat{\pi}_{\mathsf{oPSI}} = \pi_{\mathsf{oPSI}}^{\mathcal{G}_{att} \to \hat{\mathcal{G}}_{att}}$ *be the protocol where* $\mathcal{G}_{att}$ *is replaced with* $\hat{\mathcal{G}}_{att}$ *and let* $\tilde{\pi}_{\mathsf{oPSI}} = \pi_{\mathsf{oPSI}}^{\mathcal{G}_{att} \to \tilde{\mathcal{G}}_{att}}$ *be the protocol where* $\mathcal{G}_{att}$ *is replaced with* $\tilde{\mathcal{G}}_{att}$.

If Sig *is an EUF-CMA-secure signature scheme,* $\mathsf{SKE}_{\mathsf{detCPA}}$ *is a det-LoR-CPA-secure secret-key encryption scheme,* κ *is the computational security parameter and* $\lambda \in \Theta(\kappa)$ *is the statistical security parameter, then* $\hat{\pi}_{\mathsf{oPSI}}$ ξ-UC-realizes $\mathcal{F}_{\mathsf{oPSI}}$ *in the presence of* $\hat{\mathcal{G}}_{att}[\mathsf{Sig}, \mathsf{SKE}_{\mathsf{detCPA}}, \kappa], \mathcal{F}_{\mathsf{KE}}$ *under static corruptions.*

Under the same assumptions, $\tilde{\pi}_{\mathsf{oPSI}}$ ξ-UC-realizes $\mathcal{F}_{\mathsf{oPSI}}$ *in the presence of* $\tilde{\mathcal{G}}_{att}[\mathsf{Sig}, \mathsf{SKE}_{\mathsf{detCPA}}, \kappa], \mathcal{F}_{\mathsf{KE}}$ *if the adversary does not corrupt any protocol party.*

Informally, this means that π_{oPSI} is secure if a) the TEEs are almost-transparent, even if P_1 and / or P_2 are corrupted or b) if the TEEs are semi-honest and P_1 and P_2 are honest. Then, the TEEs do not learn the intersection size $|S|$.

We give a very short proof sketch.

Proof (sketch). If P_1 is corrupted, the simulator must be able to extract the inputs of P_1 and provide them to $\mathcal{F}_{\mathsf{oPSI}}$. Also, the simulator must simulate messages leading to the correct output for P_1, only knowing the intersection, but not P_2's elements that are not in the intersection.

In order to extract P_1's input, the simulator reads the ciphertexts P_1 sends to its TEE, which are encrypted with k_1. As the simulator simulates the honest party P_2, it knows k_1 and can decrypt the ciphertexts, learning P_1's input S_1.

Upon providing this input to $\mathcal{F}_{\text{oPSI}}$, the simulator learns the intersection S as well as $|S_2|$. For elements in the intersection, it can then prepare appropriate ciphertexts such that P_1 can compute the correct results. For elements not in the intersection (which the simulator does not know), it can create "dummy ciphertexts" to random values.

If P_2 is corrupted and P_1 is honest, the simulator's task is easier as it only has to extract P_2's input, which it does as described above.

If both parties are honest and the TEE is passively corrupted, the simulator learns $|S_1|$ and $|S_2|$ and can sample "dummy elements" for S_1 and S_2. Using these dummy elements, it can execute the protocol on behalf of the honest parties.

For the full proof, see the full version.

Remark 5. For the case of semi-honest corruptions of P_1 and P_2, two-sided private set intersection, *i.e.* where both P_1 and P_2 obtain the result, can be easily obtained by executing π_{oPSI} twice, once in each direction.

Remark 6. In π_{oPSI}, we encrypt the input to the TEEs. This prevents a passively corrupted TEE from learning *e.g.* a party's private input and the intersection. If one is willing to abandon these security guarantees, one could provide the TEE with the sets S_1 and S_2 in the clear and have it apply a user-defined function on the inputs, *e.g.* a perceptual hash algorithm. This way, our protocol can be adapted to different applications while retaining its efficiency and security in the presence of side-channels.

Let ℓ be a bound for the set elements' size[3]. It is easy to see that the network communication complexity is in $\Theta(\text{poly}(\kappa) + |S_2| \cdot \lambda)$, assuming that i) the key exchange protocol has a communication complexity in $\Theta(\text{poly}(\kappa))$, which holds for $\mathcal{F}_{\text{KE}}$ as well as *e.g.* for the Diffie-Hellman key exchange, ii) the length public keys and signatures of the signature scheme Sig can also bounded by a polynomial $\text{poly}(\kappa)$ and iii) the description of the UHF UHF is bounded by a polynomial $\text{poly}(\kappa)$. In particular, the communication complexity is linear in $|S_2|$ and independent of $|S_1|$ and ℓ.

The runtime complexity is in $O((|S_1| + |S_2|) \cdot \text{poly}(\kappa, \ell))$, assuming that i) $\mathcal{F}_{\text{KE}}$ resp. its instantiation can be executed in $O(\text{poly}(\kappa))$ steps, ii) the ciphertexts of plaintexts with length ℓ and keys with length in $O(\kappa)$ can be computed in $O(\text{poly}(\kappa, \ell))$ steps and have length $O(\kappa + \ell)$, iii) the sorting can be performed in $O((\kappa + \ell) \cdot |S_2|)$ resp. $O(\lambda \cdot |S|)$ steps, iv) the UHF can be sampled and evaluated (once) in $O(\text{poly}(\ell, \kappa, \lambda))$ steps and v) the signatures can be verified in $O(\text{poly}(\kappa))$ steps. If $\ell \in O(\kappa)$, we obtain a runtime complexity of $O((|S_1| + |S_2|) \cdot \text{poly}(\kappa))$.

Remark 7. Extending the above protocol to the multi-party setting is non-trivial. Let P_1 be the party that is supposed to receive the intersection and let $P_2, \ldots, P_n$ be the other parties. First, we observe that merely executing the protocol $n - 1$ times, once between P_1 and each other party, is insecure in the sense that P_1 learns more than the intersection of *all* sets.

---

[3] In $\mathcal{F}_{\text{oPSI}}$ and π_{oPSI}, we assume that $\ell = \kappa$. However, this can be easily generalized.

This problem also needs to prevented in a modified protocol: Currently, the party learning the intersection has to collect messages from each party which it can only process to compute the *joint* intersection, but not the individual ones. This seems to require a different protocol altogether and we leave the case of PSI with more than two parties in our model as future work.

5   Implementation and Evaluation

We implemented the proposed private set intersection protocol with Intel SGX enclaves on an Intel Xeon E3-1275 v6 processor.[4]

Remote attestation of SGX enclaves is more involved than modeled in the ideal functionality. While the ideal functionality just signs enclave outputs with a globally known signature key-pair, SGX enclaves complement their output with data called *attestation evidence*. However, in contrast to the formal model, this data cannot be independently verified. SGX provides two implementations of attestations: EPID and DCAP. To check the correctness of an EPID attestation, the attestation evidence needs to be submitted to an Intel-operated service, called the *Intel Attestation Service*. That service decrypts the attestation evidence and then verifies the contained group signature. The result of that check is then reported back, together with an RSA-2048 signature with a fixed key. Such a web request takes approximately 300 ms. If a protocol needs many attestations by the same enclave, the necessity of many separate interactions with the attestation service can be sidestepped by initially generating a signature key pair, then performing remote attestation with the verification key as output, and then using this keypair to sign all of the output that needed attestation before. For the evaluation, we used EPID attestations and but did not implement this optimization. ECDSA attestations realized with the Intel DCAP toolkit implicitly use this optimization, as only one initial attestation needs to be verified by the "Provisioning Certification Service" operated by Intel to attest an ECDSA signature keypair which is then used to sign and verify all further attestations. Additionally, cacheable attestation collateral needs to be downloaded from an Intel service to ensure that the attesting system is up-to-date.

For our benchmarks, we used EPID attestations, also because we found the responses from the Intel Attestations Service can be verified more easily from with enclaves than DCAP attestations. We use the RSA-2048 signature in the response from the Intel Attestation Service to check an attestation. Its required verification key is delivered into the enclaves by embedding it directly into the enclaves' code. Verifying DCAP attestations from within enclaves is more involved.

The runtime of the set intersection protocol consists of a constant part, mainly for doing the interactions with the Intel Attestation Service to confirm the validity of a remote enclave attestation and exchanging a key between the enclaves before the actual computation, and a part linear in the input size. Figure 2 shows the overall runtime for set intersection with 128-bit elements.

---

[4] For the code, see https://github.com/kastel-security/psi-with-sgx.

The protocol for the different parties was executed in the same program with a simulated `veth` device introducing 10ms of latency for all TCP packets. To intersect 2^{24} 128-bit elements with another set of 2^{24} 128-bit elements, having half of the elements in the intersection, we get a total runtime of 7.3 s of which the linear regression suggests a constant overhead of 2.0 s. For comparison the maliciously secure protocol from Rindal et al. [41] takes around 8.0 s in their paper and takes around 10.7 s when run on our hardware.

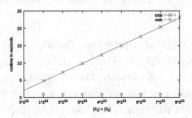

Fig. 2. Runtime of the PSI protocol, depending on the number of elements in the input sets for elements of 128 bit size. The size of S_1 and S_2 is equal and $|S_1 \cap S_2| = \frac{|S_1|}{2}$. The time is shown as total runtime including wait time for the Intel Attestation Service (roughly 0.8 s) which is also shown for reference in the "web" series. Error bars are the standard derivation over 10 measurements.

The size of the enclave memory of SGX enclaves needs to be known ahead of time and additionally cannot be increased without limits as it becomes harder to keep this memory protected with a larger enclave state. Luckily, our protocol can easily be implemented with limited enclave state size by streaming the values for encryption/hashing through the enclave, not requiring the enclave memory size to depend on the sets' size. A modification is needed for P_2's enclave, which needs to keep a large set of values as internal state, and then choose the UHF and start outputting hashes. For the correctness, it is important that P_2 needs to be committed to all the values before the enclave chooses the UHF. To eliminate the large intermediate state, the enclave can just store a collision-resistant hash (we used SHA256) of the values. Later, when the UHF needs to be evaluated on that data, the data is supplied by P_2 again. After the hashes are calculated, the attestation on the universally hashed values is only released if the collision-resistant hash on the input is unchanged, compared to the one calculated in the commit phase. As passing data into enclaves is fast (enclaves can access non-enclave memory at will), this approach brings a significant performance improvement.

For an instantiation of the UHF, we use the 64-bit variant XXHash and for choosing a random hash function we choose the 64-bit seed of XXHash uniformly at random. PSI benchmarks usually assume constant-size elements of 128-bit. Deterministically encrypting 128-bit elements can be easily done with just a single AES operation. For sorting we use an optimized variant of radix sort. As x86-64 CPUs support 128-bit unsigned integers as native types, implementing a 128-bit radix sort is straightforward.

294   F. Dörre et al.

Protocol	Runtime	Network Model
Ours	7.3s	loopback + latency
Ours	8.1s	loopback + latency + 1Gbit/s
from PaXoS [40]	69s	loopback
from VOLE [41]	10.7s	in-process memory
from VOLE [41] + sort	11.2s	in-process memory

Fig. 3. Evaluation and comparisons executed on our hardware. The runtime was measured for inputs consisting of 2^{24} 128-bit elements on the same hardware.

Figure 3 show the runtime of our PSI protocol compared to two recent maliciously secure PSI protocols [40,41]. Further information on how the protocols were executed is given in the full version. Due to implementation differences and restrictions of our evaluation setup we did not execute all PSI protocols with the exact same network abstraction. The differences that remained are noted in the column "Network Model". In our implementation we use a real TCP socket connected over a loopback adapter that simulates latency (and optionally bandwidth limitation). For the implementation based on PaXoS we did not simulate latency, the implementation based on VOLE does not use sockets at all, but communicates via an in-memory buffer. The network model for our implementation is the most pessimistic one. For the last line in the table, we adjusted [41] to not leak the input set order anymore. Details can be found in the full version.

6 Further Applications

We present further applications of the model defined in Sect. 3.

6.1 One-Sided Hamming Distance

Using a protocol that is somewhat reminiscent of our construction π_{oPSI} for one-sided PSI, parties P_1 and P_2 can compute the Hamming distance on bitstrings in a way that P_1 learns the distance, even if the TEEs are almost-transparent or passively corrupted (and P_1 and P_2 honest).

First of all, we need an additional cryptographic building block called *message authentication codes* (MACs), which can be seen as the symmetric analogue of digital signatures. As MACs are part of the attestation protocol of Intel SGX [19], we assume that MAC tags can be computed and verified securely and consider a variant of $\mathcal{G}_{att}$ that supports MACs as secure operations. In the following, we assume that MACs are *length-normal*, *i.e.* that for messages x_1, x_2 with $|x_1| = |x_2|$, the MAC tags of x_1 and x_2 have the same length.

Roughly, the protocol works as follows:

Construction 2 (Protocol π_{HD}, informal). *1. P_1 and P_2 exchange a key k_{SKE}^4 for a deterministic secret-key encryption scheme. P_2 also generates a signature key pair.*

2. For its input string $S_1 = b_1^1 || \ldots || b_1^{n_1}$, P_1 encrypts the i-th bit b_1^i of its input together with the position i, i.e. $(b_1^i || i)$ using k_{SKE}^4 and sends the resulting ciphertext set C_1 to its TEE, which stores it. As the TEE does not know k_{SKE}^4, the input of P_1 is hidden.

3. P_1 obtains keys k_{MAC} and k_{SKE}^2 from its TEE. For each position, P_1 encrypts $(0||i)$ and $(1||i)$ using k_{SKE}^4 and creates a MAC tag for each ciphertext. Then, it sorts the pairs consisting of ciphertexts and MAC tags and sends the resulting set M to P_2.

4. P_2 verifies that the ciphertexts have been correctly created (using k_{SKE}^4), signs M and sends the signature σ_M to P_1.

5. P_1 sends M and σ_M to its TEE, which checks the signature σ_M, the MAC tags and that each input provided by P_1 is contained in M. This ensures that P_1's input is correct.

6. Then, the TEE of P_1 encrypts the input ciphertexts C_1 of P_1 using a key k_{SKE}^3 that is not known by any other entity, masking the ciphertexts. It also computes MAC tags of these new ciphertexts using k_{MAC} and again encrypts the resulting ciphertexts and MAC tags first under the key k_{SKE}^2 shared with P_1 and then under a key k_{SKE}^1 that is currently only known to the TEEs of P_1 and P_2, resulting in set C_1'. The same is done for the ciphertexts in M, using k_{SKE}^2, k_{MAC} and k_{SKE}^1, resulting in M'. Both C_1' and M' are output to P_1.

7. P_1 forwards C_1' and M' to P_2, which sends (release-key) to its TEE in order to obtain k_{SKE}^1, which it uses to partially decrypt the two sets. Let C_1'' denote the first (partially decrypted) set, which contains encryptions of S_1 under k_{SKE}^4, k_{SKE}^3 and k_{SKE}^2, which is not known to P_2. Let M'' denote the second (partially decrypted) set, which contains encryptions of M under k_{Enc}^4 and k_{Enc}^3. From M'', P_2 can select the ciphertexts which belong to its input, i.e. for $(b_2^i || i)$ when the i-th bit of P_2's input is b_2^i. Let C_2 denote the resulting set. However, it cannot compare these ciphertexts to the corresponding ciphertexts of P_1, as it does not know k_{SKE}^2. P_2 sorts C_1'' and C_2 and sends both to P_1.

8. P_1 decrypts C_1'' using k_2, resulting in the set C_1'''. In order to check if P_2 has cheated, it checks that all elements in C_2 and C_1''' are unique and have correct MAC tags under k_{MAC}. As P_2 does not know k_{MAC}, it cannot fake MAC tags.

9. P_1 can now compare the ciphertexts in C_2 and C_1'''. The number of matching ciphertexts indicates the Hamming distance between the inputs of P_1 and P_2. As the ciphertexts are randomly permuted and P_1 does not know k_3, P_1 only knows how many ciphertext match, but does not know to which position they belong.

For a formal protocol description, see the full version.

6.2 Trusted Initializer

A popular application of TEEs is the use as a trusted initializer [32], which provides protocol parties with correlated randomness.

In this setting, leakage to the manufacturer is usually unproblematic, as the correlated randomness is independent of the parties' inputs and the TEEs are not used for further computation.

However, side-channels may pose a problem, as they could allow one party to learn "too much". To this end, consider the following protocol, somewhat similar to the construction in [32]. Let PRG be a pseudorandom generator and let Sig be a signature scheme.

1. Parties P_1 and P_2 are each equipped with a TEE.
2. The TEEs initially exchange keys k_0, k_1.
3. The TEE of P_1 computes $m_b = \text{PRG}(k_b)$ for $b \in \{0,1\}$ and outputs (m_0, m_1) to P_1.
4. The TEE of P_2 samples a random $b' \xleftarrow{\$} \{0,1\}$ and outputs $(b', m_{b'} = \text{PRG}(k_{b'}))$ to P_2.

This randomized OT can later be de-randomized. If the TEE of P_2 has side-channels that expose k_0 and k_1, the protocol is completely insecure, as P_2 would learn both m_0 and m_1.

We propose a construction for randomized oblivious transfer which is not only secure for semi-honest TEEs, but also for almost-transparent TEEs.

Construction 3 (Protocol π_{rOT}). *Let* Sig *be a signature scheme and* $\text{SKE}_{\text{detCPA}}$ *a deterministic secret-key encryption scheme. Let* $\kappa \in \mathbb{N}$ *be a security parameter. Let* $M = \{0,1\}^\kappa$ *be a message space. Let* $\mathcal{G}_{att} = \mathcal{G}_{att}[\text{Sig}, \text{SKE}_{\text{detCPA}}, \kappa]$.

Program prog_1 *of* P_1*'s enclave:*

1. *Receive* $(\text{mpk}, \text{eid}_1, \text{eid}_2, \text{prog}_2)$ *as first input.*
2. *Execute* $(\text{key-exchange}, \text{eid}_2)$*. Eventually, receive a message* $(\text{eid}_1', \text{eid}_2', \text{hdl})$*. Store* hdl *if* $\text{eid}_1' = \text{eid}_1$ *and* $\text{eid}_2' = \text{eid}_2$*.*
3. *On input* $(\text{init}, sid, \sigma, vk)$*:*
   (a) *Abort if* $\text{Sig.Vfy}(\text{ready}, \sigma, vk) \neq 1$*.*
   (b) *Sample* $m_0, m_1 \xleftarrow{\$} M$*.*
   (c) *Set* $c_i = \text{ske.enc}(\text{hdl}, m_i)$ *for* $i \in \{0,1\}$*.*
   (d) *Output* $(\text{ciphertexts}, sid, (c_0, c_1, vk))$*.*
   (e) *Upon the next activation, output* $(\text{result}, sid, m_0, m_1)$*.*
4. *Ignore all further messages.*

Program prog_2 *of* P_2*'s enclave:*

1. *Receive* $(\text{mpk}, \text{eid}_1, \text{eid}_2, \text{prog}_2)$ *as first input.*
2. *Eventually receive a message* $(\text{eid}_1', \text{eid}_2', \text{hdl})$*. Store* hdl *if* $\text{eid}_1' = \text{eid}_1$ *and* $\text{eid}_2' = \text{eid}_2$*.*
3. *On input* $(\text{init}, sid, (\text{ciphertexts}, sid, (c_0, c_1), vk), \sigma')$*:*
   (a) *Verify that* σ' *is a valid signature for the output* $(\text{ciphertexts}, sid, (c_0, c_1), vk)$ *of the TEE with EID* eid_1*. If the verification fails, halt.*
   (b) *Sample* $b \xleftarrow{\$} \{0,1\}$*.*
   (c) *Set* $m_b = \text{ske.dec}(\text{hdl}, c_b)$*.*
   (d) *Output* $(\text{result}, sid, (b, m_b))$*.*
4. *Ignore all further messages.*

Protocol:
If activated without input, a party yields the execution until input is received.

1. *Each party P_i (eventually) receives input (start, sid).*
2. *P_1 and P_2 each send (getpk) to $\mathcal{G}_{att}$ to obtain the master public key mpk.*
3. *P_2 generates a signature key pair $(sk_2, vk_2) \leftarrow$ Sig.Gen(1^κ) and sends vk_2 to P_1.*
4. *P_1 sends (install, sid, prog$_1$) to $\mathcal{G}_{att}$, where prog$_1$ is the program for P_1's enclave in Construction 3. It obtains eid$_1$ as answer and sends eid$_1$ to P_2.*
5. *Similary, P_2 installs an enclave with program prog$_2$, obtains eid$_2$ and sends it to P_1.*
6. *P_1 sends (mpk, eid$_1$, eid$_2$, prog$_2$) to its TEE with EID eid$_1$ via $\mathcal{G}_{att}$. Conversely, P_2 sends (mpk, eid$_1$, eid$_2$, prog$_1$) to its TEE with EID eid$_2$.*
7. *P_1 samples $r_0, r_1 \xleftarrow{\$} M$ and sends (r_0, r_1) to P_2 via $\mathcal{F}_{\text{SMT}}$, i.e. via a secure channel.*
8. *Upon receiving (r_0, r_1) via $\mathcal{F}_{\text{SMT}}$, P_2 samples a random bit $b' \xleftarrow{\$} \{0, 1\}$ and sends b' to P_1 via $\mathcal{F}_{\text{SMT}}$.*
9. *P_2 also generates a signature to the message "ready", i.e. computes $\sigma_2 \leftarrow$ Sig.Sign(sk_2, ready). Then, P_2 sends σ_2 to P_1.*
10. *Upon receiving σ_2, P_1 sends (init, sid, σ_2, vk_2) to its TEE with EID eid$_1$, receives (ciphertexts, sid, $(c_0, c_1, vk_2), \sigma_C$) as answer and forwards it to P_2.*
11. *On its next activation P_1 activates its TEE with EID eid$_1$ again and receives (result, sid, m_0, m_1). Then, P_1 outputs (result, sid, $(m_0 \oplus r_0, m_1 \oplus r_1)$ if $b' = 0$ and (result, sid, $(m_1 \oplus r_1, m_0 \oplus r_0)$ otherwise, i.e. if $b' = 1$.*
12. *Upon receiving (ciphertexts, sid, $(c_0, c_1, vk'), \sigma_C$) from P_1, P_2 asserts that $vk' = vk_2$ and verifies σ_C. In case of failure, abort. Then, P_2 sends (init, sid, (ciphertexts, sid, $(c_0, c_1, vk'), \sigma_C$)) to its TEE with EID eid$_2$ and receives (result, (b, m_b)) as answer. P_2 then outputs (result, $b \oplus b', m'_b \oplus r_b$).*

We consider the following functionality, where M is a message space.

- If P_1 is honest, choose $m_0, m_1 \xleftarrow{\$} M$ uniformly at random. If P_1 is corrupted, the adversary may provide $m_0, m_1 \in M$.
- If P_2 is honest, choose $b \xleftarrow{\$} \{0, 1\}$ uniformly at random. If P_2 is corrupted, the adversary may provide $(b, m_b) \in \{0, 1\} \times M$.
- Generate a private delayed output (m_0, m_1) to P_1 and a private delayed output (b, m_b) to P_2.

This functionality provides meaningful security for P_1 because P_2 never learns m_{1-b} and for P_2 because P_1 never learns b.

If P_1 is corrupted, the simulator simulates P_2 honestly and observes the protocol output for P_1. It sends the output to the ideal functionality as m_0, m_1.

Similarly, if P_2 is corrupted, the simulator simulates P_1 honestly and observes the output for P_2. Then, it sends this output to the functionality as (b, m_b).

If the TEE is corrupted semi-honestly, the simulator simply executes the protocol honestly on behalf of P_1 and P_2 and reports all messages from the TEE functionality.

The key insight with respect to the security in the presence of almost-transparent TEEs is the fact the TEE of P_2 *selectively* decrypts only one of the ciphertext, with the other ciphertext's plaintext remaining hidden. In a sense, this is the computational analogue of an erasure channel.

6.3 Oblivious Transfer

Construction 3 can be easily modified to directly compute oblivious transfer for user-provided inputs (m_0, m_1) of P_1 and b of P_2.

7 Conclusion

Private set intersection is an important privacy-enhancing technology with many possible applications. In this work, we have constructed and implemented a protocol for one-sided two-party PSI using trusted execution environments that is both asymptotically and practically efficient, beating the best known protocol with respect to single-threaded performance.

Instead of fully trusting the TEE, we substantially lower the required trust: Our protocol remains secure even if either i) the TEEs have side-channels and leak information to the host, except for simple cryptographic operations that remain secure or ii) the TEEs are semi-honest and leak *all* information to an entity such as the manufacturer, but not the protocol participants. This is motivated by what is assumed to be provided by current TEEs such as Intel SGX.

To show the usefulness of our model, we have also presented protocols in our model for additional tasks such as computing the one-sided Hamming distance or (randomized) oblivious transfer.

Acknowledgements. This work was supported by KASTEL Security Research Labs.

Felix Dörre: This work was supported by funding by the German Federal Ministry of Education and Research (BMBF) under the project "VE-ASCOT" (ID 16ME0275). Jeremias Mechler, Jörn Müller-Quade: This work was supported by funding from the topic Engineering Secure Systems of the Helmholtz Association (HGF).

We would like to thank Anastasia Zinkina for providing valuable feedback and laying the foundation for this work in her master's thesis [49]. We would also like to thank the anonymous referees for their valuable and very detailed feedback.

References

1. Ahmad, A., Kim, K., Sarfaraz, M.I., Lee, B.: OBLIVIATE: a data oblivious filesystem for intel SGX (2018)
2. Apple: Secure enclave (2022). https://support.apple.com/guide/security/secure-enclave-sec59b0b31ff/web. Accessed 31 Aug 2022
3. Ateniese, G., De Cristofaro, E., Tsudik, G.: (If) size matters: Size-hiding private set intersection, pp. 156–173 (2011). https://doi.org/10.1007/978-3-642-19379-8_10
4. Badertscher, C., Canetti, R., Hesse, J., Tackmann, B., Zikas, V.: Universal composition with global subroutines: capturing global setup within plain UC, pp. 1–30 (2020). https://doi.org/10.1007/978-3-030-64381-2_1

5. Bahmani, R., et al.: Secure multiparty computation from SGX, pp. 477–497 (2017)
6. Bellare, M., Desai, A., Jokipii, E., Rogaway, P.: A concrete security treatment of symmetric encryption, pp. 394–403 (1997). https://doi.org/10.1109/SFCS.1997.646128
7. Bhatotia, P., Kohlweiss, M., Martinico, L., Tselekounis, Y.: Steel: composable hardware-based stateful and randomised functional encryption, pp. 709–736 (2021). https://doi.org/10.1007/978-3-030-75248-4_25
8. Boneh, D., Shoup, V.: A graduate course in applied cryptography. Draft 0.6 (2026)
9. Camenisch, J., Drijvers, M., Gagliardoni, T., Lehmann, A., Neven, G.: The wonderful world of global random oracles, pp. 280–312 (2018). https://doi.org/10.1007/978-3-319-78381-9_11
10. Canetti, R.: Universally composable security: a new paradigm for cryptographic protocols, pp. 136–145 (2001). https://doi.org/10.1109/SFCS.2001.959888
11. Canetti, R.: Universally composable security. J. ACM 67(5), 28:1–28:94 (2020). https://doi.org/10.1145/3402457
12. Canetti, R., Dodis, Y., Pass, R., Walfish, S.: Universally composable security with global setup, pp. 61–85 (2007). https://doi.org/10.1007/978-3-540-70936-7_4
13. Canetti, R., Fischlin, M.: Universally composable commitments, pp. 19–40 (2001). https://doi.org/10.1007/3-540-44647-8_2
14. Canetti, R., Goldreich, O., Halevi, S.: The random oracle methodology, revisited (preliminary version), pp. 209–218 (1998). https://doi.org/10.1145/276698.276741
15. Canetti, R., Goldreich, O., Halevi, S.: On the random-oracle methodology as applied to length-restricted signature schemes, pp. 40–57 (2004). https://doi.org/10.1007/978-3-540-24638-1_3
16. Canetti, R., Jain, A., Scafuro, A.: Practical UC security with a global random oracle, pp. 597–608 (2014). https://doi.org/10.1145/2660267.2660374
17. Canetti, R., Krawczyk, H.: Universally composable notions of key exchange and secure channels, pp. 337–351 (2002). https://doi.org/10.1007/3-540-46035-7_22
18. Carter, J., Wegman, M.N.: Universal classes of hash functions. J. Comput. Syst. Sci. 18(2), 143–154 (1979). https://doi.org/10.1016/0022-0000(79)90044-8, https://www.sciencedirect.com/science/article/pii/0022000079900448
19. Costan, V., Devadas, S.: Intel SGX explained. Cryptology ePrint Archive, Report 2016/086 (2016). https://eprint.iacr.org/2016/086
20. Diffie, W., Hellman, M.E.: New directions in cryptography, 22(6), 644–654 (1976). https://doi.org/10.1109/TIT.1976.1055638
21. Duong, T., Phan, D.H., Trieu, N.: Catalic: delegated PSI cardinality with applications to contact tracing, pp. 870–899 (2020). https://doi.org/10.1007/978-3-030-64840-4_29
22. Garimella, G., Pinkas, B., Rosulek, M., Trieu, N., Yanai, A.: Oblivious key-value stores and amplification for private set intersection, pp. 395–425 (2021). https://doi.org/10.1007/978-3-030-84245-1_14
23. Garriss, S., Kaminsky, M., Freedman, M.J., Karp, B., Mazières, D., Yu, H.: RE: reliable email. In: Peterson, L.L., Roscoe, T. (eds.) 3rd Symposium on Networked Systems Design and Implementation (NSDI 2006), 8–10 May 2007, San Jose, California, USA, Proceedings. USENIX (2006). http://www.usenix.org/events/nsdi06/tech/garriss.html
24. Goldreich, O.: Towards a theory of software protection and simulation by oblivious RAMs, pp. 182–194 (1987). https://doi.org/10.1145/28395.28416
25. Gueron, S.: Intel advanced encryption standard (AES) new instructions set (2010)

26. Hazay, C., Lindell, Y.: Efficient protocols for set intersection and pattern matching with security against malicious and covert adversaries, pp. 155–175 (2008). https://doi.org/10.1007/978-3-540-78524-8_10

27. IBM: IBM secure execution for Linux (2022). https://www.ibm.com/downloads/cas/O158MBWG, Accessed 31 Aug 2022

28. Intel: Intel software guard extensions (intel SGX) (2023). https://download.01.org/intel-sgx/sgx-linux/2.9.1/docs/Intel_SGX_Developer_Guide.pdf

29. Johnson, S., Scarlata, V., Rozas, C., Brickell, E., Mckeen, F.: Intel software guard extensions: EPID provisioning and attestation services. White Paper **1**(1–10), 119 (2016)

30. Kulshrestha, A., Mayer, J.R.: Identifying harmful media in end-to-end encrypted communication: Efficient private membership computation. In: Bailey, M., Greenstadt, R. (eds.) 30th USENIX Security Symposium, USENIX Security 2021(August), pp. 11–13, 2021, pp. 893–910. USENIX Association (2021). https://www.usenix.org/conference/usenixsecurity21/presentation/kulshrestha

31. Kumar, A.: Active platform management demystified: unleashing the power of intel VPro (TM) technology. Intel Press (2009)

32. Lu, Y., Zhang, B., Zhou, H.S., Liu, W., Zhang, L., Ren, K.: Correlated randomness teleportation via semi-trusted hardware - enabling silent multi-party computation, pp. 699–720 (2021). https://doi.org/10.1007/978-3-030-88428-4_34

33. Marlinspike, M.: Private contact discovery for signal. https://signal.org/blog/private-contact-discovery/ (2017)

34. McCune, J.M., Parno, B., Perrig, A., Reiter, M.K., Isozaki, H.: Flicker: an execution infrastructure for tcb minimization. In: Sventek, J.S., Hand, S. (eds.) Proceedings of the 2008 EuroSys Conference, Glasgow, Scotland, UK, April 1–4, 2008. pp. 315–328. ACM (2008). https://doi.org/10.1145/1352592.1352625, https://doi.org/10.1145/1352592.1352625

35. Melotti, D., Rossi-Bellom, M., Continella, A.: Reversing and fuzzing the google titan m chip. In: Reversing and Offensive-oriented Trends Symposium, pp. 1–10 (2021)

36. Müller-Quade, J., Unruh, D.: Long-term security and universal composability, **23**(4), 594–671 (2010). https://doi.org/10.1007/s00145-010-9068-8

37. Murdock, K., Oswald, D., Garcia, F.D., Van Bulck, J., Gruss, D., Piessens, F.: Plundervolt: software-based fault injection attacks against intel SGX, pp. 1466–1482 (2020). https://doi.org/10.1109/SP40000.2020.00057

38. Nilsson, A., Bideh, P.N., Brorsson, J.: A survey of published attacks on intel SGX. CoRR abs/2006.13598 (2020). https://arxiv.org/abs/2006.13598

39. Pass, R., Shi, E., Tramèr, F.: Formal abstractions for attested execution secure processors, pp. 260–289 (2017). https://doi.org/10.1007/978-3-319-56620-7_10

40. Pinkas, B., Rosulek, M., Trieu, N., Yanai, A.: PSI from PaXoS: Fast, malicious private set intersection, pp. 739–767 (2020). https://doi.org/10.1007/978-3-030-45724-2_25

41. Rindal, P., Raghuraman, S.: Blazing fast PSI from improved OKVS and subfield VOLE. IACR Cryptol. ePrint Arch. p. 320 (2022). https://eprint.iacr.org/2022/320

42. Rindal, P., Rosulek, M.: Improved private set intersection against malicious adversaries, pp. 235–259 (2017). https://doi.org/10.1007/978-3-319-56620-7_9

43. Schwarz, M., et al.: ZombieLoad: cross-privilege-boundary data sampling, pp. 753–768 (2019). https://doi.org/10.1145/3319535.3354252

44. Stapf, E., Jauernig, P., Brasser, F., Sadeghi, A.: In hardware we trust? from TPM to enclave computing on RISC-V. In: 29th IFIP/IEEE International Conference on Very Large Scale Integration, VLSI-SoC 2021, Singapore, 4–7 October 2021, pp. 1–6. IEEE (2021). https://doi.org/10.1109/VLSI-SoC53125.2021.9606968

45. Sun, H., Su, J., Wang, X., Chen, R., Liu, Y., Hu, Q.: PriMal: cloud-based privacy-preserving malware detection, pp. 153–172 (2017)

46. Tamrakar, S., Liu, J., Paverd, A., Ekberg, J.E., Pinkas, B., Asokan, N.: The circle game: scalable private membership test using trusted hardware, pp. 31–44 (2017)

47. Tramèr, F., Zhang, F., Lin, H., Hubaux, J., Juels, A., Shi, E.: Sealed-glass proofs: using transparent enclaves to prove and sell knowledge. In: 2017 IEEE European Symposium on Security and Privacy, EuroS&P 2017, Paris, France, 26–28 April 2017, pp. 19–34. IEEE (2017). https://doi.org/10.1109/EuroSP.2017.28

48. Van Bulck, J., et al.: Foreshadow: extracting the keys to the intel SGX kingdom with transient out-of-order execution, pp. 991–1008 (2018)

49. Zinkina, A.: UC-sichere private Schnittmengenberechnung mit transparenten Enklaven. KITopen Repository of the Karlsruhe Institute of Technology (2019). https://doi.org/10.5445/IR/1000099120

Quantitative Fault Injection Analysis

Jakob Feldtkeller[1]([✉])([iD]), Tim Güneysu[1,2]([iD]), and Patrick Schaumont[3]([iD])

[1] Horst Görtz Institute for IT Security, Ruhr University Bochum, Bochum, Germany
{jakob.feldtkeller,tim.gueneysu}@rub.de
[2] DFKI, Bremen, Germany
[3] Worcester Polytechnic Institute, Worcester, USA
pschaumont@wpi.edu

Abstract. Active fault injection is a credible threat to real-world digital systems computing on sensitive data. Arguing about security in the presence of faults is non-trivial, and state-of-the-art criteria are overly conservative and lack the ability of fine-grained comparison. However, comparing two alternative implementations for their security is required to find a satisfying compromise between security and performance. In addition, the comparison of alternative fault scenarios can help optimize the implementation of effective countermeasures.

In this work, we use quantitative information flow analysis to establish a vulnerability metric for hardware circuits under fault injection that measures the severity of an attack in terms of information leakage. Potential use cases range from comparing implementations with respect to their vulnerability to specific fault scenarios to optimizing countermeasures. We automate the computation of our metric by integrating it into a state-of-the-art evaluation tool for physical attacks and provide new insights into the security under an active fault attacker.

Keywords: Fault Injection Analysis · Fault Metric · Quantitative Information Flow

1 Introduction

Since their first publication in 1997 by Boneh et *al.* [12], Fault Injection Analysis (FIA) has become a fundamental part of the threat landscape for digital systems. In FIA, a malicious attacker disturbs the intended execution flow of a sensitive system to cause a denial of service, escalate privileges, or gain secret information. Such disturbance of execution is possible through fault injection, for example, via clock glitching [1], voltage glitching [50], electromagnetic pulses [6], or focused laser beams [52]. To thwart the exploitation of FIA, system designers use shields and sensors to prevent and notice a fault injection attempt or introduce redundancy in time, space, or information to detect the propagation of faults throughout the system after successful penetration.

However, the construction of FIA-secure systems requires clear criteria of vulnerability and security for a circuit under attack to direct the deployment of countermeasures. State-of-the-art security definitions for FIA focus on the

J. Guo and R. Steinfeld (Eds.): ASIACRYPT 2023, LNCS 14441, pp. 302–336, 2023.
https://doi.org/10.1007/978-981-99-8730-6_10

observability of faulty behavior at the outputs. In particular, the fault effect is propagated through the circuit and deemed insecure when the output gets affected and dedicated countermeasures are not triggered [4,22,43]. While helpful, this criterion lacks precision for FIA aimed at information leakage. Specifically, it is overly conservative in some cases and fails to detect practical attacks in others. On the one hand, some faults may propagate undetected to the outputs without affecting security. For example, injecting a fault directly into the output of some cryptographic cipher does not affect the security but is marked insecure by the criterion. Hence, the criterion is more a measure of the effectiveness of the countermeasures than of the circuit's vulnerability. On the other hand, Statistical Ineffective Fault Analysis (SIFA) exploits the fact that a fault injection has no impact on the execution (ineffective fault) and is therefore not captured by the criterion at all while being a viable threat to implementation security. For SIFA, additional rules are introduced, such as checking the statistical dependency between secrets and fault detection behavior [31,42]. In addition, the given criterion is binary in the sense that it only offers a categorization in the buckets *secure* and *insecure*. Hence, a qualitative comparison within one of those categories is not possible.

To overcome these limitations, we need a general metric to capture the security quantitatively in the context of information-leaking FIA. In particular, such a quantitative metric universally describes the secrecy loss caused by fault injection, i.e., not by providing a specific attack but by a quantification that is independent of the used analysis method. Such a quantitative metric can be used to identify the necessity of countermeasures and measure their effectiveness more tightly, leading to more optimal secure designs. It also allows the comparison of different designs for security, enabling a trade-off between performance (area, power, latency) and security. Such a trade-off could mean that a certain level of vulnerability is willingly accepted to gain some performance. However, it requires a realistic assessment of the cost in terms of security. Similarly, a designer (or attacker) can locate the most vulnerable fault positions to prioritize development efforts where they are most effective. Also, such a quantitative metric can be used by machine learning algorithms to learn the construction of secure designs in a fine-grained manner. Since machine learning provides no guarantees for the resulting designs, security criteria are required again to assess the result.

To summarize, the overall goal is to create a framework and automated tool for the computation of fault severity that requires minimal effort from the user, with domain- and design-specific information being derived automatically or provided with ease. The tool will be used in an automatic design or evaluation framework to determine realistic fault locations, compute a quantitative security metric for the threat, and use the security assessment to optimize circuit synthesis for both performance *and* security.

Contribution. In this work, we show how to use methods of Quantitative Information Flow (QIF) analysis [3,53] to evaluate security in the context of information-leaking FIA (cf. Sect. 3). For that, we extend a commonly used fault model [44] with *probabilistic faults* and show how to model FIA based on stateless information channels. Hence, we merge results from two scientific communities to define a quantitative vulnerability metric for FIA that separates the notion of secrecy-loss due to fault injection from specific attacks against specific implementations. We provide an algorithm for precise computation, exploiting the efficient representation of boolean functions via Binary Decision Diagrams (BDDs), and integrate this approach into the state-of-the-art evaluation tool for physical security VERICA [42] (cf. Sect. 4). In our implementation, we cover deterministic information channels only. However, we show that we can transform each probabilistic channel into a deterministic channel with external random inputs and, hence, this is no restriction in generality.

The proposed quantitative FIA metric can be used to evaluate the efficiency of fault attacks (cf. Sect. 5) or the quality of countermeasures (cf. Sect. 6). We use the analysis of attacks to showcase the accuracy of our metric achieved by the tight match between theory and practice. Afterward, the analysis of countermeasures focuses on the generation of new insights to deepen our understanding of secrecy loss due to active fault injection. In particular, we show that some of the recent findings (and foundations to some security proofs) on SIFA are flawed. Also, our quantitative metric allows identifying fault locations that reduce the amount of leakage caused by other faults. This enables the implementation of new defense mechanisms, where the structure of the circuit ensures that when there is a leaking fault, there is always a leakage-reducing fault active.

While there already exist occasional works in the literature that use QIF for the evaluation of FIA, these works are non-generic and limited to specific attacks, countermeasures, or ciphers (cf. Sect. 8.1). Hence, applying those methods to other scenarios requires significant effort and expert knowledge. In contrast, we provide a general evaluation method for automatic computation.

2   Preliminaries

The important notation used throughout this work is given in Table 1. In general, we write functions in sans serif font (e.g., F) and sets as upper-case characters using a calligraphic font (e.g., $\mathcal{S}$). We denote a distribution over a set $\mathcal{S}$ by $\mathbb{D}\mathcal{S}$.

2.1   Fault Injection Analysis

Fault Injection Methods. In FIA, an adversary disrupts the normal execution of a system under attack to gain an advantage. Most fault injection methods require physical access to the attacked device and often manipulate the timing behavior of the circuit [44]. Prominent examples include clock glitching [1], which increases the clock frequency; voltage glitching [50], which increases the propagation delay of logic gates by lowering the supply voltage; electromagnetic pulses [6], which reset parts of the circuit and cause a race between clock and information signals; or focused laser beams [52], which temporarily affect the physical properties of transistors. Recently, however, more and more research has shown the ability to inject faults via software, allowing remote execution of

Table 1. Important notations used throughout this work.

Notation	Description
C	Digital logic circuit.
C	Information-theoretic channel.
$\mathcal{S}, S, s$	Set of secrets, random variable of secrets, and secret value.
$\mathcal{X}, X, x$	Set of inputs (no secrets), random variable of inputs, and input value.
$\mathcal{R}, r$	Set of random values and specific random value.
$\mathcal{Y}, Y, y$	Set of outputs, random variable of outputs, and output value.
Y', y'	Random variable of faulty output, and faulty output value.
δ	Detection flag.
k	Maximum number of simultaneous faults (security order).
τ	Fault type.
$\mathcal{F}$	Set of possible fault combinations.
V	Vulnerability metric (probability of correct guess in one attempt).
L	Leakage metric (number of leaked bits).

FIA. This can be done through the energy management system of modern Central Processing Units (CPUs) [55], through high-frequency accesses to memory locations [29], through valid but malicious bitstreams for Field-Programmable Gate Arrays (FPGAs) [28], or through randomly occurring faults in large systems [54]. In general, faults can be transient, i.e., having only a short-term effect, or permanent.

Analysis Methods. By exploiting faults, an adversary can bypass access-control mechanisms, cause denial of service, or obtain secret information. In this work, we focus on the leakage of sensitive information, where many analysis mechanisms are inspired by techniques from cryptanalysis. The first published fault attack by Boneh et al. [12] falls in the category of Algebraic Fault Analysis (AFA) [19]. It solves a system of equations depending on correct and faulty outputs and intermediate variables for the secret. Similarly, Differential Fault Analysis (DFA) [9] exploits known differentials between a correct and a faulty intermediate state to reduce the possible key space. In particular, only those key hypotheses remain where, for all pairs of correct and faulty outputs, the intermediate differential matches with the induced fault. The same idea can be applied to impossible differentials [8]. Collision-based Fault Analysis (CFA) [10] uses only correct and faulty output pairs where the output does not change despite the injected fault. The simplest example is a known fault injected into some key bit. If the output is the same for the correct and the faulty output, then the fault is a correct key guess. All the previous FIA techniques require pairs of correct and faulty outputs. The insight of biased FIA [37] is that only faulty outputs are needed if the fault injection causes some bias in an intermediate state, either because of

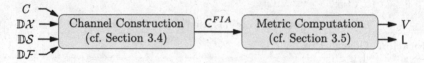

Fig. 1. Framework for quantitative fault-injection analysis.

dependencies between the secret and the fault occurrence or because of the fault itself is biased (e.g., set/reset faults). Then, only those key hypotheses remain that lead to the known bias in the intermediate state. SIFA [23] uses the same idea, but creates the bias by discarding all outputs where the fault has an effect.

2.2   Side-Channel Analysis and Masking

Another highly relevant attack is passive Side-Channel Analysis (SCA), where an adversary observes some physical characteristics such as timing [35], instantaneous power consumption [36], or electromagnetic emanations [27] to recover some processed secret, e.g., a cryptographic key. For arguing about SCA security theoretically, the d-probing model [33] was introduced, where an adversary gets access to d chosen intermediate values. As protection against such attacks, *boolean masking* [15] replaces each $x_i \in \mathbb{F}_2$ with a vector $\langle x_{i,0}, \ldots, x_{i,n-1} \rangle \in \mathbb{F}_2^n$ with $n \in \mathbb{N}$, such that knowing any set of up to d shares $x_{i,j}$ does not reveal any information about x_i, and $x_i = \bigoplus_{j=0}^{n-1} x_{i,j}$. The optimal amount of shares is $n = d+1$ (with less there is a trivial attack by probing all shares of some value). Similarly, the circuit is transformed into a *masked circuit* by transferring each operation to a set of operations that produces share vectors of the output from share vectors of the input.

3   A Vulnerability Metric for FIA

In the following, we describe the proposed vulnerability metric for FIA. For that, we start by defining our circuit, fault, and adversary models. Then we present our framework by showing how to construct an appropriate information channel and describe the actual computation of the vulnerability metric (cf. Fig. 1).

3.1   Circuit Model

Stateless Channel. We model a circuit C as a probabilistic information channel $\mathsf{C} : \mathcal{X} \times \mathcal{S} \to \mathbb{D}\mathcal{Y}$ with a secret $s \in \mathcal{S}$ and some $x \in \mathcal{X}$ as inputs that produce a (probabilistic) output $y \in \mathcal{Y}$ [3]. Thereby, the adversary tries to learn the secret s and the output y should model all information that an adversary learns by observing the execution of the circuit. In general, we describe such a channel as a matrix, where each entry $\mathsf{C}_{(x,s),y}$ gives the probability $\Pr[y \mid x, s]$. Hence, each row lists all the output probabilities given a specific input and sums up to 1. If $\mathsf{C}(x,s)$ is uniquely defined, i.e., each row has exactly one entry equal to 1, we call the circuit deterministic.

We assume a stateless channel, meaning that each input is processed independently of all previous inputs, i.e., there is no notion of time or order between different executions. In particular, the channel always accepts the same input multiple times and processes it in the same (probabilistic) way. This restriction has implications for the type of countermeasures captured by this model, as discussed below (cf. Sect. 3.4). A stateless channel does not restrict the circuit to be stateless, i.e., the circuit may contain memory elements such as registers. However, before feeding a new input to the circuit, all memory elements are reset to an initial value, so there is no dependency between different executions.

Directed Graph. To precisely model the ability of a faulting adversary, we need more internal information about the circuit than provided by a probabilistic channel. A common method in the literature is to model a circuit via a Direct Acyclic Graph (DAG) [44]. For this, we define a set of input and output gates $\mathcal{G}_{io} = \{\text{in}, \text{out}\}$ where in has no input and outputs a value from the finite field $\mathbb{F}_2$, and out does the opposite. Further, without loss of generality, we define the set of combinatorial gates to be $\mathcal{G}_c = \{\text{inv}, \text{and}, \text{nand}, \text{xor}, \text{xnor}\}$ and the set of memory gates to be clocked registers $\mathcal{G}_m = \{\text{reg}\}$. To represent probabilistic circuits, we define a randomness gate $\mathcal{G}_{rand} = \{\text{rand}\}$ with no input that outputs an independent and uniformly chosen value at each clock cycle. Then, we model a circuit C as a *directed graph* $\mathcal{C} = \{\mathcal{G}, \mathcal{W}\}$, where vertices $g \in \mathcal{G} = \mathcal{G}_{io} \cup \mathcal{G}_c \cup \mathcal{G}_m \cup \mathcal{G}_{rand}$ represent logical gates and edges $w \in \mathcal{W}$ represent wires connecting two gates and carrying a value from the field $\mathbb{F}_2$.

3.2 Fault Model

We assume a slightly modified version of the fault model from Richter-Brockmann et al. [44]. In this model, up to k faults are injected into gates, and affected gates are transformed to a different gate type specified by the fault type $\tau \in \mathcal{T}$ (cf. Fig. 2a and 2b). Typical fault types are *set*, *reset* (replacing the targeted gate with a constant one or zero, respectively), or *bit flips* (inversion of the gate). In contrast to Richter-Brockmann et al., we introduce a probabilistic notion of fault location. A fault can occur in a subset of gates $\mathcal{G}' \subseteq \mathcal{G}$. Then a fault is a tuple $f_i = (g, \tau)$ with $g \in \mathcal{G}'$ and $\tau \in \mathcal{T}$. We define a probability distribution $\mathbb{D}\mathcal{F}$ over the set $\mathcal{F}$ of all fault combinations f with up to k faults. The combination with zero faults is always in $\mathbb{D}\mathcal{F}$, potentially with probability zero. Hence, each fault combination will occur with a certain probability defined by $\Pr[f] \in \mathbb{D}\mathcal{F}$, as depicted in Fig. 2c.

This model naturally expresses transient faults, i.e., faults that affect the circuit only for a short amount of time (at one invocation). Permanent faults can be modeled by altering the underlying circuit structure according to the fault (as a fault is inherently a gate transformation).

Motivation for Probabilistic Fault Model. In the context of FIA, we consider an adversary (cf. Sect. 3.3) who is deliberate in the choice of faults that they inject. Specifically, an adversary will always try to inject faults that maximize the gain,

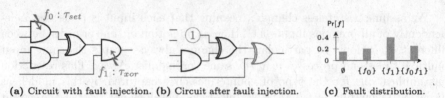

(a) Circuit with fault injection. (b) Circuit after fault injection.   (c) Fault distribution.

Fig. 2. In our fault model gates are transformed into other gate types depending on the fault type $\tau \in \mathcal{T}$. Each fault combination occurs with a probability $\Pr[f] \in \mathbb{DF}$.

i.e., maximize the leakage of some secret value. However, in practice, an adversary is restricted in the means of fault injection, resulting in a certain imprecision in the fault location. While precise methods exist, e.g., via focused laser beams [52], those methods are expensive in equipment and challenging in execution. Other fault methods, e.g., clock or voltage glitching [1,50], are much easier and cheaper but have a widely dispersed effect on the circuit. For example, the effect of clock glitching is determined by the timing behavior of each path given the current inputs together with the previously stored values of each register [44]. Similarly, a laser attack where the diameter of the laser beam is larger than the size of the transistor switches in the underlying technology may simultaneously affect multiple neighboring gates. Hence, mostly an attacker is not in total control of the effect the injected fault has on the circuit, which leads to a probabilistic fault behavior. We model this probabilistic behavior by $\mathbb{DF}$. While we extend the fault model with probabilistic faults and use $\mathbb{DF}$ in our subsequent analysis, we do not answer the question of how to come up with reasonable fault distributions. However, in practice, all fault attacks have implicit or explicit assumptions on $\mathbb{DF}$ (e.g., uniformly distributed faults) which can be used for analysis. Ideally, deriving $\mathbb{DF}$ would be part of a security-aware Electronic Design Automation (EDA) environment, which computes a reasonable approximation given some fault injection parameters. However, as this is a complex research question in its own right, we leave this for future work.

3.3 Adversary Model

The adversary $\mathcal{A}_f$ gets access to a circuit C that can be invoked exactly twice with the same input, once without manipulation and once with manipulation via fault injection. For this, $\mathcal{A}_f$ has access to the circuit structure as a directed graph and the corresponding channel matrix. The goal of $\mathcal{A}_f$ is to learn the specific input $s \in \mathcal{S}$ of which $\mathcal{A}_f$ has prior knowledge of the general distribution $\mathbb{DS}$. In addition, $\mathcal{A}_f$ knows the distribution over the other inputs $\mathbb{DX}$ (which is independent of $\mathbb{DS}$) and of the distribution over possible faults $\mathbb{DF}$.

Usually, the distribution of secrets $\mathbb{DS}$ is defined as a uniform distribution, meaning that the adversary has no prior knowledge about the secret. The distribution over the other inputs $\mathbb{DX}$ can be adjusted to model the specific scenario of interest. For example, a uniform distribution to represent other secret values $\mathcal{A}_f$ is not particularly interested in, a distribution with $\Pr[x] = 1$ for some $x \in \mathcal{X}$

to represent a known or adversary chosen input value, or something in between for scenarios where $\mathcal{A}_f$ has some knowledge about the input, e.g., because of formatting or padding.

After the invocation of C, $\mathcal{A}_f$ gets access to a fault-free output y and a faulty output y'. Providing $\mathcal{A}_f$ with the pair (y, y') marks a powerful attacker who can observe the precise effect of the injected fault. Often this is justified by an adversary who can run a circuit multiple times with the same input (as the channel C is stateless). By using probabilistic channels, our model also accounts for circuits where different probabilistic choices are used to derive y and y'. Importantly $\mathcal{A}_f$ is an information-theoretical adversary, and we do not restrict the computational power. Also, the adversary always tries to learn a secret and is not interested in behavior manipulation for other purposes, e.g., denial of service or bypassing access control.

3.4   Constructing a FIA Channel

Channel Composition. Channels can be combined into larger channels according to certain rules. In the following, we provide the composition rules for two types of two-channel compositions. Of course, these can be extended to the composition of any number of channels through iterative composition.

Parallel Composition. The simplest variant of channel composition is a parallel composition [3], where the adversary gets the output of two independent runs of two channels. The resulting channel matrix can be computed from the channel matrices being composed. In particular, given two channels $C^1 : \mathcal{X} \to \mathcal{Y}^1$ and $C^2 : \mathcal{X} \to \mathcal{Y}^2$ the entries for the parallel channel matrix can be computed as $(C^1 \parallel C^2)_{x,(y_1,y_2)} = C^1_{x,y_1} \cdot C^2_{x,y_2}$.

Composition via Internal Probabilistic Choice. Another form of composition is internal probabilistic choice [3], where the adversary gets the output of only one of two channels, but does not know which one was chosen. Again, the resulting channel matrix can be computed from the two channels. Given two channels $C^1 : \mathcal{X} \to \mathcal{Y}^1$ and $C^2 : \mathcal{X} \to \mathcal{Y}^2$ the entries for the composed channel can be computed by

$$(C^1 \oplus_r C^2)_{x,y} = \begin{cases} \Pr[C^1]C^1_{x,y} + (1 - \Pr[C^1])C^2_{x,y} & y \in \mathcal{Y}^1 \cap \mathcal{Y}^2 \\ \Pr[C^1]C^1_{x,y} & y \in \mathcal{Y}^1 \setminus \mathcal{Y}^2 \\ (1 - \Pr[C^1])C^2_{x,y} & y \in \mathcal{Y}^2 \setminus \mathcal{Y}^1 \end{cases}$$

FIA Channel. We use the above composition rules to construct a channel that represents the adversary's view and knowledge. In particular, we construct individual channels C^f for all fault combinations $f \in \mathcal{F}$, such that C^f represents the circuit C under the fault combination f. All these channels are composed by internal probabilistic choice under the distribution $\mathbb{D}\mathcal{F}$ to model a randomly

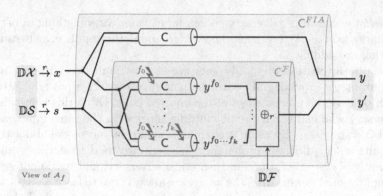

Fig. 3. Construction of a FIA information channel via composition.

selected fault scenario. The resulting channel $\mathsf{C}^{\mathcal{F}}$ is then composed in parallel with the unaltered circuit channel C, to acknowledge the leakage of pairs of correct and faulty outputs. An overview of the construction is given in Fig. 3. As a result, the overall channel matrix can be computed as

$$\mathsf{C}^{FIA}_{(x,s),(y,y')} = \mathsf{C}_{(y,s),y} \sum_{f \in \mathcal{F}} \Pr[f] \mathsf{C}^{f}_{(x,s),y'}$$

By providing the same input x and s to all channels, we can model the correct and incorrect channel executions as independent runs while still guaranteeing that the output pair (y, y') results from the same inputs.

Coverage of FIA Channel. The presented FIA channel covers a wide range of possible fault attacks and circuit structures. In particular, the channel represents all attacks that use only faulty outputs, use only correct outputs (where faulty outputs are suppressed), and use a combination of faulty and correct outputs. While the last attack scenario is trivially covered, the other two scenarios are included because the FIA channel is a composition of the channels that model the attacks where only one type of output is used. In particular, the composition strategies used do not reduce the amount of leaked information. The proposed channel is restricted in the sense that $\mathcal{A}_f$ only has access to a single output pair (y, y'). However, we argue that the analysis of leakage for a single output pair is a good enough approximation of the severity of attacks using multiple output pairs since these attacks also rely on the existence of leakage for a single output pair. Similarly, an attacker using multiple faulty outputs y'_i for each non-faulty output y relays on the existence of leakage in the case of a single faulty y'.

Since the only requirement for the channel is that it is stateless, a wide range of countermeasures can be evaluated. In particular, all countermeasures that do not depend on a stored state are covered by our model, e.g., detection, correction, and infection based on redundancy in time, space, or information. An example of a countermeasure that is out of scope is an implementation that stores all used inputs and never responds to an input a second time.

3.5   FIA Vulnerability and Leakage

Vulnerability. After constructing the appropriate channel for FIA, we can now compute the leakage of a given fault scenario and use this leakage as a metric for severity. In general, the *vulnerability* V is defined as the probability that an adversary can guess the secret in one attempt [3,53]. In particular, an adversary would always guess the most likely value to maximize the probability of success and hence $V[S] = \max_{s \in \mathcal{S}} \Pr[S = s]$. However, we are interested in the vulnerability given some output observation, which is given by the *conditional vulnerability* [3,53] with $V[S \mid Y] = \sum_{y \in \mathcal{Y}} \Pr[Y = y] \cdot \max_{s \in \mathcal{S}} \Pr[S = s \mid Y = y]$. Intuitively, the conditional vulnerability provides the expected probability that an adversary can guess the secret in one attempt, given a particular observation. Using the expected probability makes it a property of the channel rather than of a specific observation. Hence, the FIA vulnerability separates the secrecy loss caused by a fault injection from the specific attack and provides a general metric. Computing the conditional vulnerability is more practical when computed as $V[S \mid Y] = \sum_{y \in \mathcal{Y}} \max_{s \in \mathcal{S}} \Pr[Y = y \mid S = s] \Pr[S = s]$, which is equivalent using Bayes' Theorem [53]. Then, using the channel C^{FIA} defined above, we can derive the vulnerability for FIA as:

$$
\begin{aligned}
V[S \mid Y, Y'] &= \sum_{y,y'} \max_s (\Pr[s]\Pr[y, y' \mid s]) \\
&\overset{(*)}{=} \sum_{y,y'} \max_s (\sum_x \Pr[s]\Pr[x]\Pr[y, y' \mid x, s]) \\
&\overset{(**)}{=} \sum_{y,y'} \max_s (\sum_x \Pr[s]\Pr[x]\Pr[y \mid x, s] \sum_f \Pr[f]\Pr[y' \mid x, s]).
\end{aligned}
$$

* Law of total probability ** Channel decomposition

Information Leakage. Translating the vulnerability to a measure of bits leads to the *min-entropy* $H_\infty(S) = \log_2(1/V[S])$ or the *conditional min-entropy* $H_\infty(S \mid Y) = \log_2(1/V[S \mid Y])$ [3,53]. Here, the min-entropy is an expression of the residual uncertainty of the secret for the adversary. Finally, we can compute the *information leakage* L as the difference between the uncertainty before and after the circuit execution, i.e., $L[S \mid Y] = H_\infty(S) - H_\infty(S \mid Y)$ [3,53].

The information leakage is a measure of the information that an adversary can expect to learn about a secret after observing the execution of the system (in our case, the FIA channel), i.e., the leakage is weighted by the probability of occurrence. Thus, a non-integer value can be interpreted as: *There is a certain probability that some of the secret bits will be leaked to the adversary.*

3.6   Composition of Independent Fault-Channels

With the above-given definition of vulnerability, we can provide a meaningful definition of independence in the context of faults. In particular, two faults (or sets of faults) are independent of each other if the vulnerability caused by both faults can be split into the product of the individual vulnerabilities for each fault (with a correction term for the general vulnerability of the secret). Hence, the definition mirrors the definition of independent probabilities.

Definition 1. *For a given channel* C *two fault combinations* $f_0, f_1 \in \mathcal{F}$ *are independent iff*

$$V[S \mid \mathsf{C}^{f_0} \to (Y,Y')] \cdot V[S \mid \mathsf{C}^{f_1} \to (Y,Y')] = V[S] \cdot V[S \mid \mathsf{C}^{f_0 \wedge f_1} \to (Y,Y')].$$

Intuitively, this means that the impact of f_0 does not interfere with the impact of f_1 and vice versa. This gets more obvious when considering the leakage of two independent faults, which gets additive. Hence, the two faults leak different, i.e., independent, bits about the secret.

Theorem 1. *Two fault combinations* $f_0, f_1 \in \mathcal{F}$ *are independent iff* $\mathsf{L}[S|\mathsf{C}^{f_0} \to (Y,Y')] + \mathsf{L}[S|\mathsf{C}^{f_1} \to (Y,Y')] = \mathsf{L}[S|\mathsf{C}^{f_0 \wedge f_1} \to (Y,Y')].$

Proof.

$$V[S \mid \mathsf{C}^{f_0} \to (Y,Y')] \cdot V[S \mid \mathsf{C}^{f_1} \to (Y,Y')] = V[S] \cdot V[S \mid \mathsf{C}^{f_0 \wedge f_1} \to (Y,Y')]$$
$$\Leftrightarrow H_\infty(S \mid \mathsf{C}^{f_0} \to (Y,Y')) + H_\infty(S \mid \mathsf{C}^{f_1} \to (Y,Y'))$$
$$= H_\infty(S) + H_\infty(S \mid \mathsf{C}^{f_0 \wedge f_1} \to (Y,Y'))$$
$$\Leftrightarrow H_\infty(S) - H_\infty(S \mid \mathsf{C}^{f_0} \to (Y,Y')) + H_\infty(S) - H_\infty(S \mid \mathsf{C}^{f_1} \to (Y,Y'))$$
$$= H_\infty(S) - H_\infty(S \mid \mathsf{C}^{f_0 \wedge f_1} \to (Y,Y'))$$
$$\Leftrightarrow \mathsf{L}[S \mid \mathsf{C}^{f_0} \to (Y,Y')] + \mathsf{L}[S \mid \mathsf{C}^{f_1} \to (Y,Y')] = \mathsf{L}[S \mid \mathsf{C}^{f_0 \wedge f_1} \to (Y,Y')]$$

The property of independent faults can be used to analyze fault scenarios in isolation rather than in combination. Usually, the independence of faults follows from the underlying circuit structure, i.e., the propagation path of the faults does not cross. Then, the leakage can be computed independently for each circuit part and then be combined by Theorem 1 (cf. Sect. 5.1 and 5.2).

4   Methodology for Computation

Below we present how to efficiently compute the FIA vulnerability and leakage with Reduced Ordered Binary Decision Diagrams (ROBDDs) [2,13], a canonical, graph-based representation of boolean functions based on the *Shannon Decomposition* (in accordance with the literature we refer to ROBDDs as BDDs throughout this work). The transformation from a circuit to a BDD is simple but limited to DAGs. As a consequence, no looping is allowed within the circuit, and thus no iterative circuits are supported. However, such circuits can be trivially supported by simple *loop unrolling*. In addition, we restrict ourselves to deterministic circuits/channels for simplicity. However, we show below how to transform any probabilistic channel into a deterministic channel, so this is not a real limitation of our approach.

4.1   Circuit Transformation

We begin by describing some basic circuit/channel transformations required as preprocessing for our main algorithm.

Deterministic and Probabilistic Channels.   Our approach is tailored to deterministic channels. However, we show that any probabilistic channel can be transformed into an equivalent deterministic channel. As a result, the proposed analysis approach applies to *all* channels, after a preprocessing for probabilistic channels has been applied. The transformation is done by adding additional *random* input variables that externalize the random choices of the channel. The formal result is given in Theorem 2, where we use the notation $C \to y$ to indicate that the value y is an output of channel C.

Theorem 2. *Any probabilistic channel* $C^P : \mathcal{X} \to \mathbb{D}\mathcal{Y}$ *can be transformed to a deterministic channel* $C^D : \mathcal{X} \times \mathcal{R} \to \mathcal{Y}$ *with* $\Pr[C^P \to y \mid x] = \Pr[C^D \to y \mid x]$.

Proof. Let $C^P : \mathcal{X} \to \mathbb{D}\mathcal{Y}$ be a probabilistic channel with corresponding channel-matrix entries $0 \leq C^P_{x,y} \leq 1$. By definition of the channel matrix it holds that $C^P_{x,y} = \Pr[y \mid x]$. We start by defining a set of random elements $\mathcal{R}$ such that there is a distinct $r_x \in \mathcal{R}$ for each $x \in \mathcal{X}$ with $\exists y \in \mathcal{Y} : C^P_{x,y} \notin \{0,1\}$. Further, let all $r_x \in \mathcal{R}$ be of $\lceil \log_2(|\mathcal{Y}|) \rceil$ bits such that each value $r_x = i$ selects one output value $y_i \in \mathcal{Y}$. We define the distribution $\mathbb{D}\mathcal{R}$ such that $\forall r_x \in \mathcal{R}$ it holds that $\Pr[r_x = i] = C^P_{x,y_i} = \Pr[y \mid x]$. Now we define a deterministic channel $C^D : \mathcal{X} \times \mathcal{R} \to \mathcal{Y}$ with the following channel matrix entries:

$$C^D_{(x,r_x),y_i} = \begin{cases} 1, & \text{if } C^P_{x,y_i} \neq 0 \wedge r_x = i \\ 0, & \text{otherwise} \end{cases}$$

This is the required channel for the following reasons:

$$\Pr[C^D \to y_i \mid x] \overset{(*)}{=} \sum_j \Pr[y_i \mid x \wedge r_x = j]\Pr[r_x = j]$$

$$\overset{(**)}{=} \Pr[y_i \mid x \wedge r_x = i]\Pr[r_x = i]$$

$$\overset{(**)}{=} \Pr[r_x = i]$$

$$\overset{(***)}{=} \Pr[C^P \to y \mid x]$$

* Law of total probability ** Definition $C^D_{(y,r_x),y_i}$ *** Definition $\Pr[r_x = i]$

Since the adversary $\mathcal{A}_f$ has access to the channel matrix C^P, it is essential to provide $\mathcal{A}_f$ with the distribution $\mathbb{D}\mathcal{R}$ after the transformation to C^D. Otherwise, the adversary would be less powerful than before the transformation,

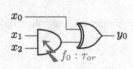

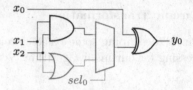

(a) Fault injected in a circuit.   (b) Circuit transformation for fault simulation.

Fig. 4. A circuit under fault injection is adapted to include a MUX that selects between the correct and the faulty behavior of the circuit.

since the details of the probabilistic choices would be missing. In addition, the computation of the vulnerability in the channel C^{FIA} changes to:

$$V[S \mid Y, Y'] = \sum_{y,y'} \max_s (\sum_{x,r} \Pr[s]\Pr[x]\Pr[r]\Pr[y \mid x, s, r] \sum_f \Pr[f]\Pr[y' \mid x, s, r])$$

(1)

Fault-Selection Variables. The adversary and fault model used allows $\mathcal{A}_f$ to select a subset of gates and change them to different gate types according to the specified fault types. A trivial algorithm would instantiate a different circuit C^f for each combination of faults $f \in \mathcal{F}$ (as indicated in Fig. 3) and change the gates accordingly. These different circuit instances can be distributed in time or space. We introduce a more efficient method by proposing a way to encode all possible fault combinations into a single circuit representation. To do this, we introduce new *fault-selection signals* sel_g for each fault location $g \in \mathcal{G}'$. Then, for each fault location $g \in \mathcal{G}'$, we add a Multiplexer (MUX) to the circuit so that the select signal of the MUX is driven by the signal sel_g. Now, the MUX will pass the output of g if $sel_g = 0$, or otherwise select a fault type. For each fault type τ, a different gate is added to the circuit so that the gate type corresponds to τ, the inputs of the gate are the same as the inputs of g, and the output is connected to the MUX. An example instantiation is shown in Fig. 4. In this way, we can evaluate different combinations of faults $f \in \mathcal{F}$ by activating the corresponding fault selection signals sel_g. Of course, this increases the size of the circuit and thus the size of the associated BDD, but it eliminates the need to create each faulty circuit individually.

4.2   Computation of FIA Vulnerability

General Idea. A naive computation of the FIA vulnerability $V[S \mid Y, Y']$ starts by deriving the channel matrix C^{FIA}, as shown in Fig. 3, by iterating over all $x \in \mathcal{X}$, $s \in \mathcal{S}$, $r \in \mathcal{R}$, and $f \in \mathcal{F}$, before computing Eq. 1. Note, however, that after transforming the probabilistic channel C^{FIA} into a deterministic channel, all entries in C^{FIA} are either one or zero. Thus, the matrix is just an encoding of valid input/output pairs that can be efficiently encoded via a BDD. When computing Eq. 1, we ensure that we only iterate over valid pairs of (y, y') by fixing

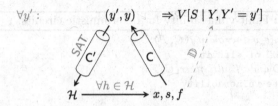

$$\forall y': \qquad (y',y) \qquad \Rightarrow V[S \mid Y, Y' = y']$$

Fig. 5. High-level overview of the principle of Algorithm 1, with $\mathcal{H} = \mathcal{X} \times \mathcal{S} \times \mathcal{R} \times \mathcal{F}$.

the faulty output y', determining all input and fault combinations that can lead to y', and computing only the corresponding non-faulty outputs y. This general principle is illustrated in Fig. 5 and can be efficiently realized using BDDs. In addition, this approach allows for parallel and probabilistic computation of $V[S \mid Y, Y']$, as we discuss below and in Appendix A.

Deterministic Computation. Our BDD-based algorithm for computing the FIA vulnerability $V[S \mid Y, Y']$ is given in Algorithm 1. The use of BDDs allows the efficient inversion of a channel since the set of satisfying assignments of a function is given by all paths ending in the true-leave of the function's BDD (without storing the entire channel matrix).

The input to Algorithm 1 is a circuit C and a set of fault combinations $\mathcal{F}$. We first extend the circuit with fault selection variables (cf. Sect. 4.1) and construct the corresponding channel BDD C'. Then, according to Fig. 5, we iterate over all possible faulty output values y' and compute the corresponding part of the vulnerability. For the actual computation, we need all inputs $x \in \mathcal{X}$, $s \in \mathcal{S}$ in addition to all fault combinations $f \in \mathcal{F}$ that can lead to the faulty output y'. This gives us the set of satisfying assignments $\mathcal{H} = \mathcal{X} \times \mathcal{S} \times \mathcal{R} \times \mathcal{F}$ of the BDD that encodes the output y'. The set of satisfying assignments also contains the specific values for $r \in \mathcal{R}$ that lead to the faulty output. However, to get all possible pairs (y, y') we consider all possible assignments to r when computing y (cf. Line 12). In addition, since we have a deterministic channel, it holds that $\Pr[y' \mid x, s, r, f] = 1$ for $(x, s, r, f) \in \mathcal{H}$ while $\Pr[y' \mid x, s, r, f] = 0$ otherwise. Given the set $\mathcal{H}$, we can compute all pairs (y, y') with $\Pr[y, y' \mid x, s, r, f] = 1$ and then compute the vulnerability $V[S \mid Y, Y' = y']$.

Since Algorithm 1 isolates the computation of $V[S \mid Y, Y' = y']$ for each y', it is easy to parallelize the computation and derive the overall vulnerability V by summing up all individual $V[S \mid Y, Y' = y']$ at the end.

Complexity. The runtime of Algorithm 1 depends on the circuit structure, the number of faults, and their locations. Without this information, it is hard to estimate the number of matching faults in Line 8 and the size of $\mathcal{L}$ in each loop iteration. This makes the impact of the fault cardinality a function of the circuit and the fault locations. However, if we inspect the algorithm considering its use with deterministic circuits, we can see that throughout all iterations of the outer loop, the for loop in Line 6 is executed for all inputs x, s, since in a deterministic

---

Algorithm 1: Fault-vulnerability for deterministic circuits.

```
 1  function fault_vulnerability(C, F):
        // Get BDD of circuit
 2      C' ← BDD[add_fault_mux(C, F)]
        // Compute vulnerability
 3      V ← 0
 4      for y' = 0 to 2^m do
            // Get satisfying assignment for given y'
 5          H ← SAT(BDD[C' = y'])
 6          L ← ∅
 7          for ∀(x, s) ∈ H do
                // Compute ∑_f Pr[f]Pr[y' | x, s]
 8              f_pr ← 0
 9              for f with matching (x, s) do
10                  ⌊ f_pr ← f_pr + Pr[f]
11              for ∀r ∈ R do
12                  y ← C(x, s, r)
                    // Sum up according to matching y
13                  if (y, s) ∈ L then
14                      ⌊ L_{y,s} ← L_{y,s} + Pr[x] · f_pr · Pr[s]
15                  else
16                      ⌊ L_{y,s} ← Pr[x] · f_pr · Pr[s]
            // Sum up everything
17          for ∀y ∈ L do
18              ⌊ V ← V + max(L_y)
19      return V
```

---

circuit all inputs result in exactly one output value. Later, and within this for loop, there is a loop over all random values r. Thus, the algorithm is at least exponential in the number of input bits (secret, non-secret, and random).

4.3 Implementation

We integrated the computation of the FIA vulnerability and leakage, as described in Sect. 4.2, into the state-of-the-art verification tool VERICA [42][1]. VERICA is a BDD-based framework for verifying the independence of secrets and probe distributions for SCA, evaluating the impact of fault propagation on the circuit output for FIA, and the combination of both for Combined Analysis (CA). In contrast to the general fault model (cf. Sect. 3.2), we also allow faults at inputs to model cases where the analysis is performed for a part of a larger design, and thus faults can be placed outside of the analyzed section.

---

[1] https://github.com/Chair-for-Security-Engineering/VERICA.

Input/Output. VERICA receives as input a Verilog netlist of the design under test, an annotation file that defines the type of input/output signals (e.g., secrets, randomness, sharing, or replication), and a definition of the fault model, i.e., the transformation of gates under faults. In addition, to compute the fault vulnerability, a fault whitelist has to be provided that specifies the fault locations (gates) and the fault probabilities (for specific gates). The tool then outputs the vulnerability (and leakage) of the given scenario.

Restrictions to the Implementation. For simplicity and ease of use, we have made the following design choices for the practical implementation. First, we assume that all faults at different fault locations are independent of each other, i.e., the probability of two faults occurring together is the product of the individual probabilities. This simplifies the definition of the fault distribution $\mathbb{D}\mathcal{F}$ since only one fault probability per fault location needs to be defined. Second, we assume that all inputs $x \in \mathcal{X}$, $s \in \mathcal{S}$, and $r \in \mathcal{R}$ are drawn from an independent and uniform distribution. For s and r, this is the most natural choice for most real-world scenarios. For x, this restriction means that $\mathcal{A}_f$ has no control or prior knowledge of the non-secret input, which limits the applicable scenarios. However, it is a reasonable assumption when x is the internal state of a cryptographic function. Both assumptions are not intrinsic to the way of computation, but a simplification to reduce the burden on the user. Of course, all of the above restrictions (Sect. 3 and Sect. 4) still apply.

5 Measuring the Efficiency of Fault Attacks

In the following section, we evaluate the described methodology for a quantitative FIA metric with respect to the match between theory and practice, by analyzing the efficiency of known fault attacks. To do so, we extend the fault model from Sect. 3.2 with additional faults on input values, i.e., each input bit can be manipulated with a *set*, *reset*, or *bit-flip* fault. While input faults have no counterpart in real-world attacks (an input fault is just another input), it is useful when analyzing only parts of circuits where input faults can occur through fault propagation. Indeed, in the following we only focus on scenarios where we analyze parts of the circuits and, hence, $\mathcal{A}_f$ has no prior knowledge of the non-secret input x. All of our circuits are synthesized using the Synopsys Design Compiler with a subset of cells in the NanGate 45 nm Open Cell Library (OCL).

We report our results using the *leakage* $\mathsf{L}[S \mid Y, Y']$. In general, vulnerability and leakage are two representations of the same quantitative metric with different advantages and disadvantages. While the vulnerability provides a standalone metric for security, the leakage is more human understandable but requires knowledge of the bit width of the secret. We decided to focus on the leakage and provide the theoretical maximum leakage where necessary for interpretation.

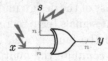

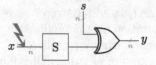

Fig. 6. Setup for key addition.   **Fig. 7.** Setup for DFA.

Table 2. Leakage after injecting faults into a key addition (cf. Fig. 6).

	Fault			Metric		
	location	$Pr[f]$	type	V^*	H_∞^*	L
input key	s_0	1.0	set	0.125	3.000	1.000
	s_0	1.0	reset	0.125	3.000	1.000
	s_0	1.0	flip	0.062	4.000	0.000
	s_0	0.5	set	0.094	3.415	0.585
input state	x_0	1.0	set	0.125	3.000	1.000
	x_0	1.0	reset	0.125	3.000	1.000
	x_0	1.0	flip	0.062	4.000	0.000
$k=2$	$s_0\ s_1$	1.0 1.0	set	0.250	2.000	2.000
	$s_0\ s_1$	1.0 0.5	set	0.188	2.415	1.585

* with $n = 4$.

Theoretical maximum: $L_{KeyAdd}^{max} = 4$.

5.1 Faulting Key Addition

We start our analysis with a simple key addition, i.e., an xor between some intermediate state x and some secret key s, as shown in Fig. 6. This is a well-understood construction with respect to FIA and serves as a trivial test of the soundness of our approach. The results for a 4-bit word are given in Table 2. As expected, *set/reset* faults on a key bit s_i lead to the leakage of one bit (the faulted key bit), while a bit flip does not reveal any secret information (because x is unknown). The reason is that for set/reset faults, the two outputs y and y' are equal if and only if the injected fault is ineffective. In contrast, a bit flip always results in an effective fault at the output. A similar effect can be achieved by corrupting a state bit x_i, as knowing two bits of an xor operation completely determines the third bit. An interesting property of the key addition is that each bit is processed individually, and thus faults injected into a key bit s_i only affect the leakage of that particular key bit. In other words, the injected faults are independent (cf. Definition 1) and it is sufficient to analyze a single construction and scale the leakage to the number of faulted key bits.

5.2 Differential Fault Analysis

One of the most common fault attacks on cryptographic ciphers is DFA [9], where an adversary $\mathcal{A}_f$ gains access to a set of correct and faulty ciphertext

Table 3. DFA against PRESENT and DEFAULT with a single S-box (cf. Fig. 7). Each fault is a bit-flip with probability $\Pr[f_i] = 1$ at the indicated input x_i. In addition, we provide the number of key candidates left after observation of one pair (y, y'), where 256×16 means that in 256 cases for (y, y') there are 16 key candidates left.

Fault location	PRESENT L	PRESENT Key Candidates	DEFAULT L	DEFAULT Key Candidates
-	0.000	256×16	0.000	256×16
$x_0\ x_1\ x_2\ x_3$	2.000	256×4	0.000	256×16
x_0	2.000	256×4	1.000	256×8
$x_0\ x_3$	2.585	$128 \times 2, 128 \times 4$	0.000	256×16
$x_1\ x_2$	2.585	$128 \times 2, 128 \times 4$	0.000	256×16
$x_0\ x_1\ x_2$	2.585	$128 \times 2, 128 \times 4$	1.000	256×8
x_3	2.585	$128 \times 2, 128 \times 4$	1.000	256×8
x_1	2.807	$192 \times 2, 64 \times 4$	1.000	256×8
x_2	2.807	$192 \times 2, 64 \times 4$	1.000	256×8
$x_0\ x_1$	2.807	$192 \times 2, 64 \times 4$	1.000	256×8
$x_0\ x_2$	2.807	$192 \times 2, 64 \times 4$	1.000	256×8
$x_1\ x_3$	2.807	$192 \times 2, 64 \times 4$	1.000	256×8
$x_2\ x_3$	2.807	$192 \times 2, 64 \times 4$	1.000	256×8
$x_0\ x_1\ x_3$	2.807	$192 \times 2, 64 \times 4$	1.000	256×8
$x_0\ x_2\ x_3$	2.807	$192 \times 2, 64 \times 4$	1.000	256×8
$x_1\ x_2\ x_3$	3.000	256×2	1.000	256×8

Theoretical maximum: $\mathsf{L}^{max}_{PRESENT} = 4$, $\mathsf{L}^{max}_{DEFAULT} = 4$.

pairs (y, y') and uses statistical analysis to reduce the search space for the secret key s. For DFA to work, $\mathcal{A}_f$ must inject bit-flip faults into an intermediate state with a subsequent nonlinear layer. For block ciphers, this is commonly done by attacking the last-round key and targeting the faults at the input of the last-round S-boxes. Hence, we have $y = S(x) \oplus s$ and $y' = S(x \oplus \Delta) \oplus s$ for an intermediate state x and a fault difference Δ (a potential last-round linear layer can be removed by choosing the corresponding output bits accordingly). More advanced attacks use the same principle but inject faults in earlier rounds to exploit fault propagation in the given cipher structure to affect multiple S-boxes at once. Therefore, to analyze the susceptibility of ciphers to DFA, it is sufficient to analyze the S-box and key addition of the last round, as shown in Fig. 7, with bit-flip faults on the input bits x_i. This simplification removes the propagation of faults to the input of the last-round S-boxes. While it removes a potential dependency between faults at the S-box input this is a common way to analyze DFA [48]. Similar to the key addition analyzed in the last section, the last-round S-boxes are also in parallel to each other, and faults injected into different S-boxes are independent of each other. Hence, we can restrict our analysis to a single instance and scale the leakage to the full set of affected S-boxes.

4-Bit S-boxes. The results for two 4-bit S-boxes are given in Table 3, along with the number of key candidates remaining after observation of one pair (y, y'). In particular, we analyze the S-boxes of PRESENT [11], a cipher with a focus on implementation efficiency in hardware, and DEFAULT [5], which is specifically designed to resist DFA. First, we observe that the leakage metric is directly related to the number of remaining key candidates. For example, for PRESENT we have a leakage of $L = 2$ when flipping the bit x_0. For the same scenario, it holds that for all possible pairs of (y, y'), 4 out of 16 key candidates remain after observing (y, y'), which means that $\mathcal{A}_f$ learns exactly 2 bits of the key. For the leakage metric, a higher value is better for the adversary, corresponding to a lower number of remaining key candidates. In addition, our metric also correctly measures the improved resistance of the DEFAULT S-box against DFA.

8-Bit S-boxes. We also analyzed AES regarding its susceptibility to DFA by using the AES S-box in the construction of Fig. 7. Interestingly, for all possible input differentials (with $\Pr[f] = 1$), we computed a leakage of $L = 6.989$ bits (where 8 is the theoretical maximum), i.e., all faults are equally bad and leak almost all possible key bits. This is confirmed by the number of key candidates left which is $1024 \times 4 \wedge 64512 \times 2$ for all fault scenarios. This behavior changes when each bit flip occurs with a probability $\Pr[f] < 1$, e.g., a bit-flip probability of $\Pr[f] = 0.5$ leads to a leakage of $L = 6$ when only bit x_7 can flip and $L = 0$ when all bits can flip. However, further analysis is needed to obtain realistic fault scenarios (cf. Sect. 8.2) and their leakage behavior.

5.3   Statistical Ineffective Fault Analysis

Another popular fault attack is SIFA [23], which exploits the knowledge that a fault is injected into some intermediate state but has no effect on the output. This is useful in situations where faulty outputs are suppressed, so $\mathcal{A}_f$ only knows correct outputs and whether a fault is ineffective (has no effect). A *sufficient* condition for a SIFA vulnerability is a statistical dependency between the detection behavior and the secret. That is if an attacker can learn something about the secret just by observing the detection behavior (in the form of a detection flag or suppression of incorrect outputs), SIFA is possible. However, contrary to claims in the literature [31], we later show that this is not a *necessary* condition for SIFA, i.e., security does not follow from the absence of dependency.

In the following, we show that our tool accurately detects leaks from SIFA when there is a statistical dependency between the detection flag and secrets. To do this, we implement two instances of a design and feed the outputs to a detection module, as shown in Fig. 8. Then, faults are injected into only one instance to maintain the correct functionality of the detection module. By considering only the detection flags as outputs, we can ensure that the only leakage detected by our metric results from a SIFA vulnerability.

For the evaluation, we selected three circuits discussed by Daemen et al. [20] based on masking (cf. Sect. 2.2). On its own, masking is not sufficient to protect

Table 4. SIFA against ISW multiplication, and χ_3 and χ_5 with masked Toffoli gates (cf. Fig. 8). All faults occur with probability $\Pr[f] = 1$ and no randomness source is faulted.

	Fault		Metric L		
	location	type	ISW	χ_3	χ_5
internal $k=1$	any	set	0.000	0.000	0.000
	any	reset	0.000	0.000	0.000
	any	flip	0.000	0.000	0.000
input max	$s_{0,0}$	set	0.585	0.000	0.000
	$s_{0,0}$	reset	0.585	0.000	0.000
	$s_{0,0}$	flip	1.000	0.000	0.000
$k=2$	$\mathsf{inv}(s_{0,1})\,\mathsf{inv}(s_{0,0})$	set	–	0.585	0.322

Theoretical maximum: $\mathsf{L}_{ISW}^{max} = 2$, $\mathsf{L}_{\chi_3}^{max} = 3$, $\mathsf{L}_{\chi_5}^{max} = 5$.

against SIFA, but it provides valuable properties by ensuring that intermediate values are independent of secrets [23]. Below, we consider the circuit's unshared inputs as secrets, use a security order $d = 1$, and implement a detection module for each share index individually to preserve the independence properties (cf. Fig. 8).

ISW Multiplication. The first circuit we analyze is the ISW multiplication [33] with additional registers to prevent SCA leakage from glitches. This circuit implements a masked and, where each input and output is masked with two shares. As can be seen in Table 4, there is no leakage for any internal fault with cardinality $k = 1$ (excluding randomness generation). However, when some input $s_{0,0}$ (first share of first input) is faulted, we see leakage due to a dependency between the secret values and the detection signal [20], i.e., $\Pr[s_0 \cdot s_1 = 1] \neq \Pr[s_0 \cdot s_1 = 1 \mid f \text{ ineffective}]$. Thus, the composition of the ISW multiplication is not SIFA-secure. From the structure of the circuit follows that faults in any input behave the same.

The inferred leakage is specific to the given implementation since implementation changes change the possible fault locations. For example, the Synopsys Design Compiler replaces and$(s_{0,0}, s_{1,1})$ with nor$(\mathsf{inv}(s_{0,0}), \mathsf{inv}(s_{1,1}))$ for timing and area optimization unless instructed otherwise. However, this potentially allows $\mathcal{A}_f$ to fault the gate $\mathsf{inv}(s_{0,0})$, which effectively introduces a fault at input $s_{0,0}$ (with the corresponding leakage behavior).

S-boxes from XOODOO and KECCAK. To protect against SIFA, Daemen et al. [20] propose circuits constructed by the composition of masked Toffoli gates. A Toffoli gate computes the term $x_0 \oplus (x_1 \cdot x_2)$ and has the property that all injected effective faults (set, reset, bit flip) are effective faults at the output. This guarantees that there is no dependency between the detection behavior

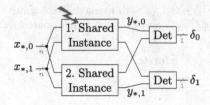

Fig. 8. Setup for SIFA.

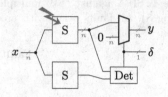

Fig. 9. Setup for analysis of detection.

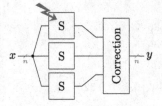

Fig. 10. Setup for analysis of correction.

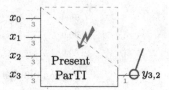

Fig. 11. Setup for CA.

and the secrets since all effective faults are always detected. Two S-boxes that can be easily implemented with Toffoli gates are those from XOODOO [21] and KECCAK [7][2]. The analyzed instances are claimed to be first-order SIFA secure, i.e., there should be no leakage for a single fault. Our metric accurately shows the independence of the detection behavior and the secrets for $k = 1$, while leakage can be seen for two injected faults (cf. Table 4).

6   Evaluating the Quality of Countermeasures

The quantitative FIA metric cannot only be used to measure the efficiency of fault attacks but also to evaluate the quality of countermeasures or the general resistance of designs against FIA. The last section used known attack vectors to highlight the close match between theory and practice. In contrast, we now show that meaningful insights can be drawn even under the constraints of scalability.

6.1   Detection/Correction

Various countermeasures against FIA have been proposed in the literature based on redundancy in time, space, or information. Common to all countermeasures is that redundancy is used either to react to the detection of faults or to directly correct faults that occur. To evaluate the effectiveness of countermeasures, we use the setting shown in Fig. 7, but with countermeasures applied. As S-box, we choose the PRESENT S-box because of its interesting leakage behavior for DFA (cf. Sect. 5.2), which we implemented according to Cassiers et al. [14].

---

[2] We implemented both S-boxes with Toffoli gates in parallel (instead of sequential, as in [20], to get the correct output) and without any registers.

Table 5. Leakage for faults injected in a PRESENT S-box & KeyAdd with counter-measures (cf. Fig. 9 and 10). All faults occurs with probability $\Pr[f] = 1$.

Fault		Metric L				
location	type	Plain	Detection (both - y, δ)	Detection (no flag - y)	Detection (flag only - δ)	Correction
x_2	set	3.000	1.000	0.954	0.000	0.000
x_2	reset	3.000	1.000	0.954	0.000	0.000
x_2	flip	2.807	0.000	0.000	0.000	0.000
$\mathsf{inv}(x_1)$	set	3.000	1.000	0.954	0.000	0.000
$\mathsf{inv}(x_1)$	reset	3.000	1.000	0.954	0.000	0.000
$\mathsf{and}(x_2, \bar{x}_1)$	flip	3.000	1.000	0.954	0.000	0.000

Theoretical maximum: $\mathsf{L}_{PRESENT}^{max} = 4$.

Detection/Correction. The most basic countermeasures are based on repetition (in space or time) of the computation, which allows comparing the result of different instances to either detect faults (inequality) or correct them directly (majority voting). To detect an arbitrary set of k faults $k + 1$ instances are required, while for correction, $2k + 1$ instances are required. In Table 5, we show the leakage behavior for countermeasures with $k = 1$ and spatial repetition, where we have chosen one of the locations with the highest leakage for a given scenario. With respect to the countermeasures, we distinguish between *plain* (no countermeasure, no repetition - cf. Fig. 7), *detection* (2 repetitions with output set to 0 on fault detection - cf. Fig. 9), and *correction* (3 repetitions with majority voting - cf. Fig. 10). To get a fine-grained analysis of the detection, we have three different versions of the detection circuit: (i) detection flag δ and output y are given to $\mathcal{A}_f$, (ii) only the output y is given to $\mathcal{A}_f$ while the detection flag is suppressed, and (iii) only the detection flag δ is given to $\mathcal{A}_f$ while the output is suppressed (cf. Sect. 5.3). We further distinguish between faults at inputs and faults in the internal structure (including the detection/correction logic).

We observe that the detection countermeasure cannot prevent all existing leaks. This is due to the occurrence of ineffective faults and the resulting biased intermediate state, as exploited by SIFA [23]. Implementing the attack in the given scenario reduces the key space to 8 out of 16, which perfectly matches the inferred leakage of $\mathsf{L} = 1$. Also, there is no leakage for bit flip faults at the inputs, since these do not introduce any bias [23] and all faults are effective faults at the output [20]. However, we observe no leakage when we look only at the detection flag, which means that there is no statistical dependency between the detection behavior and the secrets. From this, we conclude that there are designs vulnerable to SIFA whose detection behavior is independent of secrets, directly contradicting *Proposition 1* of Hadzic et al. [31] which claim the opposite. Significantly, this has implications for verification methods of SIFA security that reduce to this proposition (e.g., [31,42]). In cases where there is some leakage for detection, it is always $\mathsf{L} = 1$ (we observed the same behavior when using the AES S-box). Whether this is a coincidence or a structural property requires further investigation. For the same cases, suppressing the detection

Table 6. Leakage of faults injected in masked PRESENT S-box with key addition (Fig. 7 with masking) for $\mathcal{A}_f$ obtaining shared outputs ($L[\{s_{i,j}\} \mid y, y']$) and unshared outputs ($L[s \mid y, y']$), respectively. All faults occur with probability $\Pr[f] = 1$.

	Fault		$L[\{s_{i,j}\} \mid y, y']$		$L[s \mid y, y']$	
	location	type	*DOM*	*HPC$_2$*	*DOM*	*HPC$_2$*
input state max ($k = 1$)	$x_{2,0}$	set	2.000	2.000	2.000	2.000
	$x_{2,0}$	reset	2.000	2.000	2.000	2.000
	$x_{2,0}$	flip	2.807	2.807	2.807	2.807
	$x_{2,0} \; x_{2,1}$	set	3.170	3.170	3.000	3.000
	$x_{2,0} \; x_{2,1}$	reset	3.170	3.170	3.000	3.000
	$x_{2,0} \; x_{2,1}$	flip	1.585	1.585	0.000	0.000
secret max	$s_{0,0}$	set	0.000	0.000	0.000	0.000
	$s_{0,0}$	reset	0.000	0.000	0.000	0.000
	$s_{0,0}$	flip	0.000	0.000	0.000	0.000
	$s_{0,0} \; s_{0,1}$	set	1.000	1.000	1.000	1.000
	$s_{0,0} \; s_{0,1}$	reset	1.000	1.000	1.000	1.000
	$s_{0,0} \; s_{0,1}$	flip	0.000	0.000	0.000	0.000
rand. max	r_0	set	1.322	1.322	0.000	0.000
	r_0	reset	1.322	1.322	0.000	0.000
	r_0	flip	2.000	2.000	0.000	0.000
internal max	$\mathrm{inv}(x_{3,0})$	set	1.907	1.907	1.585	1.585
	$\mathrm{inv}(x_{3,0})$	reset	1.907	1.907	1.585	1.585
	$\mathrm{inv}(x_{3,0})$	flip	2.700	2.700	2.322	2.322
	$\mathrm{and}(x_{3,1}, \overline{x_{1,0} \oplus x_{2,0}})$	set	1.700	–	1.700	–
	$\mathrm{and}(x_{1,0} \oplus x_{2,0}, r_0)$	set	–	1.700	–	1.700

Theoretical maximum: $L^{max}_{PRESENT} = 4$.

signal only marginally reduces the leakage, since $\mathcal{A}_f$ can no longer trivially distinguish between 0 as a valid or suppressed faulty output. Finally, as expected, there is no leakage when the correction is used.

Masking. As mentioned above, masking is not a countermeasure against FIA, but against passive SCA, although it has some advantageous properties for the prevention of SIFA. However, real-world implementations must withstand a wide variety of attacks, so it is interesting to analyze masking from a FIA perspective. To do so, we consider the circuit shown in Fig. 7 with masking using $d = 1$ and instantiating the S-box with composable-secure *DOM* [24] and *HPC$_2$* [14] gadgets (i.e., small but secure subcircuits that can be securely combined). In Table 6, we show the corresponding leakage, again selecting a location with the maximum leakage for a given fault scenario (except for the two simultaneous faults in the input state x, where we selected both shares of x_2).

In general, masking does not seem to harm FIA security. In particular, faults in the input state x have the same effect as without sharing (cf. Table 5). Flipping one share results in a bit-flip in the unshared value, while flipping both shares results in no fault. If the secret itself is faulted, it is necessary to set/reset both shares of the same secret s_i, which results in resetting the unshared secret bit (cf. Sect. 5.1). Faulting random inputs r_i (required to refresh the masking after non-linear operations) does not result in a leak after observing the unshared output. This is expected since the value of the randomness has no functional impact. Also, the leakage decreases as one moves from looking at the shared outputs to the unshared outputs since there is less information in the unshared values. Finally, for this particular design, the type of gadgets has no impact on the leakage behavior. However, this may be different when considering fault combinations from real-world attack scenarios (e.g., clock glitching - cf. Sect. 8.2).

6.2 Detailed Analysis of Combined Vulnerabilities

Real-world circuits are not only exposed to FIA and SCA individually but potentially also to the combination of both attacks. While the VERICA tool [42] can verify security in such a CA setting, it does not provide a quantitative security assessment for vulnerable designs. Similar to the general FIA setting, we can also apply our quantitative metric to CA by computing $V[S \mid \mathcal{P}, \mathcal{P}']$, where the adversary receives a set of probes $\mathcal{P}$ instead of the outputs Y. Such an analysis may be more efficient than for general FIA (for a given probe set) since it is worthwhile to consider an internal subset of the design structures (which is probed) instead of the entire circuit. In general, security against CA seems to be quite expensive [25], and we hope that a dedicated quantitative analysis can instruct more efficient protection mechanisms with an acceptable leakage level.

For our case study, we chose a ParTI [49] implementation of a PRESENT S-box. ParTI is a protection scheme that combines masking (in particular Threshold Implementation (TI) [18]) with error detection codes to protect against both FIA and SCA individually. However, the scheme does not claim security against combined attacks. We use an implementation with $k = 1$ and $d = 1$, for which we ran VERICA to find a suitable probe position (output $y_{3,2}$) and removed all parts not related to that probe (cf. Fig. 7). We consider all unshared inputs as secrets.

ParTI Implementation of PRESENT Sbox. In Table 7, we show the leakage for all unshared-input bits together (s) and for each unshared-input bit individually (s_i). Concerning the fault locations, we selected locations with the maximum leakage when one input is faulted with a given fault type, the minimum leakage when two inputs are faulted with a given fault type such that the single-bit fault with the most leakage is in the fault pair and the maximum leakage for an internal fault. First, we observe that some fault locations and types leak more across all inputs than the sum of all individual leakages. For example, while $\mathsf{L}[s \mid y_{3,2}] = 0.129$ for reset faults in $s_{3,0}$ and $s_{3,1}$, the same scenario leads to $\sum_i \mathsf{L}[s_i \mid y_{3,2}] = 0,087$. Thus, $\mathcal{A}_f$ learns something about the combination of secrets even if the individual secret is securely hidden, e.g., if it is more likely that $s = \langle 0,0,0,0 \rangle$; even if the distribution over each s_i is uniform. For some of

Table 7. Leakage of Combined Analysis on ParTI implementation of the PRESENT S-box when the output $y_{3,2}$ is probed (cf. Fig. 11). All faults occur with probability $\mathsf{Pr}[f] = 1$.

	Fault		Metric $\mathsf{L}[t \mid y_{3,2}, y'_{3,2}]$				
	location	type	$t = s$	$t = s_0$	$t = s_1$	$t = s_2$	$t = s_3$
input max	$s_{3,0}$	set	0.392	0.322	0.044	0.044	0.000
	$s_{3,0}$	reset	0.392	0.322	0.044	0.044	0.000
	$s_{1,0}$	flip	0.585	0.585	0.000	0.000	0.000
	$s_{1,0}$ $s_{3,0}$	set	0.492	0.459	0.000	0.044	0.000
	$s_{1,0}$ $s_{3,0}$	reset	0.492	0.459	0.000	0.044	0.000
	$s_{0,0}$ $s_{1,0}$	flip	0.585	0.585	0.000	0.000	0.000
input min with max $k = 1$	$s_{3,0}$ $s_{0,1}$	set	0.170	0.170	0.000	0.000	0.000
	$s_{3,0}$ $s_{3,1}$	reset	0.129	0.087	0.000	0.000	0.000
	$s_{1,0}$ $s_{0,1}$	flip	0.000	0.000	0.000	0.000	0.000
internal max	$\mathsf{xor}(t_0, \overline{s_{2,0} \oplus s_{3,2}})$	set	0.833	0.807	0.000	0.000	0.000
	$\mathsf{nand}(s_{2,0}, s_{1,2} \oplus s_{3,0})$	reset	0.858	0.807	0.000	0.000	0.022
	$\mathsf{nor}(\bar{s}_{1,0}, t_1)$	flip	1.000	1.000	0.000	0.000	0.000

$t_0 = s_{2,0} \cdot (s_{1,2} \oplus s_{3,0})$; $t_1 = s_{0,1} \oplus s_{1,2} \oplus s_{3,0} \oplus x_{2,0}$.
Theoretical maximum: $\mathsf{L}^{max}_{PRESENT} = 4$.

the given fault scenarios, the sum of the individual leakages is larger than the combined leakage. However, since the difference is only marginal, we explain this by rounding errors throughout the computation.

Second, we see that adding additional faults to a fault scenario can have different effects. In Fig. 12, we provide additional insight into three of the given scenarios. Specifically, we show the leakage over the change in fault probability for two faults, where the x-axis is always the probability for a fault in $s_{1,0}$. While adding a bit-flip fault in $s_{0,0}$ has no effect (cf. Fig. 12a), a set fault in $s_{3,0}$ increases the leakage (cf. Fig. 12b). However, the reverse is also possible, i.e., a fault that reduces or even eliminates the leakage (e.g., bit-flip $s_{0,1}$ - cf. Fig. 12c). This gives us a new protection scheme against FIA by constructing a design structure that ensures that when a fault occurs in $s_{1,0}$, there is also a fault in $s_{0,1}$. Since most faults are related to the timing behavior of a circuit [44], this can be achieved by delaying some of the signals in the circuit. We can also see that, in general, for a single fault, a lower fault probability means a lower leakage, which follows directly from the equation for the vulnerability (cf. Eq. 1).

7 Performance of Prototype Implementation

In the following, we provide some insight into the performance of our implementation. We run all experiments on a 64-bit Linux Operating System (OS) environment on an Intel Xeon E5-1660v4 CPU with 16 cores, a clock frequency of 3.20 GHz, and 128 GB of RAM.

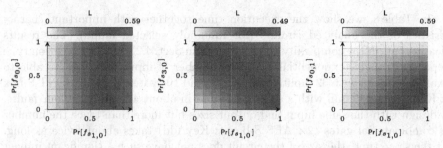

(a) Bit flip in $s_{0,0}$ and $s_{1,0}$.   (b) Set faults in $s_{1,0}$ and $s_{3,0}$.   (c) Bit flip in $s_{0,1}$ and $s_{1,0}$.

Fig. 12. Leakage behavior of fault combinations under changing fault probability.

Table 8. Execution time for vulnerability computation on a 64-bit Linux OS executing on an Intel Xeon E5-1660v4 CPU with 16 cores, a clock frequency of 3.20 GHz, and 128 GB of RAM.

	Design					Fault			Metric	
Description	$in_{x,r}$	in_s	out	comb.	reg.	k	$Pr[f]$	type	time	L
Plain	4	4	4	26	0	1	0.7	flip	0.82 s	2.561
Plain	4	4	4	26	0	4	0.7	flip	0.80 s	2.407
DOM	8	4	4	91	16	1	0.7	flip	1.15 s	0.766
DOM	8	4	4	91	16	4	0.7	flip	3.56 s	0.766
HPC_2	8	4	4	115	44	1	0.7	flip	1.16 s	1.036
HPC_2	8	4	4	115	44	4	0.7	flip	2.69 s	1.514
2×	8	8	8	52	0	1	0.7	flip	0.81 s	2.561
2×	8	8	8	52	0	4	0.7	flip	0.90 s	3.124
3×	12	12	12	78	0	1	0.7	flip	8.57 s	2.561
3×	12	12	12	78	0	4	0.7	flip	38.70 s	3.124
4×	16	16	16	104	0	1	0.7	flip	44.30 min	2.561
4×	16	16	16	104	0	4	0.7	flip	3.50 h	3.124
Plain	8	8	8	143	0	1	0.7	flip	0.84 s	7.043
Plain	8	8	8	143	0	4	0.7	flip	1.03 s	5.712
Detection	8	8	8	319	0	1	0.7	flip	0.96 s	0.000
Detection	8	8	8	319	0	4	0.7	flip	1.62 s	0.000
Correction	8	8	8	464	0	1	0.7	flip	0.97 s	0.000
Correction	8	8	8	464	0	4	0.7	flip	5.88 s	0.000
2×	16	16	16	288	0	1	0.7	flip	1.22 h	7.043
2×	16	16	16	288	0	4	0.7	flip	6.89 h	13.359
1 B. Input	0	10	10	1175	0	1	0.7	flip	1.99 s	9.743
1 B. Input	0	10	10	1175	0	4	0.7	flip	3.36 s	9.970
2 B. Input[†]	10	10	10	2392	0	1	0.7	flip	5.59 min	7.995
2 B. Input[†]	10	10	10	2392	0	4	0.7	flip	59.11 min	6.643

Left margin labels: PRESENT, AES[*], KECCAK[**]

*S-box & KeyAdd; **$b = 25$, $r = 10$; [†]single core.

328   J. Feldtkeller et al.

In Table 8, we show the execution time together with important characteristics of the analyzed circuits (for randomly selected faults). The results
clearly confirm the complexity considerations in Sect. 4.2, i.e., the execution time
depends strongly (exponentially) on the number of input bits. We are able to
analyze a design with 32 inputs, 16 outputs, and 104 gates (4× PRESENT S-box
& KeyAdd) in 45 min with a single fault and in about 4 hours with four faults.
A design with the same input and output sizes but more than twice the number
of combinatorial gates (2× AES S-box & KeyAdd) takes about twice as long.
At the same time, the size of the circuit does not have such a significant impact
on the execution time, and a design with over 2000 gates can be evaluated in
less than 6 min with one fault and in less than 1 h with four faults, even on a
single core (for 16 cores, we ran out of memory because the BDD library used
requires a copy of the BDD for each core). The parallel implementations of S-
box & KeyAdd could also be analyzed separately due to their independence with
respect to the leakage (cf. Sect. 5.1), but we show them here to give a sense of
scalability.

8 Related and Future Work

In the following section, we will discuss related and future work of the presented
methodology.

8.1 Related Work

Quantitative Information Flow. Early methods for QIF relied on *Shannon entropy* along with *mutual information* to measure the flow of information [16,17]. Intuitively, the Shannon entropy is a measure of uncertainty because
it provides the minimum number of bits required to encode a given piece of information. However, it has been shown that the security guarantees derived from
Shannon entropy do not generally provide meaningful results [53]. To better capture the information leakage, Smith proposed the *min-entropy* as a measure of
uncertainty [53], which was later refined and extended (see Alvim et al. [3] for
an overview). We, therefore, rely on the min-entropy as presented in Sect. 4.

QIF for Hardware. The first attempt at quantitative analysis in the context of
hardware was done by Mao et al. [39], who evaluated the leakage caused by the
timing behavior (in the number of cycles) of an algorithmic hardware implementation in terms of mutual information. An extension to general information flow
with automatic integration into a Hardware Description Language (HDL) was
proposed by Guo et al. with QIF-Verilog [30]. They define operation-specific rules
for leakage propagation from inputs to outputs of logical operations. These rules
are inspired by Smith's vulnerability metric V, but not an exact computation.
Later, Reimann et al. extended this approach with QFlow [41] by computing
the vulnerability V and the leakage L of subparts (groups of operations) and
combining them via a Markov chain. However, this requires the assumption of

independence for all inputs to a component of the Markov chain, which is usually not given. In contrast, we analyze the entire system at once, leading to an exact computation with weaknesses in scalability. It remains an open question how the approaches for HDLs can be tailored to the computation of V in the context of FIA.

QIF for Fault Injection Analysis. Information-theoretic metrics and QIF have also been used in the context of FIA. Sakiyama et al. [48] used Shannon entropy to determine the information leakage in DFA given a design as shown in Fig. 7. They used a handcrafted analysis to analyze and improve existing attacks against AES. Later, Liu et al. [38] extended this approach to general Substitution-Permutation Networks (SPNs) with potential FIA countermeasures. However, they assume the independence of internal signals for computational efficiency. In another line of research, Patranabis et al. [40] analyze the security of a specific infection scheme in software using the mutual information between an output differential $y \oplus y'$ and the key s. An infection scheme tries to make a faulty output y' useless for $\mathcal{A}_f$ by randomizing the effect of the fault. Hence, security is achieved when the mutual information is equal to zero. A more general methodology has been proposed by Feng et al. [26] for build-out infections, i.e., infections applied after an unmodified cipher implementation. In particular, they consider an attacker who obtains an output differential $y \oplus y'$ after a single fault injection. Using the structure of build-out infection schemes, the authors decompose the security analysis into the contribution of the unprotected cipher and the contribution of the infection scheme. In addition, common infection schemes are a composition of simple randomness-based operations that can be analyzed individually. While the methodology covers a wide range of infection schemes, the preparation must be tailored to the individual cipher and infection scheme and requires considerable expertise. In contrast to these works, we use QIF based on the min-entropy to develop a general metric for FIA not tailored to specific attacks and circuit structures. In addition, we introduce the notion of probabilistic faults into the fault model, allowing the analysis of more realistic fault scenarios.

Fault Analysis Tools. In recent years, the research community has focused on the development of automatic tools for fault susceptibility. The first set of tools focuses on the construction of potential key distinguishers for DFA, i.e., differentials between correct and incorrect intermediate states, and the evaluation of the associated attack complexity. For this purpose, XFC [34] uses classical IFA in a high-level cipher description. For the same purpose, ExpFault [47] uses system simulation in combination with data mining techniques. Of course, these methods are limited to DFA. The second set of tools takes a more general approach by analyzing the impact of faults on the output, i.e., distinguishing between detected, ineffective, and effective faults. To do this, VerFi [4] uses traditional simulation techniques to evaluate the system behavior, while FIVER [43] uses symbolic analysis based on BDDs. As an extension to FIVER, VERICA [42] compares output distributions to verify security against SIFA. Except for the SIFA extension, these tools assume that all faulty outputs are equally dangerous, and are therefore unable to make a qualitative comparison between two different fault scenarios. However, since these tools are much more efficient than the proposed FIA vulnerability calculation, they can be used as a preliminary analysis step to extract interesting fault scenarios. As a third set of tools, recent works compare ciphertext distributions with a t-test for different fault locations with fixed secrets or different secrets with fixed fault locations [45, 46]. The ciphertexts for the analysis are generated by non-exhaustive simulation and a design is classified as vulnerable to FIA when the two ciphertext distributions can be distinguished according to the t-test. Again, the result does not allow a quantitative analysis, as the t-test provides a score for the confidence of the classification and not for the difference of the distributions.

8.2 Future Work

The first and most obvious shortcoming of our proposal is scalability. While we have shown that valuable insights can be gained from essential cryptographic components of small or medium size, more efficient methods of evaluation are needed for larger structures. Thus, we need some notion of composability to reduce the complexity of a single analysis and still be able to conclude complex structures. One approach in this direction is the construction of checkpoints (as proposed by Shahmirzadi et al. [51]) that isolate two parts of a design with respect to faults. Of course, this approach imposes additional overhead on the design, and more efficient methods are desirable.

In this work, we consider an adversary who has access to exactly one pair of correct and faulty outputs (y, y'). While this seems to be a good approximation for the general vulnerability of a design to FIA, since more advanced attacks rely on the existence of leakage in this simple case, a criterion for multiple output pairs may provide more fine-grained insights. A trivial way to achieve this is to combine different FIA channels into one large channel that produces a set of output pairs (y_i, y'_i). However, since the complexity is already high for a single output pair, it is prohibitive for additional pairs and more efficient approaches are needed. In addition, we only consider state-less channels, which limits the type of circuits and countermeasures that can be analyzed. Thus, extending the concept to state-full channels is a valuable generalization.

Our fault model is based on a distribution over a set of faults $\mathbb{DF}$, without providing any instructions on how to come up with this set and distribution of faults. Indeed, this is a complex and challenging problem in itself. We envision a tool that analyzes a given circuit structure with respect to a given fault scenario and returns a set of likely fault combinations and an estimate of their distribution. Combined with our approach, this would provide a powerful tool for real-world evaluation of security in the context of FIA.

9   Conclusion

In this work, we have shown how methods from QIF can be used to establish a quantitative metric for the security of a circuit against FIA. This metric allows for fine-grained analysis of existing and new defense mechanisms, thus enabling a trade-off between performance and security. Although computationally expensive, the proposed method can provide new insights and enhance the understanding of FIA and related countermeasures. For example, we were able to find incorrect assumptions in the context of SIFA security and enable the identification of security-enhancing faults.

Acknowledgments. We would like to thank Jan Richter-Brockmann and Pascal Sasdrich for fruitful discussions on fault security and support with the tool VERICA. The work described was funded by the Deutsche Forschungsgemeinschaft (DFG, German Research Foundation) under Germany's Excellence Strategy - EXC 2092 CASA - 390781972, by the German Federal Ministry of Education and Research BMBF through the projects VE-HEP (16KIS1345) and 6GEM (16KISK038) and by the European Commission under the project CONVOLVE (101070374). This research was also supported in part by NSF Award 2219810.

A   Probabilistic Computation

A.1   Methodology

The isolated computation of $V[S \mid Y, Y' = y']$ for each $y' \in \mathcal{Y}$ allows not only the parallel computation of the vulnerability but also a probabilistic computation. Here, instead of computing the exact value of $V[S \mid Y, Y']$, we can approximate it using a subset of $\mathcal{Y}$. Specifically, we use the *Monte-Carlo method* [32], where the mean of a set of samples is used to estimate the mean of a probability distribution. This is a good approximation if the sample set is large enough and each sample is chosen independently. The quality of the approximation is given by the Confidence Interval (CI), which provides a range in which the true distribution mean lies with a certain probability (given by the confidence level).

To compute the FIA vulnerability probabilistically, we randomly select N faulty output values $y' \in \mathcal{Y}$ and compute $V[S \mid Y, Y' = y']$ (as done in Algorithm 1). We then estimate the overall vulnerability by scaling the mean of the samples by the number of existing faulty outputs y':

$$V[S \mid Y, Y'] \approx |\mathcal{Y}| \frac{\sum_{i=0}^{N} V[S \mid Y, Y' = y_i']}{N} \qquad (2)$$

Then the CI can be calculated using the Central Limit Theorem as $(\mu - z\frac{\sigma}{\sqrt{N}}, \mu + z\frac{\sigma}{\sqrt{N}})$, where μ is the sample mean, σ is the sample standard deviation, and z is the z-score of the confidence level. The z-score of common confidence levels is 1.64 for a 90% confidence level, 1.96 for a 95% confidence level, and 2.57 for a 99% confidence level. For efficient computation, an iterative formula for mean

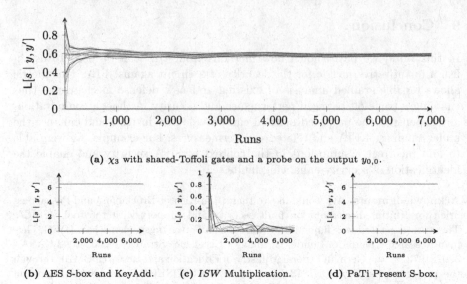

(a) χ_3 with shared-Toffoli gates and a probe on the output $y_{0,0}$.

(b) AES S-box and KeyAdd.   (c) *ISW* Multiplication.   (d) PaTi Present S-box.

Fig. 13. Leakage over the number of runs for probabilistic computation with a set fault injected to the first input (i.e., x_0 or $x_{0,0}$) Leakage is given in blue while upper and lower bounds of the confidence range (95%) are given in black. Lighter colors represent different executions. The precise leakage is marked in red. (Color figure online)

and variance can be used. The CI is defined for the mean vulnerability and therefore must be scaled up for the overall vulnerability, similar to Eq. 2. This results in a CI that grows with the number of possible output values.

A.2 Evaluation

In Fig. 13, we show the convergence of the estimated leakage to the real leakage over the number of executions for four different circuits. While the estimation improves with an increasing number of executions, several thousand executions are required to obtain a high-confidence result. Thus, this only becomes interesting for circuits with a high number of output bits, and for most of the designs we analyzed, the exact computation is faster than running the probabilistic algorithm so often. Interestingly, however, there are some cases where the probabilistic algorithm yields the exact leakage after only one iteration (cf. Fig. 13b and 13d). This is the case when the vulnerability is the same for all possible output values, i.e., the expression $\max_s(\sum_x \Pr[s]\Pr[x]\Pr[y \mid x, s] \sum_f \Pr[f]\Pr[y' \mid x, s])$ is the same for all (y, y'). Further investigation is required to determine the set of circuits for which this holds. If this can be easily determined, the computation can be accelerated significantly, e.g., running 10 iterations for the $4\times$ PRESENT S-box & KeyAdd takes only 3.87 s instead of about 3.5 h to get the exact leakage for four faults.

References

1. Agoyan, M., Dutertre, J.-M., Naccache, D., Robisson, B., Tria, A.: When clocks fail: on critical paths and clock faults. In: Gollmann, D., Lanet, J.-L., Iguchi-Cartigny, J. (eds.) CARDIS 2010. LNCS, vol. 6035, pp. 182–193. Springer, Heidelberg (2010). https://doi.org/10.1007/978-3-642-12510-2_13
2. Akers, S.B.: Binary decision diagrams. IEEE Trans. Computers **27**(6), 509–516 (1978)
3. Alvim, M.S., Chatzikokolakis, K., McIver, A., Morgan, C., Palamidessi, C., Smith, G.: The Science of Quantitative Information Flow. Information Security and Cryptography. Springer, Cham (2020). https://doi.org/10.1007/978-3-319-96131-6
4. Arribas, V., Wegener, F., Moradi, A., Nikova, S.: Cryptographic fault diagnosis using VerFI. In: HOST 2020, pp. 229–240. IEEE (2020)
5. Baksi, A., et al.: DEFAULT: cipher level resistance against differential fault attack. In: Tibouchi, M., Wang, H. (eds.) ASIACRYPT 2021, Part II. LNCS, vol. 13091, pp. 124–156. Springer, Cham (2021). https://doi.org/10.1007/978-3-030-92075-3_5
6. Beckers, A., et al.: Design considerations for EM pulse fault injection. In: Belaïd, S., Güneysu, T. (eds.) CARDIS 2019. LNCS, vol. 11833, pp. 176–192. Springer, Cham (2020). https://doi.org/10.1007/978-3-030-42068-0_11
7. Bertoni, G., Daemen, J., Peeters, M., Van Assche, G.: Keccak. In: Johansson, T., Nguyen, P.Q. (eds.) EUROCRYPT 2013. LNCS, vol. 7881, pp. 313–314. Springer, Heidelberg (2013). https://doi.org/10.1007/978-3-642-38348-9_19
8. Biham, E., Granboulan, L., Nguyen, P.Q.: Impossible fault analysis of RC4 and differential fault analysis of RC4. In: Gilbert, H., Handschuh, H. (eds.) FSE 2005. LNCS, vol. 3557, pp. 359–367. Springer, Heidelberg (2005). https://doi.org/10.1007/11502760_24
9. Biham, E., Shamir, A.: Differential fault analysis of secret key cryptosystems. In: Kaliski, B.S. (ed.) CRYPTO 1997. LNCS, vol. 1294, pp. 513–525. Springer, Heidelberg (1997). https://doi.org/10.1007/BFb0052259
10. Blömer, J., Krummel, V.: Fault based collision attacks on AES. In: Breveglieri, L., Koren, I., Naccache, D., Seifert, J.-P. (eds.) FDTC 2006. LNCS, vol. 4236, pp. 106–120. Springer, Heidelberg (2006). https://doi.org/10.1007/11889700_11
11. Bogdanov, A., et al.: PRESENT: an ultra-lightweight block cipher. In: Paillier, P., Verbauwhede, I. (eds.) CHES 2007. LNCS, vol. 4727, pp. 450–466. Springer, Heidelberg (2007). https://doi.org/10.1007/978-3-540-74735-2_31
12. Boneh, D., DeMillo, R.A., Lipton, R.J.: On the importance of checking cryptographic protocols for faults. In: Fumy, W. (ed.) EUROCRYPT 1997. LNCS, vol. 1233, pp. 37–51. Springer, Heidelberg (1997). https://doi.org/10.1007/3-540-69053-0_4
13. Bryant, R.E.: Graph-based algorithms for Boolean function manipulation. IEEE Trans. Computers **35**(8), 677–691 (1986)
14. Cassiers, G., Grégoire, B., Levi, I., Standaert, F.: Hardware private circuits: from trivial composition to full verification. IEEE Trans. Computers **70**(10), 1677–1690 (2021)
15. Chari, S., Jutla, C.S., Rao, J.R., Rohatgi, P.: Towards sound approaches to counteract power-analysis attacks. In: Wiener, M. (ed.) CRYPTO 1999. LNCS, vol. 1666, pp. 398–412. Springer, Heidelberg (1999). https://doi.org/10.1007/3-540-48405-1_26

16. Clark, D., Hunt, S., Malacaria, P.: Quantitative analysis of the leakage of confidential data. In: Workshop on Quantitative Aspects of Programming Laguages, QAPL 2001, Satellite Event of PLI 2001, Firenze, Italy, 7 September 2001, pp. 238–251 (2001)

17. Clark, D., Hunt, S., Malacaria, P.: A static analysis for quantifying information flow in a simple imperative language. J. Comput. Secur. **15**(3), 321–371 (2007)

18. Cnudde, T.D., Nikova, S.: More efficient private circuits II through threshold implementations. In: FDTC 2016, pp. 114–124. IEEE Computer Society (2016)

19. Courtois, N., Jackson, K., Ware, D.: Fault-algebraic attacks on inner rounds of DES. In: E-Smart 2010 Proceedings: The Future of Digital Security Technologies. Strategies Telecom and Multimedia (2010)

20. Daemen, J., Dobraunig, C., Eichlseder, M., Groß, H., Mendel, F., Primas, R.: Protecting against statistical ineffective fault attacks. IACR Trans. Cryptogr. Hardw. Embed. Syst. **2020**(3), 508–543 (2020)

21. Daemen, J., Hoffert, S., Assche, G.V., Keer, R.V.: The design of Xoodoo and Xoofff. IACR Trans. Symmetric Cryptol. **2018**(4), 1–38 (2018)

22. Dhooghe, S., Nikova, S.: My gadget just cares for me - how NINA can prove security against combined attacks. In: Jarecki, S. (ed.) CT-RSA 2020. LNCS, vol. 12006, pp. 35–55. Springer, Cham (2020). https://doi.org/10.1007/978-3-030-40186-3_3

23. Dobraunig, C., Eichlseder, M., Korak, T., Mangard, S., Mendel, F., Primas, R.: SIFA: exploiting ineffective fault inductions on symmetric cryptography. IACR Trans. Cryptogr. Hardw. Embed. Syst. **2018**(3), 547–572 (2018)

24. Faust, S., Grosso, V., Pozo, S.M.D., Paglialonga, C., Standaert, F.: Composable masking schemes in the presence of physical defaults & the robust probing model. IACR Trans. Cryptogr. Hardw. Embed. Syst. **2018**(3), 89–120 (2018)

25. Feldtkeller, J., Richter-Brockmann, J., Sasdrich, P., Güneysu, T.: CINI MINIS: domain isolation for fault and combined security, pp. 1023–1036. ACM CCS (2022)

26. Feng, J., Chen, H., Li, Y., Jiao, Z., Xi, W.: A framework for evaluation and analysis on infection countermeasures against fault attacks. IEEE Trans. Inf. Forensics Secur. **15**, 391–406 (2020)

27. Gandolfi, K., Mourtel, C., Olivier, F.: Electromagnetic analysis: concrete results. In: Koç, Ç.K., Naccache, D., Paar, C. (eds.) CHES 2001. LNCS, vol. 2162, pp. 251–261. Springer, Heidelberg (2001). https://doi.org/10.1007/3-540-44709-1_21

28. Gnad, D.R.E., Oboril, F., Tahoori, M.B.: Voltage drop-based fault attacks on FPGAs using valid bitstreams. In: 27th International Conference on Field Programmable Logic and Applications, FPL 2017, Ghent, Belgium, 4–8 September 2017, pp. 1–7 (2017)

29. Gruss, D., Maurice, C., Mangard, S.: Rowhammer.js: a remote software-induced fault attack in JavaScript. In: Caballero, J., Zurutuza, U., Rodríguez, R.J. (eds.) DIMVA 2016. LNCS, vol. 9721, pp. 300–321. Springer, Cham (2016). https://doi.org/10.1007/978-3-319-40667-1_15

30. Guo, X., Dutta, R.G., He, J., Tehranipoor, M.M., Jin, Y.: QIF-Verilog: quantitative information-flow based hardware description languages for pre-silicon security assessment. In: IEEE International Symposium on Hardware Oriented Security and Trust, HOST 2019, McLean, VA, USA, 5–10 May 2019, pp. 91–100 (2019)

31. Hadžić, V., Primas, R., Bloem, R.: Proving SIFA protection of masked redundant circuits. In: Hou, Z., Ganesh, V. (eds.) ATVA 2021. LNCS, vol. 12971, pp. 249–265. Springer, Cham (2021). https://doi.org/10.1007/978-3-030-88885-5_17

32. Hutchinson, M.: A stochastic estimator of the trace of the influence matrix for Laplacian smoothing splines. Commun. Stat. Simul. Comput. **19**(2), 433–450 (1990)

33. Ishai, Y., Sahai, A., Wagner, D.: Private Circuits: Securing Hardware against Probing Attacks. In: Boneh, D. (ed.) CRYPTO 2003. LNCS, vol. 2729, pp. 463–481. Springer, Heidelberg (2003). https://doi.org/10.1007/978-3-540-45146-4_27

34. Khanna, P., Rebeiro, C., Hazra, A.: XFC: a framework for eXploitable fault characterization in block ciphers. In: Proceedings of the 54th Annual Design Automation Conference, DAC 2017, Austin, TX, USA, 18–22 June 2017, pp. 8:1–8:6 (2017)

35. Kocher, P.C.: Timing attacks on implementations of Diffie-Hellman, RSA, DSS, and other systems. In: Koblitz, N. (ed.) CRYPTO 1996. LNCS, vol. 1109, pp. 104–113. Springer, Heidelberg (1996). https://doi.org/10.1007/3-540-68697-5_9

36. Kocher, P., Jaffe, J., Jun, B.: Differential power analysis. In: Wiener, M. (ed.) CRYPTO 1999. LNCS, vol. 1666, pp. 388–397. Springer, Heidelberg (1999). https://doi.org/10.1007/3-540-48405-1_25

37. Li, Y., Sakiyama, K., Gomisawa, S., Fukunaga, T., Takahashi, J., Ohta, K.: Fault sensitivity analysis. In: Mangard, S., Standaert, F.-X. (eds.) CHES 2010. LNCS, vol. 6225, pp. 320–334. Springer, Heidelberg (2010). https://doi.org/10.1007/978-3-642-15031-9_22

38. Liu, Q., Ning, B., Deng, P.: Information theory-based quantitative evaluation method for countermeasures against fault injection attacks. IEEE Access **7**, 141920–141928 (2019)

39. Mao, B., Hu, W., Althoff, A., Matai, J., Oberg, J., Mu, D., Sherwood, T., Kastner, R.: Quantifying timing-based information flow in cryptographic hardware. In: Proceedings of the IEEE/ACM International Conference on Computer-Aided Design, ICCAD 2015, Austin, TX, USA, 2–6 November 2015, pp. 552–559 (2015)

40. Patranabis, S., Chakraborty, A., Mukhopadhyay, D.: Fault Tolerant Infective Countermeasure for AES. J. Hardw. Syst. Secur. **1**(1), 3–17 (2017)

41. Reimann, L.M., Hanel, L., Sisejkovic, D., Merchant, F., Leupers, R.: QFlow: quantitative information flow for security-aware hardware design in verilog. In: 39th IEEE International Conference on Computer Design, ICCD 2021, Storrs, CT, USA, 24–27 October 2021, pp. 603–607 (2021)

42. Richter-Brockmann, J., Feldtkeller, J., Sasdrich, P., Güneysu, T.: VERICA - verification of combined attacks: automated formal verification of security against simultaneous information leakage and tampering. IACR Trans. Cryptogr. Hardw. Embed. Syst. **2022**(4), 255–284 (2022)

43. Richter-Brockmann, J., Rezaei Shahmirzadi, A., Sasdrich, P., Moradi, A., Güneysu, T.: FIVER - robust verification of countermeasures against fault injections. IACR Trans. Cryptogr. Hardw. Embed. Syst. **2021**(4), 447–473 (2021)

44. Richter-Brockmann, J., Sasdrich, P., Güneysu, T.: Revisiting fault adversary models - hardware faults in theory and practice. IEEE Trans. Computers **72**, 1–14 (2022)

45. Saha, S., Alam, M., Bag, A., Mukhopadhyay, D., Dasgupta, P.: Learn from your faults: leakage assessment in fault attacks using deep learning. J. Cryptol. **36**(3), 19 (2023)

46. Saha, S., Kumar, S.N., Patranabis, S., Mukhopadhyay, D., Dasgupta, P.: ALAFA: automatic leakage assessment for fault attack countermeasures. In: Proceedings of the 56th Annual Design Automation Conference 2019, DAC 2019, Las Vegas, NV, USA, 02–06 June 2019, p. 136 (2019)

47. Saha, S., Mukhopadhyay, D., Dasgupta, P.: ExpFault: an automated framework for exploitable fault characterization in block ciphers. IACR Trans. Cryptogr. Hardw. Embed. Syst. **2018**(2), 242–276 (2018)

48. Sakiyama, K., Li, Y., Iwamoto, M., Ohta, K.: Information-theoretic approach to optimal differential fault analysis. IEEE Trans. Inf. Forensics Secur. **7**(1), 109–120 (2012)
49. Schneider, T., Moradi, A., Güneysu, T.: ParTI – towards combined hardware countermeasures against side-channel and fault-injection attacks. In: Robshaw, M., Katz, J. (eds.) CRYPTO 2016. LNCS, vol. 9815, pp. 302–332. Springer, Heidelberg (2016). https://doi.org/10.1007/978-3-662-53008-5_11
50. Selmane, N., Guilley, S., Danger, J.: Practical setup time violation attacks on AES. In: EDCC-7 2008, pp. 91–96. IEEE Computer Society (2008)
51. Shahmirzadi, A.R., Rasoolzadeh, S., Moradi, A.: Impeccable circuits II. In: DAC 2020, pp. 1–6. IEEE (2020)
52. Skorobogatov, S.P., Anderson, R.J.: Optical fault induction attacks. In: Kaliski, B.S., Koç, K., Paar, C. (eds.) CHES 2002. LNCS, vol. 2523, pp. 2–12. Springer, Heidelberg (2003). https://doi.org/10.1007/3-540-36400-5_2
53. Smith, G.: On the foundations of quantitative information flow. In: de Alfaro, L. (ed.) FoSSaCS 2009. LNCS, vol. 5504, pp. 288–302. Springer, Heidelberg (2009). https://doi.org/10.1007/978-3-642-00596-1_21
54. Sullivan, G.A., Sippe, J., Heninger, N., Wustrow, E.: Open to a fault: on the passive compromise of TLS keys via transient errors. In: 31st USENIX Security Symposium, USENIX Security 2022, Boston, MA, USA, 10–12 August 2022, pp. 233–250 (2022)
55. Tang, A., Sethumadhavan, S., Stolfo, S.J.: CLKSCREW: exposing the perils of security-oblivious energy management. In: 26th USENIX Security Symposium, USENIX Security 2017, Vancouver, BC, Canada, 16–18 August 2017, pp. 1057–1074 (2017)

Quantum Random Oracle Model

On the (Im)possibility of Time-Lock Puzzles in the Quantum Random Oracle Model

Abtin Afshar[1], Kai-Min Chung[2], Yao-Ching Hsieh[3], Yao-Ting Lin[4(⊠)], and Mohammad Mahmoody[1]

[1] University of Virginia, Charlottesville, USA
{na6xg,mohammad}@virginia.edu
[2] Academia Sinica, Taipei, Taiwan
kmchung@iis.sinica.edu.tw
[3] University of Washington, Seattle, USA
ychsieh@cs.washington.edu
[4] UCSB, Santa Barbara, USA
yao-ting_lin@ucsb.edu

Abstract. Time-lock puzzles wrap a solution s inside a puzzle P in such a way that "solving" P to find s requires significantly more time than generating the pair (s, P), even if the adversary has access to parallel computing; hence it can be thought of as sending a message s to the future. It is known [Mahmoody, Moran, Vadhan, Crypto'11] that when the source of hardness is only a random oracle, then any puzzle generator with n queries can be (efficiently) broken by an adversary in $O(n)$ *rounds* of queries to the oracle.

In this work, we revisit time-lock puzzles in a quantum world by allowing the parties to use quantum computing and, in particular, access the random oracle in quantum superposition. An interesting setting is when the puzzle generator is efficient and classical, while the solver (who might be an entity developed in the future) is quantum-powered and is supposed to need a long sequential time to succeed. We prove that in this setting there is no construction of time-lock puzzles solely from quantum (accessible) random oracles. In particular, for any n-query classical puzzle generator, our attack only asks $O(n)$ (also classical) queries to the random oracle, even though it does indeed run in *quantum* polynomial time if the honest puzzle solver needs quantum computing.

Assuming perfect completeness, we also show how to make the above attack run in exactly n rounds while asking a total of $m \cdot n$ queries where m is the query complexity of the puzzle solver. This is indeed tight in the round complexity, as we also prove that a classical puzzle scheme of Mahmoody et al. is also secure against quantum solvers who ask $n-1$ rounds of queries. In fact, even for the fully classical case, our attack quantitatively improves the total queries of the attack of Mahmoody et al. for the case of perfect completeness from $O(mn \log n)$ to mn. Finally, assuming perfect completeness, we present an attack in the "dual" setting in which the puzzle generator is quantum while the solver is classical.

We then ask whether one can extend our *classical-query* attack to the *fully*

A. Afshar and M. Mahmoody were supported by NSF grants CCF-1910681 and CNS1936799. K.M. Chung was supported by NSTC QC project, under Grant no. NSTC 112-2119-M-001-006- and the Air Force Office of Scientific Research under award number FA2386-20-1-4066.

J. Guo and R. Steinfeld (Eds.): ASIACRYPT 2023, LNCS 14441, pp. 339–368, 2023.
https://doi.org/10.1007/978-981-99-8730-6_11

quantum setting, in which both the puzzle generator and the solver could be quantum. We show a barrier for proving such results unconditionally. In particular, we show that if the folklore simulation conjecture, first formally stated by Aaronson and Ambainis [arXiv'2009] is *false*, then there is indeed a time-lock puzzle in the quantum random oracle model that cannot be broken by classical adversaries. This result improves the previous barrier of Austrin et. al [Crypto'22] about key agreements (that can have interactions in both directions) to time-lock puzzles (that only include unidirectional communication).

1   Introduction

Time lock puzzles (TLPs) allow a puzzle generator Gen to *efficiently* generate a puzzle P for a solution s, in such a way that solving the puzzle P back into s would require *significantly more time*, even if the adversary uses multiple computers in parallel. TLPs allow "sending a message to the future" as they only allow "opening the envelope" P if a significant amount of time is spent by the solver.

The work of Rivest, Shamir, and Wagner [RSW96] both presented a construction of a time-lock puzzle and also presented applications of such primitives. Their construction was based on the assumption that repeated squaring of integers modulo RSA composites cannot be expedited even with parallel computing, unless one knows the factoring of the composite in which case they can expedite the process. Hence, the puzzle generator can find the solution by "solving the puzzle" through a shortcut, while others are forced to follow the sequential path. The work of [RSW96] also suggested using TLPs for other applications such as delayed digital cash payments, sealed-bid auctions and key escrow. Boneh and Naor [BN00] further showed the usefulness of such "sequential" primitives by defining and constructing *timed commitments* and showing their use for applications such as fair contract signing. More recently, time-lock puzzles have found more applications such as non-interactive non-malleable commitments [LPS17].

Despite their usefulness, it is still not known how to build TLPs based on more standard assumptions, and particularly based on "symmetric key" primitives. One might be tempted to use *inversion* of (say, exponentially hard) one-way functions as the process of solving puzzles. However, an adversary with k times parallel computing power can expedite the search process by a factor k through a careful splitting of the search space into k subspaces. Taking symmetric primitives to their extreme (idealized) form, one can ask whether *random oracles* can be used for constructing TLPs. The good thing about oracle models in general, and the random oracle model in particular, is that one can easily define information-theoretic notions of *time* based on the total number of queries asked to them, and also define the notion of *parallel time* based on the number of *rounds* of queries that an algorithm asks to the oracle. This means that asking, say, 10 queries in parallel to the oracle only counts as a single unit of (parallel) time.

The work of Mahmoody, Moran, and Vadhan [MMV11] proved a strong barrier against constructing TLPs from symmetric primitives by ruling out constructions that solely rely on random oracles. In particular, it was proved that if a puzzle generator asks only n queries to the random oracle and that the puzzle can be solved (honestly) with m oracle queries, then there is always a way to expedite the solving process to only $O(n)$ *rounds* of queries while the total number of queries is still poly(n, m). Note that the polynomial limit on the total number of queries is necessary to make such an attack interesting, as it is always possible to ask *all* of the (exponentially many) queries of oracle in one round and then solve the puzzle without any further queries. The attack of [MMV11] was in fact a polynomial *time* attack, though if one was willing to give up on that feature and only aim for polynomial *number of queries* (which still suffices for ruling out a ROM-based construction) they could achieve it in exactly n rounds as well.

Motivated by the developments in the area of *quantum* cryptography, in which some or all of the parties of a cryptosystem might access quantum computation, we revisit the barrier of constructing TLPs in the random oracle model. The extension of ROMs with quantum access was formally introduced in the work of Boneh et al. [BDF+11]. Therefore, one can study the existence of TLPs in the *quantum* random oracle model in which either (or both) of the puzzle generator or the puzzle solver could access the random oracle in quantum superposition. This leads us to the main questions:

Can we construct time-lock puzzles from random oracles if either or both of the puzzle generator and puzzle solver have quantum access to the random oracle?

Therefore, the question above deals with three settings: (1) only the puzzle solver is quantum, (2) only the puzzle generator is quantum, (3) both algorithms are quantum. In the first two settings, the puzzle is a classical string, as it needs to be output or read by a classical algorithm. In addition, although the first two settings are not "full-fledged quantum", we find them meaningful. Particularly, the first setting is quite natural, as it gives the extra quantum power to the *more power* entity; indeed, the puzzle generator is supposed to be the more efficient entity out of the two players of the scheme.

In a related work, Unruh [Unr14] formalizes the notion of timed-release encryption[1] in the quantum setting and shows how one can bootstrap time-lock puzzles to make them *revocable*; namely, before the puzzles are solved the solver can convince the generator, through interaction, that they are not going to find the solution after all.

1.1 Our Results

Our main result is an impossibility result that extends the result of [MMV11] to the setting in which the puzzle solver is allowed to use quantum power. In particular, we prove the following theorem.

Theorem 1 (Attacking classical-generator quantum-solver TLPs – Informally stated, see Theorem 6**).** *Any time-lock puzzle in the random oracle model with a classical-query puzzle generator and a quantum-query puzzle solver can always be broken by an attacker who asks only $O(n)$ rounds of classical queries to the random oracle, where n is the total number of oracle queries of the puzzle generator. The total number of queries of the attack will be polynomial in n, m where m is the number of (potentially quantum) oracle queries of the honest solver.*

---

[1] This is closely related to our notion of time-lock puzzles, with the difference that the puzzle solution is given to the puzzle generator at the beginning.

Note that it would be enough to find an attacker with quantum queries to the random oracle so long as the number of rounds of queries is polynomial, however, our theorem above goes one step further and shows that the quantum nature of the honest solver cannot be crucial, as there will always be an "equivalent" classical-query solver as well.

Complexity of Our Attack. Our vanilla attack is not efficient, but similarly to the work of [MMV11], we are also able to make our attack efficient, though our efficient attack will run in *quantum* polynomial time, as it will need to simulate the honest solver in its head. Note that our attack's parallel complexity is only measured by its number of rounds of queries to the oracle, and hence the (sequentially long) running time of the simulation of the honest adversary in the attacker's head is ignored in this regard. However, our result shows that basing the sequential soundness *solely* on the (quantum-accessible) random oracle is not going to be possible for constructing TLPs, even when we use extra computational assumptions. In particular, one can imagine potential TLP constructions in the ROM in which *quantum polynomial-time* adversaries cannot solve certain puzzles and would be forced to ask a large number of rounds of oracle queries. This would be similar to classical results such as [BR93] in which random oracles are used along with computational assumptions. The fact that our attack runs in quantum polynomial time rules out such approaches as well.

Optimal Attacks on Perfectly-Complete Protocols. The work of [MMV11] also presented an attack with exactly n rounds of queries. They also showed that such n-round attack is optimal, in general, by presenting an n-query puzzle generator that asks all of its queries in 1 round in such a way that it requires n rounds to be solved. The scheme is based on a construction that we refer to as a pseudo-chain. In this work, we also show that optimal-round attacks exist, at least for perfectly complete schemes.

Theorem 2 (Tight attack on classical-generator quantum-solver TLPs – Informally stated, see Theorem 4.10 in the full version). *Suppose Π is a TLP as in the setting of Theorem 1 and with perfect completeness. Then, Π can be broken in n rounds of queries and a total of $m \cdot n$ queries.*

We further observe that the n-round is indeed optimal by proving that the same pseudo-chain scheme of [MMV11] needs n rounds of queries by the solver, even if it can ask *quantum* queries to the random oracle.

Theorem 3 (A TLP with a linear difficulty gap for quantum-solver– Informally stated, see Theorem 5.3 in the full version). *Define the puzzle-generating function f to be $f^H(x_0, x_1, \ldots, x_{n+1}) := (x_0, H(x_0) \oplus x_1, \ldots, H(x_n) \oplus x_{n+1})$. Then any attacker that makes at most n rounds of quantum queries can find x_{n+1} with at most negligible probability.*

Breaking Quantum-Generator Classical-Solver Puzzles. We then turn to the next setting, in which only the puzzle generator has quantum access to the random oracle. This setting is perhaps less natural for a TLP as the puzzle generator in a TLP is usually the less resource-intensive party. However, we still find this a natural setting, in part due to its *potential applications* beyond the TLP itself. In particular, if one can break quantum-generator classical-solver TLPs in a few rounds in the ROM, it would have corollaries to the round complexity of attacks on key agreements in the ROM as well. In fact, as observed in [MMV11], the transcript T of a key agreement can be seen as a puzzle generated by the two honest parties with the solution being the agreed key k. Then, an attacker who gets T and finds k can be seen as a puzzle solver. The work of [ACC+22] showed that under the so-called polynomial compatibility conjecture, any n query perfectly complete key agreement in the quantum ROM in which the messages are classical can be broken by $\text{poly}(n)$ *classical* queries to the oracle. Hence, by interpreting the attack on the key agreement as a puzzle solver as explained above, an attack on TLPs with quantum generators and classical solvers would imply novel attacks on the key agreement protocols in the quantum ROM with $O(n)$ rounds of attack queries. In part, with such motivation in mind, we take a step towards proving such attacks on TLPs by proving the following result. Indeed we show a variant of the attack of Theorem 2 that works for the "opposite" direction of quantum-generator classical-solver TLPs.

Theorem 4 (Attacking quantum-generator classical-solver TLPs – Informally stated, see Theorem 4.6 in the full version). *Suppose Π is a TLP with perfect completeness in which the puzzle generator can ask n quantum queries to the random oracle, and the solver asks m classical queries to the random oracle. Then, Π can be broken in n rounds and a total of $m \cdot n$ oracle queries.*

Theorem 4 is also tight, in the sense that it asks exactly n rounds of queries. However, similarly to Theorem 2, it requires perfect completeness. This means that if one can improve the attack of [ACC+22] to find the key with probability 1 in $\text{poly}(m,n)$ total number of classical queries, then our Theorem 4 would immediately imply a round-optimal n-round attack.

Quantum Generators and Solvers. Finally, we turn to the case in which both puzzle generator and puzzle solver are allowed to use quantum access to the random oracle model. Note that, in general, in this setting one can imagine the puzzle itself to be a quantum object. For this setting, we are not able to present an attack. On the contrary, we identify a barrier for proving such result *unconditionally*, so long as the attack only uses classical queries to the oracle, which is the case in all of our attacks above. In particular, we show that if the so-called (folklore) "simulation conjecture" [AA14] is *false*, then there exists a TLP with a quantum puzzle generator and a quantum solver that cannot be solved by classical-query attackers, even if they ask any polynomial number of queries to the oracle.

The simulation conjecture states that for any algorithm Q that asks n *quantum* queries to a random oracle H, the probability $p_H = \Pr[Q^H = 1]$ can be ε-approximated for $1 - \varepsilon$ fraction of the random oracles H, for arbitrarily small $\varepsilon = 1/\text{poly}(n)$ using only $\text{poly}(n)$ number of *classical* queries to H. When, $p_H \in \{0, 1\}$ for all H, then this conjecture is known to be true (e.g., see [OSSS05]), but the general case is open and has resisted to be solved for more than a decade after its official exposition by [AA14].

Theorem 5 (Barrier for classically attacking fully quantum TLPs – Informally stated, see Theorem 8). *If the simulation conjecture is false, then there is a time lock* *puzzle in the quantum random oracle model that cannot be broken by classical adversaries.*

Our theorem above does not lead to an actual useful TLP in the quantum random oracle model, as it does not even offer a meaningful gap between the (true) running time of the honest solver and that of the puzzle generator. However, it has the crucial property that a classical (potentially malicious) solver is at a full disadvantage and cannot solve the puzzle even with an arbitrary polynomial number of queries, regardless of its parallel complexity. Consequently, it only serves as a barrier for extending Theorem 1 using a classical attack. Having said that, it is certainly possible that Theorem 1 could potentially be extended to the fully quantum setting using a quantum adversary. We leave this as an intriguing open question.

1.2 Technical Overview

Here we describe some of the ideas behind the proofs of our Theorems 1 and 5. We start by describing our ideas behind the attack of Theorem 1.

Ideas Behind Our Attacks of Theorem 1. Our starting points are the attacks (from the full version of) [MMV11], in which two different types of attacks on TLPs are presented: (1) computationally unbounded attacks with tight adaptivity[2] n and (2) poly-time attacks with adaptivity $O(n)$ (specifically as small as $2n$ rounds). When we move to the quantum-solver setting, we observe that their proofs suffer from incomparable issues: the first attack primarily picks its oracle queries based on the puzzle generator's algorithm, which for us is also classical, and hence the attack description is more "quantum-solver friendly". However, the *analysis* of this attack goes through conditioning on events that do not have a direct quantum variant (at least at first sight). The second attack from [MMV11] is in an opposite form: the attack's description seems to heavily rely on the solver being classical (more on this below) and hence seems to be a more challenging path to take for us here. Having said that, we show that it is indeed possible to extend a variant of the second attack to the quantum-solver setting by developing new ideas that might be useful for other contexts as well. As a bonus, we are also able to make the attack efficient (in quantum polynomial time).

The Classical Attack of [MMV11]. We start by describing the attack of [MMV11] at a high level, and then we address the challenges that arise when we move to the quantum solver setting and explain how to address them. Suppose the Gen makes n oracle queries. Then, the attacker will do the following in $3n$ rounds (of oracle queries), while in each round it learns more oracle queries encoded in a list/partial function $\mathcal{L}$ (that grows over time). In round i, the adversary will pick a full execution of the puzzle solver $\mathsf{Sol}^{H_i}(\mathrm{P}) \to \mathsf{s}_i$ over the given puzzle P to obtain the solution s_i, while H_i is a "random oracle" sampled in adversary's head conditioned on the learned list $\mathcal{L}$. Then, at the end of this round, the adversary will ask *all* of the queries asked by $\mathsf{Sol}^{H_i}(\mathrm{P})$ from the real oracle H and add this information to $\mathcal{L}$. Let $\mathcal{Q}_i$ be the queries asked in

---

[2] In fact, [MMV11] also showed that n-adaptivity is the best one can hope for, as there is a matching positive construction.

this round. The key observation is as follows: during the round-by-round executions, the adversary makes and learns more and more about the true oracle H (through the list $\mathcal{L}$). But only in n out of those $3n$ executions, the list $\mathcal{Q}_i$ can have a *new* intersection with the solver's queries $\mathcal{Q}$. So, in *most* of these executions, no such intersections exist, in which case the adversary gets a *perfectly consistent* execution of the random oracle that would be guaranteed to have the same completeness error as that of the honest solver. Therefore, in most of the rounds, the adversary finds the true answer s to the puzzle P.

Challenge: Quantum Queries Do Not Co-exist. When we move to the quantum-solver setting, the adversary still can sample a full execution $\mathsf{Sol}^{H_i}(\mathrm{P})$ conditioned on a classical list of query-answer pairs $\mathcal{L}$ that it has previously learned about the true oracle H by sampling H_i conditioned on $\mathcal{L}$ in its head and running the honest solver relative to H_i. This is despite the fact that Sol is now a *quantum* algorithm, yet this is all happening in the adversary's head. However, the real challenge is to go one step further: how can the adversary *extract* the set of queries that Sol^{H_i} is asking from its oracle H_i and ask them from the real oracle? After all, it is well-known that when we move to the quantum setting, then multiple queries asked by the same algorithm Sol might *not* coexist.

*Idea: Learning **Amplitude-Heavy** Queries, in Parallel.* Inspired by [ACC+22], our main idea for resolving the challenge above is to define a classical set of queries that are well-defined to coexist and can be learned from the real oracle *in parallel*, while at the same time, these queries will provide useful information for the attacker to succeed. In particular, for every quantum execution of Sol^{H_i}, we say that a *classical* query q is ε-amplitude heavy, if there is one of the quantum queries $\tilde{q}$ (out of the m quantum queries) of Sol^{H_i} such that, the classical query q has at least amplitude ε within $\tilde{q}$. It is easy to see that the number of such queries cannot be more than $\mathrm{poly}(m/\varepsilon)$ for every execution Sol^{H_i}, and therefore, the set $\mathcal{HQ}_\varepsilon^i$ of all ε-amplitude heavy queries of this execution will constitute a sufficiently small (i.e., polynomial-size) classical set. Our adversary will then ask all of the (classical) queries inside the ε-amplitude heavy queries set $\mathcal{HQ}_\varepsilon^i$ at the end of each round i. One can now show that if the number of rounds of the attack is, say $3n$, then again in most of the attack rounds, the attacker's heavy set of queries (that it also learns at the end of the round) will not have a new collision with the puzzle generator's set of queries $\mathcal{Q}$. It remains to show that this condition will again guarantee that the attacker will have a good chance of finding the true puzzle solution s in such rounds.

Final Touch: One-Way to Hiding. Suppose the adversary has already learned a set $\mathcal{L}$ of oracle query-answer pairs about the real oracle H, and that it makes a simulation Sol^{H_i} to obtain a candidate solution s_i by sampling the oracle H_i at random conditioned on $\mathcal{L}$. Further, suppose that we somehow have the guarantee that *none* of the ε-amplitude heavy (classical) queries of the (quantum) execution Sol^{H_i} will intersect with any of the puzzle generator's queries. In this case, we show how to use the useful one-way to hiding lemma of [AHU19], and show that the execution Sol^{H_i} will be statistically close to a *perfectly consistent* execution, in which one *also conditions* on the query-answer pairs of the puzzle generator. As a result, this execution by the adversary Sol^{H_i} would have (almost) the same chance to find the true answer, as an honest solver would.

Putting things together, this means that our attack would also succeed in finding the true answer in most of the rounds out of the $3n$ rounds of the attack, and hence it can e.g., take the majority of the obtained solutions to find the correct solution.

Learning Amplitude-Heavy Queries (Parallel) **Efficiently.** In order to make the attack efficient, the following issues need to be addressed. First, Eve cannot sample a full (exponential size) oracle to run the solver. To efficiently simulate a partially fixed quantum random oracle, we instead use $2m$-wise independent functions [Zha12], where m is the query complexity of the solver. Next, in each round, Eve cannot compute exponentially many query amplitudes of the simulated puzzle solver. Instead, we "experimentally extract" such amplitude-heavy queries. To do so, we rely on the "original version" of one-way to hiding lemma in [Unr14]. Intuitively, if a query q is of high amplitude, then running the solver until a random point and measuring the query register will output q with sufficiently large probability. Following this idea, we run such extractions many times in each *single round*, before extracting a long list of classical queries and asking them from the oracle. This leads to a quantum time-efficient algorithm to extract (almost all) ε-amplitude heavy queries, which turns out to be sufficient for the proof.

Ideas Behind the Proofs of the Tight Attacks of Theorems 2 and 4. Our attack is inspired by the classical result [BI87,Nis89,Tar89,HH87] that $D(f) \leq C_0(f) \cdot C_1(f)$, in which $f\colon \{0,1\}^N \to \{0,1\}$ is an arbitrary boolean function, D is the decision-tree complexity of f (i.e., the smallest number of adaptive queries to the N input bits to f to determine its output), and $C_b(f)$ for $b \in \{0,1\}$ is the b-certificate complexity of f (i.e., the smallest number of input bits that would provably reveal the output to be b). To see the connection, roughly speaking one has to think of the random oracle of N queries as a giant input $x = (x_1, \ldots, x_N)$ and the puzzle solution as the "output" of the function $f(x)$. (Of course, the puzzle generation is randomized, but in this simplified exposition we intentionally ignore this fact.) Below we describe our ideas first for the purely classical case, in which we quantitatively improve the query-complexity of the attack of [MMV11], and then explain the additional ideas for the quantum case.

We define two specific forms of certificates for the puzzle solution being 0 or 1. Suppose P is a puzzle and s $\in \{0,1\}$ is its solution. Consider a full execution of the puzzle generator, using the real oracle H, in which it contains the query-answer pairs $\mathcal{P}_G$ about the oracle H and at the end outputs (P, s). In this case, $\mathcal{P}_G$ serves as a certificate for s, because no solver can obtain the opposite answer $1 - $ s with respect to any oracle that is consistent with $\mathcal{P}_G$; this holds due to the perfect completeness of the scheme. Similarly, for any execution of the solver that solves P into solution s and contains query-answer pairs $\mathcal{P}_S$ about the oracle H, it holds that $\mathcal{P}_S$ serves as a certificate for the solution being s for a similar reason. We will limit ourselves to using only $\mathcal{P}_G$ for s = 0 certificates and $\mathcal{P}_S$ for s = 1 certificates.

Now, a key observation is that, in case of perfectly complete TLPs, any b-certificate, as a set of query-answer pairs, shall be *inconsistent* with any $(1 - b)$-certificate, in that they contain a similar query with different answers because otherwise, one can extend them to a full oracle in which the solver finds a wrong solution. Therefore, this leads to the following n-round attack of total mn query complexity: so long as the puzzle solution is not determined by what the attacker knows (which includes the puzzle P), the attacker would pick a 1-certificate S for *some* oracle that is consistent with attacker's knowledge about the random oracle, and then it asks all of the queries Q in S from the real oracle. The key idea is that, if the answer is still not defined, it at least holds that the effective size of any 0-certificate (among the remaining unknown queries of the oracle) will shrink by one or more. Hence, the process stops in n rounds.

Quantum Solver or Quantum Generator. For the case that either the puzzle generator or the puzzle solver is quantum, we further use inspiration from the attack on key-agreement from random oracles in [ACC+22] for the case that one party is quantum and the other one is classical. In their work, they show how to associate a degree-d polynomial over variables $x_1 \ldots x_N \in \{\pm 1\}$ (where the random oracle has a domain of size N) to the quantum state of the quantum-party conditioned on the transcript of the scheme, in which that party asks d quantum queries to the random oracle. The key idea, at a high level, that generalizes the fully-classical case described above is to replace the query-set $\mathcal{Q}_P$ of a classical party (who is now going to be a quantum algorithm) by the set of oracle queries (that correspond to variables $x_i \in \{x_1 \ldots, x_N\}$) that in turn correspond to a *maximal monomial* in the polynomial that encodes the quantum state of the quantum party (conditioned on the transcript). Then, we show that the same key idea about the inconsistency (and hence non-empty intersections of the query sets) of the 0-certificates and 1-certificates still carries to this generalized setting. This allows us to obtain a classical attack with the same round and query complexity as the fully classical case. For the case of classical puzzle solvers, the attack indeed remains the same exact (round-optimal) attack as that of the fully classical case. For the case of quantum puzzle solvers, the attacker will pick maximal monomials in the polynomial representing the solver's quantum state and ask all of the queries in that monomial in each round.

Ideas Behind the Proof of Theorem 3. Informally, the "knowledge depth" of the attacker after i rounds of queries is at x_i. Therefore, in order for the attacker to solve the puzzle better than randomly guessing x_n, the attacker must make a lucky guess. That is, there exists some $i \in [n]$ such that the attacker's queries in the i-th round hit any of $\{x_i, x_{i+1}, \ldots, x_q\}$. We use hybrid arguments to gradually collect the probabilities that the attacker makes a lucky guess in every round. Finally, we show that the attacker can only randomly guess x_n given there is no lucky guess. In particular, we design hybrids carefully in such a way that (1) in the first hybrid, the game refers to the actual real attack, (2) the last hybrid is trivial information theoretically hard to attack, as the adversary would have to guess a random string of length κ independent of its view, and (3) the neighboring hybrids are computationally indistinguishable up to certain bounds due to a standard argument. The latter relies on the fact [BBBV97,AHU19] that any quantum algorithm that makes 1 round of k-parallel quantum queries cannot distinguish whether a random oracle has been reprogrammed on S random points with advantage more than $O(\sqrt{k \cdot S/2^\kappa})$, where κ is the input length of the random oracle.

Ideas Behind the Barrier of Theorem 5. We now describe ideas behind our barrier of Theorem 5 against breaking fully TLPs classically. In fact, we prove something more general about key-agreements in the (quantum) random oracle model resisting classical attacks. Namely, we show that if the simulation conjecture is *false*, then there is a way for two (quantum) parties Alice and Bob to agree on a classical (random) key by calling a random oracle H in *quantum* superposition and Alice sending a single classical message c to Bob with the following property. Any computationally unbounded Eve who observes Alice's classical message and can query the random oracle H in $\text{poly}(\kappa)$ points *classically* has a negligible chance of finding this key. If we can construct such a protocol, it would be easy to use it to build a TLP on top of it by having Alice hide the puzzle solution using the key and send s $\oplus$ key along with the transcript (single message) c as the puzzle's description. The solver will then use Bob's algorithm to find the key, and then uncover the puzzle solution s. This protocol has the property that any classical-query adversary will have a negligible chance of solving it, establishing Theorem 5. Previously, [ACC+22] showed how to assume the simulation conjecture is false to build an *interactive* key-agreement between quantum-powered parties in the quantum-random oracle model that was secure against polynomial-classical-query adversaries. Here, in this work, we improve their result to obtain such a protocol only with one-way communication.

Idea: Classically-Secure Quantum Key-Agreement with One-Way Communication. At a high level, we use ideas from [ACC+22] to prove a similar result, but their result ended up with an *interactive* key agreement protocol. Here, it is crucial for us to obtain a *non-interactive key-agreement* protocol which we can then use to obtain a time-lock puzzle. We follow the path of [ACC+22] initially, but then the two papers diverge as follows. [ACC+22] relies on a result from [HMST22] that allows how to leverage interaction to bootstrap the obtained key agreement into one with negligible soundness and completeness error. The reduction from [HMST22] is *computational*, which is a stronger reduction but comes at the cost of interaction. On the other hand, we leverage the *information-theoretic* nature of the security of our key agreement and the fact [ACC+22] already provides a weakly secure key-agreement protocol with one-way communication that has sufficiently small completeness error.

Outline of the Technical Steps for Theorem 5. To construct a classically-secure quantum key-agreement with one-way communication we go through the following steps.

Step 0 We start off with the weak key agreement protocol from [ACC+22] (based on the simulation conjecture being false) in which Alice and Bob have quantum access to the random oracle, Alice sends a single message to Bob, and they have completeness error $\varepsilon = 1/\text{poly}(\kappa)$ and the soundness error is $\delta = \text{negl}(\kappa)$ against any adversary with a polynomial number of classical queries. As mentioned above, this completeness error $\varepsilon = 1/\text{poly}(\kappa)$ can be made arbitrarily small.

Step 1 Using Goldreich-Levin's hard-core bit lemma, we turn the above protocol into a new one in which Alice and Bob agree on a *bit* that remains indistinguishable from random, even if the adversary is given the transcript.

Step 2 Using parallel repetition, we increase the length of the key. An interesting subtle point here is that we cannot rely on the vanilla hybrid arguments to argue that this parallel repetition will increase the length of the key securely; that is because the adversary's complexity class is different from that of honest players (who will be simulated as part of the hybrid argument). Despite this subtlety, since our security notion here is *information theoretic*, the hybrid argument still goes through.

Step 3 The completeness error in all the steps above can be kept $\varepsilon' < 1/\operatorname{poly}(\kappa) < 1/2$. We finally make a final change to make the completeness error also negligible: we use another parallel repetition and this time we let Alice pick a random key key and send key $\oplus$ key$_i$ for various keys that she agrees with Bob. Bob then recovers key in most of these executions and finds key by taking a majority.

1.3 Related Work

The study of so-called sequential primitives is not limited to time-lock puzzles. A closely related primitive is a *proof of sequential work* (PoSW) [MMV13, CP18]. A PoSW also has a challenger (who takes the role of the puzzle generator) and a solver, but the solver's answer back to the challenger could be *not unique*, while its validity should be efficiently verifiable. Hence, one can interpret PoSW as a TLP with more than one possible solution, and whose exact solutions might *not* be even known to the challenger at the time of generating the challenge to the solver/prover. The works of [CFHL21, BLZ21] showed that PoSW *can* be achieved in a post-quantum world from random oracles in a strong sense that stands at the opposite of our negative result of Theorem 1: there is a TLP in which the protocol for the honest parties is classical, while its soundness holds against adversaries who are quantum powered.

Another closely related primitive to TLPs the primitive of *verifiable delay functions* [BBBF18, LW17, Pie19, Wes19]. A VDF is similar to a time-lock puzzle, in the sense that the challenger generates a puzzle/challenge with a unique solution s, but s might not be known to the challenger during the time of generation. Yet, when the solver solves the challenge, it can *prove* the validity of its answer through a verification process that is quite fast, just like the puzzle generation phase. It was shown [MSW20] that certain special forms of VDFs are impossible to achieve in the random oracle model. It is possible that using (a generalization of) our techniques one could extend our impossibility results to such classes of VDFs as well, though we leave this exploration for the full version of this paper. See [JMRR21] for a comprehensive study of the relation between the primitives above and other closely related sequential primitives.

Our work can be seen as continuing the line of work initiated by [HY20] for proving *quantum black-box separations*. Their work proved that collision-resistant hash functions cannot be based on trapdoor permutations, even through a quantum reduction. Even though we do not prove any such results explicitly, we present attacks in the random oracle model, which can provide many computational primitives for free, and so our work would also imply corresponding black-box separations. See [AHY23, AK22] for more recent works on barriers against black-box quantum constructions.

2 Preliminaries

2.1 Basic Notations

Let $\kappa \in \mathbb{N}$ denote the security parameter. For $n \in \mathbb{N}$, let $[n]$ to denote the set $\{1, 2, \dots, n\}$. Let U_n be a random variable that returns a random string of length n. By $\operatorname{negl}(\cdot)$ we denote a negligible function. For a finite set $\mathcal{S}$, by $x \xleftarrow{\$} \mathcal{S}$ we mean x

is chosen uniformly from $\mathcal{S}$. Throughout this work, we use the standard bra-ket notation for quantum objects. For the basics of quantum computing, we refer the readers to [NC10]. By $\|\cdot\|$ we denote the 2-norm.

2.2 Quantum Computation

Definition 1 (Quantum Oracle Algorithm). *A q-query quantum oracle algorithm $\mathcal{A}^{(\cdot)}$ that has access to an oracle H, defined by the unitary O_H can be specified by a sequence of unitaries $(U_q, U_{q-1}, \ldots, U_0)$. The final state of the algorithm is defined as $U_q O_H U_{q-1} \ldots O_H U_0 |0\rangle$.*

The query operator O_H is defined as $O_H |x, y\rangle \mapsto |x, y \oplus H(x)\rangle$, where we refer to the first register as the query register.

Definition 2 (Query Amplitude [BBBV97]). *Let $\mathcal{A}^{(\cdot)} = (U_q, \ldots, U_0)$ be a quantum oracle algorithm, $H : \mathcal{X} \to \mathcal{Y}$ be an oracle and $\mathcal{S} \subseteq \mathcal{X}$ be a set. The* query amplitude *$\mu(\mathcal{A}^H, \mathcal{S}) \in \mathbb{R}_{\geq 0}$ is defined as*

$$\mu(\mathcal{A}^H, \mathcal{S}) := \sum_{i=0}^{q-1} \|\Pi_\mathcal{S} |\psi_i^H\rangle\|^2,$$

where $\Pi_\mathcal{S}$ is the projector onto $\mathcal{S}$ acting on the query register of $\mathcal{A}$; each $|\psi_i^H\rangle$ denotes the state of the algorithm right before the $(i+1)^{\text{th}}$ query, i.e., $|\psi_i^H\rangle := U_i O_H \ldots O_H U_0 |0\rangle$.

If $\mathcal{S}$ is a singleton, i.e., $\{x\}$, by a slight abuse of the notation we denote it as $\mu(\mathcal{A}^H, x)$. Note that $\mu(\mathcal{A}^H, \mathcal{S})$ is at most the number of queries made by $\mathcal{A}$. Moreover, for any disjoint $\mathcal{S}_1, \mathcal{S}_2 \subseteq \mathcal{X}$, it holds that $\mu(\mathcal{A}^H, \mathcal{S}_1) + \mu(\mathcal{A}^H, \mathcal{S}_2) = \mu(\mathcal{A}^H, \mathcal{S}_1 \cup \mathcal{S}_2)$.

The following lemma is restated from a similar result in [Unr14].

Lemma 1 ([Unr14]). *For every (fixed) $H : \mathcal{X} \to \mathcal{Y}$, every (fixed) $\mathcal{S} \subseteq \mathcal{X}$, every (fixed) $z \in \{0, 1\}^*$, and every quantum oracle algorithm $\mathcal{A}^{(\cdot)}$, there exists a quantum oracle algorithm $\mathsf{Ext}(\mathcal{A}^H(z))$ that uses $\mathcal{A}^{(\cdot)}$ as subroutine and outputs an element in $\mathcal{S}$ with probability $\mu(\mathcal{A}^H(z), \mathcal{S})/q$, where q is the number of queries made by $\mathcal{A}^H(z)$.*

For completeness, the proof of Lemma 1 and the explicit description of the extractor Ext can be found in Appendix A.

Lemma 2 (One-way-to-hiding, Theorem 3 in [AHU19], restated). *Let $\mathcal{S} \subseteq \mathcal{X}$ be random. Let $F, G : \mathcal{X} \to \mathcal{Y}$ be random functions satisfying $\forall x \notin \mathcal{S}, F(x) = G(x)$. Let z be a random bitstring. $(\mathcal{S}, F, G, z$ may have arbitrary joint distribution.) Let $\mathcal{A}^{(\cdot)}$ be a q-query quantum oracle algorithm. Let*

$$P_{\text{left}} := \Pr[b = 1 : b \leftarrow \mathcal{A}^F(z)],$$
$$P_{\text{right}} := \Pr[b = 1 : b \leftarrow \mathcal{A}^G(z)],$$
$$P_{\text{guess}} := \Pr[x \in \mathcal{S} : x \leftarrow \mathsf{Ext}(\mathcal{A}^F(z))].$$

Then

$$|P_{\text{left}} - P_{\text{right}}| \leq 2q\sqrt{P_{\text{guess}}}.$$

The same holds with $\mathsf{Ext}(\mathcal{A}^G(z))$ instead of $\mathsf{Ext}(\mathcal{A}^F(z))$ in the definition of P_{guess}.

Combining Lemma 1 and Lemma 2, we obtain the following corollary.

Corollary 1. *Let* $\mathcal{S} \subseteq \mathcal{X}$ *be random. Let* $F, G : \mathcal{X} \to \mathcal{Y}$ *be random functions satisfying* $\forall x \notin \mathcal{S},\ F(x) = G(x)$. *Let* z *be a random bitstring. (*$\mathcal{S}, F, G, z$ *may have arbitrary joint distribution.) Let* $\mathcal{A}^{(\cdot)}$ *be a q-query quantum oracle algorithm. Then*

$$|P_{\text{left}} - P_{\text{right}}| \leq 2\sqrt{q\mathbb{E}\left[\mu(\mathcal{A}^F(z), \mathcal{S})\right]},$$

where the probability of the expectation is over $\mathcal{S}, F, G$ *and* z.

Proof. Note that the probability P_{guess} can be written as

$$P_{\text{guess}} = \Pr\left[x \in \mathcal{S} : x \leftarrow \text{Ext}(\mathcal{A}^F(z))\right]$$
$$= \mathbb{E}_{s,f,g,z'}\left[\Pr\left[x \in \mathcal{S} \mid \mathcal{S} = s, F = f, G = g, z = z' : x \leftarrow \text{Ext}(\mathcal{A}^F(z))\right]\right]$$
$$= \mathbb{E}_{\mathcal{S},F,G,z}\left[\frac{\mu(\mathcal{A}^F(z), \mathcal{S})}{q}\right],$$

where the last equality follows from Lemma 1. Plugging P_{guess} into Lemma 2 finishes the proof. □

2.3 Time-Lock Puzzles in the Random Oracle Model

The following definition of time-lock puzzles in the quantum world focuses on a classical puzzle generator, while the solver and the adversary are both quantum. We only allow a constant blow-up in the parallel complexity of the attacker, compared to that of the honest solver.

Definition 3 (Time-Lock Puzzle with Quantum Solver). *A time-lock puzzle scheme consists of a randomized oracle algorithm* puzzle generator $(\text{P}, \text{s}) \leftarrow \text{Gen}^H(r_G)$ *(where* P *is the puzzle and* s *is the correct solution), and a quantum oracle algorithm* puzzle solver $\text{s}' \leftarrow \text{Sol}^H(\text{P})$ *(where* s' *is the solution that the solver finds). For a puzzle generator who makes at most* n *classical queries and a puzzle solver who makes at most* m *(*$m \gg n$*) quantum queries to the oracle, we expect the following properties:*

- **Completeness:** *If the honest solver* Sol *finds the correct solution with probability* $1 - \rho$ *as follows*

$$\Pr[\text{s} = \text{s}' : (\text{P}, \text{s}) \leftarrow \text{Gen}^H(r_G), \text{s}' \leftarrow \text{Sol}^H(\text{P})] \geq 1 - \rho,$$

we say the scheme has ρ *completeness error. By default, we anticipate the completeness error to be negligible* $\rho \leq \text{negl}(\kappa)$.
- **Soundness:** *We say the scheme has* σ *soundness error, if for every quantum oracle algorithm* E *that makes* $\text{poly}(\kappa)$ *queries to the oracle* H *in* $O(n)$ *rounds,*

$$\Pr[\text{s} = \text{s}' : (\text{P}, \text{s}) \leftarrow \text{Gen}^H(r_G), \text{s}' \leftarrow \text{E}^H(\text{P})] = \sigma.$$

By default, we anticipate the scheme to have $\sigma \leq \text{negl}(\kappa)$ *soundness error.*

3   Attacks on Time-Lock Puzzles with Classical Puzzle Generators

In this section, we present attacks for time-lock puzzles with classical generators and quantum solvers (CGQS). The attacks can be seen as a quantum extension of the "efficient but non-optimal adversary" in the full version of [MMV11]. We provide two attacks: one is query-efficient and one is (quantum) time-efficient, but they are incomparable as they provide different trade-offs between parameters.

3.1   Inefficient Attacks on CGQS Time-Lock Puzzles

We now state our result about breaking classical-generator quantum-solver (CGQS) time-lock puzzles in the (quantum) random oracle model. In order to keep the notation clean, for the rest of the work, we sometimes omit the ceiling function of parameters and treat it as an integer when it is clear from the context.

Theorem 6 (Breaking CGQS Time-Lock Puzzles). *Consider any time-lock puzzle scheme in the random oracle model where the generator asks n classical queries, the solver asks m quantum queries and the completeness is $1 - \rho$ (see Definition 3). For any $\varepsilon, \delta \in (0, 1]$, there exists a randomized solver Eve (denoted by E) who asks at most q_E classical queries in at most d_E rounds and achieves the following bounds for the failure probability $\nu = 1 - \Pr[\mathrm{s} = \mathrm{s}' : (\mathrm{P}, \mathrm{s}) \leftarrow \mathsf{Gen}^H(r_G), \mathrm{s}' \leftarrow \mathsf{E}^H(\mathrm{P})]$, where the probability is over the randomness of the generator, the randomness of Eve and the random oracle H.*

1. *Small failure probability: Eve asks $q_E = \frac{4n^2 m^2}{\varepsilon \delta^2}$ queries in $d_E = n/\varepsilon$ rounds with failure probability $\nu \leq \rho + \varepsilon + \delta$.*
2. *2n adaptivity: Eve asks $q_E = \frac{8n^2 m^2}{\delta^2}$ queries in $d_E = 2n$ rounds with failure probability $\nu \leq (2n + 1)(\rho + \delta)$.*

Proof of Theorem 6. We first prove Part 1 of Theorem 6. Then we will obtain Part 2 through a modified attack and a different analysis. We first introduce some notations.

Notation. Let $\mathcal{Q}_G$ be the set of points queried by Gen^H for generating the puzzle and the solution. Let $\mathcal{P}_G$ be the set of query-answer pairs learned by Gen^H, i.e., $\mathcal{P}_G = \{(q, H(q)) \mid q \in \mathcal{Q}_G\}$. Sometimes we abuse the notation and use $(\mathcal{Q}_G, H(\mathcal{Q}_G))$ to denote the same thing $(\mathcal{P}_G)$. For a partial function $F : S \rightarrow \mathcal{Y}$ where S is a subset of the domain $\mathcal{X}$, by $\mathcal{Y}^{\mathcal{X}}|_F$ we mean the set of functions that are consistent with F. Sometimes we refer to a partial function $\mathcal{L}$ as a *list* and use $\mathcal{Q}(\mathcal{L})$ to denote its domain.

Consider the following construction:

Construction 1 (Random Stoppage Attack). *Let n, m be, in order, the number of queries made by Gen^H and Sol^H.*

- *Input: the puzzle P generated by Gen^H and parameters $\varepsilon, \delta \in (0, 1]$.*
- *Set $I = n/\varepsilon$ and initialize a list $\mathcal{L}_1 = \emptyset$.*
- *Pick $i^* \xleftarrow{\$} [I]$.*
- *For $i \in \{1, \ldots, i^*\}$, run Solve(i).*

  – *Output* s_{i^*}.

In the ith round, the subroutine $\text{Solve}(i)$ is defined in Algorithm 1. We note that Construction 1 should be understood by syntactically replacing $\text{Solve}(i)$ with the code of $\text{Solve}(i)$. Looking ahead, $\text{Solve}(i)$ will appear again in the rest of the proof.

Algorithm 1 $\text{Solve}(i)$:

  – Set $\mathcal{Q}_i = \emptyset$.
  – Sample a full oracle $H_i \overset{\$}{\leftarrow} \mathcal{Y}^{\mathcal{X}}|_{\mathcal{L}_i}$.
  – Run $\text{Sol}^{H_i}(\text{P})$ to get the solution s_i.
  – For every $x \in \mathcal{X} \setminus \mathcal{Q}(\mathcal{L}_i)$, compute the query amplitude $\mu(\text{Sol}^{H_i}(\text{P}), x)$.
  – For every $x \in \mathcal{X} \setminus \mathcal{Q}(\mathcal{L}_i)$, if $\mu(\text{Sol}^{H_i}(\text{P}), x) \geq \delta' := \frac{\delta^2}{4nm}$, then let $\mathcal{Q}_i \leftarrow \mathcal{Q}_i \cup \{x\}$.
  – Ask the classical queries $\mathcal{Q}_i$ from the real oracle to obtain $H(\mathcal{Q}_i)$.
  – Update the list by $\mathcal{L}_{i+1} \leftarrow \mathcal{L}_i \cup (\mathcal{Q}_i, H(\mathcal{Q}_i))$.

Efficiency. In each round, since the number of queries made by Sol is at most m, there are at most $\frac{m}{\delta'} = \frac{4nm^2}{\delta^2}$ points that can be added into $\mathcal{Q}_i$. Moreover, there are at most $I = \frac{n}{\varepsilon}$ rounds. Therefore, Eve's adaptivity is at most $\frac{n}{\varepsilon}$ and the total number of Eve's queries is at most $\frac{4n^2m^2}{\varepsilon\delta^2}$.

Completeness. For analysis, we introduce the following experiment which is identical to Construction 1 except that it does not stop at a random point.

Experiment 1. *Let n, m be, in order, the number of queries made by Gen^H and Sol^H.*

1. Input: the puzzle P generated by Gen^H and parameters $\varepsilon, \delta \in (0, 1]$.
2. Set $I = n/\varepsilon$ and initialize a list $\mathcal{L}_1 = \emptyset$.
3. For $i \in [I]$, run $\text{Solve}(i)$.
4. Output s_I.

    Before proving the completeness, we introduce some notations for the above experiment. By *private queries* we mean the set $\mathcal{Q}_G \setminus \mathcal{Q}(\mathcal{L}_i)$, i.e., the set of queries that are asked by the puzzle generator but not asked by Eve before the ith round. For an oracle $H : \mathcal{X} \to \mathcal{Y}$ and a set $S \subseteq \mathcal{X}$, by $H[S^{\circ}]$ we mean the oracle that is obtained by resampling the function value of every point in S uniformly from $\mathcal{Y}$. For every $i \in [I]$, define the event Heavy_i as

$$\text{Heavy}_i := \left[\mu(\text{Sol}^{H_i}(\text{P}), \mathcal{Q}_G \setminus \mathcal{Q}(\mathcal{L}_i)) \geq n\delta' \right], \tag{1}$$

i.e., the query amplitude of $\text{Sol}^{H_i}(\text{P})$ on the private queries is at least $n\delta'$ in the ith round. We say that the ith round is *heavy* if the event Heavy_i holds.
    For every $i \in [I]$, define the event Find_i as

$$\text{Find}_i := [\mathcal{Q}_i \cap (\mathcal{Q}_G \setminus \mathcal{Q}(\mathcal{L}_i)) \neq \emptyset],$$

i.e., Eve learns at least one of the private queries in the ith round.
    First, the following lemma states that the occurrence of Heavy_i implies that Eve learns some private query in the ith round.

Lemma 3. *For every* $i \in [I]$,

$$\Pr[\mathsf{Find}_i \mid \mathsf{Heavy}_i] = 1.$$

Equivalently, $\mathsf{Heavy}_i \subseteq \mathsf{Find}_i$.

Proof. Conditioned on the event Heavy_i happening, it means that the query amplitude of $\mathsf{Sol}^{H_i}(\mathrm{P})$ on the private queries $\mathcal{Q}_G \setminus \mathcal{Q}(\mathcal{L}_i)$ is at least $n\delta'$ in the ith round. Since the number of queries made by Gen is at most n, by an averaging argument, there exists $x \in \mathcal{Q}_G \setminus \mathcal{Q}(\mathcal{L}_i)$ such that $\mu(\mathsf{Sol}^{H_i}(\mathrm{P}), x) \geq \delta'$. By construction, the point x will be added into $\mathcal{Q}_i$. Thus, Eve learns at least one of the private queries in the ith round. □

Next, since the puzzle generator asks at most n queries, the number of occurring events among $\{\mathsf{Find}_i\}_{i \in [I]}$ is at most n in every execution.

Lemma 4. *For every* $i \in [I]$, *let* I_{Find_i} *be the indicator variable of* Find_i. *Then*

$$\Pr\left[\sum_{i \in [I]} I_{\mathsf{Find}_i} \leq n\right] = 1.$$

Proof. For the sake of contradiction, suppose there is a nonzero probability that all events $\mathsf{Find}_{i_1}, \ldots, \mathsf{Find}_{i_\ell}$ occur for some pairwise distinct $i_1, \ldots, i_\ell \in [I]$, where $\ell > n$. Then it means that for all $k \in [\ell]$, the set $\mathcal{Q}_{i_k} \cap \mathcal{Q}_G$ is nonempty. Moreover, all of them are pairwise disjoint since Eve never asks the same query. However, it will lead to the following contradiction

$$n < \ell \leq \bigcup_{k \in [\ell]} |\mathcal{Q}_{i_k} \cap \mathcal{Q}_G| \leq |\mathcal{Q}_G| \leq n.$$

□

The above two lemmas together imply that the number of occurring events among $\{\mathsf{Heavy}_i\}_{i \in [I]}$ is at most n in every execution.

Corollary 2. *For every* $i \in [I]$, *let* I_{Heavy_i} *be the indicator variable of* Heavy_i. *Then*

$$\Pr\left[\sum_{i \in [I]} I_{\mathsf{Heavy}_i} \leq n\right] = 1.$$

Proof. It immediately follows from Lemma 3 and Lemma 4. □

Before we move on, we rewrite Experiment 1 as the following equivalent experiment under the view of lazy evaluation:

Experiment 2

1. *Run* $(\mathrm{P}, \mathrm{s}) \leftarrow \mathsf{Gen}^{(\cdot)}(r_G)$ *by lazy evaluation.*
   // *The set* $\mathcal{P}_G$ *of query-answer pairs is sampled.*

2. Set $I = n/\varepsilon$ and initialize a list $\mathcal{L}_1 = \emptyset$.
3. For $i \in [I]$, do the following:
   - For every $x \in \mathcal{X} \setminus (\mathcal{Q}_G \cup \mathcal{Q}(\mathcal{L}_i))$, uniformly sample a value y_x from $\mathcal{Y}$.
   - Combine $\mathcal{P}_G$, $\mathcal{L}_i$, and all the query-answer pairs sampled in the previous step into a full oracle H. (Note that in each iteration H could be different.)
   - Sample $H_i \leftarrow H[(\mathcal{Q}_G \setminus \mathcal{Q}(\mathcal{L}_i))^{\circlearrowleft}]$.
                                                    // All private queries are resampled uniformly.
   - Run $\mathsf{Sol}^{H_i}(\mathrm{P})$ to obtain the solution s_i.
   - Set $\mathcal{Q}_i = \emptyset$.
   - For every $x \in \mathcal{X} \setminus \mathcal{Q}(\mathcal{L}_i)$, compute the query amplitude $\mu(\mathsf{Sol}^{H_i}(\mathrm{P}), x)$.
   - For every $x \in \mathcal{X} \setminus \mathcal{Q}(\mathcal{L}_i)$, if $\mu(\mathsf{Sol}^{H_i}(\mathrm{P}), x) \geq \delta' := \frac{\delta^2}{4nm}$, then let $\mathcal{Q}_i \leftarrow \mathcal{Q}_i \cup \{x\}$.
   - Ask the classical queries $\mathcal{Q}_i$ from the real oracle and obtain the answers.
   - Update the list by appending the query-answer pairs obtained in the previous step to get $\mathcal{L}_{i+1}$.

The distribution of H_i is consistent with that in Experiment 1 since every query beyond $\mathcal{Q}(\mathcal{L}_i)$ is independently and uniformly sampled.

We now show that, as long as the ith round is not heavy, Eve's simulation will be good enough to generate the correct solution with high probability. Formally, we have the following lemma.

Lemma 5. *For every $i \in [I]$, it holds that*

$$\Pr\left[s = s_i \wedge \neg\mathsf{Heavy}_i\right] \geq \Pr\left[s = s' \wedge \neg\mathsf{Heavy}_i\right] - \delta.$$

where the probability is defined over Experiment 2 and s' is defined to be generated by $\mathsf{Sol}^H(\mathrm{P})$ instead of using H_i in the i-th iteration.

Proof. By Corollary 1 (setting $F = H_i$, $G = H$, $\mathcal{S} = \mathcal{Q}_G \setminus \mathcal{Q}(\mathcal{L}_i)$, $z = (\mathrm{P}, s)$, and $\mathcal{A}^F(z) = \mathcal{V} \circ \mathsf{Sol}^{H_i}(\mathrm{P})$, where $\mathcal{V}(s_i) = 1$ if $s = s_i$, and 0 otherwise), we have

$$\Pr\left[s = s_i \wedge \neg\mathsf{Heavy}_i\right]$$
$$= \Pr[\neg\mathsf{Heavy}_i] \cdot \Pr\left[s = s_i \mid \neg\mathsf{Heavy}_i\right]$$
$$= \Pr[\neg\mathsf{Heavy}_i] \cdot \Pr\left[\mathcal{A}^F(z) = \mathcal{V} \circ \mathsf{Sol}^{H_i}(\mathrm{P}) = 1 \mid \neg\mathsf{Heavy}_i\right]$$
$$\geq \Pr[\neg\mathsf{Heavy}_i] \cdot \left(\Pr\left[\mathcal{A}^G(z) = \mathcal{V} \circ \mathsf{Sol}^H(\mathrm{P}) = 1 \mid \neg\mathsf{Heavy}_i\right] - 2\sqrt{mn\delta'}\right)$$
$$\geq \Pr\left[\mathcal{V} \circ \mathsf{Sol}^H(\mathrm{P}) = 1 \wedge \neg\mathsf{Heavy}_i\right] - \delta$$
$$= \Pr\left[s = s' \wedge \neg\mathsf{Heavy}_i\right] - \delta,$$

where the first inequality follows from Corollary 1 by letting the joint distribution of $(F, G, \mathcal{S}, z)$ be the conditional distribution given $\neg\mathsf{Heavy}_i$; the second inequality follows from our choice of parameter $\delta = 2\sqrt{mn\delta'}$. This finishes the proof. $\square$

Finally, with the above lemmas in hand, the completeness can be proven in the following lemma:

Lemma 6 (Completeness of Construction 1).

$$\Pr\left[s = s_{i^*} : \begin{array}{c} (P,s) \leftarrow \mathsf{Gen}^H(r_G) \\ i^* \leftarrow [I] \\ s_{i^*} \leftarrow \mathsf{Sol}^{H_{i^*}}(P) \end{array} \right] \geq 1 - \rho - \varepsilon - \delta.$$

Proof. The success probability of Eve in Construction 1 is given by

$$\Pr\left[s = s_{i^*} : \begin{array}{c} (P,s) \leftarrow \mathsf{Gen}^H(r_G) \\ i^* \leftarrow [I] \\ s_{i^*} \leftarrow \mathsf{Sol}^{H_{i^*}}(P) \end{array} \right] = \frac{1}{I} \sum_{i=1}^{I} \Pr\left[s = s_i \right]$$

$$\geq \frac{1}{I} \sum_{i=1}^{I} \Pr\left[s = s_i \wedge \neg \mathsf{Heavy}_i \right] \overset{(i)}{\geq} \frac{1}{I} \sum_{i=1}^{I} \Pr\left[s = s' \wedge \neg \mathsf{Heavy}_i \right] - \delta$$

$$\geq \frac{1}{I} \sum_{i=1}^{I} \left(\Pr\left[s = s' \right] - \Pr[\mathsf{Heavy}_i] \right) - \delta = \Pr\left[s = s' \right] - \frac{1}{I} \mathbb{E}\left[\sum_{i=1}^{I} I_{\mathsf{Heavy}_i} \right] - \delta$$

$$\overset{(ii)}{\geq} \Pr\left[s = s' \right] - \varepsilon - \delta \overset{(iii)}{\geq} 1 - \rho - \varepsilon - \delta,$$

where (i) is due to Lemma 5, (ii) follows from Corollary 2 and (iii) follows from the completeness of the puzzle.   □

This concludes the efficiency and completeness of Eve in Construction 1, and hence it finishes the proof of Part 1 of Theorem 6.

Part 2. We now move to prove Part 2 of Theorem 6. The idea is to use the *majority* of the solutions obtained in *all* rounds. Consider the following construction:

Construction 2 (Majority Vote Attack). *Let n, m be, in order, the number of queries made by* Gen^H *and* Sol^H.

- *Input: the puzzle P generated by* Gen^H *and a parameter $\delta \in (0, 1]$.*
- *Set $I = 2n$ and initialize a list $\mathcal{L}_1 = \emptyset$ and a multiset $\mathcal{S} = \emptyset$.*
- *For $i \in \{1, \ldots, I\}$, do the following:*
  - *Run* $\mathsf{Solve}(i)$.
  - *Update the solution set by $\mathcal{S} \leftarrow \mathcal{S} \cup \{s_i\}$.*
- *Sample a full oracle $H_{I+1} \overset{\$}{\leftarrow} \mathcal{Y}^{\mathcal{X}}|_{\mathcal{L}_{I+1}}$.*
- *Run one more execution* $\mathsf{Sol}^{H_{I+1}}(P)$ *to get the solution* s_{I+1}.
- *Update the solution set by $\mathcal{S} \leftarrow \mathcal{S} \cup \{s_{I+1}\}$.*
- *If there exists $s^* \in \mathcal{S}$ that has multiplicity at least $I/2 + 1 = n + 1$, output s^*. Otherwise, abort.*

Efficiency. In each round, since the number of queries made by Sol is at most m, there are at most $\frac{m}{\delta'} = \frac{4nm^2}{\delta^2}$ points that can be added into $\mathcal{Q}_i$. Moreover, there are at most $I = 2n$ rounds. Therefore, Eve's adaptivity is $2n$ and the total number of Eve's queries is at most $\frac{8n^2m^2}{\delta^2}$.

Completeness. For every $i \in [I+1]$, let $\mathsf{Success}_i$ denote the event that $\mathsf{s} = \mathsf{s}_i$. Following the same argument in Lemma 5, Eve's simulation error is at most δ conditioned on the event $\neg\mathsf{Heavy}_i$ happening. Hence, for every $i \in [I + 1]$, we have

$$\Pr[\mathsf{Success}_i \vee \mathsf{Heavy}_i] = \Pr[\neg\mathsf{Heavy}_i] \cdot \Pr[\mathsf{Success}_i \mid \neg\mathsf{Heavy}_i] + \Pr[\mathsf{Heavy}_i]$$
$$\geq 1 - \rho - \delta.$$

Equivalently, for every $i \in [I + 1]$,

$$\Pr[\neg\mathsf{Success}_i \wedge \neg\mathsf{Heavy}_i] \leq \rho + \delta.$$

Therefore, by a union bound over $i \in [I + 1]$, we have

$$\Pr\left[\bigwedge_{i \in [I+1]} (\mathsf{Success}_i \vee \mathsf{Heavy}_i)\right] \geq 1 - (I+1)(\rho + \delta).$$

Suppose the above event holds for the rest of the proof. By Corollary 2, with probability one, the number of the happening events Heavy_i is at most n, which means the number of happening events $\mathsf{Success}_i$ is at least $n + 1$. This implies the success of Eve's attack in Construction 2 and finishes the proof of Part 2 of Theorem 6.   □

3.2 Efficient Attacks on CGQS Time-Lock Puzzles

The attacks in the last subsection could be made *time*-efficient at the cost of a slightly worse query complexity. In Construction 1 and Construction 2, in order to find queries with a large amplitude, Eve needs to sample a full oracle and compute exponentially many query amplitudes. Moreover, as a quantum nature, the queries made by $\mathsf{Sol}^{H_i}(\mathsf{P})$ cannot be "recorded". Fortunately, by leveraging Lemma 1, we still have an efficient way to extract queries with a large amplitude. Although directly invoking Lemma 1 guarantees some probability for successful extraction, the probability is still too low. In this way, it will increase the number of rounds (adaptivity) by a large factor.

To overcome this issue, Eve will instead run the solver many times in each round. By choosing parameters properly, we show that Eve can find queries with a large amplitude with high probability. Lastly, the efficient simulation of a (partially fixed) quantum random oracle can be done by using $2m$-wise independent functions [Zha12]. Below, we show how to convert Construction 1 into a quantum time-efficient attack.

Theorem 7 (Efficiently Breaking CGQS Time-Lock Puzzles). *Consider any time-lock puzzle scheme in the random oracle model where the generator asks n classical queries, the solver asks m quantum queries and the completeness is $1 - \rho$ (see Definition 3). For any $\varepsilon, \delta \in (0, 1]$ and $\gamma > 1$, there exists an efficient, randomized solver Eve (denoted by E) who asks at most q_E classical queries in at most d_E rounds and in time $O(d_E \cdot T)$, where T is the running time of the honest solver, and it achieves the following bound for the failure probability $\nu = 1 - \Pr[\mathsf{s} = \mathsf{s}' : (\mathsf{P}, \mathsf{s}) \leftarrow \mathsf{Gen}^H(r_G), \mathsf{s}' \leftarrow \mathsf{E}^H(\mathsf{P})]$, where the probability is over the randomness of the generator, the randomness of Eve (including the randomness of using the quantum solver as subroutines) and the random oracle H.*

– *Small failure probability:* Eve asks $q_E = \frac{4nm^2}{\varepsilon\delta^2}\ln\left(\frac{\gamma}{\gamma-1}\right)$ queries in $d_E = n/\varepsilon$ rounds with failure probability $\nu \leq \rho + \gamma\varepsilon + \delta$.

Remark 1. *Here, we compare the parameters in Theorem 7 with the parameters in Theorem 6. Suppose we let $n = \ln\left(\frac{\gamma}{\gamma-1}\right)$ and let $n, m, \varepsilon, \delta$ be identical, then Eve's adaptivity and the number of total queries in each construction will be equivalent. In this way, we can solve the above equation and obtain $\gamma \approx 1 + e^{-n}$.*

Remark 2. *Construction 2 can be made efficient in a similar manner.*

Proof. Proof of Theorem 7. Consider the following efficient variant of Construction 1:

Construction 3 (Efficient Random Stoppage Attack). *Let n, m be, in order, the number of queries made by Gen^H and Sol^H.*

– *Input: the puzzle P generated by Gen^H and parameters $\varepsilon, \delta \in (0,1], \gamma > 1$.*
– *Set $I = n/\varepsilon$ and initialize a list $\mathcal{L}_1 = \emptyset$.*
– *Pick $i^* \xleftarrow{\$} [I]$.*
– *For $i \in \{1, \ldots, i^*\}$, do the following:*
  - *Set $\mathcal{Q}_i = \emptyset$.*
  - *Use $2m$-wise independent functions to simulate $H_i \xleftarrow{\$} \mathcal{Y}^{\mathcal{X}}|_{\mathcal{L}_i}$.*
  - *Run $\mathsf{Sol}^{H_i}(\mathrm{P})$ to get the solution s_i.*
  - *Let $\gamma' := \frac{m}{n\delta'}\ln\left(\frac{\gamma}{\gamma-1}\right)$, where $\delta' := \frac{\delta^2}{4nm}$.*
  - *For $j \in [\gamma']$, do the following:*
    * *Run $\mathsf{Ext}(\mathsf{Sol}^{H_i}(\mathrm{P}))$ to get $x \in \mathcal{X}$.*
      (Note that the oracle used in each execution is fixed, i.e., H_i.)
    * *If $x \notin \mathcal{Q}(\mathcal{L}_i) \cup \mathcal{Q}_i$, then $\mathcal{Q}_i \leftarrow \mathcal{Q}_i \cup \{x\}$.*
  - *Make classical queries to the (real) random oracle H on all points in $\mathcal{Q}_i$ and obtain $H(\mathcal{Q}_i)$.*
  - *Update the list by $\mathcal{L}_{i+1} \leftarrow \mathcal{L}_i \cup (\mathcal{Q}_i, H(\mathcal{Q}_i))$.*
– *Output s_{i^*}.*

Efficiency. In each round, the size of $\mathcal{Q}_i$ is at most $\gamma' = \frac{m}{n\delta'}\ln\left(\frac{\gamma}{\gamma-1}\right) = \frac{4m^2}{\delta^2}\ln\left(\frac{\gamma}{\gamma-1}\right)$. Moreover, there are at most $I = n/\varepsilon$ rounds. Therefore, Eve's adaptivity is at most n/ε and the total number of Eve's queries is at most $\frac{4nm^2}{\varepsilon\delta^2}\ln\left(\frac{\gamma}{\gamma-1}\right)$. Notice that the iteration of the extractor in each round can be performed in parallel. In addition, the amount of randomness for initiating a $2m$-wise independent function is $O(m) = O(T)$. Hence, Eve's running time is $O(d_E \cdot T)$.

Completeness. The following lemma is the generalization of Lemma 3. Given that the ith round is heavy, repeating the extractor in Lemma 1 many times will output a private query with high probability.

Lemma 7. *For every $i \in [I]$, it holds that*

$$\Pr[\mathsf{Find}_i \mid \mathsf{Heavy}_i] \geq \frac{1}{\gamma}.$$

Proof. Conditioned on the event Heavy_i happening, it means that the query amplitude of $\mathsf{Sol}^{H_i}(\mathrm{P})$ on the private queries $\mathcal{Q}_G \setminus \mathcal{Q}(\mathcal{L}_i)$ is at least $n\delta'$ in the ith round. By Lemma 1, the probability of obtaining $x \in \mathcal{Q}_G \setminus \mathcal{Q}(\mathcal{L}_i)$ in each iteration of the extractor is at least $n\delta'/m$. Moreover, each iteration is independent because the randomness of the extractor comes from the choice of query and the measurement. Both of them are fresh every time. Hence, after γ' iterations, the probability of obtaining $x \in \mathcal{Q}_G \setminus \mathcal{Q}(\mathcal{L}_i)$ is at least

$$1 - \left(1 - \frac{n\delta'}{m}\right)^{\gamma'} \geq 1 - e^{\ln(1-1/\gamma)} = \frac{1}{\gamma},$$

where we use $1 - x \leq e^{-x}$ for $x \in \mathbb{R}$ and $\gamma' = \frac{m}{n\delta'} \ln\left(\frac{\gamma}{\gamma-1}\right)$. $\qquad\square$

Lemma 8. *For every $i \in [I]$, let I_{Find_i} be the indicator variable of Find_i. Then*

$$\Pr\left[\sum_{i \in [I]} I_{\mathsf{Find}_i} \leq n\right] = 1.$$

Proof. The proof is the same as Lemma 4. $\qquad\square$

The following corollary is the generalization of Corollary 2.

Corollary 3. *For every $i \in [I]$, let I_{Heavy_i} be the indicator variable of Heavy_i. Then*

$$\mathbb{E}\left[\sum_{i \in [I]} I_{\mathsf{Heavy}_i}\right] \leq \gamma n.$$

Proof. From Lemma 7, we have

$$\Pr[\mathsf{Heavy}_i] \leq \gamma \Pr[\mathsf{Heavy}_i \wedge \mathsf{Find}_i] \leq \gamma \Pr[\mathsf{Find}_i].$$

By Lemma 8, it holds that

$$\mathbb{E}\left[\sum_{i \in [I]} I_{\mathsf{Heavy}_i}\right] = \sum_{i \in [I]} \Pr[\mathsf{Heavy}_i] \leq \gamma \sum_{i \in [I]} \Pr[\mathsf{Find}_i] = \gamma \mathbb{E}\left[\sum_{i \in [I]} I_{\mathsf{Find}_i}\right] \leq \gamma n.$$

$$\square$$

Finally, we have the following lemma, which is the counterpart of Lemma 6.

Lemma 9 (Completeness of Construction 3).

$$\Pr\left[s = \mathsf{s}_{i^*} : \begin{array}{c} (\mathrm{P},s) \leftarrow \mathsf{Gen}^H(r_G) \\ i^* \leftarrow [I] \\ \mathsf{s}_{i^*} \leftarrow \mathsf{Sol}^{H_{i^*}}(\mathrm{P}) \end{array}\right] \geq 1 - \rho - \gamma\varepsilon - \delta.$$

Proof. Following the same lines in the proof of Lemma 6, we have

$$\Pr\left[s = s_{i^*} : \begin{array}{c} (P,s) \leftarrow \text{Gen}^H(r_G) \\ i^* \leftarrow [I] \\ s_{i^*} \leftarrow \text{Sol}^{H_{i^*}}(P) \end{array}\right]$$

$$\geq \Pr\left[s = s' : \begin{array}{c} (P,s) \leftarrow \text{Gen}^H(r_G) \\ s' \leftarrow \text{Sol}^H(P) \end{array}\right] - \frac{1}{I}\mathbb{E}\left[\sum_{i \in [I]} I_{\text{Heavy}_i}\right] - \delta$$

$$\geq \Pr\left[s = s' : \begin{array}{c} (P,s) \leftarrow \text{Gen}^H(r_G) \\ s' \leftarrow \text{Sol}^H(P) \end{array}\right] - \gamma\varepsilon - \delta$$

$$\geq 1 - \rho - \gamma\varepsilon - \delta.$$

where the second to last inequality follows from Corollary 3.   □

This concludes the efficiency and completeness of Eve in Construction 3.   □

4   Barriers for Classical Attacks on Fully Quantum Puzzles

In this section, we present a fully quantum - i.e., quantum generator and quantum solver (QGQS) - time-lock puzzle construction that is secure against polynomial-query classical adversaries, assuming the quantum simulation conjecture does not hold.

Simulation Conjecture. Let $A^{(\cdot)}$ be a quantum oracle algorithm that outputs a single bit. For every fixed oracle H, let $p(A^H) := \Pr[1 \leftarrow A^H(1^\kappa)])$, where the probability is over the execution of A. We say an algorithm B λ-approximates an algorithm A if:

$$\mathbb{E}_H[|p(A^H) - p(B^H)|] \leq \lambda$$

The following is a weaker (asymptotic) version of the folklore Simulation Conjecture, which is stated as Conjecture 4 in [AA14].

Conjecture 1 (Quantum Polynomial-Query Simulation Conjecture). *For any constant c, there exists a constant d, such that for all κ^c-query quantum algorithm $Q^{(\cdot)}(\cdot)$, there exists a deterministic κ^d-query classical algorithm $A^{(\cdot)}(\cdot)$, such that $A(1^\kappa)$ κ^{-c}-approximates $Q(1^\kappa)$ for sufficiently large κ (when accessing a random oracle).*

We now formally define the main result of this section, which is a fully quantum time-lock puzzle that cannot be broken by classical-query adversaries, assuming that the simulation conjecture is false.

Theorem 8 (Classically breaking QGQS TLPs implies the Simulation Conjecture). *If Conjecture 1 does not hold, there exists an infinite set $\mathcal{K}$ (of security parameters κ) such that there is a protocol between two* quantum *oracle algorithms* Gen *and* Sol *that (quantumly) access a random oracle H satisfying the following:*

- *Completeness:* $\Pr[s' = s : (P,s) \leftarrow \text{Gen}^H, s' \leftarrow \text{Sol}^H(P)] \geq 1 - \text{negl}(\kappa)$.
- *Soundness: For any computationally unbounded classical adversary $\mathcal{A}$ who ask* $\text{poly}(\kappa)$ *classical queries to H, and for every $\kappa \in \mathcal{K}$, we have*

$$\Pr[s'' = s : (P,s) \leftarrow \text{Gen}^H, s'' \leftarrow \mathcal{A}^H(P)] \leq \text{negl}(\kappa).$$

The exact form of Conjecture 1 first appeared in [ACC+22, Conjecture 7.1], using which they proved the following lemma.

Lemma 10 (Weak Key Agreement with One-Way Communication [ACC+22]). *If Conjecture 1 does not hold, there exists an infinite set $\mathcal{K}$ (of security parameters κ), such that for all polynomially small $\varepsilon_0 = 1/\operatorname{poly}(\cdot)$ there is a protocol between two quantum oracle algorithms Q_A and Q_B that (quantumly) access a random oracle H satisfying the following:*

- *One-way communication: Q_A^H sends a single classical message c to Q_B^H, after which they each output $\mathsf{key}_A, \mathsf{key}_B$.*
- *Completeness: $\Pr[\mathsf{key}_A = \mathsf{key}_B : (\mathsf{key}_A, c) \leftarrow Q_A^H, \mathsf{key}_B \leftarrow Q_B^H(c)] \geq 1 - \varepsilon_0(\kappa)$.*
- *Soundness: For any computationally unbounded classical adversary $\mathcal{A}$ who ask $\operatorname{poly}(\kappa)$ classical queries to H, and for every $\kappa \in \mathcal{K}$, we have*

$$\Pr[\mathsf{key}_A = \mathsf{key}_E : (\mathsf{key}_A, c) \leftarrow Q_A^H, \mathsf{key}_E \leftarrow \mathcal{A}^H(c)] \leq \delta_0(\kappa),$$

where $\delta_0(\cdot)$ is a negligible function.

Outline of the Technical Steps. To construct a fully quantum time-lock puzzle we first show how to amplify the key agreement of Lemma 10 to a key agreement with negligible completeness and soundness error. Then we will show how to transform such a key agreement protocol into a time-lock puzzle. Here is a sketch of this process, where all the items below are with *one-way communication* (OWC).

Step 0 Start with the weak key agreement with OWC of Lemma 10.

Step 1 Construct a weakly complete and strongly sound (WCSS) single-bit key agreement with OWC. (See Construction 4.)

Step 2 Construct a weakly complete and strongly sound multi-bit key agreement with OWC. (See Construction 5.)

Step 3 Construct a strongly complete and strongly sound (SCSS) multi-bit key agreement with OWC. (See Construction 6.)

Step 4 Transform a multi-bit key agreement with OWC to a time-lock puzzle while preserving the soundness and completeness error. (See Construction 7)

Here we show how to do **Step 1**.

Construction 4 (WCSS Single-Bit Key Agreement with OWC). *Let Q_{A_0}, Q_{B_0} be a weak key agreement scheme from Lemma 10 with completeness error $\varepsilon_0(\kappa)$ and soundness error $\delta_0(\kappa)$. Let H be an oracle and define Q_{A_1} and Q_{B_1} as follows:*

- *Q_{A_1} performs the following:*
  1. *Run Q_{A_0} to get $(c_0, \mathsf{key}_{A_0}) \leftarrow Q_{A_0}^H$.*
  2. *Sample $r \leftarrow \{0, 1\}^{|\mathsf{key}_{A_0}|}$ and compute $\mathsf{key}_{A_1} = \langle r, \mathsf{key}_{A_0} \rangle$.*
  3. *Let $c_1 = c_0 \| r$.*
- *Q_{B_1} performs the following:*
  1. *Let $c_1 = c_0 \| r$.*
  2. *Run Q_{B_0} to get $\mathsf{key}_{B_0} \leftarrow Q_{B_0}^H(c_0)$.*

3. *Compute* $\text{key}_{\text{B}_1} = \langle r, \text{key}_{\text{B}_0} \rangle$.

Theorem 9 (Completeness of Construction 4). *If the construction from Lemma 10 has completeness error* $\varepsilon_0(\kappa)$, *then Construction 4 has completeness error* $\varepsilon_1 \leq \varepsilon_0$.

Proof. By the construction, if $\text{key}_{\text{A}_0} = \text{key}_{\text{B}_0}$, then $\text{key}_{\text{A}_1} = \text{key}_{\text{B}_1}$, thus $\varepsilon_1 \leq \varepsilon_0$. □

Theorem 10 (Soundness of Construction 4). *If the construction from Lemma 10 has a soundness error* $\delta_0(\kappa)$, *then Construction 4 has a soundness error* $\delta_1 \leq n^{O(1)} \cdot \delta_0^{\Omega(1)}$, *where* $n = |\text{key}_{\text{A}_0}|$. *In particular, if* $\delta_0 \leq \text{negl}(\kappa)$, *then* $\delta_1 \leq \text{negl}(\kappa)$ *as well.*

Proof. The proof is similar to the proof of the Hard-core bit lemma from [GL89]. In particular, the proof of the Hard-core bit lemma from [GL89] is black-box and transforms any adversary who guesses the hard-core bit with probability ρ, to an inverting adversary that guesses the pre-image with probability $\text{poly}(\rho/n)$, and the same reduction works even if the pre-image and image are jointly sampled (rather than the image being a deterministic function of the pre-image). □

Next, we show how to do **Step 2**.

Construction 5 (WCSS Multi-Bit Key Agreement with OWC). *Let* $Q_{\text{A}_1}, Q_{\text{B}_1}$ *be a WCSS Single-Bit key agreement scheme from Construction 4 with completeness error* $\varepsilon_1(\kappa)$ *and soundness error* $\delta_1(\kappa)$. *Let* $u = \text{poly}(\kappa)$ *(to be chosen later) be the length of the key,* H *be an oracle, and define* Q_{A_2} *and* Q_{B_2} *as follows:*

- Q_{A_2} *performs the following:*
  1. *Divide oracle* H *to* u *independent oracles* H_i *(according to some canonical division).*
  2. *For* $i \in [u]$ *run* Q_{A_1} *to get* $(c_{1,i}, \text{key}_{\text{A}_1,i}) \leftarrow Q_{\text{A}_1}^{H_i}$.
  3. *Let* $c_2 = c_{1,1} || \cdots || c_{1,u}$ *and* $\text{key}_{\text{A}_2} = \text{key}_{\text{A}_1,1} || \cdots || \text{key}_{\text{A}_1,u}$.
- Q_{B_2} *performs the following:*
  1. *Let* $c_2 = c_{1,1} || \cdots || c_{1,u}$.
  2. *Divide oracle* H *to* u *independent oracles* H_i *(according to the same canonical division).*
  3. *For* $i \in [u]$ *run* Q_{B_1} *to get* $\text{key}_{\text{B}_1,i} \leftarrow Q_{\text{B}_1}^{H_i}(c_{1,i})$.
  4. *Compute* $\text{key}_{\text{B}_2} = \text{key}_{\text{B}_1,1} || \cdots || \text{key}_{\text{B}_1,u}$.

Theorem 11 (Completeness of Construction 5). *If Construction 4 has completeness error* $\varepsilon_1(\kappa)$, *then Construction 5 has completeness error* $\varepsilon_2 \leq u \cdot \varepsilon_1$.

Proof. By the construction, if for all $i \in [u]$, $\text{key}_{\text{A}_1,i} = \text{key}_{\text{B}_1,i}$, then $\text{key}_{\text{A}_2} = \text{key}_{\text{B}_2}$. We conclude the proof by a union bound and letting $\varepsilon_2 \leq u\varepsilon_1$. □

Theorem 12 (Soundness of Construction 5). *If Construction 4 has a soundness error* $\delta_1(\kappa)$, *then Construction 5 has a soundness error (advantage)* $\delta_2 = u\delta_1$.

Proof. Suppose there exists an adversary Q_{E_2} such that:

$$| \Pr[1 \leftarrow Q_{E_2}^H(c_2, \text{key}_{A_2})] - \Pr[1 \leftarrow Q_{E_2}^H(c_2, U_u)]| \geq \delta_2.$$

We show there exists an adversary Q_{E_1} that breaks the soundness in Theorem 10 with an advantage at least δ_1. To do so define hybrids $\{\mathcal{H}_k\}_k$ for $k \in \{0, \cdots, u\}$ (where $\mathcal{H}_0$ is the experiment of Construction 5) such that in hybrid $\mathcal{H}_k$, we replace $\text{key}_{A_1,i}$ with $\text{key}'_{A_1,i} \leftarrow \{0,1\}$ when constructing key_{A_2}. Namely, in hybrid $\mathcal{H}_k$, we have $\text{key}_{A_2} = \text{key}'_{A_1,1}|| \cdots ||\text{key}'_{A_1,k}||\text{key}_{A_1,k+1}|| \cdots ||\text{key}_{A_1,u}$. Now note that in hybrid $\mathcal{H}_u$, key_{A_2} is completely random, thus an adversary has no advantage in distinguishing key_{A_2} from random. Therefore, if Q_{E_2} exists, then there is an index $k^* \in [u]$ s.t. there is a computationally unbounded classical adversary Q_{E_2,k^*} that can distinguish hybrids $\mathcal{H}_{k^*-1}$ and $\mathcal{H}_{k^*}$ with an advantage at least $\delta_2/u = \delta_1$. I.e., there is Q_{E_2,k^*} such that:

$$| \Pr[1 \leftarrow Q_{E_2,k^*}^H(c_2, \text{key}_{A_2}^{k^*-1})] - \Pr[1 \leftarrow Q_{E_2,k^*}^H(c_2, \text{key}_{A_2}^{k^*})]| \geq \delta_1,$$

where $\text{key}_{A_2}^k$ is the corresponding values of key_{A_2} in hybrid $\mathcal{H}_k$. Now construct Q_{E_1} on input (c_1'', b'') and given access to oracle H'' as follows:

1. For $i \in [u]/\{k^*\}$ sample oracles H_i'', and compute $(c_{1,i}'', \text{key}_{A_1,i}'') \leftarrow Q_{A_1}^{H_i''}$.
2. Let $(c_{1,k^*}'', \text{key}_{A_1,k^*}'') = (c_1'', b'')$.
3. Let $c_2'' = c_{1,1}''|| \cdots ||c_{1,u}''$ and $\text{key}_{A_2}'' = U_1|| \cdots ||U_1||\text{key}_{A_1,k^*}''|| \cdots ||\text{key}_{A_1,u}''$.
4. Send $(c_2'', \text{key}_{A_2}'')$ to Q_{E_2,k^*}.
5. Answer Q_{E_2,k^*}'s queries on oracle i using H'' for $i = k^*$, and H_i'' otherwise.
6. Output whatever Q_{E_2,k^*} outputs.

Now note that $(c_2'', \text{key}_{A_2}'')$ perfectly simulates $(c_2, \text{key}_{A_2}^{k^*-1})$ if $b'' = \text{key}_{A_1}$, and perfectly simulates $(c_2, \text{key}_{A_2}^{k^*})$ if $b'' \leftarrow \{0,1\}$. Thus Q_{E_1} perfectly simulates the security experiment for Q_{E_2,k^*}, therefore, has the same advantage δ_1.   □

Now we show how to do **Step 3**.

Construction 6 (SCSS Multi-Bit Key Agreement with OWC). *Let Q_{A_2}, Q_{B_2} be a WCSS Multi-Bit key agreement scheme from Construction 5. Let $t = \text{poly}(\kappa)$ (to be chosen later), H be an oracle, and define Q_{A_3} and Q_{B_3} as follows:*

- *Q_{A_3} performs the following:*
  1. *Divide oracle H to t independent oracles H_i (according to some canonical division).*
  2. *For $i \in [t]$ run Q_{A_2} to get $(c_{2,i}, \text{key}_{A_2,i}) \leftarrow Q_{A_2}^{H_i}$.*
  3. *Sample $\text{key}_{A_3} \leftarrow \{0,1\}^t$.*
  4. *For $i \in [t]$ let $\text{key}_i = \text{key}_{A_3} \oplus \text{key}_{A_2,i}$.*
  5. *Let $c_3 = c_{2,1}|| \cdots ||c_{2,t}||\text{key}_1|| \cdots ||\text{key}_t$.*
- *Q_{B_3} performs the following:*
  1. *Let $c_3 = c_{2,1}|| \cdots ||c_{2,t}||\text{key}_1|| \cdots ||\text{key}_t$.*
  2. *Divide oracle H to t independent oracles H_i (according to the same canonical division).*

3. For $i \in [t]$ run Q_{B_2} to get $\text{key}_{B_2,i} \leftarrow Q_{B_2}^{H_i}(c_{2,i})$.
4. For $i \in [t]$ compute $\text{key}_{B_3,i} \leftarrow \text{key}_i \oplus \text{key}_{B_2,i}$.
5. Compute $\text{key}_{B_3} = \text{maj}_i(\text{key}_{B_3,i})$.

Theorem 13 (Completeness of Construction 6). *If Construction 5 has completeness error $\leq 1/4$, then Construction 6 has completeness error $\varepsilon_3 \leq 2^{-t/8}$.*

Proof. By the construction, if for at least $t/2$ of $i \in [t]$ we have $\text{key}_{A_2,i} = \text{key}_{B_2,i}$, then $\text{key}_{A_3} = \text{key}_{B_3}$. Since for each of the sub-protocols the probability of $\text{key}_{A_2,i} = \text{key}_{B_2,i}$ is at least $3/4$, then by the Hoeffding inequality, the probability of *not* having the correct key in at least $t/2$ of $i \in [t]$ is at most $e^{-2\sigma^2 t}$ for $\sigma = |1/2 - 1/4| = 1/4$, which implies the error to be at most $e^{-2t/16} < 2^{-t/8}$. □

Theorem 14 (Soundness of Construction 6). *If Construction 5 has a soundness error $\delta_2(\kappa)$, then Construction 6 has a soundness error $\delta_3 = t\delta_2$.*

Proof. Suppose there exists an adversary Q_{E_3} such that:

$$|\Pr[1 \leftarrow Q_{E_3}^H(c_3, \text{key}_{A_3})] - \Pr[1 \leftarrow Q_{E_3}^H(c_3, U_u)]| \geq \delta_3.$$

We show there exists an adversary Q_{E_2} that breaks the soundness in Theorem 12 with an advantage at least δ_2. To do so define hybrids $\{\mathcal{H}_k\}_k$ for $k \in \{0, \cdots, t\}$ (where $\mathcal{H}_0$ is the experiment of Construction 6) such that in hybrid $\mathcal{H}_k$, we replace key_i with $\text{key}'_i = \text{key}_{A_3} \oplus \text{key}'_{A_2,i}$ when constructing c_3. Namely, in hybrid $\mathcal{H}_k$, we have $c_3 = c_{2,1}||\cdots||c_{2,t}||\text{key}'_1||\cdots||\text{key}'_k||\text{key}_{k+1}||\cdots||\text{key}_t$. Now note that in hybrid $\mathcal{H}_t$, there is no information about key_{A_3} in c_3, thus an adversary has no advantage in distinguishing key_{A_3} from random. Therefore, if Q_{E_3} exists, then there is an index $k^* \in [t]$ s.t. there is a computationally unbounded classical adversary Q_{E_3,k^*} that can distinguish hybrids $\mathcal{H}_{k^*-1}$ and $\mathcal{H}_{k^*}$ with an advantage at least $\delta_3/t = \delta_2$. I.e., there is Q_{E_3,k^*} such that:

$$|\Pr[1 \leftarrow Q_{E_3,k^*}^H(c_3^{k^*-1}, \text{key}_{A_3})] - \Pr[1 \leftarrow Q_{E_3,k^*}^H(c_3^{k^*}, \text{key}_{A_3})]| \geq \delta_2,$$

where c_3^k is the corresponding values of c_3 in hybrid $\mathcal{H}_k$. Now construct Q_{E_2} on input (c_2'', x'') and given access to oracle H'' as follows:

1. For $i \in [t]/\{k^*\}$ sample oracles H_i'', and compute $(c_{2,i}'', \text{key}''_{A_2,i}) \leftarrow Q_{A_2}^{H_i''}$.
2. Let $(c_{2,k^*}'', \text{key}''_{A_2,k^*}) = (c_2'', x'')$.
3. Sample a random $\text{key}''_{A_3} \leftarrow \{0,1\}^u$.
4. For $i \in [t]$ let $\text{key}''_i = \text{key}''_{A_3} \oplus \text{key}''_{A_2,i}$.
5. Let $c_3'' = c_{2,1}''||\cdots||c_{2,t}''||U_u||\cdots||U_u||\text{key}''_{k^*}||\cdots||\text{key}''_t$.
6. Send $(c_3'', \text{key}''_{A_3})$ to Q_{E_3,k^*}.
7. Answer Q_{E_3,k^*}'s queries on oracle i using H'' for $i = k^*$, and H_i'' otherwise.
8. Output whatever Q_{E_3,k^*} outputs.

Now note that c_3 perfectly simulates $c_3^{k^*-1}$ if $x'' = \text{key}_{A_2}$, and perfectly simulates $c_3^{k^*}$ if $x'' \leftarrow \{0,1\}^u$. Thus Q_{E_2} perfectly simulates the security experiment for Q_{E_3,k^*}, therefore, has the same advantage δ_2. □

Finally, we show how to do **Step 4**.

Construction 7 (QGQS Time-Lock Puzzle From Key Agreement with OWC). *Let* Q_{A_3}, Q_{B_3} *be an SCSS Multi-Bit key agreement scheme from Construction 6 with completeness error* $\varepsilon_3(\kappa)$ *and soundness error* $\delta_3(\kappa)$. *Let H be an oracle, and define* Gen *and* Sol *as follows:*

- Gen *performs the following:*
  1. *Run* Q_{A_3} *to get* $(c_3, \text{key}_{A_3}) \leftarrow Q_{A_3}^H$.
  2. *Let* $P = c_3$ *and* $s = \text{key}_{A_3}$.
- Sol *performs the following:*
  1. *Let* $P = c_3$.
  2. *Run* Q_{B_3} *to get* $\text{key}_{B_3} \leftarrow Q_{B_3}^H(c_3)$.
  3. *Let* $s' = \text{key}_{B_3}$.

Theorem 15 (Completeness of Construction 7). *If Construction 6 has completeness error* $\varepsilon_3(\kappa)$, *then Construction 7 has completeness error* $\varepsilon_4 \leq \varepsilon_3$. *Namely, we have:*

$$\Pr[s' = s : (P, s) \leftarrow \text{Gen}^H, s' \leftarrow \text{Sol}^H(P)] \geq 1 - \varepsilon_4(\kappa).$$

Proof. By the construction, if we have $\text{key}_{A_3} = \text{key}_{B_3}$, then $s' = s$, thus $\varepsilon_4 \leq \varepsilon_3$. □

Theorem 16 (Soundness of Construction 7). *If Construction 6 has a soundness error* $\delta_3(\kappa)$, *then Construction 7 has a soundness error* $\delta_4 = \delta_3 + 2^{-u}$. *Namely, we have:*

$$\Pr[s'' = s : (P, s) \leftarrow \text{Gen}^H, s'' \leftarrow Q_{E_4}^H(P)] \leq \delta_4(\kappa).$$

Proof. Suppose there exists an adversary Q_{E_4} such that:

$$\Pr[s'' = s : (P, s) \leftarrow \text{Gen}^H, s'' \leftarrow Q_{E_4}^H(P)] \geq \delta_4.$$

We show there exists an adversary Q_{E_3} that breaks the soundness in Theorem 14 with an advantage at least δ_3. Consider hybrids $\mathcal{H}_0$ and $\mathcal{H}_1$ where $\mathcal{H}_0$ is the output of Construction 7, and $\mathcal{H}_1$ is similar to $\mathcal{H}_0$ except that we replace $s = \text{key}_{A_3}$ with $s' \leftarrow \{0,1\}^u$. Note that in $\mathcal{H}_1$, no adversary can find the key with a better advantage than a random guess, so if Q_{E_4} exists, then there exists Q'_{E_4} that distinguishes $\mathcal{H}_0$ and $\mathcal{H}_1$ with an advantage at least $\delta_4 - 2^{-u} = \delta_3$. Construct Q_{E_3} s.t. on input (c_3, x), send $(P, s) = (c_3, x)$ to Q'_{E_4} and output whatever Q'_{E_4} outputs. Note that Q_{E_3} perfectly simulates $\mathcal{H}_0$ if $x = \text{key}_{A_3}$ and perfectly simulates $\mathcal{H}_1$ if $x \leftarrow \{0,1\}^u$. Thus, Q_{E_3} has the same advantage as Q'_{E_4}. □

Proof of Theorem 8. To prove this theorem we only need to determine the choice of parameters in Constructions 10, 4, 5, 6, and 7. Let κ be chosen according to $\mathcal{K}$ in Lemma 10. Let $t = u = \kappa$, $\varepsilon_0 = 1/4\kappa$ and $\delta_0 = \text{negl}(\kappa)$. Then by Theorem 9 $\varepsilon_1 \leq 1/4\kappa$, by Theorem 10 $\delta_1 \leq \text{negl}(\kappa)$, by Theorem 11 $\varepsilon_2 \leq 1/4$, by Theorem 12 $\delta_2 \leq \text{negl}(\kappa)$, by Theorem 13 $\varepsilon_3 \leq \text{negl}(\kappa)$, by Theorem 14 $\delta_2 \leq \text{negl}(\kappa)$, by Theorem 15 $\varepsilon_4 \leq \text{negl}(\kappa)$, by Theorem 16 $\delta_4 \leq \text{negl}(\kappa)$. Finally, note that ε_4 and δ_4 are the completeness and soundness errors of a QGQS time-lock puzzle. □

A   The Description of the Extractor in Lemma 1

We give a proof and the description of Ext for completeness.

Proof of Lemma 1.

Define the algorithm $\mathsf{Ext}(\mathcal{A}^H(z))$ as follows:

- Pick $i \xleftarrow{\$} [q]$.
- Run $\mathcal{A}^H(z)$ until (right before) the ith query.
- Measure the query register of $\mathcal{A}^H(z)$ in the computational basis to obtain the outcome $x \in \mathcal{X}$.
- Output x.

The probability that $\mathsf{Ext}(\mathcal{A}^H(z))$ successfully outputs $x \in \mathcal{S}$ is given by

$$\sum_{j=1}^{q} \Pr[i=j] \Pr[x \in \mathcal{S} \mid i = j : x \leftarrow |\psi_i^H\rangle] = \frac{1}{q} \sum_{j=1}^{q} \| \Pi_{\mathcal{S}} |\psi_j^H\rangle \|^2 = \frac{\mu(\mathcal{A}^H(z), \mathcal{S})}{q}.$$

$\square$

References

AA14.   Scott Aaronson and Andris Ambainis. The need for structure in quantum speedups, 2014

ACC+22.   Per Austrin, Hao Chung, Kai-Min Chung, Shiuan Fu, Yao-Ting Lin, and Mohammad Mahmoody. On the impossibility of key agreements from quantum random oracles. In Advances in Cryptology-CRYPTO 2022: 42nd Annual International Cryptology Conference, CRYPTO 2022, Santa Barbara, CA, USA, August 15–18, 2022, Proceedings, Part II, pages 165–194. Springer, 2022

AHU19.   Andris Ambainis, Mike Hamburg, and Dominique Unruh. Quantum security proofs using semi-classical oracles. In Advances in Cryptology-CRYPTO 2019: 39th Annual International Cryptology Conference, Santa Barbara, CA, USA, August 18–22, 2019, Proceedings, Part II 39, pages 269–295. Springer, 2019

AHY23.   Prabhanjan Ananth, Zihan Hu, and Henry Yuen. On the (im)plausibility of public-key quantum money from collision-resistant hash functions. Cryptology ePrint Archive, Paper 2023/069, 2023. https://eprint.iacr.org/2023/069

AK22.   Prabhanjan Ananth and Fatih Kaleoglu. A note on copy-protection from random oracles. arXiv preprint arXiv:2208.12884, 2022

BBBF18.   Dan Boneh, Joseph Bonneau, Benedikt Bünz, and Ben Fisch. Verifiable delay functions. In Advances in Cryptology-CRYPTO 2018: 38th Annual International Cryptology Conference, Santa Barbara, CA, USA, August 19–23, 2018, Proceedings, Part I, pages 757–788. Springer, 2018

BBBV97.   Charles H Bennett, Ethan Bernstein, Gilles Brassard, and Umesh Vazirani. Strengths and weaknesses of quantum computing. SIAM journal on Computing, 26(5), 1510–1523, 1997

BDF+11.   Dan Boneh, Özgür Dagdelen, Marc Fischlin, Anja Lehmann, Christian Schaffner, and Mark Zhandry. Random oracles in a quantum world. In Dong Hoon Lee and Xiaoyun Wang, editors, Advances in Cryptology - ASIACRYPT 2011, volume 7073 of Lecture Notes in Computer Science, pages 41–69. Springer, Heidelberg, December 2011

BI87. Manuel Blum and Russell Impagliazzo. Generic oracles and oracle classes. In 28th Annual Symposium on Foundations of Computer Science (sfcs 1987), pages 118–126. IEEE, 1987

BLZ21. Jeremiah Blocki, Seunghoon Lee, and Samson Zhou. On the security of proofs of sequential work in a post-quantum world. In 2nd Conference on Information-Theoretic Cryptography, page 1, 2021

BN00. Boneh, D., Naor, M.: Timed commitments. In: Bellare, M. (ed.) Advances in Cryptology - CRYPTO 2000. Lecture Notes in Computer Science, vol. 1880, pp. 236–254. Springer, Heidelberg (2000)

BR93. Mihir Bellare and Phillip Rogaway. Random oracles are practical: A paradigm for designing efficient protocols. In Dorothy E. Denning, Raymond Pyle, Ravi Ganesan, Ravi S. Sandhu, and Victoria Ashby, editors, ACM CCS 93: 1st Conference on Computer and Communications Security, pages 62–73. ACM Press, November 1993

CFHL21. Chung, K.-M., Fehr, S., Huang, Y.-H., Liao, T.-N.: On the compressed-oracle technique, and post-quantum security of proofs of sequential work. In: Canteaut, A., Standaert, F.-X. (eds.) Advances in Cryptology - EUROCRYPT 2021. Part II, volume 12697 of Lecture Notes in Computer Science, pp. 598–629. Springer, Heidelberg (2021)

CP18. Bram Cohen and Krzysztof Pietrzak. Simple proofs of sequential work. In Jesper Buus Nielsen and Vincent Rijmen, editors, Advances in Cryptology - EUROCRYPT 2018, Part II, volume 10821 of Lecture Notes in Computer Science, pages 451–467. Springer, Heidelberg, April / May 2018

GL89. O. Goldreich and L. A. Levin. A hard-core predicate for all one-way functions. In Proceedings of the Twenty-First Annual ACM Symposium on Theory of Computing, STOC '89, page 25–32, New York, NY, USA, 1989. Association for Computing Machinery

HH87. Juris Hartmanis and Lane A. Hemaspaandra. One-way functions, robustness, and the non-isomorphism of np-complete sets. In Symposium on Computation Theory, 1987

HMST22. Iftach Haitner, Noam Mazor, Jad Silbak, and Eliad Tsfadia. On the complexity of two-party differential privacy. In Proceedings of the 54th Annual ACM SIGACT Symposium on Theory of Computing, pages 1392–1405, 2022

HY20. Akinori Hosoyamada and Takashi Yamakawa. Finding collisions in a quantum world: quantum black-box separation of collision-resistance and one-wayness. In Advances in Cryptology-ASIACRYPT 2020: 26th International Conference on the Theory and Application of Cryptology and Information Security, Daejeon, South Korea, December 7–11, 2020, Proceedings, Part I 26, pages 3–32. Springer, 2020

JMRR21. Samuel Jaques, Hart Montgomery, Razvan Rosie, and Arnab Roy. Time-release cryptography from minimal circuit assumptions. In Progress in Cryptology-INDOCRYPT 2021: 22nd International Conference on Cryptology in India, Jaipur, India, December 12–15, 2021, Proceedings 22, pages 584–606. Springer, 2021

LPS17. Huijia Lin, Rafael Pass, and Pratik Soni. Two-round and non-interactive concurrent non-malleable commitments from time-lock puzzles. In Chris Umans, editor, 58th Annual Symposium on Foundations of Computer Science, pages 576–587. IEEE Computer Society Press, October 2017

LW17. Arjen K Lenstra and Benjamin Wesolowski. Trustworthy public randomness with sloth, unicorn, and trx. International Journal of Applied Cryptography, 3(4), 330–343, 2017

MMV11. Mahmoody, M., Moran, T., Vadhan, S.P.: Time-lock puzzles in the random oracle model. In: Rogaway, P. (ed.) Advances in Cryptology - CRYPTO 2011. Lecture Notes in Computer Science, vol. 6841, pp. 39–50. Springer, Heidelberg (2011)

MMV13. Mohammad Mahmoody, Tal Moran, and Salil P. Vadhan. Publicly verifiable proofs of sequential work. In Robert D. Kleinberg, editor, ITCS 2013: 4th Innovations in Theoretical Computer Science, pages 373–388. Association for Computing Machinery, January 2013

MSW20. Mohammad Mahmoody, Caleb Smith, and David J. Wu. Can verifiable delay functions be based on random oracles? In Artur Czumaj, Anuj Dawar, and Emanuela Merelli, editors, ICALP 2020: 47th International Colloquium on Automata, Languages and Programming, volume 168 of LIPIcs, pages 83:1–83:17. Schloss Dagstuhl, July 2020

NC10. Michael A Nielsen and Isaac L Chuang. Quantum computation and quantum information. Cambridge University Press, 2010

Nis89. Noam Nisan. Crew prams and decision trees. In Proceedings of the twenty-first annual ACM symposium on Theory of computing, pages 327–335, 1989

OSSS05. Ryan O'Donnell, Michael Saks, Oded Schramm, and Rocco A Servedio. Every decision tree has an influential variable. In 46th Annual IEEE Symposium on Foundations of Computer Science (FOCS'05), pages 31–39. IEEE, 2005

Pie19. Krzysztof Pietrzak. Simple verifiable delay functions. In Avrim Blum, editor, ITCS 2019: 10th Innovations in Theoretical Computer Science Conference, volume 124, pages 60:1–60:15. LIPIcs, January 2019

RSW96. Ronald L Rivest, Adi Shamir, and David A Wagner. Time-lock puzzles and timed-release crypto. Massachusetts Institute of Technology. Laboratory for Computer Science, 1996

Tar89. Gábor Tardos. Query complexity, or why is it difficult to separate $NP^A \cap coNP^A$ from P^A by random oracles A? *Combinatorica*, 9:385–392, 1989

Unr14. Unruh, D.: Revocable quantum timed-release encryption. In: Nguyen, P.Q., Oswald, E. (eds.) Advances in Cryptology - EUROCRYPT 2014. Lecture Notes in Computer Science, vol. 8441, pp. 129–146. Springer, Heidelberg (2014)

Wes19. Wesolowski, B.: Efficient verifiable delay functions. In: Ishai, Y., Rijmen, V. (eds.) Advances in Cryptology - EUROCRYPT 2019. Part III, volume 11478 of Lecture Notes in Computer Science, pp. 379–407. Springer, Heidelberg (2019)

Zha12. Mark Zhandry. Secure identity-based encryption in the quantum random oracle model. In 32nd Annual International Cryptology Conference, CRYPTO 2012, pages 758–775, 2012

Towards Compressed Permutation Oracles

Dominique Unruh[1,2]([envelope])[ORCID]

[1] RWTH Aachen, Aachen, Germany
unruh@ut.ee
[2] University of Tartu, Tartu, Estonia

Abstract. Compressed oracles (Zhandry, Crypto 2019) are a powerful technique to reason about quantum random oracles, enabling a sort of lazy sampling in the presence of superposition queries. A long-standing open question is whether a similar technique can also be used to reason about random (efficiently invertible) permutations.

In this work, we make a step towards answering this question. We first define the compressed permutation oracle and illustrate its use. While the soundness of this technique (i.e., the indistinguishability from a random permutation) remains a conjecture, we show a curious 2-for-1 theorem: If we use the compressed permutation oracle methodology to show that some construction (e.g., Luby-Rackoff) implements a random permutation (or strong qPRP), then we get the fact that this methodology is actually sound for free.

1 Introduction

The random oracle [6] is a powerful heuristic[1] for cryptographic security proofs. It allows us to abstract from the gritty details of the definition of a hash function and to imagine it to be just a random function. We can then use powerful reasoning techniques such as lazy sampling to make security proofs simpler or, in many cases, possible in the first place. (Lazy sampling refers to the technique of choosing the outputs of the random oracle "on demand", when they are first accessed). These techniques are useful even if we are not in the random oracle model. For example, when working with a pseudorandom function, the first step in a proof is often to replace it by a fictitious random function. Quite similar to the random oracle are random permutations (to model cryptographically-strong permutations), or ideal ciphers (a heuristic model for block ciphers, basically a key-indexed family of random permutations). In the standard model, random permutations occur in security proofs involving pseudorandom permutations

---

[1] In general, this heuristic is not sound: There are contrived protocols which are secure in the random oracle model but insecure when the oracle is instantiated with *any* hash function [11]. However, in practice the random oracle model has proven to be a very good heuristic. Readers who reject heuristics in security proofs may still enjoy the results in this work as a result about generic query complexity, or as a technique for security proofs involving pseudorandom permutations.

© International Association for Cryptologic Research 2023
J. Guo and R. Steinfeld (Eds.): ASIACRYPT 2023, LNCS 14441, pp. 369–400, 2023.
https://doi.org/10.1007/978-981-99-8730-6_12

(e.g., in protocols involving block ciphers). In such proofs, we often consider invertible random permutations, i.e., we also give the adversary access also to the inverse of the permutation. All of this can be handled very nicely using lazy sampling.

At least, this is the situation in classical cryptography. Once quantum (or post-quantum) cryptography enters the picture, using the random oracle becomes much harder. This is because the quantum random oracle gives the adversary superposition-access to the random oracle. That is, the adversary can query the random oracle on a superposition of many different values. Then lazy sampling as in the classical case does not work any more: The adversary could query the oracle on a superposition of all inputs already in the very first query. If we were to sample the oracle at all the sampled positions, this would mean sampling the whole function in one go. But that goes against the very idea of lazy sampling. Furthermore, we cannot just measure where the oracle is queried as this would disturb the adversary state, and we need to make sure that our technique does not influence the way in which the adversary is entangled with the random oracle (in a way that the adversary can notice).

The above does not mean that the random oracle is unusable in the quantum setting. A number of techniques have been developed for handling the random oracle (history-free reductions, $2q$-wise independent functions, semi-constant distributions, small-range distributions, one-way to hiding (O2H) theorems, polynomial method, adversary method, see the related work below). However, none of these have the general applicability of the lazy sampling method, and they are often much harder to use. Then, surprisingly, Zhandry [30] discovered that a variant of lazy sampling is actually possible with quantum random oracles, although it is not as simple (and as general) as in the classical case. We refer to this technique as Zhandry's "compressed oracle technique". (We give more details about it below).

However, when talking about (invertible) random permutations, the situation is much more limited. The abovementioned tools are specific to the random function case[2]. To the best of our knowledge, no hardness results are known about invertible random permutations, not even simple query complexity results such as the hardness of searching an input with certain properties. As a consequence, we do not know anything about the post-quantum security of cryptosystems built from invertible permutations, such as the industry-standard SHA3 [22].

The present work attempts *a first step* towards closing this gap. We present a sufficient condition for a variant of the compressed oracle technique to work also for random permutations.

The Compressed Oracle Model. Zhandry [30] presented a different way to see the random oracle. The traditional quantum random oracle is modeled by giving an adversary access to the unitary operation $|x, y\rangle \mapsto |x, y \oplus h(x)\rangle$ where h is

---

[2] Except for the O2H theorem. Some variants of the O2H theorem apply to arbitrarily distributed functions [2], in particular to invertible permutations. (An invertible permutation can be modeled as a function $f : \{0, 1\} \times \{0, 1\}^n \to \{0, 1\}^n$, uniformly sampled from the set of all functions where $f(0, \cdot)$ is a permutation and $f(1, \cdot)$ its inverse). However, we are not aware of any work that makes use of this.

a uniformly randomly chosen function. (I.e., all outputs of h are chosen independently). Given such a unitary, the adversary can evaluate h in superposition. Now Zhandry showed that the random oracle can be replaced (in an indistinguishable way) by a random oracle that keeps a lazily evaluated function in a separate register H (inaccessible to the adversary). That is, initially that register H contains $|\varnothing\rangle$ where $\varnothing$ represents the empty partial function. Then, upon a query with input $x = x_0$, the function will be updated to contain a superposition of all $|x_0 \mapsto y\rangle$ (for different y) and y will be the result of the query. (Here $x_0 \mapsto y$ is the partial function defined only at input x_0). Further queries can add more entries to this function, and if, say, H contains $|h\rangle$ and $h(x) \neq \bot$, and we query the oracle at x, we get $h(x)$. When the adversary uncomputes some information that it computed before, the corresponding output in h can become undefined again. And all of this is possible in superposition between different inputs. Now all of this is extremely simplified, and hold only up to some error terms that are annoying but necessary. The advantage of this model is that we can, within limits (due to the annoying error terms), treat the random oracles as if it did lazy sampling even in the quantum setting. We give more details in Sect. 3.

Compressed Permutations. In this work, we ask the question whether we can extend the idea above to random permutations. After all, in the classical case, lazy sampling works for random permutations is almost as easy as for random functions. However, the compressed oracle has so far withstood all attempts to be ported to the permutation setting. (See the related work below). But before we come to our contribution, let us first make explicit why we are interested in a compressed oracle for random permutations (compressed permutation oracle, CPO). There are two main ways in which we could use this technique:

- We are analyzing a cryptographic scheme that *uses* an invertible permutation. And we wish to model that permutation in an idealized way (random oracle like). E.g., we might want show that the Sponge construction [7], where the block function is an invertible permutation (as is the case with SHA3) implements a pseudorandom random function. We would then replace the invertible permutation in the proof by a CPO and then use the features of the CPO (such as "lazy sampling") to make the proof simpler.
  Analogously, we can use the technique for an analysis of a scheme using an ideal cipher. (Since the ideal cipher is simply a family of invertible permutations).
- We are analyzing a cryptographic scheme that *implements* an invertible permutation or a strong pseudorandom permutation (PRP, i.e., a secure blockcipher). For example, in the classical case, the four-round Luby-Rackoff construction [21] is known to be a strong PRP if the round function is a (noninvertible) pseudorandom function [21]; we do not know yet whether an analogous result holds in the quantum case[3]. To show this, it is sufficient to show

---

[3] We know that four rounds are not sufficient [20], but nothing excludes that, e.g., five-round Luby-Rackoff could be a strong qPRP. [18] proves that four-round Luby-Rackoff is a qPRP (but not a strong one) but their result contains a flaw and the fix is work in progress [17].

that Luby-Rackoff, using a random function as the round function, is indistinguishable from a random permutation (given queries in both directions). Now there can be different approaches for the latter, but one promising avenue for this would be: (a) Show that Luby-Rackoff is indistinguishable from a CPO (using the fact that the CPO gives us an explicit list of all queries to the random permutation in the proof). (b) Use that a CPO is indistinguishable from a random invertible permutation.

In this paper, we are specifically interested in the second use case. The problem with that use case is that, even if we show (a), we still do not know whether a CPO is indistinguishable from a random permutation (i.e., (b)). We show that this is not a problem. Specifically, we show the following almost circular seeming result:

Main contribution: If some construction (say based on a random oracle) is indistinguishable from a CPO (i.e., we have (a)), then the CPO is indistinguishable from an invertible permutation (i.e., we get (b)).

So, if we show (a), we get (b) for free!
  This has two benefits:

- If we are in the second use case, we do not need to worry whether the CPO is indeed indistinguishable from an invertible permutation. We simply can focus on the (admittedly still rather hard) problem of analyzing the construction.
- This gives a new approach towards showing that the CPO technique works – if we can show (a) for any construction (even some practically irrelevant one), then we know that the CPO is indistinguishable from an invertible permutation in general. So we can then also use it, e.g., in the first use case (say, quantum security of SHA3).

This brings us a step closer towards being able to handle invertible permutations in the quantum setting.

Related Work. Quantum Random Oracles. [19,26] showed that finding preimages in the random oracle is hard ([10] showed this in worst-case setting). [9] introduced "history-free reductions" which basically amounts to replacing the random oracle by a different function right from the start. [31] showed that random oracles can be simulated using $2q$-wise independent functions. Based on this, [26] introduces a technique for extracting preimages of the random oracle. [31] introduces the "semi-constant distributions" technique that allows us to program the random oracle in many random locations with a given challenge value without the adversary noticing. [29] improves upon this with the "small-range distribution" technique that allows us to simulate random oracles using random looking functions with a small range. [28] shows that random oracles are collision resistant (this is generalized by [4,16,23] to the case of non-uniformly distributed functions with independently sampled outputs). Collision-resistance of the random oracle is generalized to the "collapsing property" which allows us to show that measuring the output of the random oracle effectively measures the input [25]. More general methods for problems in quantum query complexity (not limited to random oracles) include the polynomial method [5] and the adversary method [1]. [3] shows that the difficulties of using the quantum random oracle are not just a matter of missing proof techniques, but that in certain cases classically secure schemes are not secure in the quantum random oracle model.

Compressed Oracles. Compressed oracles were introduced in [30] and used there to show indifferentiability of the Merkle-Damgård construction, as well as security of the Fujisaki-Okamoto transform. [12] generalizes [30] to Fourier transforms over abelian groups, thus allowing random functions with a range different from $\{0,1\}^n$. Different from [30], they do not have a compression/decompression algorithm but instead reason using invariants that are expressed in a basis different from the computational basis. They also introduce support for parallel queries. [15] generalizes [30] to non-uniformly distributed functions, but only for the case where all outputs are independently sampled. (This is similar to what we achieve in our reformulation of [30] in Sect. 3, although we additionally get rid of the Fourier transform).

Random Permutations. [28] shows that random functions are indistinguishable from (noninvertible) random permutations. This allows us to derive results for random permutations from results for random functions. [27] shows the existence of quantum-secure pseudorandom permutations (qPRP, secure under superposition-queries of the function and its inverse) from quantum one-way functions. In particular, this implies that a random invertible permutation can be efficiently simulated[4]. However, [27] does not give us any technique for analyzing schemes that *use* a qPRP. When analyzing such a scheme we would replace the qPRP by an invertible random function in the proof, and the techniques from the present paper could be helpful.

Security of the Sponge Construction. The sponge construction was proposed by [7]. In the classical random oracle model, security of the sponge construction was shown by [8], both when the sponge is based on random functions and on invertible random permutations. They showed indifferentiability, which implies many other properties such as collision-resistance, pseudorandomness, and more. In the quantum setting, collision-resistance and the collapsing property from [25] were shown in [13] in the random function case. Quantum pseudorandomness of the sponge was shown by [14] but only in the case where the underlying round function is secret (the adversary cannot query it). Indifferentiability in the quantum setting was shown by [15] in the random function case. All those results immediately imply the corresponding results in the non-invertible random permutation

---

[4] If we implement the underlying quantum one-way function using a random oracle, and we simulate that random oracle with the method from [31] or [30], then we even get a simulation without computational assumptions.

case since random functions and permutations are indistinguishable [28]. However, for invertible random permutations, no quantum results are known[5].

Organization. In Sect. 2 we introduce relevant notational conventions. In Sect. 3, we present compressed oracles for random functions. Specifically, we recap and give a new, more streamlined view on Zhandry's technique. (We recommend readers familiar with Zhandry's technique to at least skim it because it will introduce some of the formalism for later). We also give a short example how it is used. In Sect. 4, we formulate the compressed permutation oracle and give an example how to use it. In Sect. 5, we prove our main result: If some construction implements the compressed permutation oracle, then the compressed permutation oracle is indistinguishable from a random permutation.

2   Preliminaries

Total and Partial Functions. Throughout this work, we will extensively deal with total and partial functions to describe states, queries, and invariants. For sets D, R, let $D \to R$ be the *total functions* from D to R, and $D \hookrightarrow R$ the *total injections* (i.e., injective total functions) from D to R. Furthermore, $D \twoheadrightarrow R$ are the *partial functions*. For a partial function $f : D \twoheadrightarrow R$, dom $f \subseteq D$ is the domain (inputs on which f is defined) and f is the image of f.

$\varnothing$ is the *empty partial function* (defined nowhere).

Quantum-Related Notation. Quantum states are elements of a (not necessarily finite-dimensional) Hilbert space $\mathcal{H}$. We usually represent quantum states with greek letters (e.g., ψ) and use ket-notation ($|x\rangle$) to refer to basis states of the computational basis unless specified otherwise, and $\langle x|$ is the adjoint of $|x\rangle$ ($\langle x| = |x\rangle^{\dagger}$). (I.e., $|x\rangle$ for $x \in X$ form an orthonormal basis of $\mathbb{C}^X$). $\|\psi\|$ is the norm of $\psi \in \mathcal{H}$, and $\|A\|$ is the operator norm of the bounded operator $A : \mathcal{H} \to \mathcal{H}'$. For $S \subseteq \mathcal{H}$, S is the *(closed) span* of S, i.e., the smallest topologically closed subspace of $\mathcal{H}$ containing S. *Projector* always means orthogonal projector.

We will often need to consider the distance between a vector and a subspace: For two vectors $\psi, \psi' \in \mathcal{H}$, we write $\psi \overset{\varepsilon}{\approx} \psi'$ to denote $\|\psi - \psi'\| \leq \varepsilon$. And if S is a closed subspace of $\mathcal{H}$, then we write $\psi \overset{\varepsilon}{\approx} S$ to denote $\exists \psi' \in S. \; \psi \overset{\varepsilon}{\approx} \psi'^{6}$.

Quantum Oracle Queries. Throughout the paper, we will frequently refer to oracle queries. Thus, we fix some variables once and for all: D always refers to the domain and R to the range of the function. (I.e., queries are always made to a function $h :\twoheadrightarrow DR$). We will also fix once and for all the sizes of D and R as $M := |D|$ and $N := |R|$. (In particular, D, R are assumed to be finite).

We furthermore assume a commutative group operation $\oplus$ on D and on R with the property $x \oplus x = 0$. (For example, $D = R = \{0,1\}^n$ and $\oplus$ is bit-wise XOR).

---

[5] [24] has a proof of collision resistance but it was found to be flawed and withdrawn.
[6] Or equivalently: $\|(1 - P)\psi\| \leq \varepsilon$ where P is the projector onto S.

A query to a fixed function $f :\rightarrow DR$ can then be implemented by the unitary $U_f : |x\rangle|y\rangle \mapsto |x\rangle|y \oplus f(x)\rangle$. (The fact that this is unitary follows from the fact that $\oplus$ is a group operation). However, we will more often be interested in queries to a function that is also stored in a quantum register: For a set $\mathsf{Func} \subseteq D \to R$ that will always be clear from the context, define the unitary StO (for "standard oracle") on $\mathbb{C}^D \otimes \mathbb{C}^R \otimes \mathbb{C}^{\mathsf{Func}}$ by:

$$\mathsf{StO}|x\rangle|y\rangle|h\rangle = |x\rangle\, y \oplus h(x)\, |h\rangle$$

Here $y \oplus h(x)$ is defined to be y when $h(x) = \bot$. (This latter case only arises if Func contains partial functions).

Non-unitaries in Quantum Circuits. We will sometimes have operations in quantum circuits that are not unitaries (or isometries). For example, we might have a projector P as a gate. Mathematically, this simply means that the current state is multiplied with P (analogous to applying a unitary). Of course, this implies that a normalized state could become a non-normalized state. An operational interpretation of this is the following: We measure with the binary measurement $P, 1 - P$, and if the measurement fails (second outcome), we abort. The state after applying P then describes the state in the non-aborting computation path, scaled with the square-root of the probability of reaching that path.

In general the gate might not be a projector, either. (E.g., a gate $G = UP$ that is a product of a unitary U and a projector P). But the operational interpretation is still the same. (An alternative interpretation is that of a program that terminates with probability ≤ 1).

3 Compressed Function Oracles

We will now recapitulate and rephrase *Zhandry's compressed oracle technique* [30]. Trying to emphasize more the separation between implementation issues (encoding via "databases" etc.) and the core concepts. Then we proceed to give a different view on the technique that does not involve Fourier transforms and which is, in our opinion, conceptually simpler.

We will often refer to the compressed oracle as *compressed function oracle* or *CFO* to distinguish it from the compressed permutation oracle introduced later.

A reader who wishes to skip this part and to directly learn our new technique can skip ahead to the mini-summary at the end of this section (page 18).

In a nutshell, the compressed oracle technique is a way to simulate/implement a quantum random oracle (i.e., a uniformly random function $h : D \to R$ to which an adversary or quantum algorithm has superposition query access) in a way that has the following crucial features:

- *The adversary cannot distinguish between the original random oracle and the simulation.* This allows us to use the simulation in proofs instead of the original oracle.

– *The simulation uses an internal state that has a small representation.* This is
not the case for trivial implementations of the random oracle: Those would
have to pick and store the value table of the random function at the beginning.
This value table would require $|D| \cdot \log|R|$ classical bits which is infeasible for
typical size of the domain D. In contrast, the compressed oracle only requires
roughly $q(\log|D| + \log|R|)$ qubits after q queries to the random oracle.
– *The simulation keeps track where the random oracle was already queried, and
what the result of that query is.* E.g., if the adversary queries $h(x)$ (possibly in superposition between different values x), and gets $y := h(x)$, then
the simulation will keep a record that a query $x \mapsto y$ was performed (or a
superposition of such records). While this is trivial in the classical case, it is
highly surprising that this is possible in the quantum case: Naively keeping
a record of the queries would entangle the adversary's state with the state of
the compressed oracle, something the adversary might detect[7]. Having this
record is the arguably the main advantage of the compressed oracle technique
as a proof technique. For example, it allows us to formulate invariants such
as "the adversary has not yet queried an x with $h(x) = 0$".
– *The simulation is efficient.* That is, its runtime is polynomial in the number of
queries performed by the adversary, and the bitlengths of the inputs and outputs of h. This is closely related to the fact that the internal state has a small
representation. Previous approaches for efficiently implementing/simulating
the quantum random oracle either required computational assumptions (simulation via quantum pseudorandom functions [29]) or required the simulator
to know the number of queries that the adversary will perform at the outset
of the simulation (simulation via $2q$-wise independent functions [31]).

Through the rest of this section, we present our reformulation of Zhandry's
technique before considering permutations.

---

[7] For example, the adversary might initialize a register X with $\sum_x \frac{1}{\sqrt{M}}|x\rangle$, then per-
form a superposition query with input x. The compressed oracle needs to record the
query $x \mapsto y$ (in superposition between different x). Now the register X is entangled
with the compressed oracle's record. (Or, if the compressed oracle would measure
the query input, the register X would collapse to a single value). Now the adversary might wish to distinguish whether the compressed oracle records its queries or
not. For that purpose, the adversary uncomputes the previous query. Now X would
be in the original state when using the original random oracle; the adversary can
check whether this is the case. But if the compressed oracle keeps a record of the
query $x \mapsto y$, the state X will not be in its original state but entangled with the
compressed oracle. So in order to be indistinguishable, the compressed oracle needs
to forget the query (i.e., erase the record $x \mapsto y$ from its state). In other words, the
compressed oracle needs to not only record queries, but also "unrecord" queries in
case of uncomputations. Since the compressed oracle does not know a priori whether
a given query is a computation or an uncomputation (or something in between), it
would seem impossible to solve this problem. The surprising fact of the compressed
oracle technique is that it does solve this problem, almost as a side effect.

Standard Oracle. Consider the original quantum random oracle. This oracle initially classically samples a random function $h \xleftarrow{\$} (\to DR)$. And then a query to the function h is implemented by a unitary $U_f : |x\rangle|y\rangle \mapsto |x\rangle|y \oplus h(x)\rangle$ on the adversary's query registers X, Y.

It is easy to see that this is perfectly indistinguishable from the following construction (called the *standard oracle* in [30])[8]: An additional quantum register H is initialized with $\sum_{h \in \to DR} \frac{1}{\sqrt{|\to DR|}} |h\rangle$, i.e., with the uniform superposition of all possible functions. The adversary does not get access to this register H, but instead the oracle query is changed to be the unitary $\mathsf{StO} : |x\rangle|y\rangle|h\rangle \mapsto |x\rangle|y \oplus h(x)\rangle|h\rangle$ on registers X, Y, H.

To better understand the following steps, imagine that the register H consists of many separate registers H_x ($x \in D$), each H_x storing the output $h(x)$. (That is, h is represented as a value table in H with H_x being the table entries). Each H_x has Hilbert space $\mathbb{C}^R$.

Compressed Oracle. Next, we transform the oracle into yet another representation. First, we extend the registers H_x to allow for a value $|\bot\rangle$, i.e., the Hilbert space of a single H_x is $\mathbb{C}^{R \cup \{\bot\}}$. This means that the register H now contains not only total functions h, but can also contain superpositions of partial functions. ($\bot$ denoting an undefined output).

Intuitively, $|\bot\rangle$ in some H_x will mean that the corresponding h-output is not yet determined, i.e., that any value is still possible. In particular, having $|\bot\rangle$ in all registers H_x (i.e., having the empty partial function $|\varnothing\rangle$ in H) should correspond to the initial state of the random oracle.

We make this more formal by defining an encoding/decoding operation to map between states that do not use $|\bot\rangle$ (as in the standard oracle) and states that do use $|\bot\rangle$ (compressed states).

Let Q denote the quantum Fourier transform on $\mathbb{C}^R$. We extend it to work on the register H_x by defining $Q|\bot\rangle := |\bot\rangle$. (In [30], the specific case $R = \{0,1\}^n$ is considered. In this case the quantum Fourier transform is simply a Hadamard gate on each qubit in H_x. But in [12], the case for general abelian groups R is considered and other quantum Fourier transforms are used). Let $U_\bot$ be the unitary with $U_\bot|\bot\rangle = |0\rangle$, $U_\bot|0\rangle = |\bot\rangle$, $U_\bot|y\rangle = |y\rangle$ for $y \neq 0$. Let $\mathsf{Decomp}_1 := Q \cdot U_\bot \cdot Q^\dagger$ (the *decompression operation*).

In the standard oracle, H_x has initial state $\sum_y \frac{1}{\sqrt{|R|}}|y\rangle$. If we apply $\mathsf{Decomp}_1^\dagger$ to it, we get

$$\sum_y \frac{1}{\sqrt{|R|}}|y\rangle \xmapsto{Q^\dagger} |0\rangle \xmapsto{U_\bot^\dagger} |\bot\rangle \xmapsto{Q} |\bot\rangle.$$

Thus, by applying $\mathsf{Decomp}_1^\dagger$ to all registers H_x in the initial state of the standard oracle, we get $|\bot\rangle$ in every H_x. This leads to the following idea: Initialize all H_x

---

[8] The indistinguishability formally follows from the fact that the query commutes with a computational basis measurement of the register H, and the fact that if that computational basis measurement is performed at the beginning of the execution, then it is equivalent to uniformly (classically) sampling h.

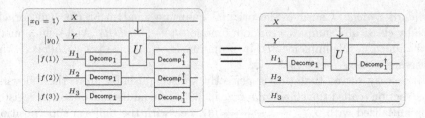

Fig. 1. Operation of CFO for fixed $x_0 := 1$. U denotes the operation $|y_0\rangle|y\rangle \mapsto |y_0 \oplus y\rangle|y\rangle$.

with $|\bot\rangle$. And whenever we want to perform an oracle query, we decompress all H_x by applying Decomp_1 (for the initial state, this gives the initial state of the standard oracle). Then we apply StO (the standard oracle)[9]. And then we compress all H_x again by applying $\mathsf{Decomp}_1^\dagger$. This will lead to exactly the same behavior as the standard oracle (since successive Decomp_1, $\mathsf{Decomp}_1^\dagger$ pairs cancel out).

In other words, we define the compressed oracle to be the oracle with the initial state $|\bot\rangle \otimes \cdots \otimes |\bot\rangle$ in register H, and that applies the following unitary to X, Y, H on each query:

$$\mathsf{CFO} := (I_X \otimes I_Y \otimes \mathsf{Decomp}^\dagger) \cdot \mathsf{StO} \cdot (I_X \otimes I_Y \otimes \mathsf{Decomp})$$

$$\text{with } \mathsf{Decomp} := \bigotimes_{x \in D} \mathsf{Decomp}_1. \quad (1)$$

Now CFO is perfectly indistinguishable from the standard oracle.

The Size of the Compressed Oracle. So far, we have seen that the compressed oracle CFO simulates the standard oracle. But why is it useful? To see this, we will think of the register H as containing partial functions: The basis states of H are $|y_{x_1}, \ldots, y_{x_N}\rangle$ for $y_{x_1} \in R \cup \{\bot\}$ where $x_1, \ldots, x_N$ are the elements of D. This is the value table of a partial function $f :\to DR$. We will identify $|y_{x_1}, \ldots, y_{x_N}\rangle$ with $|f\rangle$. In particular, the initial state of CFO is then $|\bot, \ldots, \bot\rangle = |\varnothing\rangle$. ($\varnothing$ is the completely undefined partial function).

Consider a state $|x_0\rangle|y_0\rangle|f\rangle$ before a query to the compressed oracle, with $|\mathrm{dom} f| \leq \ell$. (The initial state has $\ell = 0$).

Applying CFO to this state will decompress all H_x (which does not affect $|x\rangle$) apply StO (which does not affect H_x for $x \neq x_0$ for this particular state), and then compress all H_x again. This is illustrated in the left side of Fig. 1 for

---

[9] Since we extended the space of the register H_x to be $R \cup \{\bot\}$, StO must be well-defined also on states where one or many of the H_x are $|\bot\rangle$, i.e., on superpositions of partial functions. See the preliminaries for the precise definition for that case. Note, however, that since we start from an initial state that is a superposition of total functions, this case never arises no matter what queries to StO we perform, *unless we apply some other operations to the oracle register H directly.*

$x_0 := 1$. On all H_x with $x \neq x_0$, Decomp_1 and $\mathsf{Decomp}_1^\dagger$ cancel out (see the right side of Fig. 1). Thus, no matter what x_0, y_0, f are, the resulting state will be a superposition of f' with $f' = f$ except on x_0. In particular, $|\mathrm{dom} f'| \leq |\mathrm{dom} f| + 1 \leq \ell + 1$. Since this holds for any $|x_0, y_0, f\rangle$ with $|\mathrm{dom} f| \leq \ell$, this also holds for any superposition of such states. Thus we have shown[10] that any state of the compressed oracle that is a superposition of $|f\rangle$ of size $\leq \ell$ will, after a query, be a superposition of $|f\rangle$ of size $\leq \ell + 1$.

In particular, after q queries, the compressed oracle state is a superposition of partial functions of size $\leq q$. Such a partial function can be represented in approximately $q(\log|D| + \log|R|)$ bits, hence the state of the compressed oracle indeed has a much smaller representation. This justifies the name "compressed oracle".

And we also can see that it indeed "records" queries in some sense: if the state of the oracle contains $|f\rangle$, then every $x \in \mathrm{dom} f$ must have been queried. Otherwise we would have $f(x) = \bot$ as in the initial state. The converse does not hold, though, because queries can be uncomputed and thus removed from f.

Efficient Implementation. So far, we do not have an efficiently simulatable oracle because we represent the state of the compressed oracle by giving the complete value table for the partial functions f. (Each potential output is stored in a different register H_x). However, an algorithm implementing CFO is free to store the partial functions in a more efficient way, namely as sorted lists of input/output pairs (called a *database* in [30]), leading to a compact state. And an efficient circuit for the unitary CFO can be constructed by only applying Decomp_1 on those entries of the database that are involved in the present query. This then gives the oracle defined in [30]. We omit the details here as they are not relevant for the rest of this paper.

The advantage of separating the definition of the efficient encoding of the compressed oracle state from the conceptual encoding as a partial function is that proofs will not to consider the concrete encoding with ordered association lists only when analyzing the runtime of the simulation and can use the mathematically simpler concept of partial functions everywhere else. In particular, in information-theoretical proofs, we do not need to consider the efficient encoding at all.

Getting Rid of the Fourier Transform. So far, we have described the compressed oracle as in Zhandry's original work (although with a different presentation). As presented originally, it would seem that the Fourier transform is an integral part of the idea of the compressed oracle[11]. We will now show that there is a different view which does not involve the Fourier transform at all. Recall the definition

---

[10] Actually, we have handwavingly sketched it but a formal proof is easy and follows the same ideas.

[11] [30] considers the special case of a qubit-wise Hadamard which is the Fourier transform over the abelian group $\{0,1\}^n$. [12] generalizes this to Fourier transforms over arbitrary abelian groups.

of $\mathsf{Decomp}_1 = Q \cdot U_\perp \cdot Q^\dagger$. Using that definition, we can compute what Decomp_1 does to various basis states:

$$|\perp\rangle \xrightarrow{Q^\dagger} |\perp\rangle \xrightarrow{U_\perp} |0\rangle \xrightarrow{Q} \sum_z Q_{z0}|z\rangle =: |*\rangle$$

$$|y\rangle \xrightarrow{Q^\dagger} \underbrace{\sum_z \overline{Q_{yz}}|z\rangle}_{=Q^\dagger|y\rangle} \xrightarrow{U_\perp} \sum_z \overline{Q_{yz}}|z\rangle + \underbrace{\overline{Q_{y0}}}_{=\langle*|y\rangle}\left(|\perp\rangle - |0\rangle\right) \xrightarrow{Q} |y\rangle + \langle*|y\rangle\left(|\perp\rangle - |*\rangle\right).$$

Note that this calculation did not use that Q is the Fourier transform, only the fact that it is unitary. And the state $|*\rangle$ is simply the first column of Q. Which, in case of the Fourier transform, is of course the uniform superposition $|*\rangle = \sum_z \frac{1}{\sqrt{N}}|z\rangle$. However, any other unitary with the same first column would lead to the same result – the definition of Decomp_1 does not actually use the Fourier transform, and it only depends on the first column of Q! In fact, the above calculation works even if the first column is not the uniform superposition. For example, if we wish to analyze random oracles that use a random function h that is not uniformly chosen, but where each $h(x)$ is independently chosen according to some distribution $\mathcal{D}$, we take a unitary Q whose first column is $|*\rangle := \sum_z \frac{1}{\sqrt{\mathcal{D}(z)}}|z\rangle$, and now Decomp_1 still maps

$$\mathsf{Decomp}_1 : |\perp\rangle \mapsto |*\rangle$$
$$\mathsf{Decomp}_1 : |y\rangle \mapsto |y\rangle + \langle*|y\rangle\left(|\perp\rangle - |*\rangle\right). \tag{2}$$

In fact, we can just take this as the definition of Decomp_1 (relative to a given $|*\rangle$). The operators Q and $U_\perp$ are then just a technical tool to show that Decomp_1 is indeed unitary, and one possible way of implementing Decomp_1 efficiently, but they are not part of its definition.

We can still define an oracle CFO based on this new Decomp_1 in the same way as before via (1). Except now CFO will be indistinguishable from the standard oracle that has the initial state $|*\rangle \otimes \cdots \otimes |*\rangle$. Which is indistinguishable from the original random oracle if $|*\rangle$ is the uniform superposition. And if $|*\rangle = \sum_z \alpha_z|z\rangle$, then it is indistinguishable from the a random oracle where each $h(x)$ is sampled to be y with probability $|\alpha_y|^2$[12]. Everything discussed so far still applies. In particular, we still have that the oracle is compressed and records queries: In the compressed state, for any x that has not been queried, H_x will be in state $|\perp\rangle$ (with the intuitive meaning that the value of $h(x)$ is not sampled yet).

Thus, by removing the Fourier transform from the picture, we have generalized the compressed oracle technique to nonuniformly distributed oracles "for free"[13]. However, we stress that this approach does not yet allow us to model ran-

---

[12] We could go even farther and use a different $|*\rangle$ for every x. This would allow us to analyze oracles where $h(x)$ is picked from different distributions for different x.

[13] [15] also generalizes Zhandry's technique to non-uniformly distributed functions. (With the condition that the outputs are independently sampled, i.e., not covering permutations). However, their presentation still involves Fourier transforms.

Towards Compressed Permutation Oracles

dom permutations because a random permutation h does not have *independently* distributed $h(x)$[14].

In our opinion, this new view of the compressed oracle has multiple advantages:

- It becomes clearer what the essence of the transformation Decomp_1 is (see also the discussion below). To assume that the Fourier transform plays a relevant role in the construction may even hinder understanding of what is really happening.
- There is no need to find a group structure on the range R of the function so that it matches the operation $\oplus$ in the definition of the oracle query unitary $|x\rangle|y\rangle \mapsto |x\rangle|y \oplus h(x)\rangle$. This may lead to less requirements in proofs.
- The technique becomes more general as we are not limited to uniformly distributed functions.

For the remainder of this paper, we will not make use of this potential for generalization and assume that Q is an arbitrary unitary whose first column is the uniform superposition.

---

[14] We had one *failed* approach how to generalize this to random permutations (and possibly other function distributions). Since we believe that this approach might be natural, we shortly describe it here and why we got stuck trying to use it:

For $S \subseteq R$, we can define Decomp_1^S to be the Decomp_1 operation for the uniform distribution on S. (I.e., Decomp_1^S is defined by (2) where $|*\rangle := \sum_{y \in S} \frac{1}{\sqrt{|S|}}|y\rangle$).
Then we can define $\mathsf{Decomp}_1^{@x}$ to apply Decomp_1^M on register H_x, where M is the set of all values that are not yet used in other registers. Formally, if $D = \{x_1, \ldots, x_M\}$, $\mathsf{Decomp}_1^{@x_i}|y_1, \ldots, y_M\rangle := |y_1, \ldots, y_{i-1}\rangle \otimes \mathsf{Decomp}_1^{S_i}|y_i\rangle \otimes |y_{i+1}, \ldots, y_M\rangle$ where $S_i := R \setminus \{y_1, \ldots, y_{i-1}, y_{i+1}, \ldots, y_M\}$. (Here all $y_i \in R \cup \{\bot\}$.) And then we can define a decompression for permutations as $\mathsf{Decomp}_1^{perm} := \mathsf{Decomp}_1^{@x_M} \mathsf{Decomp}_1^{@x_{M-1}} \cdots \mathsf{Decomp}_1^{@x_2} \mathsf{Decomp}_1^{@x_1}$.
It is reasonably easy to verify that $\mathsf{Decomp}_1|\bot \ldots \bot\rangle = \sum_{h: \hookrightarrow R} \frac{1}{\sqrt{|\hookrightarrow R|}}|h\rangle$. So decompressing the initial state indeed leads to a uniform superposition of permutations (more precisely, of injections).
And it is also easy to define an oracle query in this model, namely $\mathsf{CFO}^{perm} := \mathsf{Decomp}^{perm \dagger} \otimes \mathsf{StO} \otimes \mathsf{Decomp}^{perm}$.
However, beyond that, things become difficult. First, the definition of Decomp_1 depends on the ordering of the domain D. If we would apply the $\mathsf{Decomp}_1^{@x_i}$ in a different order, we would get a different operator Decomp_1^{perm}. Second, it becomes very difficult to understand the behavior of CFO^{perm}. We were unable to give an explicit description of how it operates on a basis state. And it is not clear that CFO^{perm} maps a state $|y_1 \ldots\rangle$ where at most ℓ of the $y_i \neq \bot$ to a superposition of states $|\tilde{y}_1 \ldots\rangle$ where at most $\ell + 1$ of the $\tilde{y}_i \neq \bot$. But if this does not hold, then we do not have a compressed oracle because we have no upper bound on the size of the oracle state.
However, we do not exclude that these problems could be solved and the approach made viable. For example, it might be possible to find some operator that approximately implements CFO^{perm} and that has an easy description and that does not grow the state too much during a query. But we were unable to find such an operator.

Understanding Decomp. In order to better understand what the decompression operation does, let us have another look at the definition.

$$\mathsf{Decomp}_1 : |\perp\rangle \mapsto |*\rangle$$
$$\mathsf{Decomp}_1 : |y\rangle \mapsto |y\rangle + \underbrace{\langle *| y\rangle(|\perp\rangle - |*\rangle)}_{\text{correction term}} \tag{3}$$

And thus Decomp operates as follows:

$$\mathsf{Decomp} : |y_1 y_2 y_3 \dots\rangle \mapsto |\hat{y}_1 \hat{y}_2 \hat{y}_3 \dots\rangle + \textit{correction} \tag{4}$$

where $\hat{y} := y$ for $y \in R$ and $\hat{y} := *$ for $y = \perp$, and where *correction* is a sum of tensor products of "correction terms".

This means that in the compressed oracle state, $|\perp\rangle$ is used to denote the uniform superposition in H_x, i.e., an output that is completely undetermined so far. On the other hand, $|y\rangle$ in the compressed oracle state has a somewhat more subtle meaning. Intuitively, we might expect/want that $|y\rangle$ in the compressed oracle state means that the output is y. I.e., $|y\rangle$ in the compressed state should translate to $|y\rangle$ in the uncompressed state. In other words, the intuitively natural definition of Decomp_1 would be the definition (4) with the "correction term" removed. Unfortunately, the resulting operation would not be unitary. So the purpose of the correction terms is to stay as close to mapping $|y\rangle$ to $|y\rangle$ as possible, while keeping the operation unitary. Note that the correction terms are small because $\langle *| y\rangle = 1/\sqrt{N}^{15}$.

This leads to a different view of how Decomp_1 could be derived: Instead of constructing it bottom-up from Q and $U_\perp$, we could use the ansatz that Decomp is an operator defined as:

$$\mathsf{Decomp} : |\perp \dots \perp\rangle \mapsto |*\rangle \dots |*\rangle$$
$$\mathsf{Decomp} : |y_1 y_2 y_3 \dots\rangle \mapsto |\hat{y}_1 \hat{y}_2 \hat{y}_3 \dots\rangle + \textit{correction} \tag{5}$$

where *correction* must be chosen in such a way that Decomp becomes unitary, such that *correction* is as small as possible, and – most importantly – that the correction terms do not make the compressed oracle state bigger (i.e., when starting with $|y_1 y_2 \dots\rangle$ where there are at most ℓ non-$\perp$ entries, decompressing with Decomp, applying the oracle query operation StO, and then recompressing with $\mathsf{Decomp}^\dagger$, we should get a superposition of states $|y'_1 y'_2 \dots\rangle$ with at most $\ell + 1$ non-$\perp$ entries). The definitions of Decomp given above are then just one (although very natural) solution to this ansatz.

Mainly, we presented this approach in (5) to give a different view on the compressed oracle technique (that hopefully gives some intuition about what is going on). But maybe this approach is also one way to extend the compressed oracle

---

[15] However, the fact that they are small does not, unfortunately, mean that we can ignore them in calculations. They do, in many situations, add up to very relevant errors. In fact, Decomp_1 without the correction terms has operator norm $\sqrt{2}$ which means that the errors can be almost as big as the state itself.

technique to more complex cases such as oracles with non-independently chosen outputs or similar. We did not manage to use it for the random permutation case, but maybe future work will.

The Sanitized CFO. There is a subtle variation of the CFO that we described above. We call it the *sanitized CFO*. Recall that we use Decomp_1 to switch between two representations of the oracle state, the compressed representation (where the initial state is $|\varnothing\rangle$), and the uncompressed representation (where the initial state would be the superposition of all total functions). In the compressed representation, we make strong use of the fact that the oracle register H can contain partial functions. But in the uncompressed representation, partial functions make little sense, so the initial state in that representation is the superposition of only *total* functions. And it follows directly from the definition (1) of the CFO that throughout an execution, the uncompressed state will never contain a partial function (see also footnote 9). We arbitrarily specified the behavior of StO when it encounters $h(x) = \bot$ to do nothing. Since this case never occurs, we can also define StO differently, for example:

$$\mathsf{StO}_s|x\rangle|y\rangle|h\rangle = \begin{cases} |x\rangle\,|y \oplus h(x)\rangle\,|h\rangle & \text{if } h(x) \neq \bot, \\ 0 & \text{if } h(x) = \bot. \end{cases}$$

(Note: StO is not a unitary because it may return 0. Cf. Sect. 2, "non-unitaries in quantum circuits" for the meaning of such operations).

That is, this oracle effectively measures whether $h(x) = \bot$ before computing the query and, if so, diverges. (We call this the *sanitized standard oracle* since it removes the case where $h(x)$ is undefined in the uncompressed representation). Based on this, we can define the *sanitized CFO*:

$$\mathsf{CFO}_s := \mathsf{Decomp}^\dagger \cdot \mathsf{StO}_s \cdot \mathsf{Decomp}. \tag{6}$$

It is straightforward to verify that CFO_s and CFO are perfectly indistinguishable (by adversaries that do not touch H, and given initial state $|\varnothing\rangle$). In particular, CFO_s is also indistinguishable from a random function. Everything said above about CFO also applies to CFO_s. (Only difference: CFO_s is not unitary because it represents a potentially diverging computation).

If there is no difference between the CFO and the sanitized CFO, why consider the latter? This is because CFO_s behaves more nicely when it comes to invariant preservation. (The concept of invariant preservation will be explored in the "usage example" below).

For example, if the state of the X, Y, H registers lies in the subspace $\mathrm{Span}\{|xyh\rangle : x = 0, y = 0\}$, then after a query to CFO_s, the state is $O(1/\sqrt{N})$-close to the subspace $\mathrm{Span}\{|xyh\rangle : x = 0, y = h(0)\}$. This is very natural because it says that after a evaluating the oracle at 0, the Y-register contains the result of that evaluation. Surprisingly, we cannot show a corresponding invariant preservation for CFO[16].

CFO still performs well with invariants that do not talk about the Y register. If the CFO is invoked by the adversary, there is little to be said about the content of Y, anyway. But when the CFO is queried by an honest party or the challenger, for example, the oracle response in Y may be very relevant. So in some proofs, we might get further using $\mathsf{CFO_s}$, while in others it may not matter.

The difference between $\mathsf{CFO_s}$ and CFO will also matter in the compressed permutation case in Sect. 4.

Note: Zhandry's original work [30] defines (something very close to) the nonsanitized CFO, not the sanitized one. So their work is subject to the same limitation.

Usage Example. We will now give an example how the compressed oracle is used. We do not work out all the details (in particular, we skip some calculations) but instead focus on a high level overview required for understanding the methodology. The example works both with CFO and $\mathsf{CFO_s}$ in the same way.

Consider the following problem:

> Given quantum (i.e., superposition) access to a random oracle H, find x such that $H(x) = 0$.

We want to show that this problem is hard. We will use the compressed oracle to do so[17].

Fix an adversary A^{CFO} making polynomially many queries. Recall that H is the register of the CFO that contains the superposition of the partial functions h, and that those partial functions intuitively represent the knowledge what has been queried and what the responses were.

Consider the following invariant $\mathbf{I} := \mathrm{Span}\{|h\rangle : 0 \notin \mathrm{im} h\}$. This invariant contains all superpositions of partial functions h where 0 is not in the outputs, i.e., where A never got 0 as a result to its queries.

In an execution of A^{CFO}, the initial state of the system has $|\varnothing\rangle$ in H. Since $0 \notin \mathrm{im}\varnothing$, we have $|\varnothing\rangle \in \mathbf{I}$. Thus the initial state of the overall system (containing X, Y, and A's registers) is in $\mathbf{I}$ as well[18].

Now, when A performs a (w.l.o.g. unitary) operation on its registers, this operation does not touch H. (Recall that H is inaccessible to A). So if the state ψ before that operation is $\psi \in \mathbf{I}$, then the state ψ' after the operation is also

---

[16] For example, $|0\rangle_X |0\rangle_Y |*\rangle_{H_0}$ is in the first subspace (where the content of register H outside H_0 does not matter and is omitted here), but $\mathsf{CFO}|0\rangle_X |0\rangle_Y |*\rangle_{H_0} = |0\rangle_X |0\rangle_Y |*\rangle_{H_0}$ is not even close to the second subspace.

[17] Of course, there are many results that show that this specific problem is hard, predating the compressed oracle technique, and considerably simpler mathematically (e.g., [3,19]). This just happens to be the simplest example to demonstrate the technique.

[18] Strictly speaking, the initial state is in $\mathbf{I} \otimes \mathcal{H}_{XY\ldots}$ where $\mathcal{H}_{XY\ldots}$ is the Hilbert space of all registers besides H. We omit the $\otimes \mathcal{H}_{XY\ldots}$ for simplicity.

$\psi' \in \mathbf{I}$. In fact, if $\psi \overset{\varepsilon}{\approx} \mathbf{I}$, then $\psi' \overset{\varepsilon}{\approx} \mathbf{I}$ as well. (This follows immediately from the previous fact because the unitary performed by A has operator norm 1).

More interesting is the case when A queries the CFO. In that case, it is less obvious, but we can show:

$$\psi \in \mathbf{I} \quad \Longrightarrow \quad \psi' \overset{O\left(\sqrt{\frac{1}{N}}\right)}{\approx} \mathbf{I}.$$

(Here ψ, ψ' are the state before and after the query). We will not do the math here, see for example Zhandry's original paper [30] for a calculation, or [12] for some generic rules for bounding such invariant preservations in the CFO.

And again using that CFO has operator norm 1 and the triangle inequality for the norm, we get

$$\psi \overset{\varepsilon}{\approx} \mathbf{I} \quad \Longrightarrow \quad \psi' \overset{\varepsilon + O\left(\sqrt{\frac{1}{N}}\right)}{\approx} \mathbf{I}.$$

So by induction, we have that if the adversary does q queries, the final state is $\psi_{final} \overset{O\left(q\sqrt{\frac{1}{N}}\right)}{\approx} \mathbf{I}$. This is negligible if $q \ll \sqrt{N}$, meaning that the adversary needs around $\sqrt{N}$ queries to find a zero-preimage[19]. This concludes the analysis of zero-preimage finding in the CFO.

The advantage of the CFO is that it can be very easily adapted to a variety of different problems by changing the invariant $\mathbf{I}$. For example, if we want to show that finding a collision ($x \neq x'$ with $H(x) = H(x')$) is hard, we use the invariant

$$\mathbf{I} := \mathrm{span}\{|h\rangle : h \text{ injective}\}$$

instead. This represents the fact that the oracle as queried so far is injective, i.e., no two outputs are the same, i.e., the adversary has not found a collision. Obviously the initial state $|\varnothing\rangle \in \mathbf{I}$ again, and we can show (see, e.g., [30] again):

$$\psi \in \mathbf{I} \quad \Longrightarrow \quad \psi' \overset{O\left(\sqrt{\frac{i}{N}}\right)}{\approx} \mathbf{I} \quad \text{in the } i\text{-th query.}$$

Then the proof proceeds as above by induction, giving us $\psi_{final} \overset{O\left(\sqrt{\frac{q^3}{N}}\right)}{\approx} \mathbf{I}$. So finding a collision takes $\sqrt[3]{N}$ queries.

---

[19] There is a technicality we gloss over here: We only have shown that the oracle state does not contain a zero-preimage. To fully finish the proof, we additionally need to show that this implies that the adversary cannot guess a zero-preimage. For example, the adversary could just output something random that was not queried before and hope that it is a zero-preimage. The probability of the latter succeeding is, of course, tiny. But in a complete analysis, this all needs to be taken into account. This is important but not relevant for *illustrating* the compressed oracle technique, nor for the purposes of our paper. We refer to existing works on the compressed oracle (e.g., [30]) for details on this.

Technical Summary. The standard oracle StO operates on registers X, Y, H with Hilbert spaces $\mathbb{C}^D$, $\mathbb{C}^R$, $\mathbb{C}^{\to DR}$. It is defined as the unitary StO : $|x, y, h\rangle \mapsto |x, y \oplus h(x), h\rangle$ if $h(x) \neq \perp$ and StO : $|x, y, h\rangle \mapsto |x, y, h\rangle$ otherwise. The sanitized StO$_s$ is defined the same, except StO : $|x, y, h\rangle \mapsto 0$ when $h(x) = \perp$. The initial state of H is $\sum_{h \in \to DR} |R|^{-|D|/2} |h\rangle$ (uniform superposition of all total functions).

The compressed function oracle CFO operates the same registers X, Y, H. H can be seen equivalently as a collection of registers H_x with $x \in D$, each having Hilbert space $\mathbb{C}^{R \cup \{\perp\}}$. Q is an arbitrary unitary with $Q|0\rangle = \sum_x \frac{1}{\sqrt{N}} |x\rangle$ (e.g., the quantum Fourier transform). $U_\perp$ is the unitary mapping $|\perp\rangle \mapsto |0\rangle$, $|0\rangle \mapsto |\perp\rangle$, $|z\rangle \mapsto |z\rangle$ otherwise. Decomp$_1$:= $Q \cdot U_\perp \cdot Q^\dagger$ is the decompression unitary (for a single register H_x). Decomp is Decomp$_1$ applied to each H_x (making it an operation on H). Then the CFO is defined as Decomp $\cdot$ StO $\cdot$ Decomp†. The sanitized CFO$_s$ is defined as Decomp $\cdot$ StO$_s$ $\cdot$ Decomp†. The initial state of H is $|\varnothing\rangle$ (the empty partial function) for both CFO and CFO$_s$.

4   Compressed Permutation Oracles

In the preceding section, we considered compressed function oracles. These models the "normal" random oracle in which the adversary gets access to a uniformly random function. However, in many cases, we may be interested in uniformly random *permutations*, instead. For example, an ideal cipher is nothing but a family of random permutations (indexed by the key). Abstractly, random permutations are not a much more complicated concept than random functions (we simply pick the function from a smaller set) but they can be considerably harder to analyze. The reason for this is that in a random function, all outputs are sampled independently, while in a random permutation, this is not the case. Because of this, even simple questions relating to (superposition access to) random permutations are to the best of our knowledge not in the scope of existing techniques, such as the following conjecture:

Conjecture 1 (Double-sided zero-search). Let H be a uniformly random permutation on $\{0, 1\}^{2n}$. The following problem is hard for any adversary making polynomially many superposition queries to H and H^{-1}:
    Find $x \in \{0, 1\}^n$ such that $H(x\|0^n) = y\|0^n$ for some y.

Note that in this example, we explicitly allowed the adversary to query not only H (what we call a "forward query"), but also H^{-1} ("backward query"). If we model a non-invertible permutation (adversary can only make forward queries), random permutations are easy to handle, even in the quantum setting. Namely, we know that a random permutation is indistinguishable from a random function, even in the quantum setting [28]. So when analyzing a situation where the adversary has quantum access to a non-invertible function, we can simply replace it by a random function as the first step, and analyze from there using established techniques for random oracles (such as, for example, the CFO).

What we are interested in are, therefore, *invertible* random permutations (forward and backward queries).

In the classical setting, even invertible random permutations are quite easy to handle: The same way as we can model a random oracle via lazy sampling (i.e., pick all outputs of the oracle only when first accessed), we can also model a random permutation via lazy sampling: We pick the output to a forward query x at random, unless that query was already made, or some backward query returned x. And mutatis mutandis for backward queries. This does not give us exactly the distribution of answers that a random permutation would give, but is negligibly close. And now we have all the nice benefits of the lazy sampling of the random oracle, in particular the fact that any fresh queries give (near) uniformly random independent outputs.

Since the compressed oracle technique, roughly speaking, is a quantum analogue of lazy sampling, we might wonder whether the same is possible in the quantum setting. That is, is the following possible?

Define an oracle CPO (for "compressed permutation oracle") that keeps a superposition of partial functions as its internal state, that responds to forward and backward queries in some way that increases the length of those partial function only by 1 (or at least something small), and that is indistinguishable from having access to a permutation that is chosen uniformly at random.

It turns out that *defining* such a CPO is not too hard. What is hard (and what we will only make a step towards in this paper) is to prove that the CPO is indeed indistinguishable from a truly random permutation.

To define CPO, we need to define its behavior on forward and backwards queries. Forward queries are easy: The internal state is, like in the CFO case, a superposition of partial functions. That is, a register H with Hilbert space $\mathbb{C}^{D \to D}$. (Since we are in the permutation case, we have $D = R$ and thus $D \to R$ becomes $D \to D$). A forward query to CPO is then just handled by the oracle CFO$_s$ defined in the previous section.

(We could use the non-sanitized CFO here as well, but we use the sanitized CFO for two reasons: It tends to behave better with some invariants as explained in the previous section, and more importantly, we do not know how to prove the results in the next section with the non-sanitized one).

Backward queries are more interesting. We could define an oracle that, given an input $|x\rangle$, searches through the partial function $|h\rangle$ in H, and tries to find x in the output of h. (All of this in superposition between different $|x\rangle$ and $|h\rangle$, of course). But there is a simple trick that makes the definition (and also the use of CPO in the end) much simpler without changing its substance: Instead of searching through $|h\rangle$, we simply invert h in place, then evaluate it, and then invert it again.

More precisely: Let Flip be a linear operator such that Flip$|h\rangle = |h^{-1}\rangle$ for all injective h. We do not specify what Flip does on any $|h\rangle$ that is not injective[20]. We only require that $\|\mathsf{Flip}\| \leq 1$, that is, $\|\mathsf{Flip}\,\psi\| \leq \psi$ for all ψ. (This is to avoid strange cases where the state of the system ends up having norm greater than 1).

Then a backward query to CPO is handled by invoking the operator $\mathsf{Flip} \cdot \mathsf{CFO_s} \cdot \mathsf{Flip}$. (Inverting, evaluating, inverting back).

To summarize:

Definition 1 (Compressed permutation oracle). CPO *is a pair of oracles* $\mathsf{CFO_s}$ *and* $\mathsf{Flip} \cdot \mathsf{CFO_s} \cdot \mathsf{Flip}$ *where* $\mathsf{CFO_s}$ *is as defined in* (6) *in the previous section, and* $\mathsf{Flip}|h\rangle = |h^{-1}\rangle$ *for injective* h *(and* $\|\mathsf{Flip}\| \leq 1$*), both operating on the same registers* X, Y, H *where* H *is private to* CPO *(not accessible to the querying algorithm) and initialized in the beginning with* $|\varnothing\rangle$.

We conjecture:

Conjecture 2. For any polynomial-query algorithm A,

$$\left| \Pr[A^{\mathsf{CPO}} \Rightarrow 1] - \Pr[A^{\pi,\pi^{-1}} \Rightarrow 1 : \pi \xleftarrow{\$} (\hookrightarrow D)] \right| \text{ is negligible.}$$

(Negligible in $\log|D|$).

Usage Example. We now illustrate how the CPO can be used by showing Conjecture 1 (double-sided zero-search) using the CPO. Of course, the validity of this example rests on Conjecture 2.

The reasoning is very similar to that done for the zero-preimage search in Sect. 3. We urge the reader to recap that reasoning first.

Specifically, we first come up with some invariant that describes that the adversary has not found x, y with $H(x\|0^n) = y\|0^n$.

$$\mathbf{I} := \mathrm{Span}\{|h\rangle : \nexists xy.\ h(x\|0^n) = y\|0^n\}.$$

Obviously, the initial state of the CPO (namely $|\varnothing\rangle$ in H) satisfies $\mathbf{I}$, and unitaries evaluated by the adversary on non-H registers preserve $\mathbf{I}$.

Given a forward-query to CPO (i.e., an application of the operator $\mathsf{CFO_s}$), we have

$$\psi \in \mathbf{I} \quad \implies \quad \psi' \overset{O(2^{-n/2})}{\approx} \mathbf{I} \tag{7}$$

where ψ, ψ' are the state before/after that query. Again, we omit the details of this computation and refer the reader to existing work[21]. We only stress that intuitively, this is what we expect, since when querying the oracle on any fresh input, the output will be of the form $y\|0^n$ only with small probability.

---

[20] For example, $\mathsf{Flip}|h\rangle$ might return an h' that so that $h'(x)$ is the lexicographically smallest preimage of x under h if there are several. Or $\mathsf{Flip}|h\rangle = 0$ for non-injective h. Since a non-injective h should not happen anyway when simulating a permutation, it should not matter how Flip is defined on these, so we make sure that our results hold independent of the design choices for that case.

[21] Existing work on compressed oracles applies here since (7) refers specifically to the preservation of $\mathbf{I}$ under a query to $\mathsf{CFO_s}$ and thus is not specific to the permutation case.

The only conceptually new thing in this example is when the adversary performs a backward-query: This will execute $\mathsf{Flip} \cdot \mathsf{CFO_s} \cdot \mathsf{Flip}$. Note that if h satisfies $h(x\|0^n) = y\|0^n$, then h^{-1} satisfies it, too. So any $|h\rangle \in \mathbf{I}$ is mapped by Flip to $|h^{-1}\rangle \in \mathbf{I}$. Thus Flip preserves $\mathbf{I}$. (Meaning, if $\psi \in \mathbf{I}$, then $\mathsf{Flip}\psi \in \mathbf{I}$). Furthermore, we already know from (7) that an invocation of $\mathsf{CFO_s}$ only introduces an $O(2^{-n/2})$ distance from $\mathbf{I}$. So together with the fact that Flip preserves $\mathbf{I}$, we have that (7) also holds for backward-queries.

All in all, we then have by induction that for a q-query adversary, at the end it holds:

$$\psi_{\textit{final}} \overset{O\left(q2^{-n/2}\right)}{\approx} \mathbf{I}.$$

So to find a "doubled-sided zero", the adversary needs $\Theta(2^{n/2})$ queries.

5   Towards Compressed Permutations

As discussed in the introduction, page 4, the main contribution of our work is the following claim:

Main contribution (informal): If some construction (say based on a random oracle) is indistinguishable from a CPO, then the CPO is indistinguishable from a random invertible permutation.

To make this formal, we first need to say what exactly we mean by a construction. Specifically, we focus on constructions that implement permutations. Roughly speaking, such a construction is some deterministic algorithm C that uses one or several oracles $H_1, \ldots, H_n$ and implements two functions π and τ that are inverses of each other.

For example, in the case of three-round Luby-Rackoff[22], the algorithm C would take three oracles and implement $\pi(x_L x_R)$ as: $t_1 := H_1(x_L)$, $t_2 := H_2(x_R \oplus t_1)$, $t_3 := H_3(x_L \oplus t_2)$, return $(x_L \oplus t_2, x_R \oplus t_1 \oplus t_3)$, and $\tau(x_L x_R)$ as: $t_1 := H_3(x_L)$, $t_2 := H_2(x_R \oplus t_1)$, $t_3 := H_1(x_L \oplus t_2)$, return $(x_L \oplus t_2, x_R \oplus t_1 \oplus t_3)$. It is easy to see that π and τ are permutations with $\tau = \pi^{-1}$ for any choice of H_1, H_2, H_3.

More abstractly, a construction is some function C that takes (fixed) functions $H_1, \ldots, H_n$, and returns functions π, τ. (Deterministically. That is, for fixed $H_1, \ldots, H_n$, π, τ are fixed, too). We do not care about the algorithmic details of how C transforms the oracles $H_1, \ldots, H_n$ into functions π, τ. While it would be typical that C does this by doing a few queries to $H_1, \ldots, H_n$, this is formally not required for our result.

In addition to the algorithm/function C that specified how π, τ are implemented given the oracles, the specification of the construction also needs to tell

---

[22] We use three-round Luby-Rackoff for this example just to keep the formulas short and readable. We are aware that three-round Luby-Rackoff is not even indistinguishable from an invertible random permutation in the classical setting, let alone the quantum setting.

us what kinds of oracles $H_1, \ldots, H_n$ are. E.g., in the Luby-Rackoff case, they are random functions. In other constructions, they might be functions with some other distribution (e.g., uniformly random permutations). To be as general as possible, we simply include the desired distribution $\mathcal{D}$ of the oracles in the specification of the construction.

The following definition summarizes all this:

Definition 2. *A* permutation-construction $(C, \mathcal{D})$ *(implicitly parametrized by a security parameter λ) consists of a function C that takes a tuple of functions $\underline{H} = (H_1, \ldots, H_n)$ and returns a pair of functions $\pi, \tau : D \to D$, and of a distribution $\mathcal{D}$ (for the functions $H_1, \ldots, H_n$), and satisfies the following:*

For $\underline{H}$ distributed according to $\mathcal{D}$, with overwhelming probability, π is a permutation and $\tau = \pi^{-1}$.

Remark. We do not require that π, τ can be efficiently computed given oracle access to $\underline{H}$. In practice, one would of course require efficient constructions, but our result holds without this additional condition, so we do not include it in our definition.

Remark. Note that the definition requires that the construction produces an invertible permutation (and not, e.g., a pair of non-invertible functions) with overwhelming probability, i.e., it includes a correctness requirement. But it does not require that π and τ look random in any way.

Notation. Given $\underline{H}$, $C(\underline{H})$ is a pair of functions π, τ. If we write $A^{C(\underline{H})}$, we mean that A gets superposition access to π, τ. I.e., $A^{C(\underline{H})}$ can be read as $(\pi, \tau) := C(\underline{H}), A^{\pi, \tau}$.

We are ready to state the main result formally:

Theorem 1. *Let C be a permutation-construction. Assume that for any polynomial-query adversary A,*

$$\left| \Pr[A^{C(\underline{H})} \Rightarrow 1 : \underline{H} \xleftarrow{\$} \mathcal{D}] - \Pr[A^{\mathsf{CPO}} \Rightarrow 1] \right| \text{ is negligible.} \tag{8}$$

Then for any polynomial-query adversary A,

$$\left| \Pr[A^{\mathsf{CPO}} \Rightarrow 1] - \Pr[A^{\pi, \pi^{-1}} \Rightarrow 1 : \pi \xleftarrow{\$} (\hookrightarrow D)] \right| \text{ is negligible.} \tag{9}$$

(Recall that $\hookrightarrow D$ is the set of permutations on D).

In particular, the existence of such a construction shows Conjecture 2[23].

We present a similar result where the construction may use computational assumptions in Corollary 1 below.

---

[23] For those domains D that the construction C actually operates on. (E.g., if C only implements permutations on domains $D = \{0,1\}^{n^2}$, then this would only prove Conjecture 2 for such domains).

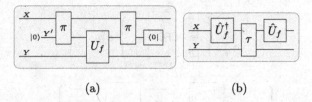

(a)   (b)

Fig. 2. Circuits implemented by B. (a) shows π', (b) shows τ'. The $\boxed{\langle 0|}$ gate denotes a multiplication with $\langle 0|$. Equivalently, this can be thought of as applying a projector onto $|0\rangle$ on Y' and then removing the register Y'. U_f is the unitary $U_f : |x, y\rangle \mapsto |x, y \oplus f(x)\rangle$. $\hat{U}_f$ is the unitary $\hat{U}_f : |x\rangle \mapsto |f(x)\rangle$. (Recall that f is bijective, so $\hat{U}_f$ is a unitary).

The (very rough) idea of the proof is simple: For a random permutation f, let $f \circ \mathsf{CPO}$ denote the CPO, but where we apply f to its outputs. (Or its inputs when doing a backward query). Then CPO and $f \circ \mathsf{CPO}$ are indistinguishable. (This follows from symmetries in the definition of CPO and does not require that CPO is actually indistinguishable from a permutation). By assumption, CPO and the construction C are indistinguishable, so $f \circ \mathsf{CPO}$ and $f \circ C$ are indistinguishable, too. (Since a distinguisher could just simulate f itself). And since C implements a permutation (not necessarily random), $f \circ C$ is a random permutation composed with permutation, thus a random permutation. So $f \circ C$ is indistinguishable from f. Taking this all together, we have that CPO is indistinguishable from f which shows the theorem.

Proof. Fix a polynomial-query adversary $A^{\pi, \tau}$ (taking two oracles π, τ). We need to show that (9) holds for this adversary.

Consider the following adversary $B^{\pi, \tau}$:

- It takes two oracles π, τ.
- It picks a permutation $f :\hookrightarrow D$ uniformly at random
- It runs $A^{\pi', \tau'}$ where π', τ' are implemented by the circuits in Fig. 2.
- It returns what A returns.

For the intuition: if π and τ are simply oracles providing superposition access to some functions π, τ, then $\pi' = f \circ \pi$ and $\tau' = \tau \circ f^{-1}$. And if moreover $\tau = \pi^{-1}$, then $\tau' = \pi'^{-1}$. However, B may be invoked with stateful oracles π, τ, so we cannot simply define π', τ' that way but instead need to give concrete circuits. (We also take care to ensure that B does not make more queries than A. Otherwise the proof of (10) below would become much harder).

We have:

$$\Pr[A^{\mathsf{CPO}} \Rightarrow 1] \approx \Pr[B^{\mathsf{CPO}} \Rightarrow 1]. \tag{10}$$

Here $\approx$ means a negligible difference. Intuitively, this follows because the definition of the CPO is symmetric, i.e., all inputs and outputs are treated the same, so permuting them should not make a difference. In reality, we need to be more careful because with small probability we can end up with oracle states on which Flip is defined arbitrarily (and possibly non-symmetrically). We defer the proof of (10) to the auxiliary Lemma 1 below.

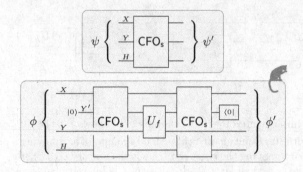

Fig. 3. Circuits C_ψ, D_ϕ in invariant preservation proof.

Since B makes the same number of queries as A, it is a polynomial-query adversary. So by assumption (8) of the lemma, we have:

$$\Pr[B^{\mathsf{CPO}} \Rightarrow 1] \approx \Pr[B^{C(\underline{H})} \Rightarrow 1 : \underline{H} \overset{\$}{\leftarrow} \mathcal{D}]. \tag{11}$$

Since C is a permutation-construction by assumption, for any fixed $\underline{H}$, $C(\underline{H}) = (\pi_H, \tau_H)$ for some functions π_H, τ_H that depend only on $\underline{H}$ (see Definition 2). We call $\underline{H}$ good if π_H is a permutation and $\tau_H = \pi_H^{-1}$. Still by definition of permutation-constructions, $\underline{H}$ is good with overwhelming probability. For a fixed good $\underline{H}$, we thus have:

$$\Pr[B^{C(\underline{H})} \Rightarrow 1] = \Pr[B^{\pi_H, \pi_H^{-1}} \Rightarrow 1] \overset{(*)}{=} \Pr[A^{f \circ \pi_H, \pi_H^{-1} \circ f^{-1}} \Rightarrow 1 : f \overset{\$}{\leftarrow} (\hookrightarrow D)]$$

$$= \Pr[A^{f \circ \pi_H, (f \circ \pi_H)^{-1}} \Rightarrow 1 : f \overset{\$}{\leftarrow} (\hookrightarrow D)]$$

$$\overset{(**)}{=} \Pr[A^{f, f^{-1}} \Rightarrow 1 : f \overset{\$}{\leftarrow} (\hookrightarrow D)] = \Pr[A^{\pi, \pi^{-1}} \Rightarrow 1 : \pi \overset{\$}{\leftarrow} (\hookrightarrow D)]$$

Here $(*)$ follows since the circuits that B computes $f \circ \pi, \tau \circ f^{-1}$ given oracles that implement fixed functions π, τ. And $(**)$ follows because for fixed permutation π_H and uniformly random permutation f, we have that $f \circ \pi_H$ has the same distribution as f.

Since this holds for any good $\underline{H}$, and $\underline{H}$ is good with overwhelming probability, by averaging we have:

$$\Pr[B^{C(\underline{H})} \Rightarrow 1 : \underline{H} \overset{\$}{\leftarrow} \mathcal{D}] \approx \Pr[A^{\pi, \pi^{-1}} \Rightarrow 1 : \pi \overset{\$}{\leftarrow} (\hookrightarrow D)]. \tag{12}$$

Equation (9) follows by (10)–(12). □

Lemma 1. *For B as defined in the proof of Theorem 1, we have*

$$\Pr[A^{\mathsf{CPO}} \Rightarrow 1] \approx \Pr[B^{\mathsf{CPO}} \Rightarrow 1].$$

Here $\approx$ means negligible difference.

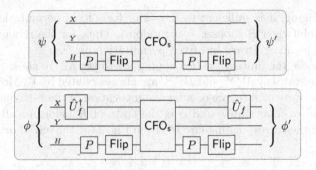

Fig. 4. Circuits D_ψ, D_ϕ in invariant preservation proof.

Proof. The basic idea in this proof is that B essentially just permutes the different possible outputs of the permutation implemented by the CPO, and since the definition of the CPO does not treat any possible output differently from any other, this permutation of outputs has no observable effect. However, this is not fully true: For example, if the oracle register H contains $|h\rangle$ where h is a non-injective partial function, the behavior of Flip is unspecified and might be asymmetric. (E.g., Flip might always pick the lexigraphically smallest string in case of ambiguities). To work around this, we first sanitize our CPO somewhat. Let P be the projection onto Span$\{|h\rangle : h$ injective$\}$ on register H. We then insert P before every call to Flip. Specifically, let CPO$'$ denote the two oracles CFO$_s$ and Flip $\cdot P \cdot$ CFO$_s \cdot$ Flip $\cdot P$. (Instead of CFO$_s$ and Flip $\cdot$ CFO$_s \cdot$ Flip as per definition of CPO). That is, CPO$'$ adds extra invocations of the projection P before each Flip[24]. The oracles making up CPO$'$ are also depicted in the top rows of Figs. 3 and 4, respectively. Then we have

$$\Pr[A^{\mathsf{CPO}} \Rightarrow 1] \approx \Pr[A^{\mathsf{CPO}'} \Rightarrow 1] \qquad \text{and} \qquad \Pr[B^{\mathsf{CPO}} \Rightarrow 1] \approx \Pr[B^{\mathsf{CPO}'} \Rightarrow 1]$$
$$(13)$$

We see this as follows: Consider the invariant $\mathbf{I} := \mathrm{Span}\{|h\rangle : h$ injective$\}$. This invariant is preserved by adversary operations on registers other than H. Queries to CFO$_s$ introduce an $O(i/N)$ error in the i-th query which is negligible. And since with h, h^{-1} is also injective, we have that Flip preserves $\mathbf{I}$. Finally, the difference between A^{CPO} and $A^{\mathsf{CPO}'}$ is that the latter has additional applications of the projector P. Since P projects onto $\mathbf{I}$ by definition, and the state is negligibly close to $\mathbf{I}$, this will change the state by a negligible amount. Therefore the final state of A differs only by a negligible amount (in the norm). Thus A's output probability also differs only by a negligible amount. Analogously for B. This shows (13).

Because of (13), to prove our lemma, it is sufficient to show:

$$\Pr[A^{\mathsf{CPO}'} \Rightarrow 1] = \Pr[B^{\mathsf{CPO}'} \Rightarrow 1].$$
$$(14)$$

---

[24] See the Sect. 2 (paragraph "non-unitaries in quantum circuits") for the meaning of applying a projection as part of a circuit.

And by averaging, it is sufficient to show this for a fixed permutation f. (Then it will also hold when B chooses f at random). Thus, for the remainder of this proof, f will be an arbitrary but fixed permutation on D.

Let V denote the unitary on H mapping $|h\rangle$ to $|f \circ h\rangle$. To show (14), we will show that the states of $A^{\mathsf{CPO}'}$ and $B^{\mathsf{CPO}'}$ are always related by V. More precisely, when ψ is the state of A before or after the invocation of the n-th query to CPO' (or the initial or final state), and ϕ is the state of B before or after the n-th invocation of the corresponding circuits from Fig. 2 (or the initial or final state), then:

$$\psi = V\phi. \tag{15}$$

For the initial state, (15) is immediate. (Recall that in the initial state, H contains $|\varnothing\rangle$, and $V|\varnothing\rangle = |f \circ \varnothing\rangle = |\varnothing\rangle$). We then proceed inductively through the execution of A and B.

Without loss of generality, A or B, respectively, interleave oracle queries and applications of some unitary operation on the adversary's state. This unitary is the same for A and B, and it trivially commutes with V (since V operates on H and H is not part of A's or B's state). Thus (15) is preserved under application of this unitary.

It remains to show that (15) is preserved under invocations of the oracle by A and B, respectively. (In the case of B, this is meant to include the wrapper circuits from Fig. 2). Let ψ, ϕ denote the state of A or B before that invocation, and ψ', π' the one after the invocation. We then need to show

$$\psi = V\phi \qquad \Longrightarrow \qquad \psi' = V\phi' \tag{16}$$

for ψ' and ϕ' being computed as in Fig. 3 or Fig. 4. (Depending whether the current query of A/B is one to its first or second oracle).

We first show (16) for ψ', ϕ' as computed in Fig. 3. Denote the operation computed by the circuit for ϕ' by C_ϕ. Then we need to show that $\psi' = \mathsf{CFO}_s\psi = \mathsf{CFO}_s V\phi \overset{!}{=} V\phi' = VC_\phi\phi$. So it is sufficient to prove $\mathsf{CFO}_s V = VC_\phi$. Since Decomp is unitary, this is equivalent to showing

$$\mathsf{Decomp} \cdot \mathsf{CFO}_s \cdot V \cdot \mathsf{Decomp}^\dagger = \mathsf{Decomp} \cdot V \cdot C_\phi \cdot \mathsf{Decomp}^\dagger. \tag{17}$$

Note that V and Decomp commute: Both V and Decomp operate on each H_x individually, namely as $\hat{U}_f$ and Decomp_1 where $\hat{U}_f$ is the unitary mapping $|z\rangle \mapsto |f(z)\rangle$, $|\perp\rangle \mapsto |\perp\rangle$. So we only need to check that $\hat{U}_f$ and Decomp_1 commute. Using the formula for Decomp_1 from (2), we compute that $\mathsf{Decomp}_1\hat{U}_f|\perp\rangle = |*\rangle$, $\hat{U}_f\mathsf{Decomp}_1|\perp\rangle = U_f|*\rangle = |*\rangle$, $\mathsf{Decomp}_1\hat{U}_f|z\rangle = \mathsf{Decomp}_1|f(z)\rangle = |f(z)\rangle + \frac{1}{\sqrt{N}}|\perp\rangle - \frac{1}{\sqrt{N}}|*\rangle$, $\hat{U}_f\mathsf{Decomp}_1|z\rangle = \hat{U}_f|z\rangle + \frac{1}{\sqrt{N}}\hat{U}_f|\perp\rangle - \frac{1}{\sqrt{N}}\hat{U}_f|*\rangle = |f(z)\rangle + \frac{1}{\sqrt{N}}|\perp\rangle - \frac{1}{\sqrt{N}}|*\rangle$. So $\hat{U}_f$, Decomp_1 commute on all basis states, hence they commute everywhere, hence V and Decomp commute.

Therefore the lhs of (17) equals $\mathsf{Decomp} \cdot \mathsf{CFO}_s \cdot \mathsf{Decomp}^\dagger \cdot V$ which is by definition $\mathsf{StO}_s \cdot V$. And the rhs equals what is drawn in Fig. 5(a). (Besides commuting Decomp and V, we also inserted Decomp, $\text{Decomp}^\dagger$ in the middle. These cancel out because they are unitary). And since $\text{StO}_s = \text{Decomp} \cdot \text{CFO}_s \cdot \text{Decomp}^\dagger$, Fig. 5(a) further simplifies to what is shown in Fig. 5(b).

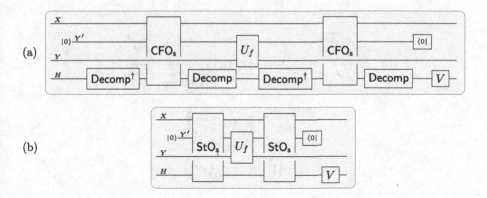

(a)

(b)

Fig. 5. Circuits in invariant preservation proof, first case.

Finally, both $\text{StO}_s \cdot V$ and the circuit from Fig. 5(b), upon input $|x, y, h\rangle$, return the state $|x, y \oplus f(h(x)), f \circ h\rangle$ when $h(x) \neq \bot$ and 0 when $h(x) = \bot^{25}$. (By elementary computation using the definitions of StO_s, U_f, V). Since they return the same state on every basis state, they are equal (by linearity). Thus the lhs and the rhs of (17) are equal; (17) holds. Hence (16) holds for ψ', ϕ' as computed in Fig. 3.

We now show (16) for ψ', ϕ' as computed in Fig. 4. Denote the circuit defining ψ' by D_ψ and the circuit defining ϕ' by D_ϕ. Then we need to show that $\psi' = D_\psi \psi = D_\psi V \phi \overset{!}{=} V\phi' = VD_\phi\phi$. So it is sufficient to prove $D_\psi V = VD_\phi$, or equivalently $D_\psi = VD_\phi V^\dagger$ (since V is unitary).

Define the unitary $W : |h\rangle \mapsto |h \circ f\rangle$ on H. (Note: compared to V, here we have $h \circ f$, not $f \circ h$).

Note that $\text{Flip}PV^\dagger = W\text{Flip}P$: For non-injective h, $\text{Flip}PV^\dagger|h\rangle$ and $W\text{Flip}P|h\rangle$ are both 0. (P projects such $|h\rangle$ to 0, and $V^\dagger$ preserves non-injectivity). For injective h, $\text{Flip}PV^\dagger|h\rangle = |(f^{-1} \circ h)^{-1})^{-1}\rangle = |h^{-1} \circ f\rangle$ and $W\text{Flip}P|h\rangle = |h^{-1} \circ f\rangle$. So $\text{Flip}PV^\dagger$ and $W\text{Flip}P$ coincide on all basis states, hence $\text{Flip}PV^\dagger = W\text{Flip}P$.

Analogously, $V\text{Flip}P = \text{Flip}PW^\dagger$.

This means that $VD_\phi V^\dagger$ can be rewritten to the circuit in Fig. 6(a). To show that that circuit is equal to D_ψ, all we need to prove is that the dashed part in Fig. 6(a) (henceforth called E_ϕ) is equal to CFO_s. And since Decomp is unitary, this in turn is equivalent to

$$\text{Decomp} \cdot \text{CFO}_s \cdot \text{Decomp}^\dagger = \text{Decomp} \cdot E_\phi \cdot \text{Decomp}^\dagger. \qquad (18)$$

---

[25] This is where we need to use the sanitized CFO. $\text{StO}_s \cdot V$ and the circuit from Fig. 5(b) (with StO instead of StO_s) return different states.

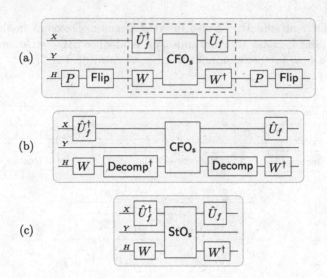

Fig. 6. Circuits in invariant preservation proof, second case.

Note further that W and $\mathsf{Decomp}^\dagger$ commute: W is just a reordering of the registers H_x (it moves H_x into $H_{f^{-1}(x)}$), and $\mathsf{Decomp}^\dagger$ applies the same unitary to each of those registers. So it makes no difference whether we apply $\mathsf{Decomp}^\dagger$ before or after reordering. Analogously $W^\dagger$ and Decomp commute.

So $\mathsf{Decomp}E_\phi\mathsf{Decomp}^\dagger$ is equal to what is depicted in Fig. 6(b). And, since $\mathsf{Decomp}\mathsf{CFO_s}\mathsf{Decomp}^\dagger = \mathsf{StO_s}$, that in turn simplifies to Fig. 6(c). (Denoted F_ϕ). So our goal (18) becomes $\mathsf{StO_s} = F_\phi$. And by elementary calculation, we get that $F_\phi|x,y,h\rangle = |x,y \oplus h(x),h\rangle$, same as $\mathsf{StO_s}$. So they coincide on basis states, so we have $\mathsf{StO_s} = F_\phi$, hence (18) holds. So (16) holds for ψ',ϕ' as computed in Fig. 4.

So (16) holds in all cases. This implies that (15) holds for the final states of A and B. The output bit of the adversary A and B is produced by the same measurement on A's and B's final state, respectively, and that measurement measures only registers belonging to the adversary (i.e., not H). So applying V on H does not change the distribution of that output bit. Hence (14) holds. By (13) the lemma follows.   □

Computational Case. Theorem 1 assumes that the construction C is indistinguishable from CPO for all polynomial-query adversaries, not just polynomial-time adversaries. If we have a construction C that is only secure under computational assumptions, Theorem 1 cannot be applied. However, the following variant of Theorem 1 applies. That is, we can at least show that CPO is computationally indistinguishable from a random invertible permutation.

Corollary 1. *Let C be a permutation-construction.* **Assume that C is efficiently implementable**[26]. **Assume that a strong qPRP with domain D exists**[27]. *Assume that for any* **polynomial-time** *adversary A,*

$$\left| \Pr[A^{C(\underline{H})} \Rightarrow 1 : \underline{H} \xleftarrow{\$} \mathcal{D}] - \Pr[A^{\mathsf{CPO}} \Rightarrow 1] \right| \text{ is negligible.} \qquad (19)$$

Then for any **polynomial-time** *adversary A,*

$$\left| \Pr[A^{\mathsf{CPO}} \Rightarrow 1] - \Pr[A^{\pi, \pi^{-1}} \Rightarrow 1 : \pi \xleftarrow{\$} (\hookrightarrow D)] \right| \text{ is negligible.} \qquad (20)$$

(The differences from Theorem 1 are highlighted in boldface).

Proof. The proof closely follows the lines of the one of Theorem 1. Fix a polynomial-time adversary $A^{\pi,\tau}$. Define $B^{\pi,\tau}$ as in the proof of Theorem 1. We assume that the unitaries $\hat{U}_f$ and $\hat{U}_f^\dagger$ in B are implemented by the following respective subcircuits:

- Initialize an extra register Z with $|0\rangle$, apply U_f to XZ, swap X, Z, apply $U_{f^{-1}}$ to XZ, and discard Z.
- Initialize an extra register Z with $|0\rangle$, apply $U_{f^{-1}}$ to XZ, swap X, Z, apply U_f to XZ, and discard Z.

These subcircuits exactly implement $\hat{U}_f$ and $\hat{U}_f^\dagger$, so this replacement does not change the behavior of B.

Since A is polynomial-time it is also polynomial-query, and thus we have by Lemma 1:

$$\Pr[A^{\mathsf{CPO}} \Rightarrow 1] \approx \Pr[B^{\mathsf{CPO}} \Rightarrow 1].$$

By assumption of the lemma, a strong qPRP $f_k : \hookrightarrow D$ exists. Let $\hat{B}$ be defined like B, with the following differences: It initially picks a key k for the strong qPRP f_k. And invocations to U_f and $U_{f^{-1}}$ are replaced by U_{f_k} and $U_{f_k^{-1}}$.

Since CFO_s and Flip can be implemented efficiently (using a compact representation of the partial functions in H), and A is polynomial-time, and f_k is a strong qPRP, it follows that

$$\Pr[B^{\mathsf{CPO}} \Rightarrow 1] \approx \Pr[\hat{B}^{\mathsf{CPO}} \Rightarrow 1].$$

Also note that $\hat{B}$ is the polynomial-time. (B was not because it picks a random permutation f. There might not be a polynomial-time implementation for that). Then by assumption (19), we have:

$$\Pr[\hat{B}^{\mathsf{CPO}} \Rightarrow 1] \approx \Pr[\hat{B}^{C(\underline{H})} \Rightarrow 1 : \underline{H} \xleftarrow{\$} \mathcal{D}].$$

---

[26] That is, we assume that there is a (potentially stateful) polynomial-time algorithm $\hat{C}$ such that $\hat{C}$ is indistinguishable from $C(\underline{H})$ with $\underline{H} \xleftarrow{\$} \mathcal{D}$ by all polynomial-query (not only polynomial-time) algorithms.

[27] See, e.g., [27] for constructions.

By assumption, C is efficiently implementable, so there is a polynomial-time $\hat{C}$ that is indistinguishable from $C(\underline{H})$ by polynomial-query adversaries, so:

$$\Pr[\hat{B}^{C(\underline{H})} \Rightarrow 1 : \underline{H} \xleftarrow{\$} \mathcal{D}] \approx \Pr[\hat{B}^{\hat{C}} \Rightarrow 1].$$

Since $\hat{C}$ is polynomial-time, we can use the strong qPRP property of f_k again and get:

$$\Pr[\hat{B}^{\hat{C}} \Rightarrow 1] \approx \Pr[B^{\hat{C}} \Rightarrow 1].$$

And since B is polynomial-query (though not polynomial-time because it picks a random permutation f),

$$\Pr[B^{\hat{C}} \Rightarrow 1] \approx \Pr[B^{C(\underline{H})} \Rightarrow 1 : \underline{H} \xleftarrow{\$} \mathcal{D}].$$

Finally, exactly as in the proof of Theorem 1, we show:

$$\Pr[B^{C(\underline{H})} \Rightarrow 1 : \underline{H} \xleftarrow{\$} \mathcal{D}] \approx \Pr[A^{\pi,\pi^{-1}} \Rightarrow 1 : \pi \xleftarrow{\$} (\hookrightarrow D)].$$

Taking all the equations together, we get (20). □

Acknowledgments. This work was supported by the ERC consolidator grant CerQuS (819317), by the Estonian Centre of Excellence in IT (EXCITE) funded by ERDF, and by PUT team grant PRG946 from the Estonian Research Council. We thank Andreas Hülsing for helpful comments.

References

1. Ambainis, A.: Quantum lower bounds by quantum arguments. J. Comput. Syst. Sci. **64**(4), 750–767 (2002). https://doi.org/10.1006/jcss.2002.1826
2. Ambainis, A., Hamburg, M., Unruh, D.: Quantum security proofs using semi-classical oracles. In: Boldyreva, A., Micciancio, D. (eds.) CRYPTO 2019. LNCS, vol. 11693, pp. 269–295. Springer, Cham (2019). https://doi.org/10.1007/978-3-030-26951-7_10
3. Ambainis, A., Rosmanis, A., Unruh, D.: Quantum attacks on classical proof systems: the hardness of quantum rewinding. In: FOCS 2014, pp. 474–483. IEEE (2014). https://doi.org/10.1109/FOCS.2014.57
4. Balogh, M., Eaton, E., Song, F.: Quantum collision-finding in non-uniform random functions. In: Lange, T., Steinwandt, R. (eds.) PQCrypto 2018. LNCS, vol. 10786, pp. 467–486. Springer, Cham (2018). https://doi.org/10.1007/978-3-319-79063-3_22
5. Beals, R., Buhrman, H., Cleve, R., Mosca, M., de Wolf, R.: Quantum lower bounds by polynomials. J. ACM **48**(4), 778–797 (2001). https://doi.org/10.1145/502090.502097
6. Bellare, M., Rogaway, P.: Random oracles are practical: a paradigm for designing efficient protocols. In: CCS 1993, pp. 62–73. ACM (1993)
7. Bertoni, G., Daemen, J., Peeters, M., van Assche, G.: Sponge functions. Ecrypt Hash Workshop (2007). https://sponge.noekeon.org/SpongeFunctions.pdf

8. Bertoni, G., Daemen, J., Peeters, M., Van Assche, G.: On the indifferentiability of the sponge construction. In: Smart, N. (ed.) EUROCRYPT 2008. LNCS, vol. 4965, pp. 181–197. Springer, Heidelberg (2008). https://doi.org/10.1007/978-3-540-78967-3_11

9. Boneh, D., Dagdelen, Ö., Fischlin, M., Lehmann, A., Schaffner, C., Zhandry, M.: Random oracles in a quantum world. In: Lee, D.H., Wang, X. (eds.) ASIACRYPT 2011. LNCS, vol. 7073, pp. 41–69. Springer, Heidelberg (2011). https://doi.org/10.1007/978-3-642-25385-0_3

10. Boyer, M., Brassard, G., Høyer, P., Tapp, A.: Tight bounds on quantum searching. Fortschr. Phys. 46(4–5), 493–505 (1998)

11. Canetti, R., Goldreich, O., Halevi, S.: The random oracle methodology, revisited. In: STOC 1998, pp. 209–218. ACM (1998)

12. Chung, K.-M., Fehr, S., Huang, Y.-H., Liao, T.-N.: On the compressed-oracle technique, and post-quantum security of proofs of sequential work. In: Canteaut, A., Standaert, F.-X. (eds.) EUROCRYPT 2021. LNCS, vol. 12697, pp. 598–629. Springer, Cham (2021). https://doi.org/10.1007/978-3-030-77886-6_21

13. Czajkowski, J., Groot Bruinderink, L., Hülsing, A., Schaffner, C., Unruh, D.: Post-quantum security of the sponge construction. In: Lange, T., Steinwandt, R. (eds.) PQCrypto 2018. LNCS, vol. 10786, pp. 185–204. Springer, Cham (2018). https://doi.org/10.1007/978-3-319-79063-3_9

14. Czajkowski, J., Hülsing, A., Schaffner, C.: Quantum indistinguishability of random sponges. In: Boldyreva, A., Micciancio, D. (eds.) CRYPTO 2019. LNCS, vol. 11693, pp. 296–325. Springer, Cham (2019). https://doi.org/10.1007/978-3-030-26951-7_11

15. Czajkowski, J., Majenz, C., Schaffner, C., Zur, S.: Quantum lazy sampling and game-playing proofs for quantum indifferentiability (2020). arXiv:1904.11477 [quant-ph]

16. Ebrahimi, E., Unruh, D.: Quantum collision-resistance of non-uniformly distributed functions: upper and lower bounds. Quantum Inf. Comput. 18(15&16), 1332–1349 (2018). https://doi.org/10.26421/QIC18.15-16

17. Hosoyamada, A., Iwata, T.: Personal communication (2021)

18. Hosoyamada, A., Iwata, T.: 4-round Luby-Rackoff construction is a qPRP. In: Galbraith, S.D., Moriai, S. (eds.) ASIACRYPT 2019. LNCS, vol. 11921, pp. 145–174. Springer, Cham (2019). https://doi.org/10.1007/978-3-030-34578-5_6

19. Hülsing, A., Rijneveld, J., Song, F.: Mitigating multi-target attacks in hash-based signatures. In: Cheng, C.-M., Chung, K.-M., Persiano, G., Yang, B.-Y. (eds.) PKC 2016. LNCS, vol. 9614, pp. 387–416. Springer, Heidelberg (2016). https://doi.org/10.1007/978-3-662-49384-7_15

20. Ito, G., Hosoyamada, A., Matsumoto, R., Sasaki, Yu., Iwata, T.: Quantum chosen-ciphertext attacks against Feistel ciphers. In: Matsui, M. (ed.) CT-RSA 2019. LNCS, vol. 11405, pp. 391–411. Springer, Cham (2019). https://doi.org/10.1007/978-3-030-12612-4_20

21. Luby, M., Rackoff, C.: How to construct pseudorandom permutations from pseudorandom functions. SIAM J. Comput. 17(2), 373–386 (1988). https://doi.org/10.1137/0217022

22. NIST. SHA-3 standard: Permutation-based hash and extendable-output functions. Draft FIPS 202 (2014). https://csrc.nist.gov/publications/drafts/fips-202/fips_202_draft.pdf

23. Targhi, E.E., Tabia, G.N., Unruh, D.: Quantum collision-resistance of non-uniformly distributed functions. In: Takagi, T. (ed.) PQCrypto 2016. LNCS,

vol. 9606, pp. 79–85. Springer, Cham (2016). https://doi.org/10.1007/978-3-319-29360-8_6

24. Unruh, D.: Compressed permutation oracles (and the collision-resistance of sponge/sha3). IACR Cryptology ePrint Archive 2021/062 (2021)

25. Unruh, D.: Computationally binding quantum commitments. In: Fischlin, M., Coron, J.-S. (eds.) EUROCRYPT 2016. LNCS, vol. 9666, pp. 497–527. Springer, Heidelberg (2016). https://doi.org/10.1007/978-3-662-49896-5_18

26. Unruh, D.: Non-interactive zero-knowledge proofs in the quantum random oracle model. In: Oswald, E., Fischlin, M. (eds.) EUROCRYPT 2015. LNCS, vol. 9057, pp. 755–784. Springer, Heidelberg (2015). https://doi.org/10.1007/978-3-662-46803-6_25

27. Zhandry, M.: A note on quantum-secure PRPs. Cryptology ePrint Archive, Report 2016/1076 (2016). https://eprint.iacr.org/2016/1076

28. Zhandry, M.: A note on the quantum collision and set equality problems. Quantum Inf. Comput. **15**(7&8), 557–567 (2015). https://doi.org/10.26421/QIC15.7-8

29. Zhandry, M.: How to construct quantum random functions. In: FOCS 2013, pp. 679–687. IEEE (2012). https://doi.org/10.1109/FOCS.2012.37

30. Zhandry, M.: How to record quantum queries, and applications to quantum indifferentiability. In: Boldyreva, A., Micciancio, D. (eds.) CRYPTO 2019. LNCS, vol. 11693, pp. 239–268. Springer, Cham (2019). https://doi.org/10.1007/978-3-030-26951-7_9

31. Zhandry, M.: Secure identity-based encryption in the quantum random oracle model. In: Safavi-Naini, R., Canetti, R. (eds.) CRYPTO 2012. LNCS, vol. 7417, pp. 758–775. Springer, Heidelberg (2012). https://doi.org/10.1007/978-3-642-32009-5_44

Tighter Security for Generic Authenticated Key Exchange in the QROM

Jiaxin Pan[1,4](✉)(iD), Benedikt Wagner[2,3](iD), and Runzhi Zeng[1](iD)

[1] Department of Mathematical Sciences, NTNU – Norwegian University of Science and Technology, Trondheim, Norway
{jiaxin.pan,runzhi.zeng}@ntnu.no
[2] CISPA Helmholtz Center for Information Security, Saarbrücken, Germany
benedikt.wagner@cispa.de
[3] Saarland University, Saarbrücken, Germany
[4] University of Kassel, Kassel, Germany

Abstract. We give a tighter security proof for authenticated key exchange (AKE) protocols that are generically constructed from key encapsulation mechanisms (KEMs) in the quantum random oracle model (QROM). Previous works (Hövelmanns et al., PKC 2020) gave reductions for such a KEM-based AKE protocol in the QROM to the underlying primitives with square-root loss and a security loss in the number of users and total sessions. Our proof is much tighter and does not have square-root loss. Namely, it only loses a factor depending on the number of users, not on the number of sessions.

Our main enabler is a new variant of lossy encryption which we call parameter lossy encryption. In this variant, there are not only lossy public keys but also lossy system parameters. This allows us to embed a computational assumption into the system parameters, and the lossy public keys are statistically close to the normal public keys. Combining with the Fujisaki-Okamoto transformation, we obtain the *first* tightly IND-CCA secure KEM in the QROM in a multi-user (without corruption), multi-challenge setting.

Finally, we show that a multi-user, multi-challenge KEM implies a square-root-tight and session-tight AKE protocol in the QROM. By implementing the parameter lossy encryption tightly from lattices, we obtain the *first* square-root-tight and session-tight AKE from lattices in the QROM.

Keywords: Authenticated key exchange · key encapsulation mechanism · quantum random oracle model · tight security · lattices

1 Introduction

Authenticated key exchange (AKE) is a fundamental primitive in cryptography. An AKE allows to establish a session key between two users. In combination with

---

Supported by the Research Council of Norway under Project No. 324235.

J. Guo and R. Steinfeld (Eds.): ASIACRYPT 2023, LNCS 14441, pp. 401–433, 2023.
https://doi.org/10.1007/978-981-99-8730-6_13

symmetric-key primitives, this allows to establish a secure channel. Many well-known AKE protocols (such as SIGMA [25] and HMQV [26]) are constructed based on the Diffie-Hellman assumption. Contrary to that, we focus on quantum-safe AKE in this paper.

KEM/PKE-BASED AKE. It is known that AKE protocols can be constructed generically from key encapsulation mechanisms (KEMs) or public-key encryption (PKE) (e.g., [9,10,19]). In particular, a quantum-safe AKE can be constructed from a quantum-safe KEM. One main advantage of such KEM-based AKE protocols is that they do not require any digital signature to authenticate the protocol transcripts explicitly. Considering the (in)efficiency of quantum-safe signature schemes, this avoids a significant overhead.

AKE IN THE QROM AND ITS NON-TIGHTNESS. The well-established random oracle model (ROM) [4] idealizes hash functions and is used to prove the security of many practical cryptographic protocols, including the aforementioned generic KEM-based AKE protocols. For quantum adversaries, however, it is more realistic to assume that they can run an "offline" primitive such as a hash function in a quantum manner. To model this, the quantum (accessible) random oracle model (QROM) has been introduced in [7]. In the QROM, a quantum adversary can query the random oracle on arbitrary superpositions. This makes it difficult to use many of the proof techniques applied in the classical ROM. In addition, it introduces a large security loss. We take the existing KEM-based AKE protocol [19] in the QROM as an example. Its security bound is[1]

$$\Theta(S^2 + S \cdot N) \cdot \left(\varepsilon_{\text{IND-CPA}} + \sqrt{Q \cdot \varepsilon_{\text{IND-CPA}}} \right), \tag{1}$$

where S, N, and Q are the numbers of total sessions, users, and random oracle queries, respectively, and $\varepsilon_{\text{IND-CPA}}$ is the advantage of breaking the underlying IND-CPA secure PKE. This is the only known bound in the QROM. Regarding the level of IND-CPA security, especially the square-root loss (i.e., the term $\sqrt{\varepsilon_{\text{IND-CPA}}}$) is undesirable. This square-root loss results from the use of the so-called oneway-to-hiding strategy in the QROM [2]. In practice, the PKE would be implemented by a standardized scheme with a 128-bit security guarantee. Even without counting other non-tight terms, the resulting AKE is only guaranteed to have 64-bit security, which is not a reasonable security margin. Even worse, for today's applications, it is easy to have $S = 2^{30}$ and $N = 2^{30}$. Hence, the security bound given by Eq. (1) provides almost no security guarantee given such a PKE implementation.

In this paper, our goal is to minimize the security loss of AKE protocols in the QROM. We emphasize that there is no known tightly secure AKE protocol in the QROM, and most tightly secure AKE protocols (e.g., [14,15,20]) are based on variants of Diffie-Hellman assumptions, which are not quantum-safe.

---

[1] For all security bounds in this section, we ignore all additive and negligible statistical terms.

1.1 Our Contributions

We propose a tighter proof for KEM-based AKE protocols in the QROM. Our proof does not have square-root loss and is tight with respect to the number of total sessions. Assuming a multi-challenge IND-CCA secure (MC-CCA) KEM (with advantage denoted as $\varepsilon_{\text{MC-CCA}}$) and a multi-user, multi-challenge IND-CCA (MUC-CCA) secure KEM (with advantage denoted as $\varepsilon_{\text{MUC-CCA}}$), our security bound for AKE in the QROM is

$$\Theta(N) \cdot \varepsilon_{\text{MC-CCA}} + \Theta(1) \cdot \varepsilon_{\text{MUC-CCA}}. \tag{2}$$

The concrete bound is given in Theorem 3. Here, the multi-user security provides an adversary with multiple users' public keys but does not allow corruption for any of the corresponding secret keys. The multi-challenge security allows an adversary to ask for multiple challenge ciphertexts under any user.

We also show that MC-CCA and MUC-CCA can be efficiently achieved either tightly or almost tightly[2] from the Decisional Learning with Errors (LWE) assumption. In combination, our bound for the resulting AKE protocol is

$$\Theta(N) \cdot \Theta(\lambda) \cdot \varepsilon_{\text{LWE}} + \Theta(\lambda) \cdot \varepsilon_{\text{LWE}}, \tag{3}$$

where λ is the security parameter, and ε_{LWE} is the advantage against the LWE assumption (cf. Corollary 2). Our AKE model is essentially the Bellare-Rogaway model [5], and additionally, it captures the key-compromise-impersonation (KCI) attacks.

PARAMETER LOSSY ENCRYPTION. Our technical tool is a more expressive and fine-grained variant of lossy encryption which we call parameter lossy encryption (PLE). (Slightly) different from the original notion of lossy encryption [16], the PLE has a system parameter that is shared among many users in the system, and each user has an independent public key. Both public keys and system parameters have a lossy mode. Under such lossy parameters and lossy public keys, ciphertexts statistically hide the encrypted messages. This enables a tight security proof as follows: Under the normal parameters, lossy public keys are statistically close to the normal ones. Further, lossy parameters are computationally indistinguishable from normal parameters. In combination, this allows us to switch from the normal to the lossy setting with a security loss that is independent of the number of keys.

TIGHT SECURITY IN THE QROM FROM PLE. Separating the system parameter from public keys can improve efficiency, since multiple users can share the same system parameter, instead of generating an independent parameter that is in a user's public key. This can largely improve the communication complexity of a KEM-based AKE, where an initiator will generate an ephemeral public key and send it to the responder (cf. Fig. 11). Moreover, separating the system parameters is important for tightness. For instance, a PLE scheme immediately implies

---

[2] This is a relaxed tightness notion from [8] where security loss is at most linear in the security parameter λ.

a multi-user, multi-challenge IND-CPA KEM tightly without random oracles, while the (original) lossy encryption can only tightly imply multi-challenge IND-CPA KEM. This is because the original lossy encryption requires computational assumptions to switch user public keys to lossy one-by-one, which introduces a security loss linear in the number of users. More importantly, the aforementioned fine-grained separation is very useful to remove the square-root loss in the QROM. When we apply the Fujisaki-Okamoto transformation [11,17] to achieve IND-CCA security, the only step that needs computational assumptions is switching normal system parameters to lossy ones, and all the other proof steps are merely statistical. The parameter-switching step does not involve random oracles. When the oneway-to-hiding lemma [2] is used, the square root function is only applied on a purely statistical term and does not affect the security loss with respect to computational assumptions. Hence, this gives us the *first* tightly secure multi-user, multi-challenge IND-CCA KEM in the QROM, which solves the open problem in [19] about a root-tight proof of IND-CCA security. We note that the work of Pan and Zeng [32] tightly implied a PKE with the same security in the classical ROM, yet it is not clear how to transform it in the QROM, since they used a lot of reprogramming.

PARAMETER LOSSY ENCRYPTION FROM LATTICES. Finally, we propose a tight construction of PLE from the LWE assumption. Our construction extends the dual Regev encryption [13,33] with lossy LWE matrices [27]. Combining with the aforementioned generic constructions, we obtain

- the first lattice-based AKE protocol in the QROM that does not have square-root security loss and is tightly secure with respect to the number of total sessions. It is not tight with respect to the number of users;
- the first tightly IND-CCA secure lattice-based KEM in the multi-user, multi-challenge setting and in the QROM.

Both results provide new insights on minimizing the security loss in the QROM, namely, PLE is a useful tool to tighten security loss in the QROM. It may be useful for future applications.

OPEN PROBLEMS. We view avoiding the square-root loss and loss concerning the number of total sessions as an important step towards tightly secure AKE in the QROM. It would be interesting to extend our techniques to construct a tightly secure AKE in the QROM. Another interesting open problem is how to construct our parameter lossy encryption from other quantum-safe assumptions, e.g., module-LWE.

1.2   More Related Work

The work of Fujioka et al. (FSXY) [9] constructed AKE generically from KEMs in the standard model. One may think that it is secure in the QROM with the same proof. However, as pointed out by Hövelmanns et al. [19], FSXY has two major drawbacks: First, it requires perfect correctness, which makes it hard to instantiate with lattices. Second, it lacks simplicity, making it overly complicated and very inefficient. Moreover, the security loss of FSXY is $\Theta(N^2 S)$ which is much larger than ours. Another work on AKE protocols in the QROM is due to Xue et al. [36] which constructed AKE from commutative supersingular isogenies. Similar to the work of Hövelmanns et al., it contains square-root-loss and depends on both the number of users and sessions. Hence, the work of Hövelmanns et al. is the most representative for our discussion. We note a very recent work on lattice-based tightly secure AKE [30] in the classical ROM, but extending it to the QROM is not trivial, since it seems difficult to extend the programming techniques of [30] to the QROM.

2 Preliminaries

For an integer n, we define the notation $[n] := \{1, \ldots, n\}$. Let $\mathcal{X}$ and $\mathcal{Y}$ be two finite sets. The notation $x \xleftarrow{\$} \mathcal{X}$ denotes sampling an element x from $\mathcal{X}$ uniformly at random. Let $\mathcal{A}$ be an algorithm. If $\mathcal{A}$ is probabilistic, then $y \leftarrow \mathcal{A}(x)$ means that the variable y is assigned to the output of $\mathcal{A}$ on input x. If $\mathcal{A}$ is deterministic, then we may write $y := \mathcal{A}(x)$. We write $\mathcal{A}^{\mathcal{O}}$ to indicate that $\mathcal{A}$ has classical access to oracle $\mathcal{O}$, and $\mathcal{A}^{|\mathcal{O}\rangle}$ to indicate that $\mathcal{A}$ has quantum access to oracle $\mathcal{O}$ All algorithms (including adversaries) in this paper are probabilistic polynomial-time (PPT), unless we state it otherwise. We use code-based games [6] to define and prove security. We implicitly assume that Boolean flags are initialized to false, numerical types are initialized to 0, sets and ordered lists are initialized to $\emptyset$, and strings are initialized to the empty string ϵ. The notation $\Pr[\mathbf{G}^{\mathcal{A}} \Rightarrow 1]$ denotes the probability that the final output $\mathbf{G}^{\mathcal{A}}$ of game $\mathbf{G}$ running an adversary $\mathcal{A}$ is 1. Let Ev be an (classical) event. We write $\Pr[\text{Ev} : \mathbf{G}]$ to denote the probability that Ev occurs during the game $\mathbf{G}$. In our security notions throughout the paper, we let N, S be numbers of users and challenges, respectively, which are assumed to be polynomial in λ.

2.1 Quantum Random Oracle Model

In the quantum random oracle model (QROM), some hash functions are modelled as publicly quantum-accessible random oracles (see [7] for more details). Unlike the classical random oracle model, the efficient reduction algorithm in the QROM cannot use lazy sampling to simulate quantum random oracles (QROs). In this paper, we do not specify the way for reduction algorithms to simulate QROs. Following the convention in [21,22,24,34], we assume that reduction algorithms (i.e., game simulators) have access to some internal quantum random oracles (which can be instantiated by quantum-secure pseudo-random functions or real-world hash functions [24,34]). Lemma 1 gives a probabilistic bound for an adversary $\mathcal{A}$ (at most q queries to $|\mathcal{O}\rangle$) to distinguish whether it is interacting with random oracle $\mathcal{O}_0$ or interacting with random oracle $\mathcal{O}_1$, where $\mathcal{O}_0 \backslash \mathcal{S} = \mathcal{O}_1 \backslash \mathcal{S}$. If $\mathcal{A}$ can distinguish, then Lemma 1 states that there exists an PPT reduction EXT that randomly measures $\mathcal{A}$'s QRO queries and outputs an element $x \in \mathcal{S}$.

Lemma 1 (OW2H, probabilities [2]). *Let $\mathcal{X}, \mathcal{Y}$, and $\mathcal{S} \subseteq \mathcal{X}$ be sets. Let $\mathcal{O}_0, \mathcal{O}_1 : \mathcal{X} \to \mathcal{Y}$ be random functions satisfying $\forall x \notin \mathcal{S}, \mathcal{O}_0(x) = \mathcal{O}_1(x)$. Let inp be some bitstring. $(\mathcal{S}, \mathcal{O}_0, \mathcal{O}_1, \mathsf{inp})$ may have arbitrary joint distribution. Let $\mathcal{A}$ be an adversary issuing at most q quantum-superposition queries to random oracle and, on input inp, it outputs either 0 or 1. Let $\mathsf{EXT}^{\mathcal{O}}$ $(\mathcal{O} = \mathcal{O}_0$ or $\mathcal{O}_1)$ be a quantum algorithm that on input inp does the following: It picks $i^* \xleftarrow{\$} [q]$, runs $\mathcal{A}^{|\mathcal{O}\rangle}(\mathsf{inp})$ until i^*th query (denoted as $|\phi\rangle$) to $\mathcal{O}$, and returns $x' :=$ $\mathrm{MEASURE}(|\phi\rangle)$. Then we have*

$$\left| \Pr[1 \leftarrow \mathcal{A}^{|\mathcal{O}_0\rangle}(\mathsf{inp})] - \Pr[1 \leftarrow \mathcal{A}^{|\mathcal{O}_1\rangle}(\mathsf{inp})] \right|$$
$$\leq 2q\sqrt{\Pr[x' \in \mathcal{S} : x' \leftarrow \mathsf{EXT}^{\mathcal{A}, |\mathcal{O}_1\rangle}(\mathsf{inp})]}$$

We consider a special case of Lemma 1. Let $\mathcal{S}$ in Lemma 1 be a randomly generated set and independent of inp. Then we have the following corollary. The proof is straight-forward since the $\mathcal{S}$ is independently random, the probability that EXT finds an element in $\mathcal{S}$ is the uniform probability $\frac{|\mathcal{S}|}{|\mathcal{X}|}$.

Corollary 1. *With the same notations and assumptions in Lemma 1, if $\mathcal{S}$ is random set generated at independently and uniformly random, then we have*

$$\left| \Pr[1 \leftarrow \mathcal{A}^{|\mathcal{O}_0\rangle}(\mathsf{inp})] - \Pr[1 \leftarrow \mathcal{A}^{|\mathcal{O}_1\rangle}(\mathsf{inp})] \right| \leq 2q\sqrt{|\mathcal{S}|/|\mathcal{X}|}$$

Lemma 2 gives a probabilistic bound for an adversary (has quantum access to oracles) to distinguish $h(k, \cdot)$ and h', where k is secret, h and h' are QRO and have the same image. When the image set is large enough, the adversary cannot distinguish these two oracles, unless it "queries" the oracle on k.

Lemma 2 ([34]). *Let s be an integer. Let $h : \{0,1\}^s \times \mathcal{X} \to \mathcal{Y}$ and $h' : \mathcal{X} \to \mathcal{Y}$ be two independent random oracles. If an unbounded time quantum adversary $\mathcal{A}$ that queries H at most q_H times, then we have*

$$\left| \Pr[1 \leftarrow \mathcal{A}^{|h\rangle, |h(k, \cdot)\rangle}() \mid k \leftarrow \{0,1\}^s] - \Pr[1 \leftarrow \mathcal{A}^{|h\rangle, |h'\rangle}()] \right| \leq 2q_H \cdot 2^{-s/2}$$

We also need the following lemma to handle PKE schemes with imperfect correctness (Definition 2). Let B_λ be the Bernoulli distribution (i.e., $\Pr[b = 1] = \lambda$ for the bit $b \leftarrow B_\lambda$). Roughly speaking, for any unbounded and quantum adversary $\mathcal{A}$, Lemma 3 bounds $\mathcal{A}$'s advantage in distinguishing whether it is interacting with a constant function or a function that follows the Bernoulli distribution B_λ. We call such a distinguishing problem as Generic quantum Distinguishing Problem with Bounded probabilities (GDPB).

Lemma 3 (GDPB [19]). *Let $\mathcal{X}$ be a finite set, and let $\lambda \in [0, 1]$. Then, for any unbounded and quantum algorithm $\mathcal{A}$ issuing at most q quantum queries,*

$$\left| \Pr[\mathsf{GDPB}^{\mathcal{A}}_{\lambda,0} \Rightarrow 1] - \Pr[\mathsf{GDPB}^{\mathcal{A}}_{\lambda,1} \Rightarrow 1] \right| \leq 8(q+1)^2\lambda,$$

where games $\mathsf{GDPB}^{\mathcal{A}}_{\lambda,b}$ are defined in Fig. 1.

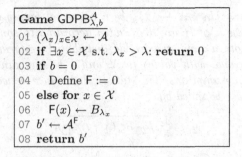

Fig. 1. Game $\mathsf{GDPB}_{\lambda,b}^{\mathcal{A}}$ used in Lemma 3.

2.2 Background About Lattices

In this section, we recall the LWE assumption and some well-known facts about Gaussians [12,29], and the lossy LWE technique and a generalized leftover hash lemma [1,23]. First, we recall the LWE assumption.

Definition 1 (LWEAssumption). *Let n, m be positive integers, q be a prime. Let χ be a distribution over $\mathbb{Z}$. All of these are implicitly parameterized by the security parameter λ. We say that the $\mathsf{LWE}_{n,m,q,\chi}$ assumption holds, if for any algorithm $\mathcal{B}$, the following advantage is negligible in λ:*

$$\mathsf{Adv}^{\mathsf{LWE}_{n,m,q,\chi}}(\mathcal{B}) := |\Pr[\mathcal{B}(\mathbf{A}, \mathbf{b}) = 1 \mid \mathbf{A} \xleftarrow{\$} \mathbb{Z}_q^{n \times m}, \mathbf{b} \xleftarrow{\$} \mathbb{Z}_q^m]$$
$$- \Pr[\mathcal{B}(\mathbf{A}, \mathbf{A}^\top \mathbf{s} + \mathbf{e}) = 1 \mid \mathbf{A} \xleftarrow{\$} \mathbb{Z}_q^{n \times m}, \mathbf{s} \xleftarrow{\$} \mathbb{Z}_q^n, \mathbf{e} \leftarrow \chi^m]|.$$

Let $s > 0$. We define the discrete Gaussian distribution over $\mathbb{Z}$ with parameter s, denoted by $D_{\mathbb{Z},s}$ to be the distribution proportional to $\rho_s(\mathbf{x}) := \exp(-\pi \|\mathbf{x}\|^2/s^2)$, restricted to $\mathbb{Z}$. Next, we recall well-known regularity lemmas and tail bounds, following [12,29].

Lemma 4. *Consider natural numbers $n, m \in \mathbb{N}$ and a prime q at least polynomial in n. Assume $m \geq 2n \log q$ and $s \geq \omega(\sqrt{\log m})$. Then, the following distributions have negligible statistical distance:*

$$\{(\mathbf{A}, \mathbf{Ae}) \mid \mathbf{A} \xleftarrow{\$} \mathbb{Z}_q^{n \times m}, \ \mathbf{e} \leftarrow D_{\mathbb{Z},s}^m\} \ and \ \{(\mathbf{A}, \mathbf{b}) \mid \mathbf{A} \xleftarrow{\$} \mathbb{Z}_q^{n \times m}, \ \mathbf{b} \xleftarrow{\$} \mathbb{Z}_q^n\}.$$

Lemma 5. *For any $s \geq \omega(\sqrt{\log m})$, and $\mathbf{x} \leftarrow D_{\mathbb{Z},s}^m$, the probability that $\|\mathbf{x}\| > s\sqrt{m}$ is at most 2^{-m+1}.*

We also make use of the lossy LWE technique. For that, we require the following lemmas from [1,23]. The lemmas make use of the so called "smooth average min-entropy" $\tilde{H}_\infty(\cdot \mid \cdot)$ [23].

Lemma 6. *Consider positive integers n, t, m, q, g, and $\beta, s' > 0$ and a distribution χ over $\mathbb{Z}$ such that $s' \geq \beta q g n m$ and $\Pr[|x| \geq \beta q \mid x \leftarrow \chi] \leq \mathsf{negl}(\lambda)$. Assume $\mathbf{s}$ is uniformly distributed over $[-g, g]^n$, and $\mathbf{e}$ is distributed according to $D_{\mathbb{Z},\mathbb{Z}}^m$. Let $\mathbf{B} \xleftarrow{\$} \mathbb{Z}_q^{n \times t}, \mathbf{C} \xleftarrow{\$} \mathbb{Z}_q^{t \times m}, \mathbf{D} \leftarrow \chi^{n \times m}$ and set $\mathbf{A} := \mathbf{BC} + \mathbf{D}$. Then, for any $\epsilon \geq 2^{-\lambda}$, we have*

$$\tilde{H}_\infty^\epsilon(\mathbf{s} \mid \mathbf{A}^\top \mathbf{s} + \mathbf{e}) \geq n \log(2g + 1) - (t + 2\lambda) \log q - \mathsf{negl}(\lambda).$$

Lemma 7. *Let $\mathcal{H} := \{h_k : \mathcal{X} \to \mathcal{Y}\}_k$ be a universal family of hash functions. Assume that the keys k of $\mathcal{H}$ are distributed according to some distribution K. Further, let U denote a random variable distributed uniformly over $\mathcal{Y}$ and X be any random variable with values in $\mathcal{X}$ and I be any random variable. Let $\epsilon \geq 0$. With these assumptions, the statistical distance between $(K, h_K(X), I)$ and (K, U, I) is upper bounded by*

$$2\epsilon + \frac{1}{2}\sqrt{2^{-\tilde{H}^\epsilon_\infty(X \mid I)} \cdot |\mathcal{Y}|}.$$

3   Parameter Lossy Encryption

In this section, we focus on public key encryption. Formally, a public key encryption (PKE) scheme PKE consists of four algorithms (Setup, KG, Enc, Dec) and a message space $\mathcal{M}$ that is assumed to be efficiently recognizable. The algorithms work as follows:

- The setup algorithm Setup, on input the security parameter λ, outputs system parameters par.
- The key generation algorithm KG, on input the parameter par, outputs a public and secret key pair (pk, sk).
- The encryption algorithm Enc, on input pk and a message $m \in \mathcal{M}$, outputs a ciphertext $c \in \mathcal{C}$.
- The decryption algorithm Dec, on input sk and a ciphertext c, outputs a message $m' \in \mathcal{M}$ or a rejection symbol $\bot \notin \mathcal{M}$.

Definition 2 (Correctness of PKE). *A PKE scheme* PKE = (Setup, KG, Enc, Dec) *with message space $\mathcal{M}$ is $(1 - \delta)$-correct if*

$$\mathbb{E}_{(\mathsf{pk},\mathsf{sk}) \leftarrow \mathsf{KG}} \left[\max_{m \in \mathcal{M}} \Pr\left[\mathsf{Dec}(\mathsf{sk}, c) \neq m : c \leftarrow \mathsf{Enc}(\mathsf{pk}, m)\right] \right] \leq \delta,$$

where the expectation is taken over par $\leftarrow$ Setup(λ), (pk, sk) $\leftarrow$ KG(par) *and randomness of* Enc. *Here $\delta := \delta(\lambda)$ is related to the security parameter λ.*

For technical reasons, we also need a bound on the probability that two public keys collide.

Definition 3 (Collision Probability of Key Generation). *We define the collision probability of* KG *of* PKE *as*

$$\eta_{\mathsf{PKE}} := \max\left[\Pr\left[\mathsf{pk}_0 = \mathsf{pk}_1 : (\mathsf{pk}_0, \mathsf{sk}_0) \leftarrow \mathsf{KG}(\mathsf{par}), (\mathsf{pk}_1, \mathsf{sk}_1) \leftarrow \mathsf{KG}(\mathsf{par})\right]\right],$$

where the maximum is taken over all $\mathsf{pk}_0, \mathsf{pk}_1$.

We can assume that η_{PKE} is negligible, as otherwise an adversary would have non-negligible probability of sampling a secret key for a given public key, which would imply that the scheme is insecure for any reasonable notion.

LOSSY ENCRYPTION. We recall the notion of lossy encryption [3,16,18]. In lossy encryption schemes, there are two modes of the public keys. Public keys in the real mode work as defined above. On the other hand, if we encrypt a plaintext using a public key in lossy mode, the ciphertext statistically hides the plaintext. Real and lossy public keys should be computationally indistinguishable. Unlike the lossy encryption in [3,18], we do not require openability here.

Definition 4 (Lossy Encryption). *Let* PKE := (Setup, KG, Enc, Dec) *be a PKE scheme with message space* $\mathcal{M}'$. PKE *is* lossy *if there is an algorithm* LKG *such that the following properties hold:*

- PKE *is correct according to Definition 2.*
- Key Indistinguishability: *We say* PKE *satisfies key indistinguishability if for any algorithm* $\mathcal{B}$, *the advantage function*

$$\mathsf{Adv}_{\mathsf{PKE}}^{\mathsf{ind\text{-}key}}(\mathcal{B}) := |\Pr\left[\mathcal{B}\left(\mathsf{par}, \mathsf{pk}\right) \Rightarrow 1\right] - \Pr\left[\mathcal{B}(\mathsf{par}, \mathsf{lpk}) \Rightarrow 1\right]|$$

is negligible, where the probability is taken over $\mathsf{par} \leftarrow \mathsf{Setup}(\lambda)$, $(\mathsf{pk}, \mathsf{sk}) \leftarrow \mathsf{KG}(\mathsf{par})$, *and* $\mathsf{lpk} \leftarrow \mathsf{LKG}(\mathsf{par})$.

- Lossiness: *For any arbitrary messages* $m, m' \in \mathcal{M}'$, *the statistical distance between the following distributions* D *and* D' *is at most* ϵ^{lo}, *where* ϵ^{lo} *is negligible:*

$$D := \left\{ (\mathsf{par}, \mathsf{lpk}, c) \,\middle|\, \begin{array}{l} \mathsf{par} \leftarrow \mathsf{Setup}(\lambda),\ \mathsf{lpk} \leftarrow \mathsf{LKG}(\mathsf{par}) \\ c \leftarrow \mathsf{Enc}(\mathsf{lpk}, m) \end{array} \right\},$$

$$D' := \left\{ (\mathsf{par}, \mathsf{lpk}, c) \,\middle|\, \begin{array}{l} \mathsf{par} \leftarrow \mathsf{Setup}(\lambda),\ \mathsf{lpk} \leftarrow \mathsf{LKG}(\mathsf{par}) \\ c \leftarrow \mathsf{Enc}(\mathsf{lpk}, m') \end{array} \right\}.$$

We refer to ϵ^{lo} *as the lossiness of* PKE.

We give a lattice-based lossy encryption in Sect. 3.3. The construction is essentially the Regev encryption scheme [33].

3.1 Parameter Lossy Encryption

We now extend the lossiness notion to a multi-user notion, where the global system parameters are also allowed to have a lossy mode. We call this new notion parameter lossy encryption.

Definition 5 (Parameter Lossy Encryption). *Let* PKE := (Setup, KG, Enc, Dec) *be a PKE scheme with message space* $\mathcal{M}'$. PKE *is* parameter lossy *if there are algorithms* LSetup *and* LKG *such that the following properties hold:*

- PKE *is correct according to Definition 2.*
- Parameter-Key Indistinguishability: *We say* PKE *satisfies parameter-key indistinguishability if for any PPT algorithm* $\mathcal{B}$, *the advantage function*

$$\mathsf{Adv}_{\mathsf{PKE}}^{\mathsf{ind\text{-}par\text{-}key}}(\mathcal{B}) := |\Pr\left[\mathcal{B}\left(\mathsf{par}, \mathsf{pk}_1, \dots, \mathsf{pk}_N\right) \Rightarrow 1\right]$$
$$- \Pr\left[\mathcal{B}(\mathsf{lpar}, \mathsf{lpk}_1, \dots, \mathsf{lpk}_N) \Rightarrow 1\right]|$$

is negligible, where N *denotes the number of users, and the first probability is taken over the experiment* $\mathsf{par} \leftarrow \mathsf{Setup}(\lambda)$, $(\mathsf{pk}_1, \mathsf{sk}_1) \leftarrow \mathsf{KG}(\mathsf{par}), \dots, (\mathsf{pk}_N, \mathsf{sk}_N) \leftarrow \mathsf{KG}(\mathsf{par})$ *and the second one is taken over* $\mathsf{lpar} \leftarrow \mathsf{LSetup}(\lambda)$, $\mathsf{lpk}_1 \leftarrow \mathsf{LKG}(\mathsf{lpar}), \dots, \mathsf{lpk}_N \leftarrow \mathsf{LKG}(\mathsf{lpar})$.

- Lossiness: *For any arbitrary messages $m, m' \in \mathcal{M}'$, the statistical distance between the following distributions D and D' is at most ϵ^{lo}, where ϵ^{lo} is negligible:*

$$D := \left\{ (\text{lpar}, \text{lpk}, c) \,\middle|\, \begin{array}{l} \text{lpar} \leftarrow \text{LSetup}(\lambda), \ \text{lpk} \leftarrow \text{LKG}(\text{lpar}) \\ c \leftarrow \text{Enc}(\text{lpk}, m) \end{array} \right\},$$

$$D' := \left\{ (\text{lpar}, \text{lpk}, c) \,\middle|\, \begin{array}{l} \text{lpar} \leftarrow \text{LSetup}(\lambda), \ \text{lpk} \leftarrow \text{LKG}(\text{lpar}) \\ c \leftarrow \text{Enc}(\text{lpk}, m') \end{array} \right\}.$$

We refer to ϵ^{lo} as the lossiness of PKE.

3.2   Parameter Lossy Encryption from Lattices

We construct a parameter lossy encryption scheme from the (Decisional) Learning With Errors (LWE) assumption. Essentially, in our encryption we extend the (dual) Regev scheme [13,33] with a lossy mode of system parameters.

SCHEME. Our scheme has message space $\{0,1\}^{\ell}$. As common for lattice-based encryption schemes, a message $m \in \{0,1\}^{\ell}$ has to be encoded on encryption and decoded on decryption. More precisely, we define the following algorithms and use them in our scheme:

- Algorithm $\text{Encode}(m)$ computes a vector $\mathbf{m}^{\top} \in \mathbb{Z}_q^{\ell}$. The ith coordinate of $\mathbf{m}^{\top}$ is given as $\lfloor q/2 \rfloor \cdot m_i$ for each $i \in [\ell]$.
- Algorithm $\text{Decode}(\mathbf{m}^{\top})$ computes a message $m \in \{0,1\}^{\ell}$ by componentwise rounding. That is, for all $i \in [\ell]$, it sets $m_i = 0$ if $\mathbf{m}_i$ is closer to 0 than to $\lfloor q/2 \rfloor$. Otherwise, it sets $m_i = 1$.

Further, our scheme makes use of parameters $n, m, q, t, g \in \mathbb{N}, s, s', s'' \in \mathbb{R}, s, s', s'' > 0$ satisfying the following conditions:

- $n = \Theta(\lambda)$, q prime
- $m \geq 2n \log q$ (for Lemma 4)
- $s, s' \geq \omega(\sqrt{\log m})$ (for Lemmata 4 and 5)
- $ss'm \leq q/4$ (for correctness)
- $s' \geq gn^2m$ (for Lemma 6, we choose $\beta q = n$)
- $n \log(2g+1) - (t+2\lambda) \log q - \text{negl}(\lambda) \geq \lambda \log q + \Omega(n)$ (for Lemma 7)

For example, a (very conservative) parameter setting that satisfies all these conditions for a given λ is

$$n := 56\lambda \qquad n^6 < q \leq n^7, \qquad g := \sqrt{n}, \qquad s := \sqrt{n},$$
$$t := \lambda, \qquad m := 2n \log q, \qquad s' := n^{2.5}m, \qquad s'' := \sqrt{n}.$$

Formally, we present our scheme in Fig. 2.

ANALYSIS. We show correctness, parameter-key indistinguishability, and lossiness. The proof of correctness follows standard arguments [33].

Lemma 8. *The scheme* PKE *in Fig. 2 is $(1 - \delta)$-correct, for negligible δ.*

Setup(λ)	KG(par $= \mathbf{A}$)	Enc(pk $= \mathbf{Y}, m$)
01 $\mathbf{A} \xleftarrow{\$} \mathbb{Z}_q^{n \times m}$	07 sk $:= \mathbf{X} \leftarrow D_{\mathbb{Z},s}^{m \times \ell}$	12 $\mathbf{s} \xleftarrow{\$} [-g, g]^n$, $\mathbf{e} \leftarrow D_{\mathbb{Z},s'}^m$
02 return par $:= \mathbf{A}$	08 pk $:= \mathbf{Y} := \mathbf{AX}$	13 $\mathbf{m}^\top := \mathsf{Encode}(m)$
	09 return (pk, sk)	14 $\mathbf{c}^\top := \mathbf{s}^\top \mathbf{A} + \mathbf{e}^\top$
LSetup(λ)		15 $\mathbf{v}^\top := \mathbf{s}^\top \mathbf{Y} + \mathbf{m}^\top$
03 $\mathbf{B} \xleftarrow{\$} \mathbb{Z}_q^{n \times t}$, $\mathbf{C} \xleftarrow{\$} \mathbb{Z}_q^{t \times m}$	LKG(lpar $= \mathbf{A}$)	16 return $c := (\mathbf{c}^\top, \mathbf{v}^\top)$
04 $\mathbf{D} \leftarrow D_{\mathbb{Z},s''}^{n \times m}$	10 lpk $:= \mathbf{Y} \xleftarrow{\$} \mathbb{Z}_q^{n \times \ell}$	Dec(sk $= \mathbf{x}, c = (\mathbf{c}^\top, \mathbf{v}^\top)$)
05 $\mathbf{A} := \mathbf{BC} + \mathbf{D}$	11 return lpk	17 $\mathbf{m}^\top := \mathbf{v}^\top - \mathbf{c}^\top \mathbf{X}$
06 return lpar $:= \mathbf{A}$		18 return $\mathsf{Decode}(\mathbf{m}^\top)$

Fig. 2. The parameter lossy encryption scheme PKE $:=$ (Setup, KG, Enc, Dec) from the LWE assumption with algorithms LSetup and LKG.

Proof. Let sk $= \mathbf{X} \leftarrow D_{\mathbb{Z},s}^{m \times \ell}$ and pk $= \mathbf{Y} = \mathbf{AX}$ be a pair of public key and secret key. Consider a message $m \in \{0,1\}^\ell$ and an honestly computed ciphertext $c := (\mathbf{c}^\top, \mathbf{v}^\top)$ for m. We have $\mathbf{c}^\top = \mathbf{s}^\top \mathbf{A} + \mathbf{e}^\top$ and $\mathbf{v}^\top := \mathbf{s}^\top \mathbf{Y} + \mathbf{m}^\top$. Now, consider $\mathbf{m}^\top$ computed during the decryption algorithm. We have

$$\mathbf{m}^\top = \mathbf{v}^\top - \mathbf{c}^\top \mathbf{X} = \mathbf{m}^\top - \mathbf{e}^\top \mathbf{X}.$$

Thus, one can see that decryption recovers m if each coordinate of $\mathbf{e}^\top \mathbf{X}$ has absolute value less than $q/4$. Fix such a coordinate, say the ith, and call it z. Except with negligible probability (see Lemma 5), we have that $\|\mathbf{e}\| \leq s'\sqrt{m}$, and the ith column $\mathbf{x}$ of $\mathbf{X}$ satisfies $\|\mathbf{x}\| \leq s\sqrt{m}$. Thus, we have

$$|z| = |\mathbf{e}^\top \mathbf{x}| \leq \|\mathbf{e}\| \|\mathbf{x}\| \leq ss'm < q/4.$$

except with negligible probability.

Lemma 9. *If the* LWE$_{t,m,q,D_{\mathbb{Z},s''}}$ *assumption holds, then the scheme* PKE *with algorithms* LSetup *and* LKG *as presented in Fig. 2 satisfies parameter-key indistinguishability. Namely, for any adversary* $\mathcal{A}$, *there is an algorithm* $\mathcal{B}$ *such that the running time of* $\mathcal{B}$ *is about that of* $\mathcal{A}$ *and*

$$\mathsf{Adv}_{\mathsf{PKE}}^{\mathsf{ind\text{-}par\text{-}key}}(\mathcal{A}) \leq n \cdot \mathsf{Adv}^{\mathsf{LWE}_{t,m,q,D_{\mathbb{Z},s''}}}(\mathcal{B}) + \mathsf{negl}(\lambda).$$

Proof. To show parameter-key indistinguishability, we need to argue that the distributions of (1) parameters and keys output by Setup and KG and (2) parameters and keys output by LSetup and LKG are computationally indistinguishable. We show this using a sequence of hybrid distributions. Namely, we start with distribution D_1, which is the distribution output by Setup and KG, namely

$$D_1 := \left\{ (\mathbf{A}, \mathbf{Y}_1, \ldots, \mathbf{Y}_N) \,\middle|\, \begin{array}{l} \mathbf{A} \xleftarrow{\$} \mathbb{Z}_q^{n \times m}, \\ \forall i \in [N] : \mathbf{X}_i \leftarrow D_{\mathbb{Z},s}^{m \times \ell}, \mathbf{Y}_i := \mathbf{AX}_i \end{array} \right\}.$$

Now, we argue that the distribution

$$D_2 := \left\{ (\mathbf{A}, \mathbf{Y}_1, \ldots, \mathbf{Y}_N) \,\middle|\, \begin{array}{l} \mathbf{A} \xleftarrow{\$} \mathbb{Z}_q^{n \times m}, \\ \forall i \in [N] : \mathbf{Y}_i \xleftarrow{\$} \mathbb{Z}_q^{n \times \ell} \end{array} \right\}$$

is statistically close to D_1. This can easily be seen using $\ell \cdot N$ applications of Lemma 4. Next, using n applications of the $\mathsf{LWE}_{t,m,q,D_{\mathbb{Z},s''}}$ assumption (one per row of $\mathbf{A}$), we see that the distribution

$$
D_3 := \left\{ (\mathbf{A}, \mathbf{Y}_1, \ldots, \mathbf{Y}_N) \;\middle|\;
\begin{array}{l}
\mathbf{B} \xleftarrow{\$} \mathbb{Z}_q^{n \times t}, \mathbf{C} \xleftarrow{\$} \mathbb{Z}_q^{t \times m}, \mathbf{D} \leftarrow D_{\mathbb{Z},s''}^{n \times m} \\
\mathbf{A} := \mathbf{BC} + \mathbf{D}, \\
\forall i \in [N] : \mathbf{Y}_i \xleftarrow{\$} \mathbb{Z}_q^{n \times \ell}
\end{array}
\right\}
$$

is computationally indistinguishable from D_2. Finally, observe that D_3 is exactly the distribution of parameters and keys output by LSetup and LKG.

Lemma 10. *The scheme* PKE *with algorithms* LSetup *and* LKG *as presented in Fig. 2 satisfies lossiness.*

Proof. Fix two arbitrary messages $m, m' \in \{0,1\}^\ell$. According to the definition of lossiness, and the specification of scheme PKE and algorithms LSetup and LKG, we need to argue that the following distributions D and D' are statistically close:

$$
D := \left\{ (\mathbf{A}, \mathbf{Y}, \mathbf{c}^\top, \mathbf{v}^\top) \;\middle|\;
\begin{array}{l}
\mathbf{B} \xleftarrow{\$} \mathbb{Z}_q^{n \times t}, \; \mathbf{C} \xleftarrow{\$} \mathbb{Z}_q^{t \times m}, \; \mathbf{D} \leftarrow D_{\mathbb{Z},s''}^{n \times m}, \\
\mathbf{A} := \mathbf{BC} + \mathbf{D}, \; \mathbf{Y} \xleftarrow{\$} \mathbb{Z}_q^{n \times \ell}, \\
\mathbf{c}^\top := \mathbf{s}^\top \mathbf{A} + \mathbf{e}^\top, \; \mathbf{v}^\top := \mathbf{s}^\top \mathbf{Y} + \mathsf{Encode}(m)
\end{array}
\right\},
$$

$$
D' := \left\{ (\mathbf{A}, \mathbf{Y}, \mathbf{c}^\top, \mathbf{v}^\top) \;\middle|\;
\begin{array}{l}
\mathbf{B} \xleftarrow{\$} \mathbb{Z}_q^{n \times t}, \; \mathbf{C} \xleftarrow{\$} \mathbb{Z}_q^{t \times m}, \; \mathbf{D} \leftarrow D_{\mathbb{Z},s''}^{n \times m}, \\
\mathbf{A} := \mathbf{BC} + \mathbf{D}, \; \mathbf{Y} \xleftarrow{\$} \mathbb{Z}_q^{n \times \ell}, \\
\mathbf{c}^\top := \mathbf{s}^\top \mathbf{A} + \mathbf{e}^\top, \; \mathbf{v}^\top := \mathbf{s}^\top \mathbf{Y} + \mathsf{Encode}(m')
\end{array}
\right\}.
$$

Observe that it is sufficient to argue that $\mathbf{s}^\top \mathbf{Y}$ is statistically close to uniform over $\mathbb{Z}_q^\ell$, given $\mathbf{A}, \mathbf{Y}, \mathbf{c}^\top$ as in D and D'. To do this, we make use of Lemma 7. Namely, we consider the hash function family $\mathbf{s} \mapsto \mathbf{s}^\top \mathbf{Y}$ parameterized by $\mathbf{Y}$. As $\mathbf{Y}$ is sampled uniformly at random in distributions D and D', and q is a prime, this family is universal. Next, we claim that $\mathbf{s}$ has a lot of entropy given $\mathbf{c}^\top$. Precisely, we use Lemma 6 and derive

$$
\tilde{H}_\infty^\epsilon (\mathbf{s} \mid \mathbf{c}) \geq n \log(2g+1) - (t + 2\lambda) \log q - \mathsf{negl}(\lambda)
$$
$$
\geq \lambda \log q + \Omega(n),
$$

where the first inequality follows from Lemma 6, and the last inequality follows from our assumptions on parameters. Now that the lower bound on the entropy of $\mathbf{s}$ is established, we use Lemma 7 with $\epsilon = 2^{-\lambda}$ and $\mathcal{Y} := \mathbb{Z}_q^\lambda$, and get that the statistical distance between $\mathbf{s}^\top \mathbf{Y}$ and uniform, given $\mathbf{A}, \mathbf{Y}, \mathbf{c}^\top$, is at most

$$
2\epsilon + \frac{1}{2}\sqrt{2^{-\tilde{H}_\infty^\epsilon(\mathbf{s} \mid \mathbf{c})} \cdot |\mathcal{Y}|} \leq 2^{-\lambda+1} + \frac{1}{2}\sqrt{2^{-\lambda \log q - \Omega(n) + \lambda \log q}} \leq \mathsf{negl}(\lambda),
$$

which finishes the proof.

3.3 Lossy Encryption from Lattices

We present a simple construction of lossy encryption from lattices. The construction is essentially Regev's public key encryption scheme [33] Formally, the public key encryption $\mathsf{PKE} = (\mathsf{Setup}, \mathsf{KG}, \mathsf{Enc}, \mathsf{Dec})$ and algorithm LKG for message space $\{0, 1\}^\ell$ is given in Fig. 3. For our description, we rely on algorithms Encode and Decode introduced in Sect. 3.2. It makes use of parameters $n, m, q \in \mathbb{N}, s, s' \in \mathbb{R}, s, s' > 0$, that should satisfy the following conditions

- $n = \Theta(\lambda)$, q prime
- $m \geq 2(n + \ell) \log q$ (for Lemma 4)
- $s, s' \geq \omega(\sqrt{\log m})$ (for Lemmata 4 and 5)
- $ss'm \leq q/4$ (for correctness)

An example non-optimized instantiation for a given security parameter λ and message length $\ell = n$ is $n := \lambda$, $n^3 < q \leq n^4$, $m := 4n \log q$, and $s := s' := \log m$.

$\mathsf{Setup}(1^\lambda)$	$\mathsf{Enc}(\mathsf{pk} = \mathbf{Y}, m)$
01 **return** par $:= \mathbf{A} \xleftarrow{\$} \mathbb{Z}_q^{n \times m}$	06 $\mathbf{x} \leftarrow D_{\mathbb{Z}, s'}^m$
	07 $\mathbf{c} := \mathbf{Ax}$
$\mathsf{KG}(\mathsf{par} = \mathbf{A})$	08 $\mathbf{v} := \mathbf{Yx} + \mathsf{Encode}(m)^\top$
02 sk $:= \mathbf{S} \xleftarrow{\$} \mathbb{Z}_q^{n \times \ell}$, $\mathbf{E} \leftarrow D_{\mathbb{Z}, s}^{m \times \ell}$	09 **return** $c := (\mathbf{c}, \mathbf{v})$
03 pk $:= \mathbf{Y} := \mathbf{S}^\top \mathbf{A} + \mathbf{E}^\top \in \mathbb{Z}_q^{\ell \times m}$	
04 **return** (pk, sk)	$\mathsf{Dec}(\mathsf{sk} = \mathbf{S}, c = (\mathbf{c}, \mathbf{v}))$
	10 $\mathbf{m} := \mathbf{v} - \mathbf{S}^\top \mathbf{c}$
$\mathsf{LKG}(\mathsf{par} = \mathbf{A})$	11 **return** $\mathsf{Decode}(\mathbf{m}^\top)$
05 **return** lpk $:= \mathbf{Y} \xleftarrow{\$} \mathbb{Z}_q^{\ell \times m}$	

Fig. 3. The lossy PKE scheme $\mathsf{PKE} := (\mathsf{Setup}, \mathsf{KG}, \mathsf{Enc}, \mathsf{Dec})$ from the LWE assumption with algorithm KG.

We now turn to the analysis of PKE. We show correctness, key indistinguishability, and lossiness.

Lemma 11. *The scheme* PKE *in Fig. 3 is* $(1 - \delta)$-*correct, for negligible* δ.

Proof. The proof is standard [13,33]. One can easily see that decryption works as long as $|\mathbf{e}^\top \mathbf{x}| < q/4$ for any column $\mathbf{e}$ of $\mathbf{E}$. By Lemma 5 and our assumption about s, s', m, and q, we have

$$|\mathbf{e}^\top \mathbf{x}| \leq \|\mathbf{e}\| \|\mathbf{x}\| \leq ss'm < q/4.$$

with overwhelming probability.

Lemma 12. *If the* $\mathsf{LWE}_{n,m,q,D_{\mathbb{Z},s}}$ *assumption holds, then the scheme* PKE *with algorithm* LKG *as presented in Fig. 3 satisfies key indistinguishability. Namely, for any algorithm* $\mathcal{A}$, *there is an algorithm* $\mathcal{B}$ *such that the running time of* $\mathcal{B}$ *is about that of* $\mathcal{A}$ *and*

$$\mathsf{Adv}_{\mathsf{PKE}}^{\mathsf{ind\text{-}key}}(\mathcal{A}) \leq \ell \cdot \mathsf{Adv}^{\mathsf{LWE}_{n,m,q,D_{\mathbb{Z},s}}}(\mathcal{B})$$

Proof. The statement follows directly from the LWE assumption, applied to each row of matrix $\mathbf{Y}$.

Lemma 13. *The scheme* PKE *with algorithm* LKG *as presented in Fig. 3 satisfies lossiness.*

Proof. Fix two arbitrary messages $m, m' \in \{0,1\}^{\ell}$. Now, according to the definition of lossiness and the specification of the scheme, we have to argue that the distributions D and D' are statistically close, where D and D' are given as

$$D := \left\{ (\mathbf{A}, \mathbf{Y}, \mathbf{c}, \mathbf{v}) \middle| \begin{array}{l} \mathbf{A} \xleftarrow{\$} \mathbb{Z}_q^{n \times m}, \; \mathbf{Y} \xleftarrow{\$} \mathbb{Z}_q^{\ell \times m} \\ \mathbf{c} := \mathbf{Ax}, \; \mathbf{v} := \mathbf{Yx} + \mathsf{Encode}(m)^{\top} \end{array} \right\},$$

$$D' := \left\{ (\mathbf{A}, \mathbf{Y}, \mathbf{c}, \mathbf{v}) \middle| \begin{array}{l} \mathbf{A} \xleftarrow{\$} \mathbb{Z}_q^{n \times m}, \; \mathbf{Y} \xleftarrow{\$} \mathbb{Z}_q^{\ell \times m} \\ \mathbf{c} := \mathbf{Ax}, \; \mathbf{v} := \mathbf{Yx} + \mathsf{Encode}(m')^{\top} \end{array} \right\}.$$

It is sufficient that in both distributions the term

$$\begin{bmatrix} \mathbf{A} \\ \mathbf{Y} \end{bmatrix} \mathbf{x}$$

is statistically close to uniform. This is guaranteed by Lemma 4.

4   CCA Secure KEMs from (Parameter) Lossy Encryption

In this section, we construct two KEM schemes KEM_1 and KEM_2 from lossy encryption and parameter lossy encryption, respectively. The schemes KEM_1 and KEM_2 have tight multi-challenge, and tight multi-user multi-challenge security, respectively, and will be used in the construction of our AKE protocol in Sect. 6. Before we describe the schemes in Sects. 4.1 and 4.2, we recall the formal definition of KEMs and define the security notions of interest.

DEFINITIONS. We recall the syntax and security definitions of a KEM. A KEM KEM consists of four algorithms (Setup, KGen, Encaps, Decaps) and a key space $\mathcal{K}$ that is assumed to be efficiently recognizable. The algorithms work as follows:

- The setup algorithm Setup, on input the security parameter λ, outputs system parameters par.
- The key generation algorithm KGen, on input the parameter par, outputs a public and secret key pair (pk, sk).
- The encapsulation algorithm Encaps, on input pk, outputs a ciphertext e and a key $K \in \mathcal{K}$.
- The decapsulation algorithm Decaps, on input sk and a ciphertext e, outputs a key $K \in \mathcal{K}$ or a rejection symbol $\perp \notin \mathcal{K}$.

In this paper, we use MC-IND-CCA secure KEM and MUC-IND-CCA secure KEM to construct AKE protocols.

Definition 6 (MC-IND-CCA Security of KEM). *Let* KEM = (Setup, KGen, Encaps, Decaps) *be a KEM. We say that* KEM *is* MC-IND-CCA *secure, if for any algorithm $\mathcal{A}$, the advantage*

Game MC-IND-CCA$^{\mathcal{A}}_{\mathsf{KEM},b}(\lambda)$	Game MUC-IND-CCA$^{\mathcal{A}}_{\mathsf{KEM},b}(\lambda)$	Oracle $\mathrm{DEC}(e)$
01 par $\leftarrow$ Setup(λ)	09 par $\leftarrow$ Setup(λ)	20 if $e \in \mathbf{e}$
02 (pk, sk) $\leftarrow$ KGen(par)	10 for $j \in [N]$	21 $\quad$ return $\perp$
03 for $i \in [S]$	11 $\quad$ (pk$_j$, sk$_j$) $\leftarrow$ KGen(par)	22 $K := $ Decaps(sk, e)
04 $\quad$ $(e, K) \leftarrow$ Encaps(pk)	12 for $i \in [S]$	23 return K
05 $\quad$ $\mathbf{e}[i] := e, \mathbf{K}_0[i] := K$	13 $\quad$ $(e, K) \leftarrow$ Encaps(pk$_j$)	Oracle $\mathrm{DEC}_{\mathsf{mu}}(j, e)$
06 $\quad$ $\mathbf{K}_1[i] \xleftarrow{\$} \mathcal{K}$	14 $\quad$ $\mathbf{e}[j, i] := e$	24 if $e \in \mathbf{e}[j, \cdot]$
07 $b' \leftarrow \mathcal{A}^{\mathrm{DEC}}(\mathsf{par}, \mathbf{pk}, \mathbf{e}, \mathbf{K}_b)$	15 $\quad$ $\mathbf{K}_0[j, i] := K$	25 $\quad$ return $\perp$
08 return b'	16 $\quad$ $\mathbf{K}_1[j, i] \xleftarrow{\$} \mathcal{K}$	26 $K := $ Decaps(sk$_j$, e)
	17 $\quad$ pk$[j] := $ pk$_j$	27 return K
	18 $b' \leftarrow \mathcal{A}^{\mathrm{DEC}_{\mathsf{mu}}}(\mathsf{par}, \mathbf{pk}, \mathbf{e}, \mathbf{K}_b)$	
	19 return b'	

Fig. 4. Games MC-IND-CCA$^{\mathcal{A}}_{\mathsf{KEM},b}$ and MUC-IND-CCA$^{\mathcal{A}}_{\mathsf{KEM},b}$ for a KEM KEM = (Setup, KGen, Encaps, Decaps). In $\mathrm{DEC}_{\mathsf{mu}}$, $\mathbf{e}[j, \cdot]$ is the list $(\mathbf{e}[j, 1], ..., \mathbf{e}[j, S])$.

$$\mathsf{Adv}^{\mathsf{MC\text{-}IND\text{-}CCA}}_{\mathsf{KEM}}(\mathcal{A}) := | \Pr[\mathsf{MC\text{-}IND\text{-}CCA}^{\mathcal{A}}_{\mathsf{KEM},0}(\lambda) \Rightarrow 1]$$
$$- \Pr[\mathsf{MC\text{-}IND\text{-}CCA}^{\mathcal{A}}_{\mathsf{KEM},1}(\lambda) \Rightarrow 1]|$$

is negligible in λ, where games MC-IND-CCA$^{\mathcal{A}}_{\mathsf{KEM},b}(\lambda)$ for $b \in \{0, 1\}$ are specified in Fig. 4.

Definition 7 (MUC-IND-CCA Security of KEM). Let KEM = (Setup, KGen, Encaps, Decaps) be a KEM. We say that KEM is MUC-IND-CCA secure, if for any algorithm $\mathcal{A}$, the advantage

$$\mathsf{Adv}^{\mathsf{MUC\text{-}IND\text{-}CCA}}_{\mathsf{KEM}}(\mathcal{A}) := | \Pr[\mathsf{MUC\text{-}IND\text{-}CCA}^{\mathcal{A}}_{\mathsf{KEM},0}(\lambda) \Rightarrow 1]$$
$$- \Pr[\mathsf{MUC\text{-}IND\text{-}CCA}^{\mathcal{A}}_{\mathsf{KEM},1}(\lambda) \Rightarrow 1]|$$

is negligible in λ, where games MUC-IND-CCA$^{\mathcal{A}}_{\mathsf{KEM},b}(\lambda)$ for $b \in \{0, 1\}$ are specified in Fig. 4.

4.1 MC-IND-CCA Secure KEM from Lossy Encryption

Let PKE = (Setup, KG, Enc, Dec) be a lossy encryption scheme with message space $\mathcal{M}'$, randomness space $\mathcal{R}'$, and ciphertext space $\mathcal{C}'$. Let s be an integer and $\mathcal{K}$ be a key space. Let H: $\mathcal{M}' \times \mathcal{C}' \to \mathcal{K}$, H': $\{0,1\}^s \times \mathcal{C}' \to \{0,1\}^s$, and G: $\mathcal{M}' \to \mathcal{R}'$ be random oracles. Our KEM scheme KEM$_1$ with KEM key space $\mathcal{K}$ is shown in Fig. 5.

KEM$_1$ has the same structure as the modular Fujisaki-Okamoto transformation FO$^{\perp}$[PKE, G, H] from [19, 21], but its underlying PKE is a lossy encryption scheme. Theorem 1 shows that, if PKE is a lossy encryption, then KEM$_1$ is a tightly IND-CCA secure KEM in the multi-challenge setting (Definition 6) in the QROM.

Theorem 1. Let S be the number of challenge ciphertexts. If PKE is $\alpha \cdot (1 - \delta)$-correct lossy encryption (Definition 4) with lossiness $\epsilon^{\mathsf{lo}}_{\mathsf{PKE}}$ and H', G, and H are

KGen$_1$(par)	Encaps$_1$(pk)	Decaps$_1$((sk, k), e)
01 (pk, sk) $\leftarrow$ KG(par)	06 $r \xleftarrow{\$} \mathcal{M}', R := G(r)$	10 $r' := \text{Dec}(\text{sk}, e)$
02 $k \xleftarrow{\$} \mathcal{M}'$	07 $e := \text{Enc}(\text{pk}, r; R)$	11 **if** $r' = \perp \vee e \neq \text{Enc}(\text{pk}, r'; G(r'))$
03 pk$'$:= pk	08 $K := \text{H}(r, e)$	12 $K := \text{H}'(k, e)$
04 sk$'$:= (sk, k)	09 **return** (e, K)	13 **else** $K := \text{H}(r', e)$
05 **return** (pk$'$, sk$'$)		14 **return** K

Fig. 5. The KEM scheme KEM$_1$ = (Setup := Setup, KGen$_1$, Encaps$_1$, Decaps$_1$) based on a lossy encryption scheme PKE = (Setup, KG, Enc, Dec), where par $\leftarrow$ Setup(λ). KEM$_1$ has implicit rejection property, namely, the decryption algorithm returns a pseudorandom KEM key if the input ciphertext is invalid.

modeled as quantum random oracles, then for any quantum adversary $\mathcal{A}$, there exists an adversary $\mathcal{B}$ such that the running time of $\mathcal{A}$ is about that of $\mathcal{B}$ and

$$\text{Adv}_{\text{KEM}_1}^{\text{MC-IND-CCA}}(\mathcal{A}) \leq 4\text{Adv}_{\text{PKE}}^{\text{ind-key}}(\mathcal{B}) + S^2 \left(\frac{1}{|\mathcal{M}'|} + \frac{1}{|\mathcal{K}|} + \frac{1}{2^s} \right)$$

$$+ \frac{S + S^2}{|\mathcal{R}'|} + 48(1 + (q_{\text{H}} + q_{\text{G}} + 2q_{\text{DEC}} + S)^2)\delta$$

$$+ 4(q_{\text{G}} + q_{\text{H}}) \sqrt{S \cdot \epsilon_{\text{PKE}}^{\text{lo}} + \frac{S}{|\mathcal{M}'|}} + 4q_{\text{H}'} \cdot 2^{-s/2},$$

where $q_{\text{H}'}, q_{\text{G}}, q_{\text{H}}$, and q_{DEC} are the numbers of $\mathcal{A}$'s queries to $\text{H}', \text{G}, \text{H}$, and DEC, respectively.

The proof of Theorem 1 is the almost identical to the one of Theorem 2, except that Theorem 1 deals with only one user and uses the key indistinguishability of lossy encryption (cf. Definition 4) instead of the parameter-key indistinguishability. By letting $N := 1$ in the proof of Theorem 2, all arguments can be adapted to the proof of Theorem 1. Thus, we refer the reader to the proof of Theorem 2.

4.2 MUC-IND-CCA Secure KEM from Parameter Lossy Encryption

Let PKE = (Setup, KG, Enc, Dec) be a parameter lossy encryption scheme with public key space $\mathcal{PK}'$, message space $\mathcal{M}'$, randomness space $\mathcal{R}'$, and ciphertext space $\mathcal{C}'$. Let s be an integer and $\mathcal{K}$ be a key space. Let $\text{H}: \mathcal{PK}' \times \mathcal{M}' \times \mathcal{C}' \to \mathcal{K}$, $\text{H}': \mathcal{PK}' \times \{0,1\}^s \times \mathcal{C}' \to \{0,1\}^s$, and $\text{G}: \mathcal{PK}' \times \mathcal{M}' \to \mathcal{R}'$ be random oracles. Fix par $\leftarrow$ Setup(λ) and our KEM scheme KEM$_2$ with KEM key space $\mathcal{K}$ is defined as in Fig. 6.

KEM$_2$ has two differences compared to the modular Fujisaki-Okamoto transformation FO$^{\perp}$[PKE, G, H] from [19, 21]. The first one is that we include a user public key into the hash function. We suppose that this change is necessary for tightness in the multi-user setting. The second difference is that our security requirement on the underlying PKE is parameter lossy. More precisely, we show in Theorem 2 that, if PKE is a parameter lossy encryption, then KEM$_2$ is a tightly IND-CCA secure KEM in the multi-user and multi-challenge setting (Definition 7) in the QROM.

KGen₂(par)	Encaps₂(pk)	Decaps₂((sk, k), e)
01 (pk, sk) ← KG(par)	06 $r \overset{\$}{\leftarrow} \mathcal{M}'$	11 $r' := $ Dec(sk, e)
02 $k \overset{\$}{\leftarrow} \{0, 1\}^s$	07 $R := $ G(pk, r)	12 if $r' = \perp$
03 pk' := pk	08 $e := $ Enc(pk, r; R)	13 $\vee e \neq$ Enc(pk, r'; G(pk, r'))
04 sk' := (sk, k)	09 $K := $ H(pk, r, e)	14 $K := $ H'(pk, k, e)
05 return (pk', sk')	10 return (e, K)	15 else $K := $ H(pk, r', e)
		16 return K

Fig. 6. KEM scheme $\mathsf{KEM_2} = (\mathsf{Setup}, \mathsf{KGen_2}, \mathsf{Encaps_2}, \mathsf{Decaps_2})$ based on a parameter lossy encryption $\mathsf{PKE} = (\mathsf{Setup}, \mathsf{KG}, \mathsf{Enc}, \mathsf{Dec})$, where par ← Setup(λ). $\mathsf{KEM_2}$ has implicit rejection property, namely, the decryption algorithm returns a pseudorandom KEM key if the input ciphertext is invalid.

Theorem 2. *Let N be the number of users and let S be the number of challenge ciphertexts. If PKE is a $(1 - \delta)$-correct parameter lossy encryption (Definition 5) with lossiness $\epsilon^{\mathsf{lo}}_{\mathsf{PKE}}$ and $\mathsf{H'}, \mathsf{G}$, and H are modeled as quantum random oracles, then for any quantum adversary $\mathcal{A}$, there exists an adversary $\mathcal{B}$ such that the running time of $\mathcal{A}$ is about that of $\mathcal{B}$ and*

$$\mathsf{Adv}^{\mathsf{MUC\text{-}IND\text{-}CCA}}_{\mathsf{KEM_2}}(\mathcal{A}) \leq 4\mathsf{Adv}^{\mathsf{ind\text{-}par\text{-}key}}_{\mathsf{PKE}}(\mathcal{B}) + 48N(1 + (q_\mathsf{H} + q_\mathsf{G} + 2q_{\mathsf{DEC}} + S)^2)\delta$$

$$+ \frac{NS + N^2S^2}{|\mathcal{R}'|} + N^2S^2 \left(\frac{1}{|\mathcal{M}'|} + \frac{1}{|\mathcal{K}|} + \frac{1}{2^s} + \eta_{\mathsf{PKE}} \right)$$

$$+ 4(q_\mathsf{G} + q_\mathsf{H})\sqrt{NS \cdot \epsilon^{\mathsf{lo}}_{\mathsf{PKE}} + \frac{NS}{|\mathcal{M}'|}} + 4Nq_{\mathsf{H'}} \cdot 2^{-s/2},$$

where $q_{\mathsf{H'}}, q_\mathsf{G}, q_\mathsf{H}$, and q_{DEC} are the numbers of $\mathcal{A}$'s queries to $\mathsf{H'}, \mathsf{G}, \mathsf{H}$, and $\mathsf{DEC}_{\mathsf{mu}}$, respectively. η_{PKE} is the collision probability of KG (Definition 3).

Proof (Theorem 2). We prove the theorem via a sequence of games, formally given in Fig. 7. Following [19, 21, 34], we assume that the game has access to some internal quantum random oracles (QROs) which are used to simulate the QROs accessed by the adversary. Namely, let $\mathsf{h'}, \mathsf{h'}_{\mathsf{pk_1}}, \ldots, \mathsf{h'}_{\mathsf{pk_N}} : \mathcal{C}' \to \mathcal{K}$ be internal QROs used to simulate $\mathsf{H'}, \mathsf{h}, \mathsf{h}_{\mathsf{pk_1}}, \ldots, \mathsf{h}_{\mathsf{pk_N}} : \mathcal{C}' \to \mathcal{K}$ be internal QROs used to simulate H, and $\mathsf{g}, \mathsf{g'}_{\mathsf{pk_1}}, \ldots, \mathsf{g'}_{\mathsf{pk_N}} : \mathcal{M}' \to \mathcal{R}'$ be internal QROs used to simulate G. Such internal QROs can be simulated be several ways [34], e.g., using $2q$-wise independent hash function (if the adversary queries the QRO at most q times) [37]. For sake of simplicity, during all our security games, we implicitly exclude collisions of users' public keys pk_i's and secret keys k_i's for implicit rejection and the collisions of the PKE messages $r_{j,i}$'s, randomnesses $R_{j,i}$'s, and KEM keys $K_{j,i}$. Excluding such collisions will add

$$N^2S^2 \left(\frac{1}{|\mathcal{M}'|} + \frac{1}{|\mathcal{K}|} + \frac{1}{|\mathcal{R}'|} + \frac{1}{2^s} + \eta_{\mathsf{PKE}} \right)$$

to the final bound. In $\mathbf{G_0}$, we use $\mathsf{g}, \mathsf{h'}$, and h to simulate $\mathsf{G}, \mathsf{H'}, \mathsf{H}$, respectively. This game is equivalent to $\mathsf{MUC\text{-}IND\text{-}CCA}^{\mathcal{A}}_{\mathsf{KEM_2}, 0}$ game (Definition 7), so we have

$$\Pr \left[\mathsf{MUC\text{-}IND\text{-}CCA}^{\mathcal{A}}_{\mathsf{KEM_2}, 0} \Rightarrow 1 \right] = \Pr \left[\mathbf{G}^{\mathcal{A}}_0 \Rightarrow 1 \right].$$

Game G_0-G_9		Oracle $\mathrm{DEC}_{mu}(j,e)$	
01 $\mathsf{par} \leftarrow \mathsf{Setup}(\lambda)$		20 if $e \in \mathbf{e}[j,\cdot]$	
02 $\mathsf{par} := \mathsf{lpar} \leftarrow \mathsf{LSetup}(\lambda)$	$/\!/ \, G_6\text{-}G_9$	21 return $\perp$	
03 for $j \in [N]$		22 $r' := \mathsf{Dec}(\mathsf{sk}_j, e)$	
04 $(\mathsf{pk}_j, (\mathsf{sk}_j, k_j)) \leftarrow \mathsf{KG}(\mathsf{par})$		23 if $r' = \perp \vee c \neq \mathsf{Enc}(\mathsf{pk}_j, r'; G(\mathsf{pk}_j, r'))$	
05 $(\mathsf{lpk}_j, \mathsf{lsk}_j) \leftarrow \mathsf{LKG}(\mathsf{par})$	$/\!/ \, G_6\text{-}G_7$	24 $K := \mathsf{H}'(\mathsf{pk}_j, k_j, e)$	
06 $(\mathsf{pk}_j, \mathsf{sk}_j) := (\mathsf{lpk}_j, \mathsf{lsk}_j)$	$/\!/ \, G_6\text{-}G_7$	25 $K := \mathsf{h}'_{\mathsf{pk}_j}(e)$	$/\!/ \, G_1\text{-}G_2$
07 for $i \in [S]$		26 else	
08 $r_{j,i} \xleftarrow{\$} \mathcal{M}'$		27 $K := \mathsf{H}(\mathsf{pk}_j, r', e)$	
09 $R_{j,i} := G(\mathsf{pk}_j, r_{j,i})$		28 $K := \mathsf{h}_{\mathsf{pk}_j}(e)$	$/\!/ \, G_3$
10 $R_{j,i} \xleftarrow{\$} \mathcal{R}'$	$/\!/ \, G_7\text{-}G_9$	29 $K := \mathsf{h}_{\mathsf{pk}_j}(e)$	$/\!/ \, G_4\text{-}G_9$
11 $e := \mathsf{Enc}(\mathsf{pk}_j, r_{j,i}; R_{j,i})$		30 return K	
12 $K_{j,i} := \mathsf{H}(\mathsf{pk}_j, r_{j,i}, e)$			
13 $K_{j,i} := \mathsf{h}_{\mathsf{pk}_j}(e)$	$/\!/ \, G_3\text{-}G_9$	Oracle $G(\mathsf{pk}, r)$	
14 $K_{j,i} \xleftarrow{\$} \mathcal{K}$	$/\!/ \, G_9$	31 if $\mathsf{pk} \in \mathbf{pk}$	$/\!/ \, G_2\text{-}G_4, \, G_8\text{-}G_9$
15 $\mathbf{e}[j,i] := e, \mathbf{K}[j,i] := K_{j,i}$		32 return $g'_{\mathsf{pk}}(r)$	$/\!/ \, G_2\text{-}G_4, \, G_8\text{-}G_9$
16 $\mathbf{pk}[j] := \mathsf{pk}_j$		33 return $g(\mathsf{pk}, r)$	
17 $b' \leftarrow \mathcal{A}^{\mathrm{DEC}_{mu}, |\mathrm{H}\rangle, |\mathrm{H}'\rangle, |\mathrm{G}\rangle}(\mathsf{par}, \mathbf{pk}, \mathbf{e}, \mathbf{K})$			
18 return b'		Oracle $\mathsf{H}(\mathsf{pk}, r, e)$	
		34 if $\mathsf{pk} \in \mathbf{pk}$	$/\!/ \, G_3\text{-}G_9$
Oracle $\mathsf{H}'(\mathsf{pk}, k, e)$		35 $\wedge e = \mathsf{Enc}(\mathsf{pk}, r; G(\mathsf{pk}, r))$	$/\!/ \, G_3\text{-}G_9$
19 return $\mathsf{h}'(\mathsf{pk}, k, e)$		36 return $\mathsf{h}_{\mathsf{pk}}(e)$	$/\!/ \, G_3\text{-}G_9$
		37 return $\mathsf{h}(\mathsf{pk}, r, e)$	

Fig. 7. Games sequence G_0-G_9 in the proof of Theorem 2. Highlighted lines are only executed in the corresponding games.

G_1: If $\mathcal{A}$ queries DEC_{mu} on (j, e) that e is invalid, then DEC_{mu} returns $\mathsf{h}'_{\mathsf{pk}_j}(e)$ instead of $\mathsf{H}'(\mathsf{pk}_j, k_j, e)$. We use Lemma 2 to bound the difference. Concretely, we apply Lemma 2 for any user $j \in [N]$, by viewing $\mathsf{H}'(\mathsf{pk}_j, \cdot)$ as oracle h in Lemma 2, and $\mathsf{h}'_{\mathsf{pk}_j}$ as oracle h' in Lemma 2. Thus, we have

$$\left| \Pr\left[G_0^{\mathcal{A}} \Rightarrow 1 \right] - \Pr\left[G_1^{\mathcal{A}} \Rightarrow 1 \right] \right| \leq 2Nq_{\mathsf{H}'} \cdot 2^{-s/2}.$$

G_2: The image set of $G(\mathsf{pk}_j, \cdot)$ is restricted to be the set only containing "good" randomnesses of pk_j. Namely, for $j \in [N]$, we define the set

$$\mathcal{R}'_{\mathsf{bad}}(\mathsf{pk}_j, \mathsf{sk}_j, r) := \{ R' \in \mathcal{R}' \mid \mathsf{Dec}(\mathsf{sk}, \mathsf{Enc}(\mathsf{pk}, r; R')) \neq r \}$$

which denotes the "bad" randomness with respect to $(\mathsf{pk}_j, \mathsf{sk}_j)$ and r. And we similarly define the "good" randomness set as $\mathcal{R}'_{\mathsf{good}}(\mathsf{pk}_j, \mathsf{sk}_j, r) := \mathcal{R}' \backslash \mathcal{R}'_{\mathsf{bad}}(\mathsf{pk}_j, \mathsf{sk}_j, r)$. and let $g'_{\mathsf{pk}_j} : \mathcal{M}' \to \mathcal{R}'$ be a quantum-accessible random oracle such that for any $r \in \mathcal{M}'$, $g'_{\mathsf{pk}_j}(r)$ is sampled uniformly from $\mathcal{R}'_{\mathsf{good}}(\mathsf{pk}_j, \mathsf{sk}_j, r)$.

We use Lemma 3 to bound the probability difference between G_1 and G_2. The proof method here is similar to the one in [19, Theorem 2]. We define

$$\delta(\mathsf{pk}_j, \mathsf{sk}_j, r) := |\mathcal{R}'_{\mathsf{bad}}(\mathsf{pk}_j, \mathsf{sk}_j, r)|/|\mathcal{R}'|,$$

$$\delta(\mathsf{pk}_j, \mathsf{sk}_j) := \max_{r \in \mathcal{M}'} \delta(\mathsf{pk}_j, \mathsf{sk}_j, r),$$

and by these notations, if PKE is $(1-\delta)$-correct, then $\delta = \mathbb{E}[\delta(\mathsf{pk}_j, \mathsf{sk}_j)]$ where the expectation is taken over $(\mathsf{pk}, \mathsf{sk}) \leftarrow \mathsf{KG}$.

Here we construct unbounded adversaries $\mathcal{B}_j$ for $1 \le j \le N$ that run in game $\mathsf{GDPB}_{\delta,b}$ ($b = 0$ or $b = 1$). For any such j, $\mathcal{B}_j$ first generates $(\mathsf{pk}_i, \mathsf{sk}_i, k_i)$ for $i \in [N]$ as in $\mathbf{G}_1$ and picks a random function f (domain and range will be clear later), and then it sets $\lambda_r := \delta(\mathsf{pk}_j, \mathsf{sk}_j, r)$ for all $r \in \mathcal{M}'$ and outputs $(\lambda_r)_{r \in \mathcal{M}'}$.

Then, $\mathcal{B}_j$ has quantum access to a function F (provided by $\mathsf{GDPB}_{\delta,b}$). It sets up the oracle $\mathsf{G}(\mathsf{pk}, \cdot)$ such that

$$\mathsf{G}'(\mathsf{pk}, r) = \begin{cases} \mathsf{Samp}(\mathcal{R}'_{\mathsf{good}}(\mathsf{pk}, \mathsf{sk}, r); f(\mathsf{pk}, r)) & \text{if } \mathsf{pk} \in \{\mathsf{pk}_1, ..., \mathsf{pk}_{j-1}\}, \\ \mathsf{Samp}(\mathcal{R}'_{\mathsf{good}}(\mathsf{pk}_j, \mathsf{sk}_j, r); f(\mathsf{pk}_j, r)), & \text{if } \mathsf{pk} = \mathsf{pk}_j \wedge \mathsf{F}(r) = 0 \\ \mathsf{Samp}(\mathcal{R}'_{\mathsf{bad}}(\mathsf{pk}_j, \mathsf{sk}_j, r); f(\mathsf{pk}_j, r)), & \text{if } \mathsf{pk} = \mathsf{pk}_j \wedge \mathsf{F}(r) = 1 \\ g(\mathsf{pk}, r), & \text{Otherwise} \end{cases},$$

and uses such G' to simulate $\mathbf{G}_1$ for $\mathcal{A}$ (namely, it replaces $\mathsf{G}(\mathsf{pk}_j, \cdot)$ by $\mathsf{G}'(\mathsf{pk}_j, \cdot)$, and other oracles like H and DEC are the same as in $\mathbf{G}_1$) and outputs $\mathcal{A}$'s final output. Here Samp is a sampling process and f is used to generate randomness for Samp (so that it can sample elements from a set uniformly at random). Since $\mathcal{B}_j$ is unbounded, it can construct such f and Samp.

If $\mathcal{B}_j$ is playing $\mathsf{GDPB}_{\delta,0}$, then $\mathsf{F}(r)$ always outputs 0, and then $\mathsf{G}'(\mathsf{pk}_j, r) = g'_{\mathsf{pk}_j}(r)$ in $\mathbf{G}_2$. If $\mathcal{B}_j$ is playing $\mathsf{GDPB}_{\delta,1}$, then $\mathsf{F}(r)$ outputs 1 with probability $\delta(\mathsf{pk}_j, \mathsf{sk}_j, r)$ and then $\mathsf{G}'(\mathsf{pk}_j, r)$ is distributed identically with $\mathsf{G}(\mathsf{pk}_j, r)$ (and $g(\mathsf{pk}_j, r)$) in $\mathbf{G}_1$.

We further let Hyb_j for $0 \le j \le N$ be a hybrid game which is almost the same as $\mathbf{G}_1$ except that, for users $j + 1$ to N, we use $g'_{\mathsf{pk}_{j+1}}, ..., g'_{\mathsf{pk}_N}$ to simulate $\mathsf{G}(\mathsf{pk}_{j+1}, \cdot), ..., \mathsf{G}(\mathsf{pk}_N, \cdot)$, respectively. By definition, $\mathsf{Hyb}_0 = \mathbf{G}_2$ and $\mathsf{Hyb}_N = \mathbf{G}_1$. By the construction of $\mathcal{B}_j$, if $\mathcal{B}_j$ plays $\mathsf{GDPB}_{\delta,1}$, then it simulates Hyb_{j-1} for $\mathcal{A}$. If $\mathcal{B}_j$ plays $\mathsf{GDPB}_{\delta,0}$, then it simulates Hyb_j for $\mathcal{A}$. We can use $\mathcal{B}_j$ for each $j \in [N]$ described above to bound the probabilities difference between Hyb_{j-1} and Hyb_j. Namely, using Lemma 3, we have

$$|\Pr[\mathbf{G}_1^{\mathcal{A}} \Rightarrow 1] - \Pr[\mathbf{G}_2^{\mathcal{A}} \Rightarrow 1]| \le |\Pr[\mathsf{Hyb}_N^{\mathcal{A}} \Rightarrow 1] - \Pr[\mathsf{Hyb}_0^{\mathcal{A}} \Rightarrow 1]|$$

$$\le \sum_{j=1}^N |\Pr[\mathsf{Hyb}_j^{\mathcal{A}} \Rightarrow 1] - \Pr[\mathsf{Hyb}_{j-1}^{\mathcal{A}} \Rightarrow 1]|$$

$$\le \sum_{j=1}^N \left|\Pr[\mathsf{GDPB}_{\delta,0}^{\mathcal{B}_j} \Rightarrow 1] - \Pr[\mathsf{GDPB}_{\delta,1}^{\mathcal{B}_j} \Rightarrow 1]\right|$$

$$\le N \cdot (\delta + 8(q_{\mathsf{H}} + q_{\mathsf{G}} + 2q_{\mathrm{DEC}} + S)^2 \delta)$$

$$= 8N(1 + (q_{\mathsf{H}} + q_{\mathsf{G}} + 2q_{\mathrm{DEC}} + S)^2)\delta$$

by Lemma 3 and $\mathcal{B}_j$ issuing $(q_{\mathsf{H}} + q_{\mathsf{G}} + 2q_{\mathrm{DEC}} + S)$ queries to F. The additional δ appears in the next to last equation is from the probability that a bad key pair with no good randomness [28,35]. For simplicity, we add the error bound δ here and exclude the event that KG outputs such bad key pair.

$\mathbf{G_3}$: In this game, we start to get rid of the secret key by using the "encrypt-then-hash" technique [19,21,34]. When $\mathcal{A}$ queries $\mathsf{H}(\mathsf{pk}, r, e)$ where $\mathsf{pk} = \mathsf{pk}_j$ for some $j \in [N]$ and $e = \mathsf{Enc}(\mathsf{pk}_j, r; \mathsf{G}(\mathsf{pk}_j, r))$, instead of returning $\mathsf{h}(\mathsf{pk}, r, e)$, the game returns $\mathsf{h}_{\mathsf{pk}_j}(e)$ (see Items. 34 to 36). For consistency, we also change the generation of challenge KEM keys (in Item 13) and $\mathrm{DEC}_{\mathsf{mu}}$ (in Item 28), since if $e = \mathsf{Enc}(\mathsf{pk}_j, r; \mathsf{G}(\mathsf{pk}_j, r))$ then $\mathsf{H}(\mathsf{pk}_j, r, e) = \mathsf{h}_{\mathsf{pk}_j}(e)$.

We claim that $\mathcal{A}$'s views in $\mathbf{G_2}$ and $\mathbf{G_3}$ are the same. This is because, starting from $\mathbf{G_2}$, $\mathsf{G}(\mathsf{pk}_j, \cdot)$ always uses "good" randomness, which implies that the map $\mathsf{Enc}(\mathsf{pk}_j, \cdot; \mathsf{G}(\mathsf{pk}_j, \cdot))$ is injective and thus $\mathsf{H}(\mathsf{pk}_j, \cdot, \mathsf{Enc}(\mathsf{pk}_j, \cdot; \mathsf{G}(\mathsf{pk}_j, \cdot)))$ behaves as a random oracle. We have

$$\Pr\left[\mathbf{G}_2^{\mathcal{A}} \Rightarrow 1\right] = \Pr\left[\mathbf{G}_3^{\mathcal{A}} \Rightarrow 1\right].$$

$\mathbf{G_4}$: We change $\mathrm{DEC}_{\mathsf{mu}}$ such that, on query (j, e), it always returns $\mathsf{h}_{\mathsf{pk}_j}(e)$ regardless of the validity of e (Item 29). We argue that this change does not affect $\mathcal{A}$'s view: On query (j, e), if e is a valid ciphertext with respect to pk_j, then $\mathrm{DEC}_{\mathsf{mu}}$ returns $\mathsf{h}_{\mathsf{pk}_j}(e)$ in both two games; If e is invalid (its decryption is $\perp$ or it cannot pass the re-encryption checking), then in $\mathbf{G_3}$, DEC returns $\mathsf{h}'_{\mathsf{pk}_j}(e)$, which is an independently random key ($\mathsf{h}'_{\mathsf{pk}_j}$ is an internal RO). Moreover, if e is invalid, $\mathsf{h}_{\mathsf{pk}_j}(e)$ is also independently random by the definition of H ($\mathcal{A}$ cannot learn $\mathsf{h}_{\mathsf{pk}_j}(e)$ from H when e is invalid). Therefore, when e is invalid with respect to pk_j, $\mathsf{h}_{\mathsf{pk}_j}(e)$ has the same distribution with $\mathsf{h}'_{\mathsf{pk}_j}(e)$, which means that the modification made by $\mathbf{G_4}$ does not change $\mathcal{A}$'s view. We have

$$\Pr\left[\mathbf{G}_3^{\mathcal{A}} \Rightarrow 1\right] = \Pr\left[\mathbf{G}_4^{\mathcal{A}} \Rightarrow 1\right].$$

$\mathbf{G_5}$: We switch back to using g to simulate G instead of using $(\mathsf{g}'_{\mathsf{pk}_1}, ..., \mathsf{g}'_{\mathsf{pk}_N})$. Similar to the gamehop from $\mathbf{G_1}$ to $\mathbf{G_2}$, we have

$$\left|\Pr\left[\mathbf{G}_4^{\mathcal{A}} \Rightarrow 1\right] - \Pr\left[\mathbf{G}_5^{\mathcal{A}} \Rightarrow 1\right]\right| \leq 8N(1 + (q_{\mathsf{H}} + q_{\mathsf{G}} + 2q_{\mathrm{DEC}} + S)^2)\delta.$$

Observe that in $\mathbf{G_5}$, we do not need to use sk_j to simulate $\mathrm{DEC}_{\mathsf{mu}}(j, \cdot)$ (where $j \in [N]$). From $\mathbf{G_6}$ to $\mathbf{G_8}$, we start to use the properties of parameter lossy encryption PKE to finish the proof.

$\mathbf{G_6}$: We switch the parameter and public keys of PKE to the lossy mode, namely, the parameter par in $\mathbf{G_6}$ is generated by LSetup (Item 02) and the public keys in $\mathbf{G_6}$ are generated by LKG (Items 05 to 06).

We construct a reduction $\mathcal{B}$ against the parameter-key indistinguishability of PKE in Fig. 8. $\mathcal{B}$'s input $(\mathsf{par}, \mathsf{pk}_1, ..., \mathsf{pk}_N)$ is from Setup and KG, then $\mathcal{B}$ perfectly simulates $\mathbf{G_5}$ for $\mathcal{A}$. If $(\mathsf{par}, \mathsf{pk}_1, ..., \mathsf{pk}_N)$ is from LSetup and LKG, then $\mathcal{B}$ perfectly simulates $\mathbf{G_6}$ for $\mathcal{A}$. Moreover, $\mathcal{B}$ outputs $\mathcal{A}$'s final output. So, we have

$$\left|\Pr\left[\mathbf{G}_5^{\mathcal{A}} \Rightarrow 1\right] - \Pr\left[\mathbf{G}_6^{\mathcal{A}} \Rightarrow 1\right]\right| \leq \mathsf{Adv}_{\mathsf{PKE}}^{\mathsf{ind\text{-}par\text{-}key}}(\mathcal{B}).$$

Reduction $\mathcal{B}(\mathsf{par}, \mathsf{pk}_1, ..., \mathsf{pk}_N)$	Oracle $\mathrm{DEC}_{\mathsf{mu}}(j, e)$
01 **for** $j \in [N]$	13 **if** $e \in \mathbf{e}$: **return** $\perp$
02 $\quad k_j \leftarrow \{0,1\}^s$	14 **return** $K := h_{\mathsf{pk}_j}(e)$
03 $\quad$ **for** $i \in [S]$	
04 $\qquad r_{j,i} \xleftarrow{\$} \mathcal{M}'$	Oracle $\mathsf{G}(\mathsf{pk}, r)$
05 $\qquad R_{j,i} := \mathsf{G}(\mathsf{pk}_j, r_{j,i})$	15 **return** $\mathsf{g}(\mathsf{pk}, r)$
06 $\qquad e := \mathsf{Enc}(\mathsf{pk}_j, r_{j,i}; R_{j,i})$	Oracle $\mathsf{H}(\mathsf{pk}, r, e)$
07 $\qquad K := h_{\mathsf{pk}_j}(e)$	16 **if** $\mathsf{pk} \in \mathbf{pk} \wedge e = \mathsf{Enc}(\mathsf{pk}, r; \mathsf{G}(\mathsf{pk}, r))$
08 $\qquad \mathbf{e}[j, i] := e$	17 $\quad$ **return** $h_{\mathsf{pk}}(e)$
09 $\qquad \mathbf{K}[j, i] := K$	18 **return** $h(\mathsf{pk}, r, e)$
10 $\quad \mathbf{pk}[j] := \mathsf{pk}_j$	
11 $b' \leftarrow \mathcal{A}^{\mathrm{DEC}_{\mathsf{mu}}, |\mathsf{H}\rangle, |\mathsf{H}'\rangle, |\mathsf{G}\rangle}(\mathsf{par}, \mathbf{pk}, \mathbf{e}, \mathbf{K})$	Oracle $\mathsf{H}'(\mathsf{pk}, k, e)$
12 **return** b'	19 **return** $h'(\mathsf{pk}, k, e)$

Fig. 8. Adversary $\mathcal{B}$ in bounding $\mathbf{G}_5$ and $\mathbf{G}_6$.

$\mathbf{G}_7$: The randomness $R_{j,i}$ of challenge ciphertext $\mathbf{e}[j, i]$ is generated by independently uniform sampling from $\mathcal{R}'$ instead of by using G (see Item 10).

In $\mathbf{G}_6$, we always have $R_{j,i} = \mathsf{G}(\mathsf{pk}_j, r_{j,i})$ for all $(j, i) \in [N] \times [S]$, while in $\mathbf{G}_7$, $R_{j,i}$'s are independent of G. Despite these $r_{j,i}$'s and $R_{j,i}$'s, oracle G behaves the same in $\mathbf{G}_6$ and $\mathbf{G}_7$. Let $\mathcal{O}_0$ be the oracle G in $\mathbf{G}_6$ and let $\mathcal{O}_1$ be the oracle G in $\mathbf{G}_7$, then we have $\mathcal{O}_0 \backslash \mathcal{S} = \mathcal{O}_1 \backslash \mathcal{S}$, where $\mathcal{S}$ is defined as follows:

$$\mathcal{S} := \{(\mathsf{pk}_1, r_{1,1}), (\mathsf{pk}_1, r_{1,2}), ..., (\mathsf{pk}_j, r_{j,i}), ..., (\mathsf{pk}_N, r_{N,S})\}, \text{ and } |\mathcal{S}| = NS$$

We use Lemma 1 to bound the difference between $\mathbf{G}_6$ with $\mathbf{G}_7$. By this lemma, there is an algorithm EXT captures the probability that $\mathcal{A}$ "learns" $r_{j,i} \in \mathcal{S}$. However, this probability cannot be directly bounded since $e_{j,i}$ is still related to $r_{j,i}$. To deal with it, we use delayed analysis. Looking ahead, we will firstly switch all challenge ciphertexts to other challenge ciphertexts that are independent of $r_{j,i}$'s (by using the lossiness of PKE) so that $r_{j,i}$'s are independently and uniformly random in $\mathcal{A}$'s view, so we can bound the winning probability of EXT and thus can bound $|\Pr[\mathbf{G}_6^{\mathcal{A}} \Rightarrow 1] - \Pr[\mathbf{G}_7^{\mathcal{A}} \Rightarrow 1]|$. For readability, we continue the proof of Theorem 2 and leave these arguments as a lemma which will be proved later.

Lemma 14. *With notations and assumptions from* $\mathbf{G}_6$ *and* $\mathbf{G}_7$ *in the proof of Theorem 2, we have*

$$|\Pr[\mathbf{G}_6^{\mathcal{A}} \Rightarrow 1] - \Pr[\mathbf{G}_7^{\mathcal{A}} \Rightarrow 1]| \leq 2(q_\mathsf{G} + q_\mathsf{H} + NS)\sqrt{NS \cdot \epsilon_{\mathsf{PKE}}^{\mathsf{lo}}} + NS/|\mathcal{M}'|.$$

$\mathbf{G}_8$: We switch the parameter and public keys of PKE to the normal mode (namely, parameter and public keys are generated by Setup and KG). Moreover, we restrict the image of $\mathsf{G}(\mathsf{pk}_j, \cdot)$ to be the set only containing "good" randomnesses of pk_j (as we did in $\mathbf{G}_2$). Similar to the game hops from $\mathbf{G}_5$ to $\mathbf{G}_6$ and from $\mathbf{G}_1$ to $\mathbf{G}_2$, there exists an adversary $\mathcal{B}$ such that

$$|\Pr\left[\mathbf{G}_7^{\mathcal{A}} \Rightarrow 1\right] - \Pr\left[\mathbf{G}_8^{\mathcal{A}} \Rightarrow 1\right]|$$
$$\leq \mathsf{Adv}_{\mathsf{PKE}}^{\mathsf{ind\text{-}par\text{-}key}}(\mathcal{B}) + 8N(1 + (q_\mathsf{H} + q_\mathsf{G} + 2q_{\mathrm{DEC}} + S)^2)\delta.$$

$\mathbf{G}_9$: We change the generation of challenge KEM keys $K_{j,i}$'s. In this game, we generate $K_{j,i} \xleftarrow{\$} \mathcal{K}$ instead of $K_{j,i} := \mathsf{h}_{\mathsf{pk}_j}(e_{j,i})$ where $e_{j,i} = \mathbf{e}[j,i]$. Since $\mathsf{h}_{\mathsf{pk}_j}$'s are internal QROs, $\mathcal{A}$ cannot trivially detect this modification.

We claim that this modification does not change $\mathcal{A}$'s view except with negligible probability. Here we firstly analyze the information about $\mathsf{h}_{\mathsf{pk}_j}(e_{j,i})$ for $(j,i) \in [N] \times [S]$ that $\mathcal{A}$ can learn from its oracle queries.

- <u>Oracles G and H$'$</u>: These two oracles do not reveal any information about $\mathsf{h}_{\mathsf{pk}_j}(e_{j,i})$ since they are independent to each other in both $\mathbf{G}_7$ and $\mathbf{G}_8$.
- <u>Oracle DEC</u>: If $\mathcal{A}$ queries $\mathrm{DEC}_{\mathsf{mu}}(j, e_{j,i})$ for $(j,i) \in [N] \times [S]$, then by the definitions of $\mathrm{DEC}_{\mathsf{mu}}$ in $\mathbf{G}_7$ and $\mathbf{G}_8$, the oracle always returns $\perp$; Otherwise, $\mathrm{DEC}_{\mathsf{mu}}$ returns a key that is independent to $\mathsf{h}_{\mathsf{pk}_j}(e_{j,1}), ..., \mathsf{h}_{\mathsf{pk}_j}(e_{j,S})$ (since $\mathsf{h}_{\mathsf{pk}_j}$ is a QRO). So, DEC does not reveal any information about $\mathsf{h}_{\mathsf{pk}_j}(e_{j,i})$.
- <u>Oracle H</u>: $\mathcal{A}$ learns $\mathsf{h}_{\mathsf{pk}_j}(e_{j,i})$ if it queries $\mathsf{H}(\mathsf{pk}_j, r, e_{j,i})$ such that $e_{j,i} = \mathsf{Enc}(\mathsf{pk}_j, r; R)$ where $R = \mathsf{G}(\mathsf{pk}_j, r)$. Since in $\mathbf{G}_8$, we already restricted $\mathsf{G}(\mathsf{pk}_j, \cdot)$ to always output good randomess, $\mathsf{Enc}(\mathsf{pk}_j, \cdot; \mathsf{G}(\mathsf{pk}_j, \cdot))$ is injective and $e_{j,i} = \mathsf{Enc}(\mathsf{pk}_j, r; R)$ means that $(r, R) = (r_{j,i}, R_{j,i})$. Since $\mathsf{G}(\mathsf{pk}_j, \cdot)$ is random oracle and $R_{j,i}$ is sampled at uniformly random from $\mathcal{R}'$, we have

$$\Pr\left[R_{j,i} = \mathsf{G}(\mathsf{pk}_j, r_{j,i})\right] = 1/|\mathcal{R}'|.$$

Since there are NS randomnesses, by a union bound, we have

$$|\Pr\left[\mathbf{G}_8^{\mathcal{A}} \Rightarrow 1\right] - \Pr\left[\mathbf{G}_9^{\mathcal{A}} \Rightarrow 1\right]| \leq NS/|\mathcal{R}'|.$$

In $\mathbf{G}_9$, the KEM keys $K_{j,i}$'s are generated at independently and uniformly random. We can undo the modifications made in $\mathbf{G}_8, ..., \mathbf{G}_1$ to achieve the game $\mathsf{MUC\text{-}IND\text{-}CCA}_{\mathsf{KEM},1}^{\mathcal{A}}$. We have

$$|\Pr[\mathbf{G}_9^{\mathcal{A}} \Rightarrow 1] - \Pr[\mathsf{MUC\text{-}IND\text{-}CCA}_{\mathsf{KEM},1}^{\mathcal{A}} \Rightarrow 1]|$$
$$\leq 24N(1 + (q_\mathsf{H} + q_\mathsf{G} + 2q_{\mathrm{DEC}} + S)^2)\delta + 2Nq_{\mathsf{H}'} \cdot 2^{-s/2}$$
$$+ 2(q_\mathsf{G} + q_\mathsf{H} + NS)\sqrt{NS \cdot \epsilon_{\mathsf{PKE}}^{\mathsf{lo}} + NS/|\mathcal{M}'|} + 2\mathsf{Adv}_{\mathsf{PKE}}^{\mathsf{ind\text{-}par\text{-}key}}(\mathcal{B}).$$

Combining all the probability differences in the games sequence, we have

$$|\Pr[\mathsf{MUC\text{-}IND\text{-}CCA}_{\mathsf{KEM},0}^{\mathcal{A}} \Rightarrow 1] - \Pr[\mathsf{MUC\text{-}IND\text{-}CCA}_{\mathsf{KEM},1}^{\mathcal{A}} \Rightarrow 1]|$$
$$\leq 4\mathsf{Adv}_{\mathsf{PKE}}^{\mathsf{ind\text{-}par\text{-}key}}(\mathcal{B}) + 48N(1 + (q_\mathsf{H} + q_\mathsf{G} + 2q_{\mathrm{DEC}} + S)^2)\delta$$
$$+ \frac{NS + N^2S^2}{|\mathcal{R}'|} + N^2S^2\left(\frac{1}{|\mathcal{M}'|} + \frac{1}{|\mathcal{K}|} + \frac{1}{2^s} + \eta_{\mathsf{PKE}}\right)$$
$$+ 4(q_\mathsf{G} + q_\mathsf{H} + NS)\sqrt{NS \cdot \epsilon_{\mathsf{PKE}}^{\mathsf{lo}} + NS/|\mathcal{M}'|} + 4Nq_{\mathsf{H}'} \cdot 2^{-s/2},$$

as stated in Theorem 2.

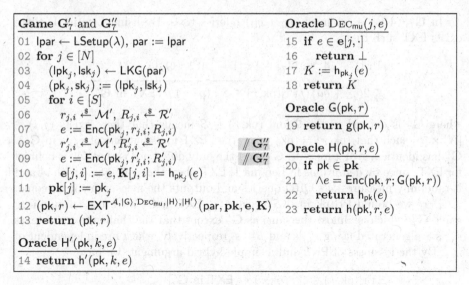

Game $\mathbf{G}_7'$ and $\mathbf{G}_7''$		Oracle $\mathrm{DEC_{mu}}(j, e)$
01 $\mathsf{lpar} \leftarrow \mathsf{LSetup}(\lambda)$, $\mathsf{par} := \mathsf{lpar}$		15 **if** $e \in \mathbf{e}[j, \cdot]$
02 **for** $j \in [N]$		16 **return** $\perp$
03 $(\mathsf{lpk}_j, \mathsf{lsk}_j) \leftarrow \mathsf{LKG(par)}$		17 $K := \mathsf{h}_{\mathsf{pk}_j}(e)$
04 $(\mathsf{pk}_j, \mathsf{sk}_j) := (\mathsf{lpk}_j, \mathsf{lsk}_j)$		18 **return** K
05 **for** $i \in [S]$		
06 $r_{j,i} \xleftarrow{\$} \mathcal{M}'$, $R_{j,i} \xleftarrow{\$} \mathcal{R}'$		Oracle $\mathsf{G}(\mathsf{pk}, r)$
07 $e := \mathsf{Enc}(\mathsf{pk}_j, r_{j,i}; R_{j,i})$		19 **return** $\mathsf{g}(\mathsf{pk}, r)$
08 $r'_{j,i} \xleftarrow{\$} \mathcal{M}'$, $R'_{j,i} \xleftarrow{\$} \mathcal{R}'$ $/\!/ \mathbf{G}_7''$		Oracle $\mathsf{H}(\mathsf{pk}, r, e)$
09 $e := \mathsf{Enc}(\mathsf{pk}_j, r'_{j,i}; R'_{j,i})$ $/\!/ \mathbf{G}_7''$		20 **if** $\mathsf{pk} \in \mathbf{pk}$
10 $\mathbf{e}[j, i] := e$, $\mathbf{K}[j, i] := \mathsf{h}_{\mathsf{pk}_j}(e)$		21 $\wedge e = \mathsf{Enc}(\mathsf{pk}, r; \mathsf{G}(\mathsf{pk}, r))$
11 $\mathbf{pk}[j] := \mathsf{pk}_j$		22 **return** $\mathsf{h}_{\mathsf{pk}}(e)$
12 $(\mathsf{pk}, r) \leftarrow \mathsf{EXT}^{\mathcal{A}, |\mathsf{G}\rangle, \mathrm{DEC_{mu}}, |\mathsf{H}\rangle, |\mathsf{H}'\rangle}(\mathsf{par}, \mathbf{pk}, \mathbf{e}, \mathbf{K})$		23 **return** $\mathsf{h}(\mathsf{pk}, r, e)$
13 **return** (pk, r)		
Oracle $\mathsf{H}'(\mathsf{pk}, k, e)$		
14 **return** $\mathsf{h}'(\mathsf{pk}, k, e)$		

Fig. 9. Games $\mathbf{G}_7'$ and $\mathbf{G}_7''$ in the proof of Lemma 14. Highlighted lines are only executed in the corresponding games.

Proof (Lemma 14). In the gamehop from $\mathbf{G}_6$ to $\mathbf{G}_7$ in the proof of Theorem 2 in Sect. 4.2, we argued that if $\mathcal{A}$ plays $\mathbf{G}_6$ then $\mathcal{A}$ is interacting with the oracle $\mathcal{O}_0$, and if $\mathcal{A}$ plays $\mathbf{G}_7$ then $\mathcal{A}$ is interacting with oracle $\mathcal{O}_1$, where $\mathcal{O}_0$ is the oracle G in $\mathbf{G}_6$, $\mathcal{O}_1$ is the oracle G in $\mathbf{G}_7$, $\mathcal{O}_0 \backslash \mathcal{S} = \mathcal{O}_1 \backslash \mathcal{S}$, and $\mathcal{S}$ is defined as follows:

$$\mathcal{S} := \{(\mathsf{pk}_1, r_{1,1}), (\mathsf{pk}_1, r_{1,2}), ..., (\mathsf{pk}_j, r_{j,i}), ..., (\mathsf{pk}_N, r_{N,S})\}.$$

We can view $\mathcal{O}_0$ and $\mathcal{O}_1$ as follows:

$$\mathcal{O}_0(\mathsf{pk}, r) = \begin{cases} R_{j,i}, & \text{if } \exists (j, i) \in [N] \times [S] \\ & \text{s.t. } (\mathsf{pk}, r) = (\mathsf{pk}_{j,i}, r_{j,i}), \\ \mathsf{g}(\mathsf{pk}, r), & \text{Otherwise} \end{cases} \qquad \mathcal{O}_1(\mathsf{pk}, r) = \mathsf{g}(\mathsf{pk}, r).$$

Therefore, we can also view the game environment of $\mathbf{G}_6$ is the same as the one of $\mathbf{G}_7$, except that the oracles G in these two games are different. That is, we can view $R_{j,i}$'s in $\mathbf{G}_6$ are also generated by independently and uniformly sampling, but then G is set up such that $\mathsf{G}(\mathsf{pk}_j, r_{j,i}) := R_{j,i}$. While in $\mathbf{G}_7$, we do not change G. So, $\mathbf{G}_6^{\mathcal{A}}$ is equivalent to $\mathcal{A}$ plays $\mathbf{G}_7$ but the oracle G it interacts with is $\mathcal{O}_0$. And thus we have

$$|\Pr\left[\mathbf{G}_6^{\mathcal{A}} \Rightarrow 1\right] - \Pr\left[\mathbf{G}_7^{\mathcal{A}} \Rightarrow 1\right]|$$
$$= |\Pr\left[1 \leftarrow \mathcal{A}^{\mathcal{O}_0} : \mathbf{G}_7\right] - \Pr\left[1 \leftarrow \mathcal{A}^{\mathcal{O}_1} : \mathbf{G}_7\right]|.$$

Here we ignore other oracles that $\mathcal{A}$ can access, since such oracles, $\mathrm{DEC}, \mathsf{H}'$, and H, are either independent of G or can be simulated by querying G.

In $\mathbf{G}_7$, $\mathcal{A}$ issues at most $(q_G + q_H)$ queries to G. By using Lemma 1, there exists EXT such that

$$\left|\Pr\left[1 \leftarrow \mathcal{A}^{\mathcal{O}_0} : \mathbf{G}_7\right] - \Pr\left[1 \leftarrow \mathcal{A}^{\mathcal{O}_1} : \mathbf{G}_7\right]\right|$$

$$\leq 2(q_G + q_H)\sqrt{\Pr[(\mathsf{pk}, r) \in \mathcal{S} : (\mathsf{pk}, r) \leftarrow \mathsf{EXT} \text{ in } \mathbf{G}_7']}$$

where $\mathbf{G}_7'$ is defined in Fig. 9 and $(\mathsf{pk}, r) \in \mathcal{S}$ means that there exists $(j, i) \in [N] \times [S]$ such that $(\mathsf{pk}, r) = (\mathsf{pk}_{j,i}, r_{j,i})$ (i.e., EXT finds out one of $r_{j,i}$'s in $\mathbf{G}_7'$). $\mathbf{G}_7'$ has identical structure with $\mathbf{G}_7$, and the only difference is that $\mathbf{G}_7'$ is defined for EXT, since by definitions in Lemma 1, EXT plays the same game with $\mathcal{A}$ and it randomly measures $\mathcal{A}$'s QRO queries and outputs the measurement outcome.

Here we bound $\Pr[(\mathsf{pk}, r) \in \mathcal{S} : (\mathsf{pk}, r) \leftarrow \mathsf{EXT} \text{ in } \mathbf{G}_7']$. We use an auxiliary game $\mathbf{G}_7''$, which is almost the same as $\mathbf{G}_7'$ except that the challenge ciphertexts $e_{j,i}$'s are generated using $r_{j,i}'$'s and $R_{j,i}'$'s, respectively, which are independent of $r_{j,i}$. By the lossiness of PKE and a simple hybrid argument, we have

$$|\Pr[(\mathsf{pk}, r) \in \mathcal{S} : (\mathsf{pk}, r) \leftarrow \mathsf{EXT} \text{ in } \mathbf{G}_7']$$
$$- \Pr[(\mathsf{pk}, r) \in \mathcal{S} : (\mathsf{pk}, r) \leftarrow \mathsf{EXT} \text{ in } \mathbf{G}_7'']| \leq NS \cdot \epsilon_{\mathsf{PKE}}^{\mathsf{lo}}.$$

In $\mathbf{G}_7''$, $r_{j,i}$'s are independent of the view of $\mathcal{A}$ (and thus independent of EXT), so we have

$$\Pr[(\mathsf{pk}, r) \in \mathcal{S} : (\mathsf{pk}, r) \leftarrow \mathsf{EXT} \text{ in } \mathbf{G}_7''] \leq \frac{NS}{|\mathcal{M}'|}.$$

Therefore, we have

$$\left|\Pr\left[\mathbf{G}_6^{\mathcal{A}} \Rightarrow 1\right] - \Pr\left[\mathbf{G}_7^{\mathcal{A}} \Rightarrow 1\right]\right| \leq 2(q_G + q_H)\sqrt{NS \cdot \epsilon_{\mathsf{PKE}}^{\mathsf{lo}} + NS/|\mathcal{M}'|},$$

as stated in Lemma 14.

5   Security Model for AKE

A two-message AKE protocol AKE consists of five algorithms Setup', KG', Init, $\mathsf{Der_R}$, and $\mathsf{Der_I}$. The setup algorithm Setup', on input security parameter 1^λ, outputs global AKE system parameters par'. For sake of simplicity, we ignore the input λ and just write $\mathsf{par}' \leftarrow \mathsf{Setup}'$. KG' takes the system parameters par' as input and outputs a key pair $(\mathsf{pk}', \mathsf{sk}')$. A user in an AKE protocol runs KG' to generate a long-term key pair for itself.

Algorithms Init, $\mathsf{Der_R}$, and $\mathsf{Der_I}$ are used to establish AKE sessions between users. Let U_i and U_j be two users with long-term key pairs $(\mathsf{pk}_i', \mathsf{sk}_i')$ and $(\mathsf{pk}_j', \mathsf{sk}_j')$, respectively. Figure 10 shows how U_i, (as initiator) shares an AKE session key with U_j (as responder). To initialize the session with U_j, U_i runs the session initialization algorithm Init, which takes sk_i', pk_j' as inputs and outputs a protocol message M_i and session state st, and then U_i sends M_i to U_j and keeps st locally. On receiving M_i, U_j runs the responder's derivation algorithm $\mathsf{Der_R}$, which takes sk_j', pk_i', and the received message M_i as inputs, to generate a response M_j and a session key SK_j. U_j sends M_j to U_i. Finally, on receiving

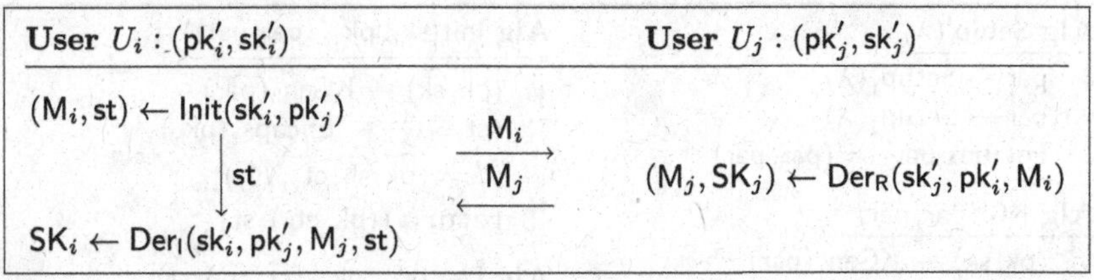

$$
\boxed{
\begin{array}{ll}
\textbf{User } U_i : (\mathsf{pk}_i', \mathsf{sk}_i') & \textbf{User } U_j : (\mathsf{pk}_j', \mathsf{sk}_j') \\[4pt]
\hline
(\mathsf{M}_i, \mathsf{st}) \leftarrow \mathsf{Init}(\mathsf{sk}_i', \mathsf{pk}_j') & \\[2pt]
\quad\Big\downarrow \mathsf{st} \qquad \xrightarrow{\;\mathsf{M}_i\;} & \\
\qquad\qquad \xleftarrow{\;\mathsf{M}_j\;} & (\mathsf{M}_j, \mathsf{SK}_j) \leftarrow \mathsf{Der_R}(\mathsf{sk}_j', \mathsf{pk}_i', \mathsf{M}_i) \\[2pt]
\mathsf{SK}_i \leftarrow \mathsf{Der_I}(\mathsf{sk}_i', \mathsf{pk}_j', \mathsf{M}_j, \mathsf{st}) &
\end{array}
}
$$

Fig. 10. Illustration for a two-pass AKE protocol execution between user U_i and U_j.

M_j, U_i runs the initiator's derivation algorithm $\mathsf{Der_I}$ which inputs $\mathsf{sk}_i', \mathsf{pk}_j'$, the received message M_j, and the local session state st generated before, to generate a session key SK_i. In two-message AKE protocols, the responder does not need to save session state since it can compute the session key right after receiving the initiator's message.

AKE SECURITY MODEL. Following [20], we define a game-based AKE security model using pseudocode. This model is a weaker version of the weak-forward-secrecy model in [20] that it does not consider the state-reveal attack and considers only one TEST query. Our motivation of considering such a model is to focus on the standard security for AKE, such as security against key-compromise-impersonation (KCI) attacks and weak forward secrecy. With state reveals, our security loss has an additional linear factor on the number of sessions, but no square-root loss, which still improves the bound of Hövelmanns et al. [19]. We stress that even in this weaker model the analysis of KEM-based AKE in the QROM of Hövelmanns et al. still has a square-root-loss. For more details, please refer to Remark 1. We move the full details of this model to our full version [31].

In this paper, we say AKE is wFS-KCI secure (weak-forward-secrecy against key-compromise-impersonation attacks) if for all adversaries $\mathcal{A}$, the advantage $\mathsf{Adv}_{\mathsf{AKE}}^{\mathsf{wFS\text{-}KCI}}(\mathcal{A})$ is negligible.

6 Session-Tight AKE Protocol

Let KEM_1 and KEM_2 be two KEM schemes with KEM key spaces $\mathcal{K}_1$ and $\mathcal{K}_2$, respectively. We construct our two-message AKE protocol $\mathsf{AKE} = (\mathsf{Setup}', \mathsf{KG}', \mathsf{Init}, \mathsf{Der_R}, \mathsf{Der_I})$ as shown in Fig. 11, where $\mathcal{SK}$ is the session key space of AKE and $\mathsf{H} : \{0,1\}^* \to \mathcal{SK}$ is a hash function which is used to derive the session key.

Theorem 3. *Let N be the number of users and S be the number of total sessions in game* wFS-KCI. *If* KEM_1 *is a MC-IND-CCA secure KEM and* KEM_2 *is a MUC-IND-CCA secure KEM and* H *is modeled as a quantum random oracle, then for any quantum adversary $\mathcal{A}$ against* AKE, *there exists quantum adversaries $\mathcal{B}_1$ and $\mathcal{B}_2$ such that the running time of $\mathcal{B}_1$ and $\mathcal{B}_2$ about that of $\mathcal{A}$ and*

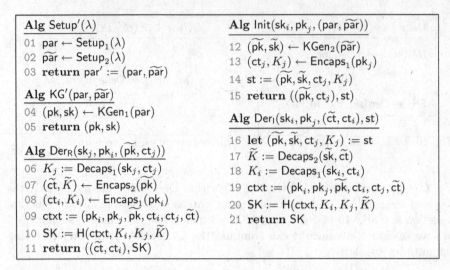

Fig. 11. Our AKE protocol AKE which is based on KEM schemes $\mathsf{KEM}_1 = (\mathsf{Setup}_1, \mathsf{KGen}_1, \mathsf{Encaps}_1, \mathsf{Decaps}_1)$ and $\mathsf{KEM}_2 = (\mathsf{Setup}_2, \mathsf{KGen}_2, \mathsf{Encaps}_2, \mathsf{Decaps}_2)$.

$$\mathsf{Adv}_{\mathsf{AKE}}^{\mathsf{wFS\text{-}KCI}}(\mathcal{A}) \leq \quad N\eta_{\mathsf{KEM}_1} + \frac{4q_{\mathsf{H}}\sqrt{SN}}{\sqrt{|\mathcal{K}_1|}} + \frac{4q_{\mathsf{H}}\sqrt{S}}{\sqrt{|\mathcal{K}_2|}}$$
$$+ 4 \cdot \mathsf{Adv}_{\mathsf{KEM}_2}^{\mathsf{MUC\text{-}IND\text{-}CCA}}(\mathcal{B}_2) + 4N \cdot \mathsf{Adv}_{\mathsf{KEM}_1}^{\mathsf{MC\text{-}IND\text{-}CCA}}(\mathcal{B}_1),$$

where q_{H} is the number of queries to H and η_{KEM_1} is the public key collision probability of KEM_1.

Combining the results from this section with the results from Sects. 3.2, 3.3, 4.1 and 4.2, we obtain the following corollary

Corollary 2. There is an AKE scheme AKE, such that for any quantum adversary $\mathcal{A}$ against AKE, there is an algorithm $\mathcal{B}$ such that the running time of $\mathcal{B}$ is about that of $\mathcal{A}$ and

$$\mathsf{Adv}_{\mathsf{AKE}}^{\mathsf{wFS\text{-}KCI}}(\mathcal{A}) \leq \quad 16k \cdot \mathsf{Adv}^{\mathsf{LWE}_{t,m,q,D_{\mathbb{Z},s''}}}(\mathcal{B})$$
$$+ 16N\ell \cdot \mathsf{Adv}^{\mathsf{LWE}_{k',m,q,D_{\mathbb{Z},s}}}(\mathcal{B}) + \mathsf{negl}(\lambda),$$

where $k = \Theta(\lambda), k' = \Theta(\lambda), \ell = \Theta(\lambda), t = \Theta(\lambda), m = o(\lambda^2)$ and $s, s'' >$ denote appropriate parameters and $\mathsf{negl}(\lambda)$ denotes a negligible statistical term.

Remark 1 (Session State Reveal). Our AKE model does not allow an adversary to reveal session states as in [19]. Considering SessionStateReveal, our security bound is no longer session-tight, since we cannot simulate the session states in a session-tight manner, given only MC-CCA or MUC-CCA security. In order to embed challenges, the security reduction has to guess which session will be tested by adversaries in advance. Hence, the bound will be

$$\varepsilon_{\mathrm{AKE}} \leq \Theta(NS) \cdot \Theta(\lambda) \cdot \varepsilon_{\mathrm{LWE}},$$

which does not contain square-root loss. It still improves the bound of Hövelmanns et al. [19] which has square-root loss on ε_{LWE} (cf. Eq. (1)).

Proof (Theorem 3). First, we assume that all users in the AKE game have different key pairs and all the messages output by the oracles are different. This will add η_{KEM_1} to the final bound. Since KEM_1 and KEM_2 are multi-challenge IND-CCA and multi-user-challenge IND-CCA secure, respectively, the probability that two different executions of Encaps_1, KGen_2, or Encaps_2 have the same output is negligible (and such probability is already considered in their multi-user-challenge or multi-challenge definitions). So, assuming different executions of SESSION_I and SESSION_R will output different protocol messages will not influence our final bound. Moreover, by this assumption, it is impossible for a session to have more than one matching or partially matching session.

To bound $\text{Adv}_{\text{AKE}}^{\text{wFS-KCI}}(\mathcal{A})$, we split up the event that the adversary wins into four cases. Let $\mathbf{G}_{x,b}$ be a game that is the same as $\text{wFS-KCI}_{\text{AKE},b}(\lambda)$ except that the test session sID^* is of type (x) (for $x \in \{1,2,3,4\}$, (cf. [31, Table 1])). That is,

$$\Pr\left[\mathbf{G}_{x,b} \Rightarrow 1\right] = \Pr\left[\text{wFS-KCI}_{\text{AKE},b}^{\mathcal{A}}(\lambda) \Rightarrow 1 \wedge \text{sID}^* \text{ is of type } (x)\right],$$

and thus we have

$$\text{Adv}_{\text{AKE}}^{\text{wFS-KCI}}(\mathcal{A}) = \left|\Pr\left[\text{wFS-KCI}_{\text{AKE},0}^{\mathcal{A}}(\lambda) \Rightarrow 1\right] - \Pr\left[\text{wFS-KCI}_{\text{AKE},1}^{\mathcal{A}}(\lambda) \Rightarrow 1\right]\right|$$

$$\leq \sum_{x=1}^{4} \left|\Pr\left[\mathbf{G}_{x,0} \Rightarrow 1\right] - \Pr\left[\mathbf{G}_{x,1} \Rightarrow 1\right]\right|.$$

Now, we can construct a security reduction according to the type of sID^*. Lemmata 15 and 16 bound $\left|\Pr\left[\mathbf{G}_{x,0} \Rightarrow 1\right] - \Pr\left[\mathbf{G}_{x,1} \Rightarrow 1\right]\right|$ for $x \in \{1,2,3,4\}$. Lemma 15 will be proved later. The proof of Lemma 16 is postponed to our full version [31].

Lemma 15. *With notations and assumptions in the proof of Theorem 3, there exists an adversary $\mathcal{B}_2$ such that its running time is about if $\mathcal{A}$ and*

$$\left|\Pr\left[\mathbf{G}_{1,0}^{\mathcal{A}} \Rightarrow 1\right] - \Pr\left[\mathbf{G}_{1,1}^{\mathcal{A}} \Rightarrow 1\right]\right| \leq 2\text{Adv}_{\text{KEM}_2}^{\text{MUC-IND-CCA}}(\mathcal{B}_2) + \frac{2q_{\text{H}}\sqrt{S}}{\sqrt{|\mathcal{K}_2|}},$$

$$\left|\Pr\left[\mathbf{G}_{2,0}^{\mathcal{A}} \Rightarrow 1\right] - \Pr\left[\mathbf{G}_{2,1}^{\mathcal{A}} \Rightarrow 1\right]\right| \leq 2\text{Adv}_{\text{KEM}_2}^{\text{MUC-IND-CCA}}(\mathcal{B}_2) + \frac{2q_{\text{H}}\sqrt{S}}{\sqrt{|\mathcal{K}_2|}}.$$

Lemma 16. *With notations and assumptions in the proof of Theorem 3, there exists an adversary $\mathcal{B}_1$ such that its running time is about if $\mathcal{A}$ and*

$$\Pr\left[\mathbf{G}_{3,0}^{\mathcal{A}} \Rightarrow 1\right] - \Pr\left[\mathbf{G}_{3,1}^{\mathcal{A}} \Rightarrow 1\right]\right| \leq 2N\text{Adv}_{\text{KEM}_1}^{\text{MC-IND-CCA}}(\mathcal{B}_1) + \frac{2q_{\text{H}}N\sqrt{S}}{\sqrt{|\mathcal{K}_1|}},$$

$$\Pr\left[\mathbf{G}_{4,0}^{\mathcal{A}} \Rightarrow 1\right] - \Pr\left[\mathbf{G}_{4,1}^{\mathcal{A}} \Rightarrow 1\right]\right| \leq 2N\text{Adv}_{\text{KEM}_1}^{\text{MC-IND-CCA}}(\mathcal{B}_1) + \frac{2q_{\text{H}}N\sqrt{S}}{\sqrt{|\mathcal{K}_1|}}.$$

Combining these lemmas, we have

$$\mathsf{Adv}_{\mathsf{AKE}}^{\mathsf{wFS\text{-}KCI}}(\mathcal{A}) = \left| \Pr\left[\mathsf{wFS\text{-}KCI}_{\mathsf{AKE},0}^{\mathcal{A}} \Rightarrow 1\right] - \Pr\left[\mathsf{wFS\text{-}KCI}_{\mathsf{AKE},1}^{\mathcal{A}} \Rightarrow 1\right] \right|$$

$$\leq N\eta_{\mathsf{KEM}_1} + \frac{4q_{\mathsf{H}}N\sqrt{S}}{\sqrt{|\mathcal{K}_1|}} + \frac{4q_{\mathsf{H}}\sqrt{S}}{\sqrt{|\mathcal{K}_2|}}$$

$$+ 4\mathsf{Adv}_{\mathsf{KEM}_2}^{\mathsf{MUC\text{-}IND\text{-}CCA}}(\mathcal{B}_2) + 4N \cdot \mathsf{Adv}_{\mathsf{KEM}_1}^{\mathsf{MC\text{-}IND\text{-}CCA}}(\mathcal{B}_1)$$

as stated in Theorem 3.

Proof (Lemma 15). We bound type (1), i.e. $\left|\Pr\left[\mathbf{G}_{1,0}^{\mathcal{A}} \Rightarrow 1\right] - \Pr\left[\mathbf{G}_{1,1}^{\mathcal{A}} \Rightarrow 1\right]\right|$. The proof for type (2), i.e. $\left|\Pr\left[\mathbf{G}_{2,0}^{\mathcal{A}} \Rightarrow 1\right] - \Pr\left[\mathbf{G}_{2,1}^{\mathcal{A}} \Rightarrow 1\right]\right|$, is identical as the one of type (1). To prove the bound, we give a game sequence $\mathbf{G}_{1\text{-}0,b}$, $\mathbf{G}_{1\text{-}1,b}$, and $\mathbf{G}_{1\text{-}2,b}$ in Fig. 12. Game $\mathbf{G}_{1\text{-}0,b}$ is the same as $\mathbf{G}_{1,b}$, and we have

$$\Pr\left[\mathbf{G}_{1,b}^{\mathcal{A}} \Rightarrow 1\right] = \Pr\left[\mathbf{G}_{1\text{-}0,b}^{\mathcal{A}} \Rightarrow 1\right] \text{ for both } b \in \{0,1\}.$$

Game $\mathbf{G}_{1\text{-}0,b}$-$\mathbf{G}_{1\text{-}2,b}$ ($b \in \{0,1\}$)

01 $\mathcal{L}_2 := \emptyset$
02 $\mathsf{cnt} := 0, \mathsf{sID}^* := \emptyset$
03 $\mathsf{par} \leftarrow \mathsf{Setup}_1(\lambda)$
04 $\widetilde{\mathsf{par}} \leftarrow \mathsf{Setup}_2(\lambda)$
05 $\mathsf{par}' := (\mathsf{par}, \widetilde{\mathsf{par}})$
06 **for** $t \in [N]$:
07 $\quad (\mathsf{pk}_t, \mathsf{sk}_t) \leftarrow \mathsf{KGen}_1(\mathsf{par})$
08 $O_1 := (\mathsf{SESSION_I}, \mathsf{DER_I}, \mathsf{SESSION_R})$
09 $O_2 := (\mathsf{COR}, \mathsf{REV}, \mathsf{TEST})$
10 $b' \leftarrow \mathcal{A}^{O_1,O_2,|\mathsf{H}\rangle}(\mathsf{par}', (\mathsf{pk}_t)_{t \in [N]})$
11 **if** $\mathsf{Fresh}(\mathsf{sID}^*) = 0 \vee \mathsf{Valid}(\mathsf{sID}^*) = 0$
12 $\quad \wedge$ sID^* is not type (1).
13 $\quad\quad$ **return** 0
14 **return** b'

Oracle $\mathsf{DER_I}(\mathsf{sID}, \mathsf{M})$

15 **if** $\mathsf{Used}[\mathsf{sID}] = 1 \vee \mathsf{St}[\mathsf{sID}] = \bot$
16 $\quad \vee \mathsf{SK}[\mathsf{sID}] \neq \bot$: **return** $\bot$
17 $\mathsf{Used}[\mathsf{sID}] := 1, \mathsf{st} := \mathsf{St}[\mathsf{sID}]$
18 $(i,j) := (\mathsf{Init}[\mathsf{sID}], \mathsf{Resp}[\mathsf{sID}])$
19 **let** $(\widetilde{\mathsf{ct}}, \mathsf{ct}_i) := \mathsf{M}$
20 **let** $(\widetilde{\mathsf{pk}}, \widetilde{\mathsf{sk}}, \mathsf{ct}_j, K_j) := \mathsf{st}$
21 $\widetilde{K} := \mathsf{Decaps}_2(\widetilde{\mathsf{sk}}, \widetilde{\mathsf{ct}})$
22 **if** $\exists K$ s.t. $(\widetilde{\mathsf{pk}}, \widetilde{\mathsf{ct}}, K) \in \mathcal{L}_2$
$\quad\quad\quad\quad\quad\quad\quad\quad\quad\quad$ ⫽ $\mathbf{G}_{1\text{-}1,b}$-$\mathbf{G}_{1\text{-}2,b}$
23 $\quad \widetilde{K} := K$ $\quad\quad\quad\quad$ ⫽ $\mathbf{G}_{1\text{-}1,b}$-$\mathbf{G}_{1\text{-}2,b}$
24 $\mathsf{ctxt} := (\mathsf{pk}_i, \mathsf{pk}_j, \widetilde{\mathsf{pk}}, \mathsf{ct}_i, \mathsf{ct}_j, \widetilde{\mathsf{ct}})$
25 $\mathsf{SK} := \mathsf{H}(\mathsf{ctxt}, K_i, K_j, \widetilde{K})$
26 $(\mathsf{R}[\mathsf{sID}], \mathsf{SK}[\mathsf{sID}]) := (\mathsf{M}, \mathsf{SK})$
27 **return** 1

Oracle $\mathsf{SESSION_I}((i,j) \in [N]^2)$

28 $\mathsf{cnt} := \mathsf{cnt} + 1, \mathsf{sID} := \mathsf{cnt}$
29 $(\mathsf{Init}[\mathsf{sID}], \mathsf{Resp}[\mathsf{sID}]) := (i,j)$
30 $\mathsf{Type}[\mathsf{sID}] := \text{"In"}$
31 $(\widetilde{\mathsf{pk}}, \widetilde{\mathsf{sk}}) \leftarrow \mathsf{KGen}_2(\widetilde{\mathsf{par}})$
32 $\mathcal{L}_2 := \mathcal{L}_2 \cup \{(\widetilde{\mathsf{pk}}, \bot, \bot)\}$ ⫽ $\mathbf{G}_{1\text{-}1,b}$-$\mathbf{G}_{1\text{-}2,b}$
33 $(\mathsf{ct}_j, K_j) \leftarrow \mathsf{Encaps}_1(\mathsf{pk}_j)$
34 $(\widetilde{\mathsf{pk}}, \widetilde{\mathsf{sk}}) \leftarrow \mathsf{KGen}_2(\widetilde{\mathsf{par}})$
35 $\mathsf{st} := (\widetilde{\mathsf{pk}}, \widetilde{\mathsf{sk}}, \mathsf{ct}_j, K_j), \mathsf{M}_i := (\widetilde{\mathsf{pk}}, \mathsf{ct}_j)$
36 $(\mathsf{I}[\mathsf{sID}], \mathsf{St}[\mathsf{sID}]) := (\mathsf{M}_i, \mathsf{st})$
37 **return** $(\mathsf{sID}, \mathsf{M}_i)$

Oracle $\mathsf{SESSION_R}((i,j) \in [N]^2, \mathsf{M})$

38 $\mathsf{cnt} := \mathsf{cnt} + 1, \mathsf{sID} := \mathsf{cnt}$
39 $(\mathsf{Init}[\mathsf{sID}], \mathsf{Resp}[\mathsf{sID}]) := (i,j)$
40 $\mathsf{Type}[\mathsf{sID}] := \text{"Re"}$
41 **let** $(\widetilde{\mathsf{pk}}, \mathsf{ct}_j) := \mathsf{M}$
42 $(\widetilde{\mathsf{ct}}, \widetilde{K}) \leftarrow \mathsf{Encaps}_2(\widetilde{\mathsf{pk}})$
43 **if** $(\widetilde{\mathsf{pk}}, \bot, \bot) \in \mathcal{L}_2$ $\quad\quad$ ⫽ $\mathbf{G}_{1\text{-}1,b}$-$\mathbf{G}_{1\text{-}2,b}$
44 $\quad \widetilde{K}_j \leftarrow \mathcal{K}_2$ $\quad\quad\quad\quad\quad$ ⫽ $\mathbf{G}_{1\text{-}2,b}$
45 $\quad \mathcal{L}_2 := \mathcal{L}_2 \cup \{(\widetilde{\mathsf{pk}}, \widetilde{\mathsf{ct}}, \widetilde{K})\}$
$\quad\quad\quad\quad\quad\quad\quad\quad\quad$ ⫽ $\mathbf{G}_{1\text{-}1,b}$-$\mathbf{G}_{1\text{-}2,b}$
46 $K_j := \mathsf{Decaps}_1(\mathsf{sk}_j, \mathsf{ct}_j)$
47 $\mathsf{ctxt} := (\mathsf{pk}_i, \mathsf{pk}_j, \widetilde{\mathsf{pk}}, \mathsf{ct}_i, \mathsf{ct}_j, \widetilde{\mathsf{ct}})$
48 $\mathsf{SK} := \mathsf{H}(\mathsf{ctxt}, K_i, K_j, \widetilde{K})$
49 $\mathsf{SK}[\mathsf{sID}] := \mathsf{SK}, \mathsf{M}_j := (\widetilde{\mathsf{ct}}, \mathsf{ct}_i)$
50 $(\mathsf{I}[\mathsf{sID}], \mathsf{R}[\mathsf{sID}]) := (\mathsf{M}, \mathsf{M}_j)$
51 **return** $(\mathsf{sID}, \mathsf{M}_j)$

Fig. 12. Games in proving Lemma 15. Oracles in O_2 are the same as in $\mathsf{wFS\text{-}KCI}_{\mathsf{AKE},b}$. The QRO H is simulated in the same way as in the proof of Theorem 2.

$\mathbf{G}_{1\text{-}1,b}$: The game first initializes a list $\mathcal{L}_2$ that will be used to store triples $(\widetilde{\mathsf{pk}}, \widetilde{\mathsf{ct}}, \widetilde{K})$ of KEM_2 generated in $\mathrm{SESSION}_I$ and $\mathrm{SESSION}_R$. Specifically, it maintains $\mathcal{L}_2$ as follows:

- In $\mathrm{SESSION}_I(i,j)$, the game simulator records $(\widetilde{\mathsf{pk}}, \perp, \perp)$ in $\mathcal{L}_2$.
- In $\mathrm{SESSION}_R(i,j,(\widetilde{\mathsf{pk}}, \mathsf{ct}_j))$, the game simulator records the tuple $(\widetilde{\mathsf{pk}}, \widetilde{\mathsf{ct}}, \widetilde{K})$ in $\mathcal{L}_2$ if $\widetilde{\mathsf{pk}}$ is generated from $\mathrm{SESSION}_I$ (i.e., generated by the game simulator).
- In $\mathrm{DER}_I(\mathsf{sID}, (\widetilde{\mathsf{ct}}, \mathsf{ct}_i))$, the game simulator gets the decryption of $\widetilde{\mathsf{ct}}$ from $\mathcal{L}_2$ (without decrypting) if its corresponding KEM key is recorded in the list.

This modification does not change $\mathcal{A}$'s view. If $\widetilde{\mathsf{pk}}$ is generated from $\mathrm{SESSION}_I$ and $\widetilde{\mathsf{ct}}$ is generated from $\mathrm{SESSION}_R$, then the game simulator knows the corresponding KEM key of $\widetilde{\mathsf{ct}}$. $\mathcal{L}_2$ is used to record such KEM keys. Therefore, these modifications are conceptual, we have

$$\Pr\left[\mathbf{G}_{1\text{-}0,b}^{\mathcal{A}} \Rightarrow 1\right] = \Pr\left[\mathbf{G}_{1\text{-}1,b}^{\mathcal{A}} \Rightarrow 1\right] \text{ for both } b \in \{0,1\}.$$

$\mathbf{G}_{1\text{-}2,b}$: We switch the KEM keys generated by KEM_2 to be independently and uniformly random. Namely, in $\mathrm{SESSION}_R(i,j,(\widetilde{\mathsf{pk}}, \mathsf{ct}_i))$, if $\widetilde{\mathsf{pk}}$ is generated from $\mathrm{SESSION}_I$ (i.e., $(\widetilde{\mathsf{pk}}, \perp, \perp) \in \mathcal{L}_2$), we sample $\widetilde{K}$ uniformly at random. Intuitively, this change will not influence the consistency of the computation of session keys, since in $\mathbf{G}_{1,b}$, all KEM keys of KEM_2 generated by the game can found in the $\mathcal{L}_2$, and the adversary cannot get the corresponding $\widetilde{\mathsf{sk}}$.

More formally, we use MUC-IND-CCA security of KEM_2 to argue that $\mathcal{A}$ cannot detect this change. To this end, we construct a reduction (against KEM_2), which works as follows: It plays the MUC-IND-CCA game with S users and S challenge ciphertexts per users (S is the number of session in the AKE game). It embeds the challenge public keys in $\mathrm{SESSION}_I$ and embed the challenge ciphertexts in $\mathrm{SESSION}_R$. This reduction $\mathcal{B}_2$ is formally given Fig. 13. The triple recorded in $\mathcal{L}_2$ are all from the inputs of $\mathcal{B}_2$. When simulating DER_I, if $(\widetilde{\mathsf{pk}}, \widetilde{\mathsf{ct}}, \widetilde{K}) \notin \mathcal{L}_2$, then $\widetilde{\mathsf{ct}}$ is not a challenge ciphertext respect to $\widetilde{\mathsf{pk}}$, and $\mathcal{B}_2$ can query $\mathrm{DEC}_{\mathsf{mu}}$ to decrypt $\widetilde{\mathsf{ct}}$. If $\mathcal{B}_2$ plays MUC-IND-CCA$_{\mathsf{KEM}_2,0}$, then it perfectly simulates $\mathbf{G}_{1\text{-}1,b}$, and if it plays MUC-IND-CCA$_{\mathsf{KEM}_2,1}$, then it perfectly simulates $\mathbf{G}_{1\text{-}2,b}$. Therefore, we have

$$\left| \Pr\left[\mathbf{G}_{1\text{-}1,b}^{\mathcal{A}} \Rightarrow 1\right] - \Pr\left[\mathbf{G}_{1\text{-}2,b}^{\mathcal{A}} \Rightarrow 1\right] \right| \leq \mathsf{Adv}_{\mathsf{KEM}_2}^{\mathsf{MUC\text{-}IND\text{-}CCA}}(\mathcal{B}_2).$$

We argue that $\mathbf{G}_{1\text{-}2,0}$ is equivalent to $\mathbf{G}_{1\text{-}2,1}$, except with a negligible probability. Let $(\mathsf{pk}_i, \mathsf{pk}_j, \widetilde{\mathsf{pk}}, \mathsf{ct}_i, \mathsf{ct}_j, \widetilde{\mathsf{ct}}, K_i, K_j, \widetilde{K})$ be the hash input of sID^*. Since sID^* is of type (1), then by definition, sID^* has a unique matching session, which means that $(\widetilde{\mathsf{pk}}, \widetilde{\mathsf{ct}}, \widetilde{K})$ is generated by the game and thus $\widetilde{K}$ is independently and uniformly random. Then, by Corollary 1, if $\mathcal{A}$ queries H at most q_{H} times, except with $\frac{2q_{\mathsf{H}}\sqrt{S}}{\sqrt{|\mathcal{K}_2|}}$ (there are at most S session keys), the session key of sID^* generated in $\mathbf{G}_{1\text{-}2,0}$ is indistinguishable from the one in $\mathbf{G}_{1\text{-}2,1}$, i.e.

$$\left| \Pr\left[\mathbf{G}_{1\text{-}2,0}^{\mathcal{A}} \Rightarrow 1\right] - \Pr\left[\mathbf{G}_{1\text{-}2,1}^{\mathcal{A}} \Rightarrow 1\right] \right| \leq \frac{2q_{\mathsf{H}}\sqrt{S}}{\sqrt{|\mathcal{K}_2|}},$$

430   J. Pan et al.

Reduction $\mathcal{B}_2^{\text{DEC}_{mu}}(\widetilde{\text{par}}, \text{pk}, \mathbf{c}, \mathbf{K})$	Oracle $\text{SESSION}_I((i,j) \in [N]^2)$
01 $\mathcal{L}_1 := \emptyset$	26 $\text{cnt} := \text{cnt} + 1, \text{sID} := \text{cnt}$
02 $\text{cnt} := 0, \text{sID}^* := \perp$	27 $(\text{Init}[\text{sID}], \text{Resp}[\text{sID}]) := (i,j)$
03 $\text{par} \leftarrow \text{Setup}_1(\lambda), \text{par}' := (\text{par}, \widetilde{\text{par}})$	28 $\text{Type}[\text{sID}] := \text{"In"}$
04 $\mathbf{for}\ t \in [N]:$	29 $\widetilde{\text{pk}} := \text{pk}[\text{sID}]$
05 $\quad (\text{pk}_t, \text{sk}_t) \leftarrow \text{KGen}_1(\text{par})$	30 $\mathcal{L}_2 := \mathcal{L}_2 \cup \{(\widetilde{\text{pk}}, \perp, \perp)\}$
06 $O_1 := (\text{SESSION}_I, \text{DER}_I, \text{SESSION}_R)$	31 $(\text{ct}_j, K_j) \leftarrow \text{Encaps}_1(\text{pk}_j)$
07 $O_2 := (\text{COR}, \text{REV}, \text{TEST})$	32 $\text{st} := (\widetilde{\text{pk}}, \widetilde{\text{sk}}, \text{ct}_j, K_j), \text{M}_i := (\widetilde{\text{pk}}, \text{ct}_j)$
08 $b' \leftarrow \mathcal{A}^{O_1, O_2, |\text{H}\rangle}(\text{par}', (\text{pk}_t)_{t \in [N]})$	33 $(\text{I}[\text{sID}], \text{St}[\text{sID}]) := (\text{M}_i, \text{st})$
09 $\mathbf{if}\ \text{Fresh}(\text{sID}^*) = 0 \vee \text{Valid}(\text{sID}^*) = 0$	34 $\mathbf{return}\ (\text{sID}, \text{M}_i)$
10 $\quad \mathbf{return}\ 0$	Oracle $\text{SESSION}_R((i,j) \in [N]^2, \text{M})$
11 $\mathbf{return}\ b'$	35 $\text{cnt} := \text{cnt} + 1, \text{sID} := \text{cnt}$
Oracle $\text{DER}_I(\text{sID}, \text{M})$	36 $(\text{Init}[\text{sID}], \text{Resp}[\text{sID}]) := (i,j)$
12 $\mathbf{if}\ \text{Used}[\text{sID}] = 1 \vee \text{St}[\text{sID}] = \perp$	37 $\text{Type}[\text{sID}] := \text{"Re"}$
13 $\quad \vee \text{SK}[\text{sID}] \neq \perp : \mathbf{return}\ \perp$	38 $\mathbf{let}\ (\widetilde{\text{pk}}, \text{ct}_j) := \text{M}$
14 $\text{Used}[\text{sID}] := 1, \text{st} := \text{St}[\text{sID}]$	39 $(\widetilde{\text{ct}}, \widetilde{K}) \leftarrow \text{Encaps}_2(\widetilde{\text{pk}})$
15 $(i,j) := (\text{Init}[\text{sID}], \text{Resp}[\text{sID}])$	40 $\mathbf{if}\ (\widetilde{\text{pk}}, \perp, \perp) \in \mathcal{L}_2$
16 $\mathbf{let}\ (\widetilde{\text{ct}}, \text{ct}_i) := \text{M}$	41 $\quad \text{Let}\ t \in [S]\ \text{s.t.}\ \widetilde{\text{pk}} = \text{pk}[t]$
17 $\mathbf{let}\ (\widetilde{\text{pk}}, \perp, \text{ct}_j, K_j) := \text{st}$	42 $\quad (\widetilde{\text{ct}}, \widetilde{K}) := (\mathbf{c}[t, \text{sID}], \mathbf{K}[t, \text{sID}])$
18 $\mathbf{if}\ \exists K\ \text{s.t.}\ (\widetilde{\text{pk}}, \widetilde{\text{ct}}, K) \in \mathcal{L}_2$	43 $\quad \mathcal{L}_2 := \mathcal{L}_2 \cup \{(\widetilde{\text{pk}}, \widetilde{\text{ct}}, \widetilde{K})\}$
19 $\quad \widetilde{K} := K$	44 $K_j := \text{Decaps}_1(\text{sk}_j, \text{ct}_j)$
20 $\mathbf{else}\ \widetilde{K} := \text{DEC}_{mu}(\text{sID}, \widetilde{\text{ct}})$	45 $(\text{ct}_i, K_i) \leftarrow \text{Encaps}_1(\text{pk}_i)$
21 $K_i := \text{Decaps}_1(\text{sk}_i, \text{ct}_i)$	46 $\text{ctxt} := (\text{pk}_i, \text{pk}_j, \widetilde{\text{pk}}, \text{ct}_i, \text{ct}_j, \widetilde{\text{ct}})$
22 $\text{ctxt} := (\text{pk}_i, \text{pk}_j, \widetilde{\text{pk}}, \text{ct}_i, \text{ct}_j, \widetilde{\text{ct}})$	47 $\text{SK} := \text{H}(\text{ctxt}, K_i, K_j, \widetilde{K})$
23 $\text{SK} := \text{H}(\text{ctxt}, K_i, K_j, \widetilde{K})$	48 $\text{SK}[\text{sID}] := \text{SK}, \text{M}_j := (\widetilde{\text{ct}}, \text{ct}_i)$
24 $(\text{R}[\text{sID}], \text{SK}[\text{sID}]) := (\text{M}, \text{SK})$	49 $(\text{I}[\text{sID}], \text{R}[\text{sID}]) := (\text{M}, \text{M}_j)$
25 $\mathbf{return}\ 1$	50 $\mathbf{return}\ (\text{sID}, \text{M}_j)$

Fig. 13. The reduction in the proof of Lemma 15. The highlighted codes show how the reduction embeds the challenges into the AKE sessions. Oracles O_2 and H are simulated in the same way with that in Fig. 12.

and in conclusion, we have

$$\left| \Pr\left[\mathbf{G}_{1,0}^{\mathcal{A}} \Rightarrow 1\right] - \Pr\left[\mathbf{G}_{1,1}^{\mathcal{A}} \Rightarrow 1\right] \right| \leq 2\text{Adv}_{\text{KEM}_2}^{\text{MUC-IND-CCA}}(\mathcal{B}_2) + \frac{2q_\text{H}\sqrt{S}}{\sqrt{|\mathcal{K}_2|}}.$$

The same arguments can be used to bound $\left| \Pr\left[\mathbf{G}_{2,0}^{\mathcal{A}} \Rightarrow 1\right] - \Pr\left[\mathbf{G}_{2,1}^{\mathcal{A}} \Rightarrow 1\right] \right|$, and we have

$$\left| \Pr\left[\mathbf{G}_{2,0}^{\mathcal{A}} \Rightarrow 1\right] - \Pr\left[\mathbf{G}_{2,1}^{\mathcal{A}} \Rightarrow 1\right] \right| \leq 2\text{Adv}_{\text{KEM}_2}^{\text{MUC-IND-CCA}}(\mathcal{B}_2) + \frac{2q_\text{H}\sqrt{S}}{\sqrt{|\mathcal{K}_2|}}.$$

References

1. Alwen, J., Krenn, S., Pietrzak, K., Wichs, D.: Learning with rounding, revisited - new reduction, properties and applications. In: Canetti, R., Garay, J.A. (eds.) CRYPTO 2013, Part I. LNCS, vol. 8042, pp. 57–74. Springer, Heidelberg (2013). https://doi.org/10.1007/978-3-642-40041-4_4
2. Ambainis, A., Hamburg, M., Unruh, D.: Quantum security proofs using semi-classical oracles. In: Boldyreva, A., Micciancio, D. (eds.) CRYPTO 2019, Part II. LNCS, vol. 11693, pp. 269–295. Springer, Cham (2019). https://doi.org/10.1007/978-3-030-26951-7_10
3. Bellare, M., Hofheinz, D., Yilek, S.: Possibility and impossibility results for encryption and commitment secure under selective opening. In: Joux, A. (ed.) EUROCRYPT 2009. LNCS, vol. 5479, pp. 1–35. Springer, Heidelberg (2009). https://doi.org/10.1007/978-3-642-01001-9_1
4. Bellare, M., Rogaway, P.: Random oracles are practical: a paradigm for designing efficient protocols. In: Denning, D.E., Pyle, R., Ganesan, R., Sandhu, R.S., Ashby, V. (eds.) ACM CCS 1993, pp. 62–73. ACM Press (1993)
5. Bellare, M., Rogaway, P.: Entity authentication and key distribution. In: Stinson, D.R. (ed.) CRYPTO 1993. LNCS, vol. 773, pp. 232–249. Springer, Heidelberg (1994). https://doi.org/10.1007/3-540-48329-2_21
6. Bellare, M., Rogaway, P.: The security of triple encryption and a framework for code-based game-playing proofs. In: Vaudenay, S. (ed.) EUROCRYPT 2006. LNCS, vol. 4004, pp. 409–426. Springer, Heidelberg (2006). https://doi.org/10.1007/11761679_25
7. Boneh, D., Dagdelen, Ö., Fischlin, M., Lehmann, A., Schaffner, C., Zhandry, M.: Random oracles in a quantum world. In: Lee, D.H., Wang, X. (eds.) ASIACRYPT 2011. LNCS, vol. 7073, pp. 41–69. Springer, Heidelberg (2011). https://doi.org/10.1007/978-3-642-25385-0_3
8. Chen, J., Wee, H.: Fully, (almost) tightly secure IBE and dual system groups. In: Canetti, R., Garay, J.A. (eds.) CRYPTO 2013, Part II. LNCS, vol. 8043, pp. 435–460. Springer, Heidelberg (2013). https://doi.org/10.1007/978-3-642-40084-1_25
9. Fujioka, A., Suzuki, K., Xagawa, K., Yoneyama, K.: Strongly secure authenticated key exchange from factoring, codes, and lattices. In: Fischlin, M., Buchmann, J., Manulis, M. (eds.) PKC 2012. LNCS, vol. 7293, pp. 467–484. Springer, Heidelberg (2012). https://doi.org/10.1007/978-3-642-30057-8_28
10. Fujioka, A., Suzuki, K., Xagawa, K., Yoneyama, K.: Practical and post-quantum authenticated key exchange from one-way secure key encapsulation mechanism. In: Chen, K., Xie, Q., Qiu, W., Li, N., Tzeng, W.G. (eds.) ASIACCS 2013, pp. 83–94. ACM Press (2013)
11. Fujisaki, E., Okamoto, T.: Secure integration of asymmetric and symmetric encryption schemes. J. Cryptol. **26**(1), 80–101 (2013)
12. Gentry, C., Peikert, C., Vaikuntanathan, V.: Trapdoors for hard lattices and new cryptographic constructions. Cryptology ePrint Archive, Report 2007/432 (2007). https://eprint.iacr.org/2007/432
13. Gentry, C., Peikert, C., Vaikuntanathan, V.: Trapdoors for hard lattices and new cryptographic constructions. In: Ladner, R.E., Dwork, C. (eds.) 40th ACM STOC, pp. 197–206. ACM Press (2008)
14. Gjøsteen, K., Jager, T.: Practical and tightly-secure digital signatures and authenticated key exchange. In: Shacham, H., Boldyreva, A. (eds.) CRYPTO 2018, Part II. LNCS, vol. 10992, pp. 95–125. Springer, Cham (2018). https://doi.org/10.1007/978-3-319-96881-0_4

15. Han, S., et al.: Authenticated key exchange and signatures with tight security in the standard model. In: Malkin, T., Peikert, C. (eds.) CRYPTO 2021, Part IV. LNCS, vol. 12828, pp. 670–700. Springer, Cham (2021). https://doi.org/10.1007/978-3-030-84259-8_23

16. Hemenway, B., Libert, B., Ostrovsky, R., Vergnaud, D.: Lossy encryption: constructions from general assumptions and efficient selective opening chosen ciphertext security. In: Lee, D.H., Wang, X. (eds.) ASIACRYPT 2011. LNCS, vol. 7073, pp. 70–88. Springer, Heidelberg (2011). https://doi.org/10.1007/978-3-642-25385-0_4

17. Hofheinz, D., Hövelmanns, K., Kiltz, E.: A modular analysis of the Fujisaki-Okamoto transformation. In: Kalai, Y., Reyzin, L. (eds.) TCC 2017, Part I. LNCS, vol. 10677, pp. 341–371. Springer, Cham (2017). https://doi.org/10.1007/978-3-319-70500-2_12

18. Hofheinz, D., Jager, T., Rupp, A.: Public-key encryption with simulation-based selective-opening security and compact ciphertexts. In: Hirt, M., Smith, A. (eds.) TCC 2016, Part II. LNCS, vol. 9986, pp. 146–168. Springer, Heidelberg (2016). https://doi.org/10.1007/978-3-662-53644-5_6

19. Hövelmanns, K., Kiltz, E., Schäge, S., Unruh, D.: Generic authenticated key exchange in the quantum random oracle model. In: Kiayias, A., Kohlweiss, M., Wallden, P., Zikas, V. (eds.) PKC 2020, Part II. LNCS, vol. 12111, pp. 389–422. Springer, Cham (2020). https://doi.org/10.1007/978-3-030-45388-6_14

20. Jager, T., Kiltz, E., Riepel, D., Schäge, S.: Tightly-secure authenticated key exchange, revisited. In: Canteaut, A., Standaert, F.-X. (eds.) EUROCRYPT 2021, Part I. LNCS, vol. 12696, pp. 117–146. Springer, Cham (2021). https://doi.org/10.1007/978-3-030-77870-5_5

21. Jiang, H., Zhang, Z., Chen, L., Wang, H., Ma, Z.: IND-CCA-secure key encapsulation mechanism in the quantum random oracle model, revisited. In: Shacham, H., Boldyreva, A. (eds.) CRYPTO 2018, Part III. LNCS, vol. 10993, pp. 96–125. Springer, Cham (2018). https://doi.org/10.1007/978-3-319-96878-0_4

22. Jiang, H., Zhang, Z., Ma, Z.: Key encapsulation mechanism with explicit rejection in the quantum random oracle model. In: Lin, D., Sako, K. (eds.) PKC 2019, Part II. LNCS, vol. 11443, pp. 618–645. Springer, Cham (2019). https://doi.org/10.1007/978-3-030-17259-6_21

23. Katsumata, S., Yamada, S., Yamakawa, T.: Tighter security proofs for GPV-IBE in the quantum random oracle model. In: Peyrin, T., Galbraith, S. (eds.) ASIACRYPT 2018, Part II. LNCS, vol. 11273, pp. 253–282. Springer, Cham (2018). https://doi.org/10.1007/978-3-030-03329-3_9

24. Kiltz, E., Lyubashevsky, V., Schaffner, C.: A concrete treatment of Fiat-Shamir signatures in the quantum random-oracle model. In: Nielsen, J.B., Rijmen, V. (eds.) EUROCRYPT 2018, Part III. LNCS, vol. 10822, pp. 552–586. Springer, Cham (2018). https://doi.org/10.1007/978-3-319-78372-7_18

25. Krawczyk, H.: SIGMA: the "SIGn-and-MAc" approach to authenticated Diffie-Hellman and its use in the IKE protocols. In: Boneh, D. (ed.) CRYPTO 2003. LNCS, vol. 2729, pp. 400–425. Springer, Heidelberg (2003). https://doi.org/10.1007/978-3-540-45146-4_24

26. Krawczyk, H.: HMQV: a high-performance secure Diffie-Hellman protocol. In: Shoup, V. (ed.) CRYPTO 2005. LNCS, vol. 3621, pp. 546–566. Springer, Heidelberg (2005). https://doi.org/10.1007/11535218_33

27. Libert, B., Sakzad, A., Stehlé, D., Steinfeld, R.: All-but-many lossy trapdoor functions and selective opening chosen-ciphertext security from LWE. In: Katz, J.,

Shacham, H. (eds.) CRYPTO 2017, Part III. LNCS, vol. 10403, pp. 332–364. Springer, Cham (2017). https://doi.org/10.1007/978-3-319-63697-9_12

28. Liu, X., Wang, M.: QCCA-secure generic key encapsulation mechanism with tighter security in the quantum random oracle model. In: Garay, J.A. (ed.) PKC 2021, Part I. LNCS, vol. 12710, pp. 3–26. Springer, Cham (2021). https://doi.org/10.1007/978-3-030-75245-3_1

29. Micciancio, D., Regev, O.: Worst-case to average-case reductions based on Gaussian measures. In: 45th FOCS, pp. 372–381. IEEE Computer Society Press (2004)

30. Pan, J., Wagner, B., Zeng, R.: Lattice-based authenticated key exchange with tight security. In: Handschuh, H., Lysyanskaya, A. (eds.) CRYPTO 2023. LNCS, pp. 616–647. Springer, Cham (2023). https://doi.org/10.1007/978-3-031-38554-4_20

31. Pan, J., Wagner, B., Zeng, R.: Tighter security for generic authenticated key exchange in the QROM. Cryptology ePrint Archive (2023). https://ia.cr/2023/1380

32. Pan, J., Zeng, R.: Compact and tightly selective-opening secure public-key encryption schemes. In: Agrawal, S., Lin, D. (eds.) ASIACRYPT 2022, Part III. LNCS, vol. 13793, pp. 363–393. Springer, Heidelberg (Dec (2022). https://doi.org/10.1007/978-3-031-22969-5_13

33. Regev, O.: On lattices, learning with errors, random linear codes, and cryptography. In: Gabow, H.N., Fagin, R. (eds.) 37th ACM STOC, pp. 84–93. ACM Press (2005)

34. Saito, T., Xagawa, K., Yamakawa, T.: Tightly-secure key-encapsulation mechanism in the quantum random oracle model. In: Nielsen, J.B., Rijmen, V. (eds.) EURO-CRYPT 2018, Part III. LNCS, vol. 10822, pp. 520–551. Springer, Cham (2018). https://doi.org/10.1007/978-3-319-78372-7_17

35. Unruh, D.: Post-quantum verification of Fujisaki-Okamoto. In: Moriai, S., Wang, H. (eds.) ASIACRYPT 2020, Part I. LNCS, vol. 12491, pp. 321–352. Springer, Cham (2020). https://doi.org/10.1007/978-3-030-64837-4_11

36. Xue, H., Au, M.H., Yang, R., Liang, B., Jiang, H.: Compact authenticated key exchange in the quantum random oracle model. Cryptology ePrint Archive, Report 2020/1282 (2020). https://eprint.iacr.org/2020/1282

37. Zhandry, M.: Secure identity-based encryption in the quantum random oracle model. In: Safavi-Naini, R., Canetti, R. (eds.) CRYPTO 2012. LNCS, vol. 7417, pp. 758–775. Springer, Heidelberg (2012). https://doi.org/10.1007/978-3-642-32009-5_44

Post-quantum Security of Key Encapsulation Mechanism Against CCA Attacks with a Single Decapsulation Query

Haodong Jiang[1(✉)], Zhi Ma[1(✉)], and Zhenfeng Zhang[2(✉)]

[1] Henan Key Laboratory of Network Cryptography Technology, Zhengzhou 450001, Henan, China
hdjiang13@gmail.com, mzh2830@163.com
[2] TCA Laboratory, State Key Laboratory of Computer Science, Institute of Software, Chinese Academy of Sciences, Beijing 100190, China
zhenfeng@iscas.ac.cn

Abstract. Recently, in post-quantum cryptography migration, it has been shown that an IND-1-CCA-secure key encapsulation mechanism (KEM) is required for replacing an ephemeral Diffie-Hellman (DH) in widely-used protocols, e.g., TLS, Signal, and Noise. IND-1-CCA security is a notion similar to the traditional IND-CCA security except that the adversary is restricted to one single decapsulation query. At EUROCRYPT 2022, based on CPA-secure public-key encryption (PKE), Huguenin-Dumittan and Vaudenay presented two IND-1-CCA KEM constructions called T_{CH} and T_H, which are much more efficient than the widely-used IND-CCA-secure Fujisaki-Okamoto (FO) KEMs. The security of T_{CH} was proved in both random oracle model (ROM) and quantum random oracle model (QROM). However, the QROM proof of T_{CH} relies on an additional ciphertext expansion. While, the security of T_H was only proved in the ROM, and the QROM proof is left open.

In this paper, we prove the security of T_H and T_{RH} (an implicit variant of T_H) in both ROM and QROM with much tighter reductions than Huguenin-Dumittan and Vaudenay's work. In particular, our QROM proof will not lead to ciphertext expansion. Moreover, for T_{RH}, T_H and T_{CH}, we also show that a $O(1/q)$ ($O(1/q^2)$, resp.) reduction loss is unavoidable in the ROM (QROM, resp.), and thus claim that our ROM proof is optimal in tightness. Finally, we make a comprehensive comparison among the relative strengths of IND-1-CCA and IND-CCA in the ROM and QROM.

Keywords: quantum random oracle model · key encapsulation mechanism · 1CCA security · tightness · KEM-TLS

1 Introduction

With the gradual advancement of NIST post-quantum cryptography (PQC) standardization, research on migration from the existing protocols to post-

J. Guo and R. Steinfeld (Eds.): ASIACRYPT 2023, LNCS 14441, pp. 434–468, 2023.
https://doi.org/10.1007/978-981-99-8730-6_14

quantum protocols with new standardized algorithms has been a hot topic. For ephemeral key establishment, one has to move the current Diffie-Hellman (DH) key-exchange to post-quantum key encapsulation mechanisms (KEMs).

The security goal required for such a substitutive KEM has been thoroughly analyzed for TLS 1.3 [15,21], KEM-TLS [37,38], Signal [9] and Noise [2]. In general, the security of these DH-based protocols is proved based on the PRF-ODH assumption [10]. But, when one uses KEM to replace DH, IND-1-CCA security is required instead, see post-quantum TLS [15,21,37,38], post-quantum Signal [9] and post-quantum Noise [2]. In addition, Huguenin-Dumittan and Vaudenay [21] pointed out that IND-1-CCA KEMs are also used in Ratcheting [4,25,32]. Roughly speaking, IND-1-CCA security says that the adversary is required to distinguish an honestly generated key from a randomly generated key by making at most a *single* decapsulation query.

IND-1-CCA security is obviously implied by IND-CCA security that has been widely studied in [6,14,16,17,19,22–24,26,35]. In general, IND-CCA-secure KEMs are obtained by applying Fujisaki-Okamoto-like (FO-like) transform to a OW/IND-CPA-secure public-key encryption (PKE). In particular, all the KEM candidates to be standardized and Round-4 KEM submissions [30] adopted FO-like construction. The current implementations of KEM-TLS [37,38], post-quantum TLS 1.3 [31] and post-quantum Noise framework [2] directly take IND-CCA-secure KEMs as IND-1-CCA-secure KEMs. However, FO-like IND-CCA-secure KEMs require re-encryption of the decrypted plaintext in decapsulation, making it an expensive operation. For instance, as shown in [21], when re-encryption is removed, there will be a 2.17X and 6.11X speedup over decapsulation in CRYSTALS-Kyber [8] and FrodoKEM [28] respectively. Moreover, the re-encryption makes the KEM more vulnerable to side-channel attacks and almost all the NIST-PQC Round-3 KEMs are affected, see [3,39]. Meanwhile, the side-channel protection of re-encryption will significantly increase deployment costs and thus complicate the integration of NIST-PQC KEMs [27]. Therefore, designing a dedicated IND-1-CCA-secure KEM without re-encryption was taken as an open problem raised by Schwabe, Stebila and Wiggers [37].

This problem was recently studied by Huguenin-Dumittan and Vaudenay [21]. They found that simple modification of the current FO-like KEMs can achieve an IND-1-CCA-secure KEM without re-encryption. In detail, they presented two constructions. One construction (called T_{CH}) is that an additional hash value of message and ciphertext is appended to the original ciphertext (usually called key-confirmation). The security of T_{CH} was proved in the random oracle model (ROM) with tightness $\epsilon_R \approx O(1/q)\epsilon_A$, and in the quantum random oracle model (QROM) with tightness $\epsilon_R \approx O(1/q^3)\epsilon_A^2$, where ϵ_R (ϵ_A, resp.) is the advantage of the reduction R (adversary A, resp.) breaking the security of the underlying PKE (the resulting KEM, resp.), and q is the number of A's queries to the random oracle (RO). Different from ROM, QROM allows the adversary to make quantum queries to the RO. To prove the post-quantum security of cryptosystem, one has to prove in the QROM [7]. Unfortunately, the QROM proof of T_{CH} in [21] relies on key-confirmation (i.e., an additional length-preserving hash is required)[1], which will leads to a ciphertext expansion.

The second construction given in [21] is T_H, where ciphertext c is obtained by encrypting a randomly message m, the key is derived by $H(m,c)$. In decapsulation, if $m' = Dec(sk,c) = \perp$, $\perp$ is returned, otherwise $H(m',c)$ is returned, where Dec is the decryption algorithm of PKE, and sk is the secret key. In fact, T_H is the same as $U^\perp$ in [17]. Note that both T_{CH} and T_H do not require re-encryption. But, compared with T_{CH}, T_H will not lead to ciphertext expansion. However, Huguenin-Dumittan and Vaudenay [21] only gave the ROM proof of T_H with tightness $\epsilon_R \approx O(1/q^3)\epsilon_{\mathcal{A}}$. The QROM proof is left open due to the challenge that a lot of RO programming property is used[2].

1.1   Our Contributions

Our contributions are as follows.

1. First, we prove the security of T_H and its implicit variant T_{RH} in both ROM and QROM. T_{RH} is the same as the T_H except that in decapsulation a pseudo-random value $H(\star,c)$ is returned instead of an explicit $\perp$ for an invalid ciphertext c such that $Dec(sk,c) = \perp$. In particular, our QROM proof will not lead to ciphertext expansion (Table 1). In the ROM, our reduction has tightness $\epsilon_R \approx O(1/q)\epsilon_{\mathcal{A}}$, which is much tighter than $\epsilon_R \approx O(1/q^3)\epsilon_{\mathcal{A}}$ given by [21] for T_H. In the QROM, our reduction achieves tightness $\epsilon_R \approx O(1/q^2)\epsilon_{\mathcal{A}}^2$, which is tighter than $\epsilon_R \approx O(1/q^3)\epsilon_{\mathcal{A}}^2$ given by Huguenin-Dumittan and Vaudenay in [21] for T_{CH} (with ciphertext expansion).
2. Then, for T_H, T_{RH} and T_{CH}, we show that if the underlying PKE meets malleability property, a $O(1/q)$ ($O(1/q^2)$, resp.) loss is unavoidable in the ROM (QROM, resp.). That is, our ROM reduction is optimal in general. Roughly speaking, the malleability property says that an adversary can efficiently transform a ciphertext into another ciphertext which decrypts to a related plaintext. In particular, such a malleability property is met by real-world PKE schemes, e.g., ElGamal, FrodoKEM.PKE [28], CRYSTALS–Kyber.PKE [8], etc.

---

[1] The length-preserving property of the additional hash is implicitly required by the QROM proof in [21] and will increase the ciphertext size by $|ct| + |m|$, where $|ct|$ is the PKE ciphertext size and $|m|$ is the message size. Very recently, Huguenin-Dumittan and Vaudenay [20] updated their ePrint version and presented a new proof for T_{CH} using the extractable RO technique [14] with improved bound $\epsilon_R \approx O(1/q^2)\epsilon_{\mathcal{A}}^2 - O(q^3/2^n) - O(q/\sqrt{2^n})$ (n is the RO-output length), which removes the length-preserving requirement. But, the additional key-confirmation is still required.

[2] At EUROCRYPT 2022, Huguenin-Dumittan and Vaudenay [21] conjectured that the popular compressed oracle technique proposed by Zhandry [42] might be of use in the QROM proof. Surprisingly, in our QROM proof, only the other two well-known techniques called one-way to hiding (O2H) [1,6] and measure-and-reprogram [12] are used.

3. Finally, we compare the relative strengths of IND-1-CCA and IND-CCA in the ROM and QROM, see Fig. 1. For each pair of notions A, B ∈{IND-1-CCA ROM, IND-CCA ROM, IND-1-CCA QROM, IND-CCA QROM}, we show either an implication or a separation, so that no relation remains open.

Remark 1. Our construction T_{RH} is essentially the construction $U^{\not\perp}$ in [17], except that the secret seed s in decapsulation is replaced by a public value $\star$ ($\star$ can be any fixed message). In fact, our proof can work for both secret seed and public value thanks to the newly introduced decapsulation simulation technique, while the current IND-CCA proofs for implicit FO-KEMs (e.g., see [17,22]) can only work for secret seed. We choose to replace secret seed by public value since it reduces the secret key size and makes the construction more concise. Moreover, from a high-assurance implementation (i.e., side-channel protected) point of view, public value is also preferable to secure seed, see comments by Schneider at NIST pqc-forum [36].

Table 1. Reduction tightness in the ROM/QROM.

Transformation	Reduction tightness	Ciphertext expansion	Re-encryption	ROM or QROM
FO [17]	$\epsilon_R \approx \epsilon_A$	N	Y	ROM
T_{CH} [21]	$\epsilon_R \approx O(1/q)\epsilon_A$	Y	N	ROM
T_H [21]	$\epsilon_R \approx O(1/q^3)\epsilon_A$	N	N	ROM
Our T_{RH} and T_H	$\epsilon_R \approx O(1/q)\epsilon_A$	N	N	ROM
FO [6,24]	$\epsilon_R \approx O(1/q)\epsilon_A^2$	N	Y	QROM
T_{CH} [21]	$\epsilon_R \approx O(1/q^3)\epsilon_A^2$	Y	N	QROM
Our T_{RH} and T_H	$\epsilon_R \approx O(1/q^2)\epsilon_A^2$	N	N	QROM

1.2 Practical Impact

An IND-1-CCA KEM is sufficient to replace Diffie-Hellman in the post-quantum migration of the widely-deployed protocols, such as TLS 1.3, Signal and Noise. Our results show that IND-1-CCA-secure KEMs can be constructed in the ROM and QROM without re-encryption and cipher-expansion. Compared with IND-CCA-secure KEMs based on FO transform, such as CRYSTALS-Kyber, the IND-1-CCA-secure KEMs based on T_H and T_{RH} do not require the re-encryption in

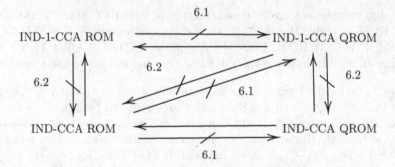

Fig. 1. The relations among notions of security for KEM. An arrow is an implication, and there is a path from A to B if and and only A $\Rightarrow$ B. The hatched arrows represent separations actually we prove. The number on an hatched arrow refers to the theorem in this paper which establishes this relationship.

decapsulation. The re-encryption is highly vulnerable to attacks and its side-channel protection will significantly increase deployment costs. Thus, from a practical point of view, removing the re-encryption of FO-like KEMs will improve the performance of embedded side-channel secure implementations. Therefore, according to our results, one can easily transform CRYSTALS-CKyber.PKE into an IND-1-CCA-secure KEM without re-encryption and cipher-expansion, and then establish post-quantum-secure variants of TLS 1.3, Signal and Noise with better performance in the embedded implementation.

1.3 Open Problem

We prove a $O(1/q)$ ($O(1/q^2)$, resp.) loss is unavoidable in the ROM (QROM, resp.) for the IND-1-CCA KEMs in this paper and [21]. Our ROM proof essentially matches this loss. However, our QROM tightness does not match $O(1/q^2)$. Thus, a natural question is can our QROM reduction tightness be further improved, or can one find a new attack that matches the QROM proof in this paper.

1.4 Technique Overview

Construction and Reduction. Re-encryption is the core feature of FO-like CCA-KEMs, which guarantees that only specific valid ciphertexts can be correctly decapsulated, and thus makes the decapsulation simulation in the ROM/QROM proof easy (see [6,14,16–19,22–24,35]). However, on the other hand, as mentioned earlier, removing the re-encryption will bring a significant speed boost in decapsulation [21,37] and reduce the risk of side-channel attacks [3,39].

However, removing re-encryption makes the current decapsulation simulation for FO-like CCA-KEMs incompatible with the KEMs in this paper and [21].

So the key in the proof is the decapsulation simulation. We note that for a valid ciphertext $\bar{c}$ such that $(Dec(sk, \bar{c}) = \bar{m} \neq \bot)^3$, the decapsulation returns $H(\bar{m}, \bar{c})$. Thus, if we reprogram $H(\bar{m}, \bar{c})$ to a random $\bar{k}$, we can simulate the decapsulation of $\bar{c}$ using $\bar{k}$ without knowledge of sk. To guarantee the consistency between the outputs of H and the simulated decapsulation, one needs to correctly guess when the adversary makes a query $(\bar{m}, \bar{c})$ to H, and perform a reprogram at that time. In the ROM, a randomly guess is correct with probability $1/q$.

In the QROM, due to adversary's superposition RO-query, it is hard to define when the adversary makes a query $(\bar{m}, \bar{c})$. Therefore, in the QROM, we argue in a different way. We find that the consistency between H and the simulated decapsulation can be guaranteed if the predicate $Decap(sk, \bar{c}) = H(\bar{m}, \bar{c})$ is satisfied. Don, Fehr, Majenz, and Schaffner [12,13] showed that a random measure-and-reprogram can keep the predicate satisfied with a high probability. However, the measure-and-reprogram in [12,13] cannot be directly applied to our case. This is due to the fact that the random measure in [12,13] is performed for all the H-queries while in our case there is an implicit (classical) H-query used in the real decapsulation that will be removed in the simulated decapsulation and thus can not be measured. In this paper, extending the measure-and-reprogram technique in [12,13], we derive a variant of measure-and-reprogram (see Lemma 3.1), which is suitable for our case. With this new measure-and-reprogram, the QROM adversary can accept the simulation of both H and the decapsulation oracle with probability at least $O(1/q^2)$.

When embedding the instance of the underlying security experiment into the IND-1-CCA instance, we successfully embed an IND-CPA instance without reduction loss in the ROM. While in [21] a OW-CPA instance is embedded with a $O(1/q)$ loss in the ROM. In the QROM, the instance embedding is very tricky. We extend the double-sided O2H technique (see Lemma 2.3) to argue the QROM instance embedding, more details please refer to the proof of Theorem 4.2.

We also remark that one can easily extend the results in this paper to the IND-q-CCA KEM case for any arbitrary constant q. But, as aforementioned, IND-1-CCA KEM is sufficient in practical protocols, e.g., TLS 1.3, KEM-TLS.

Attack and Tightness. Re-encryption in the FO-like KEMs will guarantee that only the ciphertexts generated by derandomization are identified as valid. That is, any ciphertext obtained by transforming another valid ciphertext can be identified as invalid by re-encryption check. However, for the IND-1-CCA KEMs in this paper and [21], the re-encryption check is removed. Thus, given a challenge ciphertext $c^* \leftarrow Enc(pk, m^*)$ to distinguish $K_0 = H(m^*, c^*)$ from a random K_1, if an adversary $\mathcal{B}$ can efficiently transform c^* into another ciphertext c' such that $Dec(sk, c') = f(m^*)$ for some specific function f (this property is defined as malleability), then $\mathcal{B}$ can derive a hash value $tag = Decap(sk, c') = H(f(m^*), c^*)$. Thus, $\mathcal{B}$ can search for m^* such that $tag = H(f(m^*), c^*)$ from the message $\mathcal{M}$ by querying the random oracle H, and finally use $H(m^*, c^*)$ to

---

[3] In the full proof of T_{RH}, the invalid case $Dec(sk, \bar{c}) = \bot$ is integrated into the valid case $Dec(sk, \bar{c}) \neq \bot$. while, the security of T_H is directly reduced to the security of T_{RH}.

distinguish K_0 from K_1. By detailed analysis, we show $\mathcal{B}$ can achieve advantage at least $O(q/2^\lambda)$ in the ROM ($O(q^2/2^\lambda)$ in the QROM). For a λ-bit secure PKE, any PPT adversary breaks the security of PKE with advantage at most $O(1/2^\lambda)$. Thus, we can claim that a $O(1/q)$ ($O(1/q^2)$, resp.) loss is unavoidable in the ROM (QROM, resp.) for the IND-1-CCA KEMs in this paper and [21].

Implication and Separation. By introducing a proof of quantum access to random oracle given in [40], we construct a KEM that is provably IND-CCA-secure (hence also IND-1-CCA secure) in the ROM, but cannot achieve IND-1-CCA security (hence also IND-CCA security) in the QROM. In addition, we show that applying our H_{RU} to lattice-based PKE, e.g., FrodoPKE [28], can derive an IND-1-CCA ROM (and also QROM) secure KEM. However, such a KEM cannot achieve IND-CCA security in the ROM (hence QROM). The other implication relations can be trivially obtained.

1.5 Related Work

The transformations in [21] and our paper are similar to U-transformation which is originally proposed in [11] and converts a OW-PCA-secure/deterministic PKE into an IND-CCA-secure KEM. The U-transformation has various variants, including $U_m^\perp$, $U_m^{\not\perp}$, $HU_m^\perp$, $HU^\perp$, $QU_m^\perp$, $QU_m^{\not\perp}$, $U^\perp$, $U^{\not\perp}$[4]. For $QU_m^\perp$ and $QU_m^{\not\perp}$, Hofheinz, Hövelmanns and Kiltz [17] showed that the IND-CCA security of KEM can be reduced to the OW-PCA security of PKE with tightness $\epsilon_R \approx O(1/q^2)\epsilon_{\mathcal{A}}^2$. The OW-PCA security is the same as the OW-CPA security except that the adversary can additionally access a plaintext-checking oracle that judges whether decryption of a given ciphertext is equal to a given plaintext. For implicit transformations $U_m^{\not\perp}$ and $U^{\not\perp}$, Jiang, Zhang, Chen, Wang and Ma [22] showed that the IND-CCA security of KEM can be reduced to the quantum variant of OW-PCA security of PKE or OW-CPA security of deterministic PKE (DPKE) with tightness $\epsilon_R \approx O(1/q^2)\epsilon_{\mathcal{A}}^2$, which is further improved to $\epsilon_R \approx O(1/q)\epsilon_{\mathcal{A}}^2$ by Jiang, Zhang and Ma [24], improved to $\epsilon_R \approx \epsilon_{\mathcal{A}}^2$ by Bindel, Hamburg, Hövelmanns, Hülsing and Persichetti [6], and improved to $\epsilon_R \approx O(1/q)\epsilon_{\mathcal{A}}$ by Kuchta, Sakzad, Stehlé, Steinfeld and Sun [26]. In particular, Saito, Xagawa, and Yamakawa [35] gave a tight reduction for $U_m^{\not\perp}$ from a newly introduced security (called disjoint simulatability) of DPKE to the IND-CCA security of KEM. This tight result was subsequently extended for the explicit $HU_m^\perp$ by Jiang, Zhang and Ma [23]. For $HU_m^\perp$ and $HU^\perp$, Bindel, Hamburg, Hövelmanns, Hülsing and Persichetti [6] showed that the same QROM results can be achieved as the implicit variants. Recently, Don, Fehr, Majenz and Schaffner [14] first proved the QROM security of $U_m^\perp$[5]. Note that all the U-transformations require re-encryption in decapsu-

---

[4] The symbol $\perp$ ($\not\perp$) means explicit (implicit) rejection, m (without m) means $K = H(m)$ ($K = H(m,c)$), H (Q) means an additional (length-preserving) hash value is appended into the ciphertext. In this paper, $U_m^\perp$ and $U_m^{\not\perp}$ are referred to transformations with re-encryption in decapsulation.

[5] Strictly speaking, they proved the security of $FO_m^\perp$ in the QROM. But, their proof can be translated into a proof for $U_m^\perp$.

lation except $U^\perp$ and $U^{\not\perp}$ (see [17,22]). However, the proofs for $U^\perp$ and $U^{\not\perp}$ in [17,22] require the underlying PKE satisfies OW-PCA security, which is usually obtained by using de-randomization and re-encryption.

2 Preliminaries

Symbol Description. A security parameter is denoted by λ. The set $\{0, \cdots, q\}$ is denoted by $[q]$. The abbreviation PPT stands for probabilistic polynomial time. $\mathcal{K}$, $\mathcal{M}$, $\mathcal{C}$ and $\mathcal{R}$ are denoted as key space, message space, ciphertext space and randomness space, respectively. Given a finite set X, we denote the sampling of a uniformly random element x by $x \leftarrow_\$ X$. Denote the sampling from some distribution D by $x \leftarrow D$. $x = ?y$ is denoted as an integer that is 1 if $x = y$, and otherwise 0. $\Pr[P : G]$ is the probability that the predicate P holds true where free variables in P are assigned according to the program in G. Denote deterministic (probabilistic, resp.) computation of an algorithm A on input x by $y = A(x)$ ($y \leftarrow A(x)$, resp.). Let $|X|$ be the cardinality of set X. A^H ($A^{|H\rangle}$, resp.) means that algorithm A gets classical (quantum, resp.) access to the oracle H. We present the cryptographic primitives in Supporting Material A.

2.1 Quantum Random Oracle Model

We refer the reader to [29] for basic of quantum computation. Random oracle model (ROM) [5] is an idealized model, where a hash function is modeled as a publicly accessible random oracle. Quantum adversary can off-line evaluate the hash function on an arbitrary superposition of inputs. As a result, quantum adversary should be allowed to query the random orale with quantum state. We call this quantum random oracle model (QROM) [7].

2.2 One-Way to Hiding and Its Double-Sided Variant

Lemma 2.1 (One-way to hiding (O2H)[1, Theorem 3]). *Let $S \subseteq \mathcal{X}$ be random. Let G, H be oracles such that $\forall x \notin S. G(x) = H(x)$. Let z be a random bitstring. $(S, G, H, z$ may have arbitrary joint distribution.) Let A be quantum oracle algorithm that makes at most q queries (not necessarily unitary). Let $B^{|H\rangle}$ be an oracle algorithm that on input z does the following: pick $i \in [q-1]$, run $A^{|H\rangle}(z)$ until (just before) the $(i+1)$-th query, measure all query input registers in the computational basis, output the set T of measurement outcomes. Then*

$$\left| \Pr[1 \leftarrow A^{|H\rangle}(Z)] - \Pr[1 \leftarrow A^{|G\rangle}(Z)] \right| \leq 2q\sqrt{\Pr[S \cap T \neq \emptyset : T \leftarrow B^{|H\rangle}(z)]}.$$

Lemma 2.2 ((Adapted) Double-sided O2H [6, Lemma 5]). *Let $G, H : \mathcal{X} \rightarrow \mathcal{Y}$ be oracles such that $\forall x \neq x^*. G(x) = H(x)$. Let z be a random bitstring. $(x^*, G, H, z$ may have arbitrary joint distribution.) Let A be quantum oracle algorithm that makes at most q queries (not necessarily unitary). Then, there is an* another double-sided oracle algorithm $B^{|G\rangle,|H\rangle}(z)$ such that B runs in about the same amount of time as A, and

$$\left|\Pr[1 \leftarrow A^{|H\rangle}(z)] - \Pr[1 \leftarrow A^{|G\rangle}(z)]\right| \leq 2\sqrt{\Pr[x^* = x' : x' \leftarrow B^{|G\rangle,|H\rangle}(z)]}.$$

In particular, the double-sided oracle algorithm $B^{|G\rangle,|H\rangle}(z)$ runs $A^{|H\rangle}(z)$ and $A^{|G\rangle}(z)$ in superposition, and the probability $\Pr[x^* = x' : x' \leftarrow B^{|G\rangle,|H\rangle}(z)]$ is exactly $\||\psi_H^q\rangle - |\psi_G^q\rangle\|^2/4$, where $|\psi_H^q\rangle$ ($|\psi_G^q\rangle$, resp.) is the final state of $A^{|H\rangle}(z)$ ($A^{|G\rangle}(z)$, resp.).

2.3 Search in Double-Sided Oracle

In the proof of our main Theorem 4.2, we need to bound the advantage of searching a reprogramming point in a double-sided oracle. Thus, we develop the following lemma.

Lemma 2.3 (Search in Double-sided Oracle). Let $G, H : \mathcal{X} \to \mathcal{Y}$ be oracles such that $\forall x \neq x^*$ $G(x) = H(x)$. Let z be a random bitstring. Let A be quantum oracle algorithm that makes at most q queries (not necessarily unitary). Let $B^{|G\rangle,|H\rangle}(z)$ be a double-sided oracle algorithm such that $\Pr[x^* = x' : x' \leftarrow B^{|G\rangle,|H\rangle}(z)] = \||\psi_H^q\rangle - |\psi_G^q\rangle\|^2/4$, where $|\psi_H^q\rangle$ ($|\psi_G^q\rangle$, resp.) be the final state of $A^{|H\rangle}(z)$ ($A^{|G\rangle}(z)$, resp.). Let $C^{|H\rangle}(z)$ be an oracle algorithm that picks $i \leftarrow_\$ \{1, 2, \ldots, q\}$, runs $A^{|H\rangle}(z)$ until (just before) the i-th query, measures the query input registers in the computational basis, and outputs the measurement outcome. Thus, we have

$$\Pr[x^* = x' : x' \leftarrow B^{|G\rangle,|H\rangle}(z)] \leq q^2 \Pr[x^* = x' : x' \leftarrow C^{|H\rangle}(z)].$$

In particular, if $\mathcal{X} = \mathcal{X}_1 \times \mathcal{X}_2$, $x^* = (x_1^*, x_2^*)$, x_1^* is uniform and independent of H and z, then we further have $\Pr[x^* = x' : x' \leftarrow B^{|G\rangle,|H\rangle}(z)] \leq q^2/|\mathcal{X}_1|$.

Proof. Let $|\psi_0\rangle$ be an initial state that depends on z (but not on G, H or x^*), $O_H : |x, y\rangle \to |x, y \oplus H(x)\rangle$, and U_i is A's state transition operation after the i-th query. (And analogously for $A^{|G\rangle}$.) We define $|\psi_H^i\rangle$ as $U_iO_H \cdots U_1O_H|\psi_0\rangle$, and similarly $|\psi_G^i\rangle$. Thus, $|\psi_H^q\rangle$ ($|\psi_G^q\rangle$, resp.) be the final states of $A^{|H\rangle}(z)$ ($A^{|G\rangle}(z)$, resp.). Let $P_{x^*} = |x^*\rangle\langle x^*|$, $D_i = \||\psi_H^i\rangle - |\psi_G^i\rangle\|$. Then, for $i \geq 1$, we have

$$\begin{aligned}
D_i &= \left\|U_iO_H|\psi_H^{i-1}\rangle - U_iO_G|\psi_G^{i-1}\rangle\right\| \\
&= \left\|O_H|\psi_H^{i-1}\rangle - O_G|\psi_G^{i-1}\rangle + O_G|\psi_H^{i-1}\rangle - O_G|\psi_G^{i-1}\rangle\right\| \\
&\overset{*}{\leq} \left\|(O_H - O_G)|\psi_H^{i-1}\rangle\right\| + \left\|O_G(|\psi_H^{i-1}\rangle - \psi_G^{i-1}\rangle)\right\| \\
&\overset{**}{=} D_{i-1} + \left\|(O_H - O_G)P_{x^*}|\psi_H^{i-1}\rangle\right\| \\
&\overset{***}{=} D_{i-1} + 2\left\|P_{x^*}|\psi_H^{i-1}\rangle\right\|
\end{aligned} \tag{1}$$

Here, the inequation $(*)$ uses the triangle inequality. The equation $(**)$ uses that $(O_H - O_G)P_{x^*} = O_H - O_G$ since $G(x) = H(x)$ for $\forall x \neq x^*$. The inequation

$(* * *)$ uses the fact that $(O_H - O_G)$ has operator norm ≤ 2. Note that $D_0 = \|\,|\psi_0\rangle - |\psi_0\rangle\| = 0$. From (1), we get $D_i \leq D_{i-1} + 2\left\|P_{x^*}|\psi_H^{i-1}\rangle\right\|$. This implies $D_q \leq 2\sum_{i=0}^{q-1}\left\|P_{x^*}|\psi_H^i\rangle\right\|$. Using Jensen's inequality, we get $\sum_{i=0}^{q-1}\left\|P_{x^*}|\psi_H^i\rangle\right\| \leq q\sqrt{\sum_{i=0}^{q-1} 1/q \left\|P_{x^*}|\psi_H^i\rangle\right\|^2}$.

Note that $\Pr[x^* = x' : x' \leftarrow C^{|H\rangle}(z)]$ is $\sum_{i=0}^{q-1} 1/q \left\|P_{x^*}|\psi_H^i\rangle\right\|^2$. Thus, we have $D_q \leq 2q\sqrt{\Pr[x^* = x' : x' \leftarrow C^{|H\rangle}(z)]}$. Since $\Pr[x^* = x' : x' \leftarrow B^{|G\rangle,|H\rangle}(z)]$ is exactly $\left\||\psi_H^q\rangle - |\psi_G^q\rangle\right\|^2/4 = D_q^2/4$, we have $\Pr[x^* = x' : x' \leftarrow B^{|G\rangle,|H\rangle}(z)] \leq q^2\Pr[x^* = x' : x' \leftarrow C^{|H\rangle}(z)]$. In particular, if $\mathcal{X} = \mathcal{X}_1 \times \mathcal{X}_2$, $x^* = (x_1^*, x_2^*)$, x_1^* is uniform and independent of H and z, then $\Pr[x^* = x' : x' \leftarrow C^{|H\rangle}(z)] \leq 1/|\mathcal{X}_1|$. Thus, we have $\Pr[x^* = x' : x' \leftarrow B^{|G\rangle,|H\rangle}(z)] \leq q^2/|\mathcal{X}_1|$. □

3 Extended Measure-and-Reprogram Technique

Measure-and-reprogram introduced by [12,13] shows how to reprogram the quantum random oracle adaptively at one input. In detail, for any oracle algorithm $A^{|H\rangle}$ that makes at most q queries to H and outputs a pair (x, z) such that some predicate $V(x, H(x), z)$ is satisfied, the measure-and-reprogram technique shows that there exists an another algorithm S^A that simulates H, extracts x from A^H by randomly measuring one of A's queries to H, and then reprograms $H(x)$ to a given value Θ so that z output by A^H satisfies $V(x, \Theta, z)$ with a multiplicative $O(q^2)$ loss in probability.

As we discussed in Sect. 1.4, the standard measure-and-reprogram technique in [12,13] cannot be directly applied to our case. In the proof of our main Theorem 4.2, an implicit classical H-query (this is exactly x) cannot be measured, while the random measure in [12,13] is required to be performed for all the H-queries. Thus, we extend the standard measure-and-reprogram technique and give the following lemma.

Lemma 3.1 ((Single-classical-query) Measure-and-reprogram). *Let $A^{|H\rangle}$ be an arbitrary oracle quantum algorithm that makes q queries to a uniformly random $H : \mathcal{X} \to \mathcal{Y}$, and outputs some classical $x \in \mathcal{X}$ and a (possibly quantum) output z. In particular, A's i^*-th query input state is exactly $|x\rangle$ (this is a classical state and identical with the x output by $A^{|H\rangle}$).*

Let $S^A(\Theta)$ be an oracle algorithm that randomly picks a pair $(i, b_0) \in ([q-1] \setminus \{i^* - 1\} \times \{0, 1\}) \cup \{(q, 0)\}$, runs $A^{|H_i^{i^*}\rangle}$ to output z, where $H_i^{i^*}$ is an oracle that returns Θ for A's i^*-th H-query, measures A's $(i+1)$-th H-query input to obtain x, returns A's l-th H-query using H for $l < (i + 1 + b_0)$ and $l \neq i^*$, and returns A's l-th H-query using $H_{x\Theta}$ ($H_{x\Theta}(x) = \Theta$ and $H_{x\Theta}(x') = H(x')$ for all $x' \neq x$) for $l \geq (i + 1 + b_0)$ and $l \neq i^*$.

Let $S_1^A(\Theta)$ be an oracle algorithm that randomly picks a pair $(j, b_1) \in (\{i^*, \cdots, q-1\} \times \{0, 1\}) \cup \{(q, 0)\} \cup \{(i^* - 1, 1)\}$, runs $A^{|H_j\rangle}$ to output z, where H_j is an oracle that measures A's $(j+1)$-th H-query input to obtain x, returns A's l-th H-query using H for $l < (j + 1 + b_1)$, and returns A's l-th H-query using $H_{x\Theta}$ for $l \geq (j + 1 + b_1)$.

Thus, for any $x_0 \in X$, $i^* \in \{1, \cdots, q\}$ and any predicate V:

$$\Pr_H[x = x_0 \wedge V(x, H(x), z) = 1 : (x, z) \leftarrow A^{|H\rangle}] \leq 2(2q-1)^2 \Pr_{H,\Theta}[x = x_0 \wedge V(x,$$

$$\Theta, z) = 1 : (x, z) \leftarrow S^A] + 8q^2 \Pr_{H,\Theta}[x = x_0 \wedge V(x, \Theta, z) = 1 : (x, z) \leftarrow S_1^A],$$

where the subscript $\{H, \Theta\}$ in $\Pr_H$ and $\Pr_{H,\Theta}$ denotes that the probability is averaged over a random choice of H and Θ. Moreover, if $V = V_1 \wedge V_2$ such that $V_1(x, y, z) = 1$ iff y is returned for A's i^*-th query, then $\sum x_0 \Pr_{H,\Theta}[x = x_0 \wedge V(x, \Theta, z) = 1 : (x, z) \leftarrow S_1^A] \leq \frac{1}{|\mathcal{Y}|}$.

Proof. Let $|\phi_0\rangle$ be an initial state that is independent of H and Θ[6]. $O_H : |x, y\rangle \rightarrow |x, y \oplus H(x)\rangle$. Let A_i be A's state transition operation after the i-th H-query ($i \in \{1, \cdots, q\}$).

We set $A_{i \rightarrow j}^H = A_j O_H \cdots A_{i+1} O_H$ for $0 \leq i < j \leq q$ and $A_{i \rightarrow j}^H = \mathbb{I}$ for $i \geq j$. Let $|\phi_i^H\rangle = A_{0 \rightarrow i}^H |\phi_0\rangle$ be the state of A right before the $(i+1)$-th query. The final state $|\phi_q^H\rangle$ is considered to be a state over registers X, Z and E.

Let quantum predicate V be a family of projections $\{\Pi_{x,\Theta}\}_{x,\Theta}$ with $x \in \mathcal{X}$ and $\Theta \in \mathcal{Y}$. Set $G_x^\Theta = |x\rangle\langle x| \otimes \Pi_{x,\Theta}$, where $X = |x\rangle\langle x|$ acts on register X, and $\Pi_{x,\Theta}$ acts on register Z.

Then, we have

$$\Pr[x = x_0 \wedge V(x, H(x), z) = 1 : (x, z) \leftarrow A^{|H\rangle}] = \left\| G_{x_0}^{H(x_0)} |\phi_q^H\rangle \right\|^2.$$

Since $H_{x\Theta}(x') = H(x')$ for all $x' \neq x$, we have $(A_{i+1\rightarrow q}^{H_{x\Theta}})(A_{i \rightarrow i+1}^H)(\mathbb{I} - X)|\phi_i^H\rangle = (A_{i \rightarrow q}^{H_{x\Theta}})(\mathbb{I} - X)|\phi_i^H\rangle$. Thus, $(A_{i+1\rightarrow q}^{H_{x\Theta}})|\phi_{i+1}^H\rangle$

$$= (A_{i+1\rightarrow q}^{H_{x\Theta}})(A_{i \rightarrow i+1}^H)(\mathbb{I} - X)|\phi_i^H\rangle + (A_{i+1\rightarrow q}^{H_{x\Theta}})(A_{i \rightarrow i+1}^H)X|\phi_i^H\rangle$$

$$= (A_{i \rightarrow q}^{H_{x\Theta}})(\mathbb{I} - X)|\phi_i^H\rangle + (A_{i+1\rightarrow q}^{H_{x\Theta}})(A_{i \rightarrow i+1}^H)X|\phi_i^H\rangle$$

$$= (A_{i \rightarrow q}^{H_{x\Theta}})|\phi_i^H\rangle - (A_{i \rightarrow q}^{H_{x\Theta}})X|\phi_i^H\rangle + (A_{i+1\rightarrow q}^{H_{x\Theta}})(A_{i \rightarrow i+1}^H)X|\phi_i^H\rangle.$$

Applying G_x^Θ and using the triangle equality, we have $\left\| G_x^\Theta (A_{i \rightarrow q}^{H_{x\Theta}})|\phi_i^H\rangle \right\| \leq$

$$\left\| G_x^\Theta (A_{i+1\rightarrow q}^{H_{x\Theta}})|\phi_{i+1}^H\rangle \right\| + \left\| G_x^\Theta (A_{i \rightarrow q}^{H_{x\Theta}})X|\phi_i^H\rangle \right\| + \left\| G_x^\Theta (A_{i+1\rightarrow q}^{H_{x\Theta}})(A_{i \rightarrow i+1}^H)X|\phi_i^H\rangle \right\|.$$

Summing up the above inequality over $i = 0, \cdots, q-1$, we get

$$\left\| G_x^\Theta |\phi_q^{H_{x\Theta}}\rangle \right\| \leq \left\| G_x^\Theta |\phi_q^H\rangle \right\| + \sum_{0 \leq i < q, b \in \{0,1\}} \left\| G_x^\Theta (A_{i+b\rightarrow q}^{H_{x\Theta}})(A_{i \rightarrow i+b}^H)X|\phi_i^H\rangle \right\| \quad (2)$$

---

[6] This initial state can be seen as an additional input to A. In [12, Theorem 2], it is also implicitly required that the initial state is independent of H and Θ.

Note that A's i^*-th query is classical and the query input is $|x\rangle$. Then, $X|\phi_{(i^*-1)}^H\rangle = |\phi_{(i^*-1)}^H\rangle$. Thus, there is a specific term

$$\left\| G_x^\Theta (A_{(i^*-1)\to q}^{H_{x\Theta}}) X |\phi_{(i^*-1)}^H\rangle \right\| = \left\| G_x^\Theta (A_{(i^*-1)\to q}^{H_{x\Theta}}) |\phi_{(i^*-1)}^H\rangle \right\| \tag{3}$$

on the right hand side of inequality (2).

Set $B_{j\to k}^H = A_{i^*+k} O_H \cdots A_{i^*+j+1} O_H$ for $k \geq (j+1)$ ($B_{j\to k}^H = \mathbb{I}$ for $k \leq j$.), $|\psi_0\rangle = (A_{(i^*-1)\to i^*}^{H_{x\Theta}}) |\phi_{(i^*-1)}^H\rangle$, and $|\psi_j^H\rangle = B_{0\to j}^H |\psi_0\rangle$. Then,

$$\left\| G_x^\Theta (A_{(i^*-1)\to q}^{H_{x\Theta}}) |\phi_{(i^*-1)}^H\rangle \right\| = \left\| G_x^\Theta |\psi_{q-i^*}^{H_{x\Theta}}\rangle \right\| = \left\| G_x^\Theta B_{0\to (q-i^*)}^{H_{x\Theta}} |\psi_0\rangle \right\|.$$

Since $H_{x\Theta}(x') = H(x')$ for all $x' \neq x$, we have

$$(B_{j\to(j+1)}^H)(\mathbb{I} - X)|\psi_j^H\rangle = (B_{j\to(j+1)}^{H_{x\Theta}})(\mathbb{I} - X)|\psi_j^H\rangle.$$

Thus, we can write $(B_{j+1\to(q-i^*)}^{H_{x\Theta}})|\psi_{j+1}^H\rangle$.

$$= (B_{j+1\to(q-i^*)}^{H_{x\Theta}})(B_{j\to j+1}^H)(\mathbb{I}-X)|\psi_j^H\rangle + (B_{j+1\to(q-i^*)}^{H_{x\Theta}})(B_{j\to j+1}^H)X|\psi_j^H\rangle$$

$$= (B_{j\to(q-i^*)}^{H_{x\Theta}})(\mathbb{I}-X)|\psi_j^H\rangle + (B_{j+1\to(q-i^*)}^{H_{x\Theta}})(B_{j\to j+1}^H)X|\psi_j^H\rangle$$

$$= (B_{j\to(q-i^*)}^{H_{x\Theta}})|\psi_j^H\rangle - (B_{j\to(q-i^*)}^{H_{x\Theta}})X|\psi_j^H\rangle + (B_{j+1\to(q-i^*)}^{H_{x\Theta}})(B_{j\to j+1}^H)X|\psi_j^H\rangle.$$

Rearranging terms, applying G_x^Θ and using the triangle equality, we have

$$\left\| G_x^\Theta (B_{j\to(q-i^*)}^{H_{x\Theta}})|\psi_j^H\rangle \right\| \leq \left\| G_x^\Theta (B_{j+1\to(q-i^*)}^{H_{x\Theta}})|\psi_{j+1}^H\rangle \right\| +$$

$$\left\| G_x^\Theta (B_{j\to(q-i^*)}^{H_{x\Theta}})X|\psi_j^H\rangle \right\| + \left\| G_x^\Theta (B_{j+1\to(q-i^*)}^{H_{x\Theta}})(B_{j\to j+1}^H)X|\psi_j^H\rangle \right\|.$$

Summing up the inequality over $j = 0, \cdots, q - i^* - 1$, we get

$$\left\| G_x^\Theta (A_{(i^*-1)\to q}^{H_{x\Theta}})|\phi_{(i^*-1)}^H\rangle \right\| = \left\| G_x^\Theta B_{0\to(q-i^*)}^{H_{x\Theta}} |\psi_0\rangle \right\| \leq \left\| G_x^\Theta |\psi_{q-i^*}^H\rangle \right\| +$$

$$\sum_{0\leq j<(q-i^*), b\in\{0,1\}} \left\| G_x^\Theta (B_{j+b\to(q-i^*)}^{H_{x\Theta}})(B_{j\to j+b}^H)X|\psi_j^H\rangle \right\| \tag{4}$$

According to equalities (2), (3) and (4), we get

$$\left\| G_x^\Theta |\phi_q^{H_{x\Theta}}\rangle \right\| \leq Term0 + Term1, \tag{5}$$

$$Term0 = \sum_{\substack{0 \le i < (i^*-1) \\ b_0 \in \{0,1\}}} \left\| G_x^\Theta (A_{i+b_0 \to q}^{H x \Theta})(A_{i \to i+b_0}^H) X |\phi_i^H\rangle \right\| + \left\| G_x^\Theta (A_{(i^*-1) \to q}^{H x \Theta}) X |\phi_{(i^*-1)}^H\rangle \right\|$$

$$= \sum_{0 \le i < (i^*-1), b_0 \in \{0,1\}} \left\| G_x^\Theta (A_{i+b_0 \to q}^{H x \Theta})(A_{i \to i+b_0}^H) X |\phi_i^H\rangle \right\|$$

$$+ \left\| G_x^\Theta |\psi_{q-i^*}^H\rangle \right\| + \sum_{0 \le j < (q-i^*), b_0 \in \{0,1\}} \left\| G_x^\Theta (B_{j+b_0 \to (q-i^*)}^{H x \Theta})(B_{j \to j+b_0}^H) X |\psi_j^H\rangle \right\|$$

$$= \sum_{0 \le i < (i^*-1), b_0 \in \{0,1\}} \left\| G_x^\Theta (A_{i+b_0 \to q}^{H x \Theta})(A_{i \to i+b_0}^H) X |\phi_i^H\rangle \right\|$$

$$+ \left\| G_x^\Theta (A_{i^* \to q}^H)(A_{(i^*-1) \to i^*}^{H x \Theta}) |\phi_{(i^*-1)}^H\rangle \right\|$$

$$+ \sum_{\substack{i^* \le i < q \\ b_0 \in \{0,1\}}} \left\| G_x^\Theta (A_{(i+b_0) \to q}^{H x \Theta})(A_{i \to (i+b_0)}^H) X (A_{i^* \to i}^H)(A_{(i^*-1) \to i^*}^{H x \Theta}) |\phi_{(i^*-1)}^H\rangle \right\|$$

$$Term1 = \left\| G_x^\Theta |\phi_q^H\rangle \right\| + \sum_{\substack{i^* \le i < q \\ b_1 \in \{0,1\}}} \left\| G_x^\Theta (A_{i+b_1 \to q}^{H x \Theta})(A_{i \to i+b_1}^H) X |\phi_i^H\rangle \right\|$$

$$+ \left\| G_x^\Theta (A_{i^* \to q}^{H x \Theta})(A_{(i^*-1) \to i^*}^H) X |\phi_{(i^*-1)}^H\rangle \right\|.$$

According to inequality (5), we have

$$\left\| G_x^\Theta |\phi_q^{H x \Theta}\rangle \right\|^2 \le 2 Term0^2 + 2 Term1^2.$$

Since $G_x^\Theta = G_x^\Theta X$, we get $G_x^\Theta (A_{i^* \to q}^H)(A_{(i^*-1) \to i^*}^{H x \Theta}) |\phi_{(i^*-1)}^H\rangle = G_x^\Theta (A_{(i+b_0) \to q}^{H x \Theta})$ $(A_{i \to (i+b_0)}^H) X (A_{i^* \to i}^H)(A_{(i^*-1) \to i^*}^{H x \Theta}) |\phi_{(i^*-1)}^H\rangle$ with $i = q$ and $b_0 = 0$ and $G_x^\Theta |\phi_q^H\rangle = G_x^\Theta X |\phi_q^H\rangle = G_x^\Theta (A_{i+b_1 \to q}^{H x \Theta})(A_{i \to i+b_1}^H) X |\phi_i^H\rangle$ with $i = q$ and $b_1 = 0$. Then, using Jensen's inequality, we have

$$Term0^2 \le (2q-1)\left(\sum_{0 \le i < (i^*-1), b_0 \in \{0,1\}} \left\| G_x^\Theta (A_{i+b_0 \to q}^{H x \Theta})(A_{i \to i+b_0}^H) X |\phi_i^H\rangle \right\|^2 \right.$$

$$+ \left\| G_x^\Theta (A_{i^* \to q}^H)(A_{(i^*-1) \to i^*}^{H x \Theta}) |\phi_{(i^*-1)}^H\rangle \right\|^2$$

$$+ \left. \sum_{\substack{i^* \le i < q \\ b_0 \in \{0,1\}}} \left\| G_x^\Theta (A_{(i+b_0) \to q}^{H x \Theta})(A_{i \to (i+b_0)}^H) X (A_{i^* \to i}^H)(A_{(i^*-1) \to i^*}^{H x \Theta}) |\phi_{(i^*-1)}^H\rangle \right\|^2 \right)$$

$$= (2q-1)^2 \mathbb{E}_{i, b_0} \left[\left\| \delta_{i < (i^*-1)} T_0 \right\|^2 + \left\| \delta_{i \ge i^*} T_1 \right\|^2 \right],$$

where $T_0 = (G_x^\Theta (A_{i+b_0 \to q}^{H x \Theta})(A_{i \to i+b_0}^H) X |\phi_i^H\rangle)$, $T_1 = G_x^\Theta (A_{(i+b_0) \to q}^{H x \Theta})(A_{i \to (i+b_0)}^H)$ $X(A_{i^* \to i}^H)(A_{(i^*-1) \to i^*}^{H x \Theta}) |\phi_{(i^*-1)}^H\rangle$, $\delta_{i < (i^*-1)} = 1$ if $i < (i^* - 1)$ otherwise 0, $\delta_{i \ge i^*} = 1$ if $i \ge i^*$ otherwise 0, the expectation in $Term0^2$ is over uniform $(i, b_0) \in ([q-1] \setminus \{i^* - 1\} \times \{0,1\}) \cup \{(q,0)\}$.

Thus, the probability of S outputting (x, z) such that $V(x, \Theta, z) = 1$ is exactly $\mathbb{E}_{i, b_0}\left[\left\|\delta_{i<(i^*-1)}T_0\right\|^2 + \left\|\delta_{i \geq i^*}T_1\right\|^2\right]$.

Likewise, using Jensen's inequality, we get

$$Term1^2 \leq (2q - 2i^* + 2)(\left\|G_x^\Theta|\phi_q^H\rangle\right\|^2 + \sum_{\substack{i^* \leq i < q \\ b_1 \in \{0,1\}}} \left\|G_x^\Theta(A_{i+b_1 \to q}^{H x \Theta})(A_{i \to i+b_1}^H)X|\phi_i^H\rangle\right\|^2$$

$$+ \left\|G_x^\Theta(A_{i^* \to q}^{H x \Theta})(A_{(i^*-1) \to i^*}^H)X|\phi_{(i^*-1)}^H\rangle\right\|^2)$$

$$= (2q - 2i^* + 2)^2 \mathbb{E}_{j, b_1}\left[\left\|G_x^\Theta(A_{j+b_1 \to q}^{H x \Theta})(A_{j \to j+b_1}^H)X|\phi_j^H\rangle\right\|^2\right]$$

where the expectation in $Term1^2$ is over uniform $(j, b_1) \in (\{i^*, \cdots, q-1\} \times \{0,1\}) \cup \{(q,0)\} \cup \{(i^*-1, 1)\}$.

Thus, the probability of S_1 outputting (x, z) such that $V(x, \Theta, z) = 1$ is exactly $\mathbb{E}_{j, b_1}\left[\left\|G_x^\Theta(A_{j+b_1 \to q}^{H x \Theta})(A_{j \to j+b_1}^H)X|\phi_j^H\rangle\right\|^2\right]$.

Since the initial state is independent of H and Θ, we have $\Pr_{H, \Theta}[\left\|G_x^\Theta|\phi_q^{H x \Theta}\rangle\right\|^2] = \Pr_{H, \Theta}[\left\|G_x^{H(x)}|\phi_q^H\rangle\right\|^2]$. Thus, for any $x_0 \in X$ and predicate V, we have

$$\Pr_H[x = x_0 \wedge V(x, H(x), z) = 1 : (x, z) \leftarrow A^{|H\rangle}] \leq 2(2q-1)^2 \Pr_{H, \Theta}[x = x_0 \wedge V(x,$$

$$\Theta, z) = 1 : (x, z) \leftarrow S^A] + 8q^2 \Pr_{H, \Theta}[x = x_0 \wedge V(x, \Theta, z) = 1 : (x, z) \leftarrow S_1^A],$$

as desired. Set $V_1(x, y, z) = 1$ iff y is returned for A's i^*-th query. When $V = V_1 \wedge V_2$, we get

$$\sum x_0 \Pr_{H, \Theta}[x = x_0 \wedge V(x, \Theta, z) = 1 : (x, z) \leftarrow S_1^A] \leq \Pr[H(x) = \Theta] = \frac{1}{|\mathcal{Y}|}.$$

4   IND-1-CCA-secure KEM Without Re-encryption and Ciphertext Expansion

To a public-key encryption $\text{PKE}'=(Gen', Enc', Dec')$ and a random oracle H ($H : \mathcal{M} \times \mathcal{C} \to \mathcal{K}$), we associate $\text{KEM}_H = T_H[\text{PKE}', H]$ and $\text{KEM}_{RH} = T_{RH}[\text{PKE}', H]$ as in Fig. 2. The only difference between KEM_H and KEM_{RH} is the return value for invalid ciphertexts. In detail, when a ciphertext decrypts to $\perp$, such a ciphertext will decapsulate to $\perp$ in KEM_H, and to $H(\star, c)$ in KEM_{RH}. Here, $\star$ can be any fixed public value. In the following, Theorems 4.1 and 4.2 show the IND-1-CCA security of KEM_{RH} in the (Q)ROM. In particular, Theorems 4.1 and 4.2 works for both $\star \in \mathcal{M}$ and $\star \notin \mathcal{M}$. Then, we will show that the IND-1-CCA security of KEM_H can be reduced to the IND-1-CCA security of KEM_{RH} by Theorem 4.3.

Theorem 4.1 (ROM security of T_{RH}). *If PKE' is δ-correct, for any adversary $\mathcal{B}$ against the IND-1-CCA security of $\text{KEM}_{RH} = T_{RH}[\text{PKE}', H]$ in Fig. 2,*

Gen	Encaps(pk)	Decaps(sk, c)
1: $(pk, sk) \leftarrow Gen'$	1: $m \leftarrow_\$ \mathcal{M}$	1: $m' := Dec'(sk, c)$
2: **return** (pk, sk)	2: $c \leftarrow Enc'(pk, m)$	2: **if** $m' = \perp$
	3: $K := H(m, c)$	3: **return** $\perp$ $//T_H$
	4: **return** (K, c)	4: **return** $K := H(\star, c)$ $//T_{RH}$
		5: **else return** $K := H(m', c)$

Fig. 2. $\text{KEM}_H = T_H[\text{PKE}', H]$ and $\text{KEM}_{RH} = T_{RH}[\text{PKE}', H]$

issuing at most a single (classical) query to the decapsulation oracle DECAPS and at most q_H queries to the random oracle H, there exists a OW-CPA adversary $\mathcal{A}$ and an IND-CPA adversary $\mathcal{D}$ against PKE' such that $\text{Time}(\mathcal{A}) \approx \text{Time}(\mathcal{D}) \approx \text{Time}(\mathcal{B}) + O(q_H^2)$ and

$$\text{Adv}_{\text{KEM}_{RH}}^{\text{IND-1-CCA}}(\mathcal{B}) \le q_H(q_H + 1)\text{Adv}_{\text{PKE}'}^{\text{OW-CPA}}(\mathcal{A}) \tag{6}$$

$$\text{Adv}_{\text{KEM}_{RH}}^{\text{IND-1-CCA}}(\mathcal{B}) \le 2(q_H + 1)\text{Adv}_{\text{PKE}'}^{\text{IND-CPA}}(\mathcal{D}) + 2q_H(q_H + 1)/|\mathcal{M}|.$$

If the PKE is deterministic, the bound (6) can be improved as

$$\text{Adv}_{\text{KEM}_{RH}}^{\text{IND-1-CCA}}(\mathcal{B}) \le (q_H + 1)\text{Adv}_{\text{PKE}'}^{\text{OW-CPA}}(\mathcal{A}) + \delta,$$

where $\text{Time}(\mathcal{A}) \approx \text{Time}(\mathcal{B}) + O(q_H^2) + O(q_H \cdot \text{Time}(Enc'))$.

Proof. Let $\mathcal{B}$ be an adversary against the IND-CCA security of KEM_{RH}, issuing (exactly) one classical query to DECAPS (by introducing a dummy query if necessary), and at most q_H queries (excluding the queries implicitly made in DECAPS) to H. Let Ω_H be the sets of all functions $H : \mathcal{M} \times \mathcal{C} \to \mathcal{K}$. Consider the games in Fig. 3.

GAME G_0. This is exactly the IND-1-CCA game, thus $|\Pr[G_0^{\mathcal{B}} \Rightarrow 1] - 1/2| = \text{Adv}_{\text{KEM}_{RH}}^{\text{IND-1-CCA}}(\mathcal{B})$.

GAME G_1. In game G_1, $k_0^* := H(m^*, c^*)$ is replaced by $k_0^* \leftarrow_\$ \mathcal{K}$. Thus, in G_1, the bit b is independent of $\mathcal{B}$'s view, thus $\Pr[G_1^{\mathcal{B}} \Rightarrow 1] = 1/2$. Define QUERY as the event that (m^*, c^*) is queried to H. Then, G_1 is identical with G_0 in $\mathcal{B}$'s view unless the event QUERY happens. Thus, we have

$$\text{Adv}_{\text{KEM}_{RH}}^{\text{IND-1-CCA}}(\mathcal{B}) = |\Pr[G_0^{\mathcal{B}} \Rightarrow 1] - \Pr[G_1^{\mathcal{B}} \Rightarrow 1]| \le \Pr[\text{QUERY} : G_1].$$

GAME G_2. In game G_2, we make two changes. First, we modify the DECAPS oracle, and replace $K := H(\bar{m}, \bar{c})$ by $K := \bar{k}$. Second, we reprogram the random oracle H conditional a uniform i over $[q_H]$. In particular, reprogram H to H_1^i (given by Fig. 3) when $\mathcal{B}$ makes the $(i + 1)$-th H-query $(0 \le i \le (q_H - 1))$, and then answer $\mathcal{B}$ with H_1^i for $\mathcal{B}$'s j-th query $(j \ge (i + 1))$. Let (m_i, c_i) be $\mathcal{B}$'s i-th H-query input. $H_1^i(m, c)$ returns $\bar{k}$ when $(m, c) = (m_{i+1}, c_{i+1})$ and $H_1(m, c)$

otherwise. Let $(i^* + 1)$ be the number of $\mathcal{B}$'s first query to H with $(\bar{m}, \bar{c})$, where $i^* \in [q_H - 1]$. We also denote $i^* = q_H$ as the event that $\mathcal{B}$ makes no query to H with $(\bar{m}, \bar{c})$. Note that G_2 has the same distribution as G_1 in $\mathcal{B}$'s view when the event $i^* = i$ happens. Thus, we have

$$\Pr[\text{QUERY} : G_1] \leq (q_H + 1)\Pr[\text{QUERY} : G_2].$$

Let $(pk, sk) \leftarrow Gen'$, $m^* \leftarrow_{\$} \mathcal{M}$, $c^* \leftarrow Enc(pk, m^*)$. Then, we construct an adversary $\mathcal{A}'(pk, c^*)$ that simulates $\mathcal{B}$'s view as in game G_2 and returns $\mathcal{B}$'s H-query list H-List, see Fig. 4. Note that a q_H-wise independent function is perfectly indistinguishable from a true random function for any distinguisher that makes at most q_H queries [41]. Thus, the probability of the H-List returned by $\mathcal{A}'$ contains (m^*, c^*) is exactly $\Pr[\text{QUERY} : G_2]$.

Now, we construct an adversary $\mathcal{A}$ against the OW-CPA security of the underlying PKE. If the underlying PKE is probabilistic, $\mathcal{A}$ runs $\mathcal{A}'$, and randomly selects one message in H-List as a return. Then, we have $\text{Adv}_{\text{PKE}'}^{\text{OW}-\text{CPA}}(\mathcal{A}) \geq 1/q_H \Pr[\text{QUERY} : G_2]$. Therefore, for probabilistic PKE, we have

$$\text{Adv}_{\text{KEM}_{RH}}^{\text{IND-1-CCA}}(\mathcal{B}) \leq q_H(q_H + 1)\text{Adv}_{\text{PKE}'}^{\text{OW}-\text{CPA}}(\mathcal{A}).$$

Next, we consider the case of the deterministic PKE.

GAMES $G_0 - G_2$ and $G_1^A - G_2^A$	$H(m,c)$
1 : $(pk, sk) \leftarrow Gen', j = 0, i \leftarrow_{\$} [q_H]$	1 : **if** $(m,c) = (m^*, c^*)$
2 : QUERY = **false** , $H_1 \leftarrow_{\$} \Omega_H$	2 : QUERY = **true**
3 : $\bar{k}, k_1^* \leftarrow_{\$} \mathcal{K}, b \leftarrow_{\$} \{0,1\}$	3 : **if** $j \geq i$ **return** $H_1^i(m,c)$ $//G_2, G_2^A$
4 : $m^* \leftarrow_{\$} \mathcal{M}, c^* \leftarrow Enc(pk, m^*)$	4 : $j = j + 1$ $//G_2, G_2^A$
5 : **if** COLL **return** $\perp$ $//G_1^A - G_2^A$	5 : **return** $H_1(m,c)$
6 : $k_0^* = H(m^*, c^*)$ $//G_0$	DECAPS $(sk, \bar{c} \neq c^*)$
7 : $k_0^* \leftarrow_{\$} \mathcal{K}//G_1 - G_2, G_1^A - G_2^A$	
8 : $b' \leftarrow \mathcal{B}^{H,\text{DECAPS}}(pk, c^*, k_b^*)$	1 : **if** more than 1 query **return** $\perp$
9 : **return** $b' = ?b$	2 : **return** $K := \bar{k}$ $//G_2, G_2^A$
$H_1^i(m,c)$	3 : $m' := Dec'(sk, \bar{c})$
	4 : **if** $m' = \perp$ **do** $\bar{m} = \star$
1 : **if** $(m,c) = (m_{i+1}, c_{i+1})$	5 : **else do** $\bar{m} = m'$
2 : **return** $\bar{k}$	6 : **return** $K := H(\bar{m}, \bar{c})$
3 : **else return** $H_1(m,c)$	

Fig. 3. Games for the proof of Theorem 4.1

GAME G_1^A. Define COLL as the event that there is a messages $m \neq m^*$ such that $Enc'(pk, m) = c^* = Enc'(pk, m^*)$. G_1^A is the same as G_1 except that $\perp$ is

$\mathcal{A}'(pk, c^*)$

---

1 : $k^*, \bar{k} \leftarrow_\$ \mathcal{K}, j = 0, i \leftarrow_\$ [q_H]$

2 : Pick a q_H-wise functions H_1

3 : $b' \leftarrow \mathcal{B}^{H,\mathrm{DECAPS}}(pk, c^*, k^*)$

4 : **return** H-List

$H_1^i(m, c)$

---

1 : **if** $(m, c) = (m_{i+1}, c_{i+1})$ **return** $\bar{k}$

2 : **else return** $H_1(m, c)$

$H(m, c)$

---

1 : **if** $i = q_H$ **return** $H_1(m, c)$

2 : **if** $j \geq i$ **return** $H_1^i(m, c)$

3 : $j = j + 1$

4 : **return** $H_1(m, c)$

$\mathrm{DECAPS}\ (\bar{c} \neq c^*)$

---

1 : **return** $\bar{k}$

Fig. 4. Adversary $\mathcal{A}'$ for the proof of Theorem 4.1

returned if COLL happens. Note that G_1 and G_1^A have the same distribution when COLL doe not happen (implied by the δ-correctness). Thus, we have

$$\Pr[\mathrm{QUERY} : G_1] \leq \Pr[\mathrm{QUERY} : G_1^A] + \delta.$$

GAME G_2^A. G_2^A is the same as G_1^A except that oracles DECAPS and H are modified as in G_2. Then, arguing in the same way as in G_2, we have

$$\Pr[\mathrm{QUERY} : G_1^A] \leq (q_H + 1)\Pr[\mathrm{QUERY} : G_2^A].$$

Now, we construct an adversary $\mathcal{A}$ against deterministic PKE. $\mathcal{A}$ runs $\mathcal{A}'$, selects a (m', c') from H-List such that $c' = c^*$ and $Enc(pk, m') = c^*$, and returns m'. Note that if COLL does not happen, $\mathcal{A}$ returns m^* with probability $\Pr[\mathrm{QUERY} : G_2^A]$. Thus, $\mathrm{Adv}_{\mathrm{PKE}'}^{\mathrm{OW-CPA}}(\mathcal{A}) \geq \Pr[\mathrm{QUERY} : G_2^A]$. Therefore, putting the inequalities together, we have

$$\mathrm{Adv}_{\mathrm{KEM}_{RH}}^{\mathrm{IND-1-CCA}}(\mathcal{B}) \leq (q_H + 1)\mathrm{Adv}_{\mathrm{PKE}'}^{\mathrm{OW-CPA}}(\mathcal{A}) + \delta.$$

When the underlying PKE satisfies IND-CPA security, we can construct an IND-CPA adversary $\mathcal{D}$, and derive a tighter bound. In particular, $\mathcal{D}(pk)$ samples two uniform messages m_0^* and m_1^* from $\mathcal{M}$, i.e., $m_0^*, m_1^* \leftarrow_\$ \mathcal{M}$. The IND-CPA challenger chooses a bit b, generates the challenge ciphertext $c^* \leftarrow Enc(pk, m_b^*)$ and sends c^* to $\mathcal{D}$. Then, $\mathcal{D}$ runs $\mathcal{A}'(pk, c^*)$, get $\mathcal{B}$'s H-List. If $(m_{b'}^*, *)$ is in H-List and $(m_{1-b'}^*, *)$ is not in H-List, $\mathcal{D}$ returns b'. For other cases, $\mathcal{D}$ returns a uniform b', i.e., $b' \leftarrow_\$ \{0, 1\}$. Let BAD be the event that $\mathcal{B}$ queries $(m_{1-b}^*, *)$ (that is, $(m_{1-b}^*, *)$ is in H-List). Note that m_{1-b}^* is uniformly distributed and independent from $\mathcal{B}$'s view. Thus, the events BAD and QUERY are independent, and $\Pr[\mathrm{BAD}] \leq q_H/|\mathcal{M}|$. Note that if BAD does not happen, then $\mathcal{D}$ makes a correct guess of b with probability 1 when QUERY happens, and with probability $1/2$ when QUERY does not happen. Thus, we have

$$\text{Adv}_{\text{PKE}'}^{\text{IND}-\text{CPA}}(\mathcal{D}) = |\Pr[b' = b] - 1/2|$$

$$= |\Pr[b' = b \wedge \text{BAD}] + \Pr[b' = b \wedge \neg\text{BAD}] - 1/2(\Pr[\text{BAD}] + \Pr[\neg\text{BAD}])|$$

$$\geq |\Pr[b' = b \wedge \neg\text{BAD}] - 1/2\Pr[\neg\text{BAD}]| - \Pr[\text{BAD}]\,|\Pr[b' = b|\text{BAD}] - 1/2|$$

$$\geq |\Pr[b' = b \wedge \neg\text{BAD}] - 1/2\Pr[\neg\text{BAD}]| - 1/2\Pr[\text{BAD}]$$

$$= |\Pr[b' = b \wedge \neg\text{BAD} \wedge \text{QUERY}] - 1/2\Pr[\neg\text{BAD} \wedge \text{QUERY}]| - 1/2\Pr[\text{BAD}]$$

$$= 1/2\Pr[\neg\text{BAD} \wedge \text{QUERY}] - 1/2\Pr[\text{BAD}]$$

$$\geq 1/2\Pr[\text{QUERY}] - \Pr[\text{BAD}]$$

$$\geq 1/2\Pr[\text{QUERY}] - q_H/|\mathcal{M}| = 1/2\Pr[\text{QUERY} : G_2] - q_H/|\mathcal{M}|.$$

Putting the bounds together, we have

$$\text{Adv}_{\text{KEM}_{RH}}^{\text{IND-1-CCA}}(\mathcal{B}) \leq 2(q_H + 1)\text{Adv}_{\text{PKE}'}^{\text{IND}-\text{CPA}}(\mathcal{D}) + 2q_H(q_H + 1)/|\mathcal{M}|.$$

$\square$

Theorem 4.2 (QROM security of T_{RH}). *If PKE' is δ-correct, for any adversary $\mathcal{B}$ against the IND-1-CCA security of $KEM_{RH} = T_{RH}[\text{PKE}', H]$ in Fig. 2, issuing at most one single (classical) query to the decapsulation oracle* DECAPS *and at most q_H queries to the quantum random oracle H, there exists a OW-CPA adversary $\mathcal{A}$ and an IND-CPA adversary $\mathcal{D}$ against PKE' such that* $\text{Time}(\mathcal{A}) \approx \text{Time}(\mathcal{D}) \approx \text{Time}(\mathcal{B}) + O(q_H^2)$ *and*

$$\text{Adv}_{\text{KEM}_{RH}}^{\text{IND-1-CCA}}(\mathcal{B}) \leq 6(q_H + 1)^2\sqrt{\text{Adv}_{\text{PKE}'}^{\text{OW}-\text{CPA}}(\mathcal{A}) + 1/|\mathcal{K}|}.$$

$$\text{Adv}_{\text{KEM}_{RH}}^{\text{IND-1-CCA}}(\mathcal{B}) \leq 6(q_H + 1)\sqrt{4\text{Adv}_{\text{PKE}'}^{\text{IND}-\text{CPA}}(\mathcal{D}) + 2(q_H + 1)^2/|\mathcal{M}| + 1/|\mathcal{K}|}.$$

If the PKE is deterministic, the bound can be improved as

$$\text{Adv}_{\text{KEM}_{RH}}^{\text{IND-1-CCA}}(\mathcal{B}) \leq 6(q_H + 1)\sqrt{\text{Adv}_{\text{PKE}'}^{\text{OW}-\text{CPA}}(\mathcal{A}) + 1/|\mathcal{K}|} + \delta,$$

where $\text{Time}(\mathcal{A}) \approx \text{Time}(\mathcal{B}) + O(q_H^2) + O(q_H \cdot \text{Time}(Enc'))$.

Proof Sketch: Our proof mainly consists of two steps. One is the underlying security game embedding via replacing the real key $H(m^*, c^*)$ with a random key (i.e., reprogramming H). We argue the impact of such a reprogramming by different O2H variants. When the underlying PKE is OW-CPA-secure, we follow previous proofs for $U^{\not\perp}$ in [6,22], and use general O2H (Lemma 2.1) for probabilistic PKE and double-sided O2H (Lemma 2.2) for deterministic PKE. When the underlying PKE is IND-CPA-secure, we also adopt double-sided O2H (Lemma 2.2) to argue the reprogramming impact. Since the embedded IND-CPA game is decisional, an additional game that searches a reprogramming point in double-sided oracle is introduced and we use Lemma 2.3 to argue this advantage. The other is simulation of the DECAPS oracle. As discussed in Sect. 1.4, we adopt a new DECAPS simulation that directly replaces the output $H(\bar{m}, \bar{c})$ with a random key $\bar{k}$. Intuitively, this simulation is perfect if $H(\bar{m}, \bar{c})$ is reprogrammed to be $\bar{k}$ when the adversary first makes a query $(\bar{m}, \bar{c})$. However, in the QROM, it is hard to define the first time to query $(\bar{m}, \bar{c})$. Thus, in the QROM, we argue this in a different way. We find the simulation is perfect if the predicate $\text{DECAPS}(sk, \bar{c}) = H(\bar{m}, \bar{c})$ is satisfied. Since in the simulation of DECAPS, an implicit (classical) H-query $(\bar{m}, \bar{c})$ made in the real implementation is removed and thus this specific query can not be measured. Therefore, we use a refined optional-query measure-and-reprogram technique in Lemma 3.1 to argue the simulation impact.

GAMES $G_0 - G_2$

1: $(pk, sk) \leftarrow Gen', H \leftarrow_\$ \Omega_H$

2: $k, k_1^* \leftarrow_\$ \mathcal{K}, b \leftarrow_\$ \{0, 1\}$

3: $m^* \leftarrow_\$ \mathcal{M}, c^* \leftarrow Enc(pk, m^*)$

4: $k_0^* = H(m^*, c^*)$ $//G_0 - G_1$

5: $k_0^* \leftarrow_\$ \mathcal{K}$ $//G_2$

6: $b' \leftarrow \mathcal{B}^{|H\rangle, \text{DECAPS}}(pk, c^*, k_b^*)$ $//G_0, G_2$

7: $b' \leftarrow \mathcal{B}^{|H'\rangle, \text{DECAPS}}(pk, c^*, k_b^*)$ $//G_1$

8: **return** $b' =?b$

DECAPS $(sk, \bar{c} \neq c^*)$ $//G_0 - G_2$

1: $m' := Dec'(sk, \bar{c})$

2: **if** more than 1 query **return** $\perp$

3: **if** $m' = \perp$ **do** $\bar{m} = \star$

4: **else do** $\bar{m} = m'$

5: **return** $K := H(\bar{m}, \bar{c})$

$H'(m, c)$

1: **if** $(m, c) = (m^*, c^*)$ **return** k

2: **return** $H(m, c)$

Fig. 5. Games $G_0 - G_2$ for the proof of Theorem 4.2

Proof. Let Ω_H be the sets of all functions $H : \mathcal{M} \times \mathcal{C} \rightarrow \mathcal{K}$. Let $\mathcal{B}$ be an IND-CCA adversary against KEM_{RH}, issuing a single classical query to DECAPS (if none, introduce a dummy one), and at most q_H quantum queries (excluding the queries implicitly made in DECAPS) to H. Consider the games in Fig. 5.

GAME G_0. Since game G_0 is exactly the IND-1-CCA game, $\left| \Pr[G_0^{\mathcal{B}} \Rightarrow 1] - 1/2 \right| = \text{Adv}_{\text{KEM}_{RH}}^{\text{IND-1-CCA}}(\mathcal{B})$.

GAME G_1. In game G_1, the random oracle H accessed by $\mathcal{B}$ is replaced by an oracle H' given by Fig. 5. It is easy to see that G_1 can be rewritten as game G_2.

GAME G_2. The game G_2 is the same as game G_0 except that $k_0^* := H(m^*, c^*)$ is replaced by $k_0^* \leftarrow_\$ \mathcal{K}$. Thus, in G_2, the bit b is independent of $\mathcal{B}$'s view, thus $\Pr[G_2^{\mathcal{B}} \Rightarrow 1] = 1/2$. Note that games G_1 and G_2 have the same distribution. Thus, $\Pr[G_1^{\mathcal{B}} \Rightarrow 1] = \Pr[G_2^{\mathcal{B}} \Rightarrow 1] = 1/2$. Therefore, we have

$$\text{Adv}_{\text{KEM}_{RH}}^{\text{IND-1-CCA}}(\mathcal{B}) = \left| \Pr[G_0^{\mathcal{B}} \Rightarrow 1] - \Pr[G_1^{\mathcal{B}} \Rightarrow 1] \right|. \tag{7}$$

Lemma 4.1. *There exists an adversary $\mathcal{A}$ against the OW-CPA of probabilistic PKE$'$ such that* $\text{Time}(\mathcal{A}) \approx \text{Time}(\mathcal{B}) + O(q_H^2)$ *and* $\text{Adv}_{\text{KEM}_{RH}}^{\text{IND-1-CCA}}(\mathcal{B}) \leq 6(q_H + 1)^2 \sqrt{\text{Adv}_{\text{PKE}'}^{\text{OW-CPA}}(\mathcal{A}) + 1/|\mathcal{K}|}$.

The proof of Lemma 4.1. Define games G_{3A} and G_{4A} as in Fig. 6.

Let $z1 = (pk, sk, c^*, k_b^*, b)$. Let A^O ($O \in H, H'$) be an oracle algorithm that runs $\mathcal{B}^{|O\rangle,\text{DECAPS}}(pk, c^*, k_b^*)$ to obtain b', and returns $b' =?b$. Thus, we have $\Pr[G_0^{\mathcal{B}} \Rightarrow 1] = \Pr[1 \leftarrow A^{|H\rangle}(z1)]$ and $\Pr[G_1^{\mathcal{B}} \Rightarrow 1] = \Pr[1 \leftarrow A^{|H'\rangle}(z1)]$. Let $B(z1)$ be an algorithm that randomly samples $j \in [q_H - 1]$, runs $A^{|H'\rangle}$ until (just before) the $(j+1)$-th query (In game G_{3A}, H' is rewritten to be H), measures the query input registers in the computational basis, and outputs measurement outcomes. Thus, we have $\Pr[G_{3A}^{\mathcal{B}} \Rightarrow 1] = \Pr[(m^*, *) \leftarrow B^{|H\rangle}(z1)] \geq \Pr[(m^*, c^*) \leftarrow B^{|H\rangle}(z1)]$. Therefore, according to Lemma 2.1, we have

$$\left| \Pr[G_0^{\mathcal{B}} \Rightarrow 1] - \Pr[G_1^{\mathcal{B}} \Rightarrow 1] \right| \leq 2(q_H + 1)\sqrt{\Pr[G_{3A}^{\mathcal{B}} \Rightarrow 1]}.$$

Let $C^{|H\rangle}$ be an oracle algorithm that samples pk, sk, k^*, j, m^*, c^*, and runs $\mathcal{B}^{|H\rangle,\text{DECAPS}}$ as in game G_{3A}. Let $\bar{c}$ be $\mathcal{B}$'s query to the DECAPS oracle. Let $\bar{m} = \star$ if $\bar{m}' = \perp$, and $\bar{m} = \bar{m}'$ if $\bar{m}' \neq \perp$, where $\bar{m}' = Dec'(sk, \bar{c})$. Let $x = (\bar{m}, \bar{c})$, $y = H(x)$, and $z = (z_1, z_2, z_3) = (\text{DECAPS}(sk, \bar{c}), m^*, m')$. C outputs (x, z). Let $V_1(x, y, z) = (y =?z_1)$ and $V_2 = (z_2 =?z_3)$. Instantiating the predicate V in Lemma 3.1 by $V = V_1 \wedge V_2$. Note that in G_{3A} the return of the DECAPS oracle is exactly $H(x)$. That is, $V_1 = 1$ is always satisfied. Thus, we have $\Pr[G_{3A}^{\mathcal{B}} \Rightarrow 1] = \sum x_0 \Pr_H[x = x_0 \wedge V(x, H(x), z) = 1 : (x, z) \leftarrow C^{|H\rangle}]$.

Note that C needs to implicitly query $H(\bar{m}, \bar{c})$ to simulate the DECAPS oracle. That is, C makes $q_H + 1$ H-queries in total. In the following, unless otherwise specified, the H-queries we mentioned does not include this implicit H-query. Let $S^C(\Theta)$ be an oracle algorithm that always returns Θ for C's implicit classical H-query $H(\bar{m}, \bar{c})$. S samples a uniform $(i, b) \leftarrow_\$ ([q_H - 1] \times \{0, 1\}) \cup \{(q_H, 0)\}$, runs $C^{|H\rangle}$ until the C's $(i + 1)$-th query (excluding the implicit H-query), measures the query input registers to obtain x, continues to run $C^{|H\rangle}$ until the $(i+b+1)$-th H-query, reprogram H to $H_{x\Theta}$ ($H_{x\Theta}(x) = \Theta$ and $H_{x\Theta}(x') = H(x')$ for all $x' \neq x$), and runs $A^{|H_{x\Theta}\rangle}$ until the end to output z. Let $x = (\bar{m}, \bar{c})$, $y = \Theta$, and $z = (z_1, z_2, z_3) = (\text{DECAPS}(sk, \bar{c}), m^*, m')$. S^C outputs (x, z). Note that $V_1(x, y, z) = (y =?z_1) = 1$ for S^C. Sample $\Theta = \bar{k} \leftarrow_\$ \mathcal{K}$ and $H \leftarrow_\$ \Omega_H$. Then, $S^C(\Theta)$ perfectly simulates game G_{4A} and we have $\Pr[G_{4A}^{\mathcal{B}} \Rightarrow 1] = \sum x_0 \Pr_{H,\Theta}[x = x_0 \wedge V(x, \Theta, z) = 1 : (x, z) \leftarrow S^C]$.

According to Lemma 3.1, $\sum x_0 \Pr_H[x = x_0 \wedge V(x, H(x), z) = 1 : (x, z) \leftarrow C^{|H\rangle}] \leq 2(2q_H + 1)^2 \sum x_0 \Pr_{H,\Theta}[x = x_0 \wedge V(x, \Theta, z) = 1 : (x, z) \leftarrow S^C] + 8(q_H + 1)^2 \frac{1}{|\mathcal{K}|}$. Therefore, we get

$$\Pr[G_{3A}^{\mathcal{B}} \Rightarrow 1] \leq 8(q_H + 1)^2 (\Pr[G_{4A}^{\mathcal{B}} \Rightarrow 1] + 1/|\mathcal{K}|).$$

Now, we can construct a OW-CPA adversary $\mathcal{A}(pk, c^*)$ against PKE$'$, where $(pk, sk) \leftarrow Gen', m^* \leftarrow_\$ \mathcal{M}, c^* \leftarrow Enc(pk, m^*)$. $\mathcal{A}$ samples $k^*, \bar{k}, j, i, b$ as in game

GAMES $G_{3A} - G_{4A}$

---

1 : $(pk, sk) \leftarrow Gen', H \leftarrow_\$ \Omega_H, k^*, \bar{k} \leftarrow_\$ \mathcal{K}, m^* \leftarrow_\$ \mathcal{M}, c^* \leftarrow Enc(pk, m^*)$

2 : $l = 0, j \leftarrow_\$ [q_H - 1], (i, b) \leftarrow_\$ ([q_H - 1] \times \{0, 1\}) \cup \{(q_H, 0)\}$

3 : Run $\mathcal{B}^{|H\rangle, \mathrm{DECAPS}}(pk, c^*, k^*)$ until the $(j+1)$-th query $|\psi\rangle$ // G_{3A}

4 : Run $\mathcal{B}^{|H_1^i\rangle, \mathrm{DECAPS}}(pk, c^*, k^*)$ until the $(j+1)$-th query state$|\psi\rangle$ // G_{4A}

5 : $(m', c') \leftarrow M|\psi\rangle$

   // Make a standard measure M on $\mathcal{B}$'s $(j+1)$-th query input register

6 : **return** $m^* =? m'$

DECAPS $(sk, \bar{c} \neq c^*)$ // $G_{3A} - G_{4A}$ | $H_1^i(m, c)$

1 : **if** more than 1 query **return** $\bot$ | 1 : **if** $l \geq (i + b) \wedge (m, c) = (m_{i+1}, c_{i+1})$

2 : **return** $\bar{k}$ // G_{4A} | // (m_{i+1}, c_{i+1}) is the measurement outcome

3 : $\bar{m}' := Dec'(sk, \bar{c})$ | // on $\mathcal{B}$'s $(i+1)$-th query input register

4 : **if** $\bar{m}' = \bot$ **do** $\bar{m} = \star$ | 2 : **return** $\bar{k}$

5 : **else do** $\bar{m} = \bar{m}'$ | 3 : **else return** $H(m, c)$

6 : **return** $K := H(\bar{m}, \bar{c})$ | 4 : $l = l + 1$

Fig. 6. Games G_{3A}-G_{4A} for the proof of Lemma 4.1

G_{4A}, picks a $2q_H$-wise independent function H (undistinguishable from a random function for a q_H-query adversary according to [41, Theorem 6.1]), runs $\mathcal{B}^{|H_1^i\rangle, \mathrm{DECAPS}}(pk, c^*, k^*)$ (the simulations of H_1^i, DECAPS are the same as the ones in game G_{4A}) until the $(j+1)$-th query, measures $\mathcal{B}$'s query input register to obtain (m', c'), finally outputs m' as a return. It is obvious that the advantage of $\mathcal{A}$ against the OW-CPA security of PKE' is exactly $\Pr[G_{4A}^{\mathcal{B}} \Rightarrow 1]$. Putting everything together, we have

$$\mathrm{Adv}_{\mathrm{KEM}_{RH}}^{\mathrm{IND-1-CCA}}(\mathcal{B}) \leq 6(q_H + 1)^2 \sqrt{\mathrm{Adv}_{\mathrm{PKE'}}^{\mathrm{OW-CPA}}(\mathcal{A}) + 1/|\mathcal{K}|}.$$

Lemma 4.2. *There exists an adversary $\mathcal{A}$ against the OW-CPA security of deterministic* PKE' *such that* $\mathrm{Time}(\mathcal{A}) \approx \mathrm{Time}(\mathcal{B}) + O(q_H^2) + O(q_H \cdot \mathrm{Time}(Enc'))$ *and* $\mathrm{Adv}_{\mathrm{KEM}_{RH}}^{\mathrm{IND-1-CCA}}(\mathcal{B}) \leq 6(q_H + 1) \sqrt{\mathrm{Adv}_{\mathrm{PKE'}}^{\mathrm{OW-CPA}}(\mathcal{A}) + 1/|\mathcal{K}|} + \delta$.

The proof of Lemma 4.2. Define games G_{3B}, G_{4B} and G_{5B} as in Fig. 7. Let $z1 = (pk, sk, c^*, k_0^*)$, where $(pk, sk) \leftarrow Gen'$, $k_0^* \leftarrow_\$ \mathcal{K}$, $m^* \leftarrow_\$ \mathcal{M}$, and $c^* \leftarrow Enc(pk, m^*)$. Sample $G \leftarrow_\$ \Omega_H$. Let G' be an oracle such that $G'(m^*, c^*) = k_0^*$, and $G'(x) = G(x)$ for $x \neq (m^*, c^*)$. Let $A^{|O\rangle}(z1)$ ($O \in G, G'$) be an oracle algorithm that first samples $k_1^* \leftarrow_\$ \mathcal{K}$, $b \leftarrow_\$ \{0, 1\}$, then runs $\mathcal{B}^{|O\rangle, \mathrm{DECAPS}}(pk, c^*, k_b^*)$ to obtain b' (simulating DECAPS as in games G_0 and G_1), finally returns $b' =? b$. Thus, we have $\Pr[G_0^{\mathcal{B}} \Rightarrow 1] = \Pr[1 \leftarrow A^{|G'\rangle}(z1)]$ and $\Pr[G_1^{\mathcal{B}} \Rightarrow 1] = \Pr[1 \leftarrow A^{|G\rangle}(z1)]$.

Lemma 2.2 states that there exists an oracle algorithm $\bar{B}^{|G\rangle,|G'\rangle}(z1)$ such that $|\Pr[1 \leftarrow A^{|G\rangle}(z1)] - \Pr[1 \leftarrow A^{|G'\rangle}(z1)| \leq 2\sqrt{\Pr[(m^*,c^*) \leftarrow \bar{B}^{|G\rangle,|G'\rangle}(z1)]}$. Define game G_{3B} as in Fig. 7, where $\hat{B}$ is the same as $\bar{B}$ except that $\hat{B}$ simulates $\mathcal{B}$'s DECAPS query using a given DECAPS oracle (implemented as in G_0 and G_1). Thus, it is obvious that $\Pr[(m^*,c^*) \leftarrow \bar{B}^{|G\rangle,|G'\rangle}(z1)] \leq \Pr[G_{3B}^{\hat{B}} \Rightarrow 1]$. Thus, we have

$$\mathrm{Adv}_{\mathrm{KEM}_{RH}}^{\mathrm{IND\text{-}1\text{-}CCA}}(\mathcal{B}) \leq 2\sqrt{\Pr[G_{3B}^{\hat{B}} \Rightarrow 1]}.$$

Game G_{4B} is identical to game G_{3B} except the simulation of G'. In game G_{4B}, the judgement condition $(m,c) = (m^*,c^*)$ is replaced by $c = c^* \wedge Enc'(pk,m) = c^*$ without knowledge of m^*. Define COLL as an event that there is a message $m \neq m^*$ such that $Enc'(pk,m) = c^* = Enc'(pk,m^*)$. Note that if COLL does not happen (implied by the injectivity of DPKE), then G_{4B} and G_{3B} have the same distribution. Thus, we have

$$\left| \Pr[G_{3B}^{\hat{B}} \Rightarrow 1] - \Pr[G_{4B}^{\hat{B}} \Rightarrow 1] \right| \leq \delta.$$

$G_{3B} - G_{5B}$

1 : $(pk,sk) \leftarrow Gen', G \leftarrow_\$ \Omega_H, k_0^*, \bar{k} \leftarrow_\$ \mathcal{K}, m^* \leftarrow_\$ \mathcal{M}, c^* \leftarrow Enc(pk,m^*)$
2 : $l = 0, (i,b) \leftarrow_\$ ([q_H - 1] \times \{0,1\}) \cup \{(q_H,0)\}$
3 : $(m',c') \leftarrow \hat{B}^{|G\rangle,|G'\rangle,\text{DECAPS}}(pk,c^*,k_0^*)$ //G_{3B}, G_{4B}
4 : $(m',c') \leftarrow \hat{B}^{|G_1^i\rangle,|G'\rangle,\text{DECAPS}}(pk,c^*,k_0^*)$ //G_{5B}
5 : **return** $m^* =?m'$

DECAPS $(sk, \bar{c} \neq c^*)$	$G_1^i(m,c)$
1 : **if** more than 1 query **return** $\perp$	1 : **if** $l \geq (i+b) \wedge (m,c) = (m_{i+1},c_{i+1})$
2 : **return** $\bar{k}$ //G_{5B}	// (m_{i+1},c_{i+1}) is the measurement outcome
3 : $\bar{m}' := Dec'(sk,\bar{c})$	// on $\hat{B}$'s $(i+1)$-th query input register
4 : **if** $\bar{m}' = \perp$ **do** $\bar{m} = \star$	2 : **return** $\bar{k}$
5 : **else do** $\bar{m} = \bar{m}'$	3 : **else return** $G(m,c)$
6 : **return** $K := G(\bar{m},\bar{c})$	4 : $l = l+1$

$G'(m,c)$

1 : **if** $(m,c) = (m^*,c^*)$ //G_{3B}
2 : **if** $c = c^* \wedge Enc'(pk,m) = c^*$ //$G_{4B} - G_{5B}$
3 :   **return** k_0^*//$G_{3B} - G_{5B}$
4 : **return** $G(m,c)$//$G_{3B} - G_{4B}$
5 : **return** $G_1^i(m,c)$//G_{5B}

Fig. 7. Games $G_{3B} - G_{5B}$ for the proof of Lemma 4.2

In game G_{5B}, DECAPS is modified to output a random $\Theta = \bar{k}$ for the single query $\bar{c}$, and the random oracle G is correspondingly reprogrammed conditioned on (i,b), where $(i,b) \leftarrow_\$ ([q_H - 1] \times \{0,1\}) \cup \{(q_H, 0)\}$. Using Lemma 3.1 in the same way as in Lemma 4.1, we have

$$\Pr[G_{4B}^{\hat{B}} \Rightarrow 1] \leq 8(q_H + 1)^2 (\Pr[G_{5B}^{\hat{B}} \Rightarrow 1] + 1/|\mathcal{K}|).$$

Now, we can construct a OW-CPA adversary $\mathcal{A}(pk, c^*)$ against deterministic PKE$'$, where $(pk, sk) \leftarrow Gen'$, $m^* \leftarrow_\$ \mathcal{M}$, $c^* \leftarrow Enc(pk, m^*)$. $\mathcal{A}$ samples $k_0^*, \bar{k}, i, b$ as in game G_{5B}, picks a $2q_H$-wise function G, runs $\hat{B}^{|G_1^i\rangle, |G'\rangle, \text{DECAPS}}(pk, c^*, k^*)$ (the simulations of G_1^i, G', DECAPS are the same as in game G_{5B}) to obtain (m', c'), finally outputs m' as a return. It is obvious that the advantage of $\mathcal{A}$ against the OW-CPA security of deterministic PKE$'$ is exactly $\Pr[G_{5B}^{\hat{B}} \Rightarrow 1]$. Thus, we have

$$\text{Adv}_{\text{KEM}_{RH}}^{\text{IND-1-CCA}}(\mathcal{B}) \leq 2\sqrt{8(q_H + 1)^2 (\text{Adv}_{\text{PKE}'}^{\text{OW-CPA}}(\mathcal{A}) + 1/|\mathcal{K}|) + \delta}$$

$$\leq 6(q_H + 1)\sqrt{\text{Adv}_{\text{PKE}'}^{\text{OW-CPA}}(\mathcal{A}) + 1/|\mathcal{K}| + \delta}.$$

Lemma 4.3. *There exists an adversary $\mathcal{D}$ against the IND-CPA security of probabilistic PKE$'$ such that* $\text{Time}(\mathcal{D}) \approx \text{Time}(\mathcal{B}) + O(q_H^2)$ *and*
$$\text{Adv}_{\text{KEM}_{RH}}^{\text{IND-1-CCA}}(\mathcal{B}) \leq 6(q_H + 1)\sqrt{4\text{Adv}_{\text{PKE}'}^{\text{IND-CPA}}(\mathcal{D}) + 2(q_H + 1)^2/|\mathcal{M}| + 1/|\mathcal{K}|}.$$

The proof of Lemma 4.3. Define games $G_{3C} - G_{6C}$ as in Fig. 8.

Let $z1 = (pk, sk, c^*, k_0^*)$, where $(pk, sk) \leftarrow Gen'$, $k_0^* \leftarrow_\$ \mathcal{K}$, $m_0^*, m_1^* \leftarrow_\$ \mathcal{M}$, $\bar{b} \leftarrow_\$ \{0,1\}$ and $c^* \leftarrow Enc(pk, m_{\bar{b}}^*)$. Sample $G \leftarrow_\$ \Omega_H$. Let G' be an oracle such that $G'(m_{\bar{b}}^*, c^*) = k_0^*$, and $G'(x) = G(x)$ for $x \neq (m_{\bar{b}}^*, c^*)$. Let $A^{|O\rangle}(z1)$ $(O \in G, G')$ be an oracle algorithm that first samples $k_1^* \leftarrow_\$ \mathcal{K}$, $\tilde{b} \leftarrow_\$ \{0,1\}$, then runs $\mathcal{B}^{|O\rangle, \text{DECAPS}}(pk, c^*, k_{\tilde{b}}^*)$ to obtain $\tilde{b}'$ (simulating DECAPS as in games G_0 and G_1), finally returns $\tilde{b}' =?\tilde{b}$. Thus, we have $\Pr[G_0^\mathcal{B} \Rightarrow 1] = \Pr[1 \leftarrow A^{|G'\rangle}(z1)]$ and $\Pr[G_1^\mathcal{B} \Rightarrow 1] = \Pr[1 \leftarrow A^{|G\rangle}(z1)]$.

Lemma 2.1 states that there exists an oracle algorithm $\bar{B}^{|G\rangle, |G'\rangle}(z1)$ such that $|\Pr[1 \leftarrow A^{|G\rangle}(z1)] - \Pr[1 \leftarrow A^{|G'\rangle}(z1)]| \leq 2\sqrt{\Pr[(m_{\bar{b}}^*, c^*) \leftarrow \bar{B}^{|G\rangle, |G'\rangle}(z1)]}$. Define game G_{3C} as in Fig. 8, where $\hat{B}$ is the same as $\bar{B}$ except that $\hat{B}$ simulates $\mathcal{B}$'s DECAPS query using a given DECAPS oracle (implemented as in G_0 and G_1). Thus, it is obvious that $\Pr[(m_{\bar{b}}^*, c^*) \leftarrow \bar{B}^{|G\rangle, |G'\rangle}(z1)] \leq \Pr[G_{3C}^{\hat{B}} \Rightarrow 1]$. Thus, we have

$$\text{Adv}_{\text{KEM}_{RH}}^{\text{IND-1-CCA}}(\mathcal{B}) \leq 2\sqrt{\Pr[G_{3C}^{\hat{B}} \Rightarrow 1]}.$$

In game G_{4C}, DECAPS is modified to output a random $\Theta = \bar{k}$ for the single query $\bar{c}$, and the random oracle H is correspondingly reprogrammed conditioned on (i,b), where $(i,b) \leftarrow_\$ ([q_H - 1] \times \{0,1\}) \cup \{(q_H, 0)\}$. Then, using Lemma 3.1 in the same way as in Lemma 4.1, we have

$$\Pr[G_{3C}^{\hat{B}} \Rightarrow 1] \leq 8(q_H + 1)^2 (\Pr[G_{4C}^{\hat{B}} \Rightarrow 1] + 1/|\mathcal{K}|).$$

GAMES $G_{3C} - G_{6C}$

1: $(pk, sk) \leftarrow Gen', G \leftarrow_{\$} \Omega_H, l = 0, (i, b) \leftarrow_{\$} ([q_H - 1] \times \{0, 1\}) \cup \{(q_H, 0)\}$

2: $k_0^*, \bar{k} \leftarrow_{\$} \mathcal{K}, \bar{b} \leftarrow_{\$} \{0, 1\}, m_0^*, m_1^* \leftarrow_{\$} \mathcal{M}, c^* \leftarrow Enc(pk, m_{\bar{b}}^*)$

3: $(m', c') \leftarrow \hat{B}^{|G\rangle, |G'\rangle, \mathrm{Decaps}}(pk, c^*, k_0^*) \quad // G_{3C}$

4: $(m', c') \leftarrow \hat{B}^{|G_1^i\rangle, |G'\rangle, \mathrm{Decaps}}(pk, c^*, k_0^*) \quad // G_{4C} - G_{6C}$

5: **return** $(m_{\bar{b}}^*, c^*) =?(m', c') // G_{3C} - G_{4C}$

6: **return** $(m_{1-\bar{b}}^*, c^*) =?(m', c') // G_{5C}$

7: **if** $(m_0^*, c^*) = (m', c')$ **then** $\tilde{b}' = 0$ **else then** $\tilde{b}' = 1 // G_{6C}$

8: **return** $\tilde{b}' =?\bar{b} // G_{6C}$

<table>
<tr><td>Decaps $(sk, \bar{c} \neq c^*) \; // G_{3C} - G_{6C}$</td><td>$G_1^i(m, c)$</td></tr>
<tr><td>1: **if** more than 1 query **return** $\bot$</td><td>1: **if** $l \geq (i + b) \wedge (m, c) = (m_{i+1}, c_{i+1})$</td></tr>
<tr><td>2: **return** $\bar{k} \quad // G_{4C} - G_{6C}$</td><td>$// (m_{i+1}, c_{i+1})$ is the measurement outcome</td></tr>
<tr><td>3: $\bar{m}' := Dec'(sk, \bar{c})$</td><td>$//$ on $\mathcal{B}$'s $(i + 1)$-th query input register</td></tr>
<tr><td>4: **if** $\bar{m}' =\bot$ **do** $\bar{m} = \star$</td><td>2: **return** $\bar{k}$</td></tr>
<tr><td>5: **else do** $\bar{m} = \bar{m}'$</td><td>3: **else return** $G(m, c)$</td></tr>
<tr><td>6: **return** $K := G(\bar{m}, \bar{c})$</td><td>4: $l = l + 1$</td></tr>
</table>

$G'(m, c)$

1: **if** $(m, c) = (m_{\bar{b}}^*, c^*) \quad // G_{3C} - G_{4C}$

2: **if** $(m, c) = (m_{1-\bar{b}}^*, c^*) \quad // G_{5C}$

3: **if** $(m, c) = (m_0^*, c^*) \quad // G_{6C}$

4: **return** $k_0^* // G_{3C} - G_{6C}$

5: **return** $G(m, c) // G_{3C}$

6: **return** $G_1^i(m, c) // G_{4C} - G_{6C}$

Fig. 8. Games G_{3C}-G_{6C} for the proof of Lemma 4.3

Game G_{5C} is identical to game G_{4C} except that $G'(m_{\bar{b}}^*, c^*) = k_0^*$ is replaced by $G'(m_{1-\bar{b}}^*, c^*) = k_0^*$, and correspondingly $(m_{1-\bar{b}}^*, c^*) =?(m', c')$ is returned instead of $(m_{\bar{b}}^*, c*) =?(m', c')$.

Note that game G_{4C} conditioned on $\bar{b} = 1$ has the same output distribution as game G_{4C} conditioned on $\bar{b} = 0$. Thus, we have $\Pr[G_{4C}^{\hat{B}} \Rightarrow 1 : \bar{b} = 0] = \Pr[G_{4C}^{\hat{B}} \Rightarrow 1 : \bar{b} = 1] = \Pr[G_{4C}^{\hat{B}} \Rightarrow 1]/2$. Analogously, we have $\Pr[G_{5C}^{\hat{B}} \Rightarrow 1 : \bar{b} = 1] = \Pr[G_{5C}^{\hat{B}} \Rightarrow 1]/2$. Note that $m_{1-\bar{b}}^*$ is independent of pk, c^*, k_0^* and G. Thus, according to Lemma 2.3, we have

$$\Pr[G_{5C}^{\hat{B}} \Rightarrow 1 : \bar{b} = 1] \leq (q_H + 1)^2 / |\mathcal{M}|.$$

Define game G_{6C} as in Fig. 8. Thus, $\Pr[G_{6C}^{\hat{B}} \Rightarrow 1]$

$$= 1/2\Pr[(m_0^*, c^*) = (m', c') : \bar{b} = 0] + 1/2\Pr[(m_0^*, c^*) \neq (m', c') : \bar{b} = 1]$$

$$= 1/2\Pr[(m_0^*, c^*) = (m', c') : \bar{b} = 0] + 1/2 - 1/2\Pr[(m_0^*, c^*) = (m', c') : \bar{b} = 1]$$

$$= 1/2 + 1/2\Pr[G_{4C}^{\hat{B}} \Rightarrow 1 : \bar{b} = 0] - 1/2\Pr[G_{5C}^{\hat{B}} \Rightarrow 1 : \bar{b} = 1]$$

$$= 1/2 + 1/4(\Pr[G_{4C}^{\hat{B}} \Rightarrow 1] - \Pr[G_{5C}^{\hat{B}} \Rightarrow 1])$$

Now, we can construct an IND-CPA adversary $\mathcal{D}(pk)$ against PKE$'$, where $(pk, sk) \leftarrow Gen'$. $\mathcal{D}$ samples $m_0^*, m_1^* \leftarrow_\$ \mathcal{M}$, receives challenge ciphertext $c^* \leftarrow Enc(pk, m_{\bar{b}}^*)$ ($\bar{b} \leftarrow_\$ \{0,1\}$), samples $k_0^*, \bar{k}, i, b$ as in game G_{6C}, picks a $2q_H$-wise independent function H, runs $\hat{B}^{|G_1^i\rangle, |G'\rangle, \text{DECAPS}}(pk, c^*, k_0^*)$ (the simulations of G_1^i, G', DECAPS are the same as in game G_{6C}) to obtain (m', c'), finally outputs 0 if $(m_0^*, c^*) = (m', c')$, and returns 1 otherwise. Thus, apparently,

$$\left| \Pr[G_{6C}^{\hat{B}} \Rightarrow 1] - 1/2 \right| = \text{Adv}_{\text{PKE}'}^{\text{IND-CPA}}(\mathcal{D})$$

Putting everything together, we have

$$\text{Adv}_{\text{KEM}_{\hat{R}H}}^{\text{IND-1-CCA}}(\mathcal{B}) \leq 2\sqrt{8(q_H + 1)^2(4\text{Adv}_{\text{PKE}'}^{\text{IND-CPA}}(\mathcal{D}) + 2(q_H + 1)^2/|\mathcal{M}| + 1/|\mathcal{K}|)}$$

$$\leq 6(q_H + 1)\sqrt{4\text{Adv}_{\text{PKE}'}^{\text{IND-CPA}}(\mathcal{D}) + 2(q_H + 1)^2/|\mathcal{M}| + 1/|\mathcal{K}|}.$$

$\square$

Theorem 4.3. $(T_H \to T_{RH})$. *For any adversary $\mathcal{B}'$ against the IND-1-CCA security of $KEM_H = T_H[\text{PKE}', H]$, issuing q_H queries to the random oracle H, there exists an IND-1-CCA adversary $\mathcal{B}$ against $KEM_{RH} = T_{RH}[\text{PKE}', H]^7$ that makes $q_H + 1$ queries to H such that $\text{Time}(\mathcal{B}') \approx \text{Time}(\mathcal{B})$ and*

$$\text{Adv}_{\text{KEM}_H}^{\text{IND-1-CCA}}(\mathcal{B}') \leq \text{Adv}_{\text{KEM}_{RH}}^{\text{IND-1-CCA}}(\mathcal{B}) + \epsilon_{\text{coll}},$$

where ϵ_{coll} is an advantage bound of an algorithm searching a collision of the random oracle H with q_H queries. In particular, $\epsilon_{\text{coll}} = q_H^2/|\mathcal{K}|$ in the ROM, and $\epsilon_{\text{coll}} = q_H^3/|\mathcal{K}|$ in the QROM [42, Corollary 2].

Proof. Let $\mathcal{B}'^{H, \text{DECAPS}_{T_H}}(pk, c^*, k_b^*)$ be an adversary against the IND-1-CCA security of $T_H[\text{PKE}', H]$. Construct an adversary $\mathcal{B}^{H, \text{DECAPS}_{T_{RH}}}(pk, c^*, k_b^*)$ that runs $\mathcal{B}'^{H, \text{DECAPS}'}(pk, c^*, k_b^*)$, and returns $\mathcal{B}'$'s return. The oracle DECAPS$'$ is simulated by querying DECAPS$_{T_{RH}}$. In detail, DECAPS$'(\bar{c})$ returns $\perp$ if DECAPS$_{T_{RH}}(\bar{c}) = H(\star, \bar{c})$. For other cases, DECAPS$'(\bar{c})$ just returns DECAPS$_{RH}(\bar{c})$. Note that when DECAPS$_{T_H}(\bar{c}) = \perp$, DECAPS$'(\bar{c})$ returns $\perp$ with probability 1. When DECAPS$_{T_H}(\bar{c}) \neq \perp$, $\Pr[\text{DECAPS}_{RH}(\bar{c}) = H(\star, \bar{c})] \leq \epsilon_{\text{coll}}$ since $\star \notin \mathcal{M}$. Thus DECAPS$'(\bar{c})$ returns DECAPS$_H(\bar{c})$ with probability at least $(1 - \epsilon_{\text{coll}})$. That is, for any $\bar{c}$, DECAPS$_{T_H}(\bar{c}) = \text{DECAPS}'(\bar{c})$ with probability at least $1 - \epsilon_{\text{coll}}$. Thus, we have $\text{Adv}_{\text{KEM}}^{\text{IND-1-CCA}}(\mathcal{B}') \leq \text{Adv}_{\text{KEM}}^{\text{IND-1-CCA}}(\mathcal{B}) + \epsilon_{\text{coll}}$.

---

[7] In Theorem 4.3, the return value $\star$ for invalid ciphertext in decapsulation of KEM$_{RH}$ is required not in message space (i.e., $\star \notin \mathcal{M}$).

Remark 2. The proof of Theorem 4.3 requires $\star \notin \mathcal{M}$. Theorems 4.1 and 4.2 for KEM$_{RH}$ works for both $\star \in \mathcal{M}$ and $\star \notin \mathcal{M}$. Thus, combing Theorems 4.1, 4.2, 4.3, we can directly obtain the (Q)ROM security proofs of KEM$_H = T_H[\text{PKE}', H]$ with the same tightness as KEM$_{RH} = T_{RH}[\text{PKE}', H]$.

5   Tightness of the Reductions

In this section, we will show that for $KEM = T_{RH}[\text{PKE}', H]$, a $O(q)$-ROM-loss (and q^2-loss) is unavoidable in general.

Theorem 5.1. *Let* PKE$' = (Gen', Enc', Dec')$ *be a PKE with malleability property. Let* $\mathcal{M} = \{0,1\}^n$ *be the message space of* PKE$'$. *Then, there exists a ROM (QROM, resp.) adversary* $\mathcal{B}$ *against the IND-1-CCA security of* $KEM = T_{RH}[\text{PKE}', H]$ *such that the advantage* $\text{Adv}_{\text{KEM}}^{\text{IND-1-CCA}}(\mathcal{B})$ *is about* $(1/e)\frac{q}{|\mathcal{M}|}$ $((q+1)^2/|\mathcal{M}|,$ *resp.), where* q *is the number of queries to* H *such that* $1/\sqrt{|\mathcal{M}|} \leq \sin(\frac{\pi}{6q+3})$ *and* $q \leq |\mathcal{K}|$ *(* $\mathcal{K}$ *is the key space).*

Proof. Let $(pk, sk) \leftarrow Gen'$, $m^* \leftarrow_\$ \mathcal{M}$, $c^* \leftarrow Enc(pk, m^*)$, $k_0^* = H(m^*, c^*)$, $k_1^* \leftarrow_\$ \mathcal{K}$, and $b \leftarrow_\$ \{0,1\}$. Since PKE$'$ satisfies the malleability property, there exists an algorithm $\bar{B}$ that on input (pk, c^*) outputs (f, c') such that (1) $f(m^*) = Dec(sk, c') \neq \perp$; $(2) f(\tilde{m}) \neq Dec(sk, c')$ for any $\tilde{m} \in \mathcal{M}$ and $\tilde{m} \neq m$.

Define the function $g_{c,k}^H : \mathcal{M} \rightarrow \{0,1\}$ as

$$g_{c,k}^H(m) = \begin{cases} 1 & H(f(m), c) = k \\ 0 & \text{Otherwise} \end{cases}$$

First, we consider the ROM case. Let $\mathcal{B}^{H,\text{DECAPS}}(pk, c^*, k_b^*)$ be a ROM adversary as follows.

1. Run $\bar{B}$ to obtain (f, c');
2. Query the DECAPS oracle with c' and obtain k';
3. Randomly pick $m_1, \ldots, m_q$ from $\mathcal{M}$, and compute $g_{c',k'}^H(m_i)$ for each $i \in \{1, \ldots, q\}$ by querying H;
4. If there exists an m_i such that $g_{c',k'}^H(m_i) = 1$, return $1 - (H(m_i, c^*) =?k_b^*)$, else return $\perp$.

Note that $g_{c',k'}^H(m^*) = 1$ with probability 1, and $g_{c',k'}^H(\tilde{m}) = 1$ with negligible probability $1/|\mathcal{K}|$ for $\tilde{m} \neq m^*$. We also note that $\Pr[m^* \in \{m_1, \ldots, m_q\}] = \frac{q}{\mathcal{M}}$. Thus, the ROM advantage of $\mathcal{B}$ is at least $\frac{q}{\mathcal{M}}(1 - 1/|\mathcal{K}|)^{q-1} \gtrsim (1/e)\frac{q}{\mathcal{M}}$ since $q \leq |\mathcal{K}|$.

Next, we consider the QROM case. Let $\mathcal{B}^{|H\rangle,\text{DECAPS}}(pk, c^*, k_b^*)$ be a QROM adversary as follows.

1. Run $\bar{B}$ to obtain (f, c');
2. Query the DECAPS oracle with c' and obtain k';

3. Use Grover's algorithm for q steps to try to find m^*. In details, apply Grover iteration q time on initial state $HGate^{\otimes n}|0^n\rangle$ and make a standard measurement to derive $\tilde{m}$, where Grover iteration is composed of oracle query O_g that turns $|m\rangle$ into $(-1)^{g^H_{c',k'}(m)}|m\rangle$, and diffusion operator $U = HGate^{\otimes n}(2|0^n\rangle\langle 0^n| - I_n)HGate^{\otimes n}$;

4. Return $1 - (H(\tilde{m}, c^*) =?k^*_b)$, where $\tilde{m}$ is the outcome obtained using Grover's algorithm in step 3.

Note that $g^H_{c',k'}(m^*) = 1$ with probability 1, and $g^H_{c',k'}(\tilde{m}) = 1$ with negligible probability $1/|\mathcal{K}|$ for $\tilde{m} \neq m^*$. Let $p_0 = \Pr[g^H_{c',k'}(m) = 1 : m \in \mathcal{M}] \geq 1/|\mathcal{M}|$. By q Grover iterations (requiring q quantum queries to H), the probability p_1 of finding m^* is $\sin^2((2q+1)\theta)$, where $\sin^2(\theta) = p_0$.

When $1/\sqrt{|\mathcal{M}|} \leq \sin(\frac{\pi}{6q+3})$, we have $(2q+1)\theta \leq \pi/3$. Thus, we have

$$\sin((2q+1)\theta) \geq \sin(\theta) + \frac{2q \cdot \theta}{2} \geq (q+1)\sin(\theta).$$

Therefore, we have $p_1 = \sin^2((2q+1)\theta) \geq \frac{(q+1)^2}{|\mathcal{M}|}$. Note that when m^* is obtained, one can derive b^* with probability 1 by querying $H(\tilde{m}, c^*)$. Thus, the QROM advantage of $\mathcal{B}$ is at least $\frac{(q+1)^2}{|\mathcal{M}|}$. □

Remark 3. Most IND-CPA-secure PKEs has malleability property, e.g., ElGamal, FrodoKEM.PKE [28], Kyber.PKE [8], etc. Moreover, malleability property is inherent for a homomorphic PKE. Let PKE = (Gen, Enc, Dec) be homomorphic in addition. That is, $Enc(pk, m_1 + m_2) = Enc(pk, m_1) + Enc(pk, m_2)$. Then, we can construct algorithm $\bar{B}(pk, c^*)$ $(c^* \leftarrow Enc(pk, m^*))$ that randomly picks $m \in \mathcal{M}$, computes $c' = c^* + Enc(pk, m)$, and defines $f(x) = x + m$. Note that $f(m^*) = Dec(sk, c')$ and $f(\tilde{m}) \neq Dec(sk, c')$ for $\tilde{m} \neq m$(We assume the PKE has perfect correctness for simplicity). Thus, the homomorphic property of a PKE implies the malleability property in this paper.

Remark 4. For a λ-bit IND-CPA-secure malleable public-key encryption PKE′ with message space $\mathcal{M} = 2^\lambda$ we require that any PPT adversary breaks the security of PKE′ with advantage at most $\frac{1}{2^\lambda}$. For example, such a PKE′ can be constructed based on the LWE assumption by a suitable parameter selection [34]. Theorem 5.1 shows that a ROM (QROM, resp.) adversary against the IND-1-CCA security of KEM = $T_{RH}[PKE', H]$ can achieve advantage at least $(1/e)\frac{q}{2^\lambda}$ $(\frac{(q+1)^2}{2^\lambda}$, resp.), where q is the number of adversary's queries to H. That is, a $O(1/q)$ $(O(1/q^2)$, resp.) loss is unavoidable in the ROM (QROM, resp.) for T_{RH}.

Remark 5. We remark that the output of decapsulation for an invalid ciphertext c is irrelevant to the attack given in Theorem 5.1. Thus, the aforementioned tightness results can also be applied to T_H. We also remark that such a tightness result can also be extended to the IND-1-CCA KEM construction T_{CH} given in [21], where there is tag $tag = H'(m^*, c_0^*)$ in the ciphertext $(c_0^* \leftarrow Enc(pk, m^*))$, and the key is computed by $K = H(m^*)$. The idea is that the adversary against

KEM can first search m^* such that $tag = H'(m^*, c_0^*)$ by querying H', and then query H with m^*, thus break the key indistinguishability. Following the same analysis in Theorem 5.1, one can easily derive the same tightness result for T_{CH}.

6   Relations Among Notions of CCA Security for KEM

In this section, we will compare the relative strengths of notions of IND-1-CCA security and IND-CCA security in ROM and QROM. In detail, we works out the relations among four notions. For each pair of notions $A, B \in \{$ IND-1-CCA ROM, IND-1-CCA QROM, IND-CCA ROM, IND-CCA QROM $\}$, we show one of the following:

- $A \Rightarrow B$: A proof that if a KEM meets the notion of security A then it also meets the notion of security B.
- $A \nRightarrow B$: There is a KEM construction that provably meets the notion of security A but does not meet the notion of security B.

First, according to the security definitions, one can trivially derive the relations IND-CCA QROM $\Rightarrow$ IND-1-CCA QROM $\Rightarrow$ IND-1-CCA ROM, and IND-CCA QROM $\Rightarrow$ IND-CCA ROM $\Rightarrow$ IND-1-CCA ROM. Next, we show the other nontrivial relations.

Theorem 6.1. *If the LWE assumption (Definition B.1) holds, then we have IND-1-CCA ROM$\nRightarrow$ IND-1-CCA QROM, IND-CCA ROM$\nRightarrow$IND-1-CCA QROM and IND-CCA ROM $\nRightarrow$IND-CCA QROM.*

Proof. First, if the LWE assumption holds, we can have a KEM=$(Gen, Encaps, Decaps)$ that satisfies the IND-CCA ROM security. For example, FrodoKEM [28] is such a KEM whose IND-CCA ROM security can be reduced to the LWE assumption. Let PoQRO=$(Setup, Prove, Verify)$ (Definition C.1) be a proof of quantum access to random oracle H, whose existence is based on the LWE assumption, see Lemma C.1. Here, H is independent of the KEM.

Construct a new KEM$'$=$(Gen', Encaps', Decaps')$ as in Fig. 9. Note that any efficient ROM adversary cannot find a c_2 such that $Verify^H(sk_2, c_2) = 1$ (otherwise the soundness of the PoQRO is broken). Thus, for an efficient ROM adversary, querying oracle $Decaps'$ is equivalent to querying oracle $Decaps$. Thus, KEM$'$ also meets the IND-CCA ROM security.

Meanwhile, a QROM adversary can find a c_2 such that $Verify^H(sk_2, c_2) = 1$. Thus, by querying oracle $Decaps'$ (only one time), a QROM adversary can obtain sk_1, hence break the IND-CCA security of KEM$'$. Therefore, KEM$'$ does not meet the IND-1-CCA QROM security (and also IND-CCA QROM security). Since KEM meets the IND-CCA ROM security, KEM is also IND-1-CCA-secure in the ROM. Hence, we have IND-1-CCA ROM$\nRightarrow$IND-1-CCA QROM, IND-CCA ROM$\nRightarrow$IND-1-CCA QROM and IND-CCA ROM$\nRightarrow$IND-CCA QROM.   □

Gen'	$Encaps'(pk)$	$Decaps'(sk,c)$
1 : $(pk_1, sk_1) \leftarrow Gen$	1 : **parse** $pk = (pk_1, pk_2)$	1 : **parse** $sk = (sk_1, sk_2)$
2 : $(pk_2, sk_2) \leftarrow Setup$	2 : $(K, c_1) \leftarrow_\$ Encaps(pk_1)$	2 : **parse** $c = (c_1, c_2)$
3 : $pk = (pk_1, pk_2)$	3 : $c = (c_1, \bot)$	3 : **if** $Verify^H(sk_2, c_2) = 1$
4 : $sk = (sk_1, sk_2)$	4 : **return** (K, c)	4 : **return** sk_1
5 : **return** (pk, sk)		5 : **return** $Decaps(sk_1, c_1)$

Fig. 9. Separation instance KEM$'$ for Theorem 6.1.

Theorem 6.2. *If the LWE assumption holds, then we have IND-1-CCA ROM $\nRightarrow$ IND-CCA ROM, IND-1-CCA QROM $\nRightarrow$ IND-CCA QROM, and IND-1-CCA QROM $\nRightarrow$ IND-CCA ROM.*

Proof. Let (Gen, Enc, Dec) be the key-generation, encryption and decryption algorithms of FrodoPKE [28], whose IND-CPA security can be reduced to the LWE assumption. Then, according to Theorems 4.1 and 4.2, KEM$=T_{RH}$[FrodoPKE, H] is IND-1-CCA secure in both ROM and QROM. Note that such a KEM is essentially a FO-KEM without re-encryption. Qin et al. [33] had shown such a KEM is vulnerable to key-mismatch attacks that can recover the secret key with only polynomial queries to the decapsulation oracle. That is, KEM$=T_{RH}$[FrodoPKE, H] is not IND-CCA-secure in ROM (and QROM). Hence, we have IND-1-CCA ROM $\nRightarrow$ IND-CCA ROM, IND-1-CCA QROM $\nRightarrow$ IND-CCA QROM, and IND-1-CCA QROM $\nRightarrow$ IND-CCA ROM. □

Acknowledgements. We thank anonymous reviewers for their insightful comments and suggestions. Haodong Jiang was supported by the National Key R&D Program of China (No. 2021YFB3100100), and the National Natural Science Foundation of China (Nos. 62002385). Zhi Ma was supported by the National Natural Science Foundation of China (No. 61972413).

A Supporting Material: Cryptographic Primitives

Definition A.1 (Public-key encryption). *A public-key encryption (PKE) scheme PKE consists of a triple of polynomial time (in the security parameter λ) algorithms and a finite message space $\mathcal{M}$. (1) $Gen(1^\lambda) \to (pk, sk)$: the key generation algorithm, is a probabilistic algorithm which on input 1^λ outputs a public/secret key-pair (pk, sk). Usually, for brevity, we will omit the input of Gen. (2) $Enc(pk, m) \to c$: the encryption algorithm Enc, on input pk and a message $m \in \mathcal{M}$, outputs a ciphertext $c \leftarrow Enc(pk, m)$. (3) $Dec(sk, c) \to m$: the decryption algorithm Dec, is a deterministic algorithm which on input sk and a ciphertext c outputs a message $m := Dec(sk, c)$ or a rejection symbol $\bot \notin \mathcal{M}$.*

Definition A.2 (Correctness [17]). *A PKE is δ-correct if $E[\max_{m \in \mathcal{M}} \Pr[Dec(sk, c)$*
$\neq m : c \leftarrow Enc(pk, m)]] \leq \delta$, where the expectation is taken over $(pk, sk) \leftarrow Gen$.
We say a PKE is perfectly correct if $\delta = 0$.

Note that this definition works for a deterministic or randomized PKE, but for
a deterministic PKE[8] the term $\max_{m \in \mathcal{M}} \Pr[Dec(sk, c) \neq m : c = Enc(pk, m)]$ is
either 0 or 1 for each keypair (pk, sk).

Definition A.3 (Injectivity of DPKE [6]). *A deterministic PKE (DPKE)*
is ε-injective if $\Pr[Enc(pk, *) \text{ is not injective} : (pk, sk) \leftarrow Gen] \leq \varepsilon$.

Remark 6. we observe that if DPKE is δ-correct, then DPKE is injective with
probability $\geq 1 - \delta$. That is, for DPKE, δ-correctness implies δ-injectivity.

Definition A.4 (OW-CPA-secure PKE). *Let PKE = (Gen, Enc, Dec) be a*
public-key encryption scheme with message space $\mathcal{M}$. Define OW $-$ CPA game
of PKE as in Fig. 10. Define the OW $-$ CPA advantage function of an adversary
$\mathcal{A}$ against PKE as $\mathrm{Adv}_{PKE}^{OW\text{-}CPA}(\mathcal{A}) := \Pr[OW\text{-}CPA_{PKE}^{\mathcal{A}} = 1]$.

Game OW-CPA	Game IND-CPA
1 : $(pk, sk) \leftarrow Gen, m^* \xleftarrow{\$} \mathcal{M}$	1 : $(pk, sk) \leftarrow Gen, b \leftarrow_\$ \{0, 1\}$
2 : $c^* \leftarrow Enc(pk, m^*), m' \leftarrow \mathcal{A}(pk, c^*)$	2 : $(m_0, m_1) \leftarrow \mathcal{A}(pk)$
3 : **return** $m' =?m^*$	3 : $c^* \leftarrow Enc(pk, m_b), b' \leftarrow \mathcal{A}(pk, c^*)$
	4 : **return** $b' =?b$

Fig. 10. Game OW-CPA and game IND-CPA for PKE.

Definition A.5 (IND-CPA-secure PKE). *Let PKE = (Gen, Enc, Dec) be a*
PKE scheme. Define IND $-$ CPA game of PKE as in Fig. 10, where m_0 and m_1
have the same length. Define the IND $-$ CPA advantage function of an adversary
$\mathcal{A}$ against PKE as $\mathrm{Adv}_{PKE}^{IND\text{-}CPA}(\mathcal{A}) := |\Pr[IND\text{-}CPA_{PKE}^{\mathcal{A}} = 1] - 1/2|$.

Malleability. In this paper, we say a PKE = (Gen, Enc, Dec) has a malleability
property if for any (pk, sk) generated by Gen, any $m \in \mathcal{M}$, and $c \leftarrow Enc(pk, m)$,
there exists an algorithm B that on input (pk, c) outputs (f, c') such that (1)
$f(m) = Dec(sk, c')$ $(Dec(sk, c') \neq \bot)$ (2) $f(\tilde{m}) \neq Dec(sk, c')$ for any $\tilde{m} \in \mathcal{M}$
and $\tilde{m} \neq m$.

Definition A.6 (Key encapsulation). *A key encapsulation mechanism KEM*
consists of three algorithms. (1) $Gen(1^\lambda) \rightarrow (pk, sk)$: the key generation algo-
rithm Gen outputs a key pair (pk, sk). Usually, for brevity, we will omit the

---

[8] A PKE is deterministic if Enc is deterministic.

input of Gen. (2) Encaps(pk) → (K, c): the encapsulation algorithm Encaps, on input pk, outputs a tuple (K, c), where K ∈ K and ciphertext c is said to be an encapsulation of the key K. (3) Decaps(sk, c) → K: the deterministic decapsulation algorithm Decaps, on input sk and an encapsulation c, outputs either a key K := Decaps(sk, c) ∈ K or a rejection symbol ⊥ ∉ K.

Definition A.7 (IND-CCA-secure KEM). *We define the* IND − CCA *game as in Fig. 11 and the advantage function of an adversary* $\mathcal{A}$ *against KEM as* $\mathrm{Adv}_{\mathrm{KEM}}^{\mathrm{IND\text{-}CCA}}(\mathcal{A}) := \left| \Pr[\mathrm{IND\text{-}CCA}_{\mathrm{KEM}}^{\mathcal{A}} = 1] - 1/2 \right|.$

Game IND-CCA	DECAPS(sk, c)
1: $(pk, sk) \leftarrow Gen, b \xleftarrow{\$} \{0,1\}$	1: **if** $c = c^*$ **return** ⊥
2: $(K_0^*, c^*) \leftarrow Encaps(pk), K_1^* \xleftarrow{\$} \mathcal{K}$	2: **else return**
3: $b' \leftarrow \mathcal{A}^{\mathrm{DECAPS}}(pk, c^*, K_b^*)$	3: $K := Decaps(sk, c)$
4: **return** $b' =?b$	

Fig. 11. IND-CCA game for KEM.

B   Supporting Material: Learning with Error (LWE)

Definition B.1. *Let* n, m, q *be positive integers, and let* χ *be a distribution over* $\mathbb{Z}$. *The (decision) LWE problem is to distinguish between the distributions* $(\mathbf{A}, \mathbf{As} + \mathbf{e}(\mathrm{mod}q))$ *and* $(\mathbf{A}, \mathbf{u})$, *where* $\mathbf{A} \leftarrow_\$ \mathbb{Z}_q^{n \times m}$, $\mathbf{s} \leftarrow_\$ \mathbb{Z}_q^n$, $\mathbf{e} \leftarrow \chi^m$, $\mathbf{u} \leftarrow_\$ \mathbb{Z}_q^m$.

In this paper, we refer the LWE assumption to that no quantum polynomial-time algorithm can solve the LWE problem with more than a negligible advantage.

C   Supporting Material: Proof of Quantum Access to Random Oracle (PoQRO)

Definition C.1 ([40]). *A (non-interactive) proof of quantum access to a random oracle (PoQRO) consists of the following three algorithms. (1) Setup(1^λ): This is a classical algorithm that takes the security parameter 1^λ as input and outputs a public key pk and a secret key sk. (2) Prove$^{|H\rangle}$(pk): This is a quantum algorithm that takes a public key pk as input and given quantum access to a random oracle H, and outputs a proof π[9]. (3) Verify^H(sk, π): This is a classical algorithm that takes a secret key sk and a proof π as input and given classical*

---
[9] Here, π is a classical value, and not a quantum state.

access to a random oracle H, and outputs 1 indicating acceptance or 0 indicating rejection. PoQRO is required to satisfy the following properties.

Correctness. *We have* $\Pr[Verify^H(sk, \pi) = 0 : (pk, sk) \leftarrow Setep(1^\lambda), \pi \leftarrow Prove^{|H\rangle}(pk)] \leq \mathsf{negl}(\lambda)$.

Soundness. *For any quantum polynomial-time adversary $\mathcal{A}$ that is given a classical oracle access to H, we have* $\Pr[Verify^H(sk, \pi) = 1 : Setep(1^\lambda), \pi \leftarrow \mathcal{A}^H(pk)] \leq \mathsf{negl}(\lambda)$.

Lemma C.1 ([40, **Theorem 3.3**]). *If the LWE assumption holds, then there exists a PoQRO.*

References

1. Ambainis, A., Hamburg, M., Unruh, D.: Quantum security proofs using semi-classical oracles. In: Boldyreva, A., Micciancio, D. (eds.) CRYPTO 2019, Part II. LNCS, vol. 11693, pp. 269–295. Springer, Cham (2019). https://doi.org/10.1007/978-3-030-26951-7_10

2. Angel, Y., Dowling, B., Hülsing, A., Schwabe, P., Weber, F.: Post quantum noise. In: ACM CCS 2022 (to appear) (2022). https://eprint.iacr.org/2022/539

3. Azouaoui, M., Bronchain, O., Hoffmann, C., Kuzovkova, Y., Schneider, T., Standaert, F.-X.: Systematic study of decryption and re-encryption leakage: the case of Kyber. In: Balasch, J., O'Flynn, C. (eds.) COSADE 2022. LNCS, vol. 13211, pp. 236–256. Springer, Cham (2022). https://doi.org/10.1007/978-3-030-99766-3_11

4. Balli, F., Rösler, P., Vaudenay, S.: Determining the core primitive for optimally secure ratcheting. In: Moriai, S., Wang, H. (eds.) ASIACRYPT 2020, Part III. LNCS, vol. 12493, pp. 621–650. Springer, Cham (2020). https://doi.org/10.1007/978-3-030-64840-4_21

5. Bellare, M., Rogaway, P.: Random oracles are practical: a paradigm for designing efficient protocols. In: Denning, D.E., Pyle, R., Ganesan, R., Sandhu, R.S., Ashby, V. (eds.) ACM CCS 1993, pp. 62–73. ACM (1993)

6. Bindel, N., Hamburg, M., Hövelmanns, K., Hülsing, A., Persichetti, E.: Tighter proofs of CCA security in the quantum random oracle model. In: Hofheinz, D., Rosen, A. (eds.) TCC 2019, Part II. LNCS, vol. 11892, pp. 61–90. Springer, Cham (2019). https://doi.org/10.1007/978-3-030-36033-7_3

7. Boneh, D., Dagdelen, Ö., Fischlin, M., Lehmann, A., Schaffner, C., Zhandry, M.: Random oracles in a quantum world. In: Lee, D.H., Wang, X. (eds.) ASIACRYPT 2011. LNCS, vol. 7073, pp. 41–69. Springer, Heidelberg (2011). https://doi.org/10.1007/978-3-642-25385-0_3

8. Bos, J.W., et al.: CRYSTALS - kyber: A cca-secure module-lattice-based KEM. In: EuroS&P 2018, pp. 353–367. IEEE (2018). https://doi.org/10.1109/EuroSP.2018.00032

9. Brendel, J., Fiedler, R., Günther, F., Janson, C., Stebila, D.: Post-quantum asynchronous deniable key exchange and the signal handshake. In: Hanaoka, G., Shikata, J., Watanabe, Y. (eds.) Public-Key Cryptography - PKC 2022. LNCS, vol. 13178, pp. 3–34. Springer, Cham (2022). https://doi.org/10.1007/978-3-030-97131-1_1

10. Brendel, J., Fischlin, M., Günther, F., Janson, C.: PRF-ODH: relations, instantiations, and impossibility results. In: Katz, J., Shacham, H. (eds.) CRYPTO 2017, Part III. LNCS, vol. 10403, pp. 651–681. Springer, Cham (2017). https://doi.org/10.1007/978-3-319-63697-9_22

11. Dent, A.W.: A designer's guide to KEMs. In: Paterson, K.G. (ed.) Cryptography and Coding 2003. LNCS, vol. 2898, pp. 133–151. Springer, Heidelberg (2003). https://doi.org/10.1007/978-3-540-40974-8_12

12. Don, J., Fehr, S., Majenz, C.: The measure-and-reprogram technique 2.0: multiround fiat-Shamir and more. In: Micciancio, D., Ristenpart, T. (eds.) CRYPTO 2020, Part III. LNCS, vol. 12172, pp. 602–631. Springer, Cham (2020). https://doi.org/10.1007/978-3-030-56877-1_21

13. Don, J., Fehr, S., Majenz, C., Schaffner, C.: Security of the fiat-Shamir transformation in the quantum random-oracle model. In: Boldyreva, A., Micciancio, D. (eds.) CRYPTO 2019, Part II. LNCS, vol. 11693, pp. 356–383. Springer, Cham (2019). https://doi.org/10.1007/978-3-030-26951-7_13

14. Don, J., Fehr, S., Majenz, C., Schaffner, C.: Online-extractability in the quantum random-oracle model. In: Dunkelman, O., Dziembowski, S. (eds.) Advances in Cryptology - EUROCRYPT 2022. LNCS, vol. 13277, pp. 677–706. Springer, Cham (2022). https://doi.org/10.1007/978-3-031-07082-2_24

15. Dowling, B., Fischlin, M., Günther, F., Stebila, D.: A cryptographic analysis of the TLS 1.3 handshake protocol. J. Cryptol. **34**(4), 37 (2021). https://doi.org/10.1007/s00145-021-09384-1

16. Fujisaki, E., Okamoto, T.: Secure integration of asymmetric and symmetric encryption schemes. In: Wiener, M. (ed.) CRYPTO 1999. LNCS, vol. 1666, pp. 537–554. Springer, Heidelberg (1999). https://doi.org/10.1007/3-540-48405-1_34

17. Hofheinz, D., Hövelmanns, K., Kiltz, E.: A modular analysis of the Fujisaki-Okamoto transformation. In: Kalai, Y., Reyzin, L. (eds.) TCC 2017, Part I. LNCS, vol. 10677, pp. 341–371. Springer, Cham (2017). https://doi.org/10.1007/978-3-319-70500-2_12

18. Hövelmanns, K., Hülsing, A., Majenz, C.: Failing gracefully: decryption failures and the Fujisaki-Okamoto transform. In: Agrawal, S., Lin, D. (eds.) Advances in Cryptology - ASIACRYPT 2022. Lecture Notes in Computer Science, vol. 13794, pp. 414–443. Springer, Cham (2022). https://doi.org/10.1007/978-3-031-22972-5_15

19. Hövelmanns, K., Kiltz, E., Schäge, S., Unruh, D.: Generic authenticated key exchange in the quantum random oracle model. In: Kiayias, A., Kohlweiss, M., Wallden, P., Zikas, V. (eds.) PKC 2020, Part II. LNCS, vol. 12111, pp. 389–422. Springer, Cham (2020). https://doi.org/10.1007/978-3-030-45388-6_14

20. Huguenin-Dumittan, L., Vaudenay, S.: On IND-qCCA security in the ROM and its applications - CPA security is sufficient for TLS 1.3. Cryptology ePrint Archive, Report 2021/844 (2022-12-16 version) (2021), https://eprint.iacr.org/2021/844.pdf

21. Huguenin-Dumittan, L., Vaudenay, S.: On IND-qCCA security in the ROM and its applications - CPA security is sufficient for TLS 1.3. In: Dunkelman, O., Dziembowski, S. (eds.) Advances in Cryptology - EUROCRYPT 2022. LNCS, vol. 13277, pp. 613–642. Springer, Cham (2022). https://doi.org/10.1007/978-3-031-07082-2_22

22. Jiang, H., Zhang, Z., Chen, L., Wang, H., Ma, Z.: IND-CCA-secure key encapsulation mechanism in the quantum random oracle model, revisited. In: Shacham, H., Boldyreva, A. (eds.) CRYPTO 2018, Part III. LNCS, vol. 10993, pp. 96–125. Springer, Cham (2018). https://doi.org/10.1007/978-3-319-96878-0_4

23. Jiang, H., Zhang, Z., Ma, Z.: Key encapsulation mechanism with explicit rejection in the quantum random oracle model. In: Lin, D., Sako, K. (eds.) PKC 2019, Part II. LNCS, vol. 11443, pp. 618–645. Springer, Cham (2019). https://doi.org/10.1007/978-3-030-17259-6_21

24. Jiang, H., Zhang, Z., Ma, Z.: Tighter security proofs for generic key encapsulation mechanism in the quantum random oracle model. In: Ding, J., Steinwandt, R. (eds.) PQCrypto 2019. LNCS, vol. 11505, pp. 227–248. Springer, Cham (2019). https://doi.org/10.1007/978-3-030-25510-7_13

25. Jost, D., Maurer, U., Mularczyk, M.: Efficient ratcheting: almost-optimal guarantees for secure messaging. In: Ishai, Y., Rijmen, V. (eds.) EUROCRYPT 2019, Part I. LNCS, vol. 11476, pp. 159–188. Springer, Cham (2019). https://doi.org/10.1007/978-3-030-17653-2_6

26. Kuchta, V., Sakzad, A., Stehlé, D., Steinfeld, R., Sun, S.-F.: Measure-rewind-measure: tighter quantum random oracle model proofs for one-way to hiding and CCA security. In: Canteaut, A., Ishai, Y. (eds.) EUROCRYPT 2020, Part III. LNCS, vol. 12107, pp. 703–728. Springer, Cham (2020). https://doi.org/10.1007/978-3-030-45727-3_24

27. Melissa, Az., et al.: Surviving the FO-CALYPSE: securing PQC implementations in practice. RWC 2022 (2022). https://iacr.org/submit/files/slides/2022/rwc/rwc2022/48/slides.pdf

28. Naehrig, M., et al.: FrodoKEM learning with errors key encapsulation. https://frodokem.org/files/FrodoKEM-specification-20210604.pdf

29. Nielsen, M.A., Chuang, I.L.: Quantum Computation and Quantum Information. Cambridge University Press, Cambridge (2000). no. 2

30. NIST: National institute for standards and technology. Post quantum crypto project (2017). https://csrc.nist.gov/projects/post-quantum-cryptography/round-1-submissions

31. OQS: Open-quantum-safe OpenSSL (2021). https://github.com/open-quantum-safe/openssl

32. Poettering, B., Rösler, P.: Towards bidirectional ratcheted key exchange. In: Shacham, H., Boldyreva, A. (eds.) CRYPTO 2018, Part I. LNCS, vol. 10991, pp. 3–32. Springer, Cham (2018). https://doi.org/10.1007/978-3-319-96884-1_1

33. Qin, Y., Cheng, C., Zhang, X., Pan, Y., Hu, L., Ding, J.: A systematic approach and analysis of key mismatch attacks on lattice-based NIST candidate KEMs. In: Tibouchi, M., Wang, H. (eds.) ASIACRYPT 2021, Part IV. LNCS, vol. 13093, pp. 92–121. Springer, Cham (2021). https://doi.org/10.1007/978-3-030-92068-5_4

34. Regev, O.: On lattices, learning with errors, random linear codes, and cryptography. In: Gabow, H.N., Fagin, R. (eds.) Proceedings of the 37th Annual ACM Symposium on Theory of Computing, pp. 84–93. ACM (2005). https://doi.org/10.1145/1060590.1060603

35. Saito, T., Xagawa, K., Yamakawa, T.: Tightly-secure key-encapsulation mechanism in the quantum random oracle model. In: Nielsen, J.B., Rijmen, V. (eds.) EUROCRYPT 2018. LNCS, vol. 10822, pp. 520–551. Springer, Cham (2018). https://doi.org/10.1007/978-3-319-78372-7_17

36. Schneider, T.: Implicit rejection in Kyber. NIST PQC-forum (2022). https://groups.google.com/a/list.nist.gov/d/msgid/pqc-forum/3e210b6f-08d3-48f3-9689-1d048f9b3c58n%40list.nist.gov

37. Schwabe, P., Stebila, D., Wiggers, T.: Post-quantum TLS without handshake signatures. In: Ligatti, J., Ou, X., Katz, J., Vigna, G. (eds.) ACM CCS 2020, pp. 1461–1480. ACM (2020). https://doi.org/10.1145/3372297.3423350

38. Schwabe, P., Stebila, D., Wiggers, T.: More efficient post-quantum KEMTLS with pre-distributed public keys. In: Bertino, E., Shulman, H., Waidner, M. (eds.) ESORICS 2021, Part I. LNCS, vol. 12972, pp. 3–22. Springer, Cham (2021). https://doi.org/10.1007/978-3-030-88418-5_1

39. Ueno, R., Xagawa, K., Tanaka, Y., Ito, A., Takahashi, J., Homma, N.: Curse of re-encryption: a generic power/EM analysis on post-quantum KEMs. IACR Trans. Cryptograph. Hardw. Embed. Syst. **2022**(1), 296–C322 (2021). https://tches.iacr.org/index.php/TCHES/article/view/9298, artifact available at https://artifacts.iacr.org/tches/2022/a7

40. Yamakawa, T., Zhandry, M.: Classical vs quantum random oracles. In: Canteaut, A., Standaert, F.-X. (eds.) EUROCRYPT 2021, Part II. LNCS, vol. 12697, pp. 568–597. Springer, Cham (2021). https://doi.org/10.1007/978-3-030-77886-6_20

41. Zhandry, M.: Secure identity-based encryption in the quantum random oracle model. In: Safavi-Naini, R., Canetti, R. (eds.) CRYPTO 2012. LNCS, vol. 7417, pp. 758–775. Springer, Heidelberg (2012). https://doi.org/10.1007/978-3-642-32009-5_44

42. Zhandry, M.: How to record quantum queries, and applications to quantum indifferentiability. In: Boldyreva, A., Micciancio, D. (eds.) CRYPTO 2019, Part II. LNCS, vol. 11693, pp. 239–268. Springer, Cham (2019). https://doi.org/10.1007/978-3-030-26951-7_9

Author Index

© International Association for Cryptologic Research 2023
J. Guo and R. Steinfeld (Eds.): ASIACRYPT 2023, LNCS 14441, p. 469, 2023.
https://doi.org/10.1007/978-981-99-8730-6

Printed in the United States
by Baker & Taylor Publisher Services